Lecture Notes in Computer Science 12182

More information about this series at http://www.springer.com/series/7409

Masaaki Kurosu (Ed.)

Human-Computer Interaction

Multimodal and Natural Interaction

Thematic Area, HCI 2020
Held as Part of the 22nd International Conference, HCII 2020
Copenhagen, Denmark, July 19–24, 2020
Proceedings, Part II

 Springer

Editor
Masaaki Kurosu
The Open University of Japan
Chiba, Japan

ISSN 0302-9743 ISSN 1611-3349 (electronic)
Lecture Notes in Computer Science
ISBN 978-3-030-49061-4 ISBN 978-3-030-49062-1 (eBook)
https://doi.org/10.1007/978-3-030-49062-1

LNCS Sublibrary: SL3 – Information Systems and Applications, incl. Internet/Web, and HCI

This Springer imprint is published by the registered company Springer Nature Switzerland AG
The registered company address is: Gewerbestrasse 11, 6330 Cham, Switzerland

Foreword

The 22nd International Conference on Human-Computer Interaction, HCI International 2020 (HCII 2020), was planned to be held at the AC Bella Sky Hotel and Bella Center, Copenhagen, Denmark, during July 19–24, 2020. Due to the COVID-19 coronavirus pandemic and the resolution of the Danish government not to allow events larger than 500 people to be hosted until September 1, 2020, HCII 2020 had to be held virtually. It incorporated the 21 thematic areas and affiliated conferences listed on the following page.

A total of 6,326 individuals from academia, research institutes, industry, and governmental agencies from 97 countries submitted contributions, and 1,439 papers and 238 posters were included in the conference proceedings. These contributions address the latest research and development efforts and highlight the human aspects of design and use of computing systems. The contributions thoroughly cover the entire field of human-computer interaction, addressing major advances in knowledge and effective use of computers in a variety of application areas. The volumes constituting the full set of the conference proceedings are listed in the following pages.

The HCI International (HCII) conference also offers the option of "late-breaking work" which applies both for papers and posters and the corresponding volume(s) of the proceedings will be published just after the conference. Full papers will be included in the "HCII 2020 - Late Breaking Papers" volume of the proceedings to be published in the Springer LNCS series, while poster extended abstracts will be included as short papers in the "HCII 2020 - Late Breaking Posters" volume to be published in the Springer CCIS series.

I would like to thank the program board chairs and the members of the program boards of all thematic areas and affiliated conferences for their contribution to the highest scientific quality and the overall success of the HCI International 2020 conference.

This conference would not have been possible without the continuous and unwavering support and advice of the founder, Conference General Chair Emeritus and Conference Scientific Advisor Prof. Gavriel Salvendy. For his outstanding efforts, I would like to express my appreciation to the communications chair and editor of HCI International News, Dr. Abbas Moallem.

July 2020   Constantine Stephanidis

HCI International 2020 Thematic Areas
and Affiliated Conferences

Thematic areas:

- HCI 2020: Human-Computer Interaction
- HIMI 2020: Human Interface and the Management of Information

Affiliated conferences:

- EPCE: 17th International Conference on Engineering Psychology and Cognitive Ergonomics
- UAHCI: 14th International Conference on Universal Access in Human-Computer Interaction
- VAMR: 12th International Conference on Virtual, Augmented and Mixed Reality
- CCD: 12th International Conference on Cross-Cultural Design
- SCSM: 12th International Conference on Social Computing and Social Media
- AC: 14th International Conference on Augmented Cognition
- DHM: 11th International Conference on Digital Human Modeling and Applications in Health, Safety, Ergonomics and Risk Management
- DUXU: 9th International Conference on Design, User Experience and Usability
- DAPI: 8th International Conference on Distributed, Ambient and Pervasive Interactions
- HCIBGO: 7th International Conference on HCI in Business, Government and Organizations
- LCT: 7th International Conference on Learning and Collaboration Technologies
- ITAP: 6th International Conference on Human Aspects of IT for the Aged Population
- HCI-CPT: Second International Conference on HCI for Cybersecurity, Privacy and Trust
- HCI-Games: Second International Conference on HCI in Games
- MobiTAS: Second International Conference on HCI in Mobility, Transport and Automotive Systems
- AIS: Second International Conference on Adaptive Instructional Systems
- C&C: 8th International Conference on Culture and Computing
- MOBILE: First International Conference on Design, Operation and Evaluation of Mobile Communications
- AI-HCI: First International Conference on Artificial Intelligence in HCI

Conference Proceedings Volumes Full List

1. LNCS 12181, Human-Computer Interaction: Design and User Experience (Part I), edited by Masaaki Kurosu
2. LNCS 12182, Human-Computer Interaction: Multimodal and Natural Interaction (Part II), edited by Masaaki Kurosu
3. LNCS 12183, Human-Computer Interaction: Human Values and Quality of Life (Part III), edited by Masaaki Kurosu
4. LNCS 12184, Human Interface and the Management of Information: Designing Information (Part I), edited by Sakae Yamamoto and Hirohiko Mori
5. LNCS 12185, Human Interface and the Management of Information: Interacting with Information (Part II), edited by Sakae Yamamoto and Hirohiko Mori
6. LNAI 12186, Engineering Psychology and Cognitive Ergonomics: Mental Workload, Human Physiology, and Human Energy (Part I), edited by Don Harris and Wen-Chin Li
7. LNAI 12187, Engineering Psychology and Cognitive Ergonomics: Cognition and Design (Part II), edited by Don Harris and Wen-Chin Li
8. LNCS 12188, Universal Access in Human-Computer Interaction: Design Approaches and Supporting Technologies (Part I), edited by Margherita Antona and Constantine Stephanidis
9. LNCS 12189, Universal Access in Human-Computer Interaction: Applications and Practice (Part II), edited by Margherita Antona and Constantine Stephanidis
10. LNCS 12190, Virtual, Augmented and Mixed Reality: Design and Interaction (Part I), edited by Jessie Y. C. Chen and Gino Fragomeni
11. LNCS 12191, Virtual, Augmented and Mixed Reality: Industrial and Everyday Life Applications (Part II), edited by Jessie Y. C. Chen and Gino Fragomeni
12. LNCS 12192, Cross-Cultural Design: User Experience of Products, Services, and Intelligent Environments (Part I), edited by P. L. Patrick Rau
13. LNCS 12193, Cross-Cultural Design: Applications in Health, Learning, Communication, and Creativity (Part II), edited by P. L. Patrick Rau
14. LNCS 12194, Social Computing and Social Media: Design, Ethics, User Behavior, and Social Network Analysis (Part I), edited by Gabriele Meiselwitz
15. LNCS 12195, Social Computing and Social Media: Participation, User Experience, Consumer Experience, and Applications of Social Computing (Part II), edited by Gabriele Meiselwitz
16. LNAI 12196, Augmented Cognition: Theoretical and Technological Approaches (Part I), edited by Dylan D. Schmorrow and Cali M. Fidopiastis
17. LNAI 12197, Augmented Cognition: Human Cognition and Behaviour (Part II), edited by Dylan D. Schmorrow and Cali M. Fidopiastis

38. CCIS 1224, HCI International 2020 Posters - Part I, edited by Constantine Stephanidis and Margherita Antona
39. CCIS 1225, HCI International 2020 Posters - Part II, edited by Constantine Stephanidis and Margherita Antona
40. CCIS 1226, HCI International 2020 Posters - Part III, edited by Constantine Stephanidis and Margherita Antona

http://2020.hci.international/proceedings

Human-Computer Interaction Thematic Area (HCI 2020)

Program Board Chair: **Masaaki Kurosu, The Open University of Japan, Japan**

- Salah Uddin Ahmed, Norway
- Zohreh Baniasadi, Luxembourg
- Valdecir Becker, Brazil
- Nimish Biloria, Australia
- Scott Cadzow, UK
- Maurizio Caon, Switzerland
- Zhigang Chen, P.R. China
- Ulla Geisel, Germany
- Tor-Morten Groenli, Norway
- Jonathan Gurary, USA
- Kristy Hamilton, USA
- Yu-Hsiu Hung, Taiwan
- Yi Ji, P.R. China
- Lawrence Lam, USA
- Alexandros Liapis, Greece
- Bingjie Liu, USA
- Hiroshi Noborio, Japan
- Denise Pilar, Brazil
- Farzana Rahman, USA
- Manuel Rudolph, Germany
- Emmanuelle Savarit, UK
- Damian Schofield, USA
- Vinícius Segura, Brazil
- Charlotte Wiberg, Sweden

The full list with the Program Board Chairs and the members of the Program Boards of all thematic areas and affiliated conferences is available online at:

http://www.hci.international/board-members-2020.php

HCI International 2021

The 23rd International Conference on Human-Computer Interaction, HCI International 2021 (HCII 2021), will be held jointly with the affiliated conferences in Washington DC, USA, at the Washington Hilton Hotel, July 24–29, 2021. It will cover a broad spectrum of themes related to Human-Computer Interaction (HCI), including theoretical issues, methods, tools, processes, and case studies in HCI design, as well as novel interaction techniques, interfaces, and applications. The proceedings will be published by Springer. More information will be available on the conference website: http://2021.hci.international/.

General Chair
Prof. Constantine Stephanidis
University of Crete and ICS-FORTH
Heraklion, Crete, Greece
Email: general_chair@hcii2021.org

http://2021.hci.international/

Contents – Part II

Speech, Voice, Conversation and Emotions

Multimodal Interaction

Human Robot Interaction

Gesture-Based Interaction

A Human-Centered Approach to Designing Gestures for Natural User Interfaces

Shannon K. T. Bailey[1]([✉]) and Cheryl I. Johnson[2]

[1] Immertec (Immersive Tech Inc.), Tampa, FL, USA
shannon@immertec.com
[2] Naval Air Warfare Center Training Systems Division, Orlando, FL, USA
cheryl.i.johnson@navy.mil

Abstract. As technology matures, human-computer interfaces have changed to meet the needs of interacting with more complex systems in user-friendly ways. Gesture-based interfaces, a type of natural user interface (NUI), allow users to use their bodies to interact with computers or virtual/augmented reality (VR/AR) and offer a more natural and intuitive user experience; however, most gesture-based commands have been developed not by considering the user, but rather what is easiest for a computer to interpret. This methodology may lead to users having increased mental effort and low perceived system usability. In two studies, we took a user-centered approach to determine natural gestures for a set of common computer actions, such as selecting an object and moving an object. In Study One, participants performed gestures for a list of actions, and in Study Two a different group of participants rated how natural they found the gestures produced in Study One compared to a set of arbitrary gestures. Overall, participants produced very similar gestures for the actions in Study One, and these gestures were rated as most natural in Study Two. Taken together, this research provides a user-centered methodology for determining natural gestures and building a vocabulary of gestures for system designers to use when developing gesture-based NUIs.

Keywords: Augmented reality · Human-computer interaction · Gestures · Natural user interface · Usability · Virtual reality

1 Introduction

Gesture-based interfaces, a type of Natural User Interface (NUI), allow users to interact directly with a computer system using their bodies. As advancing technology allows for gestural commands to be implemented in a growing number of computer systems, interface designers should employ a user-centered approach to developing gestures so that gestures feel natural to the user. Given the interest in using gesture-based commands in virtual or augmented reality (VR/AR), educational or training systems, and video games, it is important that designers have a vocabulary of natural gestures that do not detract from the system. If gestures are perceived as arbitrary by the user, there may be unintended effects on how the user interacts with the system, such as increased mental effort or decreased sense of system usability [1]. If users find gesture-based interactions

© Springer Nature Switzerland AG 2020
M. Kurosu (Ed.): HCII 2020, LNCS 12182, pp. 3–18, 2020.
https://doi.org/10.1007/978-3-030-49062-1_1

to lack usability or if gestures differ widely between various systems, this may cause confusion or frustration and users may take longer to learn to use a new system. These issues that result from implementing gestures that are not developed with the user in mind could be mitigated by creating a vocabulary of gesture-based interactions that are perceived as natural by users. The current set of studies utilized a human-centered approach to develop gesture-based commands for a range of common computer actions.

1.1 Human-Computer Interfaces

As technology develops, human-computer interfaces have changed to meet the needs of interacting with more complex systems in user-friendly ways. Computer interaction today commonly consists of graphical user interfaces (GUIs) in which icons on the screen visually represent computer actions that can be selected and controlled by mouse input. GUIs that utilize features such as windows, icons, menus, and pointers have been referred to as WIMPs [2]. In the mid-1980s, WIMPs replaced the command line interfaces (CLIs) of early computer systems in which the user typed commands via keyboard input to complete computer functions [3]. WIMP GUIs rapidly replaced CLIs as the mainstream computer interface, because these GUIs were more user-friendly when learning how to interact with a computer system. In 1997, Andries van Dam, a prominent computer scientist and pioneer of computer graphics, described the eras of computer interfaces as "long periods of stability interrupted by rapid change," but expressed surprise that WIMPs have dominated user interfaces for so many decades (p. 63). Van Dam argued that a "post-WIMP" era of user interface can overcome limitations in the WIMP model by incorporating additional sensory modalities, natural language, or more than one user in control. He succinctly summarized the main problem with WIMP interfaces, stating: "However user-friendly, an interface is still an intermediary between the user's intent and execution of that intent. As such, it should be considered at best a necessary evil because no matter how fluid, it still imposes a layer of cognitive processing between the user and the computer's execution of the user's intent. The ideal interface is no interface" (p. 64).

Now, recent technological advances and dropping cost of motion-tracking systems have opened the door to using gesture-based input to interact directly with computers, a form of natural user interface (NUI). The differentiating feature of NUIs compared to both GUIs and CLIs is that natural interfaces use the body as an input device to interact directly with the computer system, allowing the user to rely on existing skills of physical interaction [4]. NUIs can include gestures, speech, or touch to interact with the computer system. The purpose of NUIs is to provide the user with an interface that is easy to learn by not requiring much cognitive effort from the user. The term "intuitive" is used by human-computer interaction (HCI) researchers and product designers to describe the ease with which a new system is learned, and an intuitive user experience is a main goal of technology designers [5]. The extent to which NUIs are easy to learn and the cognitive mechanisms behind learning natural interfaces are a topical concern as these technologies become more prevalent.

1.2   What Makes a NUI Natural?

The naturalness of an interaction can be described in terms of natural mapping, or the extent to which a control matches the intended action on an object [6]. This description of naturalness between a control and object can be extended to computer interfaces. For example, a NUI may have a gesture-based command in which the user moves a hand upward to indicate the desire to move an object on the computer up. Although this example is a simple command with a correspondingly simple action, NUIs may range on a continuum of "naturalness." Describing the need for VR/AR systems to incorporate natural interactions, Steuer [7] conceptualized the naturalness of interfaces as the degree to which commands are either arbitrary movements or natural gestures. In this proposed continuum of naturalness, a control is more natural if it closely represents the intended action, such as a gesture-based command that pantomimes a physical action. This continuum is apparent in many computer interfaces, with examples of interactions across the range of natural mapping [8]. For example, double-clicking a mouse to select an object may be considered an arbitrary interaction because it does not mimic a real-world action on an object; alternatively, a NUI in which a user makes a pinching gesture to select a small object may be a more natural mapping, which has recently been utilized on the Oculus Quest VR system. The extent to which gesture-based commands are perceived as natural from the user's perspective is in the early stages of research and a vocabulary of NUI gestures has yet to be standardized.

1.3   Challenges to NUI Development

Until recently, technological challenges meant that implementing natural gestures was not feasible. A main challenge of creating gesture-based interfaces was that motion tracking technology was limited by both resolution and latency [9]. This led to the design of gesture-based commands that were based on what the motion capture system could recognize, not necessarily what the user felt was most natural [2, 10]. The limitations of previous technology may have led to the creation of gesture commands with unintended strains on the user; yet, the technology supporting NUIs is improving rapidly and becoming more widely available. As motion tracking continues to improve, the development of gesture-based commands can get closer to real-time natural interactions.

1.4   How People Interpret NUIs

Because previous developments of gesture-based NUIs were greatly limited by the technology available, research into how people interpret gesture-based NUIs was also inadequate. To mitigate these issues and propose user-centered gestures for future NUIs, Grandhi, Joue, and Mittelberg [11] conducted a study to see what gestures people produce for common mundane actions (e.g., sorting coins, closing a book) that could represent computer actions (e.g., sorting computer files, closing a computer program). The researchers found characteristics that were common among gestures and across participants, such as the use of pantomiming actions and conducting gestures from an egocentric perspective. The guidelines Grandhi and colleagues proposed can serve as useful recommendations for developers of NUIs, yet there are several limitations of this earlier work that we attempt to address in the current studies. First, participants were not told of the nature of the study and computer actions were masked as mundane actions to avoid demand characteristics in how they would determine natural gestures. Although we agree that avoiding previous knowledge of WIMP computer interactions is an important first step, it may be that asking participants to gesture mundane actions differs from how they would gesture to perform the action on a novel computer system. That is, a gesture for cutting an apple may not be the same gesture that one would use to "cut" words in a computer document. Importantly, the gestures that were produced for mundane actions were not subsequently tested for how other people interpret them. For instance, would a person be able to determine the intended computer command from watching the gesture of cutting an apple? It is unknown whether the gestures for mundane actions would be interpreted as a computer action, or even as the intended mundane action. To address the limitations of the NUI literature and determine a set of gestures for common computer actions, we asked the following research questions: What gestures do people sponta-neously think of when asked to produce a gesture representing a computer action? Are those "natural gestures" interpreted as natural by other people?

2   Study One: What Are Natural Gestures?

2.1   Methodology

Participants. Participants ($n = 17$) were students recruited from a university research participation pool, and they received class credit for completing the study. Ten were female, and seven were male. The ages ranged from 18–20 years old ($M = 18.31$, $SD = 0.60$), and all were predominantly right-handed.

Procedure. Participants signed up to participate in the in-lab study through the univer-sity research participation system. The study lasted approximately 30 min. After agreeing to an informed consent, participants were asked to stand on a mark on the floor facing a Microsoft Kinect V1 infrared motion tracker. The motion tracker was used to record video and to capture depth information and joint coordinates. The experimenter then asked participants to perform gestures to show how they would interact with a computer to complete a series of actions in a random order (Table 1). After performing a gesture for each action, participants were given a debrief page. The videos of the gestures recorded by the motion tracker were then analyzed for converging features (e.g., starting point, movement shape, and direction) to determine the most commonly performed gestures for each action.

2.2   Results

The gestures for each action were classified based on characteristics of naturalness (Table 1). The coding scheme was adapted from Grandhi et al. [11] in which features of gestures were analyzed to determine characteristics of "naturalness" and "intuitiveness." The features coded in Grandhi et al.'s analysis included: 1. Whether gestures were right or left handed, 2. Whether one or both hands were used, 3. If the gesture was pantomimed or the body was used as a tool or object, 4. Whether the gesture was static or dynamic, and 5. Whether the gesture referred to the main action (e.g., hand pantomiming cutting) or was used to set up the context of the gesture (e.g., hand pantomiming holding the object being cut). Grandhi et al. listed one more characteristic that was not used in the current study because it was not applicable to this task, "Whether or not tool or object was gestured."

Two coders rated the videos of participants gesturing for each action. The agreement between coders was 100%, highlighting the extent to which the gestures were distinct and relatively simple. A majority of participants used the same hand or hands for each gesture. Between 71%–94% used only their right hand for the actions of moving an object up, down, left, right, clockwise, counter-clockwise, and select. Both hands were predominately used for the actions enlarge and shrink. All but one of the actions were pantomimed gestures of the object manipulations, and the remaining action was selecting an object, of which 76% of participants used a pointing gesture. Every participant performed the gestures dynamically for each action, and all gestures represented the main action of object manipulation, so these two questions were not listed in Table 1 due to space limitations.

The current study extended the work by Grandhi et al. [11] by classifying additional features not included in their gesture coding scheme. Gesture features were also recorded, such as the direction of movement and shape of the hand, to narrow down the converging features of a natural gesture for each action to determine the most natural gesture-based computer commands (Table 2). The first 10% of gestures were coded by both of the same raters as above. The coding again matched, so the remainder of the gestures was coded by one coder. By recording features not coded in the scheme outlined by Grandhi et al., it was apparent that there was limited variation in the type of gestures participants performed for each action, resulting in converging gesture features for each action. For example, gestures originated from within the space of the torso area or ended at the torso. For each action, all gestures involved movement in the direction of the intended action. For example, every gesture for "move an object up" was performed in an upward motion. Likewise, all participants performed the enlarging gesture by moving hands in an outward-from-center direction. The same pattern of expected motion followed for the other actions except one; only the "select" gesture had variation on movement direction. To indicate a selecting action, all but one participant moved their hand forward either with a pointing finger or a palm press, and the remaining participant closed their hand in a grasping motion.

Variation in the gestures occurred mostly in the detailed movements. For the clockwise and counterclockwise rotating actions, gestures varied by the fulcrum point of the rotation, such that a slight majority of participants rotated the hand from the wrist and the rest rotated the entire arm from the elbow. The shrinking and enlarging gestures were all performed in the expected inward and outward directions, respectively, but they varied in whether they moved left-and-right, up-and-down, or diagonally. Although there were variations in the details of movements, these variations were limited to three or less deviations for each action, and all were performed in the overall expected direction of movement; therefore, defining the converging features for each action started from a small set of variations.

Table 1. Characteristics of natural gestures produced for each action

Action	Gesture characteristics		
	Handedness	Number of hands	Pantomime or Body-as-Object
1. Up	70.59% Right 11.76% Left 17.65% Both	82.35% One 17.65% Both	76.47% Pantomime 23.53% Body-as-Object
2. Down	94.12% Right 0% Left 5.88% Both	94.12% One 5.88% Both	70.59% Pantomime 29.41% Body-as-Object
3. Left	70.59% Right 11.76% Left 17.65% Both	17.65% Both 82.35% One	64.71% Pantomime 35.29% Body-as-Object
4. Right	88.24% Right 5.88% Left 5.88% Both	94.12% One 5.88% Both	64.71% Pantomime 35.29% Body-as-Object
5. Clockwise	82.35% Right 5.88% Left 11.76% Both	88.24% One 11.76% Both	64.71% Pantomime 35.29% Body-as-Object
6. Counter-clockwise	82.35% Right 5.88% Left 11.76% Both	88.24% One 11.76% Both	64.71% Pantomime 35.29% Body-as-Object
7. Select	94.12% Right 5.88% Left 0% Both	100% One 0% Both	23.53% Pantomime 76.47% Body-as-Object
8. Enlarge	23.53% Right 0% Left 76.47% Both	23.53% One 76.47% Both	82.35% Pantomime 17.65% Body-as-Object
9. Shrink	29.41% Right 0% Left 70.59% Both	29.41% One 70.59% Both	88.24% Pantomime 11.76% Body-as-Object

Note: Coding based on the characteristics of natural gestures defined by Grandhi et al. [11].

2.3   Discussion

This first study aimed to narrow down what natural gestures are produced by participants for common computer actions that may be implemented in a natural user interface. Participants performed gestures for nine object manipulation actions to determine what natural gestures participants would use as gesture-based computer commands. The majority of participants performed very similar gestures for each action with limited variations, making it possible to define the converging features of gestures for each action. For example, a majority of participants usually used their right hand to perform these representational gestures. This is consistent with previous research; right-handed individuals have shown a preference for using their dominant hand for gestures that represent objects or spatial relationships, but do not have this hand preference for non-representational gestures [12]. To confirm whether the most commonly performed gestures in Study One were perceived as natural by others, a second study was conducted in which a separate sample of participants rated these and other gestures on a scale from natural to arbitrary. Table 3 describes the top natural gestures performed in Study One that were included in Study Two.

Table 2. Converging features of gestures produced for each action

Action	Gesture features					
	Hand shape	Direction	Start	Stop	Detailed movements
1. Up	70.59% Open 5.88% Closed 23.53% Point	100% Up	100% Torso height	100% Head height	N/A
2. Down	64.71% Open 5.88% Closed 29.41% Point	100% Down	100% Head height	100% Torso height	N/A
3. Left	52.94% Open 11.76% Closed 35.29% Point	100% Left	100% Torso height	100% Torso height	N/A
4. Right	52.94% Open 5.88% Closed 35.29% Point	100% Right	100% Torso height	100% Torso height	N/A
5. Clockwise	64.71% Open 0% Closed 35.29% Point	100% Clockwise	100% Torso height	100% Torso height	64.71% Rotate wrist 35.29% Rotate arm
6. Counter-clockwise	64.71% Open 0% Closed 35.29% Point	100% Counter-clockwise	100% Torso height	100% Torso height	64.71% Rotate wrist 35.29% Rotate arm
7. Select	11.76% Open 11.76% Closed 76.47% Point	94.12% Forward 5.88% Closing	100% Torso height	100% Torso height	88.24% Single point 5.88% Double point 5.88% Closing hand
8. Enlarge	70.59% Open 11.76% Closed 17.65% Point	100% Outward	100% Torso height	100% Torso height	76.47% Left/Right 5.88% Up/Down 17.65% Diagonal
9. Shrink	52.94% Open 35.29% Closed 11.76% Point	100% Inward	100% Torso height	100% Torso height	70.59% Left/Right 11.76% Up/Down 17.65% Diagonal

Table 3. Most commonly produced natural gestures for each action

Action	Description
1. Up	Raise open right hand from chest height to above head with palm forward
2. Down	Lower open right hand from above head to chest height with palm forward
3. Left	Move open right hand from right to left at chest height with palm forward Move pointing right hand from right to left at chest height
4. Right	Move open right hand from left to right at chest height with palm forward Move pointing right hand from left to right at chest height
5. Clockwise	Rotate open right hand clockwise at chest height, circling from elbow Rotate open right hand clockwise at chest height, circling from wrist
6. Counter-clockwise	Rotate open right hand counterclockwise at chest height, circling from elbow Rotate open right hand counterclockwise at chest height, circling from wrist
7. Select	Point forward once with right hand at chest height Grasp with right hand at chest height
8. Enlarge	Move open hands outward left and right from center of chest Move closed hands outward left and right from center of chest
9. Shrink	Move open hands inward left and right to center of chest Move closed hands inward left and right to center of chest

3   Study Two: How Are Gestures Interpreted?

The goal of the second study was to assess quantitatively how natural the gestures produced in Study One were to a new group of participants. The converging features of the gestures produced in Study One were used to create the natural gestures for each action. A set of arbitrary gestures was also included in Study Two to have a comparison for the natural gestures produced in Study One. Arbitrary gestures were chosen from a selection of gestures that do not pantomime a real-world physical action from the motion tracker's software development kit (i.e., pre-existing gestures commands recognized by the Microsoft Kinect V1) and gesture-based commands from previous experiments [13, 14]. In Study Two, participants were asked to rate how natural or arbitrary a gesture seemed for a particular interaction. For each combination of gesture and desired computer action, participants were shown a video of an actor performing a gesture and were asked to write what happened in each video (to ensure the participants watched each video before rating the gestures) and then to rate the naturalness of each gesture-action combination. The videos included the natural gestures produced by participants from Study One as well as arbitrary gestures as a comparison to the natural gestures. It was expected that for each computer action, the gesture(s) rated as most natural would be the gestures produced for that action in Study One. It was predicted that the arbitrarily chosen gestures would be rated on the arbitrary end of the scale for each action, and gestures from Study One that did not match a computer action would also be rated as arbitrary for that combination of action and gesture. For example, the gesture of a hand moving upward from Study One should be rated as arbitrary for the action of selecting an object. The results from Study Two show whether the gestures produced in Study One were also perceived as natural when rated by others.

3.1 Methodology

Participants. A new sample of 188 participants from the same university research participant pool completed Study Two, and they were awarded class credit. Participants were excluded from participating if they were included in Study One. Participants were removed from analyses ($n = 19$) if they, 1. Did not respond to all questions, 2. Did not describe a video accurately when asked "What happened in the video" (e.g., responded "no clue"), and/or 3. Did not complete the survey on a computer as required by the instructions (i.e., used a mobile device). The following analyses included 169 participants. The sample was 68% female ($n = 115$) and 31% male ($n = 53$), and 1 participant chose the answer, "prefer not to respond." Participants were between 18–41 years old with an average age of 20.46 years ($SD = 3.90$ years). Participants reported their ethnicity and were able to select multiple options to describe themselves: 54% were White (Non-Hispanic), 24% were Hispanic/Latino, 12% were Asian/Pacific Islander, 8% were African-American, 3% were Arabian/Middle Eastern, 3% selected "Other," 0% were Native American, and 1% chose not to respond (results were rounded to the nearest percent). A majority of participants were right-handed ($n = 146$, 86%), with seventeen left-handed participants (10%) and six ambidextrous participants (4%). Mean ratings did not differ significantly by handedness, so responses were collapsed for all analyses.

Materials. Twenty-six gesture videos (3–5 s each) were presented in which an adult male actor performed each gesture. Eighteen videos corresponded with the natural gestures determined from Study One and eight arbitrary gestures were included for comparison (Table 4). A demographic survey consisted of 18 items asking for participants' age, sex, ethnicity, handedness, and educational background.

3.2 Procedure

Study Two was conducted online, and participants could respond to questions at their own pace. Participants were recruited from the university's research participation system and were directed to a survey website. After reading an informed consent and agreeing to participate, participants completed the demographic questionnaire. Participants were then informed they would be viewing a series of 26 videos (3–5 s each) depicting gesture-based commands for computer actions, and their task was to rate how natural or arbitrary each gesture was for each command. Participants could respond at their own pace and took approximately 15–30 min to complete. To reduce ambiguity in the interpretation of the terms "natural" and "arbitrary," participants were told that, "Natural means that a

Table 4. Description of gesture videos

Type	Gesture description
Natural gestures (from Study One)	1. Raise hand from chest height to head height with open right palm facing up
	2. Raise hand from chest height to head height with open right palm facing forward
	3. Lower hand from head height to waist with open right palm facing down
	4. Lower hand from head height to waist with open right palm facing forward
	5. From chest height, move right hand from right to left with open right palm forward
	6. From chest height, move right hand right to left with right hand pointing
	7. From chest height, move right hand from left to right with open right palm forward
	8. From chest height, move hand from left to right with right hand pointing
	9. From chest height, move right arm with open palm forward making a circle clockwise
	10. From chest height, move right hand with open palm forward to make a wrist rotation clockwise
	11. From chest height, move right arm with open palm forward to make a full circle counterclockwise
	12. From chest height, move right hand with open palm forward to make a wrist rotation counterclockwise
	13. Point forward once with right hand at chest height
	14. Grasp with right hand at chest height
	15. Use both open hands to move outward from center of chest
	16. Use both closed fists to move outward (left and right) from center of chest
	17. Use both open hands to move inward to center of chest starting with hands about two feet apart
	18. Use both hands with closed fists to move inward to center of chest starting with hands about two feet apart
Arbitrary gestures	19. Bring right arm up to head height making a 90-degree angle at the elbow
	20. Move right arm straight down past hip
	21. Extend straight right arm out to the right side, parallel to the ground
	22. Raise right closed fist to left shoulder
	23. From chest height, move from right to left with closed right fist
	24. From chest height, move from left to right with closed right fist
	25. Use right closed fist to press forward
	26. Right open hand wave with palm forward

gesture is more intuitive or 'makes sense' for that computer action" and that, "Arbitrary means that a gesture seems random or doesn't 'make sense' for that computer action."

Next, participants were directed to view each gesture video successively and presented in a random order. For each gesture video, participants watched the video and were asked to describe what happened in each video in a text box, which was used as a control measure to ensure participants were watching each video before rating the gesture. After describing the gesture video, the participant then rated how natural they felt the gesture was for each of the nine computer actions. The ratings were on a 6-point

Likert-type scale with endpoints "Completely Arbitrary" and "Completely Natural." The design was not fully combinatorial – not every action was rated for each of the 26 videos – because opposite gesture-action combinations were not included to avoid situations in which the action was the opposite of the gesture. For example, a gesture motioning upward was not included in possible ratings for the action of moving an object down. This was done so as not to confuse participants with opposite gesture-action combinations (i.e., "trick questions"), and because opposite movements from actions may represent another separate category of gestures (i.e., opposite actions) and should not be rated on a continuum of natural to arbitrary. After rating each gesture video for a variety of actions, participants received a post participation debriefing and were awarded class credit for their participation.

3.3 Results

For each computer action, a repeated-measures ANOVA was conducted to determine whether there were differences in naturalness ratings of the gestures. Unless otherwise noted, the Greenhouse-Geisser correction is reported for ANOVA tests and Bonferroni corrections were performed for post hoc tests. For each of the nine actions, the gestures that were rated as most natural are depicted in Fig. 1. As can be seen for each action, the gestures that were rated as most natural for each action were those gestures that were produced by participants in Study One, while the remaining gestures were rated distinctly less natural than those produced by participants in Study One, with few exceptions.

As expected, the naturalness ratings for the action "moving an object up" differed significantly, $F(10.10, 1495.32) = 155.34$, $p < .001$, $\eta p^2 = .512$. Depicted in Fig. 1a, the gestures rated most natural for the action "moving an object up" were Video 2 ($M = 5.40$, $SD = 1.17$) and Video 1 ($M = 5.24$, $SD = 1.28$). These two gestures were rated significantly more natural than all of the other gestures (all $ps < .001$), but did not differ significantly from each other ($p = .12$). The gestures shown in these two videos were those that were produced for "moving an object up" in Study One. Naturalness ratings differed among gesture videos for "moving an object down," $F(7.88, 1213.17) = 234.27$, $p < .001$, $\eta p^2 = .603$. Figure 1b shows that the most natural gestures were Video 3 ($M = 5.24$, $SD = 1.32$) and Video 4 ($M = 5.23$, $SD = 1.22$), which were rated significantly more natural than the other gestures ($ps < .001$) and did not differ from each other ($p = .11$). These videos were the gestures produced in Study One. Although the arbitrary gesture depicted in Video 19 ($M = 3.95$, $SD = 1.85$) in which the arm moves down past the hip was less natural than Videos 3 and 4, it was rated significantly more natural than the other gestures for this action (all $ps < .001$). This arbitrarily chosen gesture was likely rated more natural than the other gesture-action combinations because it looks similar to a pantomimed gesture – That is, the gesture in Video 19 looked like the pantomimed gestures in Videos 3 and 4, which were natural gestures produced in Study One; however, it is important to note that Video 19, while similar to pantomimed gestures, was rated less natural than either of the gestures from Study One.

Gesture ratings were different for the action "moving an object left," $F(7.11, 1095.51) = 234.47$, $p < .001$, $\eta p^2 = .604$. The gestures rated more natural for this action (all $ps < .001$) were Video 6 ($M = 5.40$, $SD = 1.20$) and Video 5 ($M = 5.17$, $SD = 1.34$), which were not different from each other ($p = .10$) and were both from Study One (Fig. 1c).

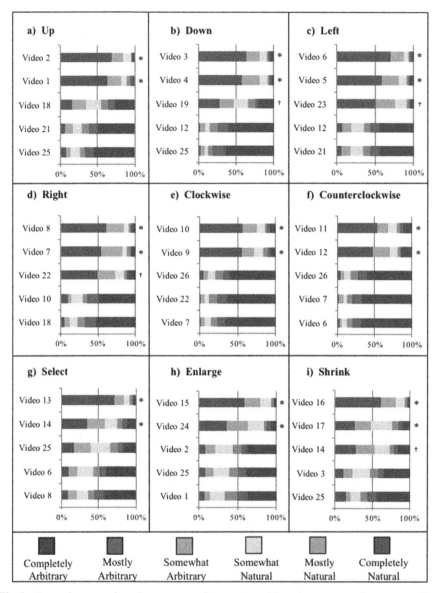

Fig. 1. For each gesture-based computer action, gesture videos that were rated most natural are graphed. The video numbers correspond to the descriptions in Table 4. Videos higher on the y-axis are seen as more natural for each action. The percentage of participant responses is presented on the x-axis. Recall that videos 1–18 were gestures from Study One, and videos 19–26 were the eight hypothesized arbitrary gestures. *Denotes that the videos showing gestures from Study One were rated significantly more natural than the other gesture videos for that action (all $p < 0.05$). † Denotes a video not from Study One that was rated significantly higher in naturalness than the other gesture videos for that action.

The naturalness rating for the arbitrary gesture in which a closed fist was moved right to left in Video 23 ($M = 5.06$, $SD = 1.29$) did not differ from the rating for Video 5, but was rated less natural than Video 6. Even though this gesture was in the arbitrary set of gestures (Table 4), it did resemble the natural gestures in Videos 5 and 6 because it made the same motion with a closed fist as opposed to an open or pointing hand. The gesture ratings also differed for "moving an object right," $F(8.26, 1304.63) = 219.30$, $p < .001$, $\eta p^2 = .581$. Shown in Fig. 1d, gestures rated most natural (all $ps < .001$) for the action "moving an object right" were Video 8 ($M = 5.26$, $SD = 1.27$) and Video 7 ($M = 5.14$, $SD = 1.33$) from Study One, and arbitrary Video 22 ($M = 4.89$, $SD = 1.56$) showing a closed fist moving right. Videos 7 and 8 did not differ at all ($p = 1.00$), and ratings for Videos 7 and 22 ($p = 1.00$) and Videos 8 and 22 ($p = .67$) were not statistically different. Comparable to the finding for "moving an object left," the arbitrary gesture that was rated closely to the natural gestures from Study One for "moving an object right" was very similar to the natural gestures.

For "rotating an object clockwise," gesture ratings differed, $F(9.81, 1510.63) = 152.78$, $p < .001$, $\eta p^2 = .498$, with Video 10 ($M = 5.26$, $SD = 1.27$) and Video 9 ($M = 5.14$, $SD = 1.33$) rated significantly more natural than other gestures (all $ps < .001$, Fig. 1e). Both gestures were from Study One and did not differ from each other ($p = 1.00$). Ratings of naturalness differed for "rotating an object counterclockwise," $F(7.40, 1132.68) = 143.80$, $p < .001$, $\eta p^2 = .485$. The gestures rated most natural for the action were from Study One (all $ps < .001$, Fig. 1f), Video 11 ($M = 4.77$, $SD = 1.72$) and Video 12 ($M = 4.71$, $SD = 1.72$). These did not differ from each other ($p = 1.00$). There was a difference in gesture ratings for "selecting an object," $F(15.44, 2408.51) = 71.68$, $p < .001$, $\eta p^2 = .315$. Shown in Fig. 1g, the naturally rated gestures for the action "selecting an object" were Video 13 ($M = 5.38$, $SD = 1.21$) and Video 14 ($M = 4.38$, $SD = 1.70$). These videos from Study One were rated more natural than all other gestures (all $ps < .001$), with Video 13 rated natural than Video 14 ($p < .001$).

Differences between the gesture ratings were also significant for "enlarging an object," $F(15.35, 2409.90) = 81.20$, $p < .001$, $\eta p^2 = .341$. Video 15 ($M = 5.24$, $SD = 1.17$) and Video 24 ($M = 4.62$, $SD = 1.52$) were rated more natural than the other gestures (all $ps < .001$), and Video 15 was significantly more natural than Video 24 ($p = .003$, Fig. 1h). Video 15 and Video 24 were gestures from Study One. Finally, the gesture ratings for "shrinking an object" were also different, $F(13.40, 2130.80) = 104.96$, $p < .001$, $\eta p^2 = .401$. The gestures rated most natural for the action "shrinking an object" were Video 16 ($M = 5.31$, $SD = 1.11$) and Video 17 ($M = 4.34$, $SD = 1.49$), but Video 16 was rated significantly more natural than Video 17 ($p < .001$; Fig. 1i). Both Video 16 and Video 17 were gestures produced in Study One.

3.4 Discussion

In Study Two, participants were asked to rate videos of the natural gestures (and arbitrary gesture distractors) on a continuum of natural to arbitrary to determine whether people interpreted as intended the gestures produced in the first study. For each action, the expected gestures (i.e., gestures produced in the Study One by participants) were rated as most natural. These results confirmed that gestures people produce when asked how they would perform a gesture-based computer action are interpreted as the intended action by a separate sample of participants. For some actions, arbitrary gestures that were similar to natural gestures were also rated as natural (above the midpoint on a continuum of arbitrary to natural), indicating that gestures that resemble pantomimed actions are considered more natural. Study Two answered the question of what natural gestures to implement in NUIs for these common computer actions by quantifying the extent to which people interpret gestures as natural. These results also corroborated that natural gestures produced by one group of people can be interpreted as natural by a different group of participants.

4   General Discussion

Across two studies, we sought to determine empirically a set of natural gestures for a range of common computer actions. The first study explored what natural gestures are spontaneously produced by participants for these actions, and the second study asked a different group of participants to rate the naturalness of the gestures that were produced. This methodology took a human-centered approach in that what a user would produce for a gesture-based computer command was considered prior to what is easiest for a computer to recognize. This research has empirical implications for the study of NUIs in that the user-centered approach to determining what gestures are natural resulted in gestures that were interpreted as natural by other users. After narrowing down the potential natural gestures for each action by choosing the most common gestures that were produced and picking the gesture rated as most natural for each action, the natural gestures were tested using the motion tracker to confirm that the gestures were possible to implement in the NUI. To summarize, future studies of NUIs can determine the natural gestures to be implemented in an interface by using a two-step process: 1. Ask participants what they think is natural and 2. Ask a second group of participants if they interpret those gestures as natural.

Additionally, we expanded upon the coding scheme outlined by Grandhi et al. [11] by including further details of each gesture necessary for system recognition and implementation, such as starting and stopping location, hand placement, etc. This extended coding scheme can be used in future research to help specify the converging features of user-produced gestures. In general, the gestures produced by participants shared clearly converging features with minimal differences among participants. In particular, the gestures produced were dynamic and pantomimed the main intended action, which supports the idea that gestural interactions should be fluid and closely mapped to the intended action as opposed to static positions or arbitrary movements, which may be easier for computers to recognize. The results of the second study confirmed that the gestures produced by the participants in the first study were rated as natural.

A limitation of conducting research on emerging technologies is that their capabilities, implementation, prevalence, and how they are perceived may change rapidly. The current state of gesture-based NUIs is that there is not yet a standard gesture vocabulary and little is known about how various gestures-based commands are perceived. As NUIs become more prevalent, particularly with the introduction of VR/AR systems that utilize gestures, people may become more accustomed to using system specific NUIs. Just as double-clicking a mouse was once an arbitrary interaction that has become ubiquitous, so too may arbitrary gestures become familiar or conventional interactions. Second, the sample of participants reported being predominately right-handed, and left-handed individuals may produce gestures using their dominate hand in contrast to the mostly right-handed gestures seen in the current sample. Additionally, the current study was conducted at a university in the United States. Some considerations going forward are that perceived naturalness of gestures may be culturally-specific [15]. Furthermore, gestures that are more physically strenuous (e.g., holding an extended arm out) may be more difficult, and thus seem less natural, for users with limited mobility. To address these limitations, future research could explore what interactions are optimal for the user.

5   Conclusion

This study determined how people would use natural gestures in a NUI by asking participants to rate the naturalness of gestures to perform common computer actions. We found that the gestures people produce when asked how they would perform a gesture-based command are also interpreted as the intended action. This research determining how people naturally gesture and how people interpret gestures is useful because it can inform the development of future NUIs and also contributes to the cognitive and human factors literatures on what makes a gesture seem "natural" versus "arbitrary."

References

1. Bailey, S.K.T., Johnson, C.I., Sims, V.K.: Using natural gesture interactions leads to higher usability and presence in a computer lesson. In: Bagnara, S., Tartaglia, R., Albolino, S., Alexander, T., Fujita, Y. (eds.) IEA 2018. AISC, vol. 826, pp. 663–671. Springer, Cham (2019). https://doi.org/10.1007/978-3-319-96065-4_70
2. Shiratuddin, M.F., Wong, K.W.: Non-contact multi-hand gestures interaction techniques for architectural design in a virtual environment. In: 5th Conference on information Technology & Multimedia, pp. 1–6. IEEE (2011). https://doi.org/10.1109/icimu.2011.6122761
3. van Dam, A.: Post-WIMP user interfaces. Commun. ACM **42**, 63–67 (1997). https://doi.org/10.1145/253671.253708
4. Roupé, M., Bosch-Sijtsema, P., Johansson, M.: Interactive navigation interface for virtual reality using the human body. Comp. Env. Urban Sys. **43**, 42–50 (2014). https://doi.org/10.1016/j.compenvurbsys.2013.10.003
5. Ullrich, D., Diefenbach, S.: From magical experience to effortlessness: an exploration of the components of intuitive interaction. In: 6th Nordic Conference on Human-Computer Interaction: Extending Boundaries, pp. 801–804. Association for Computing Machinery, NYC (2010). https://doi.org/10.1145/1868914.1869033
6. Norman, D.A.: The design of everyday things. Basic Books, NYC (2002)
7. Steuer, J.S.: Defining virtual reality: dimensions determining telepresence. J. Comm. **42**, 73–93 (1992). https://doi.org/10.1111/j.1460-2466.1992.tb00812.x
8. Schwartz, R.N., Plass, J.L.: Click versus drag: user-performed tasks and the enactment effect in an interactive multimedia environment. Comp. Hum. Beh. **33**, 242–255 (2014). https://doi.org/10.1016/j.chb.2014.01.012
9. McNamara, C., Proetsch, M., Lerma, N.: Investigating low-cost virtual reality technologies in the context of an immersive maintenance training application. In: Lackey, S., Shumaker, R. (eds.) VAMR 2016. LNCS, vol. 9740, pp. 621–632. Springer, Cham (2016). https://doi.org/10.1007/978-3-319-39907-2_59

10. Nielsen, M., Störring, M., Moeslund, T.B., Granum, E.: A procedure for developing intuitive and ergonomic gesture interfaces for HCI. In: Camurri, A., Volpe, G. (eds.) GW 2003. LNCS (LNAI), vol. 2915, pp. 409–420. Springer, Heidelberg (2004). https://doi.org/10.1007/978-3-540-24598-8_38

11. Grandhi, S.A., Joue, G., Mittelberg, I.: Understanding naturalness and intuitiveness in gesture production: Insights for touchless gestural interfaces. In: Conference on Human Factors in Computing Systems, SIGCHI, pp. 821–824. (2010). https://doi.org/10.1145/1978942.1979061

12. Sousa-Poza, J.F., Rohrberg, R., Mercure, A.: Effects of type of information (abstract-concrete) and field dependence on asymmetry of hand movements during speech. Percept. Mot. Skills **48**, 1323–1330 (1979). https://doi.org/10.2466/pms.1979.48.3c.1323

13. Bailey, S.K.T., Johnson, C.I., Schroeder, B.L., Marraffino, M.D.: Using virtual reality for training maintenance procedures. In: 17th Interservice/Industry Training, Simulation and Education Conference (2017)

14. Schroeder, B.L., Bailey, S.K.T., Johnson, C.I., Gonzalez-Holland, E.: Presence and usability do not directly predict procedural recall in virtual reality training. In: Stephanidis, C. (ed.) HCI 2017. CCIS, vol. 714, pp. 54–61. Springer, Cham (2017). https://doi.org/10.1007/978-3-319-58753-0_9

15. Mauney, D., Howarth, J., Wirtanen, A., Capra, M.: Cultural similarities and differences in user-defined gestures for touchscreen user interfaces. In: CHI Human Factors in Computing Systems, pp. 4015–4020. ACM (2010). https://doi.org/10.1145/1753846.1754095

Comparing a Mouse and a Free Hand Gesture Interaction Technique for 3D Object Manipulation

Joao Bernardes[(⊠)]

Universidade de Sao Paulo, Sao Paulo, Brazil
`jlbernardes@usp.br`

Abstract. Interacting in 3D has considerable and growing importance today in several areas and most computer systems are equipped with both a mouse or touchscreen and one or more cameras that can be readily used for gesture-based interaction. Literature comparing mouse and free-hand gesture interaction, however, is still somewhat sparse in regards to user satisfaction, learnability and memorability, which can be particularly important attributes for applications in education or entertainment. In this paper, we compare the use of mouse-based interaction with free-hand bimanual gestures to translate, scale and rotate a virtual 3D object. We isolate object manipulation from its selection and focus particularly on those three attributes to test whether the related variables show significant differences when comparing both modalities. To this end, we integrate a gesture recognition system, Microsoft's Kinect and an educational virtual atlas of anatomy, then design and perform an experiment with 19 volunteers, combining data from self-reported metrics and event logs. Our results show that, in this context, the difference is indeed significant and favors the use of gestures for most experimental tasks and evaluated attributes.

Keywords: Gesture-based interfaces · Natural user interfaces · User evaluation

1 Introduction

Interaction in virtual or augmented 3D environments has been researched at length for several years, as well as explored in areas of considerable economic importance, such as Computer Aided Design, medical imaging, rehabilitation, data visualization, training and education, entertainment etc. [8,9]. Furthermore, 3D interaction has also begun to reach a much more varied and large number of users in the last couple decades: video games are an important element in modern culture and feature 3D environments and interaction very often, being a major example of this wider reach.

Many devices and techniques were proposed and analyzed to facilitate this type of interaction beyond the use of keyboard and mouse. Since Put-That-There [4] combined pointing gestures and speech, and particularly since the first

© Springer Nature Switzerland AG 2020
M. Kurosu (Ed.): HCII 2020, LNCS 12182, pp. 19–37, 2020.
https://doi.org/10.1007/978-3-030-49062-1_2

dataglove was proposed [20], hand gestures are among these options. Image-based gesture recognition using cameras as the only sensors has become more widespread, especially in the last decade, thanks in large part to the greater availability of such image capture devices and the growth in processing power. Microsoft's Kinect sensor[1] and associated software, easily available and also providing reliable depth sensing and skeleton tracking, have intensified this trend. But the computer mouse still is one of the most used interaction devices for many tasks, including 3D interaction, despite having only two degrees of freedom to move. If, on one hand, it has this limitation, on the other a mouse or an equivalent device is present in most computer systems (with the notable and growing exception of portable devices with touch-based displays) and most users are very familiar with its use. We are now at a point in which both the mouse and some image capture devices are often already present in a large number of computer systems, making both gesture and mouse-based interaction accessible alternatives. Thus it is useful to compare these forms of interaction, particularly for 3D tasks, for which a mouse's limited degrees of freedom might be a hindrance.

Our goal, then, is to compare the use of the mouse and of free-hand, bimanual gestures in a specific major 3D interaction task: virtual object manipulation, i.e. to translate, scale and rotate a virtual object in 3D. We wish to isolate object manipulation from its selection and to focus particularly on variables that indicate satisfaction, learnability and memorability.

These three attributes often receive less attention than performance measurements, such as time for task completion, or than presence and immersion in Virtual Reality systems [8], but they can be of decisive importance in certain areas of application, such as entertainment and education [16], since these areas have certain usage characteristics in common: in most cases, users engage in either activity, playing or studying, voluntarily, without such a drive for efficiency, and they keep performing it for a period of time which is also voluntarily chosen. They also often spend only a rather limited number of hours on each application, game or subject. This usage is quite different from how users interact, for instance, with applications for work, less voluntarily and for much longer periods of time. Given the significant and growing importance of entertainment and education as areas of application for 3D interaction (as well as our experience in these areas), we believe a greater focus on these attributes beyond only traditional performance metrics can be an important contribution.

To pursue this goal, we perform and analyze data from user experiments with VIDA [12], a virtual 3D atlas of anatomy for educational use with a mouse-and-keyboard-based user interface, and adapt Gestures2Go [3], a bimanual gesture recognition and interaction system, to use depth data from Kinect and allow gesture-based interaction in VIDA.

Following this introduction, this document is organized in this manner: Sect. 2 discusses some related work, followed by Sect. 3 which briefly describes the main software systems used in our experiment as well as the techniques designed

---

[1] https://developer.microsoft.com/en-us/windows/kinect/.

and implement for both mouse- and gesture-based interaction; Sect. 4 details our experimental procedure, the results of which are presented and discussed in Sect. 5 which in turn paves the way for our conclusions in the final section.

2 Related Work

As discussed above, comparisons between interaction techniques taking advantage of conventional computer mice or similar devices and image-based gesture recognition are infrequent in literature, despite the availability of these devices. This is especially valid when applied to truly 3D interactions (and in particular object manipulation) and to evaluating learnability, memorability and subjective user satisfaction. Instead, comparisons only between different 3D interaction techniques or devices and with a focus on performance metrics are more frequent. While a systematic review of all such literature is outside the scope of this paper, we briefly discuss examples that are hopefully representative and help position our work within this context.

Poupyrev and Ichikawa [13], for instance, compare virtual hand techniques and the Go-Go technique for selecting and repositioning objects at differing distances from the user in a virtual environment and use task completion time as their primary measure of performance. Ha and Woo [6] present a formal evaluation process based on a 3D extension of Fitts' law and use it to compare different techniques for tangible interaction, using a cup, a paddle or a cube. Rodrigues et al. [15] compare the use of a wireless dataglove and a 3D mouse to interact with a virtual touch screen for WIMP style interaction in immersive 3D applications.

One example of work that actually includes mouse and keyboard along with gesture-based interaction and compares the two is presented by Reifinger et al. [14], which focuses on the translation and rotation of virtual objects in 3D augmented environments and compare the use of mouse and keyboard, tangible interactions and free-hand gestures with the user seeing his hand inserted in the virtual environments. Fifteen participants were introduced to the environment and had five minutes to explore each technique before being assigned tasks involving translation and rotations, separately or together. Experiments measured task execution times and also presented the participants with a questionnaire evaluating immersion, intuitiveness, mental and physical workload for each technique. Their results showed that, for all tasks, gesture recognition provided the most immersive and intuitive interaction with the lowest mental workload, but demanded the highest physical workload. On average all tasks, but particularly those combining translation and rotation, were performed with gestures in considerably less time than with their tangible device and also faster than when using mouse and keyboard.

Wang et al. [18] show another such example: a system that tracks the positions of both hands, without any gloves or markers, so the user can easily transition from working with mouse and keyboard to using gestures. Direct hand manipulation and a pinching gesture are used for six degrees of freedom translation and rotation of virtual objects and of the scene camera but mouse and keyboard are still used for other tasks. Movements with a single hand are mapped to translations while bimanual manipulation becomes rotations. The authors focus on performance metrics and report that, when a user who is an expert both in a traditional CAD interface and in their hybrid system, they observed time savings of up to 40% in task resolution using their gesture-based technique, mostly deriving from significantly fewer modal transitions between selecting objects and adjusting the camera.

Benavides et al. [2] discuss another bimanual technique, this time for volumetric selection, which they also show is a challenging task. The technique also involves simple object manipulation and was implemented using a head-mounted stereoscopic display and a Leap Motion sensor[2]. Their experiments indicate this technique has high learnability, with users saying they "had intuition with the movements", and high usability but did not compare their technique with other alternatives (but the authors plan to do so in future work), either with mouse and keyboard or with other devices.

In the context of education, Vrellis et al. [17] compare mouse and keyboard with gesture-based interaction using a Kinect sensor for 3D object selection and manipulation. Their manipulation, however, was limited to object translation, because a pilot study showed that including rotation made the task too difficult for their target users. In their experiments with thirty two primary school students they found that student engagement and motivation was increased when using the gesture-based interface, perhaps in part due to the novelty factor, even though, for the simple task in their experiment, that interface was found to be less easy to use than mouse and keyboard interaction, which they believe might be caused, in great measure, by sensor limitations.

Moustakas et al. [10] propose a system combining a dataglove with haptic feedback, a virtual hand representation and stereoscopic display for another application in education: a learning environment for geometry teaching. They evaluate it in experiments with secondary school students performing two relatively simple tasks in 3D and show that interaction with their system was considered highly satisfactory by users and capable of providing a more efficient learning approach, but the paper does not mention any comparison with a mouse and keyboard interface, even though it was present in the experimental setup, or aspects of interface learnability and memorability.

Despite mouse and keyboard interfaces being more than adequate and most often quite familiar for most 2D tasks, they are sometimes compared to gesture based interfaces even for these 2D tasks in certain particular contexts. Farhadi-Niaki et al. [5], for instance, explore traditional 2D desktop tasks such as moving a cursor, selecting icons or windows, resizing or closing windows and running programs, both in desktop and in large screen displays. In a study with twenty participants, they show that even though, for desktop displays, gestures are slower, more fatiguing, less easy and no more pleasant to use than a mouse, for large

---

[2] https://www.ultraleap.com/product/leap-motion-controller/.

screen displays they were considered superior, more natural and pleasing than using a mouse (although still more fatiguing as well). Juhnke et al. [7] propose an experiment to compare gestures captured with the Kinect and a traditional mouse and keyboard interface to adjust tissue densities in 3D medical images. While 3D medical image manipulation is indeed a 3D task (which is why we use an educational anatomy atlas in our experiment), this particular aspect of it, adjusting density involves manipulation in only one dimension, and all other manipulation functions are disabled in their proposed experiment. Still in the medical imaging field, Wipfli et al. [19] investigate 2D image manipulation (panning, zooming and clipping) using mouse, free hand gestures or voice commands to another person because, in the sterile conditions of an operating room, manipulating interaction devices brings complications. In an experiment with thirty users experienced with this particular 2D image manipulation, if using mouse interaction was feasible, it was more efficient and preferred by users, but using gestures was preferred to commands to another person. Once again, mouse-based techniques for 2D tasks being found superior, particularly with experienced users, comes as no surprise.

3   VIDA, Gesture Recognition and Interaction Techniques

As discussed before, we chose an educational interactive virtual atlas of anatomy, VIDA [12], to use in our experiment. As an educational tool it fits well with our goal of prioritizing learnability, memorability and satisfaction, which are often decisive for adoption and use in areas such as education and entertainment [16] and, furthermore, it is an application where isolated 3D object manipulation, without even need for selection, is actually a rather meaningful form of interaction, so students can explore and familiarize with the shown 3D anatomical structures from different angles, positions and levels of detail. VIDA was designed in a collaboration between engineers and teachers of medicine to serve both in classroom or distance learning as an alternative to the two most common ways to learn the subject. Currently, it is either learned from corpses, which are limited and present certain logistic limitations, or from static 2D images which cannot be manipulated or viewed tridimensionally, hindering the comprehension of such complex 3D structures. Another limitation of both approaches is that neither can show structures functioning dynamically, something that can only be observed in vivo during procedures by more experienced professionals, an alternative with even more logistic complications. VIDA, however, combines augmented reality by allowing the stereoscopic visualization of anatomic structures within the study environment and between user hands, animations to show their inner workings, 3D manipulation to further facilitate the comprehension of these 3D structures and dynamic behaviors and the use of gestures to make this manipulation as natural as possible, theoretically and according to the authors, freeing cognitive resources from the interaction to be employed in the learning process. shows that even for simple memorization tasks in a limited time, students who used VIDA had significantly better performances than those who only used 2D images, approximately 17% better on average. Figure 1 shows a simple visualization in VIDA of a model of the bones in the female pelvic region, without stereoscopy, textures or tags naming the structure's features.

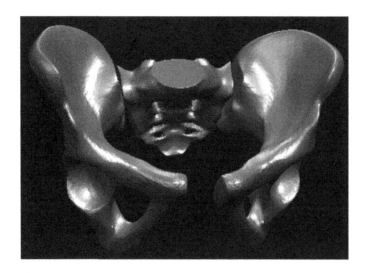

Fig. 1. Simplest visualization of an anatomical structure in VIDA

Using the mouse in VIDA, translations on the viewing plane are performed by dragging the mouse with the right button pressed (in this application, translations are actually less common than rotations, thus the choice of the right mouse button for them). Dragging with the left button pressed causes one of the two most used rotations, around the vertical axis with horizontal mouse movements and around the horizontal axis when moving vertically. Finally, the middle mouse button is used to zoom in and out by dragging vertically and dragging horizontally for the least common rotation, around the axis pointing out perpendicular to the viewing plane. With the exception of translations, the system treats diagonal mouse movements only as a horizontal or vertical, choosing the component with greater magnitude. VIDA also imposes a limitation on the maximum speed of all these transformations.

While VIDA also offers the option of manipulating objects using gestures (and that is actually an important feature in its design), its implementation at the time of the experiment, using optical flow, was somewhat limited, bidimensional, and not sufficiently robust for the experiments we wished to perform. So instead we decided to take advantage of Kinect's depth sensing for more robust segmentation and tracking of 3D movements. We did not wish to hardcode the gesture-based interface within VIDA and recompile it, however. To that end, we took advantage of the modular architecture in Gestures2Go [3] and adapted it. Gestures2Go is a system for 3D interaction based on hand gestures which are recognized using computer vision. Its main contribution is a model that defines and recognizes gestures, with one or both hands, based on certain components (initial and final hand poses, initial location relative to the user, hand movements and orientations) so that the recognition of only a few of each of these components wields thousands of recognizable gesture combinations, allowing interaction designers to pick those that make most sense to associate with each action within the user interface. The system has a modular architecture shown in Fig. 2 which simplified the implementation of the adaptations we made and the integration with VIDA. First we simply replaced the image capture and segmentation modules with new versions for the Kinect, added depth as an additional gesture parameter extracted during the analysis and extended Desc2Input for integration with VIDA. Desc2Input is a module that receives descriptions and parameters, whether from Gestures2Go or from any other source (allowing the use of other modes of interaction), and translates them as inputs to an application. In this particular case, it was extended to respond to descriptions of gestures with one or both hands by generating the same mouse events used to manipulate objects in VIDA. Using Desc2Input in this way we did not need to modify any code in VIDA to have it respond to the 3D gestures we chose for object manipulation and acquired with Kinect.

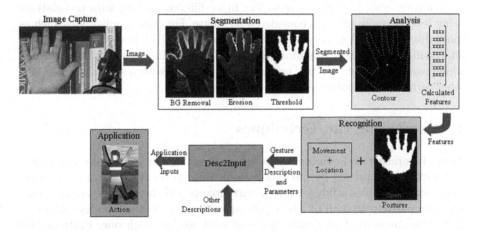

Fig. 2. Gestures2Go modules

When designing our gesture-based interaction techniques for virtual object manipulation, we elected first to use a closed hand pose, as if the users were grabbing the virtual object, to indicate their intent to manipulate it. In this way users can move their hands freely to engage in any number of other actions without interfering with the manipulation. This also includes the ability to open hands, move them to another position, close them again and continue the manipulation, allowing movements with higher amplitude, much in the same way as when keeping a button in a 2D mouse pressed but lifting the mouse from its surface to return to another position and continue the movement. We mapped movements with a single hand as translations. At first we intended this to include translations in depth, but during pilot studies we realized that, for this application, users were apparently more comfortable with restricting translations to the viewing plane and using the concept of zooming in and out instead of translation along the Z axis. We ended up mapping zooming in and out to bimanual gestures, bringing the closed hands together or pulling them apart, respectively, as if "squeezing" or "stretching" the object. Rotation around the Y axis is performed by "grabbing" the object by the sides and pulling one arm towards the body while extending the other away from it. The same movement works around the X axis, but the user must grab the object from above and below. To rotate the object around the Z axis one must also grab it by its sides, and then move one arm up and the other down, as if turning a steering wheel.

Even though the gestural interface is built upon the mouse interface, simply translating manipulation gestures as mouse events, it does not have the same limitation of only allowing one movement at a time. These mouse events are generated at a frequency of at least 15 Hz, which is sufficient to allow rotations around two or all three axes along with changes in scale all at the same time. Translation, however, cannot happen along with the other transformations, since we implemented it using the only gesture with a single hand. Since in VIDA users mostly wish to explore the object from different angles, with translations being less common, this was considered adequate. For other applications such as those discussed by Wang et al. [18] or Reifinger et al. [14], however, it should be interesting to eliminate this limitation, either by adding bimanual translation, which would be rather simple, or by adding versions with a single hand for the other forms of manipulation.

4   Comparing the Techniques

After elaborating and comprehensively documenting our experimental protocol and having it approved by our institution's human research ethics committee, we performed a pilot study with four participants and then the experiment with nineteen participants, all of whom agreed with the Free and Informed Consent (FIC) document that was presented and explained to each one. Participation was completely voluntary, anonymous and non-remunerated.

4.1   Pilot Study

Four participants (2 experienced, 1 female) went through a pilot study to help detect issues with our protocol and to estimate the average amount of time required for each experimental session. This study pointed out several improvements that were implemented in a revised experimental protocol. We already discussed how we replaced translation along the Z axis with zooming in and out and changed the associated gestures accordingly. Another important discovery was that, with the gestures we had designed for the manipulation task, users would naturally open their hands or close them into fists in several different orientations and this presented a challenge that Gestures2Go combined with Kinect was not then able to overcome robustly. Because this change in hand pose was so important for the interaction, and the only one we would use, we disabled its automatic detection and, instead, made use of Wizard of Oz experimentation and implemented a way so that a human operator could indicate to the system, using a keyboard, whether one hand, both or none were closed. Hand positions are still tracked in 3D automatically by the system. This avoided the issue of a temporary technological hindrance distorting the results about the interaction techniques. We later implemented a more robust algorithm using the same device to detect whether hands are open or not regardless of their orientation. We also determined in this phase that the stereoscopic 3D visualization offered by VIDA (which is an important part of its design and supports several devices) was not only mostly unnecessary to our experiments but also added considerable complications and additional noise to its results. First, it works best with a previous step of calibration for each user that would demand extra time in each session. Participants were distracted from the manipulation either by a well done stereoscopic display or by a poor one. Finally, some participants quickly developed visual fatigue and discomfort when we used stereoscopy. We then decided to remove stereoscopic visualization from our protocol and show the virtual object directly on a large computer monitor. Finally, due to the reduced time we determined we would have in our experimental sessions for training each participant, we decided to choose relatively simple tasks for them to perform, attempting to reduce the gap that, without such training, we realized would remain significant between users less or more experienced with 3D object manipulation or in interacting with the Kinect sensor.

4.2   Summarized Experimental Procedure

After participants, individually in each experimental session, have the opportunity to read the FIC document, have it explained verbally and ask questions about it, if they agree to participate and sign the document, they fill out a quick profile form with information relevant to the experiment. We then briefly explain and demonstrate one manipulation technique (using either mouse or gestures, chosen randomly), tell them which tasks they will have to perform and give them 5 to 10 min to engage freely with the system using that technique. We then proceed with the test itself, which consists of five tasks. Before each task begins, the object is reset to its initial position in the center of the screen. The tasks are:

1. Translation on the viewing plane: the user is asked to move the object so it touches the upper left corner of the screen, then the lower right corner and then to bring it back to the center of the screen.
2. Scaling: the user must zoom in until the object has its maximum size inside the screen without escaping its boundaries, zoom out until it has approximately half its initial dimensions and then zoom in again to reach the initial size.

3. Rotation around the X axis: the object must be rotated approximately 90° counter-clockwise, then 180° clockwise and finally 90° counter-clockwise again to return to its initial position.
4. Rotation around the Y axis and
5. Rotation around the Z axis: same procedure as around the X axis.

Participants do not need to memorize these tasks and their order. After finishing one, they are reminded of the next one even though they were initially shown all five. Rotations are not described in terms of their axis, either. Instead, they are exemplified by rotating a real object, using only one hand to avoid giving any clues about how to do it with gestures. Once the participant finishes all tasks with one technique (either mouse or gestures), they answer a questionnaire about that experience and the entire process starts again for the remaining technique, from explanation and demonstration to exploration, task execution and answering the questionnaire.

Tasks are identical for both techniques. Even though our gestural interface is capable of performing multiple transformations in response to a single gesture while the mouse interface is not, and even though this is often seen as an advantage of gesture-based interaction [14], we decided to keep the tasks simple and more comparable instead of giving gesture-based interaction this advantage it usually would have.

4.3   Metrics and Questionnaires

Like one of the experiments we discussed in Sect. 2 [15], ours can be classified as a comparison of alternative designs [1] and we also record quantitative and qualitative data, including self-reported metrics, errors or success in execution, any issues arisen during the experiments, and task completion times (despite this not being the focus in this study). Self-reported metrics are very important for us as metrics of satisfaction and ease to learn and remember. To that end, we elaborated short questionnaires using semantic differential scales to measure these attributes and to determine participant profiles (age, gender, profession, and 3 point scales to measure how frequently they interact with each of the three technologies most significant for this experiment: mouse, gesture and 3D interaction, from never or almost never, to sometimes or almost always). To evaluate satisfaction and ease of learning and remembering, we used 5 point scales, going from very unsatisfied at 1 to very satisfied at 5 and from very hard at 1 to very easy at 5. For each of three tasks (translation, scaling and rotations, which are grouped together in the questionnaire) and for each technique (based on mouse or gestures), users choose values in these scales to answer how satisfactory it was to perform the task and how easy it was to learn and remember all inputs and avoid confusing them with each other. There is also a space reserved in the questionnaire allowing users to write any qualitative observations they wish. Another metric we use to indirectly gauge ease of learning and remembering is what we called retention errors. Given our simple tasks, there were not many errors users could commit, so what we recorded as errors are more related to faulty learning or an inability to recall the inputs required in each technique to perform a task, such as using the wrong command, forgetting to hold down the mouse button or to close a hand, manipulating the object in the opposite way than desired (for instance reducing its dimensions when they should be increased) or being unable to remember which command to use and asking to be reminded of it.

4.4   Participants

In this particular experiment, we did not wish to evaluate VIDA's intended use as an aid in learning anatomy but only to compare the two interaction techniques described earlier. So since previous knowledge of or interest in anatomy was not necessary, we decided, for convenience, to recruit participants mostly from undergraduate students in our Information Systems program, many of which already held jobs in the area. Some of their family members and program faculty added a slightly wider spread of age and experience with the relevant technology. No participants from the pilot study were included in the main experiment.

5   Results and Discussion

Out of our 19 participants, 6 of them were female, ages ranged from 19 to 56 years old and averaged exactly 24. Figure 3 shows how often participants use mouse, gesture and 3D interfaces. 18 of the 19 participants were very familiar with the mouse, using it frequently or always, and the remaining one uses it sometimes, while only 1 participant used gesture-based interaction frequently and 11 never or almost never used it. 3D interaction had a less skewed spread of participants, with 8 almost never using it, 6 using it sometimes and 5 frequently.

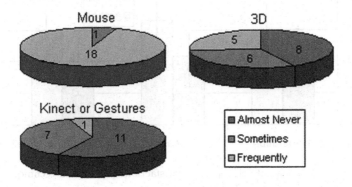

Fig. 3. Frequency of use among participants

All result distributions obtained for our metrics were checked for normality using Kolmogorov-Smirnov tests. Even with $\alpha = 0.1$ the evidence was insufficient to deny the normality of all distributions of quantitative questionnaire answers.

Retention errors were somewhat unusual and certainly were not distributed normally. For many tasks, the normality of the distribution of completion times could not be denied with $\alpha = 0.1$, but some distributions were more skewed to one extreme or the other and could only be taken as normal if $\alpha = 0.05$ (then again this was not our focus). Because of that, and because all distributions have the same number of samples (19), we used paired t-tests without testing for equal variance to calculate the probability of the averages being equal in the population for mouse interaction and for gesture interaction (which were independent, thanks in part to the randomized order in which the techniques were presented). These are the values of p discussed below and we adopted a significance level $\alpha = 0.05$ to test this hypothesis of difference between distributions.

Figure 4 shows the average values (as bars) and standard deviations (as error bars) for the answers to the questionnaires regarding subjective satisfaction for the three tasks. Satisfaction with gestures was significantly greater than that with mouse interaction for all tasks. Scaling the object was the preferred task for both mouse and gestures, but the difference was more marked with gestures. Indeed, several participants commented verbally, after the end of their experiment, that they thought "squeezing and stretching" the object with their hands to zoom in and out was the most memorable and fun task of all. Rotations in 3D were the least favorite task, which is no surprise considering that they are often cited as the most difficult aspect of 3D manipulation and one of the motivations to use more natural techniques. The fact that a single question encompassed three tasks might also have some influence in the answer. What is surprising, however, is how little difference there was between satisfaction with rotation and translation when using gestures.

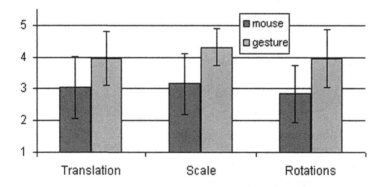

Fig. 4. Participant self-reported satisfaction by task and technique

Figure 5 shows the mean values and standard deviations for the answers to the questionnaires regarding ease to learn and remember how to use the interface for our three tasks. Once again gestures were considered easier to learn and remember for all tasks. Once again and for the same reasons discussed above, it is no surprise that rotations were considered the most difficult tasks to learn and remember. For the rotations, with our chosen α, we cannot deny the hypothesis that mouse and gestures have the same mean in the population, there is a 6% probability of that being true. We cannot be sure of the reason for this or for the large deviation in the distribution of answers for mouse rotations, but some qualitative user answers and observation hint at a hypothesis regarding our rotation gestures. These were the only gestures in which users had to move their arms back and forward along the Z axis and, particularly for the rotation around the X axis with hands grabbing the object from above and below, this was reported by many users as the most difficult gesture to execute. One user also reported in his qualitative comments that he imagined the virtual objects between his or her hands (which is as we intended) and wanted to naturally move the hands circularly around the object, but noticed that the implementation favored more linear movements. It really does, due to the equations we used to map the 3D bimanual movements into linear mouse movements. So we believe that our gesture-based technique for 3D rotations was indeed nearly as difficult to learn as VIDA's mouse-based technique, albeit for different reasons, physical rather than cognitive. This also appears to agree with the observations about cognitive and physical load of gestures reported in previous work [14].

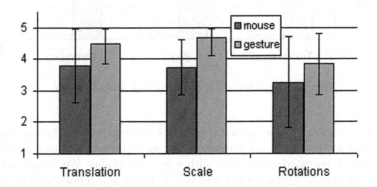

Fig. 5. Participant self-reported ease to learn and remember by task and technique

Figure 6 shows the percentage of retention errors for mouse and gestures. This percentage is calculated as the ratio between the sum of retention errors incurred by all participants and the total number of successful and failed attempts, which in turn is nothing but the total number of participants, since all eventually had success in all tasks, plus the number of errors for failed attempts. This figure shows perhaps the most impressive (and somewhat unexpected) result of our experiments. For all 19 participants completing all 5 tests, we did not witness a single retention error when using gestures. We did notice what we believe were users momentarily forgetting what gesture to use, for instance when, after being told what task they should accomplish (but not reminded about how to go about it), they would hesitate and sometimes even look at their hands or move them slightly while thinking, before closing them to start the manipulation.

But eventually, before making any mistakes or asking for assistance, they could always figure out which gesture to use to achieve their desired action, and in the correct orientation, regardless of their previous experience or lack thereof with 3D or gestural interaction. We believe this is a very strong indicator of the cognitive ease to learn and remember this sort of gesture-based 3D manipulation technique (or to figure it out when forgotten) for all tasks we evaluated. With VIDA's mouse-based technique, however, errors varied between approximately 21% and 24%, proving the technique was confusing for users with as little training or experience with the technique as our participants.

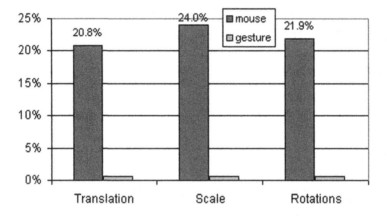

Fig. 6. Logged retention errors by task and technique

Using Pearson's product-moment correlation coefficient, we found only negligible correlation between participants previous experience and most other variables we have discussed up to now, with a few exceptions. We found moderate positive correlations (between 0.4 and 0.5) between self-reported ease to learn rotations using gestures and previous experience with both 3D and gestures, and also between satisfaction with this same task and previous experience with gestures. This becomes more significant when we recall that rotations were the tasks reported as most difficult to learn and remember and least satisfactory to perform and leads us to believe that, as the experience of users with both gesture-based interfaces and 3D interaction in general increases, we may find an even greater advantage to the use of gestures for these difficult tasks. It also goes somewhat against the idea that a large portion of user satisfaction with gestures is due to their novelty and thus should decrease with increasing experience. Then again, these were not strong correlations and we had a single user that was very experienced with gestures, so our evidence for these speculations is not strong. But they do suggest interesting future experiments to try to prove or disprove them. Given the fact that only one of our participants was not very experienced in the use of computer mice, it comes as no surprise that we could not find significant correlations between that variable and any others. But it is curious that, when using VIDA's mouse-based technique, we could find no correlation between experience with 3D interaction and any other variables either, unlike what happened between gestures and rotations. This might suggest that, for 3D manipulation, even for users experienced with using a mouse, its use within the technique, and not the user's previous experience with 3D interaction, was the dominant factor in their satisfaction and ease to learn and remember.

Finally, Fig. 7 shows the mean values of completion times, in seconds, for all tasks, not grouping rotations together for once. These times were measured from the moment when users started the manipulation (by clicking or closing their hand), using the correct command to do it, to the moment when the task was completed. Scaling was not only the preferred task but also the fastest to perform. Given that we had calibrated the system to use ample gestures and that we did not explore one of the main advantages of gestures regarding execution times, that it is easier to perform several transformations at once using them, we expected gestures to show greater execution times than mouse. This was indeed true for three tasks, scaling and rotating around X and Y, which showed an advantage between 1.1 s and 1.9 s or 15% and 20% for mouse interaction, always with $p < 0.05$ (which also came as somewhat of a surprise). For translation using only one hand, however, gestures were significantly faster than using a mouse (31% faster, $p < 0.05$). Results for rotation around Z are interesting. Using a mouse it took slightly longer on average, but with nearly identical means and distributions. The other two rotations, around X and Y, were considered by users the most difficult to perform, physically, because they demanded moving the arms back and forward along the Z axis (in the future we will try to avoid this). Without facing the same problem, rotations around Z were completed as quickly with gestures as with a mouse.

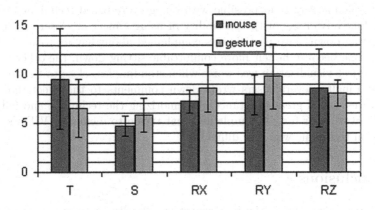

Fig. 7. Logged task completion times (in seconds) by task and technique

We took note of a couple of issues during the experiments but believe they had only a mild influence in our results, if any. The first was that, sometimes (6 times in the entire experiment, in fact), VIDA's display would lock up for a small but noticeable period of time, which ended up increasing completion time for some tasks. This problem affected both mouse and gestures sporadically. The second is that some users would repeat the same movement several times, either because they enjoyed it or because they wanted to get the object at just the right position, which was rather subjective and difficult to ascertain, since only that single object was shown on the screen. This happened only 4 times, but always with gestures.

Finally, some of the qualitative comments from participants also bring up interesting points. Two of them complained that VIDA's upper limit for trans-formation speeds was particularly annoying when using gestures but did not make the same comment regarding mouse interaction. Given the greater phys-ical effort involved in the use of gestures, it is not a great surprise that being forced to act slower than one would like causes greater annoyance in this case. We believe this effort is the same reason why two other participants complained that moving the arms was "harder" than moving the mouse (even though one said closing the hand to "grab" was much better than clicking a mouse button) and one reported being hindered in some of the gestural manipulations by a shoul-der which had been broken in the past. Another participant criticized our use of ample gestures. It is interesting to notice that, except for the rotation around X, all gestures could have been performed while following advice to create more ergonomic gestural interfaces [11]: keeping elbows down and close to the body. We, however, calibrated the system favoring precision over speed, in a way that, without using ample gestures with arms further away from the body, tasks would require more repeated movements, grabbing and releasing the object more often. We also always demonstrated gestures with arms well extended when explaining the technique to participants, inducing them to do the same. It is interesting to notice that, with just these two actions, we induced all 19 users to interact in a less ergonomic way than possible with our gesture-based technique. We also did not take advantage of the possibility of using Kinect at closer distances or while sitting down. Two participants complained about having to stand to use gestures, one because he felt more comfortable sitting down, the other because he said object visualization was worse when standing less close to the computer monitor. Finally, several users wrote down comments to the effect that using the gestures was of great assistance in memorizing the technique and felt more natural, intuitive or fun, or complained that trying to memorize VIDA's mouse interaction technique was very difficult.

6   Conclusions

To our knowledge, this is the first report specifically comparing gesture-based and mouse-based interaction for virtual object manipulation in 3D with a focus in satisfaction, learnability and memorability rather than mostly or only in met-rics of performance such as task completion time. The gesture-based technique we designed and implemented for this task, as well as the design of our experi-ment, had several points unfavorable to gestures. We forgot to ask participants about their handedness and, although we could have easily implemented functionality to allow the use of their dominant hand for translations, we did not and instead forced all to use the right hand (when later we realized that, we were surprised that no participants complained about it, even though we did observe a few that were left-handed). Our implementation using the Kinect sensor forced participants to use gestures only while standing, although that should not have been a technical necessity, and to stand further away from our display than needed. Our gesture system calibration for precision over speed and our technique demonstrations to participants induced them to use ample gestures which were less ergonomic. VIDA's upper limit for transformation speeds, which is not at all a necessary component for either technique, was perceived more negatively when using gestures than with a mouse. Users imagined virtual objects between their hands and wanted to naturally move them circularly around the object, but our implementation favored more linear gestures because of the equations we used to map 3D bimanual movements into linear mouse movements. Finally, our experimental tasks did not allow gestures to benefit from one of their greatest advantages in 3D manipulation, the ability to combine several transformations in one gesture with far more ease than with most mouse-based techniques. Clearly, there are several improvements we can strive for in future works to design and implement a gesture-based interaction technique with much greater usability, not to mention new experiments we could design to play up to gestural interaction strengths. And yet, despite all these disadvantages imposed to the gesture-based interaction, we believe our greatest contribution with this work is to show unequivocally that there is indeed a statistically significant difference between the use gestures and mouse for 3D manipulation regarding user satisfaction and interface learnability and memorability, and that for all subtasks of manipulation this difference clearly favors the use of gestures, at least with the techniques we evaluated and most likely with similar alternatives. Our log of retention errors constitutes rather impressive evidence for this advantage. With mouse-based interaction, these errors, nearly always derived from failures in learning or remembering a technique correctly, varied between approximately 21% and 24% of all interactions, but for all 19 participants completing all 5 tests, we did not witness a single retention error when using gestures. While we suspect some participants may indeed have forgotten which gesture to use in certain tasks, they could always quickly remember or figure them out again on their own, without asking for assistance or first making any mistakes. Our experiments also pointed out several ways in which we can improve our gesture-based interaction techniques. Finally, while at first we believed that part of the advantage of using gestures was in its novelty and should fade with time, as users became more experienced with them, the correlations between previous participant experience and the rest of the questionnaire gives some evidence to the contrary, showing positive correlations between experience with gestures and both satisfaction and ease to learn and remember, indicating that as users become more experienced in the use of gestures, they might come to be more satisfied with them, not less so.

References

1. Albert, W., Tullis, T.: Measuring the User Experience: Collecting, Analyzing, and Presenting Usability Metrics. Newnes, Oxford (2013)
2. Benavides, A., Khadka, R., Banic, A.: Physically-based bimanual volumetric selection for immersive visualizations. In: Chen, J.Y.C., Fragomeni, G. (eds.) HCII 2019. LNCS, vol. 11574, pp. 183–195. Springer, Cham (2019). https://doi.org/10.1007/978-3-030-21607-8_14
3. Bernardes, J., Nakamura, R., Tori, R.: Comprehensive model and image-based recognition of hand gestures for interaction in 3D environments. Int. J. Virtual Reality **10**(4), 11–23 (2011). https://doi.org/10.20870/IJVR.2011.10.4.2825. https://ijvr.eu/article/view/2825
4. Bolt, R.A.: "Put-that-there": voice and gesture at the graphics interface. SIGGRAPH Comput. Graph. **14**(3), 262–270 (1980). https://doi.org/10.1145/965105.807503
5. Farhadi-Niaki, F., GhasemAghaei, R., Arya, A.: Empirical study of a vision-based depth-sensitive human-computer interaction system. In: Proceedings of the 10th Asia Pacific Conference on Computer Human Interaction, pp. 101–108 (2012)
6. Ha, T., Woo, W.: An empirical evaluation of virtual hand techniques for 3D object manipulation in a tangible augmented reality environment. In: 2010 IEEE Symposium on 3D User Interfaces (3DUI), pp. 91–98. IEEE (2010)
7. Juhnke, B., Berron, M., Philip, A., Williams, J., Holub, J., Winer, E.: Comparing the microsoft kinect to a traditional mouse for adjusting the viewed tissue densities of three-dimensional anatomical structures. In: Medical Imaging 2013: Image Perception, Observer Performance, and Technology Assessment, vol. 8673, p. 86731M. International Society for Optics and Photonics (2013)
8. Kim, Y.M., Rhiu, I., Yun, M.H.: A systematic review of a virtual reality system from the perspective of user experience. Int. J. Hum.-Comput. Interact. 1–18 (2019). https://doi.org/10.1080/10447318.2019.1699746
9. LaViola Jr., J.J., Kruijff, E., McMahan, R.P., Bowman, D., Poupyrev, I.P.: 3D User Interfaces: Theory and Practice. Addison-Wesley Professional, Boston (2017)
10. Moustakas, K., Nikolakis, G., Tzovaras, D., Strintzis, M.G.: A geometry education haptic VR application based on a new virtual hand representation. In: 2005 IEEE Proceedings, VR 2005, Virtual Reality, pp. 249–252. IEEE (2005)
11. Nielsen, M., Störring, M., Moeslund, T.B., Granum, E.: A procedure for developing intuitive and ergonomic gesture interfaces for HCI. In: Camurri, A., Volpe, G. (eds.) GW 2003. LNCS (LNAI), vol. 2915, pp. 409–420. Springer, Heidelberg (2004). https://doi.org/10.1007/978-3-540-24598-8_38
12. dos Santos Nunes, E.P, Nunes, F.L.S., Roque, L.G.: Feasibility analysis of an assessment model of knowledge acquisition in virtual environments: a case study using a three-dimensional atlas of anatomy. In: Proceedings of the 19th Americas Conference on Information Systems - AMCIS 2013, Chicago, USA (2013)
13. Poupyrev, I., Ichikawa, T.: Manipulating objects in virtual worlds: categorization and empirical evaluation of interaction techniques. J. Vis. Lang. Comput. **10**(1), 19–35 (1999)
14. Reifinger, S., Laquai, F., Rigoll, G.: Translation and rotation of virtual objects in augmented reality: a comparison of interaction devices. In: 2008 IEEE International Conference on Systems, Man and Cybernetics, pp. 2448–2453. IEEE (2008)
15. Rodrigues, P.G., Raposo, A.B., Soares, L.P.: A virtual touch interaction device for immersive applications. Int. J. Virtual Reality **10**(4), 1–10 (2011)

16. Shneiderman, B., et al.: Designing the User Interface: Strategies for Effective Human-Computer Interaction. Pearson, Essex (2016)
17. Vrellis, I., Moutsioulis, A., Mikropoulos, T.A.: Primary school students' attitude towards gesture based interaction: a comparison between microsoft kinect and mouse. In: 2014 IEEE 14th International Conference on Advanced Learning Technologies, pp. 678–682. IEEE (2014)
18. Wang, R., Paris, S., Popović, J.: 6D hands: markerless hand-tracking for computer aided design. In: Proceedings of the 24th Annual ACM Symposium on User Interface Software and Technology, pp. 549–558 (2011)
19. Wipfli, R., Dubois-Ferriere, V., Budry, S., Hoffmeyer, P., Lovis, C.: Gesture-controlled image management for operating room: a randomized crossover study to compare interaction using gestures, mouse, and third person relaying. PLoS ONE **11**(4) (2016)
20. Zimmerman, T.G., Lanier, J., Blanchard, C., Bryson, S., Harvill, Y.: A hand gesture interface device. ACM SIGCHI Bull. **18**(4), 189–192 (1986)

Research on Gesture Interaction Design for Home Control Intelligent Terminals

Bin Jiang, Xuewei Wang$^{(\boxtimes)}$, and Yue Wu$^{(\boxtimes)}$

School of Design Art and Media, Nanjing University of Science and Technology, Nanjing, Jiangsu, People's Republic of China
624908221@qq.com, 631603555@qq.com

Abstract. With the development of artificial intelligence, more and more attention has been paid to ho me intelligent terminal products. Compared with the common products, the family control intelligent terminal products are more complex in functional architecture and hierarchy, and the existing interactive gestures can not meet the functional requirements. The aim of this paper is to design a new interaction gesture for home control intelligent terminal. Analyzes the need and feasibility of using gesture interaction in this type of product and explores several factors that affect the accuracy of gesture interaction. We obtained user needs for product functions through questionnaire surveys, and then proposed four principles for gesture design for smart home products based on home control and designed a set of interactive gestures based on this criterion. Finally, we use Kinect V2 to perform gesture recognition experiments and issue a Likert scale questionnaire to obtain users' subjective experience. The recognition rate of the gesture system is more than 80%, and it has good recognition ability. 0.5 m–4.5 m is the best recognition area. When the distance increases, the accuracy will decrease. However, due to the limitation of family space, there are few areas over 4.5 m. The subjective scores of users are over 9 points, indicating that the gesture system of the device has good recognition and user experience.

Keywords: Gesture interaction · Interaction design · Intelligent terminals · Usability · Kinect V2

1 Introduction

With the continuous progress of science and technology, artificial intelligence has made great progress in recent years. Artificial intelligence has been widely used in many areas of our life: face recognition, intelligent wearable devices, speech recognition, deep learning, intelligent robots and so on. Gesture interaction, as an important research area of artificial intelligence, has been applied in VR, somatic games, intelligent wearable devices and interface interaction of automobile, such as Kinect V2, which accomplishes specific tasks by identifying the user's actions [1]. Compared with the traditional use of game handle, the use of gesture interaction can greatly enhance the user's interactivity, let the user have the feeling of immersive experience, and improve the user's use experience (Fig. 1).

© Springer Nature Switzerland AG 2020
M. Kurosu (Ed.): HCII 2020, LNCS 12182, pp. 38–56, 2020.
https://doi.org/10.1007/978-3-030-49062-1_3

Fig. 1. Kinect V2 somatic device

Home control intelligent terminals have been available for a long time. As an important part of the smart home [2], most of these products use multi-channel interaction methods such as hardware interaction, interface interaction, voice interaction, to perform real-time monitoring and data sharing of various smart devices in the home environment. It is also responsible for the management and control of home smart devices, and completes tasks assigned by users. Taking Changhong's home intelligent terminal product as an example, the product classifies the commonly used devices in home life: light management, surveillance camera, device control, safety protection, and centralized management. Users can operate most functions in the home environment as long as they use the product, which provides great convenience for users (Fig. 2).

Fig. 2. Changhong home intelligent terminal products

In the family environment, smart terminal products mainly use APP to interact with the machine interface [3], and some of them use intelligent voice interaction. There are few such products that use gesture interaction. However, gesture interaction, which is an important development trend of future human-computer interaction, combined with smart terminal products will bring a completely new interactive experience. Although the existing research has some research on the application of gesture interaction in three-dimensional environment, but is limited to simple gesture interaction, use static gestures for interactive operations and have not conducted in-depth research on the use of gestures in products with complex functional levels, such as control-type smart terminals (Fig. 3).

We propose a new gesture design method: Giving basic gestures layer by layer, and finally combine basic gestures bound at different levels to form dynamic gestures. And it is applied to home control intelligent terminals to control the turning on and off of the

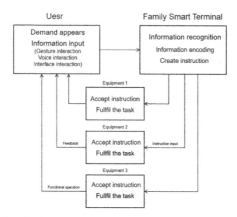

Fig. 3. Home control smart terminal work process

device, so that users can clearly understand the specific meaning of the gestures they make, forming a clear hierarchical concept in the user's mind.

The rest of this paper is structured as follows. Section 3 introduces the existing architecture of home control intelligent terminal products and conducts a hierarchical analysis. Section 4 conducts in-depth design research on gesture interaction of home control smart terminals, analyzes functional requirements, based on the four dimensions of nature, difference, simplicity, and efficiency, a set of interactive gestures was designed according to the architecture level. Sections 5 and 6 conducted experiments on gesture interactions, processed and analyzed the obtained data, and finally introduced our conclusions.

2   Related Works

There are many scholars doing research on gesture interaction. JI, R [4] studied the application of natural interaction in family life, and proposed four natural interaction design strategies for smart homes, including anthropomorphic interaction objects and inclusive operation space, but did not propose specific gesture interaction design solutions.

Wan, H, G [5] studied three-dimensional scene-oriented freehand gesture interaction methods and put forward: user requirements principle, user experience principle, environment limitation principle, and designed the gesture model. Using static gestures to complete the static gesture movement and rotation Responsive action. Although this type of gesture can achieve the expected result very well, but it is only suitable for gesture interaction with simple function commands, and is not suitable for systems with complex functional levels. Wu, H. [6] designed a set of gesture interaction models for watching TV. They collected the common functions and operations in TV, and adopted the translation and rotation of different basic gestures to achieve the corresponding functions. Ntoa, S [7] studied the user experience of using gesture interaction in large screen devices. Ram Pratap Sharma [8] researched the gesture interaction by recognizing the shape and orientation of the hand to generate a static gesture image.

Li, X [9] studied the user experience of gesture interaction and voice interaction in smart TVs and found that the operation of the selection process requires high efficiency, so most users like gesture interaction. It shows that when designing a TV interface for selection and control, gesture interaction should be strengthened, and home control intelligent terminals mainly control different devices, and all perform control operations, which are also applicable to gesture interaction.

Min Li [10] researched the home intelligent interactive terminal system and analyzed the characteristics of smart home. By using a computer, mobile phone, and intelligent interactive terminal to control monitors, Smart Appliances, and using smart switches to control normal appliances, to achieve the purpose of controlling all the equipment in the home.

3   Hierarchical Analysis of Home Control Intelligent Terminal

Home control intelligent terminals need to control a large number of home devices, and have more complex information architecture and functional levels than ordinary products. The first level of architecture needs to be representative, which can summarize the second level. We refer to the existing Changhong's home intelligent terminal architecture, and classify the functional devices commonly used in family life according to the types of devices involved and the nature of their functions [10]. Then divided the first level of the information architecture into 4 subsystem:

1. Lighting system: responsible for switching control and brightness adjustment of all lighting-related equipment in the home environment.
2. Home electrical system: responsible for regulating the switches, functions, etc. of various household devices
3. Door and window system: responsible for the opening and closing of door locks, opening and closing of curtains, opening and closing of windows, etc.
4. Dialing system: Responsible for telephone contact with family members, and is equipped with emergency dialing and other help functions.

The above 4 systems basically cover the functions of the equipment involved in the home. The second level under each system is the control operation of specific equipment, for example, the lighting system includes: kitchen lights, toilet lights, living room lights, etc. switches and brightness control (Fig. 4).

In designing gesture interaction of such complex information systems, we must fully consider factors such as control functions, number of gestures, interaction efficiency, and gesture fluency. Because gesture interaction requires simple and fast implementation, the complex functions of some devices are more sophisticated and require multiple gestures to complete. The increase in gestures will affect the device's recognition burden, increase the user's learning costs and the interactive experience.

There are many devices in family life, but not all of them are used frequently. Many devices may only be turned on once long. If gesture binding is performed on all products, the total number of gestures is increased and users rarely use. This gesture causes a waste of resources; and because some devices are closely related to our lives, they need to be

Fig. 4. Home control intelligent terminal architecture

used frequently. Designing gestures for such devices can effectively help users complete tasks in daily life. Therefore, in the process of designing gestures in this paper, the functions of different devices are screened based on the frequency and importance of use, and gestures are mainly designed for functions with high frequency and importance. For example, in a lighting system, gesture interaction is responsible for controlling the switching of lights in different home areas without the need to control the adjustment of brightness.

4 Research on Gesture Interaction Design for Home Control Intelligent Terminal

4.1 Design Principle of Gesture Interaction for Intelligent Control Terminal

Yang Li's research [11] shows that when dealing with any project related to ergonomics, we should consider the relationship among human, machine and environment, and take health, safety, comfort and efficiency as the starting point of our design [12]. Because recognition efficiency and user interaction experience are affected by gestures, this article considers the following four perspectives when designing gesture interaction:

1. Naturalness: Gesture interaction is the most natural and the most human instinct in all interaction modes. We should focus on the normal interaction habits of people in the design of gesture model [13], so that the gesture is consistent with people's daily behavior process of completing specific matters, and integrate the user's daily behavior into the involved gesture model. It enables users to connect natural gestures

with gesture models to reduce the difficulty of gesture learning and improve their user experience [14]. And the design of gesture should also conform to people's own natural physiological structure, reasonably control the interaction time, reduce the user's long-time hand lifting, and avoid doing some gestures that do not conform to people's physiological structure, such as: wrist bending for a long time; if dynamic gesture is designed, the range of action should be considered reasonably to avoid excessive damage to the user's body and reduce user and family control The fatigue in the interaction process of manufacturing intelligent terminal products.

2. Difference: The latest gesture-based devices have improved the recognition accuracy and effective recognition distance, but when the gesture modeling design is relatively similar, it will still cause system error recognition, increase the number of errors, and seriously affect the user experience. Therefore, designers should pay more attention to the differences between each gesture in the process of gesture model design, and make the designed gesture have a greater differentiation on the basis of meeting people's interaction habits.

3. Simplicity: Compared with other interaction methods, the biggest feature of gesture interaction is that it can give instructions and complete related tasks naturally, quickly and efficiently, so some complex gestures should be avoided in the design process; in the process of gesture system design, the realization of a certain instruction may need to combine multiple gestures, and the increase of gestures will inevitably improve the learning difficulty and efficiency of users Cognitive load, so the number of corresponding gestures is also a key factor to be considered in the design of gesture model. On the premise of successfully realizing gesture recognition, strive to be concise and minimize the number of gestures required for a single command.

4. Efficiency: If a command needs two or more gesture combinations to express, we need to focus on the fluency and recognition efficiency of each gesture [15]. When the two gestures are obviously uncomfortable or the hand muscles are uncomfortable during the conversion process, it means that there is a problem in the fluency of the combined gesture, and one of the gestures needs to be replaced. If there is a recognition error in the connection process of one gesture and other gestures, it is necessary to analyze the gesture, and decide whether to redesign or not according to the reasons The ultimate goal of giving up the gesture is to make gesture interaction more efficient, user interaction more comfortable, machine recognition smoothly, and improve interaction efficiency.

4.2 Gesture Design for Home Control Intelligent Terminal

We studied the products and functions commonly used in family life, and based on the above four gesture interaction design factors, we considered the user's psychology, interaction environment, and operation efficiency to design gesture models.

Product Functional Requirements Survey. We studied 13 types of functional devices commonly used in households, focus on the importance and frequency of features and products. A questionnaire survey was conducted on 47 users of different ages and cultural backgrounds, including teachers; students; takeaway delivery staff; cleaners; porters, aged 19 to 58 years. The importance and frequency of different functional devices in family life are scored according to a scale of 10 points (Fig. 5).

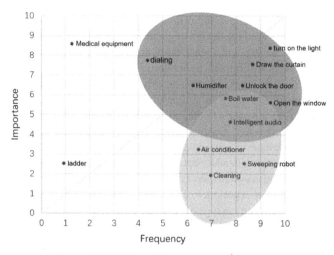

Fig. 5. Distribution of importance and frequency

The horizontal axis of each point in the figure above is the score of frequency of use, and the vertical axis is the score of importance. A higher score indicates that the device is more important and used more frequently. It can be seen that the functions in the upper right circle have higher usage frequency scores and importance scores.

Table 1. Functional architecture of home control intelligent terminal

Name	First level	Second level
Home intelligent terminal	Lighting system	Kitchen
		Living room
		Balcony
		TOILET
		Balcony
		Bedroom
		.....
	Household electrical appliances	Intelligent air conditioning
		Intelligent audio
		Sweeping robot
		Humidifier
		Heater
		.....
	Door and window system	Electric curtain
		Door lock
	Dialing system	Number 1
		Number 2
		Emergency number

Among them, the functions in the blue circle, such as light control, door and window control, need to be considered as important factors in family life. Medical devices and other devices are important because they are used too frequently. No related gesture design. According to the information architecture related content discussed in Sect. 3, the functional architecture of intelligent products and related equipment with high frequency and importance is established (Table 1).

Basic Gesture Design. We propose a new gesture design pattern: layer basic gestures, and finally combine basic gestures bound at different levels to form dynamic gestures. Due to the complex information architecture of home control intelligent terminal products, there are many functions that need to be controlled. This mode is applied to such complex information architecture products to enable users to clearly understand the specific meanings of the gestures they make. A clear hierarchy concept is formed in the user's mind. One gesture corresponds to one hierarchy, instead of blindly imitating the complex gestures provided, thereby reducing the user's learning cost.

The existing gesture interaction models are mainly divided into two types: static gesture and dynamic gesture [16]. Static gestures are the most basic gestures, while dynamic gestures are arranged and combined on the basis of static gestures. According to the architecture of home intelligent terminal, we designed 8 basic gestures, and then designed a new dynamic gesture by translating, rotating, and combining the 8 gestures. Then we designed dynamic gestures by performing operations such as panning and combining the 8 gestures, and inductively integrated all static gestures and dynamic gestures to form a set of gesture models for home control intelligent terminals.

According to the functional architecture table of the home control terminal, the control intelligent terminal product is divided into two levels. The first level contains four systems: lighting control system, home appliance control system, security control system, and dial system. It is the foundation of the entire gesture interaction system. The gesture design in this part needs to be simple and convenient for the machine to quickly recognize; The second level of information is detailed into the specific functions of the device. Gesture design should be based on the correlation between gestures and real actions on the basis of ensuring recognition. Also, if the conditions allow, it can provide a higher degree of freedom, allowing users to bind the second-level functions according to personal preferences and the actual needs of the family, such as interactive gestures to turn on the light, and can be used for bedrooms and living rooms. Sequence coding, which corresponds to the sequence of numbers to the corresponding gesture.

According to the functional positioning of the first level and the second level, the items of each level are individually bound to the basic gestures. Considering that the use of hand shape changes for long-distance gesture interaction may reduce the accuracy of recognition. Too many gestures and complicated gestures will increase the user's memory burden. The arm has a larger range of motion than the hand type and requires less recognition accuracy, can improve the efficiency of camera capture. Using the movement changes between the torso of the arm for gesture design (Table 2).

Dynamic Gesture Design. During the dynamic gesture design process, the smoothness of the connection between the first-level gesture and the second-level gesture is carefully considered, and the two gestures are converted in accordance with the four factors of

Table 2. Static gesture design

Number	Explanation	Gesture model	手势演示
Basic gesture①	Clench your right hand and extend your arms forward and up		
Basic gesture②	Clench with one hand, extend the arm 45° above the right		
Basic gesture③	Clench your right hand and extend your arm horizontally to the right		
Basic gesture④	Clench with right hand, extend the arm 45° below the syncline		
Basic gesture⑤	Clench your right hand and extend your arms down		
Basic gesture⑥	Clench your right hand, keep the forearm vertical and upward, and keep the forearm close to the inside of the body		
Basic gesture⑦	Clench your right hand and extend your arm horizontally forward		
Basic gesture⑧	Clench your right hand and point to your temple		

nature, difference, simplicity, and efficiency. First, bind the four items in the first level with the basic gestures based on the connection between the gestures and the items. Among the eight static gestures, select gesture 1, gesture 6, gesture 7, and gesture 8 as the corresponding four subsystems in the first level. Gestures, and then perform gesture binding on the second level of each subsystem, and combine the remaining seven gestures with the second-level devices to form the final dynamic gesture, as shown in Table 3:

Table 3. Dynamic gesture design

Name	First level	Basic gesture	Second level	Basic gesture	Dynamic gesture
Home intelligent terminal	Lighting system	⑦	Kitchen	②	⑦ + ②
			Living room	③	⑦ + ③
			Balcony	④	⑦ + ④
			TOILET	⑤	⑦ + ⑤
	Household electrical appliances	⑥	Intelligent air conditioning	②	⑥ + ②
			Intelligent audio	③	⑥ + ③
			Sweeping robot	④	⑥ + ④
	Door and window system	①	Electric curtain	②	① + ②
			Door lock	⑤	① + ⑤
	Dialing system	⑧	Number 1	②	⑧ + ②
			Emergency number	③	⑧ + ③

4.3 Interactive Area Analysis

The interaction distance of indoor space will affect the accuracy of gesture recognition to a certain extent. The home intelligent control terminal uses the device's own camera and cameras placed in the family living room, study, etc. for gesture capture. It needs to meet the interactive distance requirements of each space, so it is necessary to analyze the distance of the indoor environment. Zhu, M.B's research [17] shows that the per capita living space in China's cities is about 39 m^2, and the per capita area in rural housing is 47 m^2. Based on 2–3 people per household, the housing area of most Chinese families is 70 m^2, -130 m^2.

The space is mainly divided into six parts: bedroom, kitchen, balcony, living room, dining room and bathroom. The living room covers an area of about 30% of the entire building surface, between 20 m^2 and 40 m^2 (Fig. 6).

With reference to the living room related scale standard, this article uses 11 m as the maximum length of the living room, sets the camera in the center of the space, and divides the test distance into three levels: short distance (0.5 m–1.5 m), middle

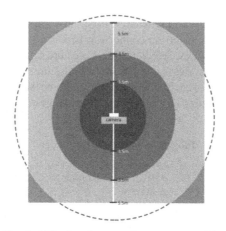

Fig. 6. Effective distance of gesture recognition

distance (1.5 m–3.5 m), Long distance (3.5 m–5.5 m), and use the above three distances as variables to experiment the usability of interactive gestures.

5   Gesture Interaction Experiment

5.1   Purpose

In order to verify the usability of hand gesture interaction model for home control terminals in actual use, the specific situation of the designed hand gesture ensemble in actual use, including the accuracy of hand gesture recognition, error rate of hand gesture recognition, user's subjective feeling when using a certain hand gesture. For practical use of home control intelligent terminal products.

5.2   Participant Selection

The participants selected 47 people, aged from 18 to 56 years, and their occupations were: teacher; student; shopper; cleaners; porters. All have long-term family life experience, with height between 158 cm and 187 cm, without any physical or psychological illness. There were 25 male participants and 22 female participants.

5.3   Experimental Variables

Interaction distance is one of the important factors affecting the accuracy of gesture recognition. The accuracy of gesture recognition is different at different distances. Therefore, according to the previous analysis of environmental factors in the family, the test distance is divided into three levels: close distance (0.5 m–1.5 m), middle distance (1.5 m–3.5 m), and long distance (3.5 m–5.5 m). For each of these three distances, the usability test of the gesture model is performed.

5.4 Experimental Equipment

Kinect V2; Windows 10 System; Unity3D 5.5; Kinect Manager.

5.5 Experimental Place

This experiment was carried out in the laboratory of Nanjing University of Science and Technology.

5.6 Experiment Process

1. 47 participants were numbered from 1 to 47, and the corresponding gender was recorded.
2. Before the test, provide 30 min for the participants to learn the hand gesture interaction ensemble, and make sure that the participants master all the interaction gestures skillfully.
3. The participants were brought into the test room to familiarize themselves with the test environment for 15 min, and then the main subjects were informed of the relevant requirements, experimental methods and precautions in the experiment.
4. Connect Kinect V2, calibrate the instrument and open the software for experiment.
5. The participants were asked to do a test to focus the lens, and then enter the formal experiment.
6. According to the distance, it can be divided into three points: near, middle and far, and the three points are tested respectively. Each gesture provides 15 s of experimental time. If the recognition is still not successful after 15 s, it indicates that the interactive gesture may have usability problems. If unrecognized phenomena occur in multiple test subjects, you need to analyze the two gestures, whether they are in the connection process or gestures. There is a problem with its own recognition, and then it is determined whether the gesture needs to be replaced or redesigned according to the reason. At the end of each gesture test, there will be a voice prompt, and then two seconds for the next gesture test. There are special personnel to record the number of errors, correct recognition time and other data in each test.
7. At the end of the test, participants were invited to score the four indicators of all static gestures and dynamic gestures by completing the five-point Likert scale questionnaire [18]: natural A1, difference A2, simple A3, and high efficiency A4. Fill in 9 points if you think a gesture is very good, and 1 point if you think a gesture is very bad. After that, the next participant was invited to enter the test room, and repeat the above steps for gesture interaction test until the end of the experiment (Table 4).

Table 4. Scoring criteria for the Likert scale

	Very bad	Not good	Common	Good	Very good
Score	1	3	5	7	9

6   Experimental Results

6.1   Analysis of Experimental Data

Analyzing the data of 47 participants in the static gesture experiment, as shown in Fig. 7. The recognition rate of eight basic gestures is relatively high, among which gesture 7 has the lowest recognition accuracy, 91.48%, higher than 90%. It shows that eight basic gestures are very good in the recognition of single body, and can be used for smooth gesture recognition.

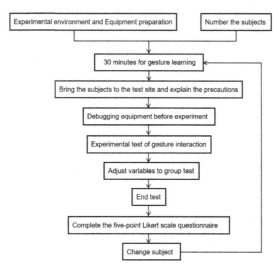

Fig. 7. Experiment flow chart

The data of dynamic gesture recognition shows that during close-range and medium-range gesture interactions, the overall recognition of gestures is greater than 80%, of which the minimum recognition rate of close-range gesture interaction is 87.23%, and the average recognition rate is 90.9%; The recognition rate of gestures at medium distances is not much different from the recognition rate of short distances. The average recognition rate is 89.5%, which indicates that the recognition accuracy of the designed gesture model in middle and short distances is less affected by distance. When the distance becomes longer, the accuracy of gesture recognition is significantly reduced, which indicates that the accuracy of gesture recognition is affected by the increase of distance in the range of 3.5 m–5 m (Figs. 8 and 9).

6.2   Analysis of Questionnaire Data

Analytic Hierarchy Process. AHP [19] deals with complex decision-making problems in a hierarchical manner, calculates the feature vector of the judgment matrix, and calculates the final weighted weights to obtain an evaluation model for each dimension of gesture interaction availability.

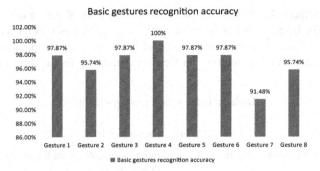

Fig. 8. Basic gestures recognition accuracy

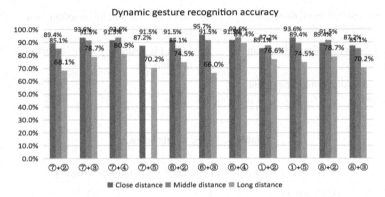

Fig. 9. Dynamic gesture recognition accuracy

We constructs a judgment matrix, compares the importance of each pair of evaluation indicators under the same criteria, and scores the indicators according to their importance levels. Finally, a judgment matrix is constructed based on the results of the questionnaire. As a result of comparing element i and element j according to importance, the judgment matrix has the following properties: $a_{ij} = 1/a_{ji}$.

Construct a judgment matrix R = (a_{ij}) $n_1 \times n_1$, i = 1, 2, ..., n1 j = 1, 2, ..., n1, n1 is the number of evaluation indexes

$$R = \begin{bmatrix} a_{11} & a_{12} & \cdots & a_{1j} \\ a_{21} & a_{22} & \cdots & a_{2j} \\ \vdots & \vdots & \ddots & \vdots \\ a_{i1} & a_{i2} & \cdots & a_{ij} \end{bmatrix}.$$

Index Weight Calculation. Use AHP to analyze the data collected by the five-point Likert scale to obtain the overall score of each gesture [20].

First set the weights of the four evaluation indicators based on naturalness A1, difference A2, simple A3 and high efficiency A4. Referring to the scoring standards in Table 5, compare the importance of the four indicators of naturalness, difference, simplicity, and efficiency, and invite two experts to score the index weights of the above four indicators. Take the approximate value of the average of all the scoring results, optimize the index weights, and sort out the final specific scores, as shown in Table 6.

Table 5. Index weight scoring standard

Importance level	Value	Importance level	Value
Both indicators are equally important	1	Index j is slightly more important than Index i	1/3
Index i is slightly more important than Index j	3	Index j is more important than Index i	1/5
Index i is more important than Index j	5	Index j is much more important than Index i	1/7
Index i is much more important than Index j	7	Index j is absolutely more important than Index i	1/9
Index i is absolutely more important than Index j	9		

Table 6. Index weight score

A	Naturalness	Difference	Simplicity	Efficiency
Naturalness	1	3	1	1/5
Difference	1/3	1	1/3	1/3
Simplicity	1/1	3	1	1/3
Efficiency	5	3	3	1

Establish a judgment matrix:

$$R = \begin{bmatrix} 1 & 3 & 3 & 5 \\ 1/3 & 1 & 1/3 & 3 \\ 1/3 & 3 & 1 & 3 \\ 1/5 & 1/3 & 1/3 & 1 \end{bmatrix}$$

Sum calculation for each column of the judgment matrix R:

$$R_j = \sum_{i=1}^{n} r_{ij}$$

The normalization process is performed on each column of the judgment matrix R, and the new matrix B is obtained as:

$$B = \frac{r_{ij}}{R_j}$$

Sum the indexes of each row of the matrix B to obtain the feature vector T_i as:

$$T_i = \sum\nolimits_{j=1}^{n} b_{ij}$$

Normalize the feature vector Ti to get the index weight value Wi as:

$$W_i = |T_i| / \sum |T_i| \quad i = 1, 2, \ldots n$$

Table 7. AHP analysis results

Factor	Weight
A1- Naturalness	0.17929180008150933
A2- Difference	0.08936792491161455
A3- Simplicity	0.20371481550143006
A4- Efficiency	0.527625459505446

Calculate the maximum characteristic root $\lambda_{\max}$ of the judgment matrix R:

$$\lambda_{\max} = \frac{1}{n} \sum (R \cdot W)_i / W_j \quad n \in Z^+$$

Calculate the consistency index CI of the judgment matrix R:

$$CI = \frac{\lambda - n}{n - 1}$$

When CI is close to 0, there is satisfactory consistency; the larger the CI, the more inconsistent; when CI = 0, there is 100% consistency. To measure the size of CI, a random consistency indicator RI is introduced:

$$RI = \frac{CI_1 + CI_2 + \cdots + CI_n}{n}$$

When constructing a judgment matrix, the evaluation of the weight relationship will be affected by human subjective limitations. In order to establish a reasonable multi-level index weight model, it is necessary to systematically check the consistency of the judgment matrix. The test results will be fed back to the previous step. The matrix system thus optimizes the weights (Table 7).

Calculation formula for consistency correlation detection:

$$CR = \frac{CI}{RI}$$

Calculated:

$$CI = 0.08680791252208753$$
$$CR = 0.09753698036189609 < 0.1$$
$$\lambda_{\max} = 4.260423737566263$$

The CR value is less than 0.1, and the consistency test passes. The weights shown in the table below can be used for analysis and calculation.

Finally, the weight of each indicator and the user's score are multiplied to get the number of scores of a single indicator, and then the individual scores of these four indicators are added to get the overall subjective score of the gesture (Fig. 10).

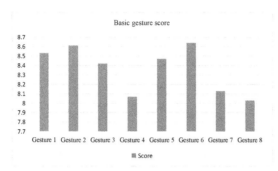

Fig. 10. Score for basic gestures

The user comprehensive scores of basic gesture and overall gesture are all above 7 points, which indicates that the interactive gesture designed in this paper has a good user experience. The highest score of gesture 1 + 2 (control electric curtain) is 8.73 points, which may be due to the combination of gesture and user's normal use habits; the lowest score of gesture 6 + 3 is 7.87 points, which indicates that the gesture needs to be re optimized (Fig. 11).

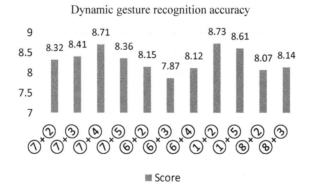

Fig. 11. Comprehensive score of dynamic gesture

7 Discussion

This article is aimed at home control intelligent terminal products. Based on its complex information architecture, a new gesture design method is proposed: basic gestures are layered, and basic gestures bound at different levels are combined to form dynamic gestures. According to the standards of the first level and the second level, the functional information of the control-type intelligent terminal products is divided. Draw up 8 static gestures, follow the four design principles to bind the static gestures of the commands at each level, and then combine the functions of the two levels to design a set of dynamic gesture interaction models based on the hierarchical architecture. User interviews and questionnaires verify the feasibility of this gesture set. The experimental results prove that the accuracy rate of the gesture recognition is higher in the three distances of middle, near and far distances, and the user has good feedback during the use, which initially proves the usability of the interactive gesture.

In the subsequent research, the gesture model will be deeply optimized. It is hoped that the gesture design concepts and gesture schemes proposed in this article can be adopted by home control intelligent terminal products, and also use gestures in such products Interactive research provides some reference.

8 Conclusion

This paper proposes a new gesture design method for home control intelligent terminal products based on its complex information architecture: Basic gestures are bound according to levels, and finally, basic gestures bound at different levels are combined to form dynamic gestures. According to the standards of the first level and the second level, the functional information of the control-type intelligent terminal products is divided. Draw up 8 static gestures, follow the four design principles to bind the static gestures of the commands at each level, and then combine the functions of the two levels to design a set of dynamic gesture interaction models based on the hierarchical architecture. User interviews and questionnaires verify the feasibility of this gesture set. The experimental results prove that the accuracy rate of the gesture recognition is higher in the three distances of middle, near and far distances, and the user has good feedback during the use, which initially proves the usability of the interactive gesture.

In the subsequent research, we will carry out deep optimization on this gesture model. We hope that the gesture scheme proposed in this article can be adopted by home control smart terminal products and also used in home control smart terminal products in the future. The research on gesture interaction provides some reference.

References

1. Panger, G.: Kinect in the kitchen: testing depth camera interactions in practical home environments. In: CHI 12 Extended Abstracts on Human Factors in Computing Systems (2012)
2. Mittal, Y., Toshniwal, P., Sharma, S., Singhal, D., Gupta, R., Mittal, V.K.: A voice-controlled multi-functional smart home automation system. In: 2015 Annual IEEE India Conference (INDICON), New Delhi, pp. 1–6 (2015)
3. Miroslav, B., Ondrej, K.R.: Vision of smart home point solution as sustainable intelligent house concept. IFAC Proc. Vol. 46(28), 383–387 (2013). ISSN 1474-6670, ISBN 9783902823533

4. Ji, R., Gong, M.S.: Application of natural interaction design in smart home. Packag. Eng. **40**(22), 208–213 (2019)
5. Wan, H.G., Li, T., Feng, L.W., Chen, Y.S.: An approach to free-hand interaction for 3D scene modeling. Trans. Beijing Institute Technol. **39**(02), 175–180 (2019)
6. Wu, H., Wang, J., Zhang, X.: User-centered gesture development in TV viewing environment. Multimed Tools Appl. **75**, 733–760 (2016)
7. Ntoa, S., Birliraki, C., Drossis, G., Margetis, G., Adami, I., Stephanidis, C.: UX design of a big data visualization application supporting gesture-based interaction with a large display. In: Yamamoto, S. (ed.) HIMI 2017. LNCS, vol. 10273, pp. 248–265. Springer, Cham (2017). https://doi.org/10.1007/978-3-319-58521-5_20
8. Ram, P.S., Verma, G.K.: Human computer interaction using hand gesture. Procedia Comput. Sci. **54**, 721–727 (2015). ISSN 1877-0509
9. Li, X., Guan, D., Zhang, J., Liu, X., Li, S., Tong, H.: Exploration of ideal interaction scheme on smart TV: based on user experience research of far-field speech and mid-air gesture interaction. In: Marcus, A., Wang, W. (eds.) HCII 2019. LNCS, vol. 11584, pp. 144–162. Springer, Cham (2019). https://doi.org/10.1007/978-3-030-23541-3_12
10. Min, L., Gu, W., Chen, W., He, Y., Wu, Y., Zhang, Y.: Smart home: architecture, technologies and systems. Procedia Comput. Sci. **131**, 393–400 (2018). ISSN 1877-0509
11. Li, Y., Huang, J., Tian, F., Wang, H.-A., Dai, G.-Z.: Gesture interaction in virtual reality. Virtual Reality Intell. Hardware **1**(1), 84–112 (2019). ISSN 2096-5796
12. Grandhi, S.A., Joue, G., Mittelberg, I.: Understanding naturalness and intuitiveness in gesture production: insights for touchless gestural interfaces. In: Proceedings of the SIGCHI Conference on Human Factors in Computing Systems, pp. 821–824. ACM (2011)
13. Wigdor, D., Wixon, D.: Brave NUI World: Designing Natural User Interfaces for Touch and Gesture. Elsevier, Amsterdam (2011)
14. Shin, Y.K., Choe, J.H.: Remote control interaction for individual environment of smart TV. In: IEEE International Symposium on Personal. IEEE Xplore (2011)
15. Annelies, K., Sujit, S.: Language ideologies on the difference between gesture and sign. Lang. Commun. **60**, 44–63 (2018). ISSN 0271-5309
16. Dinh, D.-L., Jeong, T.K., Kim, T.-S.: Hand gesture recognition and interface via a depth imaging sensor for smart home appliances. Energy Procedia **62**, 576–582 (2014). ISSN 1876-6102
17. Zhu, M.B., Li, S.: The housing inequality in China. Res. Econ. Manag. **39**(09), 91–101 (2018)
18. Khaoula, B., Majida, L., Samira, K., Mohamed, L.K., Abir, E.Y.: AHP-based approach for evaluating ergonomic criteria. Procedia Manuf. **32**, 856–863 (2019). ISSN 2351-9789
19. Gil, M., Lubiano, M., de la Rosa de Sáa, S., Sinova, B.: Analyzing data from a fuzzy rating scale-based questionnaire. A case study. Psicothema **27**, 182–191 (2015)
20. Camargo, M., Wendling, L., Bonjour, E.: A fuzzy integral based methodology to elicit semantic spaces in usability tests. Int. J. Ind. Ergon. **44**, 11–17 (2014)

A Comparative Study of Hand-Gesture Recognition Devices for Games

Ahmed S. Khalaf[1]([✉]), Sultan A. Alharthi[1], Ali Alshehri[2], Igor Dolgov[3],
and Phoebe O. Toups Dugas[1]

[1] Play and Interactive Experiences for Learning Lab,
Computer Science Department, New Mexico State University, Las Cruces, NM, USA
khalaf@nmsu.edu, phoebe.toups.dugas@acm.org
[2] Electrical Engineering Department,
New Mexico State University, Las Cruces, NM, USA
[3] Psychology Department, New Mexico State University, Las Cruces, NM, USA

Abstract. Gesture recognition devices provide a new means for natural human-computer interaction. However, when selecting these devices to be used in games, designers might find it challenging to decide which gesture recognition device will work best. In the present research, we compare three vision-based, hand-gesture devices: Leap Motion, Microsoft's Kinect, and Intel's RealSense. The comparison provides game designers with an understanding of the main factors to consider when selecting these devices and how to design games that use them. We developed a simple hand-gesture-based game to evaluate performance, cognitive demand, comfort, and player experience of using these gesture devices. We found that participants preferred and performed much better using Leap Motion and Kinect compared to using RealSense. Leap Motion also outperformed or was equivalent to Kinect. These findings were supported by players' accounts of their experiences using these gesture devices. Based on these findings, we discuss how such devices can be used by game designers and provide them with a set of design cautions that provide insights into the design of gesture-based games.

Keywords: Hand-gesture · Games · Game design · Leap Motion · Kinect · RealSense · Vision-based

1 Introduction

The proliferation of gesture-recognition technology enables players to interact with games in new ways [13,36,57]. Such devices enable players to use different parts of their body as a controller, increasing physical immersion and enabling designers to explore novel game mechanics and interaction methods [36,47].

Human hands are one of the most expressive body parts [14,40,43]. To detect the different hand movements and gestures, several technologies have been developed and employed for various domains and applications: education [60,62], entertainment [12,15,63], navigation [28], and training games [51,52]. However,

© Springer Nature Switzerland AG 2020
M. Kurosu (Ed.): HCII 2020, LNCS 12182, pp. 57–76, 2020.
https://doi.org/10.1007/978-3-030-49062-1_4

the accuracy and performance of these technologies vary greatly [7], and in some cases the characteristics of the technologies may be incompatible with the game design [8,32].

When selecting hand-gesture recognition devices, game designers might find it challenging to decide which device will work best for their game. The present research enables game designers to understand the differences between these devices, how to select them, and how to incorporate them within their games. Based on our motivation and prior research, we evaluate three commonly used hand-gesture recognition devices: Leap Motion (LM), Intel RealSense (RS), and Microsoft Kinect (MK). This comparison develops an understanding of the main factors that influence their performance and use in games. Based on our study of prior work [29,35,41,46,50,56,58], we hypothesized that LM would outperform MK and that MK would outperform RS in games across the following measures:

H1–H4: Game performance (H1: overall completion time, H2: completion time for small objects, H3: completion time for large objects, H4: error rate): LM > MK > RS.

H5–H10: NASA Task Load Index (NASA-TLX) [18,19] workload measurement item scores (H5: mental demand, H6: physical demand, H7: temporal demand, H8: effort, H9: frustration, H10: performance[1]): LM < MK < RS.

H11–12: Perceived comfort (H11) and accuracy (H12): LM > MK > RS.

To test our hypotheses, we developed a simple hand-gesture game, *Handy*. In this game, players move an embodiment [6] on the screen with the gesture device and collect gems by performing a "grab" hand gesture when the embodiment is over them. The goal of the game is to collect all the gems as fast as possible. The development of the game identified issues in developing cross-platform gesture-based systems. In a mixed methods, within-subjects study, 18 participants played *Handy* using the three different hand-gesture recognition devices: LM, MK, and RS. We investigated the impact of these devices on game completion time, error rate, cognitive workload, and player experience.

We found that players performed better and felt most comfortable when they used LM and MK. Players also reported that LM and MK are more accurate, and they felt most comfortable using these devices. Through this work, we contribute:

1. a comparative study of three different vision-based hand-gesture recognition devices and analyzed how they might impact performance, cognitive load, and player experience in games; and
2. provide a set of design *cautions* that game designer can take into consideration when working and designing with hand-gesture recognition devices.

In the reminder of this paper, we synthesize background on gesture-based interaction, prior hand-gesture studies, and gesture-based interaction in games. We then provide a description of the methodology, the design of the game *Handy*,

---

[1] In the NASA-TLX, the performance score is reverse-coded so that, like the other scores, a higher score is worse, thus, a high score on performance indicates worse perceived performance.

and the user study. Finally, we discuss our results and provide a set of design cautions for future hand-gesture based games.

2 Background

In this section, we synthesize prior research on gesture-based interaction, discuss prior hand-gesture comparative studies, and provide an overview of prior designs and studies of gesture-based interaction in games.

2.1 Gesture-Based Interaction

Gesture-recognition technology enables users to interact with systems and games with their body in novel ways [13,36,57]. For example, users can use their hands to create different mid-air gestures to perform a number of actions, such as scrolling through an application window, flipping a page in a digital book, or pointing and selecting a folder in a computer desktop [16,40]. Such natural human-computer interaction has being shown to be useful and effective in a number of domains, such as in education [60,62], entertainment [12,15,63], navigation [28], and training games [51,52].

To enable such gesture-based interaction, a number of technologies have been designed and developed that utilize different techniques and sensors. Based on prior work [1,2,11,43,57], these devices can be divided into three types: vision-based (e.g., Leap Motion [25]), sensor-based (e.g., Myo Armband [23]), and hybrid-based (e.g., Electronic Speaking Glove [2]).

Gestures can be divided into *dynamic* or *static* [16,43]. A dynamic gesture consists of the movement of the hand, arm, and/or fingers over time (e.g., waving, writing in the air), whereas a static gesture involves the hand remaining in a certain posture at a point in time (e.g., fist, open palm) [44]. Vision-based systems need three phases: *hand detection, hand tracking*, and *gesture recognition* [43]. Infrared (IR) sensing is one of the technologies that vision-based recognition devices use to detect gestures. Some IR sensors depend on an IR projector which projects different dots on the recognized object within the range of the device; then captures the different movements with a camera [54].

While these devices provide designers and users with a set of different affordance that can enable novel ways to interact with applications and games, they pose new challenges and limitations that are worth investigating. In this work, we focus on investigating the differences between three vision-based hand-gesture recognition devices in the context of games.

2.2 Prior Hand-Gesture Comparative Studies

Prior studies have addressed how gesture-based interaction compares to more traditional approaches [45,46], as well as investigated the performance of specific devices [9,58]. For example, Sambrooks and Wilkinson [45], conducted a comparative study between MK, mouse, and touchscreen, in which they concluded

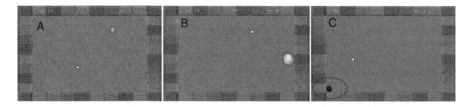

Fig. 1. The hand-gesture game *Handy*; the player collects gems of various sizes by moving their embodiment (a hand cursor) over the gem and executing a grab gesture. A: Collecting a small gem (green) near the top. B: Collecting a large gem (yellow) to the right. C: Collecting a small gem (black, circled in red) in the lower-right corner; in some cases, gems are placed in difficult areas that might require players to be more precise when moving their hand and making the grab gesture. (Color figure online)

that the performance of MK was much worse than mouse and touch screen for simple computer tasks. Furthermore, Seixas et al. [46] compared between LM, mouse, and touchpad, and found that LM performed poorly in pointing tasks compared to both mouse and touchpad. These studies together provide insights into the performance and usability of mid-air gesture device compared to traditional input modalities for 2D pointing tasks.

On the other hand, comparing between different mid-air hand gesture devices showed that these devices perform differently and can be selected based on the specific tasks [9,58]. Carvalho et al. [9], conducted a comparative study that considers LM and MK to evaluate their performance with relation to the user's age difference. Overall, device performance was consistent when comparing both devices side-by-side with specific groups of users; however, there was a significant difference in terms of performance of each device between some of the age groups. The authors reported that the performance of mid-air gesture devices could be varied based on age of the users. Furthermore, Weichert et al. [58] investigated the accuracy and robustness of LM. The authors conducted an experiment with an industrial robot to look at static gestures to drive the robot and dynamic ones to draw a path. The authors stated that the level of accuracy of LM is higher than other gesture devices within its price range, such as MK.

These studies together point to the advantages and disadvantages of these input modalities and provide insights into the performance of various gesture-recognition devices. However, they do not focus on vision-based gesture devices, do not provide enough insight into how such devices can be used in games, and are, thus, unable to assist game designers in making sound decisions about how to design and work with hand-gesture devices in games.

2.3   Gesture-Based Interaction in Games

Within the context of games, prior work investigated the performance and usability of different hand-gesture devices [30]. Correctly performing gestures in games can be part of the main mechanics, challenges, and experience of playing these games

[42,57]. However, hand-gesture recognition devices need to be responsive, consistent, intuitive, and comfortable for them to be used successfully in games [57].

Delays or lack of accuracy can negatively impact the experience of playing games. Moser and Tscheligi [35], examined the accuracy of LM when playing the physics-based game *Cut the Rope*, and found out that using gesture devices provided a positive player experience, however, a number of accuracy and orientation issues materialized when playing such games with a mid-air gesture device when compared to touch screens.

Muscle-controlled games, such as *The Falling of Momo* [51,52] have been developed to explore novel ways to utilize gesture recognition devices in physical therapy and training, and have been shown to be an effective mode of interaction.

Recognizing players hands is one of most common ways to enable interaction in virtual reality games [4,22,27,64]. Prior research investigated the use of such devices in VR games and how they influence players experience and the ability to perform different mid-air gestures correctly [24,26].

While prior research provides an understanding of how gesture recognition devices can be used in games, and sheds light on the challenges of using these devices, they do not provide game designers with an understanding of the differences between these gesture recognition devices and what they need to consider when designing games using this type of interaction.

3 Methodology

In this section, we explain the methods used to evaluate our hypotheses. We provide a detailed description of the process of recruiting participants, our hypotheses and experimental design, measures used, the game design, and study protocol.

3.1 Participants

We invited participants from New Mexico State University to volunteer for the formal study. Data collection occurred over a four-week period in the summer of 2018. 18 participants ($n = 18$, 3 female, 15 male; $M_{age} = 30.83$ years, $SD_{age} = 8.87$) were recruited. All participants were right-handed and were current computer science students.

3.2 Experimental Design

We used a within-subjects design with one independent variable (IV), device type, with three factors (i.e., LM, MK, RS). The dependent variables (DVs) were time taken to collect all objects, gesture recognition error rate, and workload. Game experience was taken as a co-variate (CV) (Table 1).

Participants played the game three times with each of the three devices. To rule out order effects, a complete counterbalance of the factors was achieved. With three conditions in this within-subject experiment, the total number of sequences required to achieve a complete counterbalance was six. We had a total of three participants in each sequence.

Fig. 2. Vision-based hand-gesture recognition devices compared in the present study. Left: Leap Motion (LM); middle: Intel RealSense (F200) (RS); right: Microsoft Kinect v2 (Windows Version) (MK).

Table 1. Description of the variables in this within-subject study.

Variable	Description
Hand-gesture devices (IV)	LM, RS, and MK
Game completion time (DV)	Time spent collecting all game objects in seconds
Error rate (DV)	Number of unrecognized hand-gestures
Cognitive workload (DV)	NASA-TLX used to assess workload
Game experience (CV)	Questionnaire used to assess game experience

Measures. Game completion time accounts for how long it took players to move from each gem to the next, performing the gesture accurately. We captured this data automatically with a logging system built into the game software, which separates how long it took the player to collect each goal.

Gesture error rate was determined by observing the player during gameplay. One researcher performed the observation and recorded false positives and negatives from the gesture system.

To assess cognitive workload, we used the NASA Task Load Index (NASA-TLX) [19], one of the most commonly used and the most widely validated of the various tools available for measuring workload [18]. NASA-TLX consists of six items measuring different aspects of workload (i.e., mental demand, physical demand, temporal demand, performance, effort, frustration) on a 100-point scale. Overall, higher values are worse, indicating that the participant found the task taxing or perceived low performance. In this study, the weighting component of NASA-TLX was omitted to reduce the time it took to complete the questionnaire [34].

To gauge subjective experience, after each session, we asked participants about the perceived accuracy of each device, perceived comfort, preference, and overall experience.

3.3   Research Artifact: *Handy*

To compare between the three hand-gesture devices, we designed *Handy*, a hand-gesture-based single-player game, in which the player uses their hand movements and gestures to play. The goal is to collect 36 objects that appear in a sequence and come in two different sizes (i.e., small, large) (Fig. 1). These objects need

Table 2. The hand gestures supported by each device.

Device	Supported hand gesture
LM	Different hand gestures can be defined using a detection utility [25]
RS	Open hand, close hand, grab, thumb up, thumb down, 'V' sign, two fingers pinch, full pinch, tap, wave, swipe, fingers spread
MK	Open hand, close hand, lasso

to be collected by placing the player's embodiment over the gem and using a "grab" gesture as fast as possible. The player's hand position is presented as a hand-shaped cursor embodiment on a 2D space. To successfully collect one object in the game, players need to perform the following:

- move their hand in any direction using hand movements with an open palm gesture and try to position their hand over the visible game object; then
- perform the "grab" gesture to successfully collect the game object.

On each play through, the player first has 6 randomly positioned targets, which do not count for score, followed by 30 that are pre-positioned. The pre-positioning was accomplished with an algorithm to randomly position the objects a consistent distance apart; the results were saved and used for each game round. This design enables the player to have a tutorial with the new device, followed by a consistent set of targets. Players are scored based on the time it takes them to collect each object. The gesture devices can be interchanged in the game for the purpose of this study.

3.4 Apparatus

Participants played *Handy* in a laboratory using a Windows PC (processor: Intel Core i7-5960X 3.00 GHz; RAM: 16 GB; graphics: NVIDIA GeForce GTX 980 Ti; monitor: 4K LED 27-in., wide screen), which was sufficient to run the game without performance issues. In each condition, the participants played the game with a different hand-gesture device. These vision-based hand-gesture recognition devices were selected based on their popularity and wide use within games:

- **Leap Motion**[2] (LM; Fig. 2, left): a small device for detecting hand position and gestures released in 2012. It is placed on a surface in front of a monitor, then can detect hands above it using IR sensors. The device contains two IR cameras and three IR LEDs [58]. We use LM SDK Orion Beta v3.2 to process captured data.
- **Intel RealSense**[3] (RS; Fig. 2, middle): a device for tracking human bodies, hands, and faces released in 2015. We use the F200 model, which uses an

---

[2] https://www.leapmotion.com.

[3] https://downloadcenter.intel.com/product/92255.

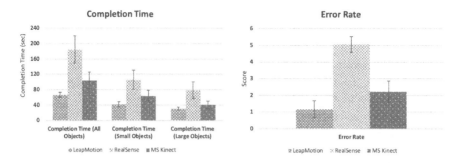

Fig. 3. Data plotted for completion time and error rate. Error bars represent 95% confidence intervals.

IR depth camera and RGB camera (1080p resolution) to capture imagery 20–120 cm from the device. We use the RS SDK version 2016 R2.

- **Microsoft Kinect**[4] (MK; Fig. 2, right): a motion-sensing input device by Microsoft for Xbox 360 and Xbox One video game consoles and Windows PCs, originally introduced in 2009, then upgraded in 2013 [55]. MK projects an IR dot pattern into the environment, which is uses for an IR depth camera; it also includes an RGB camera. For our study, we use the Kinect for Windows v2 and Kinect SDK v2.0.

3.5 Study Protocol

Before the beginning of the experiment, participants read and signed a consent form. Participants were then asked to complete the demographics questionnaire and asked about their prior experience with hand-gesture devices. Participants then played each of the three rounds of the game, with each of the different hand-gesture recognition devices. Between each round, they completed the NASA-TLX and the two Likert-scale-based questions. When participants finished the last session of the experiment, they were asked two open-ended questions to assess their overall experience.

4   Results

In this section, we present both the quantitative and qualitative results from our mixed methods within-subjects user study and discuss the main findings.

4.1 Performance

Repeated-measures analyses of variance (ANOVAs; IV: device) were used to evaluate the impact of using LM, RS, and MK on game performance, including completion time (overall, large objects, small objects) and error rate. The sphericity

---
[4] https://developer.microsoft.com/en-us/windows/kinect.

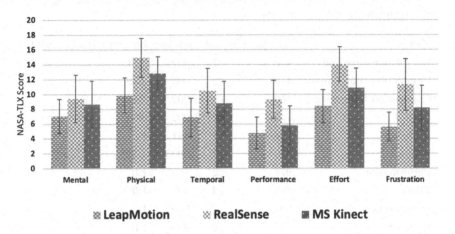

Fig. 4. Data plotted for cognitive workload. Error bars represent 95% confidence intervals.

assumption was violated for each of the completion time metrics (see Table 3), so we used the Hyunh-Feldt correction for degrees of freedom and significance in the corresponding ANOVAs.

As noted in Table 4 the main effect of device was significant across all of the behavioral measures; effect sizes were all very large. Pairwise comparisons showed RS to be worse than LM and MK across all measures ($p < 0.05$ in all cases). Pairwise comparisons also showed LM outperformed MK in measures of overall completion time, completion time for small objects, and error rate ($p < 0.05$ in all cases; see Fig. 3). So, hypotheses **H1–H4** were generally supported, except in instances where LM and MK performed similarly.

4.2   Cognitive Workload

Repeated-measures ANOVAs (IV: device) were used to evaluate the impact of using LM, RS, and MK on the measures included in the NASA-TLX. The sphericity assumption was only violated for temporal demand (see Table 3), so we used the Hyunh-Feldt correction for degrees of freedom and significance in the corresponding ANOVA.

As noted in Table 4, the main effect of device was significant across all of the TLX; effect sizes ranged from medium to small. Pairwise comparisons showed LM to be better than RS across all measures ($p < 0.05$ in all cases). Pairwise comparisons also showed MK to be better than RS across measures of perceived performance ($p < 0.05$) and marginally better ($p < 0.10$) in frustration. Additionally, pairwise comparisons showed LM to be similar to MK other than in temporal demand where LM performed better ($p < 0.05$) (Fig. 4). So, hypotheses **H5–H10** were generally supported, except in instances where self-reports of LM and MK use were similar.

Table 3. Mauchly's Test of Sphericity. When the sphericity assumption was violated ($p < 0.05$), we used the Hyunh-Feldt correction for degrees of freedom and significance in the corresponding analyses of variance.

Measure	Mauchly's W	DF	p-value	Epsilon (Hyunh-Feldt)
Completion time (all)	.460	2	.002	.681
Completion time (small)	.476	2	.003	.689
Completion time (large)	.460	2	.002	.681
Mental	.742	2	.092	.864
Physical	.898	2	.421	1.0
Temporal	.370	2	.0003	.637
Performance	.971	2	.790	1.0
Effort	.889	2	.391	1.0
Frustration	.994	2	.950	1.0
Comfort	.947	2	.646	1.0
Accuracy	.973	2	.802	1.0
Error Rate	.993	2	.944	1.0

Table 4. Results of the one-way ANOVAs for each of the DVs.

Measure	Treat. DF	Error DF	F value	p-value	η_p^2
Completion time (all)	1.361	23.144	28.915	<.0001	.630
Completion time (small)	1.379	23.439	14.862	.0003	.466
Completion time (large)	1.361	23.138	16.524	.0002	.493
Mental	2	34	1.689	.199	.09
Physical	2	34	6.154	.005	.266
Temporal	1.273	21.644	4.887	.030	.223
Performance	2	34	9.294	.0006	.353
Effort	2	34	7.462	.002	.305
Frustration	2	34	9.563	.0005	.360
Comfort	2	34	26.039	<.0001	.605
Accuracy	2	34	24.924	<.0001	.595
Error Rate	2	34	53.334	<.0001	.758

4.3   Perceived Comfort and Accuracy

We considered the responses to the questionnaire and coded the response values 1–5, with positive responses being higher. Repeated-measures ANOVAs (IV: device) were used to evaluate the impact of using LM, RS, and MK on measures of perceived comfort and accuracy. The sphericity assumption was not violated (see Table 3).

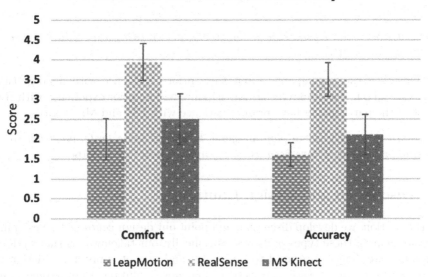

Fig. 5. Data plotted for perceived comfort and accuracy. Error bars represent 95% confidence intervals.

As noted in Table 4, the main effect of device was significant across both measures and the effect sizes were both large. Pairwise comparisons showed RS to be significantly worse than LM and MK across both measures ($p < 0.05$), whereas LM and MK did not differ from one another ($p < 0.05$) (Fig. 5). So, hypotheses **H11–H12** were partially supported.

4.4 Player Experience

We examined the participants' reflections on their experiences using these different hand-gesture devices in the game. Players stated that the accuracy of the three gestures devices varied:

> *I prefer Leap Motion because I could handle objects with better accuracy than Kinect which would be second choice.* [P15]

Players reported that they were more comfortable during the game when they used certain devices.

> *I was more comfortable when I used the first device [LM] to play the game.* [P17]

Some participants were more comfortable using MK:

> *I prefer Kinect because it was way more comfortable compared to other two devices.* [P13]

In contrast, players reported that they felt tired when they used RS to play the game.

I felt tired when I worked with the second device [RS], also, with it I lost the accuracy. [P7]

We asked the participants about their prior experience with hand-gesture devices, and our data showed that participants had no prior experience with RS. Most of the participants have prior experience with LM and MK devices.

I liked to use Kinect to play the game because it is accurate and I am so familiar with it. I have been using it for three years now. [P16]

5   Discussion and Design Cautions

In this section, we develop discussion and point out design *cautions* for designing and developing these types of games. Specifically, our take-away is that mid-air hand gesture devices are hard to design for and do not support the design of cross-platform games. Designers need to find novel solutions to overcome some of the challenges they may face when designing hand-gesture based games to provide players with an overall positive experience. The objective of this study was to compare three hand gesture recognition devices (LM, MK, RS) in the context of games and to provide insights and point to solutions for designing hand gesture-based games. Our results show that LM has better performance and accuracy compared to MK and RS, and players felt more comfortable when they played the game using LM and MK. These results align with prior research [49,58]. In the following, we present a number of cautions when designing and working with hand gesture-based devices. Attending to these cautions will help designers to improve their game design and player experience.

5.1   Arm and Body Fatigue

Our data showed that players felt tired when they played the hand-gesture game. We observed that some players experienced hand and arm fatigue. To overcome this, they switched to their left hand to support their right hand and to be able to continue playing the game. This problem is known as the "gorilla-arm effect" [20]. The reason for this problem is that participants had to raise and extend their arms and keep it in the air for extended periods while they were playing the game. This type of input modality is not suitable for long-term and extended use [5].

Designers of hand-gesture-based games need to understand the potential degrees of freedom for arms and hands [33,37,48], and be able to distinguish between which hand gestures are perceived as natural or easy to perform. Allowing players to use both hands to interact with the game can help players to switch between both hands during the game, which helps them rest and reduce any fatigue. An alternative solution is to position the gesture recognition device so that players do not raise their arms high. For example, a player could wear a small gesture recognition device, such as LM, and strap it to their thigh [28], allowing the arms to hang naturally at the sides of the body, reducing the need to raise their hands.

Another solution is to manipulate the level of interaction required by these games. For example, instead or requiring players to constantly interact with the game using their hands, the game can shift between different periods of active and regular hand-gesture interaction to periods of idling with essentially no interaction, allowing players to rest between these periods. This shift in interaction levels has shown to be effective in reducing *click fatigue* in clicker and idle games [3,39].

We observed that some of these devices worked best while a player is standing instead of seating. Such differences in how these devices can be interacted with may cause not only arm fatigue, but also whole body fatigue. When selected these devices, designers need to consider whether the designed game is intended to be player while seating or standing to ensure that such design can be better supported by the device.

5.2   Challenges with Designing Hand-Gesture Games

Designing games that can be played using hand gestures poses challenges. Not all gesture-recognition devices support the same set of hand gestures. For example, RS can recognize multiple predefined hand gestures (e.g., thumbs up, two fingers pinch, full pinch), on the other hand, MK and Myo Armband do not support these gestures by default (see Table 2). Some of these devices enable designers to create their own set of hand gestures using SDKs, detection utilities, and toolkits, making it possible to build cross-platform and cross-device games. Designers need to make sure that their designs and gestures used are supported, this calls for a unified set of predefined gestures that devices need to support by default.

During the iterative process of designing our game *Handy*, we experimented with three different hand gestures (i.e., open hand, close hand, 'V' sign) that map to particular gems to be collected, which were color-coded. The problem with such a design is that it does not provide a natural mapping [38] between the action that the player is performing (i.e., collecting objects), and the hand gesture itself (e.g., 'V' sign) which could impact the performance of the players. Thus, avoiding unnatural gestures and mapping is critical to ensure the usability and comfort of such games. One solution is to focus on designing and supporting hand *microgestures* [10], or simple gestures that can be created in small interaction spaces. Further research is encouraged to provide game designers with a set of clearly identified natural mapped hand gestures and their possible uses within games (e.g., upward finger flick can be mapped to jumping) [48].

5.3   Size and Position of Game Objects

Our results showed that participants collected large game objects faster than small ones. We believe the reason for this is that using mid-air gesture devices is difficult when interacting with small objects. These results align with prior research [35], and are consistent with Fitts's Law [53]. Game designers should consider designing game objects that players and gesture devices can easily recognize and interact with.

Each vision-based gesture recognition device has a fixed detection range. For example, the detection range of RS for hand tracking and gesture recognition is 20–60 cm [21], if a player moves their hand closer to the camera, where the distance between the player hand and the device less than 20 cm (e.g., playing a 3D game), the device will stop detecting the player's hand. Thus, game designers need to take into consideration the detection range of these devices and make sure that the interaction space aligns with it.

5.4   Usability Considerations

Another caution is whether this kind of technology can be usable, responsive, intuitive, and comfortable within the context of games and how designer can find solutions for any usability problems. Our data indicated that participants were more accurate and perceived themselves to be more accurate when using some devices over others. We observed that such devices can easily lose track of the players' hands and fail to recognize the performed gestures. Due to such low accuracy level of most of these devices, designers need to make sure to provide appropriate feedback and awareness cues [17,59] to enable players to be aware if their hand gestures were correctly recognized or not. Objects that players need to interact with in the game should be made as obvious and accessible as possible. For example, avoiding the edges of the screen can help players maintain the position of their embodiment within the game.

While we only recruited right-handed players in this work, designers are encouraged to support both right and left-handed players to improve accessibility in games [61]. Our results indicated that participants preferred to use some devices over others for playing hand-gesture games, such preference was attributed to the accuracy, comfort, and familiarity with these devices. Designers of such games can make it possible for players to define or select their own gestures to play these games.

Finally, while providing players with the ability to interact with games using hand gestures can improve player experience and enjoyment [35], designers need to make sure that their games can still be played using other interaction modes if necessary.

6   Conclusions

In this study, we investigated three different vision-based gesture devices, LM, RS, and MK, in a computer game context to understand the differences in accuracy and performance between these devices. We found that participants preferred and performed better using the LM and MK than using the RS device. LM also outperformed MK along some metrics but not others, where they were equivalent. These findings were supported by players' accounts of their experiences using these gesture devices. Additionally, we found that participants preferred to used either LM or MK to play the game because of their improved accuracy (over RS) and prior familiarity with these devices.

While gesture devices proliferate and are capable of impressive hand tracking, they are still in a nascent stage. We found it challenging to develop similar experiences across multiple devices and ran into a number of issues with tracking errors in practice (even when playing in ideal conditions). We provide game designers with a set of design cautions and solutions to overcome some the challenges they might face when designing hand gesture games. It is our expectation that, as these technologies improve, these issues will get better.

7   Limitations

We acknowledge that this work is limited, and not intended to provide a complete analysis of the differences between hand-gesture devices for games. Here we focus on providing an initial understanding of how these devices might be different and how these differences might influence how they are used in games, which can help game designers to be aware of the challenges these hand-gesture devices might impose.

Our study was conducted with a small, specific sample (computer science students) which may limit the generalizability of the findings. Further research is encouraged to evaluate a wider range of devices with a larger sample of players using different off-the-shelf games in a more ecologically valid environment. We also did not conduct an analysis using Fitts's Law [31], doing that would have enabled us to conduct a more robust analysis, however, due to the design of the game and the collected data, such analysis is not possible. While the findings of this study provide insights and suggest a number of design cautions, they must be viewed within the limitations of the study.

References

1. Ahmed, M.A., Zaidan, B.B., Zaidan, A.A., Salih, M.M., Lakulu, M.M.B.: A review on systems-based sensory gloves for sign language recognition state of the art between 2007 and 2017. Sensors (Basel, Switzerland) **18**(7) (2018). http://europepmc.org/articles/PMC6069389
2. Ahmed, S.F., Ali, S.M.B., Qureshi, S.S.M.: Electronic speaking glove for speechless patients, a tongue to a dumb. In: 2010 IEEE Conference on Sustainable Utilization and Development in Engineering and Technology, pp. 56–60, November 2010
3. Alharthi, S.A., Alsaedi, O., Toups Dugas, P.O., Tanenbaum, T.J., Hammer, J.: Playing to wait: a taxonomy of idle games. In: Proceedings of the 2018 CHI Conference on Human Factors in Computing Systems, CHI 2018, pp. 621:1–621:15. ACM, New York (2018). https://doi.org/10.1145/3173574.3174195
4. Alimanova, M., et al.: Gamification of hand rehabilitation process using virtual reality tools: using leap motion for hand rehabilitation. In: 2017 First IEEE International Conference on Robotic Computing (IRC), pp. 336–339, April 2017

5. Bachynskyi, M., Palmas, G., Oulasvirta, A., Steimle, J., Weinkauf, T.: Performance and ergonomics of touch surfaces: a comparative study using biomechanical simulation. In: Proceedings of the 33rd Annual ACM Conference on Human Factors in Computing Systems, CHI 2015, pp. 1817–1826. ACM, New York (2015). https://doi.org/10.1145/2702123.2702607

6. Bayliss, P.: Beings in the game-world: characters, avatars, and players. In: Proceedings of the 4th Australasian Conference on Interactive Entertainment, IE 2007, pp. 4:1–4:6. RMIT University, Melbourne (2007). http://dl.acm.org/citation.cfm?id=1367956.1367960

7. Boulabiar, M.-I., Coppin, G., Poirier, F.: The issues of 3D hand gesture and posture recognition using the kinect. In: Kurosu, M. (ed.) HCI 2014. LNCS, vol. 8511, pp. 205–214. Springer, Cham (2014). https://doi.org/10.1007/978-3-319-07230-2_20

8. Cabreira, A.T., Hwang, F.: An analysis of mid-air gestures used across three platforms. In: Proceedings of the 2015 British HCI Conference, British HCI 2015, pp. 257–258. ACM, New York (2015). http://libezp.nmsu.edu:4009/10.1145/2783446.2783599

9. Carvalho, D., Bessa, M., Magalhães, L., Carrapatoso, E.: Performance evaluation of gesture-based interaction between different age groups using Fitts' law. In: Proceedings of the XVI International Conference on Human Computer Interaction, Interacción 2015, pp. 5:1–5:7. ACM, New York (2015). http://libezp.nmsu.edu:4009/10.1145/2829875.2829920

10. Chan, E., Seyed, T., Stuerzlinger, W., Yang, X.D., Maurer, F.: User elicitation on single-hand microgestures. In: Proceedings of the 2016 CHI Conference on Human Factors in Computing Systems, CHI 2016, pp. 3403–3414. ACM, New York (2016). https://doi.org/10.1145/2858036.2858589

11. Cheng, J., Bian, W., Tao, D.: Locally regularized sliced inverse regression based 3d hand gesture recognition on a dance robot. Inf. Sci. **221**, 274–283 (2013)

12. Cook, H., Nguyen, Q.V., Simoff, S.: Enabling finger-gesture interaction with kinect. In: Proceedings of the 8th International Symposium on Visual Information Communication and Interaction, VINCI 2015, pp. 152–153. ACM, New York (2015). http://libezp.nmsu.edu:2763/10.1145/2801040.2801060

13. Doliotis, P., Stefan, A., McMurrough, C., Eckhard, D., Athitsos, V.: Comparing gesture recognition accuracy using color and depth information. In: Proceedings of the 4th International Conference on PErvasive Technologies Related to Assistive Environments, PETRA 2011, pp. 20:1–20:7. ACM, New York (2011). http://libezp.nmsu.edu:2763/10.1145/2141622.2141647

14. Erol, A., Bebis, G., Nicolescu, M., Boyle, R.D., Twombly, X.: Vision-based hand pose estimation: a review. Comput. Vis. Image Underst. **108**(1), 52–73 (2007). Special Issue on Vision for Human-Computer Interaction. http://www.sciencedirect.com/science/article/pii/S1077314206002281

15. Freeman, W.T., Ichi Tanaka, K., Ohta, J., Kyuma, K.: Computer vision for computer games. In: FG (1996)

16. Gardner, A., Duncan, C.A., Selmic, R., Kanno, J.: Real-time classification of dynamic hand gestures from marker-based position data. In: Proceedings of the Companion Publication of the 2013 International Conference on Intelligent User Interfaces Companion, IUI 2013 Companion, pp. 13–16. ACM, New York (2013). http://libezp.nmsu.edu:2763/10.1145/2451176.2451181

17. Gutwin, C., Greenberg, S.: A descriptive framework of workspace awareness for real-time groupware. Comput. Support. Coop. Work (CSCW) **11**(3), 411–446 (2002). https://doi.org/10.1023/A:1021271517844

18. Hart, S.G.: Nasa-task load index (NASA-TLX); 20 years later. Proc. Hum. Fact. Ergon. Soc. Annu. Meet. **50**(9), 904–908 (2006). https://doi.org/10.1177/154193120605000909
19. Hart, S.G., Staveland, L.E.: Development of NASA-TLX (task load index): results of empirical and theoretical research. Adv. Psychol. **52**, 139–183 (1988). Human Mental Workload. http://www.sciencedirect.com/science/article/pii/S0166411508623869
20. Hincapié-Ramos, J.D., Guo, X., Moghadasian, P., Irani, P.: Consumed endurance: a metric to quantify arm fatigue of mid-air interactions. In: Proceedings of the SIGCHI Conference on Human Factors in Computing Systems, CHI 2014, pp. 1063–1072. ACM, New York (2014). http://libezp.nmsu.edu:2763/10.1145/2556288.2557130
21. Intel RealSense Technology: Intel RealSense, March 2016. https://software.intel.com/en-us/articles/intel-realsense-data-ranges
22. Khundam, C.: First person movement control with palm normal and hand gesture interaction in virtual reality. In: 2015 12th International Joint Conference on Computer Science and Software Engineering (JCSSE), pp. 325–330, July 2015
23. Labs, T.: Myo gesture control armband (2015). https://support.getmyo.com/hc/en-us/articles/203398347-Getting-started-with-your-Myo-armband
24. LaViola Jr., J.J.: Context aware 3D gesture recognition for games and virtual reality. In: ACM SIGGRAPH 2015 Courses, SIGGRAPH 2015, pp. 10:1–10:61. ACM, New York (2015). https://doi.org/10.1145/2776880.2792711
25. Leap Motion: Detection Utilities, March 2016. https://developer-archive.leapmotion.com/documentation/v2/unity/unity/Unity_DetectionUtilities.html
26. Lee, P.W., Wang, H.Y., Tung, Y.C., Lin, J.W., Valstar, A.: Transection: hand-based interaction for playing a game within a virtual reality game. In: Proceedings of the 33rd Annual ACM Conference Extended Abstracts on Human Factors in Computing Systems, CHI EA 2015, pp. 73–76. ACM, New York (2015). http://libezp.nmsu.edu:2763/10.1145/2702613.2728655
27. Lee, S., Park, K., Lee, J., Kim, K.: User study of VR basic controller and data glove as hand gesture inputs in VR games. In: 2017 International Symposium on Ubiquitous Virtual Reality (ISUVR), pp. 1–3, June 2017
28. Liu, M., Nancel, M., Vogel, D.: Gunslinger: subtle arms-down mid-air interaction. In: Proceedings of the 28th Annual ACM Symposium on User Interface Software & Technology, UIST 2015, pp. 63–71. ACM, New York (2015). http://libezp.nmsu.edu:2763/10.1145/2807442.2807489
29. Lu, W., Tong, Z., Chu, J.: Dynamic hand gesture recognition with leap motion controller. IEEE Signal Process. Lett. **23**(9), 1188–1192 (2016)
30. Lv, Z., Halawani, A., Feng, S., Ur Réhman, S., Li, H.: Touch-less interactive augmented reality game on vision-based wearable device. Pers. Ubiquitous Comput. **19**(3–4), 551–567 (2015). https://doi.org/10.1007/s00779-015-0844-1
31. MacKenzie, I.S.: Fitts' law as a research and design tool in human-computer interaction. Hum. Comput. Interact. **7**(1), 91–139 (1992). https://doi.org/10.1207/s15327051hci0701_3
32. Matthies, D.J.C., Müller, F., Anthes, C., Kranzlmüller, D.: Shoesolesense: proof of concept for a wearable foot interface for virtual and real environments. In: Proceedings of the 19th ACM Symposium on Virtual Reality Software and Technology, VRST 2013, pp. 93–96. ACM, New York (2013). http://libezp.nmsu.edu:4009/10.1145/2503713.2503740
33. Morasso, P.: Spatial control of arm movements. Exp. Brain Res. **42**(2), 223–227 (1981). https://doi.org/10.1007/BF00236911

34. Moroney, W.F., Biers, D.W., Eggemeier, F.T., Mitchell, J.A.: A comparison of two scoring procedures with the NASA task load index in a simulated flight task. In: Proceedings of the IEEE 1992 National Aerospace and Electronics Conference, NAECON 1992, pp. 734–740. IEEE (1992)
35. Moser, C., Tscheligi, M.: Physics-based gaming: exploring touch vs. mid-air gesture input. In: Proceedings of the 14th International Conference on Interaction Design and Children, IDC 2015, pp. 291–294. ACM, New York (2015). http://libezp.nmsu.edu:4009/10.1145/2771839.2771899
36. Mueller, F.F., Byrne, R., Andres, J., Patibanda, R.: Experiencing the body as play. In: Proceedings of the 2018 CHI Conference on Human Factors in Computing Systems, CHI 2018, pp. 210:1–210:13. ACM, New York (2018). https://doi.org/10.1145/3173574.3173784
37. Napier, J., Napier, J.R., Tuttle, R.H.: Hands, vol. 9. Princeton University Press, Princeton (1993)
38. Norman, D.: The Design of Everyday Things: Revised and Expanded Edition. Basic Books, Revised 2013 edn. (2013)
39. Paavilainen, J., Hamari, J., Stenros, J., Kinnunen, J.: Social network games: players' perspectives. Simul. Gaming 44(6), 794–820 (2013). https://doi.org/10.1177/1046878113514808
40. Peixoto, P., Carreira, J.: A natural hand gesture human computer interface using contour signatures (2005)
41. Pino, A., Tzemis, E., Ioannou, N., Kouroupetroglou, G.: Using kinect for 2D and 3D pointing tasks: performance evaluation. In: Kurosu, M. (ed.) HCI 2013. LNCS, vol. 8007, pp. 358–367. Springer, Heidelberg (2013). https://doi.org/10.1007/978-3-642-39330-3_38
42. Rautaray, S.S., Agrawal, A.: Interaction with virtual game through hand gesture recognition. In: 2011 International Conference on Multimedia, Signal Processing and Communication Technologies, pp. 244–247, December 2011
43. Rautaray, S.S., Agrawal, A.: Vision based hand gesture recognition for human computer interaction: a survey. Artif. Intell. Rev. 43(1), 1–54 (2015). https://doi.org/10.1007/s10462-012-9356-9
44. Reifinger, S., Wallhoff, F., Ablassmeier, M., Poitschke, T., Rigoll, G.: Static and dynamic hand-gesture recognition for augmented reality applications. In: Jacko, J.A. (ed.) HCI 2007. LNCS, vol. 4552, pp. 728–737. Springer, Heidelberg (2007). https://doi.org/10.1007/978-3-540-73110-8_79
45. Sambrooks, L., Wilkinson, B.: Comparison of gestural, touch, and mouse interaction with Fitts' law. In: Proceedings of the 25th Australian Computer-Human Interaction Conference: Augmentation, Application, Innovation, Collaboration, OzCHI 2013, pp. 119–122. ACM, New York (2013). http://libezp.nmsu.edu:4009/10.1145/2541016.2541066
46. Seixas, M.C.B., Cardoso, J.C.S., Dias, M.T.G.: The leap motion movement for 2D pointing tasks: characterisation and comparison to other devices. In: 2015 International Conference on Pervasive and Embedded Computing and Communication Systems (PECCS), pp. 15–24, February 2015
47. Spanogianopoulos, S., Sirlantzis, K., Mentzelopoulos, M., Protopsaltis, A.: Human computer interaction using gestures for mobile devices and serious games: a review. In: 2014 International Conference on Interactive Mobile Communication Technologies and Learning, IMCL 2014, pp. 310–314, November 2014
48. Sridhar, S., Feit, A.M., Theobalt, C., Oulasvirta, A.: Investigating the dexterity of multi-finger input for mid-air text entry. In: Proceedings of the 33rd Annual ACM

Conference on Human Factors in Computing Systems, CHI 2015, pp. 3643–3652. ACM, New York (2015). https://doi.org/10.1145/2702123.2702136

49. Staretu, I., Moldovan, C.: Leap motion device used to control a real anthropomorphic gripper. Int. J. Adv. Rob. Syst. **13**(3), 113 (2016). https://doi.org/10.5772/63973

50. Svoboda, J., Bronstein, M.M., Drahansky, M.: Contactless biometric hand geometry recognition using a low-cost 3D camera. In: 2015 International Conference on Biometrics (ICB), pp. 452–457, May 2015

51. Tabor, A., Bateman, S., Scheme, E., Flatla, D.R., Gerling, K.: Designing game-based myoelectric prosthesis training. In: Proceedings of the 2017 CHI Conference on Human Factors in Computing Systems, CHI 2017, pp. 1352–1363. ACM, New York (2017). https://doi.org/10.1145/3025453.3025676

52. Tabor, A., Kienzle, A., Smith, C., Watson, A., Wuertz, J., Hanna, D.: The falling of momo: a myo-electric controlled game to support research in prosthesis training. In: Proceedings of the 2016 Annual Symposium on Computer-Human Interaction in Play Companion Extended Abstracts, CHI PLAY Companion 2016, pp. 71–77. ACM, New York (2016). https://doi.org/10.1145/2968120.2971806

53. Tognazzini, B.: First principles of interaction design. Interaction design solutions for the real world, AskTog (2003)

54. Ververidis, D., Karavarsamis, S., Nikolopoulos, S., Kompatsiaris, I.: Pottery gestures style comparison by exploiting myo sensor and forearm anatomy. In: Proceedings of the 3rd International Symposium on Movement and Computing, MOCO 2016, pp. 3:1–3:8. ACM, New York (2016). http://libezp.nmsu.edu:4009/10.1145/2948910.2948924

55. Vokorokos, L., Mihal'ov, J., Chovancová, E.: Motion sensors: gesticulation efficiency across multiple platforms. In: 2016 IEEE 20th Jubilee International Conference on Intelligent Engineering Systems (INES), pp. 293–298, June 2016

56. Vrellis, I., Moutsioulis, A., Mikropoulos, T.A.: Primary school students' attitude towards gesture based interaction: a comparison between microsoft kinect and mouse. In: 2014 IEEE 14th International Conference on Advanced Learning Technologies, pp. 678–682, July 2014

57. Wachs, J.P., Kölsch, M., Stern, H., Edan, Y.: Vision-based hand-gesture applications. Commun. ACM **54**(2), 60–71 (2011). http://libezp.nmsu.edu:2763/10.1145/1897816.1897838

58. Weichert, F., Bachmann, D., Rudak, B., Fisseler, D.: Analysis of the accuracy and robustness of the leap motion controller. Sensors **13**(5), 6380–6393 (2013). http://www.mdpi.com/1424-8220/13/5/6380

59. Wuertz, J., et al.: A design framework for awareness cues in distributed multiplayer games. In: Proceedings of the 2018 CHI Conference on Human Factors in Computing Systems, CHI 2018, pp. 243:1–243:14. ACM, New York (2018). https://doi.org/10.1145/3173574.3173817

60. Yao, Y., Chiu, P.T., Fu, W.T.: A gestural interface for practicing children's spatial skills. In: Proceedings of the 22nd International Conference on Intelligent User Interfaces Companion, IUI 2017 Companion, pp. 43–47. ACM, New York (2017). http://libezp.nmsu.edu:2763/10.1145/3030024.3038265

61. Yuan, B., Folmer, E., Harris, F.C.: Game accessibility: a survey. Univers. Access Inform. Soc. **10**(1), 81–100 (2011). https://doi.org/10.1007/s10209-010-0189-5

62. Zhang, K., Zhai, Y., Leong, H.W., Wang, S.: An interaction educational computer game framework using hand gesture recognition. In: Proceedings of the 4th International Conference on Internet Multimedia Computing and Service, ICIMCS

2012, pp. 219–222. ACM, New York (2012). http://libezp.nmsu.edu:2763/10.1145/2382336.2382398

63. Zhang, X., Chen, X., Wang, W.H., Yang, J.H., Lantz, V., Wang, K.Q.: Hand gesture recognition and virtual game control based on 3D accelerometer and EMG sensors. In: Proceedings of the 14th International Conference on Intelligent User Interfaces, IUI 2009, pp. 401–406. ACM, New York (2009). http://libezp.nmsu.edu:2763/10.1145/1502650.1502708

64. Zhu, Y., Yuan, B.: Real-time hand gesture recognition with kinect for playing racing video games. In: 2014 International Joint Conference on Neural Networks (IJCNN), pp. 3240–3246, July 2014

The Social Acceptability of Peripheral Interaction with 3D Gestures in a Simulated Setting

Sara Nielsen[1], Lucca Julie Nellemann[1], Lars Bo Larsen[1,2(✉)], and Kashmiri Stec[2]

[1] Aalborg University, Aalborg, Denmark
snie@cs.aau.dk, LuccaJNellemann@outlook.dk, lbl@es.aau.dk
[2] Bang and Olufsen, Struer, Denmark
ksh@bang-olufsen.dk

Abstract. We investigate the effects of social context on the acceptability of 3D (touchless) gestures used to control a music system. We also focus on the extent to which gesture control can be regarded as peripheral interaction [3]. We first identified six gestures for player control to use in the social acceptability study. Next, we used a Wizard-of-Oz design to investigate social acceptability by inviting user dyads (N = 24 participants) to a living room setting where they were assigned the roles of host or guest. The host used gestures to control the music system responding to cues while the guest engaged them in a distractor task. We video recorded the interaction and interviewed participants separately about their experiences. We found no reservations from either male, female, mature or young users about gesture interaction, and no distinction between groups with respect to social acceptability. Taken together, this suggests that gesture control is socially acceptable for all users. We analysed gaze direction when gesturing based on the video recordings. Using this as an indicator for user attention we also found evidence that gesture control can indeed exist in the periphery of attention.

Keywords: Gesture interfaces · Social acceptability of gestures · Peripheral interaction with gestures · Gestures for music player control · Natural interfaces · Human centric · User experience · Age group comparison

1 Introduction

3D (touchless) gesture interaction to control content has long been the focus of user studies. The research has addressed a number of issues, from the identification of appropriate use cases and system functions, which can best take advantage of the strengths of gesture control [35, 37], to the means by which gestures should be created by designers [21, 23, 43]. Other studies have aimed to elicit gestures selected by users [46, 47, 54], to the acceptability of gesture control in various social settings [9, 32, 44].

In this study, we take as a starting point a limited use case (basic music player control) and use it to investigate social acceptability and peripheral interaction, a kind of calm technology [52]. Social acceptability is the dynamic, real-time processing of personal

© Springer Nature Switzerland AG 2020
M. Kurosu (Ed.): HCII 2020, LNCS 12182, pp. 77–95, 2020.
https://doi.org/10.1007/978-3-030-49062-1_5

and physical experiences combined with a higher-level interpretation and reflection of the interaction [19, 53]. Peripheral interaction is the perception of and physical interaction with devices in the periphery of attention [3]. Inspired by Cabreira and Hwang [11], we do this by comparing two groups of users: young users (aged 30 or below) and mature users (31 or above). This group comparison is important to ensure that in adopting a user-centred approach [18, 46], we are as inclusive in our design and usability considerations as possible [14, 24].

Although few products with gestures for basic player control exist today, interest is steadily growing. Samsung's SmartTV (2013) [45] accepts 3D gestures for basic player control; so do BMW in their 7-series cars (2015) [7], where 3D gesture interaction can control the in-car infotainment system. Further, at the time of writing, several projects have been funded on kickstarter which promise basic player control, e.g. Ninja Blocks, Hayo and Bixi [6, 22, 36]. Piccolo [40], a start-up funded by Y Combinator, envisages a visual assistant which accepts gesture input to control domestic experiences much like the voice assistants on offer from Google, Amazon and Apple do. Apple has not announced 3D gesture-controlled devices, but was awarded a patent in 2013 for "Three Dimensional User Interface Session Control" [18].

What Piccolo, Bixi and others working with gesture input share is a focus on use cases: basic interactions that can meet a majority of user needs. When designed appropriately, they take full advantage of both the strengths of gesture interaction, and the promise of peripheral interaction. As the technology matures and is able to meet user needs for usability and design, it's increasingly crucial that gesture interaction is comfortable and appropriate for users of all ages, and socially acceptable despite the changes in audience or setting that come with in-home use [37].

Because of this, our aim is to investigate the social acceptability of 3D gesture control in situ, using a naturalistic setting. This is important as most studies focus on single users in laboratory settings [11, 13, 46, 47], a situation which is never encountered in real life. As technology is advancing to meet human usability needs, it's increasingly necessary to design and test these systems in situ, where users will make use of them as part of ordinary interactions in their everyday life (see, e.g. [38]). Because of this growing need, we created a living room environment and invited pairs of friends to test the gesture interaction in the form of an everyday scenario: we asked respondents to engage in a role play, where one friend played "the host", and was responsible for using gestures to control a music system, and the other friend played "the guest", and was responsible for keeping the pair "on task" as they planned a holiday together. The gesture controlled music player was placed in the living room environment. Unbeknownst to the guest, the host interacted with the system according to a set of cues which were edited into the playlist. In this way, we were able to assess the effects of gesture control on both the user and spectator, as well as the extent to which peripheral interaction influences interaction with the device.

We emphasize that our experiment emulates a naturalistic setting only to a certain degree. Although the setting resembles a living room, it is not the home of the host. The holiday will not take place, and the cues for the host are consequences of the experimental design, and do not necessarily reflect the user's true desire for controlling music playback. In Sect. 5.1 we will return to these issues and discuss the impact on the validity of the findings.

We simulate the gesture detection using Wizard-of-Oz to achieve error-free gesture interaction. Thus, we create a best-case scenario, that will be hard to achieve with current gesture recognition technology. However, as our goal is to verify whether gesture control is a credible and socially acceptable candidate for peripheral interaction in the home, it is necessary to first investigate the "best case" in a controlled environment. Indeed, if this best-case scenario fails to be socially acceptable, there is no need to invest in developing either the technology or commercial products utilizing it to a high-performance level, as they are not likely to be used.

In the best-case scenario, we report on here, we expect that if gesture control truly qualifies as peripheral interaction, then, over time, the hosts should reduce the number of times they look at the device while gesturing to it and the guests should reduce the number of times they look at the host performing the gestures. Further, we expect that because gesture control has the potential to be less intrusive than other types of interaction (compared, e.g., to voice or mobile phone apps), it has a high likelihood of being socially acceptable for all participants – provided the gestures meet standards for social acceptability. This is indeed what we look for.

In this paper, we report on the results and implications from this study. In so doing, we provide a methodology for assessing some of the group comparisons, which are necessary when designing for a wide audience, as well as a methodology for investigating peripheral interaction and social acceptability with respect to 3D gesture control. In this way, we contribute to a growing body of knowledge on 3D, freehand gesture interactions by investigating the effects of the user's social context on their interactions with systems that have gesture control.

In the following, we describe relevant work from human-human gesture studies, user-centred methods for eliciting and selecting 3D gestures for smart devices, the importance of considering social context both with respect to social acceptability and age group comparisons, and the role of peripheral interaction in gesture control. This is followed by a presentation of our methodology and findings. We close with a discussion of the implications of these results for the products with gesture control.

2 Related Work

2.1 Gestures as Emblems

The gestures we consider in this project have variously been referred to as 3D gestures, freehand gestures, 3D gestures and air gestures as they are made by the hands moving in free space. This contrasts to semaphores, which are arbitrary hand and arm movements that create limited languages such as those used when taxying an aircraft or coordinating work in noisy factories [21, 26]. Whereas semaphores are purposefully made to be unnatural so as to maximize their communicative value in the workplace, gesture control for the home environment seeks to pair handshapes (also called hand forms or poses) to maximize feelings of intuitiveness and naturalness for the user. In this sense, they are emblems [16, 30]: hand and finger movements whose meaning is easily verbalized, easily produced, easily understood and, crucially, naturally makes sense to a community of users because they draw on either community standards [16] or an iconic relationship between the gesture and its intended meaning [39].

2.2 Gestures for Content Control

Gesture interaction for the smart home has typically investigated the context of TV control, where special focus is given to identifying appropriate gestures and mapping those gestures to functions, e.g. [17, 41, 56]. Typically, the functions of interest include play, pause, next and previous track/song/channel/chapter, and volume up/down. Depending on the project, other functions may also be included, e.g. size of the viewing screen, menu, favourite(s), point, select or confirm and undo or cancel. As only the first six functions ("basic player control") are relevant for controlling audio playback, we focus our study on them.

Following Wobbrock et al. [54] and Norman [37], who both point out the problems of relying on the expertise of designers at the expense of the user's experience, many of these studies involve users in the design process, e.g. [27, 29, 47, 54, 56]. While this approach solves some challenges, it creates others. For example, many people are unconscious of the gestures they naturally produce with their hands during conversation [31] and so may be unable to either propose or reflect on appropriate gestures to control their interactions with a device. Further, asking users to create gestures in an experimental setting can lead to the creation of an "accepted" gesture set which relies on artefacts from past experiences rather than taking full advantage of the new modality, e.g. a trace of the letter "M" for Menu or a trace of the letter "O" for Open menu on a smart TV, as in [56]. While these gestures clearly demonstrate a link between domains of use, they fail to take advantage of the spatial modality offered by gesture interaction and risk being inappropriate on a global scale. Because of this, for each function, we asked (N = 18) users to rank their preferred gestures (top 3, bottom 1). In our study, the selected gestures are a combination of those found in scientific literature (e.g. [46]) and those created by the first and second authors of this study [34] using the aforementioned method. This is described in detail in the following section. We use these user-selected gestures to investigate our main area of interest: the social acceptability of gesture interaction.

2.3 Social Context Matters

Any device that enters the home will be used in a social setting. Because of this, assessing the social acceptability of an interaction modality (in general) and instantiation (specific gesture forms) in a naturalistic or simulated setting is crucial to understanding whether the system will be adopted, loved and used regularly in the home [15, 28]. In this context, location, audience and type of gestures all play important roles [42, 49, 53], with European users exhibiting strong preferences for discrete gestures performed in the presence of family or friends [42].

Although familiarity and social acceptability are dynamic processes which change as users become more familiar with the system [48], the social acceptability of an initial encounter is important as it may make or break the chance for adoption [12]. Both Brewster et al. and Montero et al. [9, 32] suggest that any investigation into social acceptance should take into account the user's and the spectator's (or observer's) social acceptance of the interaction, as social acceptability tends to improve when it is obvious that the user is interacting with a device and not, e.g., doing something strange or weird [1, 44, 53]. In short, designers should strive to make users feel good about the interaction – and, to the extent possible, prevent users from feeling like dorks in their own homes.

To the best of our knowledge, only two studies have compared young and mature users in the context of 3D gesture interaction: Bobeth et al. [8] conclude that older users can and will perform gestures, but with uncertainty. Similarly, Cabreira and Hwang [11] compare evaluations of first-time use, and find that while all users could perform the gestures, only younger users were confident and comfortable doing so. As this raises obvious questions about social acceptability for mature users, we include an age group comparison so that our results are more generalizable both with respect to user population and scope of applicability.

2.4 Peripheral Interaction Enables Gesture Control

One of the strengths of 3D gesture interaction is its ability to shift interaction into the periphery – of attention, interactional space, etc. – and enable the kind of calm computing envisioned by Weiser and Brown [52]. This is particularly true when compared to other interaction modalities: voice interaction interrupts and restructures conversations (see Brown, [10]), while apps require shifting focused visual attention to a screen. Most work in this area has focused on the role of micro-gestures which can be performed by small finger movements, e.g. [2, 55]. We hypothesize that 3D gestures enable peripheral interaction, and investigate it in our study in two ways: first, by noting the visual attention participants (both hosts and guests) give to the gestures in our study, and second, by directly asking participants about the extent to which gesture control enabled or prevented the user's involvement in the distractor task. Observing the visual attention (i.e. the gaze direction) only constitutes indirect evidence of peripheral interaction. However, as humans are predominantly visually oriented (see e.g. Juola p. 40 [25]), we argue that direction of visual attention can be used as an indication of at least a relaxation of the attention [25].

3   Methods

We begin this section with our research questions. Next, we briefly describe the elicitation task which identified the six gestures used in the social acceptability study. Following this, we describe the experimental design of the social acceptability study, including the selection of participants. Throughout, we adopt a user-centric approach [18, 46, 54].

Research Questions. Our research questions are: (1) What is the social acceptability of a media player controlled by 3D gestures in the home, presuming optimal gesture detection? (2) Can gesture control be used in the periphery of attention (i.e. as a peripheral interaction modality)? (3) Does the user's age affect answers to either RQ1 or RQ2?

Gestures for Player Control. The gestures used in this study are depicted in Fig. 1. The figure shows the gestures for basic player control: Play (a), Volume up (b), Next track (c), Pause (d), Volume down (e) and Previous track (f). We focus on these functions as they

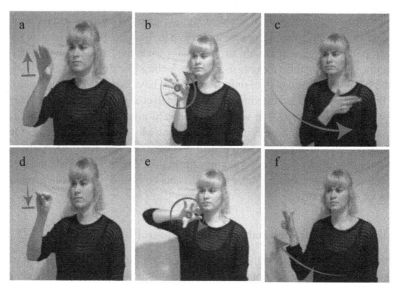

Fig. 1. User-selected gestures for player control: Play (a), Volume up (b), Next track (c), Pause (d), Volume down (e) and Previous track (f). The arrows indicate direction of the movement.

are most often used, and therefore hypothesised to be the best suited for investigating the role of gestures with respect to peripheral interaction.

We identified these gestures using an elicitation task with 18 young (age 30 or younger) users recruited from Aalborg University [34]. Apart from one left-handed user, each participant self-identified as right-handed with normal hearing. In the task, users were first shown short videos which demonstrated each gesture with the appropriate functional feedback; users were presented with 7–9 options per function. After each of the gestures had been presented for a given function, users were presented with a visual summary of the gestures and asked to rank their preferences (top 3 and bottom 1), to talk about what they liked and disliked about the gesture forms, and to propose alternates. Alternates could be variations of one of the gestures they had seen (e.g. number of fingers used or tension in the hand) or a new gesture entirely. The gestures presented in Fig. 1 are the winning gestures from this study.

Social Acceptability Study Design. Twenty-four (15 male and 9 female) participants from Aalborg University participated in this study. Of these, 12 were young (30 years or younger; mean age 23 years, range 21–27 years; 4 female) and 12 were mature (31 years or older; mean age 51 years, range 36–80 years; 5 female). We make this distinction because other studies indicate there may be differences in gesture acceptance according to age group [8, 11]. All dyads knew each other; this was an important inclusion criteria for ensuring comfortable, naturalistic behaviour, (see Müller et al. [33]). Young participants were recruited from students in the social sciences faculty. Students from design- or technical programmes were viewed as potentially biased and excluded.

Mature participants were recruited among the administrative and scientific staff at Aalborg University. Further, all participants were native Danish speakers and self-identified their handedness.

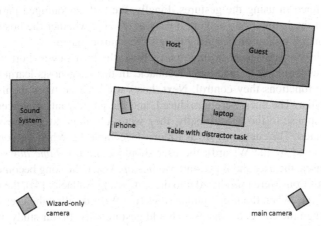

Fig. 2. The setting for the social acceptability study (walls, door and window not shown). The host and guest are sitting in a couch. The computer and phone are on a coffee table in front of them.

Right-handed participants were always assigned the role of host; guests could be either left- or right-handed. To maximize visibility of the gestures, all sessions were recorded with the main camera angled at approximately 45° with respect to the participants [33] as this improves gesture visibility during analysis.

The setting for the social acceptability study is shown in Fig. 2. The room evokes a typical living room with couch, coffee table, sound system and windows (not shown in the figure). The sound system (a Beosound 3200 [5]) is located to the user's right, away from the guest. For a right-handed user performing gestures, this is the ideal setup for peripheral interaction with a device, as it is furthest from the interaction space shared by the host and guest [50, 51]. The Wizard's camera is located near the sound system so that the Wizard can see "what the system would see". The host was trained and interviewed in this room. A smaller room with a couch and window was used by the guest to prepare the distractor task and for the guest's post-task interview.

The study consists of three parts: training, task and interview. During training (15 min), the host learned to perform the gestures and to use them in response to cues built into the soundtrack. At the same time, the guest prepared a distractor task (holiday planning). During the task (15 min), the guest engaged the host in holiday planning. At the same time, the sound system played music which was controlled by the host's gestures, according to a set of cues described below. Finally, the host and guest were interviewed separately about their experiences (15 min). The entire study was designed to take 45 min.

The distraction task was carefully selected. Firstly, planning a holiday is a common task for friends to engage in; because of this, we could expect our participants to have experience with the activity. The task was also considered realistic for the timeframe of the experiment. Secondly, having a semi-structured activity helps to create presence in an experimental setting. This was needed to ensure a familiar social setting [30]. Thirdly, preparing the holiday trip also provided an activity for the guests during the time the hosts were trained in using the gestures. Finally, the task encouraged participants to concentrate on the laptop, thus making it easy to observe whether the hosts' attention was focused on the task or on gesturing towards the music player.

Training the host consisted of three parts. First, the host saw a short video showing the gestures paired with functional feedback. In this way, hosts learnt the gesture forms and the functions they control. Next, hosts tried the gestures themselves with a training playlist. The cues were introduced, and the participants practiced using the gestures in response to the cues. Finally, they were left alone to gesture whenever a cue was presented. The cues used are as follows (see Table 1). When the sound volume increases (initiated by the Wizard), the user should gesture *volume down*. When the volume decreases, the user should gesture *volume up*. When the song becomes distorted (30 s-long distortions were introduced into the song using Audacity [4]), the user should gesture *next track*. When the user's phone rings (the Wizard calls), the user should gesture *pause*. When the call ends, the user should gesture *play*. In our study, we omit the gesture for *previous track* both because of its similarity to *next track* and because in pilot testing, the cues created more confusion than opportunities to observe it. In total, the playlist comprised 7 tracks of music and the host received 24 gesture cues throughout the testing session, for approx. 15 min of playback time.

Table 1. The cues used to elicit gesture control during the social acceptability task.

Agent	Cue	Gesture to perform
Wizard	Phone call	*Pause*
User	Hang up phone	*Play*
Wizard	Volume goes up	*Volume down*
Wizard	Volume goes down	*Volume up*
Edited into song	Distortion in the song	*Next track*

While the host received training, the guest was given a laptop and asked to brainstorm three types (budget, average and luxury) of two-week long holidays they could go on with the host. They were given a budget for each type of holiday and asked to make plans accordingly.

During the task, the host and guest were left alone in the living room environment shown in Fig. 1 and discussed plans for the three types of holidays they could take together. At the same time, the host used gestures to respond to the cues in the playlist and control the sound system. The Wizard used the phone calls as an opportunity to give the host instructions, e.g. if the host failed to react to cues repeatedly. Hosts were given a mobile phone which the experimenter called.

Finally, each participant was interviewed separately in the room where they had prepared the task: the host in the main room and the guest in the alternate room.

4 Results

This section presents the results of the study and is organized such that we first present information derived from observations of the participants followed by a discussion of the post-test interviews. Due to the nature of the study, our analysis is primarily qualitative and does not include extended statistical analyses or hypothesis testing. Where applicable, we summarise the findings numerically. For each topic, we include both young and mature respondents, and any similarities or differences we found, according to the research questions outlined in the previous section. We refer to hosts and guests with the prefixes "Y" for young, "M" for mature, "H" for host and "G" for guest, followed by a number. We include illustrative quotes from participants where appropriate. These are freely translated from Danish and are indicated using italics. The data is analysed with respect to age group, as previous studies indicate there might be differences between young and mature respondents, see [8, 11]. Where relevant, we report other demographic distinctions, such as male/female.

Table 2. Breakdown of age distribution and task time for young and mature respondents

	Young	Mature
Avg. age, st.dev, range	23.2 1.6 (21–27) years	51.0 12.7 (36–80) years
Familiarisation time	15 min	20 min
Task time	16 min	14 min
Post test interview time	8 min	8 min
Total time, st.dev, range	38 1.35 (37–42) min	42 5.21 (38–54) min

The 24 respondents were split into two age groups, young (up to 30 years) and mature (31 and above). Table 2 Shows the age and time distribution for the participants. Time variation was larger for mature participants (SD = 5:21 min) than for young ones (SD = 1:35 min), probably due to this being a less homogeneous group.

4.1 Results Related to Gesture Reproduction and Peripheral Interaction

Gesture Reproduction. For young hosts, the Wizard could interpret and react to all gestures. However, the hosts still made mistakes. YH3, YH4 and YH5 all made errors where they used a full hand for the next gesture instead of just two fingers (see Fig. 1). In some cases, this gesture was also produced with a single finger (YH4, YH5). YH3 generally started the next gesture correctly but ended it with a full hand (denoted as "lazy hand"). YH3 reproduced the gesture correctly in the familiarisation phase, so this is likely an effect of gaining confidence during the test and thus a relaxing of gesture reproduction (similar to McNeill's notion of catchment [31]). The young hosts generally reacted correctly to the cues, although, e.g., YH1 repeatedly missed cues for Volume Up/Down and Play/Pause, remarking that he usually didn't turn off the music because of a phone call.

We saw a similar pattern for the mature hosts. The Wizard could identify all control gestures. The only gesture that exhibited variation was *next*, which some users produced with either a full hand or three fingers (MH1, MH4, MH6). However, the mature hosts exhibited some problems recognising and understanding the cues, especially the distortion which was edited into the tracks.

When the hosts were asked how they had experienced the interaction using gestures, all said the gestures had been easy to learn and remember – a fact which is also confirmed by the low observed number of errors. Young hosts made a total of two gesture errors and mature hosts made 8. The total expected number of gestures for each host is 24 gestures. Young hosts found the gestures very intuitive and related them to gestures known from smartphones (YH3, YH4, YH5) and *"the swipe culture"* (YH4, MH5). All hosts claimed to have reproduced the gestures correctly, and said they could manage both the gesture interaction and the distraction task simultaneously without the gestures being disruptive. In contrast to this, nearly all hosts and guests mentioned that the gesture cues had been quite disruptive, especially the phone calls (the cue for "pause"). A majority of mature hosts (MH2, MH3, MH5, MH6) and two young hosts (YH1, YH6) mentioned the volume up/down gestures as *"the least comfortable"* gesture to reproduce. Only one host (MH3) mentioned problems remembering the gestures *"a little in the beginning"*. All respondents had prior experience with 2D gestures (e.g. from smartphones), but only one had tried 3D gestures (for gaming).

Peripheral Interaction. To determine whether the hosts exhibited signs of peripheral interaction, we observed whether hosts looked at the sound system while performing the control gestures. These results are summarised in Fig. 3 below. We find that hosts exhibit quite different individual behaviours in this regard. If the test protocol was strictly followed, the task required 24 gestures in total. However, not all hosts did that (e.g. YH3 performed at least 25 gestures, as seen in Fig. 3), so some findings are reported as percentages for comparison. Figure 3 shows marked individual differences: four users – two young and two mature (YH1, YH2, MH3 and MH5) – almost never look at the device while gesturing. In contrast, six users – two young and four mature (YH3, YH4, MH1, MH2, MH4, MH6) – almost always looked.

To investigate the extent that guests were aware of the hosts' gestures, we observed how often they looked at the hosts performing the gestures. This is shown in Fig. 4.

Figure 4 displays percentages rather than numbers as it was not always possible to observe the guests' gaze direction from the video recordings, and thus the number of observations differs between guests. Excluding MG1, who closely observed the host throughout the task, the guests saw 18% of the hosts' gestures on average.

Finally, as part of the post-test interview, we asked all guests to produce the control gestures used by the host. These results are summarised in Fig. 5.

Figure 5 shows that most guests were able to reproduce the gestures correctly, though with some observable differences. For example, the *volume up/down* (Fig. 1b, e) gestures were produced correctly or partly correctly by all guests. *Next* (Fig. 1c) was often

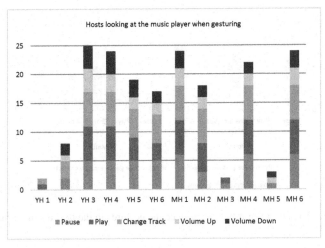

Fig. 3. The number of times the hosts looked at the music system when gesturing.

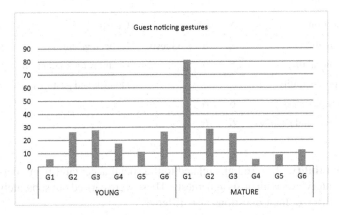

Fig. 4. Percentage of times the guests noticed the hosts' gestures.

produced with the correct movement component but an incorrect handshape, with a full hand instead of the two fingers indicated in Fig. 1c. For mature guests in particular, *next*, *pause* and *play* (Fig. 1c, d, a) seemed to be harder to reproduce than *volume up/down* (Fig. 1b, e).

This is consistent with the interview data. Indeed, all guests noticed that the hosts used gestures to control the sound system. However, when asked if they felt the gestures took attention from the planning task, all young guests, and the majority of the mature guests, answered they didn't feel so. MG1 felt the gestures had interfered and MG4 also expressed this, but to a lesser degree. Nearly all hosts and guests mentioned that the cues used to trigger the hosts' gestures had been much more noticeable. All guests agreed that the hosts could manage both the planning task and the gestures, though YG1 remarked that YH1 sometimes lost focus. The answers are summarised in Table 3.

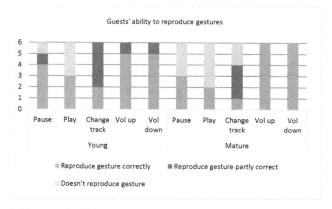

Fig. 5. The guest's ability to reproduce the gestures in the post test interview.

Table 3. Summary of Guests' and Hosts' answers about gesturing. There were 6 respondents in all cells. The numbers indicate answers displaying a positive attitude to gesture interaction

	Question	Y	M		Question	Y	M
Hosts	Learnability	6	6	Guests	Noticed gestures	6	6
	Memorability	5	5		Gestures took attention	6	4
	Reproducibility	5	5		Do task and gestures	6	6
	Disruptiveness	6	6				
	Do task and gestures	6	6				

Social Acceptability. The findings related to the social acceptability are derived from the post-test interviews with hosts and guests. These were carried out separately. As their experiences differed, their questions also differed.

Guests' Attitudes to Gesture Interaction in a Social Context

These interview questions were focused on gestures in a real-life context. We asked four questions about social acceptability;

- Q1. How would you feel, if you saw your friend do the gestures (in a real-life situation)?
- Q2. Would it make a difference who you are with?
- Q3. Do you think the gestures could work in a social context?
- Q4. Could you see yourself using gestures to control a music system?

All guests said they would be comfortable seeing a friend using the gestures to control a sound system. Likewise, the overall reply to Q2 was "*No*", (i.e. they would be comfortable regardless of who else was present) except YG4, MG4, and MG5, who remark that it depends on who's in control of the device. All guests said they would expect gesture interaction to be comfortable in a social setting. However, some guests (YG1, YG2, and all MG) expressed reservations about a party situation, where control was considered problematic. Finally, all guests could see themselves using gesture control as experienced in the experiment in the future.

Hosts' Attitudes to Gesture Interaction in a Social Context

We asked the hosts four questions related to the social acceptability of gesture interaction;

- Q1. How do you think gesture interaction will work alone and in a social context?
- Q2. Will the location make a difference?
- Q3. Were there any gestures that made you feel uncomfortable?
- Q4. Could you see yourself using gestures to control a music system?

All hosts responded positively to Q1, but also thought the location made a difference (Q2). However, just like the guests, many hosts expressed doubts whether gesture interaction would work in a party situation (YH1, YH5, YH6, and MH5). MH1, MH2, and MH3 expressed doubts about gesturing in "public spaces" and MH2 was concerned that humans gesturing to each other (not the device) may confuse the system. MH1 noted that *"gestures are less awkward than spoken commands"*. YH3 remarked that *"doing gestures might make one look ridiculous in a social context"*. Answers to Q3 were all related to the physical (dis)comfort of producing the gestures, not whether they felt socially awkward: YH1, YH6, MH3, MH5, MH6 all felt the volume up/down gestures were harder to produce than the other gestures. MH1 found the next (track) gesture uncomfortable. Finally, like the guests, all hosts said they would use gestures in the future when it becomes available. However, young hosts expressed greater enthusiasm, e.g. YH1: *"it's better than a remote"*, YH3: *"Yes, definitely"*, YH5: *"gestures would be fun"*, YH6: *"a cool gadget, I want one"* and *"I would use gestures for everything"*. At the same time, some hosts expressed reservations, e.g. YH1: *"I wouldn't pay extra for it"*, and MH6: *"I would only use gestures, e.g., if my hands were dirty"* (Table 4).

Table 4. Summary of Guests' and Hosts' answers to social acceptability. There were 6 respondents in all cells. The numbers indicate answers with a positive attitude to gesture interaction

	Question	Young	Mature		Question	Young	Mature
Hosts	Q1	6	5	Guests	Q1	5	6
	Q2	5	4		Q2	4	2
	Q3	6	5		Q3	5	3
	Q4	5	6		Q4	6	6

Table 4 summarizes the respondents' attitudes towards gestures. For the Hosts' Q1, the answer is interpreted as a "yes" to both alone and in a social context.

5 Discussion

This section discusses the results as well as the experimental design and limitations.

5.1 Experimental Design Considerations

As mentioned in the previous section, not all hosts strictly followed the experimental protocol. In some instances, they missed (or deliberately ignored) a cue. In others, the host changed tracks or adjusted the volume without being given a cue. As the focus of the study is on social acceptability, we chose to limit interference with the participants when performing the task to the extent possible, and therefore corrected the hosts as little as possible.

The participants were not made aware of the Wizard-of-Oz setup. Despite this, they did not comment on this or the presence of the cameras when interviewed. The setting, although situated at Aalborg University, closely resembled a living room. We therefore posit a high ecological validity regarding the physical environment. However, the configuration of the room and the setting was ideal for gesture interaction as the hosts were placed with the music system to their right and the guest to the left. Thus, the hosts could use their dominant hand (right for all hosts) without interfering with the personal space of the guests.

During the interviews, all hosts and guests commented on the cues for the gestures, which they found annoying and disruptive. This is hard to avoid in an experimental situation, as we needed an incentive for the hosts to perform a high number of gestures in a short period of time (24 gestures in 15 min). This clearly had an impact on the social interaction for the host and guest as they tried to complete the planning task. The question arises, whether the impact of the cues could in fact dominate the experience to the extent that participants felt the gestures to be less intrusive than they would feel in a real-life scenario. This is a possibility that must be taken into account, when interpreting the findings.

All decoding and interpretation of the gestures were carried out error-free by the Wizard. Therefore, the participants experienced only a best-case scenario. In real life, errors will occur, and thus have the possibility to create a substantially negative impact on the experience. This ideal scenario is intended and indeed a goal of the study. But care must be taken when evaluating the overall positive attitudes towards gesture interaction.

5.2 Peripheral Interaction

Our experiment revealed several indications which point towards the potential for free-hand gestures to be used as peripheral interaction. This is evidenced by the observations of hosts' and guests' gaze directions during the interaction. Four of 12 hosts (YH1, YH2, MH3, MH5, see Fig. 3) performed most gestures without redirecting their visual attention from the planning task. Guests directed their attention towards the hosts for less than 20% of the gestures, even though their comments in the post-test interviews revealed they were very well aware of the cues initiating the gestures. Still, guests were capable of reproducing the gestures during the post-test interview. As peripheral interaction is closely related to routine and period of exposure [3], we cannot expect the present experiment to reveal evidence of truly peripheral interaction. Hosts were only trained for 15 min prior to the task, and the task itself lasted only 15 min. However, we remain confident the behaviour exhibited by some of the hosts can be expected to be more widely adopted over a prolonged period of time, such as with periodic repeated use in the home or with a repeated-measures task design.

5.3 Social Acceptability

The social acceptability of gesture interaction was investigated through post-test interviews. This revealed no major objections to gesture interaction for either young nor mature hosts and guests. Indeed, responses were remarkably consistent across users, regardless of age group or role. While young participants described gesture interaction using phrases like "*cool gadget*", mature participants were more neutral in their expressions. The only expressed concerns about gesturing in a social setting were about a party context, where participants speculated about a chaotic situation if a larger group of people tried to control the sound system (multi-user scenarios). They were also concerned that gestures not directed to the sound system could accidentally trigger the device (false positives). These concerns did not impair the social acceptability of gesturing as such, but were more practical concerns that can inform system design.

5.4 Limitations

The study is designed and implemented as a Wizard-of-Oz simulation, with perfect, error-free gesture recognition. Thus, we cannot report on the impact of gesture detection errors, which would have been valuable and surely would impact both the social acceptance and the potential peripheral interaction of the gesture interaction. However, our goal was to verify if gesture interaction is indeed acceptable in the ideal case. If that's not the case, then efforts to develop robust, high performance gesture recognition systems may be wasted.

As Don Norman observes [37], gesture interaction "is not natural" per se: gestures must be learned and remembered, and the interaction carefully designed with appropriate signifiers and feedback. For example, in this study we only provided functional feedback (music stopping and starting, volume going up and down, etc.). However, in the present case the hosts didn't report difficulties remembering the proposed gestures. Their focus was less on remembering and reproducing the gestures than the social impact of doing them.

In order to force hosts to perform the gestures, we introduced cues to the audio tracks. While these would certainly also occur in a natural setting, the frequency is greatly exaggerated and, to a certain extent, annoyed our participants. The disruptive effect of the cues may thus have overshadowed the disruptions created by the gestures and led to overly positive responses in the interviews. This must be considered, when interpreting our findings and conclusions. Still, the observations we made of several hosts performing the gestures without changing their visual attention, even in their initial session, leads us to a strong belief that gesture interaction is definitely suitable for peripheral interaction.

6 Conclusion

This study addressed two issues in relation to human-system gesture interaction: The acceptability of gesture interaction in a social context, and the extent to which gesture interaction has the potential to support peripheral interaction.

We investigated these questions through a user experiment, where pairs of participants carried out a planning task, while one of them also interacted with a music player. We used a simulated (Wizard-of-Oz) setup. Six dyads were recruited from two age groups (young users aged 30 or below, and mature users aged 31 or above), in total 24 participants (15 male and 9 female). Observations during the test and post-test interviews comprise the data collected.

Our results point towards a confirmation of the research questions. We found no evidence from either age group indicating that gesture interaction is not socially acceptable – this despite the fact that some participants expressed concerns about alternate user cases, e.g. in multiuser scenarios such as parties. We found evidence supporting the hypothesis that gesture interaction is a strong candidate for peripheral interaction. Finally, we did not observe differences between the age groups.

However, there are some limitations to the study that must be taken into account. First, the sample is limited to 24 persons with all participants drawn from the same cultural, geographic and linguistic area. This was done to minimize cultural confounds – but to be useful to a global audience, the study should be broadened to include different cultures before drawing firm conclusions.

Second, the gesture interaction was simulated, and thus the participants experienced only a "best case" interaction. There were no false positives, false negatives or other mis-classifications of the users' control gestures (or gestures in general). In a real-life situation, there will be technological limitations which will most likely have a negative impact on the user experience and will test users' tolerance of the system.

Taking this into account, the present study still offers an important contribution to the field of gesture and peripheral interaction, demonstrating that when the right circumstances are present, gesture interaction is a strong candidate for future natural human-system communication. Indeed, if the opposite had been the case, it would have been doubtful whether investments in robust, high-performance gesture recognition systems would be advisable.

6.1 Future Work

To continue this line of work and ensure a reliable validity of social acceptability, future studies should investigate cultural and situational variability. In order to further investigate the potential for peripheral interaction, a study could be carried out where users are exposed over a period of time, e.g. in their home, allowing for familiarisation and routines to develop. Finally, cross-cultural studies and state-of-the-art automatic gesture detection should be investigated to determine the impact of imperfect performance on users' acceptance of the device in a social context.

Acknowledgements. Most of the reported study was carried out by the first two authors as their bachelor's thesis project at Aalborg University [34]. We wish to thank all participants for lending us their time, as well as Aalborg University and Bang and Olufsen for financial support.

References

1. Ahlström, D., Hasan, K., Irani, P.: Are you comfortable doing that? Acceptance studies of around-device gestures in and for public settings. In: Proceedings of the 16th International Conference on Human-Computer Interaction with Mobile Devices & Services, pp. 193–202. ACM Press, New York (2014)
2. ATAP: project soli (2018). https://atap.google.com/soli
3. Bakker, S., Hausen, D., Selker, T. (eds.): Peripheral Interaction: Challenges and Opportunities for HCI in the Periphery of Attention. Springer, Cham (2016). https://doi.org/10.1007/978-3-319-29523-7
4. Audacity: Free, open source, cross-platform audio software. https://www.audacityteam.org
5. Beocentral: Beosound 3200 (2018). https://beocentral.com/beosound3200
6. Bixi Remote (2018). https://bixi.io
7. BMW: Using gesture controls (2015). https://www.youtube.com/watch?v=ttTBJkE-6fs
8. Bobeth, J., Schmehl, S., Kruijff, E., Deutsch, S., Tscheligi, M.: Evaluating performance and acceptance of older adults using freehand gestures for TV menu control. In: Proceedings of the 10th European Conference on Interactive TV (EuroITV 2012). ACM Press, New York (2012)
9. Brewster, S., Murray-Smith, R., Crossan, A., Vasquez-Alvarez, Y., Rico, J.: The GAIME project: gestural and auditory interactions for mobile environments. British Computer Society (2009)
10. Brown, J.N.A.: "Unseen, yet crescive": the unrecognized history of peripheral interaction. In: Bakker, S., Hausen, D., Selker, T. (eds.) Peripheral Interaction. HIS, pp. 13–38. Springer, Cham (2016). https://doi.org/10.1007/978-3-319-29523-7_2
11. Cabreira, A.T., Hwang, F.: How do novice older users evaluate and perform mid-air gesture interaction for the first time? In: Proceedings of NordiCHI 2016 (2016)
12. Casey, T., Wilson-Evered, E.: Predicting uptake of technology innovations in online family dispute resolution services: an application and extension of the UTAUT. Comput. Hum. Behav. **28**(6), 2034–2045 (2012)
13. Chattopadhyay, D., Bolchini, D.: Touchless circular menus: toward an intuitive UI for touchless interactions with large displays. In Proceedings of (AVI 2014) (2014)
14. Clarkson, P.J., Coleman, R., Keates, S., Lebbon, C.: Inclusive Design: Design for the Whole Population. Springer, Cham (2013)
15. Comtet, H.: Acceptance of 3D-gestures based on age, gender and experience. Master's thesis, Gjøvik University College, Gjøvik, Norway (2013)
16. Ekman, P., Friesen, W.V.: Hand movements. J. Commun. **22**(4), 353–374 (1972)
17. Freeman, W.T., Weissman, C.D.: Television control by hand gestures. In: Proceedings of IEEE International Workshop on Automatic Face and Gesture Recognition, Zurich (1995)
18. Galor, M., Pokrass, J., Hoffnung, A.: Three dimensional user interface session control. Apple Corp. United States Patent No: US 8,933,876 B2 (2013)
19. Giddens, A.: The Constitution of Society: Outline of the Theory of Structuration. University of California Press, Berkeley (1986)
20. Grandhi, S.A., Joue, G., Mittelberg, I.: To move or to remove? A human-centric approach to understanding gesture interpretation. In: Proceedings of DIS'2012 (2012)
21. Harrison, S.: The production line as a context for low metaphoricity. Exploring links between gestures, iconicity, and artefacts on a factory shop floor. In: Herrmann, J., Berber Sardinha, T. (eds.) Metaphor in Specialist Discourse: Investigating Metaphor Use in Technical, Scientificnad Popularized Discourse Contexts, pp. 131–161. John Benjamins, Amsterdam (2015)
22. Hayo (2018). https://hayo.io

23. Hurtienne, J., et al.: Physical gestures for abstract concepts: Inclusive design with primary metaphors. Interact. Comput. **22**, 475–484 (2010)
24. Inclusive Design Toolkit (2018). https://www.inclusivedesigntoolkit.com/whatis/whatis.html
25. Juola, J.F.: Theories of focal and peripheral attention. In: Bakker, S., Hausen, D., Selker, T. (eds.) Peripheral Interaction. HIS, pp. 39–61. Springer, Cham (2016). https://doi.org/10.1007/978-3-319-29523-7_3
26. Karam, M., Schraefel, M.C.: A taxonomy of gestures in human computer task interactions. In: Proceedings of (CHI 2005), pp. 1961–1964. ACM Press, New York (2005)
27. Lim, J.H., Jo, C., Kim, D.-H.: Analysis on user variability in gesture interaction. Convergence and hybrid information technology. In: Proceedings of the International Conference on Hybrid Information Technology, pp. 295–302. ACM Press, New York (2012)
28. Malhotra, Y., Galletta, D.F.: Extending the technology acceptance model to account for social influence: theoretical bases and empirical validation. In: Proceedings of the 32nd Annual Hawaii International Conference on System Sciences (HICSS-32) (1999)
29. Mauney, D., Howarth, J., Wirtanen, A., Capra, M.: Cultural similarities and differences in user-defined gestures for touchscreen user interfaces. In: Proceedings of CHI 2010 Extended Abstracts on Human Factors in Computing Systems (CHI EA 2010), pp. 4015–4020. ACM Press, New York (2010)
30. McNeill, D.: Hand and Mind: What Gestures Reveal About Thought. University of Chicago Press, Chicago (1992)
31. McNeill, D.: Gesture & Thought. University of Chicago Press, Chicago (2005)
32. Montero, C.S., Alexander, J., Marshall, M.T., Subramanian, S.: Would you do that? Understanding social acceptance of gestural interfaces. In: Proceedings of the 12th International Conference on Human Computer Interaction with Mobile Devices and Services, pp. 275–278. ACM Press, New York (2010)
33. Müller, C., Cienki, A., Fricke, E., Ladewig, S., McNeill, D., Teßendorf, S. (eds.): Body-Language-Communication. de Gruyter Mouton, Berlin (2013)
34. Nellemann, L., Nielsen, S.: Perifer interaktion med et musikanlæg. B.Sc. thesis, Aalborg University, Aalborg, Denmark (2017)
35. Nielsen, M., Störring, M., Moeslund, T.B., Granum, E.: A procedure for developing intuitive and ergonomic gesture interfaces for HCI. In: Camurri, A., Volpe, G. (eds.) GW 2003. LNCS (LNAI), vol. 2915, pp. 409–420. Springer, Heidelberg (2004). https://doi.org/10.1007/978-3-540-24598-8_38
36. Ninja Blocks (2015). https://ninjablocks.com
37. Norman, D.: Natural user interfaces are not natural. Interactions **17**(3), 6–10 (2010)
38. Panger, G.: Kinect in the kitchen: testing depth camera interaction in practical home environments. In: Proceedings of CHI 2012 Work-in-Progress. ACM Press, New York (2012)
39. Perniss, P., Vigliocco, G.: The bridge of iconicity: from a world of experience to the experience of language. Phil. Trans. Roy. Soc. B **369**(1651), 20130300 (2014)
40. Piccolo Labs (2018). https://www.piccololabs.com
41. Rautaray, S.S., Agrawal, A.: A vision based hand gesture interface for controlling VLC media player. Int. J. Comput. Appl. (2010) ISSN 0975-8887
42. Rico, J.: Evaluating the social acceptability of multimodal mobile interactions. In: Proceedings of CHI 2010 Extended Abstracts on Human Factors in Computing Systems (CHI EA 2010), pp. 2887–2890. ACM Press, New York (2010)
43. Rempel, D., Camilleri, M.J., Lee, D.L.: The design of hand gestures for human-computer interaction: lessons from sign language interpreters. Int. J. Hum.-Comput. Stud. **72**, 728–735 (2014)
44. Rico, J., Brewster, S.A.: Usable gestures for mobile interfaces: evaluating social acceptability. In: Proceedings of the SIGCHI Conference on Human Factors in Computing Systems. ACM Press, New York (2010)

45. Samsung: SmartTV Guide Book (2013). http://www.samsung.com/ph/smarttv/common/guide_book_3p_si/waving.html
46. Vatavu, R.-D.: User-defined gestures for free-hand TV control. In: Proceedings of the 10th European Conference on Interactive TV and Video (EuroITV 2012), pp. 45–48. ACM Press, New York (2012)
47. Vatavu, R.-D., Wobbrock, J.O.: Formalizing agreement analysis for elicitation studies: new measures, significance test, and toolkit. In: Proceedings of the 33rd Annual ACM Conference on Human Factors in Computing Systems, pp. 1325–1334. ACM Press, New York (2015)
48. Venkatesh, V., Davis, F.D.: A theoretical extension of the technology acceptance model: four longitudinal field studies. Manag. Sci. 46(2), 186–204 (2000)
49. Verma, S., Bansal, H., Sorathia, K.: A study for investigating suitable gesture based selection for gestural user interfaces. In: Proceedings of the 7th International Conference on HCI (IndiaHCI), pp. 47–55. ACM Press, New York (2015)
50. Sweetser, E., Stec, K.: Maintaining multiple viewpoints in gaze. In: Dancygier, B., Wei-lun, L., Verhagen, A. (eds.) Viewpoint and the Fabric of Meaning: Form and Use of Viewpoint Tools across Languages and Modalities, pp. 237–257. Mouton de Gruyter, Berlin (2016)
51. Taniberg, A., Botin, L., Stec, K.: Context of use affects the social acceptability of gesture interaction. In: Proceedings of NordiCHI 2018, the 10th Nordic Conference on Human-Computer Interaction, pp. 731–735 (2018)
52. Weiser, M., Brown, J.S.: The coming age of calm technology. In: Denning, P.J., Metcalfe, R.M. (eds.) Beyond Calculation: The Next Fifty Years of Computing, pp. 75–85. Springer, New York (1997). https://doi.org/10.1007/978-1-4612-0685-9_6
53. Williamson, J.R.: User experience, performance, and social acceptability: usable multimodal mobile interaction. Ph.D. dissertation, University of Glasgow, Glasgow, Scotland (2012)
54. Wobbrock, J.O., Morris, M.R., Wilson, A.D.: User-defined gestures for surface computing. In: Proceedings of CHI 2009. ACM Press, New York (2009)
55. Wolf, K.: Microgestures—enabling gesture input with busy hands. In: Bakker, S., Hausen, D., Selker, T. (eds.) Peripheral Interaction. HIS, pp. 95–116. Springer, Cham (2016). https://doi.org/10.1007/978-3-319-29523-7_5
56. Zaiți, I.-A., Pentiuc, Ş.-G., Vatavu, R.-D.: On free-hand TV control: experimental results on user-elicited gestures with Leap Motion. Pers. Ubiquit. Comput. 19(5–6), 821–838 (2015)

Research of Interactive Gesture Usability of Navigation Application Based on Intuitive Interaction

Zhicheng Ren[(✉)], Bin Jiang, and Licheng Deng

School of Design Art and Media,
Nanjing University of Science and Technology, Nanjing 210094,
Jiangsu, People's Republic of China
956821843@qq.com, jb508@163.com, 532958737@qq.com

Abstract. With the development of gesture recognition technology, gesture control will be more and more widely used in every scene of life. As for map applications or applications, which people need to use more and more in daily travel, the operation mode of it still needs to be improved. Applying gesture control technology to map applications will provide a better user experience than the original operation mode in a specific scene. Actually, there are many gestures that may not conform to the users' intuition. With the maturity of non-contact gesture interaction technology, the daily operation of map by gesture will have more advantages than the original operation mode. In this study, users' intuitive gestures for different map functions are extracted through experiments. And summarized the gestures that were used the most times or the most intuitive gestures corresponding to each function. Finally form a set of intuitive gestures suitable for map applications. The research also analyzes the relationship between users' intuitive gestures and map tasks. Also analyzes the relationship between users' intuitive gestures and their previous experience of using intelligent devices, to discuss the impact of the using experience of intelligent devices on users' intuitive gestures. We conducted gesture research experiments with participants, and we learned about the gestures they chose when facing different tasks and why they chose them. We found similarity between a part of intuitive gestures in experiment and the daily gestures during using intelligent devices.

Keywords: Intuitive interaction · Non-contact gestures · Map navigation

1 Introduction

With the development of transportation network in China and the increase of people's daily travel demand, mobile map has become an indispensable product in people's daily life. In the third quarter of 2019, the total number of active users in mobile map APP market of China was 784 million, down 1.9% month on month, up 3.9% year on year [1]. The scale of active users in the mobile map industry, especially in the leading map platform, has become stable, while the subsequent competition of each platform for the

© Springer Nature Switzerland AG 2020
M. Kurosu (Ed.): HCII 2020, LNCS 12182, pp. 96–105, 2020.
https://doi.org/10.1007/978-3-030-49062-1_6

stock market is to provide a full range of multi-scenario services, so as to improve service quality and enhance user viscosity.

Besides providing users with more comprehensive traffic information through big data, the navigation function, as one of the traditional core functions of map applications, is still the core competitiveness of mobile map APPs. As for the existing map navigation operation mode, on-skin touch gesture, which is limited by the existing technology and equipment, so many gestures may not conform to the users' intuition and have high learning cost. With the development of gesture recognition technology, gesture control will be more and more widely used in every scene of life. On the one hand, gesture control can enhance the immersion experience, on the other hand, it can also reduce people's attention in secondary task. On the premise of meeting relevant ergonomic requirements, non-contact intuitive gesture control may make human-computer interaction safer, more comfortable and more intuitive [2]. Therefore, for the map applications that people need to use more and more in daily travel, its operation mode still needs to be improved. Applying intuitive gestures to map applications, and combining voice control technology properly, will make map applications provide better user experience than the original operation mode in specific scenes.

2 Related Work

The non-contact gesture recognition technology is to capture the image sequence including the operator's gesture through the camera and recognize the image area analysis. The equipment price is low and the operation method is simple. And the current camera can not only obtain the two-dimensional scene map in front of it, but also capture the depth information of the scene. The accuracy of gesture recognition is greatly improved compared with the previous. For example, Kinect, a somatosensory device developed by Microsoft, can simultaneously acquire color images, depth images, human bone data, etc. of the scene to separate the target objects, and its recognition process is not affected by light intensity, background, object color, texture, etc. Huawei mate 30 pro, launched in 2019, integrates gesture recognition technology into mobile phones to realize space separation gesture operation. Users can flip the page by waving up and down, and quickly screen capture by grabbing.

Although the social acceptance of contact gesture interaction is higher [3], the future non-contact gesture interaction on mobile phones is still needed in specific scenarios. Some of its advantages are higher than touch gesture interaction.

For intuitive gestures, intuition is a cognitive process, usually unconscious, and uses stored empirical knowledge. Intuitive interaction involves the use of knowledge gained from other products and/or experiences. K. R. Popper has an opinion that all human activities carry and reflect the acquired knowledge [4]. Blackler et al. found through two experiments that prior contact with products with similar functions can help participants complete experimental tasks faster and use familiar functions more intuitively than unfamiliar ones. Another of their experiments confirmed that performance is influenced by a person's familiarity with similar technologies [5].

Michael Kipp et al. put forward a set of algorithms to integrate the users' behavior characteristics and create a new set of gestures, so as to realize more natural gesture combination [6]. Chaklam et al. designed a set of gestures for video game, by asking the participants to make gestures to execute game actions/commands, in addition, they also designed a set of other parts of the body in the same way to replace/assist hand gestures [7].

It is found that users have stronger memory for their own defined gestures. Miguel A. Nacenta et al. verified by experiments that the memory integrity of users for their own defined gestures after two days is much higher than that provided by the author [8].

3   Method

The gesture design process is divided into three parts (see Fig. 1). In the first part, the common functions of map applications are extracted, and the daily use process is divided into independent operations. The subjects are asked to propose their own intuitive gestures according to their intuitive feelings for different functions, summarize the experimental results, and summarize the intuitive gestures with a large number of users. In the second part, the summarized gestures and their corresponding functions are displayed at the same time, and the subjects are asked to make gestures, In the third part, the subjects were asked to remember the gestures related to the map function, and to test whether the intuitive gestures summarized in the first part were easy for users to remember.

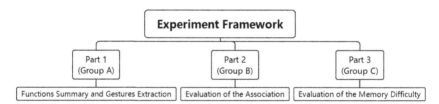

Fig. 1. Experiment framework

3.1   Common Functions of Map Applications and Gesture Extraction

In this study, Baidu map, the map applications with the highest monthly population, was selected as the experimental material to screen the daily functions of the map applications and separate out various functions related to navigation requirements. And sort the usage frequency of various functions, extract and split the navigation related functions frequently used by users in daily life, and get 14 independent operations, which are zoom in, zoom out, move up, move down, move right, move left, select location, select route, start navigation, change route (in navigation), confirm switch route, slide up browse and view location related information, return to superior (see Fig. 2).

22 drivers with C1 driving license and more than 1-year driving experience (group A) were recruited to participate in the experiment. The age of subjects ranged from 22 to 50 years old, including 16 males and 6 females. All the subjects have smart phones and 12 had experience of using tablet computers.

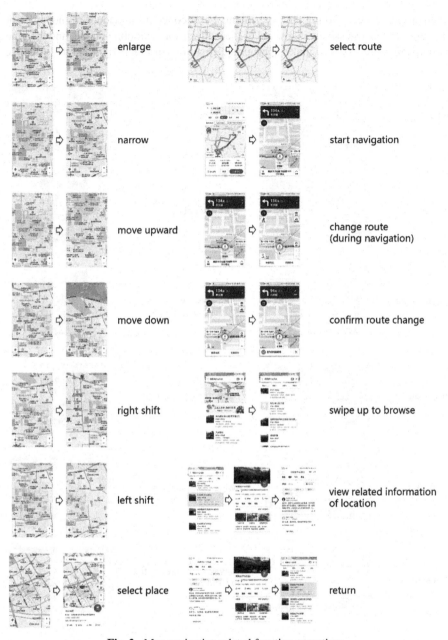

enlarge

select route

narrow

start navigation

move upward

change route
(during navigation)

move down

confirm route change

right shift

swipe up to browse

left shift

view related information
of location

select place

return

Fig. 2. Map navigation related function operation

At the beginning of the experiment, each subject was required to sit in a designated seat, with a distance of 30 cm between the front chest and the edge of the table, and put his hands on the table, and stand the mobile phone in front of the right of the subject to simulate the relationship between the seat and the location of the mobile phone when driving the car. During the experiment, 14 video recording videos of independent operation were successively displayed to the subjects on the mobile phone, and then the participants were asked to make appropriate gestures with their right hands to realize

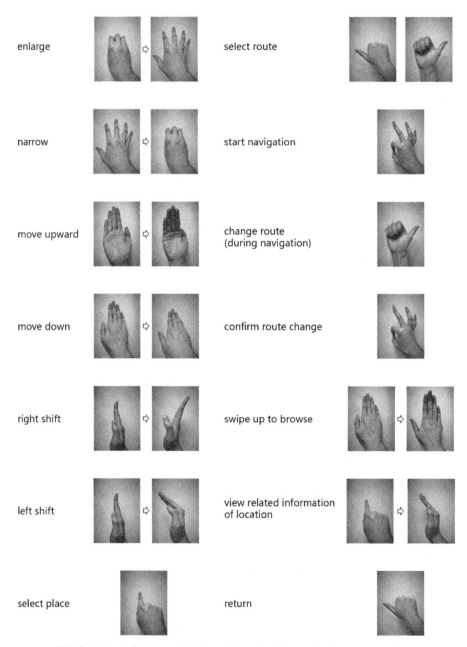

Fig. 3. Map navigation related functions operation and final selected gestures

the operation, and then video recording was performed for the gestures proposed by the subjects in turn. After the experiment, the subjects were interviewed to find out why they proposed the corresponding gestures for each operation.

The 308 gestures collected in the previous part of the experiment were sorted out. For each operation, the gestures were sorted according to the number of times, and 14 gestures with the largest number of people were selected (see Fig. 3).

3.2 Evaluation of the Association Degree of Intuitive Gesture

In the second part, another 20 subjects (group B) were invited to participate in the experiment to show them 14 gestures and 14 operations in disorder order. Participants were required to observe the gestures and then associate their corresponding specific operations. For each gesture, record the proportion of subjects who can associate the actual operation represented by the gesture (see Table 1).

Table 1. Proportion of correct association of different gestures

Operation	Proportion of correct association/%
Enlarge	100
Narrow	95
Move upward	90
Move down	90
Right shift	95
Left shift	90
Select place	75
Select route	45
Start navigation	55
Change route (in navigation)	30
Confirm route change	55
Swipe up to browse	75
View related information of location	50
Return	45

Then, the gestures and their corresponding operations are displayed to the participants at the same time, and they are required to score the relevance degree of the two. The scoring method is in the form of Likert scale 1–5 points respectively represent very strong relevance, strong relevance, weak relevance, weak relevance and no relevance (see Table 2).

Table 2. Score of gesture correlation degree

Operation	Average score
Enlarge	4.5
Narrow	4.3
Move upward	4.1
Move down	4.8
Right shift	4.5
Left shift	4.4
Select place	4.6
Select route	3.9
Start navigation	4.2
Change route (in navigation)	3.5
Confirm route change	4.0
Swipe up to browse	4.2
View related information of location	3.2
Return	3.8

Table 3. Proportion of memory accuracy of different gestures

Operation	Proportion of memory accuracy/%
Enlarge	100
Narrow	95
Move upward	90
Move down	90
Right shift	95
Left shift	90
Select place	80
Select route	75
Start navigation	85
Change route (in navigation)	75
Confirm route change	80
Swipe up to browse	85
View related information of location	70
Return	80

3.3 Evaluation of the Memory Difficulty of Intuitive Gesture

Twenty subjects (Group C) were invited to learn and memorize the 14 gestures selected in the second part, and completed the memory work within the specified time. After the participants memorized, the video recording of different operations was displayed on the screen, and the participants were required to make corresponding gestures and record at the same time. 14 gestures of each subject were compared with the most representative 14 gestures selected in the second part. The higher the accuracy, the less difficult the intuitive gesture memory (see Table 3).

4 Findings and Discussion

4.1 Impact of Smart Device Experience

Through interviews, it was found that when participants were asked why they chose a gesture for an operation, they often mentioned using mobile phones, tablet computers and other operations in daily life, such as zooming in or zooming out, which would be realized by hand opening and closing.

However, 82.14% of the gestures made by the participants were related to their experience in daily operation of smart electronic devices such as mobile phones, while the rest of the smaller gestures were more than 44 years old. It is reasonable to speculate that they used less functions in daily use of mobile phones and other devices.

4.2 Difference of Interaction with Contact Gesture

Although the previous experience of using smart devices will enable users to adopt similar gestures when facing similar tasks, the gestures will still have some changes when changing from contact interaction to non-contact interaction. In the first phase of the experiment, it was found that most of the participants (70%) used hand gestures when moving maps and flipping up and down, rather than finger movements when using intelligent electronic devices. In the interview, we learned that there are three main reasons for using the palm to complete some operations: first, the gesture of a single finger is not easy to be recognized; second, with the separation of the fingertip and the screen, the participants think it needs more power to operate the software; third, the size of the moving object has a psychological hint to the experimental participants, the map is close to the whole screen, giving a person an implication that it's hard to drag. This is consistent with the research results of Yubo Kou and others, that is, users will use different gestures due to the different target sizes of their operations [9].

At the same time, we also observed that for some operations with weak directional characteristics, the gesture chosen by users is quite different, such as returning to the superior. This kind of operation is limited by the interaction mode, which can not directly transplant the daily click operation on the mobile phone to the non-contact operation, and it is also difficult to find similar actions in life [2]. However, after the user remembers the gesture, it also shows a high accuracy, so it is necessary to establish a set of highly predictable gesture system so that the user can learn and master it more easily.

For other operations, such as selection, non-contact gesture interaction brings great uncertainty to the user, which makes the experimental participants sometimes unable to determine whether they have selected the right object. As Florian et al. Showed in the experiment, there are more errors when using airtap gestures [10]. Therefore, in this case, the designer should propose a non-contact interactive feedback mechanism (such as cursor) to increase the user's certainty on the selection target. On the other hand, it can also be solved by combining voice control.

According to Norman, gesture interaction adds an active pleasure to fingers with low click rate. However, due to the lack of gesture consistency and easy triggering of some unrecoverable operations, system availability will be affected [11]. Therefore, in the gesture design, we should consider adding gesture operation similar to forced return to ensure the real-time availability of the system.

5   Conclusion

The results of this study show that from the perspective of users, the navigation function of map applications can be summed up a set of intuitive hand system for large-scale users, and most of the gestures and functions are more in line with user psychology. The recognition of the intuitive gesture needs to be further tested by gesture recognition equipment.

This study also found that the daily touch gesture operation on smart devices such as mobile phones and tablets has become a source of inspiration for some users when they face non-contact gesture interaction, while it has little impact on users who have smart devices but use less functions. Although the touch gesture has been widely used in the present, it still has the possibility of innovation, For non-contact gesture interaction, its biggest feature is non-contact. If only the contact operation is transplanted into the non-contact operation, it will greatly increase the users' self-confidence, that is, the uncertainty of the target. This kind of uncertainty will greatly reduce the user experience, and in the real world.

For non-contact gesture operation, the users' behavior habits in daily life will also have an impact on the users' gesture. This impact is reflected in the fact that when users operate intelligent devices in the face of scenes similar to daily life on the screen, they are likely to use gestures similar to actions in life, rather than a simple operation of a finger. At the same time, on the premise that gesture recognition technology can meet the function, designers should pay more attention to the impact of non-contact gesture interaction on users' psychology. Give users more real and timely feedback when their fingers leave the screen.

References

1. Mobile map analysis industry digital process analysis. https://www.analysys.cn/. Accessed 5 Dec 2019
2. Stecher, M., et al.: Tracking down the intuitiveness of gesture interaction in the truck domain. Procedia Manuf. **3**, 3176–3183 (2015). Tareq Ahram, Waldemar Karwowski, Dylan Schmorrow (eds.)

3. Havlucu, H., Ergin, M.Y., Bostan, İ., Buruk, O.T., Göksun, T., Özcan, O.: It made more sense: comparison of user-elicited on-skin touch and freehand gesture sets. In: Streitz, N., Markopoulos, P. (eds.) DAPI 2017. LNCS, vol. 10291, pp. 159–171. Springer, Cham (2017). https://doi.org/10.1007/978-3-319-58697-7_11
4. Popper, K.R.: Philosophy of Science (History and Philosophy of Science: Conjectures and Refutations. The growth of scientific knowledge). Science (140)
5. Blackler, A., Popovic, V., Mahar, D.: Investigating users' intuitive interaction with complex artefacts. Appl. Ergon. **41**(1), 72–92 (2010)
6. Kipp, M., Neff, M., Kipp, Kerstin H., Albrecht, I.: Towards natural gesture synthesis: evaluating gesture units in a data-driven approach to gesture synthesis. In: Pelachaud, C., Martin, J.-C., André, E., Chollet, G., Karpouzis, K., Pelé, D. (eds.) IVA 2007. LNCS (LNAI), vol. 4722, pp. 15–28. Springer, Heidelberg (2007). https://doi.org/10.1007/978-3-540-74997-4_2
7. Chaklam, S.: Jump and shoot: prioritizing primary and alternative body gestures for intense gameplay. In: Proceedings of the SIGCHI Conference on Human Factors in Computing Systems, Kochi University of Technology, pp. 951–954 (2014)
8. Nacenta, M.A., Kamber, Y., Qiang Y., Kristensson, P.O.: Memorability of pre-designed and user-defined gesture sets. In: Proceedings of the SIGCHI Conference on Human Factors in Computing Systems 2013 (CHI 2013), pp. 1099–1108. ACM Press, NewYork (2013)
9. Kou, Y., Kow, Y.M., Cheng, K.: Developing intuitive gestures for spatial interaction with large public displays. In: Streitz, N., Markopoulos, P. (eds.) DAPI 2015. LNCS, vol. 9189, pp. 174–181. Springer, Cham (2015). https://doi.org/10.1007/978-3-319-20804-6_16
10. van de Camp, F., Schick, A., Stiefelhagen, R.: How to click in mid-air. In: Streitz, N., Stephanidis, C. (eds.) DAPI 2013. LNCS, vol. 8028, pp. 78–86. Springer, Heidelberg (2013). https://doi.org/10.1007/978-3-642-39351-8_9
11. Norman, D.A., Nielsen, J.: Gestural interfaces: a step backward in usability. Interactions **17**, 46–49 (2010)

Gesture-Based Interaction: Visual Gesture Mapping

Kasper Rise$^{(\boxtimes)}$ and Ole Andreas Alsos$^{(\boxtimes)}$

Norwegian University of Science and Technology, Trondheim, Norway
risekasper@gmail.com, oleanda@ntnu.no

Abstract. Gesture-based interaction allows for interacting with computers, machines and robots in an intuitive way without direct physical contact. The challenge is that there are no agreed-upon interaction patterns for gesture-based interaction in VR and AR environments. In this paper we have developed a set of 10 gestures and corresponding visualizations in the following categories of gestures: (1) directional movement, (2) flow control, (3) spatial orientation, (4) multifunctional gestures, and (5) tactile gestures. One of the multifunctional gestures and its visualization were selected for usability testing (N = 18) in a 3D car track simulator. We found that the visualization made it faster and easier to understand the interaction made the interaction more precise. Further, we learned that the visualization worked well as guidance to learn to control the car but could be removed after a while as the user had learned the interaction. By combining gestures from the library, gesture-based interaction can be used to control advanced machines, robots and drones in an intuitive and non-strenuous way.

Keywords: Gesture-based interaction · Virtual reality · Gesture control

1 Introduction

Keyboards, touch screens, buttons, levers and joysticks are common ways of controlling and interacting with computers, machines and robots. In most cases these conventional ways of interacting with computers are sufficient, but sometimes they restrict our interaction. Gesture control, defined as the ability to recognize and interpret movements of the human body in order to interact with and control a computer system without direct physical contact (Gesture Control 2019), removes the input controller device and allows the user to interact directly with the machine, using their hands or body. Gesture-control can, therefore, offer a more intuitive and natural interaction than conventional interaction.

In robotics, there are several advantages of implementing gesture-based interaction (Rise 2020). Firstly, replacing advanced controllers with simple and intuitive gestures can lead to a clear improvement of intuitiveness and reduce the time it takes to learn the system. Additionally, controlling robotics with discrete hand gestures can be highly beneficial in environments where the body is physically restrained. However, we have found no agreed-upon interaction patterns for gesture-based interaction in VR and AR environments. Therefore, we have in this study developed a set of 10 gestures that can

© Springer Nature Switzerland AG 2020
M. Kurosu (Ed.): HCII 2020, LNCS 12182, pp. 106–124, 2020.
https://doi.org/10.1007/978-3-030-49062-1_7

solve many common interaction patterns in domains where gestures can be used to interact with systems. We hope that these gestures can be a starting point for a standard convention for gesture-based interaction in a real, virtual (VR) and augmented reality (AR).

The purpose of the study was to (1) develop a set of intuitive gestures that are simple, logically mapped and non-strenuous, (2) design corresponding visualization-feedback based on design principles, and (3) evaluate if visualization feedback helps the user learn and understand the gestures.

We have limited our focus to active gestures, i.e. gestures giving continuous feedback and not gestures that are a part of a «gesture language» where one gesture, or combination of gestures in sequence, is mapped to one system command. We have used an iterative design approach in developing the gestures, using a range of methods such as literature review, co-design with experts on gesture-based interaction of drones, usability testing, surveys and post-test interviews with novices.

In the rest of the article, we present further details on the theoretical foundation and background, describe the methods used, describe the 10 gestures developed, present data from one of the usability tests and discuss the findings from the test.

2 Background

2.1 Gesture-Based Interaction

The term *Gesture control* is used in a wide range of contexts and can be interpreted differently. In Gartner Glossary gesture control is defined as "(…) the ability to recognize and interpret movements of the human body in order to interact with and control a computer system without direct physical contact" ("Gesture Control 2019). Although this definition covers any movements of the human body, we will in this article focus on hand gestures.

Applications of Gesture-Based Interaction. Even though gesture-based interaction is a relatively new interaction method, it has emerged in several domains already. TeMoto, a teleoperation system has been developed, using a Leap Motion sensor to track gestures to control a rover (Valner et al. 2018). Gestix uses vision-based gesture tracking for navigation and manipulation of electronic medical records (EMR) (Wachs et al. 2008). Using gesture control to operate a robotic microscope in surgery (Antoni et al. 2015), laparoscopic instruments (Arkenbout et al. 2018) and for controlling operating light (Hartmann and Schlaefer 2013) have also been explored in the healthcare domain. Research has been done using sensor gloves to control a snake-like robot in space (Liu et al. 2016) and in the field of military technology a so-called "real-time soldier-robot teaming" have been developed using multimodal interaction, combining gesture control and speech (Barber et al. 2016). We also see gesture-based interaction emerge in the consumer market, such as in premium smartphones (Google's Pixel 4) and cars (BMW).

2.2 Design Theory

Gesture-based interaction in a real or VR/AR environment is not different from other forms of interaction; it has to follow the basic rules of interaction design. This means that *visibility, feedback, constraints, mapping* and *affordance* need to be considered when designing these. In this section, Norman's design principles (Norman 2013) will be explained and put in the context of gesture-based interaction.

Visibility and Feedback. Gesture-based interaction is not a conventional interaction pattern that everybody is familiar with. Therefore, if you are using it for the first time, you would need the proper visual clues to aid you in knowing what to do and how to do it right. In a real environment, it can be challenging to provide this feedback, especially when operating IoT devices, where the user interface often is very limited or only accessible through a smartphone or computer. In augmented reality (AR) or virtual reality (VR), it is easier to provide visual interaction feedback inside the virtual model.

There are several ways of giving interaction feedback. The feedback can be sound, light, vibrations, screen-based visuals or text, etc. AR and VR both provide gesture-based interaction with the visual feedback that is needed to obtain an intuitive interaction. In this study, we have developed visualization that provides the necessary visual feedback to the users.

Dynamic feedback is one type of feedback that stands out as being highly valuable in the context of gesture-based interaction scenario. Dynamic feedback means giving constant feedback based on the movement of the gestures, in contrast to summative feedback given only when an interaction is performed and successfully interpreted by the system. In a VR environment where physical hand controls are used, this is often displayed as a pair of virtual hands floating in mid-air showing which buttons are pressed or not (ref). By using gesture tracking, one can get constant input from the users' gestures, and give feedback accordingly to what they are doing. This increases the intuitiveness of the interaction. The goal is to give enough feedback to allow the user to interact with the system without the need for instructions.

Constraints. When designing physical or digital objects, giving physical or visual constraints one can give the user the hints needed to intuitively understand how to (and not to) interact with the object. Real-world examples are garbage bins with different openings depending on the categorization of the trash is a common example of constraints that forces the user to throw the trash in the correct bin (Norman 2013).

When designing for gestures one has to consider biomechanics and ergonomics. Bodily constraints, such as how you rotate your arm, fingers and wrist, are important to take into consideration when designing for physical controls, such as keyboards, joysticks and throttle controls. Constraints can also be used as an aid when designing visualizations for a VR/AR environment. By emphasizing biomechanics and the bodily constraint in the visualization, the user will intuitively understand the boundaries of the gestures, knowing what is maximum and minimum. An example from the physical world is the power throttle of a boat. Based on its physical restrictions the user knows when the throttle is on max because the throttle can not move any further forward.

Mapping. Natural mapping is when there is a clear and obvious relationship between the controls and the object to be controlled. The gesture being used to determine an action should be mapped correspondingly to the action being executed. In a study on gesture control in VR they discovered that:

> *The gesture/action should be well mapped to the content being learned. An example of this could be mapping changing gears in a car. The action should be similar to moving the gear stick rather than pushing a toggle up or down. By performing actions, it stimulates the motor system and also strengthens the memory traces associated with newly learned concepts* (Johnson-Glenberg 2018).

Every visualization should, therefore, be mapped according to the position of the hand, considering physical restrictions as well. Intuitive metaphors should also be used both when choosing the gesture and the visualization. An example could be an axial plane describing the movement of a drone.

Affordance. Affordance refers to an attribute of an object that allows people to know how to use it. Essentially, *to afford* means to give a clue. As you intuitively know how to open a door by looking at where its hinges and door knob are located, affordances can be used to design visualizations for gestures that work as a «hint» of how it should be used. This could be translated into direct visual elements that indicate something or when choosing visual elements already known. An example could be choosing known geometry that has the affordances of what you want to convey. A cylinder has the affordance of being rotated along its axis and a sphere or a ball has the affordance of scaling about origo (Norman 2013).

2.3 Guidelines

Combined with design theory, having certain guidelines as a framework when designing for gestures, is beneficial. The guidelines in this chapter is based on literature research, taking knowledge from different research-domains. Some of the guidelines are also requirements from relevant stakeholders that work as a framework.

Gesture as Assessment. In a study using gesture control in VR for education, Johnson-Glenberg states that designing for gestures should reveal the state of the learner's mental model, both during learning (called formative or in-process) and after the act of learning (called summative). She gives the example;

> *Prompt the learner to demonstrate negative acceleration with the swipe of a hand controller. Does the controller speed up or slow down over time? Can the learner match certain target rates? This is an embodied method to assess comprehension that includes the added benefit of reducing guess rates* (Johnson-Glenberg 2018, p. 16).

Although this literature is mainly focusing on gestures for learning, this idea can be applied to any case of designing for gestures. In our case, the visualizations should give a clue what the user is supposed to do before doing an action, meanwhile doing the action (formative) and give a response after an action has been done (summative). These three steps should be covered with constraints, affordances, feedback and good mapping as discussed in the previous section.

One theory that further underlines this concept is that using gestures requires motor planning and this activates multiple simulations even before the action is taken. Hostetter and Alibali (2008) posit that:

> *Gestures first requires a mental simulation before movement commences, at that time motor and premotor areas of the brain are activated in action-appropriate ways. This pre-action, covert state of imaging an action appears to stimulate the same collaries as the overt action i.e., motor cortex, the cerebellum, and basal ganglia (Jeannerod 2001). The combination of planning and then performing may lead to more motor and pre-motor activity during encoding, which might lead to a stronger learning signal and memory trace.*

Enabling User-Defined Gestures. In a paper that discusses the ability of users to remember the gestures and their meanings (Nacenta et al. 2013), the authors considered user-defined gestures, pre-designed gestures and randomly assigned gestures and concluded that user-defined gestures are preferable and more memorable than the other types. The authors recommended 'enabling user-defined gestures' as well as paying attention to the relationship between the gesture and the action that it invokes. This coheres with other recent work on natural user interfaces (NUIs) (Malizia and Bellucci 2012; O'hara et al. 2013).

This theory is the core concept of designing a library of different gestures. By making a library instead of imposing gestures where they are unnatural or might not fit the purpose, users can choose the gestures and corresponding visualizations that fit the use case.

3   Developing a Gesture Library

In this section, we present the process and results of developing a gesture library and corresponding visualizations, which could be used as interaction feedback in a AR and VR setting.

3.1   Method

The design theory and literature review presented above worked as a framework when selecting gestures and design the gesture visualizations presented later in this paper. Even though the gestures were chosen rather than "designed", they had to follow the previously established guidelines and correspond with the visualization. It was, therefore, two elements that had to be designed together. The first step was to create a framework of criteria that was crucial for the success of the project. The second step was to understand what kind of gestures different use-cases would need. A co-design workshop with designers, drone experts and pilots, VR-experts and computer engineers was conducted focusing on establishing categories of gestures that could be used in an real or AR/VR setting.

The criteria were established based on prior experience working on the topic of gesture control of drones, requirements from stakeholders and takeaways from use-cases. The process then continued with mapping out several use cases, creating user-journeys to understand which type of interaction that would best suit the different case.

3.2 Categories of Gestures

From the workshop, we came up with 3 main categories: (1) gestures for *directional movement*, e.g. steering a rover, (2) gestures for *flow control*, e.g. controlling the speed of a rover (3) gestures for *spatial orientation,* e.g. positioning a robotic arm. While these categories were sufficient to cover simple (meaning single output) gestures, they did not cover combinations or variations of gestures. Therefore, two subcategories were developed: (4) *multifunctional* gestures, e.g. controlling the path *and* speed of a rover, and (5) *tactile* gestures, e.g. selecting the power-level or gears. A description of each category is presented in Table 1.

Table 1. Description of each gesture-category

Gesture category	Description
Gestures for directional movement	Gestures related to directional movement and does not deal with the control of altitude etc.
Gestures for flow control	Gestures related to controlling the amount of any output value
Gestures for spatial orientation	Gestures related to three-dimensional orientation and movement in 3 degrees of freedom (DOF) along the x, y and z-axis
Multifunctional gestures	Gestures controlling more than one input at the time and therefore combine gestures from the other categories
Tactile gestures	Gestures using the body itself as tactile feedback. These gestures are not unique on their own but can be merged with the other gestures in cases where tactile feedback is required

When the categorization was established, the process of designing specific gestures for each category started. Using the use cases that were discovered in the workshop and the background from research and design theory, a set of gestures were designed for each of the three main categories. Then these gestures were used to implement new gestures for the use-cased that required more than one control output or would benefit from more tactile feedback.

When a gesture library was established, they were reviewed in a second co-design workshop with the same experts on VR and gesture interaction with competence in both interaction design, computer science and artificial intelligence. The group gave feedback on design and interaction, technical implementation, input algorithms and possible use scenarios. With the feedback and new scenarios, some gestures were iterated, some discarded and new ones were designed. Finally, a gesture library comprising of 10 gesture visualizations were designed. One gesture was chosen for further development and testing on the background of being one of the most valuable as well as relatively simple to implement and test in a VR environment. Details on the user test presented in the section Usability Evaluation.

3.3 Criteria for Designing Gestures

Based on the scope of the project and the use case, certain criteria can be formulated to narrow down the research area. The criteria, compared to the guidelines, are not based on literature or research, but rather on input from experts.

The Gesture Should be Unique and Non-Overlapping. The participants of the co-design workshops reported that when controlling robotics, several inputs are required. Designing gestures that are unique would, therefore, make it possible to control several mechanics with a few distinct gestures. The gestures should, in that case, be designed in a way that they do not overlap to avoid them being interpreted as two things at once. One example the participants used was controlling a drone using your palm, where the power is adjusted by bending your fingers. To activate the automatic landing function of the drone, one has to make a fist. In this case, when making a fist to land, the input will firstly be to increase the power, making the drone go up, before registration the fist gesture making it activate the landing function.

Gestures Should Require as Little Movement as Possible. When designing for interaction using hand gestures, one has to consider biomechanics and the physical strain on the body. As a guideline, one should therefore always try to avoid bodily movements that are physically demanding or that will cause strain or fatigue over time. An argument for using gestures to control robotics could be that it is used in scenarios where the human body is physically constrained, thereby using facile gestures is beneficial.

3.4 Developing a Gesture-Library

In addition to the gesture categories, we developed two gestures in each of the five categories, giving a total of 10 gestures. A detailed description of the gesture categories and gestures is presented in the following subsections.

Gestures for Directional Movement. Controlling the directional movement is related to any steering mechanism. Mechanical steering is often more constrained than flow control and spatial orientation, and should, therefore, be used with gestures that follow these constraints.

Gesture 1. Pointing Arrow. In use cases where a more directional (rather than rotational) visualization is more intuitive can the pointing gesture be applied. Making a flat hand with straight fingers, moving around the wrist, one can point in the desired direction. The gesture is constrained to a certain degree which is also added in the visualization (Fig. 1).

Fig. 1. Gesture 1: *Pointing Arrow* gesture and visualization

The visualization consists of an arrow pointing in the direction of the gesture. The arrow has the affordance of direction and the circle at its root indicates rotation. Adding a stapled line in the center makes it easy to indicate where the neutral position is.

Gesture 2. Rotating Cylinder. The gesture of rotating your wrist around the axis of your hand gives you close to 180 degrees of rotational freedom. This matches the mechanical constraints of steering. In this case, the hand gesture, either it is a palm or fist, is not that important, which gives it the benefit of being combined with other gestures (which will be further explored in Multifunctional Gestures section) (Fig. 2).

Fig. 2. Gesture 2: *Rotating Cylinder* gesture and visualization

The cylinder has the affordance of rotation. To give the cylinder an index of the rotational position, a vertical plane is added. This plane represents the position of the hand, where the «flatness» of the hand is mapped to the plane. The cylinder itself is mapped in the direction of the arm, making it an abstract illustration of the user's own arm. To make the physical constraints cohere with the visualization, two balls are added to stop the rotation where the hand can not be rotated anymore.

Gestures for Flow Control. Controlling the flow could be any control unit measuring an amount from 0 to a limit (i.e. power, volume, throttle, etc.). Simple gestures that represent this control unit can be used either alone, combined with two hand gestures (another gesture for the other arm), or combined with other controls in the same gesture (see Multifunctional gestures). By making the visualization in 3D it gives a better representation as it can be better mapped to the direction of the gesture.

Gesture 3. Cylinder Flow Bar. The gesture of extending and closing the fingers follows the same constraints as the visualization. A fully stretched out hand can not be extended anymore, making it a natural max point. A closed palm, therefore, represents the minimum point as the gesture can not contract any further. The gesture is also ergonomic and non-straining and has a sufficient span to give control over fine adjustments (Fig. 3).

The cylinder has clear constraints by having a defined height/length, determining the max and min. It also has clear visual dissemination of filling up a cylindrical container and works as a metaphor for filling up a glass. Being in 3D, the visualization can be mapped to the direction of the gesture, making the dynamic feedback even more intuitive.

Fig. 3. Gesture 3: *Cylinder Flow Bar* gesture and visualization

Gesture 4. Ball in Sphere. The gesture of opening and closing the fist is similar to the previous gesture, but represents a ball rather than a cylinder. The gesture also has the constraints of being at the min with a closed fist and at max with a fully extended hand. The gesture is also ergonomic and non-straining (Fig. 4).

Fig. 4. Gesture 4: *Ball in Sphere* gesture and visualization

The visualization of a ball in the sphere follows the hand being mapped as a ball when being a fist. As the user extend the fist/ball gesture the ball will scale up until it reaches its map being when the hand is fully extended (but still mimicking a ball). The sphere around the ball represents the max.

Gestures for Spatial Orientation. Spatial orientation, meaning positional orientation in a three-dimensional space, is harder to design for, as there are fewer common metaphors to represent the controls. One could argue that spatial orientation is harder than previous mentioned orientations and a well-designed visualization can, therefore, provide even more value.

Gesture 5. Plane Gesture. Some control units do not have limited directional navigation but can have 360-degree navigation. A plane is a good metaphor to represent navigation on one level. A flat hand can then be used to represent the plane resulting in a good mapping. To give feedback on the power being applied in the direction, a grid system can be used to visualize how much power and in what direction the power is applied. By moving the hand like a plane, the visualization will correspond showing the corresponding visualization (Fig. 5).

Fig. 5. Gesture 5: *Plane gesture* and visualization

The visualization is designed as a grid system, where the power and direction are indicated by coloring the squares according to the gesture. The borders of the grid work as a constraint indicating the maximum of power. The black square in the middle indicates the neutral position.

Gesture 6. XYZ Gesture. While the gesture plane gesture gives 360 degrees of navigation, it only covers the x and y-axis. In situations where you want to position or control something in all directions (along the *x*, *y* and *z*-axis) the XYZ gesture can be valuable. The distinct gesture of simulating the XYZ axis with your fingers makes it intuitive and well mapped (Fig. 6).

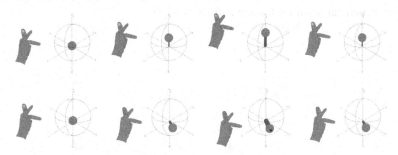

Fig. 6. Gesture 6: XYZ gesture and visualization

The visualization includes four elements; a ball, a cylinder, an XYZ axis and a sphere. The ball represents the hand's position in the real space. The cylinder visualizes the power being applied as its thickness increases as it gets further away from the origin (the point set when activating the gesture). The XYZ axis is there as a visual aid to show which direction and position in space the force is being applied. And the sphere is there as a constraint to visualize the maximum of power one is able to apply.

Multifunctional Gestures. The gestures presented so far have been considered simple, and mainly focused on one control output. Combining different gestures will show the true potential of gesture-based interaction. Being able to control a complex control system with single gestures that control several outputs and then put in a sequence of non-overlapping gestures can be very valuable.

Gesture 7. Rotating Cylinder with Flow. By combining the cylinder directional gesture with the gesture for flow control, one has a multifunctional gesture that gives the user the possibility to control flow and direction with one hand. Also in this case can the flow control be calibrated so that negative flow is possible (reverse etc.). The test of this gesture and visualization can be read in the next chapter (Fig. 7).

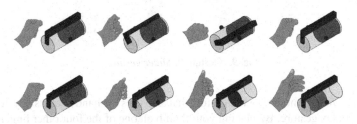

Fig. 7. Gesture 7: *Rotating Cylinder with Flow* gesture and visualization

Gesture 8. 3D Plane. As mentioned in the chapter of spatial orientation, the plane gesture does not give an opportunity to control something in the z-axis. By merging the content of the bar gesture in the chapter of Flow Control, one can use the two gestures simultaneously. Using your flat palm (as a plane) to control the direction and folding your fingers to control the power. The power can be calibrated to a neutral point making it possible to have negative flow as well. This visualization and gesture combination can be highly beneficial when controlling a drone (Fig. 8).

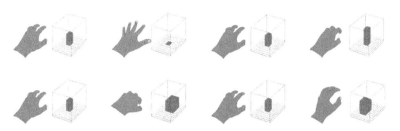

Fig. 8. Gesture 8: *3D Plane* gesture and visualization

Tactile Gestures. Dynamic feedback gives a very responsive interaction but can in some cases make it hard to keep constant control at a certain point, especially when combining several controls in one gesture. By using tactile gestures where the hand itself is used as physical feedback, it can make it easier to remember where the level is set at you the brain not only have visual feedback but also a physical one as you can feel the interaction on your body.

9. Slider Gesture. One tactile gesture could be sliding your thumb along the inside of your index finger, which can represent a slider controlling the amount of flow. This gesture is inspired by Google's work on gesture control for the Soli chip (Lien et al. 2016). This gesture gives the opportunity to control flow continuously, as well as making it easy to keep the flow at a continuous state. The downside to this gesture, and why someone might choose «non-tactile» gesture is that it is not as responsive and dynamic as other mentioned gestures (Fig. 9).

Fig. 9. Gesture 9: *Slider gesture*

10. Index Gesture. Another tactile gesture that also uses the hand itself as physical feedback is the index gesture. By placing your thumb on one of the four other fingers, it can represent different levels. This gesture is beneficial in cases where the control of flow is more step-based. As with the slider-gesture (see the section above), this is not optimal if continuous flow control is required (Fig. 10).

Fig. 10. Gesture 10: *Index gesture*

4   Method: Usability Evaluation

To verify if the gestures could be used in practice, we selected one of the gestures and performed a usability test. The selected gesture was the multifunctional gesture (#7) *Rotating Cylinder with Flow*. The rationale behind this was that the gesture was a combination of two gestures, the *cylinder directional gesture* (#2) and the *flow control gesture* (#3). This made it one of the most demanding gestures on the list for the users.

4.1   Setup and Preparation

The goal of the user test was to (1) test the selected gesture and (2) test the importance of visualization feedback in aiding users to understand the interaction. In preparation for the user test, the gesture visualization was implemented in a car game developed with the computer game engine *Unreal*. The visualization and the car controls were linked with the input from a gesture tracking glove, the *Manus-VR glove*. The glove was equipped with a number of sensors, such as gyroscope, accelerometer, degree of finger bend, etc. In this study, we used glove data from two sensor points in the gloves middle finger and used the average as input to control power and reverse, while the glove's gyroscope gave input for the cars turning. Two test tracks were designed, one to test fine motor skills and another to test speed and control (Fig. 11).

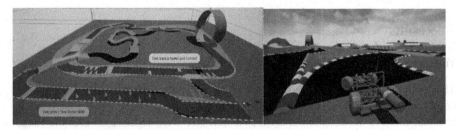

Fig. 11. *Left:* The test track tested the participants' fine motor skills, as well as abilities for speed and control. *Right:* The track and the car with visualization

4.2 Procedure

18 test participants were recruited for the study. All of them were students at a national technological university but from different study programs and nationalities. The test group consisted of 9 male and 9 female students aged from 21 to 28. None of the participants knew anything about the project before the usability test and only one had any experience with gesture control. To get valid test results on the effect of the visualization, the test group of 18 participants was divided into two subgroups, where one group tested the gesture *with* the visualization, while the other group tested *without* the visualization.

The users were first asked to fill out a consent form giving permission to use the data from the user test (including video and photo). While putting on, setting up and calibrating the glove, the participant was placed facing away from the screen, unable to get any clues of what they were supposed to do. They were then told to turn around and try to control the car in the game without any further instruction. They were instructed to talk aloud during the experiment and to explain the controls to the facilitator when they thought they had understood how to interact with the car. The facilitator took the time from the participant turned towards the screen until they understood how to control the car. Additionally, both groups were asked to complete the two different test tracks, while recording the time of completion. At the end of the user test, a short interview was conducted to get more detailed feedback on their experience (Fig. 12).

Fig. 12. The setup and glove used in the experiment

5 Results

The usability test revealed a number of insights, as presented below.

The Visualizations were Useful. 14 out of 18 who participated in the user test were positive in using the visualization to aid them in steering. Two were indifferent to having a visualization or not and did not use it as a tool. Two were negative towards the visualization and would rather drive without it as it was more disturbing than helpful. Several of the test subjects that started out without visualization believed that the visualization would have made them understand how to control the car earlier (which cohere with the test results as well). Several also stated that the visualization was a great tool to learn the controls, but might be removed when they had learned and adapted to the controls.

When taking the time from starting the experiment until the test subject gained control over the car, we measured that the *with-visualization* group was on average 41 s (34%) faster, that the *without-visualization* group. However, due to the variation in completion time, the differences were not significant (Fig. 13).

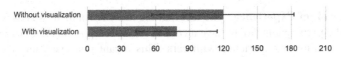

Fig. 13. Seconds for test subject to gain control over the car on the first try

Assuming Starting Position. Several users assume that a flat hand is the natural start position. Some say it is because the hand is mapped in relation to the hand, others say that the vive-tracker on top of the glove made them want to balance it and therefore keeping a flat hand as neutral. When they understood and/or was being described that the natural position was a vertical hand, they agreed that it is more ergonomic. For some of the users with this mapping in mind, the plane in the visualization did not make it clear how to adjust the hand to a neutral starting position.

Observations and Feedback. Many felt that the system was uncalibrated to their mental model. A takeaway from this could be to add more visual clues to the visualization to make it more understandable that the flat plane is representing the hand's position.

Other than the data gathered, several valuable observations were done during the user test. Firstly, we observed how different people reacted to the visualization (either if they started with it or if it was added later). Some participants did not pay any attention to it and assumed it was a part of the car. More commonly though, participants found the visualization very helpful. One of the participants said: «*Oh, that was much better. It feels like it gets less sensitive. I have much more control now.*» Another said: «*I understood how to control the car after a while, but the visualization helped me adjust my hand position. I can calibrate the hand gesture correctly to the steering.*»

It was also interesting to see the level of control the user gained, once they understood the controls. 12 out of the 18 participants managed to complete the first track with an average time of 42 s on a fairly technical and challenging track. These numbers do not conclude anything, but it shows that the gesture that was tested was intuitive and understandable, and gave the user a high sense of control and precision.

5.1 Sources of Error

Even though the user test was conducted successfully and with a sustainable amount of participants, there were some sources of error to be considered when evaluating the results.

Inaccurate Measurements. Trying to get a clear and precise data point for when someone understands something is difficult. In the experiment, the test subject was given no instructions on how to control the car, and had to find it out by himself/herself. The single facilitator, following a protocol based on observations and the test subjects' responses, decided when they had understood the interaction and stopped the time. This gives us only an indication of the value of the visualization. Further testing needs to be done to verify the finding.

Different Levels of Experience. The fact that the test environment was as a car game meant that the participants would have a certain relationship to this kind of interaction either from gaming or experience with cars. This meant that everyone did not start from zero, but some might have a better starting point for understanding the interaction. To examine this further, the participants were asked to complete a survey describing their experience with cars and gaming. This revealed that test subjects who had «some experience» or «a lot experience» with gaming spent less time to get control over the car compared with test subjects with «no experience» or «a little experience» with gaming. However, due to the low number of participants in each category, these findings are not significant. However, it provides a possible explanation of the time differences (Fig. 14).

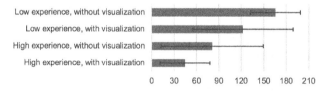

Fig. 14. Seconds for test subject to gain control over the car on the first try

Glove Setup Might Have Influenced Test Results. In the setup phase, where the users had the back to the screen, they were told to move their fingers so that the facilitator could check if the glove was calibrated correctly. Some users mentioned after the test that this helped in knowing what types of inputs the glove looked at. Although this could have affected some results, mainly the general time it took to understand the interaction, the same procedure was done for every user and should therefore not make that big of an impact when it comes to the difference in times.

6 Discussion

In this study we have found 5 gesture categories and developed 10 specific gestures that are simple, logically mapped and non-strenuous. Further, we have designed corresponding visualization-feedback based on design principles. At last, we have evaluated one of the gestures and the corresponding visualization and found indications that it improves the learning time of controlling a car in a simulated setting.

6.1 Benefits of Using Gesture-Based Interaction

By assisting gesture-based interaction with corresponding visualizations one can achieve a more instinctive and intuitive interaction. By instinctive interaction, we mean that a user should be able to know how to interact with a system without any prior knowledge or instructions. When achieving this, one could introduce gesture-based interaction in domains with advanced (and often unintuitive) controls and making the job easier and more efficient, as well as reducing training costs. The study on TeMoto (Valner et al. 2018) that tests a fairly simple gesture-interaction demonstrates that this can be the case.

In several cases, it is advantageous to interact using hand gestures rather than conventional controllers due to factors that are specific for certain domains. In the domain of healthcare, hygiene is a vital factor when it comes to interacting with computers and robotics, and can, therefore, benefit a lot from taking advantage of gesture-based interaction. In other domains, like space exploration or scuba diving, where the body is restricted and using conventional controllers are almost impossible, gesture-based interaction can be highly valuable.

6.2 Combining Gestures

Gesture-based interaction has the highest potential when several gestures are combined to form a gesture sequence. When done correctly, using non-overlapping gestures, one can create highly advanced interaction patterns that would be very hard to imitate with conventional controllers. By choosing different gestures to control different outputs, one can create intuitive yet advanced control systems. As an example; by combing the *Directional Cylinder with Flow control gesture (#7)* and the *XYZ gesture (#6)* one can control advanced machines and robots with only one hand. The user could drive the rover by using the *Directional Flow Cylinder* and when the desired position is reached, the user could simply change his/her gesture to the *Xyz Gesture* and control the robotic arm. The same principles could be applied for drone-steering where the user could swap between steering controls depending on the use case (e.g. fast traveling or detailed inspection) (Fig. 15).

Fig. 15. Combining Gestures

6.3 Visual Gesture Mapping Makes Interaction Easier to Learn

Looking at the results presented in the usability evaluation we can argue that having a visualization does make it faster and easier to understand the interaction as well as making the interaction more precise. Feedback from the test subjects also indicate that the visualization worked well as guidance to learn how to properly interact with the car simulator, and that it could be removed after a while when the user had learned the interaction pattern. This can be interpreted both as the visualization being helpful but also that the gesture itself was intuitive enough for the user to quickly learn how to use it. Examples of this were found in the results; users who first was presented with the visualization and then having it removed, did not lose control or forget how to interact with the car simulator.

Although the visual elements in the gesture visualization was proven to be effective, it was not perfect. The design process gave the foundation of a gesture-hypothesis that was made on the basis of design theory, research and expert-reviews. The usability evaluation was, in that case, a test of that hypothesis (Fig. 16).

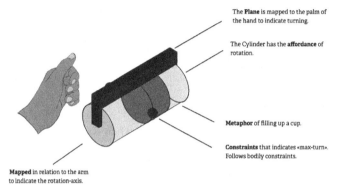

Fig. 16. Design hypothesis of *Rotating Cylinder with Flow* visualization

The hypothesis of mapping a flat palm to a flat plane and that the cylinder should indicate the hand direction were both understandable, but not intuitive enough that this was obvious without explanation. These elements were vital to quickly understand how to calibrate the gesture (in this case the steering). The visualization seemed to be too abstract for the user to intuitively understand that the plane represents their hand, and should rather be designed with a closer resemblance to the hand/palm. The mapping of the cylinder to the user's hand was probably the most crucial element of the hypothesis, as it determines if the user managed to steer accurately. Several test subjects managed to steer and control the car to a certain degree but complained about inaccuracy. The reason why was usually that they did not understand that the steering was supposed to be around the axis of their hand instead of a more common assumption of turning the hand as they would turn a steering wheel.

To summarize, the visual gesture mapping was indeed helpful and did make the interaction more intuitive compared to having no visualization at all. But the visualization has to be improved to reach the goal of being self-explanatory and result in an *instinctive* interaction.

7 Conclusion

In this study we have found 5 gesture categories and developed 10 specific gestures that are simple, logically mapped and non-strenuous. Further, we have designed corresponding visualization-feedback for each of the gestures. At last, we have evaluated one of the gestures and the corresponding visualization and found indications that it made it faster and easier for the test subjects to understand the interaction, gave them better control, and improved the learning time of controlling a car in a simulated setting. The gesture library is not a finished product, but a foundation for further work in the field of gesture-based interaction. Further testing of the gesture library and refinement of the corresponding visualizations is necessary. By combining gestures from the library, gesture-based interaction can be used to control advanced machines, robots and drones in an intuitive and non-strenuous way.

References

Antoni, S.-T., Sonnenburg, C., Saathoff, T., Schlaefer, A.: Feasibility of interactive gesture control of a robotic microscope. In: Current Directions in Biomedical Engineering, vol. 1, p. 164 (2015)

Arkenbout, E.A., de Winter, J.C.F., Ali, A., Dankelman, J., Breedveld, P.: A gesture-based design tool: assessing 2DOF vs. 4DOF steerable instrument control. PLoS ONE **13**(7) (2018). https://doi.org/10.1371/journal.pone.0199367. urn: issn: 1932-6203

Barber, D., Howard, T., Walter, M.: A multimodal interface for real-time soldier-robot teaming (2016)

Gesture Control: Gartner Glossary (2019)

Hartmann, F., Schlaefer, A.: Feasibility of touch-less control of operating room lights. Int. J. Comput. Assist. Radiol. Surg. **8**(2), 259–268 (2013). https://doi.org/10.1007/s11548-012-0778-2

Hostetter, A.B., Alibali, M.W.: Psychon. Bull. Rev. **15**, 495 (2008). https://doi.org/10.3758/PBR.15.3.495

Jeannerod, M.: Neural simulation of action: a unifying mechanism for motor cognition. NeuroImage **14**(1), S103–S109 (2001). https://doi.org/10.1006/nimg.2001.0832

Johnson-Glenberg, M.C.: Immersive VR and education: embodied design principles that include gesture and hand controls (2018)

Lien, J., et al.: Soli: ubiquitous gesture sensing with millimeter wave radar. ACM Trans. Graph. **35**(4), 1–19 (2016). https://doi.org/10.1145/2897824.2925953

Liu, J., Luo, Y., Ju, Z.: An interactive astronaut-robot system with gesture control. (Research Article) (Report). Comput. Intell. Neurosci. (2016). https://doi.org/10.1155/2016/7845102

Malizia, A., Bellucci, A.: The artificiality of natural user interfaces. Commun. ACM **55**(3) (2012). https://doi.org/10.1145/2093548.2093563

O'hara, K., Harper, R., Mentis, H., Sellen, A., Taylor, A.: On the naturalness of touchless: Putting the & ldquo; interaction & rdquo; back into NUI. ACM Trans. Comput. Hum. Interact. **20**(1), 1–25 (2013). https://doi.org/10.1145/2442106.2442111

Nacenta, M.A., Kamber, Y., Qiang, Y., Kristensson, P.O.: Memorability of pre-designed and user-defined gesture sets. In: Paper presented at the Proceedings of the SIGCHI Conference on Human Factors in Computing Systems, Paris, France (2013)

Norman, D.A.: The Design of Everyday Things (Rev. and exp. ed. ed.). Basic Books, New York (2013)

Rise, K.: The Potential of Gesture-based Interaction (2020)

Valner, R., Kruusamäe, K., Pryor, M.: TeMoto: intuitive multi-range telerobotic system with natural gestural and verbal instruction interface. Robotics **7**(1), 9 (2018). https://doi.org/10.3390/rob otics7010009

Wachs, J.P., et al.: A gesture-based tool for sterile browsing of radiology images. J. Am. Med. Inform. Assoc. **15**(3), 321–323 (2008). https://doi.org/10.1197/jamia.M2410

The Potential of Gesture-Based Interaction

Kasper Rise[✉] and Ole Andreas Alsos[✉]

Norwegian University of Science and Technology, Trondheim, Norway
risekasper@gmail.com, ole.alsos@ntnu.no

Abstract. Gesture control has been a topic of research and development since the 1970s. As hands are humans' native tool for interaction, it is natural to look at gesture control when talking about next-generation human-computer interaction. Throughout history many have tried to take advantage of the potential of gesture control, without huge success. Gesture-based interaction for consumer electronics have been widely explored using gesture to control TVs, mobile phones and drones, without making it a preferred interaction pattern. It is hard to argue that screen-based media is a preferred application for gesture-based interaction due to the lack of clear benefits of changing a known interaction pattern. Digital objects without screen interfaces show potential for use of gesture control but lacks the possibility of giving proper feedback to make it intuitive. Considering design principles as visibility, feedback and constraints, VR and AR stands out as the most promising medias to apply gesture-based interaction. The potential is not only determined by the medium, but also in what domain it is applied to. Domains like education, healthcare, robotics, heavy industry and space show clear benefits. When designing for the global market (B2C), social acceptance, cultural differences and timing are complications one has to consider. What goes for any case applying this technology; gesture-based interaction should not be used because it is possible, but because it is needed.

Keywords: Gesture-based interaction · Gesture control · Virtual Reality · Augmented Reality

1 Introduction

The advent of the Macintosh in 1984 was an important event in the history of human-machine interface and computation in general. Since then, people fundamentally changed the way people thought of computers and how to interact with them. Ever since this shift in human-computer interaction (HCI), technology in general has drastically evolved. Memory capacity, processing speeds and graphics power have skyrocketed. The Web and, more recently, the cloud have revolutionized the way we interact with computers. Interfaces have though yet to change (Underkoffler 2010).

Humans still mainly interact with digital media using mouse and keyboard, sticks, levers, buttons or touch, with everything displayed on a screen. We are seeing a shift in how we interact with digital media though. Voice control combined with artificial intelligence is becoming more and more implemented in people's interaction patterns.

© Springer Nature Switzerland AG 2020
M. Kurosu (Ed.): HCII 2020, LNCS 12182, pp. 125–136, 2020.
https://doi.org/10.1007/978-3-030-49062-1_8

But as for now, it only works as a supplement to screen-based interfaces and can't replace them completely.

Humans' instinctive way of interacting with objects is using their hands. It is, therefore, logical to look at gesture control when we talk about the next generation of HCI. Gesture control is not something new. Steven Spielberg's movie Minority Report where Tom Cruise is controlling a futuristic gesture-based interface is often used as a reference in these discussions. And with good reasons; the movie producers actually hired a team of designers and engineers to design the interface as an R & D (Underkoffler 2010). The movie premiered in 2002 and ever since have different companies tried to make use of this technology and revolutionize how we interact with digital media.

To discuss the potential of gesture-based interaction this article will firstly look at some key milestones in the history of gesture control, then look at different domains and digital media where gesture control can be applied.

2   Background

2.1   Method

The article relies mostly on reviewing literature that was relevant to the subject. Articles in domains of computer science, psychology, robotics, engineering and interaction design were focused on. It was important to understand the technical challenges of gesture-based interaction by looking at articles from computer science, engineering and robotics but also get an understanding of what had been done in terms of research and testing, therefore looking at articles from psychology and interaction design.

2.2   Gesture Control Defined

The term *Gesture control* is used in a wide range of contexts and can be interpreted differently. In Gartner Glossary it is defined as: "Gesture control is the ability to recognize and interpret movements of the human body in order to interact with and control a computer system without direct physical contact" (Gesture Control 2019).

The definition above covers "movements of the human body", where this article will merely focus on hand gestures. Combinations of controller inputs and gestures (i.e. VR controllers) will neither be in the scope of this article.

2.3   Brief History of Gesture Control

To get an understanding of the future of gesture control, one has to look at where gesture control has been used in the past. This section will mention some key milestones in the history of gesture control.

The first prototype of a gesture tracing glove emerged in 1977 and was called the Sayre Glove. It used flexible tubes with a light source at one end and a photocell at the other, which were mounted along each finger of the glove. When you bent your fingers, the light passing through the tubes would decrease. Later in the 70s and the 80s several different prototypes of gloves emerged, using different types of sensors (Premaratne 2014).

The use of cameras to recognize hand gestures started very early along with the development of the first wearable sensor gloves. There were many hurdles at that time in interpreting camera-based gestures. Coupled with significantly low computing-power available only on mainframe computers, cameras offered very poor resolution along with color inconsistency. Despite these hurdles, the first computer vision gesture recognition system was reported in the 1980s (Premaratne 2014). The MIT-LED glove was developed at the MIT Media Laboratory in the early 1980s as part of a camera-based LED system to track body and limb position for real-time computer graphics animation (Sturman and Zeltzer 1994). The first instance of a hand recognition system that totally relied on computer vision without markers was reported by Rehg and Kanade in 1993 and was called DigitEyes (Rehg and Kanade 1994).

Throughout history the gaming industry has been one of the leading forces to bring gesture control to the consumer market. From the Nintendo Power Glove in 1989, marketed as the future of game controller (Lee 2011) to the PlayStation Eye Toy in 2003, the Nintendo Wii in 2006 and the Xbox Kinect in 2009. Even though these devices do not fit the given definition of gesture control, they are still worth mentioning.

Around 2008 several companies start to focus on gesture control for the consumer electronics(CE) market. In IFA 2008, the second-largest CE show in the world (behind CES), Toshiba showed gesture control for TVs. Samsung, JVC and Hitachi presented TVs with gesture control at CES in 2008 and in 2009 (Shan 2010). Gesture control has also been implemented in mobile phones over the years. Sony Ericsson launched its Z555 in 2008 with the ability to mute or snooze the alarm by waving the hand to the build-in camera (Shan 2010). In 2019 Google launched the Pixel 4 that supports gesture control.

Leap Motion launched its sensor in 2011, that lets users control their computer by using gestures. The Dji Spark drone (nicknamed the "Selfiedrone") launched in 2017, allows users to control the drone by using their hand instead of a controller.

2.4 Technologies for Tracking Gestures

Gesture control requires advanced technology and several different approaches have been tested over the years. This article will give an overview of the general approaches in the technology of gesture control (Fig. 1).

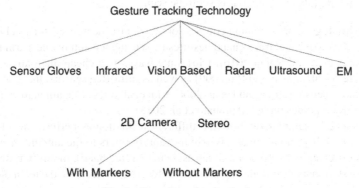

Fig. 1. Overview of technologies

Sensor Gloves. Sensor Gloves was the first technology made for gesture control already back in 1970s. Sensor glove in essence is a wired interface with certain tactile or other sensory units that were attached to the fingers or joints of the glove, worn by the user (Premaratne 2014). These gloves offer high accuracy but are also highly intrusive compared to other technologies.

Vision-Based Gesture Recognition. In recent years, more and more research is concentrated on vision-based hand gesture recognition. Compared to sensor gloves, vision-based recognition is more natural and comfortable- able, as it does not constrain the flexibility of hand movements (Premaratne 2014). The downside to this technology is that it lacks the accuracy that modern sensor gloves provide.

2D Cameras: With camera sensors becoming low-cost and pervasive in CE products, vision technologies receive increasing attention, which allow unobtrusive and passive gesture sensing (Shan 2010). By using markers on your hands, either as colored gloves or as stickers on your fingers, the camera is able to track your hand gestures accurately (Premaratne 2014). The problem with this approach is that using gloves makes it more intrusive and might be ineffective in certain use cases. As camera technology advances, many examples occur of gesture tracking using algorithms to track gestures without using markers, delivering high accuracy. A problem with 2D camera tracking is that one might lose accuracy due to self-occlusion, where the hand from certain angels overlaps itself (Premaratne 2014).

Stereo Cameras: Astereo camera is a camera with two or more lenses and can simulate human binocular vision. Today stereo cameras are implemented in high-end smartphones, but previously required a stationary setup with several cameras. With stereo camera setups for gesture tracking one has to use several cameras to get a 3D tracking of the hand and bypass the problem of self-occlusion (Premaratne 2014). Stereo cameras are more expensive than 2D cameras.

Radar Technology. More recently, products using radar technology to track hand gestures have been released. Soli, Google's gesture recognition radar chip is an example of this. It is a high-resolution, low- power, miniature gesture sensing technology. It is based on millimeter-wave radar that operates on the principle of reflection and detection of radiofrequency electromagnetic waves (Lien et al. 2016). Even though this technology is very promising, its full potential is yet to be seen.

Other Technologies. Electromagnetic Sensors have also been used for tracking gestures. The Myo wristband tracks hand gestures by sensing tension in one's arm muscles (Sathiyanarayanan and Rajan 2016). Ultrasonic waves is a cheap alternative to track hand gestures (Kalgaonkar and Raj 2009) as well as Infra-Red sensors, that can be used as a standalone sensor (Hillebrand et al. 2006; Kim et al. 2012; Megalingam et al. 2016) or combined with other inputs (Abraham et al. 2018).

The (Table 1) summarizes how the different technologies perform in relation to movability, mobility and accuracy. Where movability refers to the amount of intrusion for the user (i.e. a glove will be more intrusive than a free hand), mobility refers to the setup being stationary or mobile and accuracy refers to how accurate the technology can track your hand gestures. The classification of low, medium and high is in relation to each other, meaning that low in accuracy does not necessarily mean that it is inaccurate but less accurate than the others.

Table 1. Movability, Mobility and Accuracy of the given technologies

Technology	Movability	Mobility	Accuracy
Sensor Glove	Low	High	High
2D VB with markers	Medium	Medium	Medium
2D VB without markers	High	Medium	Low
VB Stereo Camera	High	Low	Medium
Radar	High	Medium	High
Ultrasound	Medium	High	Low
EM Sensors	High	Low	Low

3 Findings

3.1 Gesture Control in Different Media

Gesture control can be used in a range of different domains, as presented below.

Gesture Control for Virtual Reality. Gesture control for Virtual Reality (VR) has a huge potential as it can give visual feedback to the user. Many VR systems are depending on hand controllers to interact in the virtual world. These controllers try to give as much feedback to the user as possible by tracking some hand gestures as rotation and some finger movements but restrict the user's movability. By using accurate gesture control technology one can map physical hands in VR 1-1, giving the user the feeling of embodiment in the virtual world (Haans and Ijsselsteijn 2012).

Research has shown that by engaging the user's motoric system via the hand leads to a reduction in simulator sickness, which can be used as an argument for gesture control in VR (Stanney and Hash 1998).

Gesture Control for Augmented Reality. In Augmented Reality (AR) visual information is layered on top of the world one sees. A visual representation of your hands is therefore not needed. But by using gestures to control something in the real world, AR can be highly beneficial for giving visual feedback that is needed.

Gesture Control for Screens. Many examples of gesture control for screens have been given in the chapter about history (2.2). As humans have developed a well-known interaction pattern for interacting with screens, the arguments for adapting to another type of interaction have to be substantial. Don Norman argues that:

> *Gestures will form a valuable addition to our repertoire of interaction techniques, but they need time to be better developed, for us to understand how best to deploy them, and for standard conventions to develop so the same gestures mean the same things in different systems* (Norman 2010).

Gesture Control for Digital Objects. Interacting with objects using your hands is a natural part of human behavior. Using your hands to interact with digital objects and smart devices is therefore natural as well. Digital objects are in this article defined as devices that do not have a designated interface. This can be electronics and devices in a smart home such as lights, ovens speakers etc. These digital objects often go under the term Internet of Things (IoT) and Talal H. Noor argues that "Gesture control can help IoT services' users to have a better experience when controlling the IoT products" (Noor 2018, p. 3894). In his article he explores the technical possibility of controlling IoT products by making signs with their fingertips (Noor 2018). By recognizing the user's eyes and finger, gestures can be used to interact with a screen. This method makes the HCI more secure than a touch-based interface (Xu et al. 2018).

3.2 Potential Domains for Gesture Control

Gesture control has been explored in several different domains. This section will look at some domains where gesture control can have a big impact.

Gesture Control in Robotics. Telerobotics allows operators to execute tasks from a safe distance and have been proven successful in many situations. But many tasks are still completed by human operators despite the presence of hazards and the costs associated with protective gear, training and additional waste disposal. Gesture control can in this example have a great advantage as workers still have performance and cognitive advantages over remote systems. This includes work-rate, adaptability, dexterity and minimal delay and latency issues during task planning and execution (Valner et al. 2018).

TeMoto is a teleoperation system that combines gesture control with voice control and a physical turn knob to interact with a telerobot. The system was tested on different robots in different scenarios; threading a needle with a robotic arm and navigating a rover and controlling its arm. The results show that untrained operators can quickly understand and use TeMoto as well as the well-established mouse input, even to run systems too complex to be efficiently operated with only a mouse input (Valner et al. 2018).

Gesture Control in Healthcare. A domain that can benefit a lot from gesture control is the healthcare sector by offering a major advantage in sterility (Wachs et al. 2008) as well as aiding health professionals in situations where conventional interfaces might not be sufficient. In a case study, researchers gathered ethnographic evidence from surgeons about the concept of gesture-based control over the display of their patients' radiographic scan data during surgery. This gave the surgeons direct access to their patients' scan data without compromising their sterile working field and without needing to rely on other clinicians to interpret display instructions (Stevenson et al. 2016). Another example of gesture control in health care is Gestix, a vision-based hand gesture capture and recognition system that interprets in real-time the user's gestures for navigation and manipulation of images in an electronic medical record (EMR) database (Wachs et al. 2008). Ultigesture is another example; a low-cost wristband able to track hand gestures for simple navigation. (Zhao et al. 2019). Using gesture control to operate a robotic microscope in surgery (Antoni et al. 2015), laparoscopic instruments (Arkenbout et al.

2018) and for controlling operating light (Hartmann and Schlaefer 2013) have also been explored.

Gesture Control for Space and Military. Domains that leads to physical restrictions to bodily movement will have clear incentives for taking advantage of gesture control. Astronauts in Space are one example of this. Research has been done using sensor gloves to control a snake-like robot in space (Liu et al. 2016). More recently, Ntention, a start-up at the Norwegian University of Science and Technology, collaborated with NASA and the SETI Institute to make a glove that controls a drone by only using hand gestures specifically for use in space exploration (McDonald 2019). Using multimodal interaction, combining gesture control and speech, has been researched in the field of military technology to develop so-called "real-time solider-robot teaming" (Barber et al. 2016).

Gesture Control in Automotive Sector. Gesture control has been increasingly applied to the automotive industry to reduce the distraction caused by in-vehicle interactions to the primary task of driving (Ma et al. 2016). Studies show that gesture control indeed required less attention off the road (gaze aversion) (Ma et al. 2016; Zöller et al. 2018). On the other hand, the types of gestures that are necessary/wanted while driving are important to consider. Users prefer not to use gestures to control functions that are directly related to their safety (as adjusting rearview mirror) or require high precision (as controlling air vent) (Ma et al. 2016).

Gesture Control in Heavy Industry. A huge that domain can benefit from gesture-based interaction is the heavy industry. In construction, cranes can improve their control system by using gesture control (Pietrusewicz 2014). Mobile robotic system for remote leak sensing and localization can also benefit from gesture-based interaction (Soldan et al. 2012).

Gesture Control for Enhanced Learning. An area where gesture control can be highly beneficial is when used for educational purposes. It is shown that gestures activate larger portions of the sensori-motor system and motoric pre-planning pathways than the other two systems and gestures may, therefore, lead to stronger memory traces (Goldin-Meadow 2011). Taking advantage of modern VR technology gives the possibility to simulate situations and visualizations in 3D to make the learner acquire knowledge faster and show better retention compared to 2D (Jeffrey 2011). By using hands as controls with gestures, the learner is given the possibility not only to get 3D visualizations but also to interact with the content. This follows the concept of "learning by doing" which works as a strong argument for gesture control in education. Engelkamp and Zimmer performed a task literature where they found that when participants performed short tasks, the task-associated words were better remembered compared to conditions where the participants read the words, or saw others perform the tasks (Engelkamp and Zimmer 1994). When learners take physical decisions about the placement of content using representational gestures, they become "active learners", which has shown an increase of STEM grades by 20% (Waldrop 2015). This research can both argue for using gesture-based interaction directly for educational purposes, but also as an argument for using gesture control over conventional controllers for enhanced learning effect.

4 Discussion

4.1 Changing Conventional Interaction Patterns Requires Good Incentives

Looking back at history, we have seen that gesture control is not something new. Trying to implement gesture-based interaction in the consumer market has been tried several times without making a substantial impact. Gesture control for TVs had incentives for implementing this technology; to solve the problem of losing the remote or having to get out of the sofa to find it. However, the incentives where not impactful enough for people to learn this new way of interaction. Additionally, using inaccurate and immature technology are arguably reasons why we do not see this type of interaction in TVs today. Mobile phones, computers and any screen-based CE serves even fewer incentives for implementing gesture-based interaction. The Magic Leap did a serious attempt at changing how we interact with computers, but it serves more as a tool for designers and researchers on the topic of gesture control rather than a consumer product. Looking at these examples one could argue that gesture control should not be applied where humans have already a well-established interaction pattern if it is not enough incentives to change it.

4.2 What Medium Has the Biggest Potential for Gesture-Based Interaction?

Most screen-based interfaces lack the incentives to adapt to gesture-based interaction, but there are some examples where this is not the case. In healthcare, where sterility often is required, gesture-based interaction can aid health professionals to interact with the same tools without compromising their work- or hygienic environment.

Digital objects and IoT do not have an established interaction pattern and therefore are tablets and computers often used to control these units. In this case, it is plenty of incentives to implement a new and more effective way of interacting. The problem is that without any interface, the user does not get the feedback that is needed. Layering information and feedback with AR can solve this problem, but as AR technology is not a common possession for the general consumer, it might not be the right time to apply this technology.

The need for feedback is one of 6 design principles by Norman (the other being: visibility, affordance, mapping, constraints and consistency) (Norman 2013). These principles can be used as a reference when discussing the right medium to apply gesture-based interaction. Doing so, one can argue that VR and AR stand out as the preferred medium as it provides better visibility and affordance.

4.3 Where Should Gesture-Based Interaction Be Applied?

Some domains show clearer incentives of applying gesture-based interaction than others. Healthcare have already been mentioned as an interesting domain due to sterility, but many of its examples also overlaps with the domain of robotics. Controlling robots, in any industry, usually relies on advanced controllers with sticks and levers. If designed correctly, gesture-based interaction can in these cases offer a more natural and intuitive form of interaction. Studies also show that by using gestures compared to controllers it leads to faster learning and better memorability (Goldin-Meadow 2011; Valner et al. 2018; Waldrop 2015).

In situations where the human body is physically restrained also shows several incentives for applying gesture-based interaction. That could be operating drones in a pressurized spacesuit, controlling equipment under water, in hazardous environments or used in military combat. Gesture-based interaction serves the benefit of only require small movements of hand gestures and requires only one hand.

Gesture-based interaction in the automotive industry have some incentives for being useful and is implemented in several modern cars. Despite arguments for less gaze-aversion while driving and lower operating times of dashboard controllers (Zöller et al. 2018) the award of learning this way of interaction is only when operating minor controls in the car (i.e. volume, audio tracks, heat, etc.). One can therefore argue that even though there are incentives for applying gesture-based interaction it is not where it has the biggest potential. One can also speculate if cars will drive by themselves in the near future and will not need human interaction at all.

4.4 What Complications Need to Be Considered When Designing for Gesture-Based Interaction?

Gestures are highly related to our culture. In some countries thumbs up means good, while it might mean something completely different somewhere else. Cultural differences are something designers have to take into account when designing for gestures. In a study to test gesture control on TVs across different countries they concluded that their findings support the possibility of creating a global gesture language for most basic TV interactions (Meier et al. 2014). The aspect of taking account for cultural differences mainly applies when designing for products that will reach the global market. On the other hand it is shown that user-defined gestures are preferable and more memorable than the other types (Malizia and Bellucci 2012); (O'hara et al. 2013) which might solve the problem of cultural differences.

Social acceptance is also something to consider when designing for gesture control. When talking about consumer electronics many would be uncomfortable using gestures in public spaces (Rico and Brewster 2010). Also, people will always be reluctant to learn something new. As argued before, it should be a clear incentive for people to switch from conventional interaction to gesture-based interaction.

The technology also has to be mature enough for gesture control to be accepted by the public. It is reasonable to argue that gesture tracking technology will be highly accurate and non-intrusive in a couple of years. Until then the technology being used should fit the purpose of the application. If one is depending on high accuracy but mobility is not a necessity, then a sensor glove might be the right technology to use However, if movability is required but only simple gestures are being tracked, then a camera-based technology might be suitable. The technology we have today is definitely good enough to be considered a reliable tool for gesture-based interaction. Some technologies though, like AR and VR, are well developed, but still expensive and not a common possession for the general consumer. This makes these technologies more usable when designing for a few experts (B2B) in certain domains than for the general public (B2C).

Although the technology is mature, the market has to be as well. Timing and execution are therefore a major aspect to consider when releasing new technology. The technology has to be released at a time when the market is ready for it and executed properly. The Nintendo Power Glove is a good example of a great concept but lacked both the mature technology (as the glove was highly inaccurate and unresponsive) and the execution (the Nintendo platform was not designed for this type of interaction). Decades later, they managed to deliver a technology that was mature enough and executed properly with the, greatly successful, Nintendo Wii (Lee 2011).

The lack of physical feedback using gestures contradicts with Norman's design principles and can be used as an argument when interacting against the use of gesture-based interaction. Studies of controlling surgical robot they concluded that a touch-based interface was better suited for the task than gesture interaction due to lack of force-feedback provided by contact with a surface, thus leading to a lack of precision, sensitivity, and context (Zhou et al. 2016). With this in mind, gesture-based interaction might, in certain areas, not be suitable before better technology (as sensor gloves with haptic feedback) are available.

5   Conclusion

This article has looked at the history of gesture control and how and where it has been used in the past. Different media where gesture control can be used have been mentioned. And lastly, it has presented promising domains where gesture control can make an impact.

There is no doubt that gesture-based interaction has a large potential, but it has to be used in areas where it has clear incentives for changing a well-established interaction pattern. Different media and domains offer different challenges and possibilities. Designers and researchers have to consider this when making products for gesture control. When designing gesture controlling for global consumers, one has to take into account social acceptance, cultural diversity and the burden of learning something new. In all cases applying this technology one has to consider the following; gesture-based interaction should not be used because it is possible, but because it is needed.

References

Abraham, L., Urru, A., Normani, N., Wilk, M., Walsh, M.: Hand tracking and gesture recognition using lensless smart sensors. Sensors 18(9) (2018). https://doi.org/10.3390/s18092834

Antoni, S.-T., Sonnenburg, C., Saathoff, T., Schlaefer, A.: Feasibility of interactive gesture control of a robotic microscope. In: Current Directions in Biomedical Engineering, vol. 1, pp. 164 (2015)

Arkenbout, E.A., de Winter, J.C.F., Ali, A., Dankelman, J., Breedveld, P.: A gesture-based design tool: assessing 2DOF vs. 4DOF steerable instrument control. PLoS ONE 13(7) (2018). https://doi.org/10.1371/journal.pone.0199367. urn: issn: 1932-6203

Barber, D., Howard, T., Walter, M.: A multimodal interface for real-time soldier-robot teaming (2016)

Engelkamp, J., Zimmer, H.D.: Motor similarity in subject-performed tasks. Psychol. Res. 57(1), 47–53 (1994). https://doi.org/10.1007/bf00452995

Gesture Control: Gartner Glossary (2019)

Goldin-Meadow, S.: Learning through gesture. Wiley Interdisc. Rev. Cogn. Sci. **2**(6), 595–607 (2011). https://doi.org/10.1002/wcs.132

Hartmann, F., Schlaefer, A.: Feasibility of touch-less control of operating room lights. Int. J. Comput. Assist. Radiol. Surg. **8**(2), 259–268 (2013). https://doi.org/10.1007/s11548-012-0778-2

Hillebrand, G., Bauer, M., Achatz, K., Klinker, G.: Inverse kinematic infrared optical finger tracking (2006)

Haans, A., Ijsselsteijn, W.A.: Embodiment and telepresence: toward a comprehensive theoretical framework. Interact. Comput. **24**(4), 211–218 (2012). https://doi.org/10.1016/j.intcom.2012.04.010

Jeffrey, J.: Digital dome versus desktop display in an educational game: gates of Horus. Int. J. Gaming Comput. Mediated Simul. (IJGCMS) **3**(1), 13–32 (2011). https://doi.org/10.4018/jgcms.2011010102

Kalgaonkar, K., Raj, B.: One-handed gesture recognition using ultrasonic Doppler sonar. In: Paper Presented at the 2009 IEEE International Conference on Acoustics, Speech and Signal Processing, 19–24 April 2009

Kim, D., et al.: Digits: freehand 3D interactions anywhere using a wrist-worn gloveless sensor. In: Paper Presented at the Proceedings of the 25th Annual ACM Symposium on User Interface Software and Technology, Cambridge, Massachusetts, USA (2012)

Lee, J.C.: Know Your Platform-Chapter 22. Elsevier Inc. (2011)

Lien, J., et al.: Soli: ubiquitous gesture sensing with millimeter wave radar. ACM Trans. Graph. **35**(4), 1–19 (2016). https://doi.org/10.1145/2897824.2925953

Liu, J., Luo, Y., Ju, Z.: An interactive astronaut-robot system with gesture control (Research Article) (Report). Comput. Intell. Neurosci. **2016** (2016). https://doi.org/10.1155/2016/7845102

Ma, J., Xu, M., Du, Y.: A Usability Study on In-Vehicle Gesture Control, vol. 2016 (2016)

Malizia, A., Bellucci, A.: The artificiality of natural user interfaces. Commun. ACM **55**(3) (2012). https://doi.org/10.1145/2093548.2093563

McDonald, R.: An Astronaut Smart Glove to Explore The Moon, Mars and Beyond [Press release] (2019). https://www.seti.org/press-release/astronaut-smart-glove-explore-moon-mars-and-beyond

Megalingam, R.K., Rangan, V., Krishnan, S., Alinkeezhil, A.B.E.: IR sensor-based gesture control wheelchair for stroke and SCI patients. IEEE Sens. J. **16**(17), 6755–6765 (2016). https://doi.org/10.1109/JSEN.2016.2585582

Meier, A., Goto, K., Wörmann, M.: Thumbs up to gesture controls? A cross-cultural study on spontaneous gestures, vol. 8528, pp. 211–217 (2014)

Noor, T.H.: A gesture recognition system for gesture control on Internet of Things services. J. Theoret. Appl. Inf. Technol. **96**(12), 3886–3895 (2018)

Norman, D.A.: The way I see it: Natural user interfaces are not natural. Interactions **17**(3) (2010). https://doi.org/10.1145/1744161.1744163

Norman, D.A.: The design of everyday things (Rev. and exp. ed. ed.). Basic Books, New York (2013)

O'hara, K., Harper, R., Mentis, H., Sellen, A., Taylor, A.: On the naturalness of touchless: putting the "interaction" back into NUI. ACM Trans. Comput. Hum. Interact. **20**(1), 1–25 (2013). https://doi.org/10.1145/2442106.2442111

Pietrusewicz, K.: Gestures can control cranes. Control Engineering, n/a (2014)

Premaratne, P.: Historical development of hand gesture recognition. Human Computer Interaction Using Hand Gestures, pp. 5–29. Springer, Singapore (2014). https://doi.org/10.1007/978-981-4585-69-9_2

Rehg, J.M., Kanade, T.: DigitEyes: vision-based hand tracking for human-computer interaction. In: Paper Presented at the Proceedings of 1994 IEEE Workshop on Motion of Non-rigid and Articulated Objects, 11–12 November 1994

Rico, J., Brewster, S.: Usable gestures for mobile interfaces: evaluating social acceptability. In: Paper presented at the Proceedings of the SIGCHI Conference on Human Factors in Computing Systems, Atlanta, Georgia, USA (2010)

Sathiyanarayanan, M., Rajan, S.: MYO armband for physiotherapy healthcare: a case study using gesture recognition application (2016)

Shan, C.: Gesture control for consumer electronics. In: Shao, L., Shan, C., Luo, J., Etoh, M. (eds.) Multimedia Interaction and Intelligent User Interfaces: Principles, Methods and Applications, pp. 107–128. Springer, London (2010). https://doi.org/10.1007/978-1-84996-507-1_5

Soldan, S., Bonow, G., Kroll, A.: RoboGasInspector - a mobile robotic system for remote leak sensing and localization in large industrial environments: overview and first results. IFAC Proc. Volumes 45(8), 33–38 (2012). https://doi.org/10.3182/20120531-2-NO-4020.00005

Stanney, K.M., Hash, P.: Locus of user-initiated control in virtual environments: influences on cybersickness. Presence Teleoperators Virtual Environ. 7(5), 447–459 (1998). https://doi.org/10.1162/105474698565848

Stevenson, D., et al.: Evidence from the surgeons: gesture control of image data displayed during surgery. Behav. Inf. Technol. 35(12), 1063–1079 (2016). https://doi.org/10.1080/0144929x.2016.1203025

Sturman, D.J., Zeltzer, D.: A survey of glove-based input. IEEE Comput. Graphics Appl. 14(1), 30–39 (1994). https://doi.org/10.1109/38.250916

Underkoffler, J.: Pointing to the future of UI. In: Paper presented at the TED2010 (2010). https://www.ted.com/talks/john_underkoffler_drive_3d_data_with_a_gesture

Valner, R., Kruusamäe, K., Pryor, M.: TeMoto: intuitive multi-range telerobotic system with natural gestural and verbal instruction interface. Robotics 7(1), 9 (2018). https://doi.org/10.3390/robotics7010009

Wachs, J.P., et al.: A gesture-based tool for sterile browsing of radiology images. J. Am. Med. Inform. Assoc. 15(3), 321–323 (2008). https://doi.org/10.1197/jamia.M2410

Waldrop, M.M.: Why we are teaching science wrong, and how to make it right. Nature 523(7560), 272–274 (2015). https://doi.org/10.1038/523272a

Xu, J., Zhang, X., Zhou, M.: A high-security and smart interaction system based on hand gesture recognition for Internet of Things. Secur. Commun. Netw. 2018, 11 (2018). https://doi.org/10.1155/2018/4879496

Zhao, H., Wang, S., Zhou, G., Zhang, D.: Ultigesture: a wristband-based platform for continuous gesture control in healthcare. Smart Health 11, 45–65 (2019). https://doi.org/10.1016/j.smhl.2017.12.003

Zhou, T., Cabrera, M.E., Wachs, J.P., Low, T., Sundaram, C.: A comparative study for telerobotic surgery using free hand gestures. J. Hum. Robot Interact. 5(2), 1–28 (2016). https://doi.org/10.5898/jhri.5.2.zhou

Zöller, I., Bechmann, R., Abendroth, B.: Possible applications for gestures while driving. Automot. Engine Technol. 3(1), 11–20 (2018). https://doi.org/10.1007/s41104-017-0023-7

Detecting Gestures Through a Gesture-Based Interface to Teach Introductory Programming Concepts

Lora Streeter[✉] and John Gauch[✉]

University of Arkansas, Fayetteville, AR 72701, USA
{lstrothe,jgauch}@uark.edu

Abstract. The goal of this research is to find an algorithm that is capable of recognizing gestures drawn in a visual and gesture-driven interface used to teach introductory programming concepts. Our system combines components from Google's Blockly, a visual programming language with a drag-and-drop puzzle piece interface, and Microsoft's Xbox Kinect which is used to perform skeletal tracking. We focus on two supervised machine learning clustering algorithms, centroid matching and medoid matching, to detect gestures.

Keywords: Blockly · Gesture matching · Kinect · Programming · Supervised machine learning · Medoid matching · Centroid matching · Visual programming

1 Introduction

Computer programming is an integral part of a technologically driven society, so there is a tremendous need to teach programming to a wider audience. One of the challenges in meeting this demand for programmers is that most traditional computer programming classes are targeted to university/college students with strong math backgrounds. To expand the computer programming workforce, we need to encourage a wider range of students to learn about programming.

This project uses Microsoft's Xbox Kinect to perform skeletal tracking, and is built on top of Google's Blockly, a visual block programming language with drag-and-drop puzzle pieces. We use the Kinect to capture the movements of new programmers as they use our system, then our software tracks and interprets student hand movements in order to recognize specific gestures which correspond to different programming constructs, and uses this information to create and execute programs using the Google Blockly visual programming framework.

We have implemented and evaluated a number of gesture matching algorithms. One challenge is that the size, shape, and path of the gestures varied considerably, so data has to be normalized for any comparisons. We discovered that paring down the coordinates to a predefined number provided no discernible loss of precision when matching. We focus on various gesture recognition algorithms to interpret user data as specific gestures, specifically supervised machine learning clustering algorithms for this paper.

© Springer Nature Switzerland AG 2020
M. Kurosu (Ed.): HCII 2020, LNCS 12182, pp. 137–153, 2020.
https://doi.org/10.1007/978-3-030-49062-1_9

We are aiming to create and evaluate a visual and gesture-driven interface to teach programming to non-traditional programmers, typically school-age children. We want to make learning how to program enjoyable and fun to engage the students and increase their attention span. The goal of this project is to find an algorithm that can accurately detect a drawn gesture.

2   Background and Related Work

Two categories of research that are relevant to our project are visual and gesture-based programming languages. We'll also briefly discuss human-computer interaction (HCI) systems that make use of the Kinect and/or gesture recognition as input. We will be incorporating elements of both in the design and implementation of our own system.

2.1   Visual Programming Languages

A visual programming language is designed so that the user manipulates program elements graphically instead of using traditional text oriented systems. Many visual languages are designed to appeal to non-traditional programmers by giving goal oriented tasks (e.g. "Make your character skate and create a snowflake") or by encouraging storytelling instead of text-driven computations that are seen in many introductory programming classes. We will look at two visual programming languages that have been very successful.

Google Blockly
Google has created a web-based visual editor that enables users to create programs by using a mouse to drag-and-drop connecting puzzle piece blocks together to accomplish a set of goals. An example of the Google Blockly programming interface is shown in Fig. 1. After the user has completed a goal, Blockly shows them how many lines their program would have taken in JavaScript (or any other language that is built in). There are eight different games listed on Google's site to help teach programming. These games are written in such a way to enable self-teaching. Each task the user is given can be

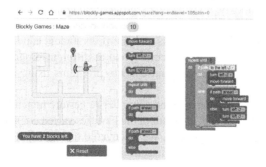

Fig. 1. Blockly IDE

solved with the information they have been provided, and each puzzle builds on the previous in each game.

MIT's Scratch

Created by the Lifelong Kindergarten Group at the MIT Media Lab and released to the public in 2007, Scratch is a web-based visual language specifically designed to easily create stories, games and animations. Although the software was targeted to young children through mid-teenagers, people of all ages use it. Scratch is built to encourage young people to think creatively, learn reasoning skills, and work together with others. Scratch features color-coded drag-and-drop puzzle pieces that click together with pull-down menus and fill-in-the-blanks on form options. An example of the Scratch programming interface is shown in Fig. 2.

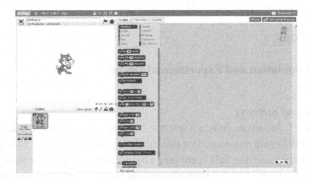

Fig. 2. Scratch IDE

2.2 Gestural Programming Languages

A gestural programming language is one that takes input as a movement of the hands, face or other parts of the body instead of keyboard or mouse input [1]. Consumer devices, like mobile phones, tablets, and controller-free sensors such as the Kinect and Leap Motion, equipped with many sensors, like cameras and multi-touch screens, have driven the need to develop gestural programming languages to better interact with these commercially available items.

There have been several advances made to gestural programming languages, although the Kinect has not been seriously considered as a gestural language input device since it is still a relatively new sensor. Gestural languages have generally involved taking input other than from a typical mouse-and-keyboard setup. Some take input from multiple fingers making movements on a screen [2], while others take an image or video and analyze the components on the screen to determine the operation being specified [3, 4]. Another way to read and interpret gestures is to use a data glove [5], although only certain pre-defined gestures are recognized.

Communicating audibly or through keyboard commands is not always a practical solution for programmers. For instance, to control an underwater robot, it makes more sense to send instructions through a visual interface instead [6]. The human operator can select a card with symbolic tokens that the robot will interpret as various pre-programmed commands. These communication cards could be considered as special cased of static gestures where different poses are used to represent different concepts or actions.

2.3 Kinect

The Kinect is a popular, inexpensive, three-dimensional camera that has revolutionized human-computer interaction by having depth and RGB cameras in the same easy-to-use unit. Although the Kinect was originally developed for video game input, it has been used as an input device for a wide range of applications, both because it provides a hands-free interface and because it provides physical engagement for users. There are many applications that use the Kinect in medicine [7–9], entertainment [10, 11], art [12], and other motion tracking applications [13–17].

3   Methodology

3.1   Student Population and Experimental Design

Student Input and Surveys
The University of Arkansas runs a variety of engineering summer camps for 6-12th graders in three different sessions. For this study, we worked with 124 students taking part in the computer science and computer engineering camps over three consecutive summers. Since we were working with minors, the surveys and proposed gesture capture system were approved by an institutional review board on human subjects research before starting. Some of these students came in with absolutely no programming experience, while others had used one or more programming languages already. Very few, if any, of the students had used Blockly before, although around half of the students had utilized Scratch in the past.

The students taking part in our study were instructed for several hours on how to program with Scratch and/or Blockly. After completing a number of activities, the students then filled out a survey at the end of the session about the platforms used and the concepts learned. Not all students filled out the surveys, and for those who did, not everyone answered every question.

First, students were asked their favorite and least favorite features of each programming platform, and how well they understood the following concepts after using each platform:

- Sequences of Actions/Steps
- For Loops
- While Loops
- If Statements
- If/Else Statements
- Functions

In order to focus our user interface design efforts, we demonstrated the Microsoft Kinect to the students, and then asked them to imagine themselves creating programs using gestures instead of the mouse and keyboard. We then asked students what type of gestures they would prefer for programming – standing and using full body motions, or sitting and using only hand gestures – and why. Students who completed the survey were then asked to devise gestures that they thought represented the following six programming concepts:

- If statement
- If/else statement
- For loop
- While loop
- Run program
- Undo previous action

The questions were left relatively open-ended to allow the students to either describe in words the gestures/movements they would make, or to draw the path of the gesture, or a combination of both.

Student Gesture Capture
After filling out paper surveys, students had an opportunity to capture and record their gestures into the computer using the Kinect. In order to do this, we implemented a gesture capture program written in Processing that interfaces with the Kinect to capture the (x, y, z) coordinates of all fifteen user joints at 30 frames/sec as users make gestures. This program tracks full body motions, so users are able to draw gestures with either hand, or other parts of their body if desired. Our program saves the (x, y, z) coordinates of each joint into a text file for subsequent analysis. At the same time, our program displays the path each joint takes on the screen as the user makes their gesture. Finally, a screen shot of this path is saved as a jpg image.

The joints are color-coded as seen in Figs. 3a and 3b below for easier tracking with the human eye. There is also a set of checkboxes in the corner that allow the computer operator to choose which of the user's joints they are viewing. All joints are still being tracked and the coordinates are being saved, but it allows the user to only view the relevant joints on the screen.

In our student gesture capture experiments, the student would indicate that they were ready to start, and the operator would press a key to record their gesture. When the student completed their gesture, they told the operator, who stopped recording. The program recorded the (x, y, z) coordinates of each of the user's fifteen joints, even though all of our data was drawn one-handed, and made note of which joints were intended to comprise the gesture path (typically just the right or left hand).

The only processing that the program does to the coordinates before saving is to make sure that the exact same coordinate is not saved twice in a row. Instead of checking to make sure that coordinates differed for at least one of fifteen joints, the assumption was made (using collected student data) that the user would be moving at least one of their hands at least a little bit at any given time. Therefore, the program compares the previous coordinate of the left hand to the current left hand coordinate, and compares the

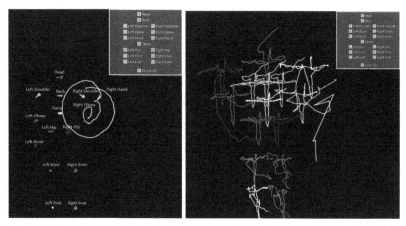

Fig. 3. a (left). Capture gesture interface with joints labeled; the user is drawing a loop with their right hand. **b (right).** Capture gesture interface where the user jumped up and down, then moved left to right to show full skeletal tracking.

previous coordinate of the right hand to the current right hand coordinate, and as long as one of the x, y, or z coordinates is different than the previous of one of the hands, the new coordinate is recorded. This mainly prevents the initial searching for the skeletal tracking from recording multiple identical sets of coordinates, or the instances when the user gets too close to the Kinect and the tracking is lost, so the last set of coordinates is continually recorded until the skeleton is rediscovered. No other processing of the coordinates took place at the time of data gathering, and no other user data was recorded.

Common Gestures Among Students

While the students were given relatively open-ended prompts to generate gesture shape information, there were six distinct gestures that appeared consistently throughout the student surveys: circle, spiral, thumbs up, wave, figure-eight, and infinity symbol. The rest of the gestures described or drawn were less common or unique.

The spiral is very similar to a circle, so for the sake of simplicity and distinct gestures, we decided not to focus on it. The Microsoft Kinect software we are currently using for skeletal tracking does not track individual fingers, and we are looking more towards dynamic gestures instead of static poses, so the thumbs up gesture was also discarded.

In order to obtain more gesture data for testing purposes, we performed a smaller scale experiment with around twenty-five young adults interesting in computing. In this case, we asked each of these students to draw each of our final four gestures (circle, infinity symbol, figure-eight, and wave). Students were not told where to start the shape, which direction to go, or which hand to use. The (x, y, z) coordinates for all fifteen joints were saved for each of these gestures in text files, and screen shots of the gesture paths were saved as images for future review.

Other Observations

Although our instructions to students were intentionally open-ended, we found that the gestures that students invented were surprisingly consistent in many ways. First of all, the majority of gestures were drawn with one hand, regardless of if the student was sitting or standing. We had expected more two handed gestures with hands coming towards each other from different angles or moving together to represent different operations. We also expected a variety of gestures with feet or legs, but only a few students proposed kicking gestures.

Secondly, most of the student gestures involved two-dimensional motions, with one hand or the other tracing a path on an imaginary plane half way between the user and the computer screen. Again, we had expected the students to create more three-dimensional gestures with their hands/feet moving forwards and backwards relative to the computer screen. For example, the student using their hand push an on/off button in mid-air in front of them.

Another common concept for gestures was to use the letter of the command or construct as the gesture, for instance tracing an 'R' in mid-air for 'Run'. Upon further consideration, we decided that this approach would cause more frustration because of the variances in handwriting styles, and some letters require multiple brush strokes to complete which is challenging when drawing in mid-air.

3.2 Software/Hardware System Design

Our system design consists of hardware and software components that work together to enable programmers to create and execute programs using hand gestures to control mouse movement. For user input, we are using the Microsoft Kinect since it is capable of capturing the locations of the user's hands and other joints in real-time. To make our system visually engaging, we are writing our code to interact with Google Blockly to show the game, intended tasks, and finished animation, and a smaller window to the side

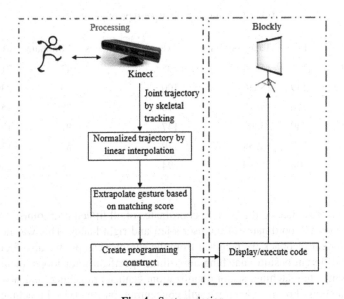

Fig. 4. System design

for the Processing application to show the joints that are being tracked and give visual cues when a gesture has been recognized.

The Processing application captures user motions from the Kinect and processes this information to track hand motions and recognize user gestures. The output of this Processing application is a sequence of mouse motions and actions that are used to communicate with the visual programming framework, Blockly. We chose this framework for students to create and execute programs after seeing its success during the summer camps. The high level design of our hardware and software is illustrated in Fig. 4 above.

4   Gesture Matching Algorithms

An important part of controlling the computer with gestures is the ability to recognize when a gesture has been drawn. By far, the most popular gesture created by students was a circle motion for a loop gesture. So to refine the gesture matching algorithms, it was decided to concentrate on matching the loop gesture first.

Using the data collected in 608 gesture files, we did a statistical analysis of the lengths of these five gestures shown in Table 1. The minimum length and maximum length for each gesture covered a large range, with the shortest gesture at 38 coordinates and the longest gesture at 230 coordinates. There was also a wide range in average gesture length for the five gestures, with loops averaging 78 coordinates and spirals averaging almost twice as many coordinates with 147. The overall average length of all gestures was around 94 coordinates. When this system is implemented with live data (instead of saved gesture files), we should be able to look at a window of around 150 coordinates at a time to decide whether the person's movement contains a recognizable gesture.

Table 1. Number of files per type of gesture

Gesture type	Files	Total coordinates	Average coordinates	Minimum	Maximum
Figure-eight	172	16454	95	42	211
Infinity symbol	179	18026	100	39	230
Loop	190	14872	78	38	157
Spiral	40	5890	147	97	193
Wave	27	2138	79	53	131
All	608	57380	94	38	230

Although we collected the (x, y, z) coordinates of all fifteen user joints, we focused only on the (x, y) coordinates of the user's left and right hands. This was determined from the student feedback we received from the summer camps. We also focused on a number of different gesture matching algorithms specifically for loops, including two forms of template matching, sector quantization, centroid matching, and two forms of medoid matching. For this paper, we will concentrate on supervised machine learning in the form of centroid and medoid matching.

4.1 Centroid and Medoid Matching

K-nearest neighbors classification has been used successfully in a wide range of machine learning and artificial intelligence applications. In order to apply this technique to gesture matching, we must first define the centroid/medoid for gesture data, and then develop appropriate methods to measure the "nearness" of gestures to these centroids/medoids.

The centroid of a set of figures is simply the mean figure of a set of data points, while a medoid is the best matching figure of the data set that has the least dissimilarity from all other members of the data set. For training data, we took around 70% of the files of each gesture type's file data randomly chosen from our pre-gathered data to calculate the centroid of each gesture shape (Table 2). We used the remaining 30% of our pre-gathered data for testing. We tried both using all five gesture shapes for this classification for a more accurate representation of types of figures we might see, and also only testing for figure-eights, infinity symbols, and loops since we did not obtain enough training data for the spiral and the wave. We are also attempting to answer beyond the shadow of a doubt whether a loop and a spiral are centroidally distinguishable from each other.

Table 2. How the files were split for training versus testing

Gesture type	Training		Testing		Total
	Num files	Percent	Num files	Percent	
Figure-eight	120	69.77%	52	30.23%	172
Infinity symbol	125	69.83%	54	30.17%	179
Loop	133	70.00%	57	30.00%	190
Spiral	28	70.00%	12	30.00%	40
Wave	19	70.37%	8	29.63%	27
Total	425	69.90%	183	30.10%	608

We tried three different techniques: 1.) nearest centroid classification, 2.) nearest medoid classification with aligned gestures, and 3.) nearest medoid classification with point-set distances. For each of these techniques, we first converted all of the gestures from N coordinates to 50 coordinates so our gesture representations would all be the same size. To pare the coordinates down, first the gestures had missing coordinates interpolated (the speed at which the gesture was drawn effects the number of coordinates recorded and the spacing of those coordinates), and then fifty coordinates were chosen, spaced evenly around the figure.

For the nearest medoid classification algorithms, we evaluated two different methods of matching between both the align-compare and point-set distance algorithms. Since there was limited data for spirals and waves, we compared our test data to all five gestures, and also only to the gestures for which we had enough data to accurately train the models (figure-eights, infinity symbols, and loops). Our method of evaluation was to do a modified k-nearest neighbors algorithm where k = 1.

4.2   Nearest Centroid Classification

For our first experiment, we calculated the sample-by-sample average (x, y) coordinate for all of the loops in the training data. The first point on this average shape was the average of all first points, the second point was the average of all second points, and so on. Unfortunately, this technique does not take into consideration the different starting points for the gesture, nor the direction in which the gesture was drawn so many of our "average" gestures are barely recognizable. The figure-eight centroid was relatively recognizable, since that is a common symbol that is taught in grade school. There were still differences and variations amongst users, but for the most part, the centroid looks similar. Unfortunately, the loop gesture and infinity symbol failed terribly. This is primarily because students are taught to draw these shapes in different ways, some students drew shapes in clockwise order while others drew them in counter-clockwise order. Students also had multiple different starting points for these shapes. We can see the results in Fig. 5.

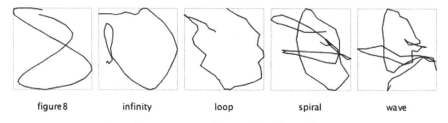

figure 8   infinity   loop   spiral   wave

Fig. 5. Gesture centroids, pared to 50 coordinates

Since centroids do not take into consideration the starting points or direction of travel, a pure centroid calculation failed terribly. Because the centroids were not recognizable as the figures they were supposed to represent, other than the figure-eight, we did not pursue this experiment any further. Instead, we chose to use a nearest medoid classification, in two uniquely different ways.

4.3   Nearest Medoid Classification with Aligned Gestures

Our next gesture classification method is based on aligned gesture matching – using the medoid gesture. Our first step was to calculate the distance between all gestures in the training set to each other using aligned differences. There is a one-to-one relationship between each figure's coordinates. If we compare the first gesture's first coordinate to the second gesture's first coordinate, it is not necessarily going to be the best match (see Fig. 6a).

However, when we shift which coordinate is being compared from the first gesture to the second gesture, we can see that the distance between each set of coordinates is significantly smaller (see Fig. 6b). We continued shifting the starting point of the second figure until every coordinate was compared with every other coordinate (Eq. 1). We

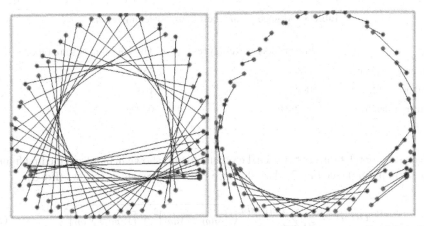

Fig. 6. a (left). Two loop gestures compared by starting point to starting point. **b (right).** Two loop gestures compared by attempting to align their coordinates

also reversed the order of the second figure's coordinates to check for clockwise versus counter-clockwise comparisons.

$$D(i, j, \textit{offset}) = \frac{1}{50} \sum_{p=0}^{49} \sqrt{\left[x_{i(p)} - x_{j((p+\textit{offset})\%50)}\right]^2 + \left[y_{i(p)} - y_{j((p+\textit{offset})\%50)}\right]^2} \quad (1)$$

After running these calculations, we then chose three medoids of each gesture type as the gestures with the lowest total distances to all other gestures in that category (Eq. 2).

$$D(i, j) = \frac{\arg\min}{\textit{offset}} D(i, j, \textit{offset}) \quad (2)$$

These medoids were then used for nearest medoid classification by calculating the aligned distance between all of the testing set gestures and the medoids chosen above.

For k-nearest neighbors where k = 1, we compared each test data file against each of the fifteen best match medoids (three medoids for each of the five gesture types). If the best aligned match gesture type was the same as the test gesture type, then it was successful. We had 178 out of the 183 test files match correctly (97.27% accuracy) (see Table 3). We also compared each test data file against the nine best match medoids representing only figure-eights, infinity symbols, and loops and got a slightly better match rate at 159 files match of the 163 test files (97.55%).

4.4 Nearest Medoid Classification with Point-Set Distances

Finally, we calculated nearest medoids with point-set distances. In this case, we calculated the distances between all of the gestures in the training set by calculating the sum of the distances between the closest points for two gestures. This calculation represents

Table 3. Aligned gesture best figure matching results

	Five medoid gesture types	Three medoid gesture types
Accurate matches	178	159
Number of files	183	163
Percent accurate	97.27%	97.55%

a many-to-one relationship between the second figure (shown in blue) and the first figure (shown in purple) (see Fig. 7). This distance can be expressed as follows (Eq. 3):

$$D(i,j) = \frac{1}{50} \sum_{p=0}^{49} \underset{q}{\arg \min} \sqrt{\left[x_{i(p)} - x_{j(q)}\right]^2 + \left[y_{i(p)} - y_{j(q)}\right]^2} \tag{3}$$

This searches for a point q on our test data file that is closest to point p on our medoid training data file.

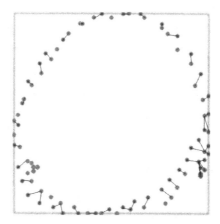

Fig. 7. Two loop gestures compared with point-set differences. (Color figure online)

We again calculated the best three medoids for each gesture type so we have a set of fifteen best medoids to train against, and performed nearest medoid classification using the point-set differences. We tried the same two methods of matching as the align-compare algorithm above, with all of the training and testing data, and also with a subset of each, removing the wave and spiral gestures.

We were very surprised to see that the best figure match came in at only 59.56% accuracy (109 out of 183 files) (see Table 4). Even using a subset of the data and only checking for figure-eights, infinity symbols, and loops brought the accuracy up to 93.87% (153 out of 163 files).

We were initially expecting this to yield a significantly higher match percentage than the align-compare algorithm since these points were finding the closest point and

Table 4. Point-set distance best figure matching results

	Five medoid gesture types	Three medoid gesture types
Accurate matches	109	153
Number of files	183	163
Percent accurate	59.56%	93.87%

the distance should be much lower. However, because we were not forcing our test data points to correspond to points in the same order as those in the gesture itself, multiple test data points would cluster around the most convenient nearest coordinate in the medoid, which may or may not be the correct one corresponding to the equivalent one in the correct medoid gesture type. As we can see below, the spiral in Fig. 8 has many points spread over the matching area, as does the infinity symbol in Fig. 9.

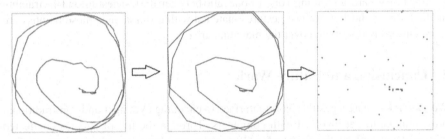

Fig. 8. A spiral pared to 50 coordinates, plotted as points

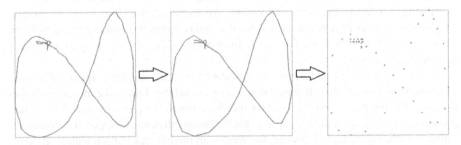

Fig. 9. An infinity symbol pared to 50 coordinates, plotted as points

In fact, out of our 183 test files, 85 of them (46.45% of them) matched as a spiral since those points are scattered rather evenly over the entire matching area so it is very easy for any shape to match to the closest spiral coordinate. See Fig. 10 as an example. The infinity symbol incorrectly maps to the spiral because the points can cluster around the spiral points instead of following an infinity symbol path.

Fig. 10. An infinity symbol in correctly mapped to a spiral medoid

Because we are not forcing a one-to-one ratio between the test gesture and the training medoid, over a third of our test gestures matched with a spiral since those points were more uniformly distributed over the matching area.

5 Conclusion and Future Work

We set out to create a gesture-based interface to encourage younger and non-traditional programmers to get involved with computers. Through the use of surveys conducted with students between the sixth and twelfth grades, we chose to implement our interface on top of Google's visual programming language, Blockly. We also discovered that the majority of students would prefer to sit and program using only their hands instead of standing and using full body movement. We were surprised that overwhelmingly students created gestures that were one-handed and two-dimensional instead of making use of the space around them. This paper focuses on finding the best way to recognize gestures when they were drawn.

We used some machine learning algorithms for gesture matching, specifically centroid and medoid matching. Because the centroid matching didn't take into account the different starting points, directions, and speeds at which the gestures were drawn, the produced centroids were unrecognizable for the gesture they were supposed to represent (other than the figure-eight). Instead, we went with medoid calculation with shift-align and point-set distances. We split all of our data into a 70% training set and a 30% testing set to see how effective the algorithms were.

We improved upon the centroid matching by trying to align our training gestures first. Once we got the gestures aligned, we found the top three figures that had the most similarity amongst the same gesture types (figure-eight, infinity symbol, loop, spiral, and wave), resulting in fifteen medoids of five different gesture types. Then, we compared our testing data to the fifteen medoids with a one-to-one relationship between the points and found the medoid with the most similarity and pulled a 97.27% accuracy rate with all five gesture types.

We also attempted to do point-set distances between the training medoids and the testing data, but because the points were not held to a strict adherence to the intended gesture path, they ended up clustering around the closest point which caused problems. This was especially apparent with the training spiral data since those points were uniformly spread across the matching area.

After implementing and comparing multiple different gesture matching algorithms, medoid matching of aligned gestures has proven to be the most effective for our application.

Future Work

Along with creating a gesture-based programming interface and being able to accurately detect drawn gestures, we must also think ahead to how we will test its effectiveness. To do so, we will have groups of students use the tool we developed to perform various tasks and observe their performance. We will develop surveys and skill tests to be taken both before and after activities to measure their interest levels towards programming, the amount of material learned, and the effectiveness of this interface for teaching difficult concepts.

We have developed two similar, but unique approaches to gathering information on the effectiveness of our gesture-based programming framework. For both evaluation plans, we will split the students into several groups using different programming methods, labeled as below:

a. Gesture-based interface using the Kinect
b. Mouse-and-keyboard version of the same interface
c. Traditional textual programming

The first plan requires three groups of students randomly assigned to groups a, b, or c. They would learn 'x' number of basic programming skills using the assigned method. Once they have completed the assigned method, we will have all groups continue onto the same second step using traditional textual programming, learning one or two slightly more advanced programming skills. An advantage to this method would be our ability to use the students who start with group c as a control group, since that is the way traditional introduction to programming classes are taught. We would also be able to judge the degree of improvement and comprehension since all students will do the same second task using the same method. However, a distinct disadvantage would be that those who start with text programming will have an advantage going into step two, while the students who started out using the gesture interface will need to learn things like variable declaration and semicolons at the end of almost every line. That may be alleviated by showing the gesture interface students what their code snippet would look like after they complete a task. Depending on the age levels of the students, and their attention spans, that may help the transition from gesture to text interfaces go smoother.

Our second plan is to randomly split the students into four groups to learn the same programming skills using two different methods. Since we will be judging the effectiveness of the gesture-based interface, we would start two groups of students on set a, transitioning half of them to set b, and the other half to set c. The other two groups of students would be split to start on set b and set c respectively, before both transitioning to set a. Learning the same thing with two different methods will help reinforce the concepts, but many students will prefer the first method they learn more than the second – we will need to find a way to compensate for those biases.

Part of our evaluation plan will be to judge which option out of the three listed above worked better, which helped their understanding, and which one is easier to use. We will also want to determine which group can accomplish tasks faster and which method leads to the least amount of frustration and highest accuracy. We will want to find out if learning programming on a gesture-based interface has helped or hurt them when they switch over to text programming. Since most programming jobs available in the real world take place in an office, or even just a cubicle, it is not currently practical to keep programmers only on a gesture-based interface.

Not only do we need to know how we are planning to evaluate this tool, we need to think ahead to who we will be evaluating it on. Since our main goal is to be able to increase interest in programming by non-traditional programmers, that includes a younger audience (middle and high school students), non-computer science/computer engineering majors, and more broadly, non-engineers. Engineering majors are taught how to problem solve, so providing this tool to non-engineers will give some good insight about its effectiveness as well. We will defer this decision until we have a pilot application working, at which time we will determine the appropriate audience.

We would also like to update the hardware we are using in this project. The Xbox 360 Kinect was discontinued by Microsoft in April 2016, and the Xbox One Kinect was discontinued in October 2017. While Microsoft made the decision not to pursue Kinect development in regards to a gaming device, they are still developing the platform for developers, and the Azure Kinect launched last year. It is very compact and has some of Microsoft's best artificial intelligence sensors in a single device.

References

1. Hoste, L., Signer, B.: Criteria, challenges and opportunities for gesture programming languages. In: Proceedings of EGMI, pp. 22–29 (2014)
2. Lü, H., Li, Y.: Gesture coder: a tool for programming multi-touch gestures by demonstration. In: Proceedings of the SIGCHI Conference on Human Factors in Computing Systems, pp. 2875–2884. ACM (2012)
3. Kato, J.: Integrated visual representations for programming with real-world input and output. In: Proceedings of the Adjunct Publication of the 26th Annual ACM Symposium on User Interface Software and Technology, pp. 57–60. ACM (2013)
4. Kato, J., Igarashi, T.: VisionSketch: integrated support for example-centric programming of image processing applications. In: Proceedings of the 2014 Graphics Interface Conference, pp. 115–122. Canadian Information Processing Society (2014)
5. Kavakli, M., Taylor, M., Trapeznikov, A.: Designing in virtual reality (desire): a gesture-based interface. In: Proceedings of the 2nd International Conference on Digital Interactive Media in Entertainment and Arts, pp. 131–136. ACM (2007)
6. Dudek, G., Sattar, J., Xu, A.: A visual language for robot control and programming: a human-interface study. In: 2007 IEEE International Conference on Robotics and Automation, pp. 2507–2513. IEEE (2007)
7. Tani, B., Maia, R., von Wangenheim, A.: A gesture interface for radiological workstations. In: 2007 Twentieth IEEE International Symposium on Computer-Based Medical Systems, CBMS 2007, pp. 27–32. IEEE (2007)

8. Gallo, L., Placitelli, A., Ciampi, M.: Controller-free exploration of medical image data: experiencing the kinect. In: 2011 24th International Symposium on Computer-Based Medical Systems (CBMS), pp. 1–6. IEEE (2011)
9. O'Hara, K., et al.: Touchless interaction in surgery. Commun. ACM **57**(1), 70–77 (2014)
10. Zhang, H., Song, Y., Chen, Z., Cai, J., Lu, K.: Chinese shadow puppetry with an interactive interface using the kinect sensor. In: Fusiello, A., Murino, V., Cucchiara, R. (eds.) ECCV 2012. LNCS, vol. 7583, pp. 352–361. Springer, Heidelberg (2012). https://doi.org/10.1007/978-3-642-33863-2_35
11. Held, R., et al.: 3D puppetry: a kinect-based interface for 3d animation. In: UIST, Citeseer, pp. 423–434 (2012)
12. Murugappan, S., Piya, C., Ramani, K.: Handy-potter: rapid 3D shape exploration through natural hand motions. In: ASME 2012 International Design Engineering Technical Conferences and Computers and Information in Engineering Conference, pp. 19–28. American Society of Mechanical Engineers (2012)
13. Tian, J., et al.: KinWrite: handwriting-based authentication using kinect. In: NDSS (2013)
14. Huang, J.: Kinerehab: a kinect-based system for physical rehabilitation: a pilot study for young adults with motor disabilities. In: The Proceedings of the 13th International ACM SIGACCESS Conference on Computers and Accessibility, pp. 319–320. ACM 2(011)
15. Roith, J., et al.: Gestairboard: a gesture-based touch typing keyboard using the kinect camera. In: Gesellschaft für Informatik eV (GI), p. 137 (2013)
16. Giovanni, S., Choi, Y.C., Huang, J., Khoo, E.T., Yin, K.: Virtual try-on using kinect and HD camera. In: Kallmann, M., Bekris, K. (eds.) MIG 2012. LNCS, vol. 7660, pp. 55–65. Springer, Heidelberg (2012). https://doi.org/10.1007/978-3-642-34710-8_6
17. Avancini, M., Ronchetti, M.: Using kinect to emulate an interactive whiteboard. In: MS in Computer Science, University of Trento (2011)

A Mouth Gesture Interface Featuring a Mutual-Capacitance Sensor Embedded in a Surgical Mask

Yutaro Suzuki[✉], Kodai Sekimori, Yuki Yamato, Yusuke Yamasaki,
Buntarou Shizuki, and Shin Takahashi

University of Tsukuba, Tsukuba, Japan
{ysuzuki,sekimori,yamato,yusukeyamasaki,shizuki,
shin}@iplab.cs.tsukuba.ac.jp

Abstract. We developed a mouth gesture interface featuring a mutual-capacitance sensor embedded in a surgical mask. This wearable hands-free interface recognizes non-verbal mouth gestures; others cannot eavesdrop on anything the user does with the user's device. The mouth is hidden by the mask; others do not know what the user is doing. We confirm the feasibility of our approach and demonstrate the accuracy of mouth shape recognition. We present two applications. Mouth shape can be used to zoom in or out, or to select an application from a menu.

Keywords: Mouth gesture interface · Surgical mask · Mutual-capacitance sensor · Wearable device · Non-verbal input

1 Introduction

Touch is the most popular input to mobile devices. This requires one or both hands, which are not available in a crowded train or when holding luggage. Voice input is a useful alternative but may not work well in noisy public spaces [1,2]. Non-verbal mouth/tongue gestures are not affected by noise, but are nonetheless useful inputs. Prior studies have recognized mouth/tongue gestures using a smartphone camera [3], pressure sensors [4], and myoelectric potential sensors [5].

We developed a mouth gesture interface featuring a mutual-capacitance sensor embedded in a surgical mask. In East Asia, mask-type interfaces are acceptable; many people wear surgical masks on a daily basis. Our interface recognizes non-verbal mouth gestures. Thus, it is robust for acoustic noise, and others cannot eavesdrop on anything the user does with the user's device. The mask covers the user's mouth; others do not know what the user is doing. Here, we introduce the mouth gesture interface and its implementation. We evaluate mouth shape recognition accuracy and offer some useful applications.

© Springer Nature Switzerland AG 2020
M. Kurosu (Ed.): HCII 2020, LNCS 12182, pp. 154–165, 2020.
https://doi.org/10.1007/978-3-030-49062-1_10

2 Related Work

We employed mouth gesture interfaces featuring mutual-capacitance sensors to control mobile/wearable devices. We explored mouth shapes, hands-free inputs to mobile/wearable devices, and mutual-capacitance sensing.

2.1 Recognizing Mouth Shapes

Cameras recognize mouth shape and position. Azh et al. [6] operated a mobile device using camera-captured lip shapes. Lyons et al. [7] combined lip shapes and Japanese character inputs to control mobile devices. Vowels were obtained from lip shapes and consonants from keystrokes. Chan et al. [8] detected mouth shapes using a head-mounted camera; mouth movement and a hand-operated pen were used to draw pictures. Koguchi et al. [9] used touch-free lip shape inputs; a camera recognized shaped vowels.

In addition, some studies have exploited tongue movements. Miyauchi et al. [10] identified mouth regions by reference to Kinect depth and RGB data and evaluated tongue protrusion during training of children with Down's syndrome. Crawford et al. [11] identified mouth areas using a web camera and recorded tongue protrusions in real-time by reference to color and textural characteristics. Tongue movement has also been evaluated without a camera. Cheng et al. [4] used a fabric, pressure sensor array attached to the outside of the cheek to this end. Sasaki et al. [5] estimated tongue movement by measuring the myoelectrical potentials of multichannel electrodes attached to the lower jaw. Similarly, Zhang et al. [12] recorded tongue movements using six myoelectric potential sensors attached to the chin and two attached to the cheeks. Goel et al. [13] used a headset featuring three (forward, left, and right) X-band motion detectors to record tongue movement. Li et al. [14] placed three micro-radar (forward, left and right) sensors around the mouth to detect tongue movement using the Doppler effect.

2.2 Mutual-Capacitance Sensing

Capacitive sensing is important in the field of human-computer interaction (HCI) [15]; such sensing is employed by mobile, wearable, and stationary devices. Zimmerman et al. [16] used capacitive sensing to detect humans. Dietz et al. [17] developed the DiamondTouch system that simultaneously detects the touches and gestures of many people; the sensors are arrayed. Hinckely et al. [18] attached capacitive touch sensors to a mouse and a trackball. Rekimoto [19] developed the SmartSkin system for detecting changes in capacitance at multiple positions when the human body touched electrode meshes on a horizontal plane. Sato et al. [20] developed the Touché system that recognizes grip using only a single electrode; the impedance frequency characteristics change by the touching mode employed. Tsuruta et al. [21] developed a single-connection, RootCap capacitive sensor that was activated when multiple electrodes were touched. Wang et al. [22] distinguished the driver from a passenger when an in-vehicle screen was touched, exploiting the capacitances of sensors in the seats and the screen. No study has yet used capacitive sensing to identify mouth shape.

3   A Mouth Gesture Interface Featuring a Mask-Type Sensor

Figure 1 shows a schematic of our mouth gesture interface. The user wears a surgical mask featuring a mutual-capacitance sensor that recognizes mouth gestures and maps them to commands controlling applications. As the mouth is hidden by the mask, others do not know what the user is doing. For example, a user can unlock a smartphone without password leakage.

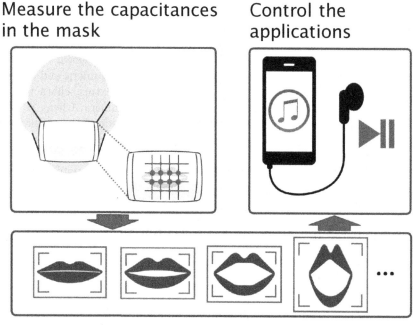

Measure the capacitances in the mask

Control the applications

Recognize the mouth gestures

Fig. 1. An overview of our approach. The mask sensor measures capacitances that correspond to user mouth gestures; these control the applications.

3.1   Mutual-Capacitance Sensing

We use mutual-capacitance sensing to recognize mouth shape. When a user moves the mouth, the capacitances of touched or approached intersections change; the interface thus recognizes mouth gestures.

A mutual-capacitance sensor features multiple intersecting electrodes [19,23]; those facing in one direction collectively serve as a transmitter delivering a sine wave and those facing in the opposite direction as the receiver. The transmitter and receiver create an electrical field. When an element approaches the intersections, that element interacts with the electrical field and the intersection capacitances change. The voltages at each receiver electrode thus also change.

3.2 Mouth Gestures

Mouth gestures can serve as interface inputs in many ways. One of the simplest mouth gesture sets includes only the open and closed mouth; these gestures are robustly recognized. The extent of mouth-opening (to which a numerical value may be assigned using a slider) may serve as an input. We use multiple mouth shapes as inputs. The gesture set contains six mouth shapes: 'n' (the neutral state) and the Japanese vowels 'a,' 'i,' 'u,' 'e,' and 'o' (Fig. 2). This allows simple character input triggering a command or operation. The five gestures other than 'n' can select and move a cursor up, down, left, or right; the gesture set can also execute an application that is pre-planned by sequentially changing mouth shape. For example, the sequence 'a-e-a' activates a smartphone camera ('camera' in Japanese is pronounced 'ka-me-ra,' thus with the vowel sequence 'a-e-a').

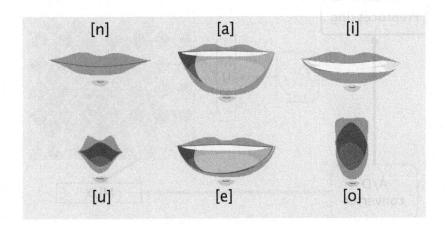

Fig. 2. The six mouth shapes. 'n' is the neutral state and 'a,' 'i,' 'u,' 'e,' and 'o' are Japanese vowels.

4   Implementation

We confirmed the feasibility of mouth gesture recognition via a mutual-capacitance sensor embedded in a surgical mask. The system features a sensing circuit and software (Fig. 3). In the sensing circuit, a sine wave is applied to the transmitter electrodes; then the voltages at the receiver electrodes are measured.

We used an Analog Discovery 2 instrument[1] to both apply the sine wave and measure voltages. The analyzer is connected to a laptop via a cable and sends defined voltages to the software. The laptop performs signal pre-processing and recognizes mouth gestures using a machine-learning algorithm.

Four horizontal wires serve as transmitter electrodes and five vertical wires serve as receiver electrodes; 49 $1\,cm^2$ copper foils are attached to the wires (Fig. 4). The horizontal wires are connected to a waveform generator via a multiplexer and the vertical wires are connected to an A/D converter via another multiplexer. The generator and converter are included in the Analog Discovery 2 instrument. The wire intersection points are insulated using thin transparent tape. The sensor is covered with plastic wrap to prevent direct mouth contact. A sine wave of 10 $V_{peak-to-peak}$ is delivered at 100 kHz to the transmitter electrodes; the voltages of all intersections are sampled 1,000 times and the data sent to Python software.

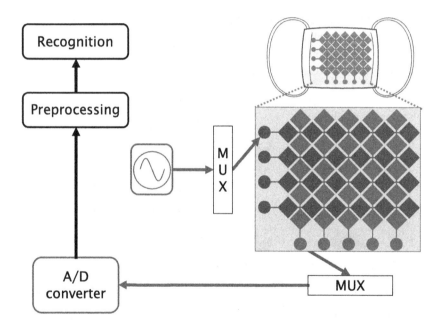

Fig. 3. Our implemented system. A mutual-capacitance sensor is embedded in the mask. The transmitter electrodes are shown in red and the receiver electrodes in blue. (Color figure online)

The signals are first pre-processed and then recognized. During pre-processing, the software removes noise using a band-pass filter that blocks signals

---

[1] https://reference.digilentinc.com/reference/instrumentation/analog-discovery-2/start.

of frequencies other than 90 to 110 kHz. We used the SciPy[2] "buttord" function to this end. Next, the software calculates the root mean square voltage (V_{rms}) at each intersection using the 1,000 sets of voltage values corresponding to capacitances. The V_{rms} values of all 20 intersections are considered a single frame; the process requires about 0.18 s. Recognition employs the Random Forest (RF) classifier of the scikit-learn library[3].

5   Preliminary Experiment

We performed a preliminary experiment to determine where the mouth touched the sensor and to evaluate the accuracy of mouth shape recognition. Three male volunteers (mean age 23.3 years) participated.

5.1   Procedure

We used the six mouth shapes shown in Fig. 2 (those made while mouthing the neutral 'n' and the five vowels 'a,' 'i,' 'u,' 'e,' and 'o'). As participants wore the mask, we told them to shape their mouths as instructed and to hold the shapes

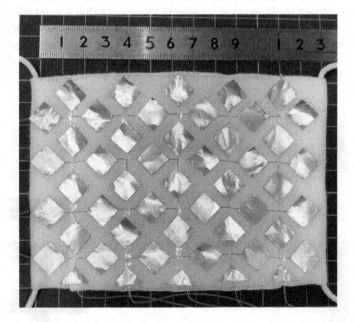

Fig. 4. The mutual-capacitance sensor used in the preliminary experiment. The horizontal electrodes served as transmitters and the vertical electrodes as receivers. Copper foil was cut into 1 cm^2 and placed on the wires at 2 cm intervals.

---

[2] https://docs.scipy.org/.
[3] https://scikit-learn.org/.

for about 3 s. We randomized the mouth shape order and acquired 20 frames for each shape. All participants completed five consecutive sessions each featuring all six mouth shapes. We thus acquired 600 frames [5($sessions$) × 6($shapes$) × 20($frames$)] per participant.

5.2   Results and Analyses

Figure 5 shows heatmaps representing the sums of the 20($frames$) × 5($sessions$) V_{rms} values at each intersection for the mouth shapes of Participant 1. The deeper blue points reflect higher V_{rms} values; the mouth often touched these points strongly.

We used principal component analysis (PCA) to calculate the contributions of all intersections (Fig. 6). The most significant points were (in order) [0, 2], [2, 2], [0, 3], [3, 3], [1, 2], and [3, 1]; points [1, 0], [1, 1], [1, 3], and [1, 4] made only small contributions. Thus, the central regions of the vertical wires well-captured mouth shapes; the edges of the wires did not. Thus, the edges of the vertical wires and the second horizontal wire from the top are redundant; their removal would accelerate data collection and implementation.

We trained the RF classifier to recognize mouth shapes. We randomly chose 80% of the data (480 frames) for training and used the remaining 20% (120 frames) to evaluate recognition accuracy; the average value was 99.2% (Table 1).

Then we performed *Leave-One-session-Out Cross-Validation* (*LOOCV*); the average recognition accuracy was 75.4% (Table 1), less than that of random validation. Changes in mask positions between sessions may explain the difference. We will collect more training data when the mask is worn in different positions.

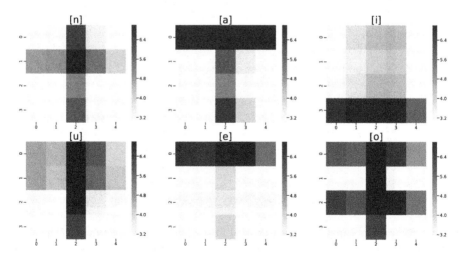

Fig. 5. Heatmaps showing the 100-frame V_{rms} sums at each intersection for each mouth shape of Participant 1. The darker blue points are associated with higher V_{rms} values; the mouth often touched these points strongly. (Color figure online)

Table 1. The recognition accuracies for each participant.

Participant	1	2	3	Average
Random (%)	99.17	98.33	100.0	99.17
LOOCV (%)	83.67	78.83	63.83	75.44

6 Application Examples

6.1 Zooming in or Out

Zooming in or out is very common; mobile devices employ pinch-in/-out systems. In our application, the user zooms in using the mouth shape 'u' and zooms out employing 'o.' In Fig. 7, the user mouths different vowels, but others do not know what he is doing.

6.2 Executing Commands

Application or command selection is often desirable. We used the mask-type interface to move through menus. We assigned the mouth shapes to commands. The user moves the cursor up by forming a 'u,' down by forming an 'o,' right by forming an 'i,' left by forming an 'a,' and selects the item using 'e' (Fig. 8). Thus, a desired application or command can be chosen in a hands-free manner.

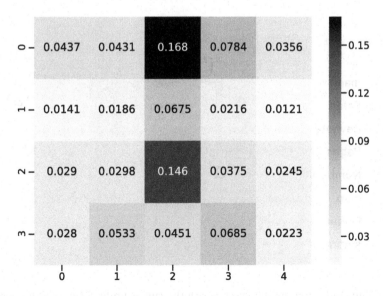

Fig. 6. The contribution ratio of each PCA intersection to the mouth shapes of Participant 1.

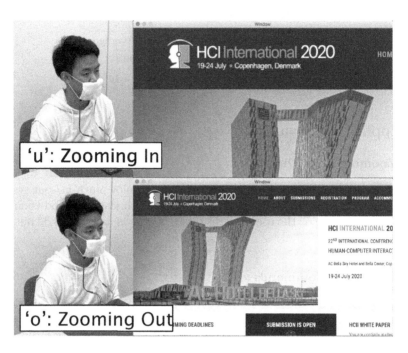

Fig. 7. A zooming application. The user zooms in using the mouth shape 'u' and zooms out employing 'o.'

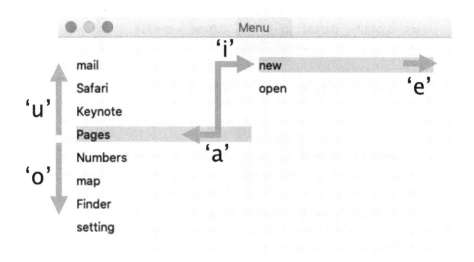

Fig. 8. Command selection. The user moves the cursor up by forming a 'u,' down by forming an 'o,' right by forming an 'i,' left by forming an 'a,' and selects the item using 'e.'

6.3   Preliminary Evaluation of the Applications

Zooming three-class classification worked well in terms of command execution; six-class classification did not. Real-time recognition accuracy must be improved. The vowel mouth shapes are not completely different: 'a' and 'e' are similar. Subtle variation in mouth shape caused by changes in facial expression and breathing patterns triggered misrecognition even when the mouth shape was correct. We will collect more data. We plan to use a sliding window to stabilize real-time classification, and to identify mouth shapes that facilitate robust classification.

7   Conclusion and Future Work

We developed a mouth gesture interface; a mutual-capacitance sensor is embedded in a surgical mask. This wearable hands-free interface recognizes non-verbal mouth gestures; others cannot eavesdrop on anything the user does with the user's device. As the mouth is hidden by the mask, others do not know what the user is doing. We confirmed the feasibility of our approach, and showed that the mutual-capacitance sensor performed well. We explored two applications. Mouth shape was used to zoom in and out and to select from a menu of applications. In the future, we will develop a low-cost, disposable mutual-capacitance sensor. We will also replace the copper foils and wires with conductive cloth and threads. Real-time recognition accuracy will be improved. We will also define a recognizable set of mouth shapes.

References

1. Fukumoto, M.: SilentVoice: unnoticeable voice input by ingressive speech. In: Proceedings of the 31st Annual ACM Symposium on User Interface Software and Technology, UIST 2018, pp. 237–246. ACM, New York (2018)
2. Ronkainen, S., Häkkilä, J., Kaleva, S., Colley, A., Linjama, J.: Tap input as an embedded interaction method for mobile devices. In: Proceedings of the 1st International Conference on Tangible and Embedded Interaction, TEI 2007, pp. 263–270. ACM, New York (2007)
3. Sun, K., Yu, C., Shi, W., Liu, L., Shi, Y.: Lip-Interact: improving mobile device interaction with silent speech commands. In: Proceedings of the 31st Annual ACM Symposium on User Interface Software and Technology, UIST 2018, pp. 581–593. ACM, New York (2018)
4. Cheng, J., et al.: On the tip of my tongue: a non-invasive pressure-based tongue interface. In: Proceedings of the 5th Augmented Human International Conference, AH 2014, pp. 12:1–12:4. ACM, New York (2014)
5. Sasaki, M., et al.: Tongue interface based on surface EMG signals of suprahyoid muscles. ROBOMECH J. 3 (2016). Article number: 9. https://doi.org/10.1186/s40648-016-0048-0
6. Azh, M., Zhao, S.: LUI: lip in multimodal mobile GUI interaction. In: Proceedings of the 14th ACM International Conference on Multimodal Interaction, ICMI 2012, pp. 551–554. ACM, New York (2012)

7. Lyons, M.J., Chan, C.-H., Tetsutani, N.: MouthType: text entry by hand and mouth. In: CHI 2004 Extended Abstracts on Human Factors in Computing Systems, CHI EA 2004, pp. 1383–1386. ACM, New York (2004)
8. Chan, C., Lyons, M.J., Tetsutani, N.: Mouthbrush: drawing and painting by hand and mouth. In: Proceedings of the 5th International Conference on Multimodal Interfaces, ICMI 2003, pp. 277–280. ACM, New York (2003)
9. Koguchi, Y., Oharada, K., Takagi, Y., Sawada, Y., Shizuki, B., Takahashi, S.: A mobile command input through vowel lip shape recognition. In: Kurosu, M. (ed.) HCI 2018. LNCS, vol. 10903, pp. 297–305. Springer, Cham (2018). https://doi.org/10.1007/978-3-319-91250-9_23
10. Miyauchi, M., Kimura, T., Nojima, T.: A tongue training system for children with down syndrome. In: Proceedings of the 26th Annual ACM Symposium on User Interface Software and Technology, UIST 2013, pp. 373–376. ACM, New York (2013)
11. Crawford, C.S., Bailey, S.W., Badea, C., Gilbert, J.E.: Using Cr-Y components to detect tongue protrusion gestures. In: Proceedings of the 33rd Annual ACM Conference Extended Abstracts on Human Factors in Computing Systems, CHI EA 2015, pp. 1331–1336. ACM, New York (2015)
12. Zhang, Q., Gollakota, S., Taskar, B., Rao, R.P.N.: Non-intrusive tongue machine interface. In: Proceedings of the SIGCHI Conference on Human Factors in Computing Systems, CHI 2014, pp. 2555–2558. ACM, New York (2014)
13. Goel, M., Zhao, C., Vinisha, R., Patel, S.N.: Tongue-in-cheek: using wireless signals to enable non-intrusive and flexible facial gestures detection. In: Proceedings of the 33rd Annual ACM Conference on Human Factors in Computing Systems, CHI 2015, pp. 255–258. ACM, New York (2015)
14. Li, Z., Robucci, R., Banerjee, N., Patel, C.: Tongue-n-cheek: non-contact tongue gesture recognition. In: Proceedings of the 14th International Conference on Information Processing in Sensor Networks, IPSN 2015, pp. 95–105. ACM, New York (2015)
15. Grosse-Puppendahl, T., et al.: Finding common ground: a survey of capacitive sensing in human-computer interaction. In: Proceedings of the 2017 CHI Conference on Human Factors in Computing Systems, CHI 2017, pp. 3293–3315. ACM, New York (2017)
16. Zimmerman, T.G., Smith, J.R., Paradiso, J.A., Allport, D., Gershenfeld, N.: Applying electric field sensing to human-computer interfaces. In: Proceedings of the SIGCHI Conference on Human Factors in Computing Systems, CHI 1995, pp. 280–287. ACM Press/Addison-Wesley Publishing Co., New York (1995)
17. Dietz, P., Leigh, D.: DiamondTouch: a multi-user touch technology. In: Proceedings of the 14th Annual ACM Symposium on User Interface Software and Technology, UIST 2001, pp. 219–226. ACM, New York (2001)
18. Hinckley, K., Pausch, R., Goble, J.C., Kassell, N.F.: Passive real-world interface props for neurosurgical visualization. In: Proceedings of the SIGCHI Conference on Human Factors in Computing Systems, CHI 1994, pp. 452–458. ACM, New York (1994)
19. Rekimoto, J.: SmartSkin: an infrastructure for freehand manipulation on interactive surfaces. In: Proceedings of the SIGCHI Conference on Human Factors in Computing Systems, CHI 2002, pp. 113–120. ACM, New York (2002)
20. Sato, M., Poupyrev, I., Harrison, C.: Touché: enhancing touch interaction on humans, screens, liquids, and everyday objects. In: Proceedings of the SIGCHI Conference on Human Factors in Computing Systems, CHI 2012, pp. 483–492. ACM, New York (2012)

21. Tsuruta, M., Nakamae, S., Shizuki, B.: RootCap: touch detection on multi-electrodes using single-line connected capacitive sensing. In: Proceedings of the 2016 ACM International Conference on Interactive Surfaces and Spaces, ISS 2016, pp. 23–32. ACM, New York (2016)
22. Wang, E.J., Garrison, J., Whitmire, E., Goel, M., Patel, S.: Carpacio: repurposing capacitive sensors to distinguish driver and passenger touches on in-vehicle screens. In: Proceedings of the 30th Annual ACM Symposium on User Interface Software and Technology, UIST 2017, pp. 49–55. ACM, New York (2017)
23. Pourjafarian, N., Withana, A., Paradiso, J.A., Steimle, J.: Multi-touch kit: a do-it-yourself technique for capacitive multi-touch sensing using a commodity microcontroller. In: Proceedings of the 32nd Annual ACM Symposium on User Interface Software and Technology, UIST 2019, pp. 1071–1083. ACM, New York (2019)

Speech, Voice, Conversation and Emotions

The Effects of Body Gestures and Gender on Viewer's Perception of Animated Pedagogical Agent's Emotions

Justin Cheng, Wenbin Zhou, Xingyu Lei, Nicoletta Adamo[(⊠)], and Bedrich Benes

Purdue University, West Lafayette, IN 47906, USA
nadamovi@purdue.edu

Abstract. The goal of this research is to develop Animated Pedagogical Agents (APA) that can convey clearly perceivable emotions through speech, facial expressions and body gestures. In particular, the two studies reported in the paper investigated the extent to which modifications to the range of movement of 3 beat gestures, e.g., both arms synchronous outward gesture, both arms synchronous forward gesture, and upper body lean, and the agent's gender have significant effects on viewer's perception of the agent's emotion in terms of valence and arousal. For each gesture the range of movement was varied at 2 discrete levels. The stimuli of the studies were two sets of 12-s animation clips generated using fractional factorial designs; in each clip an animated agent who speaks and gestures, gives a lecture segment on binomial probability. 50% of the clips featured a female agent and 50% of the clips featured a male agent. In the first study, which used a within-subject design and metric conjoint analysis, 120 subjects were asked to watch 8 stimuli clips and rank them according to perceived valence and arousal (from highest to lowest). In the second study, which used a between-subject design, 300 participants were assigned to two groups of 150 subjects each. One group watched 8 clips featuring the male agent and one group watched 8 clips featuring the female agent. Each participant was asked to rate perceived valence and arousal for each clip using a 7-point Likert scale. Results from the two studies suggest that the more open and forward the gestures the agent makes, the higher the perceived valence and arousal. Surprisingly, agents who lean their body forward more are not perceived as having higher arousal and valence. Findings also show that female agents' emotions are perceived as having higher arousal and more positive valence that male agents' emotions.

Keywords: Affective pedagogical agents · Body gestures · Gender · Valence · Arousal

1 Introduction

Research has shown that animated pedagogical agents (APA) can be effective in promoting learning [1], but many questions still remain unanswered, particularly concerning their emotional design. With the growing understanding of the complex interplay

© Springer Nature Switzerland AG 2020
M. Kurosu (Ed.): HCII 2020, LNCS 12182, pp. 169–186, 2020.
https://doi.org/10.1007/978-3-030-49062-1_11

between emotions and cognition, there is a need to develop life-like agents that not only provide effective expert guidance, but also convincing emotional interactions with the learner [2–4].

One goal of our research is to develop APAs that can convey clearly perceivable emotions through speech, facial expressions and body gestures. The studies reported in the paper are steps in this direction. They focus on how emotions are conveyed through body cues and, in particular, they examine the extent to which modifications to the range of movement of a set of beat gestures affects viewer' perception of the agent's emotional state. An important issue in bodily expression of emotion research concerns the distinction between a person's encoding of emotion in physical behavior versus an observer's decoding of emotion from observations of the person's behavior. We are concerned with the latter, and whether the observed perceptual effects are moderated by viewer's characteristics such as gender, age, ethnicity and educational level.

There has been considerable debate as to whether posture and movement reliably convey emotions, or rather convey only the intensity of the emotion [5, 6]. We examine how body gestures might convey both the quality of the emotion and its level of activation. We use Russell's [7] model of core affect in which any particular emotion can be placed along two dimensions, valence (ranging from positive to negative), and arousal (ranging from activation to deactivation) and investigate whether and how changes in the motion parameters of a set of body gestures affect the perception of the agent's emotion along both dimensions. We also examine whether the agent's gender has an effect on viewer's perception of the emotional content.

Our studies are important because they may advance not only research on representation of emotion in affective embodied agents, but also psychology research on bodily expression/perception of emotion in general.

2 Background

2.1 Animated Pedagogical Agents

Several studies suggest that the presence of pedagogical agents can improve learning [8, 9]. A meta-analysis by Schroeder showed that lessons with animated pedagogical agents led to statistically significant learning improvements compared to lessons without them [2]. Studies also suggest that APAs could be employed in e-learning environments to enhance users' attitude towards online courses [10]. Agents interacting using multiple modalities appear to lead to greater learning than agents that interact only in a single channel [11, 12].

One reason why pedagogical agents might help to facilitate learning could be that the viewers find them engaging because of their "human-like" personalities [13]. A study by Poggiali showed that students found "animated videos with agents easier to learn from, in part because they held their attention" [14]. The agent's personality helped to contribute towards the student's engagement; study participants reported that the agent's outgoing personality helped them relate to it the same way they relate to an outgoing human instructor. These findings emphasize the importance of establishing a social connection between the agent and the learner. Incorporating emotional design within the pedagogical agents improved learning outcomes within a lesson [15], demonstrating the need for the agents to have recognizable emotions.

Some researchers have investigated the effect of different APA's features on student's learning, engagement, and perception of self-efficacy. Mayer and DaPra [16] examined whether the degree of embodiment of an APA had an effect on students learning of science concepts. Findings showed that students learned better from a fully embodied human-voiced agent that exhibited human-like behaviors and emotions than from an agent who did not communicate using these human-like actions. A study by Gulz and Haake [17] revealed that female students preferred as a learning companion an agent that developed social relationship during the learning activities rather than an agent that was strictly task oriented. Additional empirical studies showed that peer-like agents helped enhance positive affect and motivation for females who learned STEM topics [2, 4]. Other experiments suggest that agent's features such as voice and appearance [18, 19], visual presence [20], non-verbal communication [21] and communication style [22] could impact learning and motivation.

2.2 Expression/Perception of Agents' Emotion and Personality from Body Gestures

The agent's gestures are crucial in conveying its emotional state and personality, as non-verbal cues potentially can make up to 93% of the communication during conversation [23]. A study by Anasingaraju et al. [24] showed that body gestures were the biggest contributors to perceiving the agent's emotion, rather than the character's facial animation and lip sync.

Despite gestures playing a crucial role in conversation, identifying emotions from body gestures alone is not straightforward. Some emotions are easily perceivable from body gestures only, such as anger, sadness, and happiness [25]. However, there are also emotions that are difficult to express with body language alone. Surprise, disgust, and fear are the most difficult emotions to convey from arm movements alone [26]. A study by Atkinson suggests that sadness and disgust were most easily misclassified for each other [27]. A study by Ennis showed that body gestures only without the face caused confusion in differentiating emotions with high arousal [28]. Ennis concluded that body gestures alone caused difficulties in identifying between happy and angry gestures, but in contrast sadness and fear were more identifiable from each other. Karg argues that high valence and low arousal gestures, such as content, were not easy to express from gestures alone [25]. While gestures may help to differentiate between emotions with high and low valence, arousal was more easily identifiable by agent's movement than from still poses.

Several studies that examine agent's expression of personality through body cues can be found in the literature. Compared to an emotion, a personality is defined as a set of permanent or long-lasting complex characteristics that make up how the agent interacts with the environment [29]. In this section we review primarily prior research that compared between extroverted and introverted personalities and that are relevant to our studies. In general, an extroverted agent is likely to express emotions that have positive valence and high arousal, whereas an introverted agent is more likely to show emotions that have negative valence and low arousal.

An agent with an extroverted personality is more likely to show interest and friendliness towards the viewer [30, 31]. As a result, the agent tends to amplify a sense of space [32] by having more horizontal and open arms/hands movements, rotating out the elbows and raising the shoulders. An agent that expresses friendliness, tends to consistently make eye contact with the viewer [32] and stretch the arms towards the viewer [33]. Furthermore, an extroverted character asserts more dominance than an introverted character. This gives the extroverted character an additional incentive to both directly make eye-contact towards the viewer and to amplify a larger sense of space [32].

An agent with an introverted personality tends to show disinterest towards the viewer. As a result, the agent is more likely to focus on minimizing their body size [29]. The upper torso is more likely to stand upright or to lean slightly backwards, whereas the hands are prone to close and touch the agent's own body [32]. When comparing the horizontal spread of the agent's gestures, the introverted agent's horizontal spread is only 10% to 60% of the extroverted agent's horizontal spread [32]. Considering that the introverted agent is more prone to minimizing occupied space, the agent tends to perform fewer out-directing gestures, leading to the introverted character showing more submissiveness [30].

Findings from the studies listed above, as well as best practices in character animation that suggest that high valence/arousal characters are characterized by open and forward body gestures [34] form the basis of the hypotheses of our 2 experiments.

3   Methods

We hypothesize that modifications to the range of movement of 3 beat gestures, e.g., both arms synchronous outward gesture (OG), both arms synchronous forward gesture (FG), and upper body lean (BL), and the agent's gender (G) have significant effects on viewers' perception of the agents' emotion in terms of valence and arousal. More specifically, based on prior research and on best practices in character animation we hypothesize the following:

- Ha(FG): the more forward the gesture, the higher the perceived arousal
- Ha(OG): the more open the gesture, the higher (e.g., more positive) the perceived valence
- Ha(BL): the more forward the body lean, the higher the perceived arousal and perceived valence
- Ha(G): the emotions of female agents are perceived as having higher arousal and higher valence than those of male agents

The 3 beat gestures selected for the study are gestures that are commonly produced by instructors while lecturing and have been shown to convey some information about the speaker's emotional state, personality or status [35]. For each gesture the range of movement is varied at 2 discrete levels. Table 1 lists the factors and levels used in the studies.

Two experiments were conducted; one study used a within-subjects design and metric conjoint analysis; the other study used a between-subject design and linear regression.

Table 1. Factors and levels

Factor	Level 1	Level 2
OG	Arms/hands are close to body on the sides	Arms/hands are spread apart horizontally
FG	Hands are right in front of the body	Arms/hands are stretched in front of the agent
BL	Body leans backwards	Body leans forwards
G	Agent is male	Agent is female

The stimuli for both studies were sets of 12-s animation clips generated using partial factorial designs; each clip showed a different combination of body gestures and ranges of motion. 120 subjects participated in the first study and 300 subjects participated in the second one. In the first study subjects were asked to watch the stimuli clips and rank them from highest to lowest arousal and valence. In the second study subjects were divided into two groups: one group was assigned the clips featuring the female agent and one group the clips featuring the male agent. All subjects were asked to watch the stimuli clips and rate the valence and arousal of each clip using a 7-point Likert scale.

The stimuli in both studies were two sets of 12-s animation clips; in each clip an animated agent who speaks and gestures, gave a lecture segment on binomial probability. All animation clips were assembled within the Unity game engine and the gesture animations and slide timings were manually synced using the Unity's Timeline feature. The agents were framed from thigh-up, at a ¾ view towards the viewer so that FG and BL levels were clearly visible.

Both agents are commercially available 3D character rigs whose joint structure was modified in order to be compatible with Unity's character animator feature. The agents' gestures were motion captured and manually blended together; the agents' lip-sync animations were generated with a Unity script. Camera angle, background, lighting, and speech were kept the same in every clip. The agent's faces were blurred out to eliminate potential confounding variables.

The full quote that the agents spoke was the following: "A success is defined by you as one or more of the possible outcomes. For example, a success of rolling a die could be that you rolled a number greater than four." While the agent was speaking the first sentence, the agent would point towards the viewer with his or her left hand. This gesture was not modified and remained the same in all animation clips. During the second sentence, the agent would smoothly transition to another gesture, modified by the offset script with parameters that varied in each clip, which involved the agent opening out his or her hands and leaning his or her body. The agent returned to a neutral standing position at the end of each gesture.

The labelling format for the clips was in the form of [G]_OG[x]-FG[x]-BL[x], where [G] was replaced by the gender initial of M or F, and [x] was replaced by 1 or 2 to indicate level.

4 Study 1

4.1 Design

A metric conjoint analysis and a partial factorial design were used for the first study. As the study included 4 different factors (the 3 gestures + agent's gender) each varied at 2 levels, a full factorial design would have required 16 different clips. Such number of animations would have been difficult to rank. Hence, 8 representative combinations of the factors were created according to a fractional factorial design generated with JMP PRO 14 statistical software. This design allowed us to examine main effects as well as 2-factor interactions. The 8 representative combinations of the factors and levels are listed in Table 2. Figure 1 shows frames extracted from the 8 animation clips used in the first study.

The evaluation instrument was an online survey designed using Qualtrics software. In the survey, subjects were presented with 2 ranking tasks: (1) rank the 8 clips in terms of arousal and (2) rank the 8 clips in terms of valence from highest to lowest. For each ranking task, all eight clips were simultaneously loaded, with the clip order randomized. Participants needed to drag and drop the clips in order to rank them, with the clips that had highest perceived valence or arousal placed at the top of the page. Demographic information such as the participant's age, gender, and highest level of completed education were also collected. The survey's time limit was set to 20 min. The study used simple random sampling and anyone over the age of 18 was eligible to participate. 120 subjects were recruited through Amazon Mechanical Turk but only 103 responses were considered. The subjects' demographics were the following: male (66), female (37); 18–30 years old (45), 30+ years old (57); no-degree (32) and degree (71).

A 4-way ANOVA test and a linear regression model were applied to test for main effects and two-way interactions. A Chi-squared test was applied to test the independence of the valence and arousal rankings. The study assumed that the data distribution was normal, and all ranking entries were independent.

Table 2. Factors and levels combinations

#	Label	OG	FG	BL	G
1	M_OG2-FG1-BL2	2	1	2	M
2	M_OG1-FG1-BL1	1	1	1	M
3	M_OG1-FG2-BL2	1	2	2	M
4	M_OG2-FG2-BL2	2	2	1	M
5	F_OG1-FG1-BL2	1	1	2	F
6	F_OG2-FG2-BL2	2	2	2	F
7	F_OG1-FG2-BL1	1	2	1	F
8	F_OG2-FG1-BL1	2	1	1	F

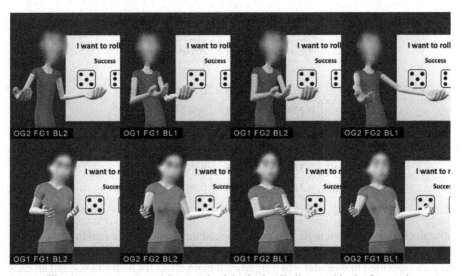

Fig. 1. Frames extracted from each of the 8 stimuli clips used in the first study

4.2 Results

A total of 120 study participants completed the survey, however only 103 responses were considered. 17 responses were discarded because completion times were below our 22 s time filter. Table 3 shows the average mean rankings and standard deviations, and Table 4 shows the statistical analysis results (p for p-value and β for linear regression model coefficient). A higher mean rank meant that clip had lower perceived valence or arousal.

Table 3. Primary study full results mean rankings

Clip	Valence M	Valence SD	Arousal M	Arousal SD
M_OG1-FG1-BL1	5.05	2.16	4.32	2.2
M_OG1-FG1-BL1	4.98	2.09	4.43	2.29
M_OG1-FG2-BL2	5.03	2.2	3.97	2.29
M_OG2-FG2-BL1	5.04	2.36	4.5	2.33
F_OG1-FG1-BL2	4.27	2.47	4.59	2.36
F_OG2-FG2-BL2	3.77	2.23	4.93	2.2
F_OG1-FG2-BL1	4.03	2.27	4.69	2.23
F_OG2-FG1-BL1	3.83	2	4.56	2.32

Gender (G) was a significant main effect for perceived valence (p = nearly 0.000) and for perceived arousal (p = 0.015). OG was close to statistical significance, (p = 0.083) for perceived valence. According to the linear regression model for valence and

Table 4. Primary study full results statistical analysis test

Factor	Valence p	Valence β	Arousal p	Arousal β
OG	0.319	−0.156	0.083	−0.276
FG	0.663	−0.068	0.808	−0.038
BL	0.709	0.058	0.927	−0.014
G	0	−1.048	0.015	−0.388
OGxFG	0.852	0.03	0.447	−0.122
OGxBL	0.575	−0.088	0.273	−0.174
FGxBL	0.213	−0.194	0.784	−0.044

arousal, changing G from male to female changed the mean valence ranking by nearly a full rank ($\beta = -1.048$), and about four-tenths of an arousal rank ($\beta = -0.388$). Overall, the data supported that gender was a significant main effect for both valence and arousal rankings; the clips featuring the female agent were ranked significantly higher for valence and arousal than the clips featuring the male agent.

Table 5. P values for perceived valence for demographic subsets – study 1

Factor	Age subset		Gender subset		Education level subset	
	18–30	30+	Female	Male	Degree	No-degree
OG	0.034	0.675	0.166	0.845	0.281	0.864
FG	0.449	0.967	0.166	0.612	0.710	0.820
BL	0.042	0.181	0.878	0.725	0.528	0.776
G	0.000	0.000	0.001	0.000	0.000	0.000
OGxFG	0.421	0.530	0.538	0.482	0.911	0.608
OGxBL	0.570	0.209	0.538	0.242	0.656	0.088
FGxBL	0.603	0.225	0.412	0.349	0.081	0.690

In regard to the demographic subsets, Table 5 and Table 6 report the results of the statistical analyses for perceived valence and arousal respectively. For the valence rankings OG, BL, and G were significant main effects for the 18–30 years old group. OG and BL had β values of −0.5 and 0.478 respectively. For the 30+ years old subset for valence, only G was a significant main effect; no significant main effects were found for arousal.

In the male participants subset, only G was a significant main effect for valence. In the female participants group, G was significant for valence, as well as for arousal.

In regard to the 'no degree' subset only G was a significant main effect for valence; no significance was found for arousal. In the degree subset, G was a significant main effect for valence; no significance was found for arousal.

Table 6. P values for perceived arousal for demographic subset – study 1

	Age subset		Gender subset		Education level subset	
Factor	18–30	30+	Female	Male	Degree	No-degree
OG	0.153	0.166	0.244	0.193	0.256	0.157
FG	0.381	0.596	0.685	1.000	0.883	0.513
BL	0.213	0.271	0.761	0.733	0.420	0.174
G	0.019	0.254	0.023	0.185	0.062	0.115
OGxFG	0.356	0.775	0.648	0.544	0.256	0.744
OGxBL	0.644	0.308	0.960	0.161	0.085	0.549
FGxBL	1.000	0.744	0.418	0.791	0.304	0.301

The reported R-squared values for both the full dataset and all of the subsets had a minimum of 0.044 (Degree) to a maximum of 0.115 (No Degree) for valence, and 0.011 (Male) to 0.04 (18–30 y/o). As for the Chi-square test, significance was found in both the full dataset ($p = 0.037$) and the male subset ($p = 0.011$).

4.3 Discussion

Results of the statistical analyses support our hypothesis that gender is a significant main effect across all subjects and for each demographic subset: the clips featuring the female agent were ranked significantly higher for valence and arousal than the clips featuring the male agent.

When examining different demographic subsets, results show that for the 18–30 years old group OG and BL were significant main effects for valence rankings, with OG raising the valence ranking ($\beta = -0.5$) and BL decreasing valence ranking ($\beta = 0.478$) when the factor levels changed from level 1 to level 2 for both factors. This suggests that for the 18–30 years old group increasing the agent's OG from level 1 to level 2 (e.g., extending the agent's arms/hands outward more) results in higher perceived valence. This finding supports our OG hypothesis. However, leaning the agent's body forward decreases perceived valence; this finding does not support our BL hypothesis.

As for arousal rankings, only the 18–30 years old subset and the female subset suggests that G influences the arousal rankings ($P = 0.019$ and 0.023). According to the linear regression model, modifying G from male to female for the listed groups would result in higher perceived arousal (β values of -0.566 and -0.608).

The Chi-squared test that was performed on the main dataset, yielded a p-value of 0.037, suggesting that the valence and arousal rankings were not-independent of each other for the full dataset. This was also shown for the male subset, where the p-value was 0.011.

It should be noted that for all the datasets, the reported R-squared values were very low. From the main dataset, the valence R2 value was 0.056 and the arousal R2 value was 0.013. The R2 values from the subsets all did not exceed 0.150. The low R2 suggests that even if the data points suggest a relationship between factors and perceived valence/arousal, the exact relationship may differ from the suggested linear model.

5 Study 2

5.1 Design

After a careful review of the findings from study 1, we identified two potential issues with the experiment design. First, we realized that the agent design, e.g., appearance and voice, may have introduced gender comparison biases. In other words, subjects might have ranked the clips featuring the female agent higher in valence and arousal because of the intrinsic characteristics of the female agent design and because of the quality of her voice, rather than because of the mere difference in gender. Second, subjects commented that the ranking tasks were quite difficult to perform and rating the clips in terms of perceived valence and arousal would have been easier than ranking them. These issues prompted us to conduct a follow- up experiment; we refer to this second experiment as study 2.

Table 7. Study 2 clip combinations

#	Label	OG	FG	BL	G
1	M_OG2-FG1-BL2	2	1	2	M
2	M_OG1-FG1-BL2	1	1	2	M
3	M_OG2-FG2-BL2	2	2	2	M
4	M_OG1-FG2-BL2	1	2	2	M
5	M_OG1-FG1-BL1	1	1	1	M
6	M_OG2-FG2-BL1	2	2	1	M
7	M_OG1-FG2-BL1	1	2	1	M
8	M_OG2-FG1-BL1	2	1	1	M
9	F_OG2-FG1-BL2	2	1	2	F
10	F_OG1-FG1-BL2	1	1	2	F
11	F_OG2-FG2-BL2	2	2	2	F
12	F_OG1-FG2-BL2	1	2	2	F
13	F_OG1-FG1-BL1	1	1	1	F
14	F_OG2-FG2-BL1	2	2	1	F
15	F_OG1-FG2-BL1	1	2	1	F
16	F_OG2-FG1-BL1	2	1	1	F

Study 2 used a between-subjects design with 300 participants; the stimuli were 16 12-s animation clips. Subjects were recruited through Amazon Mechanical Turk and divided into 2 groups of 150 participants each: one group viewed only the 8 clips featuring the male agent and one group viewed only the 8 clips featuring the female agent. Study 2 used a partial factorial design generated using JMP Pro 14 statistical software. Table 7 lists the clip combinations and Fig. 2 shows frames extracted from each one of the 16 stimuli clips.

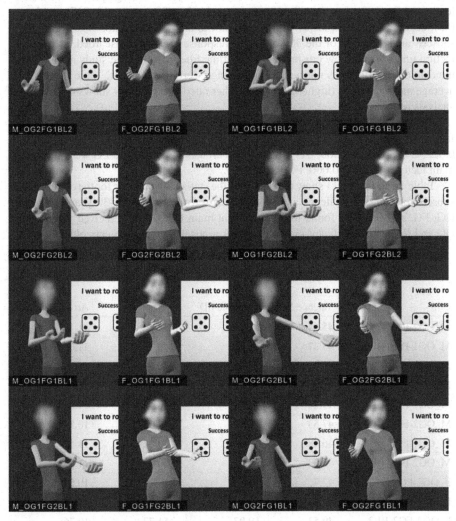

Fig. 2. Frames extracted from the 16 stimuli clips used in study 2

The evaluation instrument was an online survey designed using Qualtrics software. In the survey, subjects in each group were asked to watch the 8 video clips (presented in randomized order) and rate each clip for valence and arousal using a 7-pointLlikert scale (1 = low arousal; 7 = high arousal; 1 = highly negative valence; 7 = highly positive valence).

The same set of statistical tests and hypotheses as in study 1 were used. In study 2, a higher number (rating) meant that the clip had higher perceived valence/arousal.

5.2 Results

A total of 300 subjects completed the survey; the subjects' demographics were the following: male (182), female (89), 18–30 years old (53), 30+ years old (217), no degree (83), degree (186). Responses with "prefer not to answer" were not considered in the subsets' analyses. Out of the 300 collected responses, 27 were discarded, as the completion times were below our predesignated time filter of 11 s. The study assumed that the data distribution was normal, and all ratings were independent. Table 8 shows the average mean rankings (higher M means higher rated), and Table 9 shows the statistical analysis results.

Results of a 4-way ANOVA test performed across all subjects showed that all main factors were significant for perceived valence (OG $P = 0.003$, FG $P = 0.012$, BL $P = 0.022$, G P = nearly 0.000). As for perceived arousal, only OG and FG were significant main factors (OG $P = 0.000$, FG $P = 0.017$).

Table 10 and Table 11 show the results of the statistical analyses for the demographic subsets for perceived valence and arousal, respectively. In the 18–30 years old subset OG, FG, and BL were found to be significant main factors for perceived valence, and OG and BL were significant main factors for arousal. In the 30+ years old subset OG,

Table 8. Mean and standard deviation values for study 2

Clip	Valence M	Valence SD	Arousal M	Arousal SD
M_OG2-FG1-BL2	45.64	10.02	49.85	11.14
M_OG1-FG1-BL2	45.27	9.86	49.54	11.09
M_OG2-FG2-BL2	46.3	10.19	50.31	10.19
M_OG1-FG2-BL2	45.61	9.94	48.03	12.36
M_OG1-FG1-BL1	45.24	10.23	48.15	10.86
M_OG2-FG2-BL1	47.53	10.7	52.27	10.31
M_OG1-FG2-BL1	46.48	9.53	49.82	11.51
M_OG2-FG1-BL1	46.62	10.15	50.32	11.09
F_OG2-FG1-BL2	47.76	10.2	49.22	10.54
F_OG1-FG1-BL2	47.04	10.69	48.11	11.86
F_OG2-FG2-BL2	49.53	9.97	51.77	10.76
F_OG1-FG2-BL2	47.83	9.56	48.35	11.61
F_OG1-FG1-BL1	47.04	9.88	47.67	11.34
F_OG2-FG2-BL1	50.6	9.49	51.76	11.21
F_OG1-FG2-BL1	49.32	8.99	50.32	10.82
F_OG2-FG1-BL1	49.97	10.2	50.76	10.6

Table 9. p and β values for study 2

Factor	Valence p	Valence β	Arousal p	Arousal β
OG	0.003	1.272	0	2.038
FG	0.012	1.082	0.017	1.136
BL	0.022	−0.982	0.12	−0.74
G	0	2.548	0.932	−0.04
OGxFG	0.839	−0.086	0.451	0.358
OGxBL	0.355	−0.396	0.601	−0.25
FGxBL	0.667	−0.184	0.152	−0.684

FG, and G were significant main factors for perceived valence and OG and FG were significant main factors for perceived arousal.

Table 10. P values for perceived valence for demographic subsets – study 2

	Age subset		Gender subset		Education level subset	
Factor	18–30	30+	Female	Male	Degree	No-degree
OG	0.080	0.014	0.013	0.037	0.039	0.010
FG	0.055	0.063	0.322	0.014	0.041	0.108
BL	0.001	0.337	0.079	0.144	0.136	0.041
G	0.100	0.000	0.000	0.024	0.000	0.045
OGxFG	0.255	0.360	0.991	0.672	0.958	0.528
OGxBL	0.675	0.192	0.930	0.250	0.401	0.609
FGxBL	0.463	0.360	0.835	0.699	0.878	0.580

For gender, in the male subset OG, FG, and G were significant main factors for perceived valence, whereas OG and FG were significant for perceived arousal. In the female subset OG and G were significant main factors for perceived valence, while only OG was significant for arousal. G had a surprising β of 5.084.

In regard to the level of education subsets, in the no degree subset OG, BL and G were significant main factors for perceived valence, while OG and FG were significant for perceived arousal. In the degree subset OG, FG and G were significant main factors for perceived valence, while OG only was significant for arousal.

The reported R-squared values for both the full dataset and all of the subsets had a minimum of 0.013 (Male) to the maximum of 0.073 (Female) for valence, and 0.013 (Full and Degree) to 0.33 (18–30 y/o).

Table 11. P values for perceived arousal for demographic subsets – study 2

	Age subset		Gender subset		Education level subset	
Factor	18–30	30+	Female	Male	Degree	No-degree
OG	0.082	0.000	0.004	0.001	0.001	0.006
FG	0.364	0.019	0.215	0.030	0.093	0.004
BL	0.008	0.836	0.094	0.504	0.075	0.965
G	0.246	0.859	0.035	0.058	0.836	0.577
OGxFG	0.193	0.991	0.304	0.950	0.622	0.654
OGxBL	0.823	0.408	0.672	0.416	0.506	0.977
FGxBL	0.503	0.208	0.603	0.175	0.355	0.201

5.3 Discussion

Findings from the statistical analyses show that all main factors were significant for perceived valence; OG and FG were significant main factors for perceived arousal. Results support 3 of our hypotheses, e.g., OG, FG, and G affect perceived valence, and OG and FG affect perceived arousal. After applying the linear regression model to the full dataset, the model still shows that G is the most influential factor for perceived valence ($\beta = 2.548$) and perceived valence increases when G is changed from male to female. OG and FG increase the valence rating by a smaller amount when the levels are changed from 1 to 2, with OG $\beta = 1.272$ and FG $\beta = 1.082$. As for arousal, OG is the most influential factor when increased from level 1 to level 2 ($\beta = 2.038$). FG also increases perceived arousal when changed from level 1 to 2 ($\beta = 1.136$). Although BL was found to be a significant main effect, BL's $\beta = -0.982$, hence perceived valence decreases when BL changes from level 1 to level 2. This finding does not support our BL hypothesis.

The same significant main effects were found for the different data subsets with a few exceptions. All subgroups except the 18–30 years old group demonstrated that OG is a significant factor for influencing perceived valence and perceived arousal. FG was a significant factor for the male subset and the degree subset for valence and was a significant main effect for the 30+ years old subset and the no degree subset for arousal. BL was only significant for the 18–30 years old subset and the no degree subset for valence, and the 18–30 years old subset for arousal. G was a significant factor for the 30+ years old subset, female subset, no degree subset, and degree subset for valence, and a significant main factor for arousal for the female subset.

The linear regression models performed on the subsets in study 2 aligned with the models performed in study 1 for many of the factors. Two notable exceptions were BL for valence ratings for the 18–30 years old subset, and G for valence rating for the female subset. According to the regression models, modifying BL from level 1 to level 2 would result in $\beta = -3.34$ in comparison to the first study BL's $\beta = -0.982$. As for the female subset, modifying G from male to female results in $\beta = 5.084$ compared to the first study G's $\beta = 2.548$.

Overall, the R-squared values were low. The full dataset's R^2 was 0.025 for valence and 0.013 for arousal. The largest R^2 value when looking at the data subset was 0.073, which was still very low. Just like Study 1, the low R^2 suggests that even if the data points suggest a relationship between factors and perceived valence/arousal, the exact relationship may differ from the suggested linear model.

6   Conclusion and Future Work

The findings from the two studies are consistent in part with results of prior experiments reported in the literature review. They provide evidence that a positive-valence, high arousal pedagogical agent tends to display open body gestures, e.g., he/she tends to open the arms and hands more outwards, as in study 2 OG was tested to be significant in affecting both perceived valence and arousal. The linear regression models showed that there was a positive relationship between the arms opening out and the viewer's perceived valence and arousal. Both the female and male agent's OG2-FG2-BL1 clips in study 2 were perceived as having either the highest valence or arousal, the arms were forward and spread out in both those clips. Findings also provided evidence that a positive-valence, high-arousal pedagogical agent tends to reach out to the viewer more with arms and hands, as FG was a statistically significant main effect for both perceived valence and arousal in study 2. The linear regression models showed a positive relationship between stretching the arms forward and the perceived valence and arousal. The clips with the highest perceived valence or arousal were also the OG2-FG2-BL1 clips as mentioned above.

The studies did not support prior research findings according to which highly active/engaged pedagogical agents would tend to lean their body forward more. While BL was tested to be significant in study 2 (both valence and arousal from the 18/30+ years old subset and just valence from the full dataset), the linear regression model suggested that leaning the body forward decreased the viewer's perceived valence and arousal of the agent. One possible explanation is that modifying BL via the Unity custom script would modify the agent's body lean independently from the hand locations. For example, if BL was adjusted backward, the hands and arms would not be dragged with the body too. As a result, the backwards leaning motion of the agent could have been perceived more as a balancing action than an intentional action of the agent trying to reach out towards the viewer. This was further demonstrated in study 2 as the clips with the highest mean valence and arousal rating were both M_OG2-FG2-BL1 and F_OG2-FG2-BL1 clips; in these clips the agent's hands were spread wide open and towards the viewer while the agent's body was leaned backwards.

Gender was the most significant main factor for both perceived valence and arousal in both studies. Study 1 showed that G was the most significant factor for valence rankings. G was also shown to be significant in study 2 for valence, with the linear regression model stating that G influenced the valence and arousal ratings more than any of the body gesture factors.

The results of our studies in part support findings from prior studies which suggest that female agents are perceived as more supportive/positive. The female clips had the highest perceived mean valence rankings or ratings in both studies. As for male agents being perceived to be more engaging/active (high arousal) [36], both studies' findings were not able to statistically support this claim, despite the fact that the clips with the highest perceived arousal were all male clips. Prior findings that suggest that participants find agents of opposite gender more engaging were not supported by our studies. Study 2 suggested that for the female subset G was a significant main effect and female clips had significant higher perceived arousal.

While the studies also attempted to determine if two-way factor interactions OGxFG, OGxBL, and FGxBL were significant, data analyses from both the first and second studies were unable to confirm if these interactions influenced valence or arousal perception. Only main effects OG, FG, BL and G had significance.

Our studies focused on body poses only, other important factors such as gesture frequency and movement speed were not considered. In future experiments we will examine how these variables affect perception of the agent's emotions. In addition, in future work we will also investigate which specific visual features of an agent and degree of embodiment and personalization influence perception of the agent and for which types of learners.

Our research aims to develop APAs that can display believable and convincing personality and emotions through life-like gestures, speech, body movements, and facial expressions, and hence be an effective alternative to expert and caring human tutors or learning companions. The main goal is to generate evidence-based guidelines for how to incorporate affective (or emotional) features in APAs, in order to improve learning. The studies reported in the paper are first steps in this direction.

Acknowledgements. The work reported in the paper is supported in part by NSF – Cyberlearning Collaborative Research: Multimodal Affective Pedagogical Agents for Different Types of Learners, Award Number: 1821894. We thank Purdue Statistical Consulting Services for their help with the statistical analyses.

References

1. Schroeder, N., Adesope, O.O., Barouch Gilbert, R.: How effective are pedagogical agents for learning? A meta-analytic review. J. Educ. Comput. Res. **49**(1), 1–39 (2013)
2. Kim, Y., Baylor, A.L.: Pedagogical agents as social models to influence learner attitudes. Educ. Technol. **47**(01), 23–28 (2007)
3. Zhou, W., Cheng, J., Lei, X., Benes, B., Adamo, N.: Deep learning-based emotion recognition from real-time videos. In: Proceedings of HCI International 2020, Copenhagen, Denmark (2020, in press)
4. Kim, Y., Lim, J.: Gendered socialization with an embodied agent: creating a social and affable mathematics learning environment for middle-grade females. J. Educ. Psychol. **105**(4), 1164–1174 (2013)
5. Ekman, P., Friesen, W.: The repertoire of nonverbal behavior: categories, origins, usage, and coding. Semiotica **1**(1), 49–98 (1969)
6. Lhommet, M., Marsella, S.: Expressing emotion through posture and gesture. In: Calvo, R., D'Mello, S., Gratch, J., Kappas, A. (eds.) The Oxford Handbook of Affective Computing, pp. 273–285. Oxford University Press, Oxford (2015)
7. Russell, J.A.: Core affect and the psychological construct of emotion. Psychol. Rev. **110**, 145–172 (2003)

8. Johnson, W.L., Lester, J.C.: Face-to-face interaction with pedagogical agents, twenty years later. Int. J. Artif. Intell. Educ. **26**(1), 25–36 (2016)
9. Martha, A.S.D., Santoso, H.B.: The design and impact of the pedagogical agent: a systematic literature review. J. Educ. Online, **16**(1) (2019)
10. Annetta, L.A., Holmes, S.: Creating presence and community in a synchronous virtual learning environment using avatars. Int. J. Instr. Technol. Distance Learn. **3**, 27–43 (2006)
11. Alseid, M., Rigas, D.: Three different modes of avatars as virtual lecturers in elearning interfaces: a comparative usability study. Open Virtual Reality J. **2**, 8–17 (2010)
12. Lusk, M.M., Atkinson, R.K.: Varying a pedagogical agent's degree of embodiment under two visual search conditions. Appl. Cogn. Psychol. **21**, 747–764 (2007)
13. Dehn, D.M., Van Mulken, S.: Impact of animated interface agents: a review of empirical research. Int. J. Hum. Comput. Stud. (2000). https://doi.org/10.1006/ijhc.1999.0325
14. Poggiali, J.: Student responses to an animated character in information literacy instruction. Library Hi Tech **36** (2018). https://doi.org/10.1108/lht-12-2016-0149
15. Mayer, R.E., Estrella, G.: Benefits of emotional design in multimedia instruction. Learn. Instr. **33**, 12–18 (2014)
16. Mayer, R.E., DaPra, C.S.: An embodiment effect in computer-based learning with animated pedagogical agents. J. Exp. Psychol. Appl. **18**(3), 239–252 (2012)
17. Gulz, A., Haake, M.: Social and visual style in virtual pedagogical agents. In: Proceedings of the Workshop on Adapting the Interaction Style to Affective Factors, 10th International Conference on User Modelling (2005)
18. Domagk, S.: Do pedagogical agents facilitate learner motivation and learning outcomes? The role of the appeal of agent's appearance and voice. J. Media Psychol. **22**(2), 84–97 (2010)
19. Mayer, R.E.: Principles based on social cues in multimedia learning: personalization, voice, image, and embodiment principles. In: Mayer, R.E. (ed.) The Cambridge Handbook of Multimedia Learning, 2nd edn, pp. 345–368. Cambridge University Press, New York (2014)
20. Rosenberg-Kima, R.B., Baylor, A.L., Plant, E.A., Doerr, C.E.: Interface agents as social models for female students: the effects of agent visual presence and appearance on female students' attitudes and beliefs. Comput. Hum. Behav. **24**, 2741–2756 (2008)
21. Baylor, A.L., Kim, S.: Designing nonverbal communication for pedagogical agents: when less is more. Comput. Hum. Behav. **25**(2), 450–457 (2009)
22. Wang, N., Johnson, W.L., Mayer, R.E., Rizzo, P., Shaw, E., Collins, H.: The politeness effect: pedagogical agents and learning outcomes. Int. J. Hum. Comput. Stud. **66**, 98–112 (2008)
23. Larsson, P.: Discerning emotion through movement – a study of body language in portraying emotion in animation, pp. 6–7, May 2014. http://www.diva-portal.org/smash/get/diva2:723 103/FULLTEXT01.pdf
24. Anasingaraju, S., Popescu, V., Adamo, N., Wu, M.L.: Digital learning activities delivered by eloquent instructor avatars: scaling with problem instance. In: Proceedings of SIGGRAPH Asia 2016 – Education Symposium. ACM Digital Library (2016)
25. Karg, M., Samadani, A.A., Gorbet, R., Kühnlenz, K., Hoey, J., Kulić, D.: Body movements for affective expression: a survey of automatic recognition and generation. IEEE Trans. Affect. Comput. **4**(4), 341–359 (2013)
26. Sawada, M., Suda, K., Ishii, M.: Expression of emotions in dance: relation between arm movement characteristics and emotion. Percept. Mot. Skills **97**, 697–708 (2003)
27. Atkinson, A.P., Dittrich, W.H., Gemmell, A.J., Young, A.W.: Emotion perception from dynamic and static body expressions in point-light and full-light displays. Perception **33**(6), 717–746 (2004). https://doi.org/10.1068/p5096
28. Ennis, C., Hoyet, L., Egges, A., McDonnell, R.: Emotion capture: emotionally expressive characters for games. In: Proceedings of Motion on Games (2013). https://doi.org/10.1145/2522628.2522633

29. André, E., Klesen, M., Gebhard, P., Allen, S., Rist, T.: Exploiting models of personality and emotions to control the behavior of animated interactive agents. In: Workshop on "Achieving Human-Like Behavior in Interactive Animated Agents" in Conjunction with the Fourth International Conference on Autonomous Agents, pp. 3–7 (2000)

30. Allbeck, J., Badler, N.: Toward representing agent behaviors modified by personality and emotion. In: Embodied Conversational Agents at AAMAS, vol. 2, pp. 15–19 (2002). https://doi.org/10.1.1.19.2054

31. Mehrabian, A.: Analysis of the big-five personality factors in terms of the PAD temperament model. Aust. J. Psychol. (1996). https://doi.org/10.1080/00049539608259510

32. Neff, M., Wang, Y., Abbott, R., Walker, M.: Evaluating the effect of gesture and language on personality perception in conversational agents. In: Allbeck, J., Badler, N., Bickmore, T., Pelachaud, C., Safonova, A. (eds.) IVA 2010. LNCS (LNAI), vol. 6356, pp. 222–235. Springer, Heidelberg (2010). https://doi.org/10.1007/978-3-642-15892-6_24

33. Ball, G., Breese, J.: Relating personality and behavior: posture and gestures, pp. 196–203 (2006). https://doi.org/10.1007/10720296_14

34. Roberts, S.: Character Animation in 3D. Focal Press, Oxford (2004)

35. Cui, J., Adamo, N., Popescu, V.: Charismatic and eloquent instructor avatars with scriptable gesture. In: Proceedings of SIGGRAPH 2014 - Talks, Vancouver, August 2014 (2014)

36. Kim, Y.: Pedagogical agents as learning companions: the effects of agent affect and gender on learning, interest, self-efficacy, and agent persona. Ph.D. thesis, FSU (2003). https://diginole.lib.fsu.edu/islandora/object/fsu:181467/datastream/PDF/view

Integrating Language and Emotion Features for Multilingual Speech Emotion Recognition

Panikos Heracleous[1]([⊠]), Yasser Mohammad[2,3], and Akio Yoneyama[1]

[1] KDDI Research, Inc., 2-1-15 Ohara, Fujimino-shi, Saitama 356-8502, Japan
{pa-heracleous,yoneyama}@kddi-research.jp
[2] Data Science Laboratories, NEC, Tokyo, Japan
[3] Assiut University, Asyut, Egypt
yasserm@aun.edu.eg

Abstract. The current study focuses on multilingual speech emotion recognition using realistic emotional speech extracted from English, Italian, and Spanish films. Two novel methods are proposed, which exploit language information and emotion information. In the first method, features specific to the three languages are concatenated with emotion-specific features and applied using a common extremely randomized trees (ERT) classifier to recognize five emotions. In the second method, a stacked generalization ensemble (SGE) with two ERTs for language and emotion are employed. On top, another ERT is used as a meta-classifier for the final recognition of five emotions. Using the feature fusion-based method, a 73.3% unweighted average recall (UAR) was achieved. This result is very promising and superior to the UAR obtained by human evaluation (71.8% for Italian instances). When using the SGE-based method, a 69.2% UAR was achieved, which is closely comparable to the human evaluation results.

Keywords: Multilingual speech emotion recognition · Feature fusion · Stacked generalization ensemble · Extremely randomized trees

1 Introduction

Speech emotion recognition serves an important role in human-machine interaction and is attracting a substantial amount of attention because it can be used in several real-world applications [1]. Emotion recognition can be applied in human-robot interaction when robots communicate with humans according to the detected emotions. Speech emotion recognition can be employed in call centers in the case of emergencies (e.g., hospitals and police) or to identify the level of customer satisfaction of provided services.

In this study, multilingual emotion recognition based on speech was experimentally investigated. Using English, Italian, and Spanish emotional corpora, multilingual emotion recognition experiments were conducted with extremely

M. Kurosu (Ed.): HCII 2020, LNCS 12182, pp. 187–196, 2020.
https://doi.org/10.1007/978-3-030-49062-1_12

randomized trees [2] and the i-vector paradigm framework [3]. The data in the experiments consist of speech utterances extracted from films. The advantage of using these data is that the speech samples were produced in similar conditions enabling a more natural solution to the task of multilingual speech emotion recognition. In this study, the EmoFilm [4] multilingual emotional corpus was employed.

In this study, two methods for multilingual speech emotion recognition that exploit language information are proposed and evaluated. In the first method, features extracted from the emotions are concatenated with the corresponding features of the language spoken. The concatenated feature vectors are used to train a common multilingual model set that is able to simultaneously recognize five emotions produced in English, Italian, and Spanish. In the second method, two parallel classifiers are being used with a meta-classifier to combine the prediction probabilities of the two classifiers. This stacked generalization ensemble-based method consists of a language classifier and a multilingual classifier that operates in parallel.

2   Related Work

Previously, many studies addressed the problem of speech emotion recognition using different classifiers and various feature extraction methods. A study on emotion recognition based on hidden Markov models (HMMs) was introduced in [5]. Emotion recognition using neural networks (NN) was reported in [6]. Support vector machines (SVMs) are among the most popular classifiers in speech emotion recognition [7]. Recent approaches include speech emotion recognition based on deep neural networks (DNNs) [8,9]. Concerning the feature extraction techniques, mel-frequency cepstral coefficients (MFCC) [10] and its derivatives are extensively employed in speech emotion recognition. In many recent studies, low-level descriptors (LLD) and functionals [11] are extensively applied.

The majority of studies in speech emotion recognition solely focused on a single language, while cross-corpus speech emotion recognition was addressed in only a few of the studies [12,13]. In [14], experiments on emotion recognition were described using comparable speech corpora collected from American English and German interactive voice response systems, and the optimal sets of acoustic and prosodic features for mono-, cross-, and multilingual anger recognition were computed. Cross-language speech emotion recognition based on HMMs and GMMs was reported in [15]. Four speech databases for cross-corpus classification with realistic, non-prompted emotions and a large acoustic feature vector were reported in [16].

In [17], the authors reported on monolingual speech emotion recognition using convolutional neural networks (CNN). Furthermore, in [18], the authors reported on multilingual speech emotion recognition based on a two-pass classification scheme that also exploited spoken language identification. In the current study, the methods were further improved and simplified by integrating language and emotion information on the feature level to perform multilingual speech emotion recognition in a single pass using naturalistic emotional speech data.

3   Methods

3.1   Data

In the current study, the EmoFilm multilingual emotional speech corpus was used. The corpus consists of 1115 instances extracted from 43 films in English, Italian, and Spanish. Five emotions were considered: anger, disgust, happiness, fear, and sadness. Compared with acted speech or multilingual emotion studies using data collected in different conditions, EmoFilm offers a more reliable and natural solution for this task. Note that multilingual emotional speech corpora are not very common [19]. Usually, in studies that address multilingual speech emotion recognition, data recorded under different conditions are used, which causes a decrease in the performance of a classifier. The data from each language were randomly split into two sets: 80% for training and 20% for testing. The corresponding sets from the three languages were pooled to form the multilingual training and test data.

3.2   Feature Extraction and Classification Approaches

Twelve MFCC features were extracted from the emotional speech signal every 10 ms with a window-length of 20 ms. Due to the effectiveness of the shifted delta cepstral (SDC) [20] feature vectors in language identification, SDC coefficients concatenated with the basic features were also used to form the feature vectors. The parameter configuration of SDC was optimized to 11,1,3,3. Figure 1 shows the extraction of SDC feature vectors.

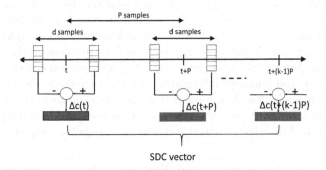

Fig. 1. Computation of shifted delta cepstral (SDC) coefficients.

Gaussian mixture models (GMMs) with universal background models (UBMs) are extensively applied in speaker recognition. In this case, each speaker model is created by adapting a UBM using maximum a posteriori (MAP) adaptation. A GMM supervector is constructed by concatenating the means of the adapted model. Similar to speaker recognition, GMM supervectors can be used for emotion recognition.

The main disadvantage of GMM supervectors is the high dimensionality, which imposes high computation and memory costs. In the i-vector paradigm, the limitations of high dimensional supervectors were overcome by modeling the variability contained in the supervectors with a small set of factors. An input utterance can be modeled as follows:

$$\mathbf{M} = \mathbf{m} + \mathbf{Tw} \tag{1}$$

where $\mathbf{M}$ is the emotion-dependent supervector, $\mathbf{m}$ is the emotion-independent supervector, $\mathbf{T}$ is the total variability matrix, and $\mathbf{w}$ is the i-vector. Both the total variability matrix and the emotion-independent supervector are estimated from the complete set of training data.

The MFCC features with SDC coefficients were used to extract i-vectors with 100 dimensions for modeling and classifying emotions. The number of Gaussian components in UBM was set to 128.

For classification, the extremely randomized trees classifier (ERT) was used, which is similar to random forests [21], but with random tree splitting. Previous studies showed the effectiveness of using ERT in the case of a small amount of data and low dimensional feature vectors, which was also the case in the current study.

3.3   Proposed Methods for Multilingual Speech Emotion Recognition

The proposed methods are based on the idea that when language and emotion information are integrated, the intra- and inter- discrimination ability of the emotion models across languages will be increased due to additional and more relevant information. This premise is analogous to the independent operation of three monolingual classifiers. In this study, however, two complete systems are being proposed to simultaneously recognize five emotions produced in three different languages. Furthermore, only one set of multilingual emotion models is being employed, and language information is being exploited. The advantage of the current scheme is that deterministic language identification is not a requirement, as in [18,22], which prevents a decrease in performance when the language identification module fails to correctly recognize the spoken language.

Feature Fusion of Language and Emotions. In this approach, two feature extractors are being used for languages and emotions, as shown in Fig. 2. After the i-vector extraction, linear discriminant analysis (LDA) with Fisher criterion [23] is performed to produce language- and emotion-relevant feature vectors. LDA is used to perform supervised dimensionality reduction by projecting the input data to a linear subspace that consists of the directions that maximize the separation between classes. The dimension of the produced feature vectors is $C - 1$, where C is the number of classes. The corresponding language and emotion labels are used when performing LDA, which generates different final feature vectors. Using the training data, the LDA transformation matrix

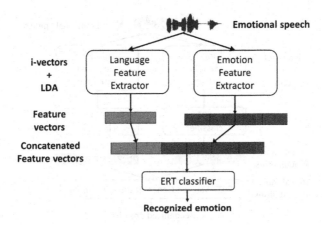

Fig. 2. Language and emotion feature fusion

is computed, which is also used during the testing phase. Following LDA, the produced feature vectors are concatenated and applied by an ERT classifier for emotion recognition.

Stacked Generalization Ensemble (SGE). In this proposed approach, two parallel ERT classifiers are used for language and emotion classification. The concatenated prediction probabilities of the two classifiers are used to train an ERT meta-classifier for the final emotion prediction. The same procedure in the previous method was used to extract the i-vectors and perform LDA. The meta-classifier receives the outputs of the subclassifiers as input and attempts to learn how to best combine the input predictions to make a better emotion prediction. To overcome the problem of overfitting, the total training dataset was split to train the validation sets (70%–30%). The two subclassifiers were trained on the training set, and the meta-classifier was trained on the validation set. Note that the proposed method differs from the conventional stacking approach, where the subclassifiers usually make decisions on the same classes. The proposed method is aimed at improving the emotion recognition by incorporating language information in the emotion classifier. Figure 3 shows the proposed method based on the stacked generalization ensemble.

4   Results

Table 1 shows the results obtained when using feature fusion in comparison with results of human evaluation and baseline systems. When only emotion features were used, the UAR was 62.5%. When language information was also applied, a 73.3% UAR was obtained showing a 29% relative improvement. This results is very promising and even higher than the rates obtained by human evaluation. Additionally, the emotions anger and sadness were recognized with the highest

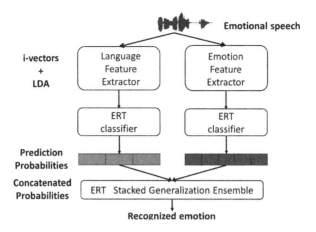

Fig. 3. Stacked generalization ensemble

Table 1. Recalls for individual emotions when using feature (early) fusion [%].

Classifier	Emotion					
	Anger	Disgust	Fear	Happy	Sadness	Average
Human evaluation (Italian instances) [4]	83.5	58.0	60.0	75.5	80.0	71.8
Extremely randomized trees (Emotion features only)	87.5	66.7	45.8	41.7	70.8	62.5
Extremely randomized trees (Emotion + language features)	95.8	75.0	54.2	54.2	87.5	73.3
Extremely randomized trees (Emotion + language features) (Italian instances)	87.5	75.0	75.0	75.0	100.0	82.5

recalls in all cases. Furthermore, when the ERT classifier with integrated features was used, the order of individual emotions' recalls using only Italian instances are consistent with the human evaluation, but significantly higher.

Table 2 shows the precisions in the case of feature fusion. As is shown, the precisions show the same tendency as the recalls. When using only emotion features, the average precision was 62.4%. When language features were also concatenated, the average precision improved to 73.0%. When only Italian instances were considered, the average precision was 84.7%.

The F1-scores when using feature fusion are shown on Table 3. The average F1-score when using emotion features was 62.0%. When language features were also added, a 72.4% average F1-score was obtained. The results show that the differences in recalls, precisions, and F1-scores are not significant indicating a high performance of the classifier.

Table 2. Precisions for individual emotions when using feature (early) fusion [%].

Classifier	Emotion					
	Anger	Disgust	Fear	Happy	Sadness	Average
Human evaluation (Italian instances) [4]	70.5	64.8	75.9	76.25	72.4	72.0
Extremely randomized trees (Emotion features only)	80.8	51.6	50.0	55.6	73.9	62.4
Extremely randomized trees (Emotion + language features)	74.2	69.2	68.4	72.2	80.8	73.0
Extremely randomized trees (Emotion + language features) (Italian instances)	77.8	85.7	60.0	100.0	100	84.7

Table 3. F1-scores for individual emotions when using feature (early) fusion [%].

Classifier	Emotion					
	Anger	Disgust	Fear	Happy	Sadness	Average
Human evaluation (Italian instances) [4]	76.4	61.2	75.7	68.3	75.9	71.5
Extremely randomized trees (Emotion features only)	84.0	58.2	47.8	47.6	72.3	62.0
Extremely randomized trees (Emotion + language features)	83.6	72.0	60.5	61.9	84	72.4
Extremely randomized trees (Emotion + language features) (Italian instances)	82.4	80.0	66.7	85.7	100.0	83.0

The recalls obtained when stacked generalization ensemble was used are shown on Table 4. As is shown, the rates are lower compared to feature fusion. Possible reasons include that feature fusion performs integration from the beginning of the procedure, correlation between emotion features and language features is also considered. Additionally, in feature fusion a single classifier is being used with easier hyper-parameters tuning. The UAR using emotion and language features was 69.2%. In the case of Italian instances only, the average recall was 72.5%, which was higher compared with the recall achieved by human evaluation.

Table 5 shows the precisions in the case of stacking approach. The rates are closely comparable with the recalls, and the differences are not statistically significant. The F1-scores are shown on Table 6. In this integration approach, recalls, precisions, and F1-scores do not show significant differences.

Table 4. Recalls for individual emotions when using stacked generalization ensemble [%].

Classifier	Emotion					
	Anger	Disgust	Fear	Happy	Sadness	Average
Extremely randomized trees (Emotion + language features)	95.8	70.8	54.2	58.3	66.7	69.2
Extremely randomized trees (Emotion + language features) (Italian instances)	87.5	75.0	62.5	62.5	75.0	72.5

Table 5. Precisions for individual emotions when using stacked generalization ensemble [%].

Classifier	Emotion					
	Anger	Disgust	Fear	Happy	Sadness	Average
Extremely randomized trees (Emotion + language features)	82.1	63.0	61.9	58.3	80.0	69.1
Extremely randomized trees (Emotion + language features) (Italian instances)	87.5	60.0	55.6	83.3	85.7	74.4

Table 6. F1-scores for individual emotions when using stacked generalization ensemble [%].

Classifier	Emotion					
	Anger	Disgust	Fear	Happy	Sadness	Average
Extremely randomized trees (Emotion + language features)	88.5	66.7	57.8	58.3	72.7	68.8
Extremely randomized trees (Emotion + language features) (Italian instances)	87.5	66.7	58.8	71.4	80.0	73.0

5   Discussion

In the current study, an emotional speech corpus consisting of utterances from films was applied in emotion recognition experiments. Although the used corpus provides a more natural approach, the speech produced might still be considered as acted emotional speech. On the other hand, the speech extracted from films was produced in conversations and could be considered as spontaneous emotional speech. A disadvantage of the Emofilm corpus is that neutral speech is not included, and perfect comparisons with similar studies are not possible. However, considering the very few multilingual emotional corpora existing, the current study and the proposed methods show that multilingual speech emotion recognition with high performance is still possible even in the case of speech extracted from films.

For comprehensive analysis and experiments, a larger number of languages is required. This task is currently under investigation and consideration. The current study will be extended to also deal with standard, state-of-the-art corpora commonly applied in speech emotion recognition.

6 Conclusions

In the current study, two methods were presented from multilingual speech emotion recognition. The methods are based on the idea that when language features are additionally applied to emotion features, the performance of a multilingual speech emotion recognition system will improve due to the additive and relevant information. In the first method, the emotion features were concatenated with language features to form multilingual feature vectors applied by a single ERT classifier to simultaneously recognize five emotion from English, Italian, and Spanish languages. The UAR obtained was 73.3%, which was a very promising result and higher than the UAR obtained by human evaluation.

In the second approach, two parallel ERT classifiers were applied for language and emotion, respectively. On top, another ERT meta-classifier was used, to best combine the prediction probabilities of the two subclassifiers and to provide the final emotion prediction. In this case, the UAR was 69.2%, which is still comparable with human evaluation results. Currently, evaluating the proposed methods using a larger number of languages is in progress.

References

1. Busso, C., Bulut, M., Narayanan, S.: Toward effective automatic recognition systems of emotion in speech. In: Gratch, J., Marsella, S. (eds.) Social Emotions in Nature and Artifact: Emotions in Human and Human-Computer Interaction, pp. 110–127. Oxford University Press, New York (2013)
2. Geurts, P., Ernst, D., Wehenkel, L.: Extremely randomized trees. Mach. Learn. **63**(1), 3–42 (2006)
3. Dehak, N., Kenny, P.J., Dehak, R., Dumouchel, P., Ouellet, P.: Front-end factor analysis for speaker verification. IEEE Trans. Audio Speech Lang. Process. **19**(4), 788–798 (2011)
4. P-Cabaleiro, E., Costantini, G., Batliner, A., Baird, A., Schuller, B.: Categorical vs dimensional perception of Italian emotional speech. In: Proceedings of Interspeech, pp. 3638–3642 (2018)
5. Schuller, B., Rigoll, G., Lang, M.: Hidden Markov model-based speech emotion recognition. In: Proceedings of the IEEE ICASSP, vol. I, pp. 401–404 (2003)
6. Nicholson, J., Takahashi, K., Nakatsu, R.: Emotion recognition in speech using neural networks. Neural Comput. Appl. **9**(4), 290–296 (2000)

7. Pan, Y., Shen, P., Shen, L.: Speech emotion recognition using support vector machine. Int. J. Smart Home **6**(2), 101–108 (2012)
8. Stuhlsatz, A., Meyer, C., Eyben, F., Zielke1, T., Meier, G., Schuller, B.: Deep neural networks for acoustic emotion recognition: raising the benchmarks. In: Proceedings of ICASSP, pp. 5688–5691 (2011)
9. Han, K., Yu, D., Tashev, I.: Speech emotion recognition using deep neural network and extreme learning machine. In: Proceedings of Interspeech, pp. 2023–2027 (2014)
10. Sahidullah, M., Saha, G.: Design, analysis and experimental evaluation of block based transformation in MFCC computation for speaker recognition. Speech Commun. **54**(4), 543–565 (2012)
11. Schuller, B.W., et al.: The INTERSPEECH 2016 computational paralinguistics challenge: deception, sincerity & native language. In: Proceedings of Interspeech, 2001–2005 (2016)
12. Feraru, S.M., Schuller, D., Schuller, B.: Cross-language acoustic emotion recognition: an overview and some tendencies. In: International Conference on Affective Computing and Intelligent Interaction (ACII), 125–131 (2015)
13. Li, X., Akagi, M.: Improving multilingual speech emotion recognition by combining acoustic features in a three-layer model. Speech Commun. **110**, 1–12 (2019)
14. Polzehl, T., Schmitt, A., Metze, F.: Approaching multi-lingual emotion recognition from speech-on language dependency of acoustic prosodic features for anger detection. In: Proceedings of Speech Prosody (2010)
15. Bhaykar, M., Yadav, J., Rao, K.S.: Speaker dependent, speaker independent and cross language emotion recognition from speech using GMM and HMM. In: 2013 National Conference on Communications (NCC), pp. 1–5. IEEE (2013)
16. Eyben, F., Batliner, A., Schuller, B., Seppi, D., Steidl, S.: Crosscorpus classification of realistic emotions - some pilot experiments. In: Proceedings of the Third International Workshop on EMOTION (Satellite of LREC) (2010)
17. Heracleous, P., Mohammad, Y., Yoneyama, A.: Deep convolutional neural networks for feature extraction in speech emotion recognition. In: Kurosu, M. (ed.) HCII 2019. LNCS, vol. 11567, pp. 117–132. Springer, Cham (2019). https://doi.org/10.1007/978-3-030-22643-5_9
18. Heracleous, P., Yoneyama, A.: A comprehensive study on bilingual and multilingual speech emotion recognition using a two-pass classification scheme (2019). https://doi.org/10.1371/journal.pone.0220386
19. Ververidis, D., Kotropoulos, C.: Emotional speech recognition: resources, features, and methods. Speech Commun. **48**(9), 1162–1181 (2006)
20. Bielefeld, B.: Language identification using shifted delta cepstrum. In: Fourteenth Annual Speech Research Symposium (1994)
21. Ho, T.K.: Random decision forests. In: Proceedings of the 3rd International Conference on Document Analysis and Recognition, pp. 278–282 (1995)
22. Sagha, H., Matejka, P., Gavryukova, M., Povolný, F., Marchi, E., Schuller, B.W.: Enhancing multilingual recognition of emotion in speech by language identification. In: Proceedings of Interspeech, pp. 2949–2953 (2016)
23. Fukunaga, K.: Introduction to Statistical Pattern Recognition, 2nd edn. Academic Press, New York (1990). Ch. 10

A New Approach to Measure User Experience with Voice-Controlled Intelligent Assistants: A Pilot Study

Félix Le Pailleur[✉], Bo Huang, Pierre-Majorique Léger, and Sylvain Sénécal

HEC Montréal, Montréal, Canada
{felix.le-pailleur,bo.huang,pierre-majorique.leger,
sylvain.senecal}@hec.ca

Abstract. Voice-controlled intelligent assistants use a conversational user interface (CUI), a system that relies on natural language processing and artificial intelligence to have verbal interactions with end-users. In this research, we propose a multi-method approach to assess user experience with a smart voice assistant through triangulation of psychometric and psychophysiological measures. The approach aims to develop a richer understanding of what the users experience during the interaction, which could provide new insights to researchers and developers in the field of voice assistant. We apply this new approach in a pilot study, and we show that each method captures a part of emotional variance during the interaction. Results suggest that emotional valence is better captured with psychometric measures, whereas arousal is better detected with psychophysiological measures.

Keywords: Human-Computer Interactions · Conversational user interface · User experience · Vocal assistant · Arousal · Valence · Emotion

1 Introduction

Voice assistants (e.g., Alexa, Google Assistant, Siri) are voice-controlled devices that allow consumers to use their voice to make queries such as listening to music, accessing the latest news, or answering general questions. In the U.S., it is estimated that conversational user interface (CUI) users will surpass 123 million by 2021, which represents an increase of 44% since 2017 (Petrock 2019). In addition, a recent study shows that Amazon has sold 75 million dollars' worth of smart speakers around the globe in 2018, a growth of 600% over the last year (Tung 2018).

Although voice assistants have become omnipresent in our phones, vehicles, and homes, to date, academic research that aims at developing methods to study these increasingly popular technologies is still lacking (Nass 2005; Sciuto et al. 2018; Lopatovska and Oropeza 2018; Lopatovska and Williams 2018; Jiang 2015). In fact, not all traditional methods for evaluating the user experience appears to be suited to the context of interaction with intelligent voice assistants. For instance, the "Think Aloud" method

© Springer Nature Switzerland AG 2020
M. Kurosu (Ed.): HCII 2020, LNCS 12182, pp. 197–208, 2020.
https://doi.org/10.1007/978-3-030-49062-1_13

(Fonteyn et al. 1993) where the researcher asks the participant to verbalize what he or she is doing and thinking while performing a task does not apply in this context since the participant is already using his/her voice to interact with the device.

Therefore, the goal of this paper is to propose a new approach to evaluate user experience during vocal interactions with voice assistants. Specifically, we propose to bonify self-reported measures used *before* and *after* the task with psychophysiological measures (i.e., electrodermal activity and micro facial expressions) to investigate the automatic and non-conscience reaction *during* the interaction. To test the feasibility of our new approach, we conducted a laboratory experiment in which participants (N = 11) were instructed to interact with Alexa. To elicit emotional reactions from participants, we designed a set of tasks likely to generate a wide range of discrete emotions.

The article is structured as follows. We first review existing research using self-reported measures in the context of voice assistant, then we discuss related work on psychophysiological measurement in the HCI literature. Next, we explain our research methodology as well as summarize the results and their interpretations in the discussion.

2   Current Research on Voice Assistants Using Self-reported Measures

Past research on user interaction with voice assistants has been using both qualitative and quantitative research methods such as questionnaires, diaries, and interviews.

Questionnaires are a widely used tool since they allow researchers to manage a large amount of data from participants quickly and inexpensively (De Singly 2016). There are several forms in which questionnaires can be presented. For example, using Likert scales, questionnaires can be quickly presented to participants before or after completing a task without hindering the flow of the experiment. In a study conducted by Jiang et al. (2015), participants were asked to complete a sequence of 10 tasks using the vocal assistant Cortana on a smartphone, and a questionnaire was used to assess frustration, success, effort, and reuse intentions. For every task, the participant only had to answer a questionnaire regarding their experience using a standard 5-point Likert scale, the most commonly used question model for measuring affective variables (Brown 2000; Burns and Grove 2005).

Similarly, diaries have also been used frequently as a method for qualitative research because it provides access to users' subjective impressions and more importantly, reflections on their interactions. This technique is advantageous since studies have shown that the presence of a stranger, e.g., researcher, might affect the way a user will interact with a voice assistant since it is mainly used in a private or comfortable context (e.g., home, with friends or alone) (Easwara Moorthy and Vu 2015). Hence, diaries offer a suitable alternative or an addition for qualitative research that might be affected by the presence of a researcher in a laboratory (Nicholl 2010). Researchers have used this method in a variety of contexts to user experience after the use of a voice assistant. For instance, Lopatovska and Williams (2018) used a diary log in studying user personification of Alexa. The study data were collected primarily through a structured online diary, which participants were asked to complete once a day for four days. The diary was also the primary method in Lau et al. (2018)'s study on users' privacy concerns when interacting with voice assistant. Through the analysis of the diary logs, they found that many non-users did not see the utility of smart speakers or did not trust speaker companies. Other studies went further. They found innovative ways to conduct data collections to understand how Alexa was used in participant's households with multiple members on a long period in a more natural way without having to report their interactions in a diary (Sciuto et al. 2018; Lopatovska and Oropeza 2018). For example, a recent study by Porcheron et al. (2018) used a Conditional Voice Recorder (CVR), a device that is activated when Alexa is turned on, to record the interaction. That way, it is possible to record multiple interactions with the voice assistant and family members in a natural context of use.

As a common tool in the HCI literature, interviews are often used as a complementary method in conjunction with the above-discussed methods. For example, in order to study user sharing practices of voice assistants, Garg and Moreno (2019) used semi-structured interviews in addition to diary logs. In a similar vein, in-depth interviews were conducted to have a better understanding of the collected conversational logs with voice assistants in investigating of Alexa's in-homer usage pattern (Sciuto et al. 2018).

Finally, observations are the only traditional methods providing a way to record user behavior during the interaction directly. For instance, in a recent study examining user interaction with voice assistants in public spaces, the area around Alexa was observed at different times of the day and different days for one week, totalling 5.5 observation hours and 132 persons observed (Lopatovska and Oropeza 2018). However, observation provides little insight on how the user feels emotionally and cognitively during the interaction.

3 Psychophysiological Measures in HCI

As presented above, most studies used qualitative or quantitative methods, mostly relying on self-reported measures. Although they provide extensive and informative results on user interaction with voice assistants, these methods alone may suffer from not precisely measuring what the user really experienced at the moment of the interaction. Researchers are calling for multi-method approaches that consider what the users really experience and perceive (Vom Brocke et al. 2020). For instance, it is possible that these results mainly "assess the user's reflection on the interaction, but not the interaction itself" (Georges et al. 2017, p. 91). Therefore, we posit that what users have really experienced might be different from their subjective evaluation of their experience.

Research in Human-Computer Interaction (HCI) has used psychophysiological measures as a viable indicator of cognitive and emotional states such as cognitive effort or frustration (Rowe et al. 1998; De Guinea et al. 2013, 2014; Giroux-Huppé et al. 2019; Beauchesne et al. 2019; Lourties et al. 2018; Agourram et al. 2019; Maunier et al. 2018). The literature has shown that user's emotional and cognitive states can also be inferred using psychophysiological signals, such as electrodermal activity (EDA), heart rate, eye-tracking, and facial expressions (see Riedl and Léger 2016 and Riedl et al. 2020).

By using self-reported measures only, researchers can face various cognitive biases such as social desirability (de Guinea et al. 2014). For example, psychologists suggest that the presence of a stranger (e.g., researcher) can change the way one will interact and, in our case, use a voice assistant to respond in the most socially desirable way (Piedmont

2014, p. 6036–6037). For example, by asking participants their likelihood to use a voice assistant in multiple environments (e.g., alone at home, in the metro or at work), Easwara and Vu (2015) found that the social context in which the interaction occurs, influence the information transmitted to the vocal assistant. Hence, psychophysiological measurement tools can contribute to overcoming bias coming from self-reported measures or observations (Xiong and Zuo 2020).

Thus, in the context of assessing the experience of users while they are interacting with a voice assistant, psychophysiological tools are an interesting add-on because they make it possible to complement traditional means of measurements (e.g., questionnaires, interviews), but especially to bring a precision on a specific emotional state, in time, to which a user cannot remember (Lourties et al. 2018). For example, it might be difficult for a participant, in the context of evaluating an intelligent voice assistant, to remember how he/she felt at a particular moment of the interaction (e.g., when he/she felt frustrated after the CUI gave an irrelevant answer to his/her question).

How users react at the moment of interacting with a device comes from unconscious and automatic mechanisms (De Guinea et al. 2013). The most accurate way to assess how they felt at one particular moment is with the psychophysiological response to the stimuli rather than their perception of what motivates their reaction (Dijksterhuis and Smith 2005).

In this research, we contribute to the literature on human interaction with voice assistants by proposing a multi-method approach to study user experience with a voice assistant by combining both psychological and psychophysiological measures, which could provide insights to researchers and developers in the field of intelligent assistants Specifically, this study leverages electrodermal activity and micro facial expressions based on Ekman's universal facial expressions (Ekman 1997) (happy, sad, angry, surprised, scared, disgusted) and emotional valence (positive-negative) in studying user experience with intelligent assistants. In the next section, we show how psychophysiological measures can offer interesting additional information to conventional self-reported measures.

3.1 Arousal

Arousal is an emotional state related to psychophysiological activity, which is linearly manifested from "calm" to "aroused" (Deng and Poole 2010; Russell 2003). Being aroused by a specific stimulus results typically in a feeling of alertness, readiness, or mobility (e.g. body movement, deep breath) (Boucsein 2012). This emotional state can be measured with Electrodermal Activity (EDA), which can assess the changes in the skin conductance response (SCR) from the nervous system functions (Braithwaite et al. 2013; Dawson et al. 2000; Bethel 2007). It is an easy to use and reliable psychophysiological measure that has been widely used in NeuroIS research (Léger et al. 2014; Brocke et al. 2013; Giroux-Huppé et al. 2019; Lamontagne et al. 2020). Arousal can also be measured perceptually by using the self-reported measure such as the Self-Assessment manikin rating (SAM), in which users report their perceived emotional state for a specific stimulus, such as excited, wide-awake, neutral, dull, calm (Bradley and Lang 1994).

However, the main advantage of using a psychophysiological measure to assess arousal is that it is not invasive, requires no overt behaviour to be recorded, and offers an ecologically valid portrait of the user's arousal, at any time during an experiment

(Dirican and Göktürk 2011). For instance, in a study on child-robot interaction, Leite et al. (2013) measured user's arousal through skin conductance and found that such a method is valuable and reliable for capturing interaction with social robots. Also, it can be used to complement and validate traditional survey methods (e.g. questionnaires).

Moreover, in a study measuring the effects of time pressure and accuracy using a computer mouse, participants were asked to paint rectangles with a decreasing time limit. Heiden et al. (2005) found that there was a significant difference in electrodermal data between task difficulty levels. Finally, in a study providing a systematic assessment of IS construct validity, de Guinea et al. (2013) found that the convergent validity of arousal was evidenced by the significant correlation between the SAM scale and the electrodermal data.

3.2 Valence

Emotional valence refers to the emotional response, with negative emotions (e.g., fear, anger, sadness) on one side of the spectrum and positive emotions (e.g., joy, surprise) on the other, to a specific stimulus (Lane et al. (1999). Valence can easily be measured perceptually with self-reported measure (e.g., SAM Scale) as the intensity of positive emotions minus the intensity of negative emotions expressed within a range from − 1 to 1 (Bradley and Lang 1994). Another way to measure valence is by interpreting facial expressions, which are expressed by the micro-movements of facial muscles (e.g. frowning when angry) (Ekman 1993). It used to be that the only way to interpret facial expressions was via a trained observer who would observe and note changes in facial expressions based on the Facial Action Coding System (FACS) by Ekman and Friesen (1997).

Today, this time-consuming method is replaced with automatic facial analysis tools (AFA), which can automatically recognize the small changes in facial action units (e.g. raising a brow, chin raise, jaw drop, etc.) and interpret data based on the FACS (Cohn and Kanade 2007, Ekman 1997).

This technology allows us to accurately detect facial expressions in real-time by distinguishing between a set of discrete emotions such as angry, happy, disgusted, sad, scared, surprised. For example, Danner et al. (2014) used this technology to examine participants' facial reactions when tasting orange juice samples to compare implicit measures from the tool with explicit measures from the questionnaire. They found that the software was accurate to report changes in the participant's micro facial expressions between the different samples. Zaman and Shrimpton-Smith (2006) found that, compared to a user questionnaire, data captured by facial micro-expressions is more effective in measuring instant emotions and fun of use. Also, their results suggest that questionnaire data was instead a reflection of the outcome of a task, than a genuine self-reflection of how the user felt when accomplishing the task. Similarly, in a recent study, Lourties et al. (2018) explored the convergent validity of self-reported measures with psychophysiological measures. Their results suggest that the experience lived by a participant is not the same as it is reported. Users self-evaluate their emotional valence more accurately at the end than at the beginning of a task, while they evaluate their arousal more accurately only at the beginning of a task.

To the best of our knowledge, no studies have yet used automatic facial analysis in conjunction with the precise triangulation of electrodermal activity to study user experience with a voice assistant. The proposed triangulated method could provide new insights for this learning or evaluation context using voice only.

4   Method

To test the feasibility of using psychophysiological measures in conjunction with psychometric measures to evaluate user experience with voice assistant, we conducted a pilot laboratory experiment where participants were invited to actively interact with Alexa through Amazon's (Amazon Inc, Seattle, WA) Echo Dot (3rd generation) device by completing a series of tasks. A total of 11 subjects participated in the experiment (4 males, 7 females, mean age = 24; sd = 5.48) and received a $20 gift card as compensation. This project was approved by the IRB of our institution.

4.1   Participants and Design

Since this is a feasibility study, and we wanted to generate as much as variance in the data, we designed a within-subject experiment where each participant was instructed to perform a sequence of interactions. The experiment has one factor with two conditions: impossible tasks (i.e., queries that Alexa was unable to complete) and possible tasks (i.e., queries that Alexa was able to complete) in order to induce negative emotions such as frustration. Participants were randomly assigned to two different sets of tasks wherein one condition, they completed possible tasks before impossible tasks and in the other condition, we reversed the sequence. During the experiment, participants completed a set of 8 interactions in total.

4.2   Procedure and Measures

Participants were informed that they would have to complete a total of 8 tasks. The goal of each task was explained under the form of pictograms on a tablet.

Participants completed a short questionnaire after each interaction as well as a final questionnaire at the end of the study, followed by a brief interview. To measure user perceptions, the 5-point Self-Assessment Manikin (SAM) scale (Bradley and Lang 1994) was used. The tool allows to directly measure a person's perceived emotional reaction to a stimulus, such as valence and arousal. Respectively, the scales range from sad (1) happy (5) and calm (1) to excited (5).

For the psychophysiological arousal measure, we collected EDA with a Biopac MP-160 (Biopac, Goleta, USA) device with pre-gel sensors placed on the palm of the participant's non-dominant hand to capture changes in skin conductivity.

Electrodermal measures were standardized using as a reference a baseline captured on each participant before the experiment. The baseline consists of measuring the normal electrodermal activity unique to each participant, so that variations from the baseline can be compared. Also, results were rescaled from -1 to 1 for analysis purpose.

Finally, psychophysiological emotional valence was captured via micro facial expressions with the software FaceReader (Noldus, Wageningen, Netherlands). This nonobtrusive method can detect up to six emotions: happy, sad, angry, surprised, scared, and disgusted. Valence value was calculated by subtracting the value of the "happy" emotion and the value of the highest negative emotion (Noldus, FaceReader).

Since the objective of this study is to investigate user experience at the moment of interaction with a voice assistant, only psychophysiological measures that were captured at the moment of listening to Alexa's answers were retained for analysis. It is the participant's reactions to the response given by the voice assistant that interests us.

4.3 Material and Apparatus

The apparatus was installed in a quiet room with a mirror window, to reduce noise or external stimulation to make sure there was no interruption and that our psychophysiological data would be good quality (see Fig. 1 for a detailed setup).

Fig. 1. Experimental setup

Our experimental setup was composed of an Alexa device, a microphone, mounted with a camera, and a digital tablet was installed. During the experiment, participants were interacting with the device. Facial expressions during the experiment were captured using a Logitech camera (Newark, USA), and recorded with the software Media Recorder (Noldus, Wageningen, Netherlands). The software Observer XT (Noldus, Wageningen, Netherlands) and CubeHX (Montréal, Canada) was used to precisely and temporally synchronize all psychophysiological measurements, in line with the guidelines proposed by Léger and colleagues (Léger et al. 2014, 2019; Courtemanche et al. 2018). Statistics were performed using the Statistical Analysis System 9.4 (SAS Inst., U.S.A.).

5   Results

To analyze the data, we first performed several linear mixed-effects regressions where each of the measures was entered as a dependent variable (see Table 1 for detailed results). For self-reported measures, namely the valence and arousal, we found that participants reported significantly more positive valence in the possible tasks, compared to impossible tasks (t (76) $= -3.77$, p $< .001$), which was expected. This suggests that participants felt more positive emotions than negative emotions when having successful interactions with the voice assistant. However, arousal did not show a significant difference (t (76) $= 0.54$, p $= .59$, NS) between the two task sets.

Table 1. Summary of results: means standard deviation and linear regression

	Possible tasks	Impossible tasks	Estimate	Std. error	t-value	p-value
Valence (self-reported)	3.65 (0.96)	3 (0.83)	−0.65	0.18	−3.77	p < .001
Arousal (self-reported)	2.45 (0.96)	2.36 (0.93)	−.09	0.17	−0.54	p = .59
Arousal (Psychophysiological)	−0.01 (0.33)	0.07 (0.30)	0.08	0.01	7.46	p < .0001
Valence (Psychophysiological)	0.03 (0.35)	0.004 (0.31)	0.01	0.01	−0.94	p = 0.35

Note: Standard deviations are reported in parentheses.

For psychophysiological measures, arousal results suggest that impossible tasks generate much higher EDA than possible tasks (t (2638) $= 7.46$, p $< .0001$). This means that participants experienced a much higher aroused emotional state when they were having difficulties during their interactions. However, in terms of the valance, we did not find a significant difference between possible and impossible tasks (t (1776) $= -0.94$, p $= .35$, NS). The following table presents the descriptive statistics and regression results.

In order to understand the relationship between the two self-reported measures and the psychophysiological measures, we conducted two additional linear mixed-effects regression analyses. The results showed that the self-reported arousal is positively correlated with psychophysiological arousal (t (2638) $= 3.82$, p $< .0001$). However, surprisingly, our analysis revealed that self-reported valence was negatively correlated with psychophysiological valence (t (1776) $= -5,09$ $\rho < .0001$).

6 Discussion

Our main contribution with this methodological paper is through the triangulation of psychological and psychophysiological measures since, to the best of our knowledge, this study is the first to compare results from both psychophysiological and self-reported measures in the context of user interaction with a voice assistant. Specifically, we found that for arousal, results from EDA showed a significant difference between possible tasks and impossible tasks (but the self-reported measure did not capture such difference). In contrast, for valence, the self-reported measure was more effective than the automatic facial analysis (AFA) in detecting variance in valence. Since previous studies mainly used self-reported measures in studying user interaction with voice assistant, our study contributes by showing the benefit of a multimethod approach in this context, as each method captures a distinct emotional dimension. This suggests that during interaction with a voice assistant, what users experienced might not be exactly the same as reported by themselves. We note that this finding is in line with previous research that combining both methods in studying similar emotional states (i.e., arousal and valence) (Lourties et al. 2018).

Also, the results suggest that the self-perceived arousal was consistent with the psychophysiological responses measured with electrodermal activity when combing both task sets, as they showed a significant positive correlation. These results support previous findings in HCI research using EDA and extend these findings in user interaction context with voice assistants. For example, De Guinea et al. (2013) found that the convergent validity of arousal was evidenced by the significant correlation between the SAM scale measure and the electrodermal measure. Such correlation was evidenced in the current research as well.

Moreover, our results indicate that the emotions inferred from the user's facial expressions by AFA during the interaction complement the self-perceived emotional valence reported by the users. However, we note that there is a discrepancy between valence inferred based on AFA and the reported by questionnaire. For example, they are negatively correlated in general when combining both tasks. To investigate this surprising result, we conducted further observation analysis by analyzing the video recordings of our participants performing the tasks. We found a tendency of several participants smiling when they were not able to complete an impossible task, but a smile emanating from frustration rather than joy, which would be aligned with self-reported valence results.

As a future research avenue, researchers have found a way to overcome this kind of situation by focusing on a new set of emotions called epistemic. For example, D'Mello and Calvo (2013) report in their E-learning study with students that "boredom," "confusion," "curiosity," "happiness," and "frustration" where the most common affective states felt during learning and reading situations. In particular, the affective state of "confusion" might be interesting to test in our context since there can be much discrepancy between what the participant expects to get as an answer and the actual answer given by the intelligent voice assistant since speech recognition is not yet optimal. We are currently running a new study where we are considering the affective states "boredom," "confusion," and "curiosity."

Our experience is limited by the fact that it took place in a user experience laboratory. Thus, the user experience may have been slightly different than if it had taken place in a more natural setting. Future research could extend the current study to other real-life settings such as home and office where interaction with voice assistant is more frequent. In addition, our experiment only measured EDA and facial expressions, while many other tools and measurements suggested by the literature still need to be tested in our specific study context. Hence, it would be interesting for future research to consider a more natural set up and to add more psychophysiological tools. Also, rarely do voice assistant users use their device without performing other tasks at the same time. The main advantage of this tool is that it allows the user to perform a vocal command when he can perform something else simultaneously (e.g. walking, driving or listening to television). In our opinion, the idea of adding pupillometry to measure cognitive load (Sirois and Brisson 2014; Léger et al. 2018) in a multi-tasking context using a vocal assistant would be an excellent contribution to the research in HCI.

References

Agourram, H., Alvarez, J., Sénécal, S., Lachize, S., Gagné, J., Léger, P.-M.: The relationship between technology self-efficacy beliefs and user satisfaction – user experience perspective. In: Kurosu, M. (ed.) HCII 2019. LNCS, vol. 11568, pp. 389–397. Springer, Cham (2019). https://doi.org/10.1007/978-3-030-22636-7_29

Beauchesne, A., et al.: User-centered gestures for mobile phones: exploring a method to evaluate user gestures for UX designers. In: Marcus, A., Wang, W. (eds.) HCII 2019. LNCS, vol. 11584, pp. 121–133. Springer, Cham (2019). https://doi.org/10.1007/978-3-030-23541-3_10

Bradley, M.M., Lang, P.J.: Measuring emotion: the self-assessment manikin and the semantic differential. J. Behav. Ther. Exp. Psychiatry 25(1), 49–59 (1994)

Braithwaite, J.J., Watson, D.G., Jones, R., Rowe, M.: A guide for analyzing electrodermal activity (EDA) & skin conductance responses (SCRs) for psychological experiments. Psychophysiology 49(1), 1017–1034 (2013)

Brocke, J.V., Riedl, R., Léger, P.M.: Application strategies for neuroscience in information systems design science research. J. Comput. Inf. Syst. 53(3), 1–13 (2013)

Brown, J.D.: What issues affect Likert-scale questionnaire formats. Shiken JALT Test. Eval. SIG Newslett. 4(1), 27–30 (2000)

Burns, N., Grove, S.K.: The Practice of Nursing Research: Conduct, Critique and Utilization. Elsevier, Amsterdam (2005)

Bethel, C.L., Salomon, K., Murphy, R.R., Burke, J.L.: Survey of psychophysiology measurements applied to human-robot interaction. In: 16th IEEE International Symposium on Robot & Human Interactive Communication (2007)

Nass, C.: Wired for Speech: How Voice Activates and Advances the Human-Computer Relationship. MIT Press, Cambridge (2005)

Cohn, J.F., Kanade, T.: Use of automated facial image analysis for measurement of emotion expression. In: Handbook of Emotion Elicitation and Assessment, pp. 222–238 (2007)

Courtemanche, F., Léger, P.-M., Dufresne, A., Fredette, M., Labonté-LeMoyne, É., Sénécal, S.: Physiological heatmaps: a tool for visualizing users' emotional reactions. Multimedia Tools Appl. 77(9), 11547–11574 (2018)

Danner, L., Sidorkina, L., Joechl, M., Duerrschmid, K.: Make a face! Implicit and explicit measurement of facial expressions elicited by orange juices using face reading technology. Food Qual. Prefer. 32, 167–172 (2014)

De Guinea, A.O., Titah, R., Leger, P.M.: Explicit and implicit antecedents of users' behavioral beliefs in information systems: a neuropsychological investigation. J. Manag. Inf. Syst. 30(4), 179–210 (2014)

Guinea, D., Ortiz, A., Titah, R., Léger, P.-M.: Measure for measure: a two study multi-trait multimethod investigation of construct validity in IS research. Comput. Hum. Behav. 29(3), 833–844 (2013)

De Singly, F.: Le questionnaire, 4th edn. Armand Colin, Paris (2016)

Dirican, A.C., Göktürk, M.: Psychophysiological measures of human cognitive states applied in human-computer interaction. Procedia Comput. Sci. 3, 1361–1367 (2011)

Easwara Moorthy, A., Vu, K.-P.L.: Privacy concerns for use of voice activated personal assistant in the public space. Int. J. Hum.-Comput. Interact. 31(4), 307–335 (2015)

Ekman, P.: Facial expression and emotion. Am. Psychol. 48(4), 384 (1993)

Ekman, P., Keltner, D.: Universal facial expressions of emotion. In: Segerstrale, U., Molnar, P. (eds.) Nonverbal Communication: Where Nature Meets Culture, pp. 27–46. Lawrence Erlbaum Associates, Inc., Mahwah (1997)

Fonteyn, M.E., Kuipers, B., Grobe, S.J.: A description of think aloud method and protocol analysis. Qual. Health Res. 3(4), 430–441 (1993)

Georges, V., Courtemanche, F., Sénécal, S., Léger, P.M., Nacke, L., Pourchon, R.: The adoption of psychophysiological measures as an evaluation tool in UX. In: International Conference on HCI in Business, Government, and Organizations, pp. 90–98. Springer, Cham, July 2017

Giroux-Huppé, C., Sénécal, S., Fredette, M., Chen, S.L., Demolin, B., Léger, P.-M.: Identifying psychophysiological pain points in the online user journey: the case of online grocery. In: Marcus, A., Wang, W. (eds.) HCII 2019. LNCS, vol. 11586, pp. 459–473. Springer, Cham (2019). https://doi.org/10.1007/978-3-030-23535-2_34

Jiang, J., et al.: Automatic online evaluation of intelligent assistants. In: Proceedings of the 24th International Conference on World Wide Web - WWW 2015. Presented at the 24th International Conference (2015). https://doi.org/10.1145/2736277.2741669

Lamontagne, C., et al.: User test: how many users are needed to find the psychophysiological pain points in a journey map? In: Ahram, T., Taiar, R., Colson, S., Choplin, A. (eds.) IHIET 2019. AISC, vol. 1018, pp. 136–142. Springer, Cham (2020). https://doi.org/10.1007/978-3-030-25629-6_22

Lane, R.D., Chua, P.M., Dolan, R.J.: Common effects of emotional valence, arousal and attention on neural activation during visual processing of pictures. Neuropsychologia 37(9), 989–997 (1999)

Lau, J., Zimmerman, B., Schaub, F.: Alexa, are you listening? Privacy perceptions, concerns and privacy-seeking behaviors with smart speakers. In: Proceedings of the ACM on Human-Computer Interaction, vol. 2, no. CSCW, pp. 1–311 (2018)

Léger, P.-M., Courtemanche, F., Fredette, M., Sénécal, S.: A cloud-based lab management and analytics software for triangulated human-centered research. In: Davis, F.D., Riedl, R., vom Brocke, J., Léger, P.-M., Randolph, A.B. (eds.) Information Systems and Neuroscience. LNISO, vol. 29, pp. 93–99. Springer, Cham (2019). https://doi.org/10.1007/978-3-030-01087-4_11

Léger, P.M.,Davis, F.D., Cronan, T.P., Perret, J.:Neuropsychophysiological correlates of cognitive absorption in an enactive training context. Comput. Hum. Behav. 34, 273–283 (2014)

Léger, P.-M., Charland, P., Sénécal, S., Cyr, S.: Predicting properties of cognitive pupillometry in human–computer interaction: a preliminary investigation. In: Davis, F.D., Riedl, R., vom Brocke, J., Léger, P.-M., Randolph, A.B. (eds.) Information Systems and Neuroscience. LNISO, vol. 25, pp. 121–127. Springer, Cham (2018). https://doi.org/10.1007/978-3-319-67431-5_14

Lopatovska, I., Oropeza, H.: User interactions with "Alexa" in public academic space. Proc. Assoc. Inf. Sci. Technol. 55(1), 309–318 (2018). https://doi.org/10.1002/pra2.2018.14505501034

Lopatovska, I., Williams, H.: Personification of the Amazon Alexa: BFF or a mindless companion. In: Proceedings of the 2018 Conference on Human Information Interaction & Retrieval, pp. 265–268. ACM, March 2018

Lourties, S., Léger, P.-M., Sénécal, S., Fredette, M., Chen, S.L.: Testing the convergent validity of continuous self-perceived measurement systems: an exploratory study. In: Nah, F.F.-H., Xiao, B.S. (eds.) HCIBGO 2018. LNCS, vol. 10923, pp. 132–144. Springer, Cham (2018). https://doi.org/10.1007/978-3-319-91716-0_11

Maunier, B., et al.: Keep calm and read the instructions: factors for successful user equipment setup. In: Nah, F.F.-H., Xiao, B.S. (eds.) HCIBGO 2018. LNCS, vol. 10923, pp. 372–381. Springer, Cham (2018). https://doi.org/10.1007/978-3-319-91716-0_29

Dawson, M.E., Schell, A.M., Filion, D.L.: The electrodermal system. In: Cacioppo, J.T., Tassinary, L.G., Berntson, G.G. (eds.) Handbook of Psychophysiology, vol. 2. Cambridge University Press, Cambridge (2000)

Nicholl, H.: Diaries as a method of data collection in research. Paediatr. Care 22(7), 16–20 (2010). https://doi.org/10.7748/paed2010.09.22.7.16.c7948

Noldus FaceReader methodology. https://info.noldus.com/free-white-paper-on-facereader-methodology

Petrock, V.: Voice Assistant Use Reaches Critical Mass. Retrieved from e-Marketer database, 15 August 2019

Piedmont, R.L.: Social desirability bias. In: Encyclopedia of Quality of Life and Well-Being Research, pp. 6036–6037 (2014). https://doi.org/10.1007/978-94-007-0753-5_2746

Riedl, R., Fischer, T., Léger, P.-M., Davis, F.: A decade of NeuroIS research: progress, challenges, and future directions. Data Base Adv. Inf. Syst. **51** (2020, in press)

Rowe, D.W., Sibert, J., Irwin, D.: Heart rate variability: indicator of user state as an aid to human-computer interaction. In: Proceedings of the SIGCHI Conference on Human Factors in Computing Systems, pp. 480–487. ACM Press/Addison-Wesley Publishing Co, January 1998

Sciuto, A., Saini, A., Forlizzi, J., Hong, J.I.: Hey Alexa, what's up? In: Proceedings of the 2018 on Designing Interactive Systems Conference 2018 - DIS 2018. Presented at the 2018 (2018). https://doi.org/10.1145/3196709.3196772

Sirois, S., Brisson, J.: Pupillometry. Wiley Interdisc. Rev. Cogn. Sci. **5**(6), 679–692 (2014)

Tung, L.: Amazon: We sold tens of millions of Echo devices in 2018, and Alexa has now 70 000 skills. Retrieved from ZDnet database, 20 December 2018

Vom Brocke, J., Hevner, A., Léger, P.M., Walla, P., Riedl, R.: Advancing a NeuroIS research agenda with four areas of societal contributions. Eur. J. Inf. Syst. **29**, 9–24 (2020)

Xiong, J., Zuo, M.: What does existing NeuroIS research focus on? Inf. Syst. **89**, 101462 (2020). https://doi.org/10.1016/j.is.2019.101462

Zaman, B., Shrimpton-Smith, T.: The FaceReader: measuring instant fun of use. In: Proceedings of the 4th Nordic Conference on Human-Computer Interaction: Changing Roles, Chicago, pp. 457–460. ACM, October 2006

D'Mello, S., Calvo, R.A.: Beyond the basic emotions: what should affective computing compute? In: CHI 2013 Extended Abstracts on Human Factors in Computing Systems, pp. 2287–2294 (2013)

Heiden, M., Lyskov, E., Djupsjöbacka, M., Hellström, F., Crenshaw, A.G.: Effects of time pressure and precision demands during computer mouse work on muscle oxygenation and position sense. Eur. J. Appl. Physiol. **94**(1–2), 97–106 (2005)

Leite, I., Henriques, R., Martinho, C., Paiva, A.: Sensors in the wild: exploring electrodermal activity in child-robot interaction. In: 2013 8th ACM/IEEE International Conference on Human-Robot Interaction (HRI), pp. 41–48. IEEE, March 2013

Boucsein, W.: Electrodermal Activity, 2nd edn. Springer, Boston (2012). https://doi.org/10.1007/978-1-4614-1126-0

Russell, J.A.: Core affect and the psychological construction of emotion. Psychol. Rev. **110**(1), 145 (2003)

Deng, L., Poole, M.S.: Affect in web interfaces: a study of the impacts of web page visual complexity and order. MIS Q, 711–730 (2010)

Dijksterhuis, A., Smith, P.K., Van Baaren, R.B., Wigboldus, D.H.: The unconscious consumer: effects of environment on consumer behavior. J. Consum. Psychol. **15**(3), 193–202 (2005)

Garg, R., Moreno, C.: Exploring everyday sharing practices of smart speakers. In: IUI Workshops, January 2019

Porcheron, M., Fischer, J.E., Reeves, S., Sharples, S.: Voice interfaces in everyday life. In: Proceedings of the 2018 CHI Conference on Human Factors in Computing Systems, pp. 1–12 April 2018

Riedl, R., Léger, P.M.: Fundamentals of NeuroIS. Studies in Neuroscience, Psychology and Behavioral Economics. Springer, Heidelberg (2016). https://doi.org/10.1007/978-3-662-45091-8

Comparing the User Preferences Towards Emotional Voice Interaction Applied on Different Devices: An Empirical Study

Qinglin Liao, Shanshan Zhang, Mei Wang[✉], Jia Li, Xinrong Wang, and Xuemei Deng

School of Mechanical Engineering, Sichuan University, Chengdu 610065, China
sc_wm@263.net

Abstract. Voice interaction has been widely used. Designers hope to use artificial intelligence technology to create humanlike voice assistants, which not only help users handle the daily chores, but also provide emotional support and communication. Voice interaction has been utilized for both mobile and home automation, and many researchers have studied the emotional voice interaction of various devices. As different voice interaction products have diversified orientations and the functions integrated in them varies, users may prefer to use them under different operating conditions or interaction modes. This paper chooses mobile phone voice assistant and smart home voice assistant as study subjects, representing mobile and stand-alone voice assistant respectively. A 2 (voice assistant type: mobile phone assistant V.S. smart home assistant) × 3 (interaction level: low V.S. medium, V.S. high) between-subjects experiment was conducted. Then the influences of different devices and voice interaction modes on user emotional experience were discussed. Thus it provides reference and guidance for the voice interaction design of corresponding products.

Keywords: Voice interaction · Mobile phone voice assistant · Smart home voice assistant · Emotional design · Human-computer interaction · User experience

1 Introduction

In the past few years, the Internet and various intelligent technologies have been developing vigorously, and intelligent human-computer interactions continue to spring up with the advent of manifold new sensors. As the intelligent terminals rapidly popularized, intelligent voice interaction has played an important role in the Internet era. Since it is the most natural way of human communication, voice has more advantages in the interaction with machines. It can lower the threshold for users, reduce the time and cost of learning, and free the operator's hands. The development of voice interaction technology has led human-computer interaction into a new stage. Traditional graphical user interface (GUI) has been extended to voice user interface (VUI), which has been widely

---

The first two authors Liao and Zhang are designated as co-first authors of this article.

© Springer Nature Switzerland AG 2020
M. Kurosu (Ed.): HCII 2020, LNCS 12182, pp. 209–220, 2020.
https://doi.org/10.1007/978-3-030-49062-1_14

used in product design and interaction design [1, 2]. Intelligent voice assistant is one of the typical applications regarding voice interaction. Virtual personal assistants in mobile terminals like Apple's Siri, Microsoft's Cortana, or Samsung's S-voice are commonly used. And conversational agents integrated in home automations or other stand-alone devices like Amazon Echo or Google home are also prevailing. Voice interaction is gradually entering people's lives, making the application scenarios of voice interaction technology more common and enriching the interactive experience.

Voice conversation is the most convenient and natural way of communication among people. In addition to semantic information, there is also a lot of emotional information in voice. As for voice interaction, emotional information conveyed by voice and language has a profound impact on user experience. Norman [3] integrated cognitive psychology and depicted emotional design in three levels: the visceral, behavioral and reflective level. These levels interact with each other. In terms of voice interaction, the sound and character in the visceral level and the interaction in behavior level are usually unified. The visceral level will leave users a psychological expectation and impression for the behavior level, while the design of the behavior level will also conversely strengthen the characteristics of the visceral level. Also, the interaction in behavior level can create emotions and experiences in the reflective level. And the reflective level will then give feedback to the behavior level during the interaction process between user and the product, promoting more interactive behaviors.

However, there are some differences between diverse voice interaction products and their own levels. Different designs, especially those in the interaction aspect, may create various emotional experiences. Therefore, this study takes mobile phone voice assistant and smart home voice assistant as research subjects. An experiment was conducted to explore the voice interactions and emotional designs of different devices.

2   Related Works

2.1   Emotional Voice Interaction

Most people prefer sounds that were more natural [4]. Studies on human-computer emotional interaction and emotional voice interaction initially focused on pattern recognition and affective computing [5–7]. The "emotion" of a robot was synthesized through algorithm and a variety of emotion model, and then conveyed to the user via voice, text, or facial expression, which focused more on the basic properties of sound like frequency, duration, quality and clarity. However, with the development and application of deep neural network and concatenative speech synthesis technology, the research scope of voice interaction is no longer limited to the naturalness and flexibility of speech synthesis, but pays more attention to emotional expression in human-computer interaction [8, 9]. Xue et al. [10] developed a speech synthesis system that could convert neutral voice into voice with various degrees of emotions.

Users can have better impressions on conversational agents when emotions were added appropriately into the dialogue [11]. Niculescu et al. [12] concluded that for service-oriented social robots, humor and compassion were needed for improving their affections and user participations, and a high-pitched voice can convey more "emotions". Braun et al. [13] concluded that when drivers were in an angry or sad mood, an empathic voice assistant may help. Bickmore et al. [14] found that voice assistants can better accomplish tasks through small talk and conversational storytelling, which can also help with building trust and relationship with users.

From a user-centered perspective, emotional interaction involves two dimensions: the emotion conveyed by the robot to the user, and the emotional feedback from the user. The former is embodied in perceived social support and perceived emotional support, while the latter is embodied in the subjective emotional representation of users during the interaction. Some researches on emotional design of voice interaction try to convey emotions through personality or basic attributes of voice [12, 15–17], and some also adopt different response strategies by monitoring user's emotions [14, 18, 19]. Corresponding to the three levels of emotional design proposed by Norman [3], the visceral level could set an emotional tone for users, and the behavior level could improve user experience in emotional interaction by affecting the reflective level.

2.2 Emotional Design of Different Voice Assistants

As one of the most common applications of voice interaction, the design of intelligent voice assistants has long become a hot topic for studies. Many researches combined different types of voice assistants together [8, 14, 20, 21], in order to draw a general conclusion. But more research focuses on a specific type of intelligent voice assistant, among which mobile terminal and home automation are most frequently discussed.

Carolus et al. [22] found that smartphone voice assistants that responded politely were rated higher than those responded impolitely. Through interviews and observations with human senior assistants, Ghosh et al. [23] concluded that smartphone voice assistants should be controllable, expressive, and rapid in response, and need to show some empathy for user's emotions at the same time. Luge et al. [24] interviewed with experienced users of Siri and Google Now, and found that there was a huge gap between user expectations for interacting with the voice assistant and their actual experiences. Users were reluctant to use their mobile phone voice assistants for complex or sensitive activities.

Lopatovska et al. [25] collected some user data about Alexa usage and found that the interaction experience of Alexa was more important to users than the content of interaction output. Lutfi et al. [26] found that adding emotions into the design of domestic voice assistants can effectively reduce users' frustrations and improve user satisfaction. Purington et al. [27] drew on user reviews of the Echo that were published to Amazon.com. The study showed that the personification level of the device can predict user satisfaction, and that users who rated Echo as highly personified reported more social interactions with it. Sun et al. [18] studied how smart speakers alleviated users' sadness with tone and interaction strategies, and improved user experience through empathic care. Ge et al. [19] found that when a smart speaker made a mistake, it was necessary to apologize to the user as soon as possible and not to be humorous; otherwise it would appear insincere and cause negative emotions of the user.

Thus it leaves a question whether these conclusions can be generalized, or is there any difference between the designs of different voice assistants? The main factors influencing user satisfaction of intelligent voice assistants differ in situations, and the property and complexity of the current task can also affect user satisfaction [28]. Braun et al. [15] found that even in car driving scenarios, users had different preferences for interaction when they used the voice assistant for distinct functions. The perceived usefulness and pleasure of virtual assistants have a significant impact on whether users are willing to use them [29]. Different types of products vary in functions and usage scenarios, and the highlight of perceived usefulness and usability design may not be the same. For different kinds of voice assistants, user preferences of interaction design and emotional design may vary as well. Therefore, the following hypotheses are proposed:

H1: User satisfaction of varying kinds of voice assistants differ in the extent to interaction levels;

H2: Perceived emotional support of varying kinds of voice assistants differ in the extent to interaction levels;

H3: Users' emotional feedback for varying kinds of voice assistants differ in the extent to interaction levels.

3 Method

3.1 Experiment Design

In this study, a 2 (voice assistant type: mobile phone assistant V.S. smart home assistant) × 3 (interaction level: low V.S. medium, V.S. high) between-subjects experiment was conducted. The voice assistants of different interaction levels only differed in conversational patterns and dialogue scripts, while the tone and volume of each voice assistant remained the same. The AI persona of each voice assistant is shown in Table 1. To avoid the subjective evaluations of participants getting disturbed by certain kinds of tasks, the scripts contain both entertainment and task-oriented dialogues.

Table 1. AI persona of voice assistants.

Name of the assistants	Interaction level	Interactive features
Xiaoyu	Low	With warm tips, no supplementary recommendation, no initiating dialogue, and no relevant information recording
Xiaoxue	Medium	With warm tips, supplementary recommendation, no initiating dialogue, and with relevant information recording
Xiaobai	High	With warm tips, supplementary recommendation, initiating dialogue, and relevant information recording

The voice assistants used in the experiment were developed with the automatic speech recognition and speech synthesis technology supported by Baidu, and the natural language processing technology supported by Turing Robot. The graphic user interface of the mobile phone assistants was designed utilizing Adobe Photoshop. Combing with the Wizard of Oz technique, the experiment was conducted in a studio where a homey mood was created.

3.2 Pre-test

The purpose of the pre-test, on the one hand, was to test the naturalness and fluency of the scripts avoiding irrelevant factors affecting the subjective assessments of participants, and to check the setting of each experimental group and questionnaire items on the other.

Firstly, an experienced user and a voice interaction expert were invited to verify whether the dialogue scripts were fluent and in harmony with the scenarios. Secondly, five users joined to help modify the experiment design and questionnaires until the experiment operators (wizards) could complete the operations smoothly and all users could distinguish the experimental groups from different interaction levels.

3.3 Participants

76 participants were recruited, aging from 18 to 30. They were also interested in new technology, which matches with the characteristics of the target users of voice interaction.

3.4 Procedure

As mentioned above, there were six experimental groups, and all participants were assigned randomly to one group. The whole experiment mainly consisted of three parts. Firstly, a small talk was made to help the participants get familiar with the basic operations and ease their anxiety, and some basic information of participants was collected.

Secondly, a scenario was given to the participants depicting that they were going to Shanghai for business the next day. And then they were invited to perform specific tasks, including 3 entertainment tasks and 3 work-related tasks, such as setting an alarm, checking the weather, setting a reminder, searching for local food and playing music. All of these tasks are frequently used in intelligent voice assistant [30, 31], and they are all linked with one another. For example, if you tell the voice assistant that you are going to Shanghai where the temperature will be a bit lower the next day, when you check the weather of Shanghai, the assistant may kindly remind you to bring more clothes when departing. The dialogue samples are shown in Table 2. No matter whether the assistant

Table 2. Dialogue samples.

Identity	Script
User	What's the weather in Shanghai tomorrow?
Xiaoyu	Shanghai will be fine tomorrow with light rain and breeze, with a minimum temperature of 15 degrees and a maximum temperature of 20 degrees. Don't forget to bring an umbrella
Xiaoxue	Shanghai will be fine tomorrow with light rain and breeze, with a minimum temperature of 15 degrees and a maximum temperature of 20 degrees. Remember to bring an umbrella and more clothes when departing
Xiaobai	Shanghai will be fine tomorrow with light rain and breeze, with a minimum temperature of 15 degrees and a maximum temperature of 20 degrees. Don't forget to bring an umbrella. Do you need me to remind you to bring more clothes?

was integrated in mobile phone or smart home, the experiment tasks and dialogue scripts kept the same. The order of entertainment tasks and work-related tasks were random.

After finishing the tasks, participants would fill out a questionnaire rated mainly on seven-point Likert scale. Measurement items included the satisfaction of the voice assistant, perceived anthropomorphism, perceived emotional support and users' emotional feedback.

Finally, a semi-structured interview was conducted to gather more information about this experiment, including the reasons why they liked or disliked the voice assistant; whether they would use this assistant in certain circumstances; the subjective perception of task duration and their engagements, etc.

4 Results

4.1 Preliminary Analysis

In all, 76 valid questionnaire responses were collected (M: F = 1:1), aged between 18 and 30. All of them were college students who were familiar with voice interaction products. A majority of the participants had used intelligent voice assistant for more than 3 months.

The Cronbach's alpha coefficient of the questionnaire data all reached 0.8, which indicated that the items had relatively high internal consistency, and the reliability of the questionnaire was considered acceptable. Meanwhile, each group of data satisfied the homogeneity of variance assumption. Thus further analysis could be conducted.

4.2 Hypotheses Testing

According to the experimental design and preliminary analysis, two-way ANOVA was conducted to analyze the data of each experimental group.

The descriptive statistics of user satisfaction are shown in Table 3. The results showed that, for user satisfaction, the main effect of voice assistant type was not significant ($p = 0.254 > 0.05$). And the main effect of interaction level was not significant ($p = 0.123 > 0.05$). But there was a significant interaction effect ($p < 0.001$). Neither the user satisfactions of different voice assistants nor those of different interaction levels showed significant difference. For varying interaction levels of different voice assistants, however, there were significant differences in user satisfaction, as shown in Fig. 1. Therefore, hypothesis 1 was supported.

The simple effect analysis of the interaction effect showed that there was a significant difference between the two types of voice assistants with the low interaction level in user satisfaction ($p = 0.380 < 0.05$). And the two assistants with the high interaction level were also significantly different in user satisfaction ($p < 0.001$). While the difference between the assistants of medium interaction level was not significant ($p = 0.747 > 0.05$).

The descriptive statistics of perceived emotional support are shown in Table 4. There was no significant difference in perceived emotional support among different types of voice assistants ($p = 0.218 > 0.05$), but the main effect of interaction level was significant ($p < 0.001$). And a significant interaction effect was verified ($p = 0.003 < 0.05$). For

Table 3. Descriptive statistics of user satisfaction

Voice assistant type	Interaction level	M (S.D)	N
Mobile phone voice assistant	Low (Xiao Yu)	5.520 (0.530)	14
	Medium (Xiao Xue)	5.726 (1.005)	12
	High (Xiao Bai)	4.631 (1.244)	12
			Total 38
Smart home assistant	Low (Xiao Yu)	4.806 (0.889)	14
	Medium (Xiao Xue)	5.612 (0.968)	14
	High (Xiao Bai)	6.171 (0.409)	10
			Total 38

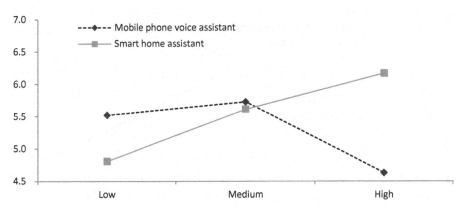

Fig. 1. Interaction profile plot of user satisfaction.

varying interaction levels of different voice assistants, user perceptions of emotional support showed significant differences, as shown in Fig. 2, thus supported hypothesis 2.

The simple effect analysis of the interaction effect showed that the difference of perceived emotional support between different types of voice assistants with the high interaction level was very significant (p < 0.001). There was no significant difference between voice assistants with the low interaction level (p = 0.248 > 0.05), and those with the medium interaction level also showed no significant difference (p = 0.278 > 0.05).

The descriptive statistics of emotional feedback are shown in Table 5. Regarding user's emotional feedback, the main effect of voice assistant type was not significant (p = 0.676 > 0.05), nor was interaction level (p = 0.075 > 0.05), but their interaction effect was significant (p < 0.001). In other words, for different interaction levels of different voice assistants, the emotional feedback form user had a significant difference, as shown in Fig. 3. So that hypothesis 3 was supported.

According to the simple effect analysis of the interaction effect, the voice assistants with a lower interaction level were significantly different in the emotional feedback from users (p = 0.001). And assistants with a higher interaction level were also significantly

Table 4. Descriptive statistics of perceived emotional support

Voice assistant type	Interaction level	M (S.D)	N
Mobile phone voice assistant	Low (Xiao Yu)	5.410 (0.648)	14
	Medium (Xiao Xue)	6.188 (0.978)	12
	High (Xiao Bai)	5.125 (1.170)	12
			Total 38
Smart home assistant	Low (Xiao Yu)	5.036 (0.831)	14
	Medium (Xiao Xue)	5.821 (0.857)	14
	High (Xiao Bai)	6.600 (0.357)	10
			Total 38

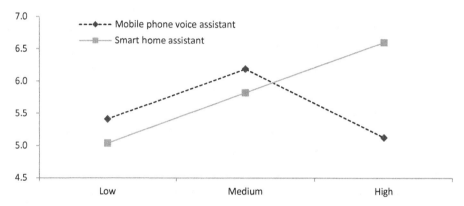

Fig. 2. Interaction profile plot of perceived emotional support.

different (p < 0.001). While the assistants with the medium interaction level showed no significant difference (p = 0.652 > 0.05).

In addition, intelligent voice assistants with different interaction levels showed significant differences in terms of perceived anthropomorphism, but the interaction effect was not significant.

5   Discussion

The analyses of experimental data prove that all three hypotheses proposed previously are supported. With the increase of interaction level, the user satisfaction, perceived emotional support and emotional feedback of smart home voice assistants were rated higher. But these trends are not coincident with those of mobile phone voice assistants. When voice assistant with the low interaction level (Xiaoyu) was applied on the smart home product, user satisfaction is significantly lower than when it was applied on the mobile phone. While the user satisfaction of the voice assistant with high interaction level

Table 5. Descriptive statistics of emotional feedback

Voice assistant type	Interaction level	M (S.D)	N
Mobile phone voice assistant	Low (Xiao Yu)	6.595 (0.456)	14
	Medium (Xiao Xue)	6.652 (0.539)	12
	High (Xiao Bai)	5.791 (0.899)	12
			Total 38
Smart home assistant	Low (Xiao Yu)	5.761 (0.976)	14
	Medium (Xiao Xue)	6.536 (0.486)	14
	High (Xiao Bai)	6.933 (0.086)	10
			Total 38

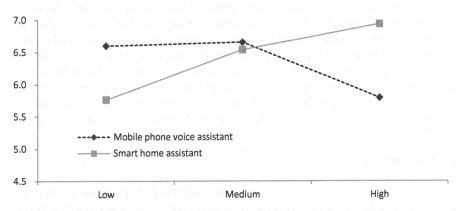

Fig. 3. Interaction profile plot of emotional feedback.

(Xiaobai) applied on the smart home product was significantly higher than that applied on the mobile phone. The voice assistant with a medium interaction level (Xiaoxue) performed well in both types of devices, and the differences of all measurement items were not significant.

Combing with users' comments on each group of voice assistants and the interviews after the experiment, "Xiaoyu" can accomplish user's instructions and provides appropriate warm tips, but will not recommend or respond with supplementary information for users. For mobile terminal users, although the perceived emotional support of it is rather low, it can still satisfy the basic needs of users and finish tasks efficiently, thus achieving better user satisfaction and emotional feedback. But for smart home users, voice assistant with the low level of interaction seems to be a bit disappointing. They considered it "just answer a question and then nothing", "sounds inflexible", "lack of vitality", and they expected it to be capable of more communication.

In addition to completing basic commands, "Xiaoxue" can also provide information that may be needed in the context, which makes it more vivid than "Xiaoyu". Therefore, it was rated highly in both types of devices. The function that it recorded the previous dialogue was generally praised by the participants as "considerate and practical". But there were also some users who thought it was "a little talkative", "machinelike" and "wish it can be more interesting".

"Xiao bai", the voice assistant with a higher interaction level, owns another function of initiating dialogue on the basis of the former voice assistants, which will guide users to continue the current conversation. Users from the mobile phone group showed some resistance towards it, complaining that "it talks too much" and "it is a waste of time". During the experiment, some participants even interrupted the voice assistant repeatedly. Most users from the smart home group, however, said "it is nice of it to remind me something I haven't thought about or have forgotten ". And they expressed strong desires to engage in such communication, even expecting that "the personality of the voice assistant can be more distinctive and interesting".

The difference between a mobile phone voice assistant and a smart home voice assistant lies in the different entities that carry them. For such products as mobile phones, voice is not the major way humans interact with them. Users will use many other functions in a smart phone, so the efficiency of voice interaction may be more important for a mobile phone user. While for stand-alone products, such as home automations, voice has become the main way and even the only way of interaction, and their functions are relatively concentrated and simple. In other words, the mobile phone voice assistant is more like an accessory of the product, while the smart home assistant creates an impression that it represents the product itself. Therefore, in terms of voice interaction and emotional experience, users have different expectations and preferences for these two products.

6 Conclusions

The results of the experiment show that users have different preferences and perceptions for the interaction of mobile phone voice assistant and smart home voice assistant. Users expect the mobile voice assistants to complete tasks concisely and efficiently, and could expand the answers properly or record relevant information. But users don't want them to initiate a conversation. As a result for smart home assistants, users are inclined to communicate with them the way real people do, and wish to gather more interactions and emotional communications.

Therefore, there should be particular focus on interaction design, especially emotional interaction for different intelligent voice assistant designs, which cannot be generalized. Otherwise, it is liable to lose the positive impressions from users, and even result in some negative emotions. Meanwhile, some users in the experiment have different preferences from what most people have. And even in the majority groups, there are also slight individual differences. Each user has his or her own judgement about emotional interaction, and it should be taken into account. That's why personalization is encouraged in voice interaction design and intelligent voice assistant design.

Although the fixed and default design paradigm will not make any mistakes, it can no longer meet the deeper emotional needs of users and their desires for novelty. Designers wish to pursue the ultimate user experience to make their products more competitive. But it requires specific analysis to significantly improve the usability and ease of use for products, as well as the experience in emotions.

References

1. Tucker, P., Jones, D.M.: Voice as interface: an overview. Int. J. Hum. Comput. Interact. **3**(2), 145–170 (1991)
2. Porcheron, M., Fischer, J.E., Reeves, S., Sharples, S.: Voice interfaces in everyday life. In: Conference on Human Factors in Computing Systems - Proceedings of CHI 2018, pp. 1–12. ACM (2018)
3. Norman, D.A.: Emotional Design: Why We Love (or Hate) Everyday Things. Basic Books, New York (2004)
4. Romportl, J.: Speech synthesis and uncanny valley. In: Sojka, P., Horák, A., Kopeček, I., Pala, K. (eds.) TSD 2014. LNCS (LNAI), vol. 8655, pp. 595–602. Springer, Cham (2014). https://doi.org/10.1007/978-3-319-10816-2_72
5. Chen, L., Su, W., Feng, Y., Wu, M., She, J., Hirota, K.: Two-layer fuzzy multiple random forest for speech emotion recognition in human-robot interaction. Inf. Sci. **509**, 150–163 (2020)
6. Xie, Y., Liang, R., Liang, Z., Huang, C., Zou, C., Schuller, B.: Speech emotion classification using attention-based LSTM. IEEE/ACM Trans. Audio Speech Lang. Process. **27**(11), 1675–1685 (2019)
7. Tebbi, H., Hamadouche, M., Azzoune, H.: TTS-SA (A text-to-speech system based on Standard Arabic). In: 4th International Conference on Digital Information and Communication Technology and its Applications, DICTAP 2014, pp. 337–341. IEEE Press, Bangkok (2014)
8. Becker, C., Kopp, S., Wachsmuth, I.: Why emotions should be integrated into conversational agents. In: Conversational Informatics: An Engineering Approach, pp. 49–67. Wiley (2007)
9. Torrey, C., Fussell, S.R., Kiesler, S.: How a robot should give advice. In: 8th ACM/IEEE International Conference on Human-Robot Interaction (HRI), pp. 275–282. IEEE Press (2013)
10. Xue, Y., Hamada, Y., Akagi, M.: Voice conversion for emotional speech: rule-based synthesis with degree of emotion controllable in dimensional space. Speech Commun. **102**, 54–67 (2018)
11. Kase, T., Nose, T., Ito, A.: On appropriateness and estimation of the emotion of synthesized response speech in a spoken dialogue system. In: Stephanidis, C. (ed.) HCI 2015. CCIS, vol. 528, pp. 747–752. Springer, Cham (2015). https://doi.org/10.1007/978-3-319-21380-4_126
12. Niculescu, A., Dijk, B., Nijholt, A., Li, H., See, S.L.: Making social robots more attractive: the effects of voice pitch, humor and empathy. Int. J. Soc. Robot. **5**(2), 171–191 (2013)
13. Braun, M., Schubert, J., Pfleging, B., Alt, F.: Improving driver emotions with affective strategies. Multimodal Technol. Interact. **3**(1), 21 (2019)
14. Bickmore, T.W., Cassell, J.: Small talk and conversational storytelling in embodied interface agents. In: Proceedings of the AAAI Fall Symposium on Narrative Intelligence, pp. 87–92 (1999)
15. Braun, M., Mainz, A., Chadowitz, R., Pfleging, B., Alt, F: At your service: designing voice assistant personalities to improve automotive user interfaces a real world driving study. In: Conference on Human Factors in Computing Systems - Proceedings of CHI 2019. ACM, New York (2019)
16. Ehrenbrink, P., Osman, S., Möller, S.: Google now is for the extraverted, Cortana for the introverted: investigating the influence of personality on IPA preference. In: 29th Australian Conference on Human-Computer Interaction, pp. 257–265. ACM, New York (2017)
17. Doyle, P.R., Edwards, J., Dumbleton, O., Clark, L., Cowan, B.R.: Mapping perceptions of humanness in intelligent personal assistant interaction. In: 21st International Conference on Human-Computer Interaction with Mobile Devices and Services, MobileHCI 2019. ACM, New York (2019)
18. Sun, Y., et al.: Attempts to leverage interaction design to mimic emotional care and empathy-based feedback on smart speakers. In: Rau, P.-L.P. (ed.) HCII 2019. LNCS, vol. 11577, pp. 354–369. Springer, Cham (2019). https://doi.org/10.1007/978-3-030-22580-3_26

19. Ge, X., Li, D., Guan, D., Xu, S., Sun, Y., Zhou, M.: Do smart speakers respond to their errors properly? A study on human-computer dialogue strategy. In: Marcus, A., Wang, W. (eds.) HCII 2019. LNCS, vol. 11584, pp. 440–455. Springer, Cham (2019). https://doi.org/10.1007/978-3-030-23541-3_32

20. Lee, S.S., Lee, J., Lee, K.P.: Designing intelligent assistant through user participations. In: Proceedings of the 2017 ACM Conference on Designing Interactive Systems, DIS 2017, pp. 173–177. ACM, New York (2017)

21. Jiang, J., et al.: Automatic online evaluation of intelligent assistants. In: 24th International Conference on World Wide Web, WWW 2015, pp. 506–516. ACM (2015)

22. Carolus, A., Muench, R., Schmidt, C., Schneider, F.: Impertinent mobiles - effects of politeness and impoliteness in human-smartphone interaction. Comput. Hum. Behav. **93**, 290–300 (2019)

23. Ghosh, S., Pherwani, J.: Designing of a natural voice assistants for mobile through user centered design approach. In: Kurosu, M. (ed.) HCI 2015. LNCS, vol. 9169, pp. 320–331. Springer, Cham (2015). https://doi.org/10.1007/978-3-319-20901-2_29

24. Luger, E., Sellen, A.: "Like having a really bad PA": the gulf between user expectation and experience of conversational agents. In: Conference on Human Factors in Computing Systems - Proceedings of CHI 2016, pp. 5286–5297. ACM (2016)

25. Lopatovska, I., et al.: Talk to me: exploring user interactions with the Amazon Alexa. J. Librarianship Inform. Sci. **51**(4), 984–997 (2019)

26. Lutfi, S.L., Fernández-Martínez, F., Lorenzo-Trueba, J., Barra-Chicote, R., Montero, J.M.: I feel you: the design and evaluation of a domotic affect-sensitive spoken conversational agent. Sensors **13**(8), 10519–10538 (2013)

27. Purington, A., Taft, J.G., Sannon, S., Bazarova, N.N., Taylor, S.H.: "Alexa is my new BFF": social roles, user satisfaction, and personification of the Amazon Echo. In: Conference on Human Factors in Computing Systems - Proceedings of CHI 2017, vol. Part F127655, pp. 2853–2859. ACM (2017)

28. Kiseleva, J., et al.: Understanding user satisfaction with intelligent assistants. In: Proceedings of the 2016 ACM Conference on Human Information Interaction and Retrieval, CHIIR 2016, pp. 121–130. ACM (2016)

29. Yang, H., Lee, H.: Understanding user behavior of virtual personal assistant devices. IseB **17**(1), 65–87 (2019)

30. Ammari, T., Kaye, J., Tsai, J.Y., Bentley, F.: Music, search, and IoT: how people (really) use voice assistants. ACM Trans. Comput. Hum. Interact. **26**(3) (2019)

31. Sciuto, A., Saini, A., Forlizzi, J., Hong, J.I.: "Hey Alexa, what's up?": studies of in-home conversational agent usage. In: Proceedings of the 2018 Designing Interactive Systems Conference, DIS 2018, pp. 857–868. ACM (2018)

Research on Interaction Design of Artificial Intelligence Mock Interview Application Based on Goal-Directed Design Theory

Yingying Miao, Wenqian Huang, and Bin Jiang[✉]

Nanjing University of Science and Technology, Xiaolingwei 200, Nanjing, Jiangsu, China
398991222@qq.com, 375572014@qq.com, jb508@163.com

Abstract. In recent years, the employment problems confronted with the graduates become a livelihood issue in China. How to build an effective mock interview platform to provide more practical interview experience for graduates is an important direction for employment guidance. The gradual maturity of artificial intelligence technology provides technical support, but in academic research, it still focuses on system architecture design and artificial intelligence algorithm development, and few people have studied the improvement of the system user experience. This paper aims to use the goal-directed design theory to research the applications of artificial intelligence mock interview, identity user goals and needs. Propose interaction design principles and strategies to provide ideas and reference for the future design of such products. First, conduct theoretical research and elaborate related concepts to provide a basic theoretical framework for subsequent research; then, follow the design process provided by goal-directed theory to conduct research, modeling, and requirements construction of mock interview applications; and finally according to the user goals and artificial intelligence application interaction design trends, this paper proposes some principles and strategies of interaction design for artificial intelligence mock interview applications.

Keywords: Goal-directed design theory · Mock interview · Interaction design

1 Introduction

The lack of work experience and job-hunting ability is one of the reasons for the difficulty of employment for college students. Under the situation that the number of college students is increasing year by year and the pressure of job competition is increasing, it is important for college students to practice more in the interview process before applying for a job to improve the success rate. Through mock interviews, job seekers can know where they need to improve, and make adjustments in a short time. At present, some universities have added mock interview activities to their student employment guidance. However, due to the limited time, lack of information and weak pertinence for each position and individual, the activities often fail to achieve the expected results.

© Springer Nature Switzerland AG 2020
M. Kurosu (Ed.): HCII 2020, LNCS 12182, pp. 221–233, 2020.
https://doi.org/10.1007/978-3-030-49062-1_15

A small number of applications have applied artificial intelligence technologies based on natural language processing and deep learning to the interview process. But research still focuses on technology development, and few people have studied the improvement of the system user experience. Therefore, although existing applications can implement functions, the interaction mode is relatively rigid and single. Poor user experience makes users unwilling to use them. Goal-directed theory is often used to guide interaction design and provides scientific processes and methods for interaction design. Based on the design method flow of goal-directed design theory, this paper studies the interaction design of artificial intelligence mock interview application.

2   Research on Goal-Directed Design

2.1   Goal-Directed Design Concepts and Design Processes

Goal-directed design is behavior-oriented design, the purpose of which is to study and satisfy the user's goals and motivations. When designing the interface, it is necessary to pay attention to the goal that the user wants to achieve through the interface operation. A human-machine interface with a good user experience can only be achieved if the user's goals are met. The premise of understanding goal-oriented design is to fully research and understand user goals and how to guide the design of interactive behaviors through the researched user goals [1].

The process of user target recognition is roughly divided into the following six stages: research, modeling, defining requirements, defining frameworks, refinement and support, as shown in Fig. 1 [1]. These phases follow the five components of interaction design: understanding, abstraction, architecture, presentation, and detail.

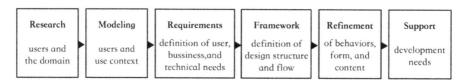

Fig. 1. Goal-directed interaction design process.

2.2   Types and Relationships of User Goals

On the basis of years of cognitive research, Donald A. Norman proposed that the product should solve three different levels of cognitive and emotional processing, namely the visceral, behavioral, and reflective level [2]. Mapping three emotion cognitive processes to user goals to guide the establishment of user models. User goals can be divided into experience goals, ultimate goals and life goals. The relationship model between different targets is shown in Fig. 2 [3].

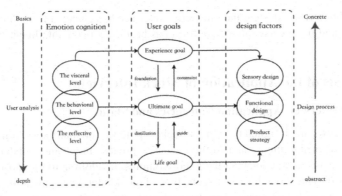

Fig. 2. User target relationship model.

3   Interaction Design in the Context of Artificial Intelligence

The development of interaction design is closely related to interaction technology. Artificial intelligence is one of the important interaction technologies, which has expanded the horizon and dimension of interaction design. Artificial intelligence has played a huge role in pushing forward the breakthrough of product interaction design thinking, the innovation of traditional product interaction forms, the enhancement of emotional interaction between human and machine, the optimization of interactive information architecture, and the expansion of the limitations of traditional interface design [4].

For example, in terms of design thinking, from the need for users to come to input requirements, to actively inquire about user requirements, is a microcosm of the transformation of interactive design thinking in the era of artificial intelligence. In the form of interaction, the earliest input was perforated paper. In the era of keyboard interaction, the command line interface (CLI) has appeared. After that, Apple introduced the graphical user interface (GUI) operating system, and developed the interactive method of touch screen on smart devices. The WYSIWYG input is more in line with human intuition and has become a very important interaction method on mobile devices. As the deep learning algorithms in artificial intelligence have gradually matured, voice and visual-based interactions have become mainstream. As long as you speak to the machine, it can understand what people say and turn into operations. As long as you make some gestures to the camera, the machine can recognize your operation intention. In terms of interactive emotions, traditional human-computer interaction cannot understand and adapt to human moods, and lacks the ability to understand and express emotions. Therefore, it is difficult to expect human-computer interaction to be truly harmonious and natural. In the era of artificial intelligence, it is measured by sensors. User emotion data and autonomous machine learning can recognize the user's emotional state and take corresponding actions to achieve human-machine emotional resonance. In terms of interactive information architecture, artificial intelligence greatly improves the accuracy of the recommendation system, the cost of finding content is reduced. Artificial intelligence can also undertake more complex operations, and the use process will be reduced accordingly. These make the product no longer need a complex architecture to carry different content, and the information architecture becomes flatter. In terms of the expansion of design limitations, the design has gradually realized from "bordered" design to "borderless" design, the interactive interface has changed from "tangible" to "invisible", and the precise interactive form has become a fuzzy intelligent interactive form.

4 Analysis of the Application of Mock Interview

4.1 Mock Interview Application Categories and Status

Mock interviews are designed to help job seekers practice job interviews. It make them clear personal positioning, adapt to the interview process in advance, understand the focus of each link and understand their shortcomings. In addition to the most common form of role-playing mock interviews, one type of mock interview applications is online live-matching mock interviews. This type of application includes online matching of two job applicants to each other using the interview questions provided by the system (such as Pramp), online interview with specialized interviewers (such as gainlo.co) and other forms. Although these applications can simulate real interviews online, according to user feedback, the former has difficulties in matching, and the capabilities of the users are different. The latter has the disadvantages of high prices and cumbersome processes. With the development of artificial intelligence technologies based on natural language processing and deep learning, many companies began to try to use artificial intelligence interview, aiming to free recruiters from highly repetitive tasks prior to recruitment. At the same time, some artificial intelligence mock interview applications have also been generated to help job seekers improve their interview skills. The forms of artificial intelligence mock interview applications that have been developed in China include avatar video interviews, multiple choice interviews and chat-bot interviews, as shown in Fig. 3.

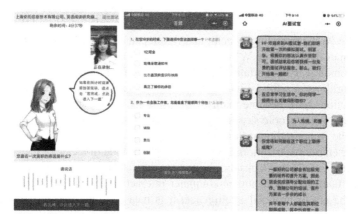

Fig. 3. Representative forms of some artificial intelligence mock interview applications in China.

4.2 Advantages and Disadvantages of Artificial Intelligence Mock Interview

Applying artificial intelligence to the field of mock recruitment interviews is very appropriate. First, artificial intelligence is "on call" and is very suitable for job seekers to start their own exercises anytime, anywhere, without being constrained by space and other people's time. Second, digital feedback can better help job seekers understand their strengths and weaknesses. Artificial intelligence collects data on the interviewer's expressions, language organization, and behavioral patterns during the interview, analyzes the interviewee's potential, career suitability, and lack of interviews, and generates visual reports, which are easy for users to record and reflect. Third, directly using artificial intelligence mock interview can enable candidates to adapt to the situation that more and more companies are now using "artificial intelligence interviewers" in advance. Although the technology is feasible, there are still many problems with existing applications. Multiple choice interviews and chat-bot interviews can only be used for text analysis. I think that it is just a more advanced way to have a "written test", which is difficult to achieve the effect of simulating the real interview scene. At present, the avatar video interview is a better solution, but the use experience still needs to be improved. The interaction is still not natural. Take China's first officially launched AI interview robot "AI RecruiTas" as an example. Camera and microphone are used to collect user data, however, in addition to answering questions, the remaining actions still take the form of touch screen input, and there is no immediate feedback after collecting biological data. It is not smooth enough to use, and it is difficult to stimulate user emotions. Improving system usability and achieving natural interaction will definitely be the future. Studying the interaction design of artificial intelligence mock interview application under this background has great practical guiding significance.

5   Artificial Intelligence Mock Interview Application User Target Recognition

5.1 Research

Subject Matter Experts Interview. Subject matter expert interviews are also known as SME interviews. Experts are authoritative persons in the product's field. They will provide us with valuable views in their professional field. For the field of job interviews, we define the experts as human resources specialists. The purpose of the interview was to understand the company's recruitment process, the length and structure of regular interviews, interview focus and common scoring methods.

In SME interview, two human resources specialists were invited for interviews. They worked for a private enterprise and a state-owned enterprise in China. The results of the interview are summarized in Table 1. This information has a great effect on the overall framework construction of the application.

User Interviews and Experiments. The purpose of user interviews and observations is to initially understand user status, including the user's basic situation and knowledge background, related product use experience, usage scenarios, etc. Collect user information and users' general expectations to facilitate the mining of user emotions.

The target users of the mock interview application are those who may need a job in the near future and need interview practice. Based on the positioning of the product, the interviewees of this paper are five fresh undergraduates, two graduate students, and two workplace freshmen who have worked for 1–2 years and want better job opportunities.

Table 1. Summary of SME interview.

Problem	Summary of results
Corporate recruitment process	Corporate recruitment is divided into campus recruitment and social recruitment. The recruitment process of each company is generally similar, and it can be summarized as follows: first, online or on-site resume delivery, and then job seekers will conduct an online professional personality assessment. After passing the written test, job seekers can enter the interview session. If the interview is successful, they will receive an offer and enter the probation period. After successfully passing the probationary period, they can officially enter the job
Regular interview duration and structure	The number of interviews varies from two to five, depending on the company and position. Forms include group interviews, professional knowledge interview, comprehensive ability interview, and some positions will also have English tests. The total length of the discussion without a leader group is controlled in about an hour. Professional knowledge interview and comprehensive ability interview are generally one-to-one or two-to-one, and the length of each one ranges from 20 min to 40 min
Employers' focus and common scoring methods	During the interview, the company mainly examines the applicant's learning ability, logical analysis ability, professional knowledge, subjective initiative, etc. Through interview communication, the interviewer will score job applicants in these dimensions, and finally all scores are entered into the computer system to sort the final selected personnel

These interviewees included five men and four women. From the credibility of the interview results, the nine interviewees did have an interview demand recently, so selection of target users was initially correct. These users can be divided into two categories: no actual interview experience and have previous interview experience. Therefore, this article classifies them into two categories: "interviewing novice users" and "interview improved users". Based on the interview results, the behavior variables of different categories of users are summarized in Table 2.

After the previous interview, all interviewees were invited to experiment with two existing artificial intelligence mock interview applications with high attention in China, one is a WeChat applet application for comprehensive interviews, and the other is a web application for IT technology interviews. Make user observations, observe the process of using these applications and the problems existing in the process. Conduct further questionnaire surveys and interviews on the details of the use process and interaction. Do not make any guiding or evaluating utterances during user use to ensure authenticity.

Post-Study System Usability Questionnaire (PSSUQ) was used for quantitative analysis after the experiment. PSSUQ is often used to quantify user experience. Through the corresponding question group of this questionnaire, the system quality, information quality, and interface quality of the tested system can be obtained, and the overall application evaluation can be obtained. Each result has a score between 1 and 7, with lower scores indicating higher satisfaction. After modifying and deleting the standard questionnaire for this research, all test users were asked to fill in the questionnaires separately for the two applications. The modified questionnaire fill-in results were analyzed by SPSS. The Kronebach coefficient α are all above 0.9. This indicates that the reliability of the questionnaire is high. The experimental results are shown in Fig. 4. The mean value of 3.5 is

Table 2. Summary of interview user behavior variables.

User behavior	Interviewing novice users	Interview improved users
What questions did you have before or during the interview	I don't know what ability does the company expect me to master; Insufficient knowledge of the position; Lack of interview experience and skills; Easy to be nervous and not fluent enough	I don't know whether my experience meets the company standards; I don't know how to show my advantages in a short time
How to prepare for an interview	Find the company's business model online; Ask seniors for interview experience; Search for common interview questions for this position; Simulate interview scenarios with others	Targeted search company and job keywords; Rearrange the framework and knowledge of previous project; Simulate responses based on the original interview experience
Where to prepare for the interview	Dormitory; Classroom; Library	Home; Subway
Attitude towards artificial intelligence mock interviews	Provide interview opportunities to facilitate self-improvement; Can avoid leaving bad records during formal interviews	Flexible time, can go home to practice by myself, without delaying work time
Expect style of AI interviewer	Friendly and relaxed	Professional and calm
Expectations for AI mock interview applications	Let me be familiar with the entire interview process; Let me know what I lacked during the interview; Allow me to fill in gaps in professional knowledge; Let me understand the degree of match between my position and my resume; Can recommend a suitable company for me based on my ability	Questions are more targeted and efficient; Can adjusted to corresponding interview style according to the company I like; Have feedback on the questions at each link, and finally give a total data feedback; Ability to properly switch topics based on the interviewee's expressions and actions

the cut-off point of agreement and disagreement. The score of the existing application in the experiment is not ideal either in terms of the score of overall quality or in terms of the score of each variable.

Get the details after observing their operations and ultimately interviewing them. There are many problems during the use of the Wechat applet, such as the lack of prompt sound, the simplistic interface visual design, the lack of professional interview atmosphere due to the excessive cartoon information, the lack of feedback after answering questions, and the confusion of jump relations. The user experience of the web application is slightly better than the previous one, and the process is clearer and more complete. However, there are also many problems. Such as tedious resume filling in, long waiting for the end of the countdown to submit answers, and the lack of immediate feedback. The final data report can only be viewed by returning to multiple pages. According to the summary of experimental data and interview results, the application of artificial intelligence mock interview need to be further studied in aspect of visual design, information architecture, interaction and feedback mechanism. Although the technology of machine interview has been realized, most users still feel that these applications are not "intelligent" enough due to the poor user experience.

number	Questionnaire	Average (Measured WeChat Mini-Program)	Average (Measured web application)
1	Overall, I am satisfied with how easy it is to use this application.	3.56	3.22
2	It was simple to use this application.	3.00	3.11
3	Using the application, I could effectively complete a mock interview.	3.11	3.56
4	I felt comfortable using this application.	4.00	3.11
5	It was easy to learn to use this application.	3.00	3.56
6	I believe I can use this application to improve my interview skills quickly.	4.11	3.78
7	The application gave error messages that clearly told me how to fix problems.	4.00	3.22
8	Whenever I made a mistake using the application, I could recover easily and quickly.	4.44	4.00
9	The information (such as interview status and results) provided with this system was clear.	3.22	3.00
10	It was easy to find the information I needed.	3.22	3.11
11	The information was effective in helping me complete the mock interview.	3.22	3.00
12	The organization of information on the application screens was clear.	3.56	3.11
13	The interface of this application was pleasant.	3.78	3.33
14	The layout of the application's interface is reasonable.	3.56	3.00
15	This application has all the functions and capabilities I expect AI mock interview to have.	3.56	3.44
16	Overall, I am satisfied with this application.	3.33	3.11

field	Field scoring rules		
System quality	The average of items 1 minus 6	3.46	3.39
Information quality	The average of items 7 minus 12	3.61	3.24
Interface quality	The average of items 13 minus 15	3.63	3.25

Fig. 4. Results data sheet.

5.2 Modeling

Persona Construction. In order to vividly express user needs, explain the relationship between products and users, help designers better understand user goals, and promote design transformation, it is necessary to create a typical persona. First, according to user research, summarize the different levels of goals for the two types of users, as shown in Table 3.

Table 3. Different levels of goals for typical users.

User goals	Performance level	Interviewing novice users	Interview improved users
Experience goal	The visceral level	Text or voice prompts are easy to understand; The image and voice of the interviewer is friendly and relaxed; The visual design is clear and beautiful; the layout is easy to operate; the system is smooth and agile	Text or voice prompts are accurate and efficient; the image and voice of the interviewer is calm and professional; the visual design is simple and elegant; the layout is easy to operate; the system is smooth and agile
Ultimate goal	The behavioral level	The interview process is clear and complete; Generate complete interview reports; Propose improvement suggestions; Mock interview record storage and share; Match resume and position; Position recommendation; Have a comprehensive question bank; Interview experience sharing; The interaction forms are convenient and natural; Reduce data input; Reasonable information structure	Targeted interview process; Instant feedback and interaction at each session; Personalized interview process; A large number of professional question banks; Simple and efficient interaction; Reduced data input; Reasonable information architecture
Life goal	The reflective level	Improve myself through mock interviews and help achieve my ambitions; increase self-confidence in practice	Recognize myself through mock interviews to better demonstrate my strengths; gain self-affirmation in practice

In general, artificial intelligence mock interviews are functional applications that help users improve themselves and recognize themselves in order to achieve the goal of successful job search. For the two types of typical users, the needs of interviewing novice users are more basic and comprehensive. Therefore, this paper regards interviewing novice users as the main group of applications and interviewing advanced users as the secondary group. Create persona for these two groups (see Fig. 5) and use them to represent observed user motivations, behaviors, attitudes, abilities, psychology, activity processes, and goals.

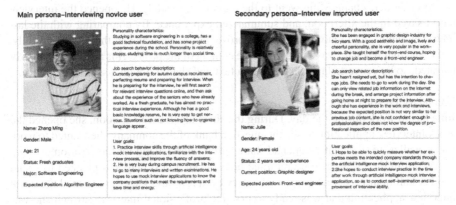

Fig. 5. Persona.

User Scenario Script Construction. Constructing a scenario script can really integrate the character with the entire design process. In the construction process, use scenarios to simulate the user's product use process under ideal conditions, and design the framework according to these needs. Scenarios are based on the main points of contact between persona and the system during a day or other meaningful period of time.

Main Persona: Zhang Ming

Zhang Ming is currently preparing for autumn campus recruitment. At 9 am, Zhang Ming arrived at the library to prepare for professional knowledge. On the mock interview application, he searched the question bank for algorithm engineers, researched each question, and marked out the important questions for later review. At 11 am, He was a little tired and went to the library hallway to get some air. He learned other people's interviewing experience and skills on mock interview application, and collects helpful information.

After lunch break, Zhang Ming opened the mock interview application in the dormitory. He uploaded his revised resume, adjusted the lighting and put on headphones to avoid being disturbed by the roommate's voice. In order to get familiar with the entire process of company interviews, artificial intelligence mock interviews were conducted on all aspects. At first he was a little nervous, but the virtual interviewer was very friendly and gave a timely affirmation after he answered correctly. Zhang Ming gradually entered the interview state through conversation. After the interview, Zhang Ming got a complete report of the interview results. The report told him that he had a good understanding of professional knowledge, but in the comprehensive ability interview, his answers were illogical, lack of confidence. The expression is not natural enough and need more practice. Through comparing the excellent resumes of the algorithm positions with his resume, the application gave revisions to his uploaded resume. Because his classmates called him to dinner, he only glanced at it and kept the report in the interview record.

After dinner, Zhang Ming went to the classroom to study. He opened the interview report saved in the afternoon, and summarized experience. By comparing with the last interview report, he found that he has improved a lot. He watched the report carefully, and it said that when he was asked about the content of the project, his answer was poorly narrated, so he converted his answer into a text and shared it with a senior for advice.

Secondary Persona: Julie
Julie has to work during the day. During the short lunch break at noon, she opened the mock interview application to see the question bank of the company she wanted to work for, as well as to see what others had shared after interviewing for the position.

At ten in the evening, Julie returned home from a busy day and planned to spend another half hour preparing for her job interview a few days later. She opened the mock interview application and was ready to practice professional interview, which she was least confident of. The application suggested that the front-end engineer's professional mock interview took about 20 min, which was in line with her time planning. Since she uploaded a resume yesterday, she chose to skip it when the application asked her if she needed to update her resume. On professional questions, the virtual interviewer discussed with her, giving her a deeper understanding of these questions. The report showed that her interview skills were very good, and she was ready to interview front-end engineers.

5.3 Requirement

According to the product usage scenario description of the personas, combined with the previous research results, the core functional requirements of users for artificial intelligence mock interview applications can be summarized. The core needs of the main persona include: uploading and modifying resumes, the whole process mock interview, generating and storing complete interview reports, classified question banks by position, and sharing interview experience; the core requirements of secondary persona include: uploading and modifying resumes, conduct mock interviews for each session, classified question banks by enterprise, generation and storage of complete interview reports, and sharing interview experience. Other requirements include interview audio to text, interview results sharing, resume and position matching, position recommendation, etc. For all the requirements, the information architecture model design is shown in Fig. 6.

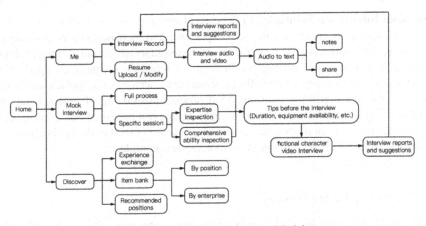

Fig. 6. Information Architecture Model.

6 Interaction Design Principles and Strategies of Artificial Intelligence Mock Interview Application

6.1 Interaction Design Principles

Behavior Feedback Effectiveness Principle. Feedback is a way for users to communicate with applications. The feedback allows users to know their location and task status in real time, and also prevents and corrects operation errors. In particular, the feedback design of artificial intelligence applications needs to be fast and timely, so that users can feel a good sense of interaction during use. Interview is a scene that requires communication. In particular, it is necessary to optimize the feedback process after user input to reduce the negative emotions such as distrust of the machine and confusion and anxiety caused by waiting. Bring a good interactive experience to users through optimized design. In conversation design, natural language processing is performed on the user's response voice, multi-round dialogue mechanism is used to track the conversation state. The machine helps users achieve user goals through the mechanism of inquiries and confirmations, and provides timeline and receipt.

Strong Correlation and Streamlining of Interactive Processes. The connection between each step of the user's operation is reasonable and consistent with user logic. Reduce page jumps across logical levels. For example, reduce the number of steps in the mock interview operation, and try to show the results of the operation through the current page refresh and animation. Design major functions in detail, simplify minor functions. During the interaction process, too many steps and too many form filling will make users feel bored during the operation, and it will also cause users to feel fear. For example, in the resume filling module, job seekers often have edited resume documents themselves. In the application, if users are forced to use forms to fill in information, it will make users troublesome. Two methods can be provided for uploading and filling for users to choose, to streamline user operations as much as possible.

Emotional Interaction Principle. In the case of meeting user goals, the use of emotional interaction can ensure a better user experience and increase the user viscosity of the product. But the premise is that it must meet the usage scenarios and user psychology, otherwise it may be counterproductive. In the mock interview scenario, the application plays the role of a recruiter, while in the personal center scenario, the application should play the role of a user's job assistant. Find product positioning of professional and friendly, use visual, animation, conversational tone and response methods to bring users into the situation, so that users gradually develop a sense of trust in the application, and ultimately achieve the user's life goals to increase self-confidence.

6.2   Interaction Design Strategy

Multi-modal Interaction. Multi-modal interaction is the comprehensive use of multiple input channels and output channels to provide services in the most appropriate way to meet user needs. In the mock interview process, a combination of microphone, camera, touch screen input, display screen, and speaker output are used. For example, during a mock interview, the user can adjust the camera angle and fix the phone and sit at a proper distance from the camera. After answering the questions, the user can directly say "My answer is complete" or make an "OK" gesture. The application can analyze and recognize the microphone or camera information to respond directly, without having to click the touch screen to jump to the next link. It is more convenient and natural to use.

Flexible Interface Layout. The layout design of the interface is not just a simple arrangement of interface elements, but a process of unifying the interface and functions based on the requirements of the information architecture. In artificial intelligence mock interview applications, the layout of the interface can be more flexible, and adjusted according to the user's focus on the current page. For example, in the preparation stage after the user enters the mock interview, the user often needs to adjust the camera, organize his manners, and so on. When the user starts to answer, the user's focus is often on the interview questions themselves. Under the premise of conforming to the user's visual and operating habits, flexibly adjusting the size of the controls on the interface can often help users better achieve their current goals.

7   Conclusion

With the maturity of artificial intelligence technology, more and more "AI+" applications will appear in our lives. How to design reasonable interactions for artificial intelligence applications and efficiently help users achieve their goals is the primary problem to be considered after the technology is achieved. This paper studies the application of artificial intelligence mock interview by using the method of goal-directed design, sorts out the goals and expectations of users in the whole process of using, and puts forward the interactive design principles and strategies corresponding to different levels. It is hoped that it can provide some inspiration for future "AI+" design and create more natural and efficient application through the research of interaction design.

References

1. Cooper, A., Reimann, R., Cronin, D., Noessel, C.: About Face 4: The Essentials of Interaction Design, 1st edn. Publishing House of Electronics Industry, Beijing (2015)
2. Donald, A.: Norman: The Design of Everyday Things, 3rd edn. CITIC Publishing House, Beijing (2011)
3. Chen, M.: Research on object-oriented interactive design of fitting app. Shandong University (2017)
4. Yuqi, L., Songyang, L., Jing, W.: Application of artificial intelligence technology in product interaction design. Packag. Eng. **40**(16), 14–21 (2019)

The Effect of Personal Pronouns on Users' Emotional Experience in Voice Interaction

Jianhong Qu[1], Ronggang Zhou[1,2(✉)], Liming Zou[3], Yanyan Sun[3], and Min Zhao[3]

[1] School of Economics and Management, Beihang University, Beijing, China
[2] Beijing Advanced Innovation Center for Big Data Brain Computing,
Beihang University, Beijing, China
zhrg@buaa.edu.cn
[3] Baidu, Beijing, China

Abstract. There is a growing tendency that users expect voice assistants can recognize and follow some principles in interpersonal communication to enhance emotional experience. Therefore, we study how personal pronouns should be used in the response of voice assistants for Chinese users. We conducted a quantitative experiment. The independent variable is the use of personal pronouns in the intelligent voice assistants, including three levels: no personal pronouns, singular first-person pronouns and singular second person pronouns. 24 participants listened to dialogues between users and the voice assistant and evaluated the perception of emotional experience. It is found in the results that the use of personal pronouns by voice assistants can affect users' emotional experience. Compared with non-use of personal pronouns and use of first-person pronouns, users would have more trust in the voice assistants when it responded in the second person pronouns, and users were more satisfied with the response of the voice assistants in the second person pronouns. These results can inform the design of voice interaction and it is possible to design response strategies for machines based on the theory of interpersonal communication and pragmatics.

Keywords: Personal pronouns · Voice assistants · User emotional experience

1 Introduction

In this developing country, China, ever since the launch of the first batch of digital home assistants of Chinese brands, such as Tmall Genie and Du digital home assistant in 2017, the digital home assistant market in China has risen rapidly. According to statistics, the sales volume of digital home assistants in China will exceed 60 million by the end of 2019 [1]. At the same time, Huawei, Xiaomi and other mobile phone brands have also launched voice assistants. Popular social networking platforms TikTok and Weibo have witnessed very high click-through rates (for example: # Xiaodu helps me turn on the air conditioner #) on funny videos related to voice system, which demonstrates that voice interaction has been gradually integrated into people's daily life. However, through the usability test and interview earlier in this article (n = 100), we found that, in addition to

© Springer Nature Switzerland AG 2020
M. Kurosu (Ed.): HCII 2020, LNCS 12182, pp. 234–243, 2020.
https://doi.org/10.1007/978-3-030-49062-1_16

other uses, people will often interact with the digital home assistant only when they just buy it, and a few days later users merely use it to listen to the music, check the weather, etc., and there is few continuous in-depth interaction.

Scholars in the field of human-computer interaction has always been focusing on the human-to-technology communication [2–4]. Cassell (2001) proposed to concentrate on social and linguistic intelligence "conversational smarts" [5], so as to make people more willing to use intelligent voice system. In current researches, the commonly used research method is to observe the user's use behavior in various ways, conduct conversational analysis, and then do the interview so as to provide the designer with fresh and constructive perspectives. The research questions can be divided into two categories. One is to analyze how users respond to different situations in human-computer interaction, such as error reporting scenarios [6, 7], interruption scenarios [2], and multi-people participation scenarios [4]. The other is to analyze the differences of different types of users' usage patterns and emotional experiences in voice interaction, such as computer level [3, 8] and user experience [8].

At the same time, it is found that people would use social language when interacting with powerful and idealized conversational interfaces [9]. This means that although people will constantly adjust their language to adapt to the interaction with the machine, it does not mean that they do not have higher expectations for the intelligence degree of the machine's speech expression [3]. For humans, interpersonal function is one of the important functions of linguistics [10]. Different linguistic features (content features, physical attributes) represent different emotional expressions [11]. Therefore, we want to know how to use the linguistic features to improve the user's experience in human-computer interaction.

In our research, we blend two fields of study: human computer interaction and pragmatics. We choose the personal pronouns in pragmatics to study the following problems. Firstly, this paper reviews the literature on pragmatics and personal pronoun use. And then we report an experiment and analyze the impact of pronouns on user experience through quantitative methods.

2 Personal Pronouns

The use of personal pronouns can affect the emotion conveyed by a sentence. A sentence is made up of two words, content word and functional word. Functional words are responsible for connecting and organizing content words, such as pronouns, prepositions and conjunctions [12]. Personal pronoun is an important functional word, including the first-person pronoun, the second-person pronoun and the third-person pronoun and it denotes a reference [13]. Subtle changes in personal pronouns can bring a lot of emotional experience, which can be used to analyze a person's personality. For example, the use of pronouns in writing is related to psychological state [14]. By observing how people use functional words such as personal pronouns, we can learn what they are thinking and how they relate to others [12]. This means that the use of pronouns affects how people relate to others. These conclusions are not only found in the field of education, but also confirmed by other studies. In the field of marketing, people use smart personal pronouns to repair the relationship with lost customers [15] and improve the reliability of online reviews [16]. In a marital relationship, the pronouns a spouse uses in conflict resolution discussions provide insight into the quality of their interactions and marriage [17]. The use of personal pronouns plays an important role in education, marketing and educational psychology. What these areas have in common is that they are all about improving human relationships. This is exactly what is needed in the field of human interaction today. This paper mainly analyzes the singular of the first-person pronoun and the singular of the second-person pronoun so it is about the one-to-one conversation between the voice system and the user.

The same sentence can be expressed in either the first or second-person pronoun. In a one-on-one conversation, the speaker can express different emotions from the orientation of the other person or from himself. The subtle differences between the two are reflected in the flexible use of pronouns in language expression. The same answer, if it starts with "you", which means the second-person pronoun is used as the subject, it refers to other-focused, whereas the first-person pronoun, "I", means it starts from the speaker [18]. For example, in a marital relationship, spouses who use more second-person pronouns are more negative in the interaction, while spouses who use more first-person plural pronouns will propose more positive solutions to problems [17]. For example, when the user asks voice assistants guide about dress, voice assistants answer "down jacket" which is to provide information directly, centering all information on clothing guideline. Yet "I think it is ok to wear a down jacket" is one of the suggestions from the voice assistant perspective. The sentence "you can wear a down jacket" is not a straight answer but a step forward from voice assistant as the main body to the user as the main body, providing the user with an action command.

First-person pronouns are biased and subjective compared to not using them. Users will find it less efficient, and therefore less helpful; secondly, the perception of the relevance of comments will be reduced [16], which will be regarded as the speaker wants to express his own views rather than provide the information the listener really wants. For example, "Beijing cuisine includes" will be more objective than "I think Beijing cuisine includes". Past studies of human-computer interaction have found that because voice assistants are non-human, "I" is a human word, so if the voice assistant uses "I" to answer, it will cause the user's cognitive dissonance [11].

The second personal pronoun can form a self-reference [13] to enhance persuasion. Adding a second person pronoun to the description can enhance people's self-reference. The central aspect of self-reference is that the self-acts as a background or setting against which incoming data are interpreted or coded. This process involves an interaction between the previous experience of the individual (in the form of the abstract structure of self) and the incoming materials [19]. Self-reference can prompt people to wake up the previous experience, and then it is easier to produce purchase behavior, which can increase persuasion. When consumers receive information that is relevant to them, they will respond more positively to the message. This effect is more pronounced in declarative situations [20] and voice assistants respond in declarative sentence. Thus, for voice assistants, it might be more convincing to use second-person pronouns.

In our research, we blend two fields of study: human computer interaction and pragmatic and try to answer the following problems. (1) Should intelligent voice assistants use personal pronouns? (2) Which personal pronouns should they use? (3) How can the use of personal pronouns improve the user experience? What has affected users' emotional experience?

3 Method

We conducted a study about the use of personal pronoun in voice assistants on the perception of emotional experience. We use a qualitative method to carry out the experiment. Participants are asked to rate the conversations they hear between the user and the voice system (more on that later).

The independent variable is the response mode of the voice system, and there are three levels of them, first person pronoun singular, second person pronoun singular, no personal pronoun. It should be noted that there are two forms (word-forms) in Chinese regarding the singular of the second personal pronoun in the independent variable, the commonly used one is "ni" and the other is "nin". "nin" represents a more respectful "you" in Chinese culture.

In the experimental design, given that voice assistants are now primarily positioned to serve users, the second personal pronoun singular level in the independent variable is "nin" rather than "ni."

3.1 Experimental Material and Stimulus Preparation

The material in this experiment is pre-recorded voice conversations, that is, one to one one-round answer that simulates the user asking and then the voice assistant answering. Interactive scenarios of weather query and travel query were selected as experimental scenarios in this study. Each scenario involved a script with three dialogues at different levels of independent variables. See the Table 1 below for details.

These dialogues were finally determined through predictive tests and internal discussions. The Baidu AI open platform was used to make voice dialogues between users and voice assistants in advance. The speech speed is medium, about 280 words/min. Synthetic sounds are used in this study. Participants rated the results after listening to the recorded conversation.

In addition to the independent variables, we also control for other variables. First, personal pronouns are located in the subject part of the sentence, i.e. the first part of the sentence, and no personal pronouns are found in other parts of the sentence. Second, in actual use, users may also use different forms of personal pronouns to interact with the voice system, so this study sets that users do not use personal pronouns in the dialogue.

3.2 Design of Affective Experience Satisfaction Scale

Which aspect of user experience is affected by the use of personal pronouns? Through the literature review, we found that there are some scales in the field of human-computer interaction and user experience, such as the attrakdiff scale in user experience. In human-computer interaction, there are mood scales for PAD and SUS scales for synthetic sounds. However, the objective of this paper is to explore the experience of pronoun use, which involves linguistics. Therefore, some indicators in interpersonal communication are considered to be introduced. Therefore, this study did not use existing questionnaires, but designed several questions to understand the emotional experience of users.

In this paper, 4 user experience researchers and 1 user experience professor were invited to discuss and determine the measurement of emotional experience. After discussing the five questions designed in this paper, the subjective experience of the subjects was measured. Firstly, the naturalness index. Because the experimental material in this paper adopts the synthetic audio frequency [21]. For the synthetic sound, naturalness is an important measurement index in speech interaction. Secondly, considering that the design of personal pronouns itself comes from pragmatics, this paper selects two indicators of closeness index and trust index in speech research based on theories related to interpersonal speech [22]. Also, the index of trust plays an important role in human-computer interaction [24]. Thirdly, the design of personal pronouns focuses on enjoyment rather than practicality in user experience. Therefore, this paper also adds the fondness index [23], and finally adds the satisfaction index as the overall evaluation of users' emotional experience [23].

The dependent variable is user's real feeling towards the voice system response, which is measured from the following five dimensions: "the response of voice response is pleasant", "the response of voice system is natural", "the response of voice system is trustworthy", "the response of the voice system can close the distance between me and the voice system" and "the response of the voice system is satisfying". Participants rated all cues by completing a 7-point Likert scale, from totally disagree to totally agree.

3.3 Experimental Procedure: Rating

The experiment was conducted in a quiet computer room, with a pair of headphones placed in front of each computer for participants to use. The specific process is as follows: participants first enter the E-prime system, read the experimental instructions presented on the screen independently, and then enter the rehearsal stage of the formal experiment (the rehearsal part can be done repeatedly). After comprehending the experiment process, combining with their real feelings, the participants will be asked to rate the conversations between the user and the voice system. The experimental instruction is as follows:

"Next, you will do a voice evaluation experiment. After entering the experiment, you will hear a dialogue between the user and the voice system. The male voice is for the user and the female voice is for the voice system. Please pay attention to the content difference of every conversation. At the end of the conversation, you will need to evaluate this dialogue in multiple dimensions and record the score according to the instructions. The system will automatically jump to the next page when you finish recording."

Selection of dependent variables: after listening to each dialogue, participants evaluated their feelings from six dimensions through a 7-point scale (1 = Strongly disagree, 7 = Strongly agree).

Table 1. Tasks' contents (conditions where users do not use personal pronouns and the digital home assistants use different personal pronouns.)

Task	User's instruction	Voice assistant's response
Weather query	Xiao Du Xiao Du, what kind of clothes are suitable for tomorrow?	The temperature in Beijing will be comfortable tomorrow. **YOU CAN** wear a T-shirt and a thin coat and pay attention to the temperature difference between morning and evening
	Xiao Du Xiao Du, what kind of clothes are suitable for tomorrow?	The temperature in Beijing will be comfortable tomorrow. **I THINK IT OK TO** wear a T-shirt and a thin coat and pay attention to the temperature difference between morning and evening
	Xiao Du Xiao Du, what kind of clothes are suitable for tomorrow?	The temperature in Beijing will be comfortable tomorrow. PLEASE wear a T-shirt and a thin coat and pay attention to the temperature difference between morning and evening
Travel query	Xiao Du Xiao Du, what are the interesting tourist attractions in Singapore?	**YOU CAN** Tourist attractions in Singapore include Sentosa, Universal Studios and Merlion Park
	Xiao Du Xiao Du, what are the interesting tourist attractions in Singapore?	**I THINK** Tourist attractions in Singapore include Sentosa, Universal Studios and Merlion Park
	Xiao Du Xiao Du, what are the interesting tourist attractions in Singapore?	Tourist attractions in Singapore include Sentosa, Universal Studios and Merlion Park

Task order: participants evaluate all three voice dialogues in the same scene, and then evaluate the voice dialogues in the other scene. Two dialogue scenes are randomly presented, and three audio dialogue materials from the same scene are randomly presented. Participants will grade after listening to each dialogue.

The experiment has passed the ethical review of the institution. Participants were required to sign the informed consent form before the start of the experiment. There were 24 participants, including 11 male subjects, 13 female subjects, 12 working subjects and 12 students. Participants shall at least have used intelligent voice assistant, and the one with intelligent speaker experience is preferred. This was the final sample after 6 participants were excluded from the study (because they were abnormal values).

4 Result

This paper adopts the single factor analysis of variance (one - way ANOVA) to do the analysis. The results find that overall, the participants of the experiment of speech synthesis have given a generally high score to the emotional experience of dialogue (all index score of 5.40 or higher), belonging to the acceptable range. Combined with the data analysis, we can draw the conclusion that on all emotional experience index, use of "nin" to the phonetic system has yielded the highest score, the second is not using personal pronouns and using first-person pronouns (Fig. 1).

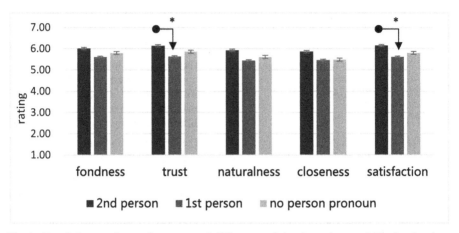

Fig. 1. Result in experiment the score and difference of the dependent variable for the three response in the two scenarios. *p < .05.

In the index of trust, the second-person pronoun singular score (6.13) is significantly higher ($F(2,141) = 3.30$, $p = .040$) than the first-person pronoun singular score (5.63). It means that using the second personal pronoun response makes it easier for the voice assistant to build trust with the user; in the emotional experience index of fondness, the mean score of voice assistant using the second personal pronoun singular is 6.00, and the mean score of voice assistant answering with and without the first personal pronoun singular is 5.60 and 5.79, respectively. In the naturalness index, the mean score of the voice assistant using the second personal pronoun singular is 5.92, while the mean score of the voice assistant answering with and without the first personal pronoun singular is 5.44 and 5.60, respectively. In the closeness index, the mean score of the voice assistant using the second personal pronoun singular is 5.85, while the mean score of the voice assistant answering with and without the first personal pronoun singular is 5.46 and 5.48, respectively.

In terms of overall satisfaction, the second personal pronoun singular score (6.15) is significantly higher ($F(2,141) = 3.21$, $p = .043$) than the first personal pronoun singular score (5.60). This suggests that users are generally more satisfied with second-person pronoun responses, and the reason for this may be that voice assistant is more likely to build trust when using second-person pronoun responses.

5   Discussion

This paper studies the effect of personal pronouns on users' emotional experience in voice interaction. The results showed that when personal pronouns appeared in the response of the voice system, the emotional experience of users changed. In general, when the second personal pronoun was added to the assistant's response, users trusted the response more and were more satisfied with the response. However, not all personal pronouns could help improve users' emotional experience. Compared with no personal pronouns, the use of second personal pronouns can indeed improve users' emotional experience, while the addition of first personal pronouns can have adverse impact on users' emotional experience. This was also analyzed in the previous literature review. The same sentence can begin with either a first-person pronoun or a second-person pronoun, the difference being whether from the speaker's or the listener's perspective. For the response starting with the first-person pronoun, for one thing, it can be seen from the research results in other fields that the information contains the subjective view of the speaker, which will reduce the objectivity of the information and distract the user from understanding the information. Previous human-computer interaction, for another, the study found that users believe that machines can communicate but not human beings; to express and to begin with "I", it is considered that the speaker needs to have their own independent personality, and this is contradictory to the identity of the machine, so when the machine using "I", will allow the user to produce psychological reaction of cognitive dissonance. As for the second personal pronoun, from the perspective of pragmatics and psychology, starting with the second personal pronoun in the presentation of information will trigger the listener's self-reference behavior, stimulate the user's memory related to the past, and thus improve the persuasiveness of the information.

This paper also further verifies the reason why the second person can improve users' emotional experience and satisfaction. In this study, users were asked to evaluate the responses of voice assistants from five aspects: naturalness, fondness, trust, closeness, and satisfaction, among which the satisfaction index was put at the end as the overall evaluation. Finally, it was found that for the responses starting with the second-person pronouns, the first-person pronouns and with no personal pronouns, there were no significant differences in naturalness, fondness and closeness; the users' evaluation of differences embodied in trust and satisfaction. It further illustrates that the user satisfaction is higher because users have more trust in responses with the second-person pronoun. Trust in automated systems has been extensively studied. Trust is one example of the important influence of affect and emotions on human-technology interaction. Trust is also one example of how affect-related considerations should influence design of complex, high consequence systems [24]. This paper further verified the important role of trust in human-computer interaction design. For the future human-computer interaction design, this paper suggests that the conclusion of pragmatics can be considered to improve user experience, and user trust should be taken into account when improving user experience.

6   Limitation

The experimental tasks selected in our quantitative experiment are from 2 scenarios. In order to control the variables, the queries and responses between 2 scenarios were consistent, which made the content of some tasks more verbose than that of daily life. The sample this time is limited to 24, and only in China. The scope and scale of the sample will be expanded in the future.

References

1. Hannah, RM., Pelikan, Broth, M.: Why that Nao: How humans adapt to a conventional humanoid robot in taking turns-at-talk. In: Proceedings of the 2016 CHI Conference on Human Factors in Computing Systems, pp. 4921–4932. ACM (2016)
2. Beneteau, E., Richards, OK., Zhang, M., Kientz, J.A., Yip J., Hiniker, A.: Communication breakdowns between families and Alexa. In: Proceedings of the 2019 CHI Conference on Human Factors in Computing Systems, p. 243. ACM (2019)
3. Luger, E., Sellen, A.: Like having a really bad PA: the gulf between user expectation and experience of conversational agents. In: Proceedings of the 2016 CHI Conference on Human Factors in Computing Systems, pp. 5286–5297. ACM (2016)
4. Porcheron, M., Fischer, J.E., Sharples, S.: Do animals have accents?: talking with agents in multi-party conversation. In: Proceedings of the 2017 ACM Conference on Computer Supported Cooperative Work and Social Computing, pp. 207–219. ACM (2017)
5. Cassell, J., Bickmore, T., Campbell, L., Hannes, V., Yan, H.: Conversation as a System Framework: Designing Embodied Conversational Agents. The MIT Press, Cambridge (2000)
6. Jiang, J., Jeng, W., He, E.: How do users respond to voice input errors? lexical and phonetic query reformulation in voice search. In: Proceedings of the 36th international ACM SIGIR Conference on Research and Development in Information Retrieval, pp 143–152. ACM (2013)
7. Murray, I.R., Arnott, J.L.: Toward the simulation of emotion in synthetic speech: a review of the literature on human vocal emotion. J. Acoust. Soc. Am. **93**(2), 1097–1108 (1993)
8. Chen, M., Wang, H.: How personal experience and technical knowledge affect using conversational agents. In: Proceedings of the 23rd International Conference on Intelligent User Interfaces Companion, p. 53. ACM (2018)
9. Large, D.R., Clark, L., Quandt, A., Burnett, G., Skrypchuk, L.: Steering the conversation: a linguistic exploration of natural language interactions with a digital assistant during simulated driving. Appl. Ergon. **63**, 53–61 (2017)
10. Liu, J., Shu, N., Zhang, Q.: Interpersonal interpretation of personal pronoun in marriage advertising. Res. J. Eng. Lang. Lit. **3**(1), 18–25 (2015)
11. Nass, C.I., Brave, S.: Wired for Speech: How Voice Activates and Advances the Human-Computer Relationship. MIT Press, Cambridge (2005)
12. Pennebaker, J.W.: The secret life of pronouns. New Sci. **211**(2828), 42–45 (2011)
13. Levinson, S.: Pragmatics (1983)
14. Campbell, R.S., Pennebaker, J.W.: The secret life of pronouns: flexibility in writing style and physical health. Psychol. Sci. **14**(1), 60–65 (2003)
15. Packard, G., Moore, S.G., McFerran, B.: (I'm) Happy to help (you): the impact of personal pronoun use in customer-firm interactions. J. Mark. Res. **55**(4), 541–555 (2018)
16. Wang, F., Karimi, S.: This product works well (for me): The impact of first-person singular pronouns on online review helpfulness. J. Bus. Res. **104**, 283–294 (2019)
17. Simmons, R.A., Gordon, P.C., Chambless, D.L.: Pronouns in marital interaction: what do "you" and "I" say about marital health? Psychol. Sci. **16**(12), 932–936 (2005)
18. Ickes, W., Reidhead, S., Patterson, M.: Machiavellianism and self-monitoring: as different as "me" and "you". Soc. Cogn. **4**(1), 58–74 (1986)
19. Rogers, T.B., Kuiper, N.A., Kirker, W.S.: Self-reference and the encoding of personal information. J. Pers. Soc. Psychol. **35**(9), 677 (1977)
20. Escalas, J.E.: Self-referencing and persuasion: narrative transportation versus analytical elaboration. J. Consum. Res. **33**(4), 421–429 (2006)
21. Adiga, N., Prasanna, S.R.M.: Acoustic features modelling for statistical parametric speech synthesis: a review. IETE Tech. Rev. **36**(2), 130–149 (2019)

22. Street, R.L.: Evaluation of noncontent speech accommodation. Lang. Commun. **2**(1), 13–31 (1982)
23. Brill, T.M., Munoz, L., Miller, R.J.: Siri, Alexa, and other digital assistants: a study of customer satisfaction with artificial intelligence applications. J. Mark. Manag. **35**(15–16), 1401–1436 (2019)
24. Lee, J.D., See, K.A.: Trust in automation: designing for appropriate reliance. Hum. Factors **46**(1), 50–80 (2004)

The Effect of Naturalness of Voice and Empathic Responses on Enjoyment, Attitudes and Motivation for Interacting with a Voice User Interface

Jacqueline Urakami$^{(\boxtimes)}$ ⓘ, Sujitra Sutthithatip, and Billie Akwa Moore

Tokyo Institute of Technology, 2-12-1 Ookayama, Meguro-Ku, Tokyo 152-8552, Japan
urakami.j.aa@m.titech.ac.jp

Abstract. In human-computer interaction much attention is given to the development of natural and intuitive Voice User Interfaces (VUI). However, previous research has shown that humanlike systems will not necessarily be perceived positive by users. The study reported here examined the effect of human likeness on users' rating of enjoyment, attitudes and motivation to use VUI in a Wizard-of-Oz experiment. Two attributes of human likeness, voice of the system (humanlike vs. machinelike) and social behavior of the system (expressing empathy vs. neutral) were manipulated. Regression analyses confirmed that perceived empathy of the VUI improved interaction enjoyment, attitude towards the system, and intrinsic motivation but no effect of voice was found. Session order also affected participants' evaluation. In the second session, participants rated the VUI as more negative than in the first session. The results indicate that a VUI that expresses social behavior (e.g. showing empathy) is perceived as more favorable by the user. Furthermore, changing user expectations pose a challenge for the design of the VUI. The dynamics of user interactions must be taken into account when designing the VUI.

Keywords: Voice user interface · Empathy · Human likeness

1 Introduction

Voice User Interfaces (VUI) are widely used and are incorporated in many commercial applications such as home appliances like washing machines and dish washers, automobiles or computer operating systems. Artificial Intelligence (AI) and Deep learning has opened the door to more advanced applications of VUI such as intelligent agents that process customer requests and automated service attendants that take orders, make reservations or give directions. It is in the interest of the service provider that users can communicate with VUI in a positive way and are motivated to use the system again.

The central goal in designing VUI that act as conversational agents has been to create a natural and intuitive interaction between the user and the technical system. It is still disputed in the literature whether humans treat such systems like other social partners,

© Springer Nature Switzerland AG 2020
M. Kurosu (Ed.): HCII 2020, LNCS 12182, pp. 244–259, 2020.
https://doi.org/10.1007/978-3-030-49062-1_17

applying social rules and expectations to them as described in Reeves and Nass [1] media-equation hypothesis. According to this view human-computer interaction improves when the system provides many social cues and shows humanlike attributes in its behavior and appearance. In contrast the theory of human-automation assumes that humans respond to machines in a unique and specific way proposing that humans judge and evaluate machines fundamentally different [2, 3].

Goal of the study presented here is to test how users evaluate the human likeness of a VUI in regard to interaction enjoyment, attitude and intrinsic motivation. For VUI used in the service setting it is imperative that users have a positive impression of the system and are willing to engage with the system again in the future. The VUI is also seen as a representative of the company and evaluation of such a system likely will affect users' perception of the company employing it [4].

Previous studies have especially focused on human likeness in appearance of computer agents. The unique aspect of the study presented here is that the focus is not only on appearance (voice) but also considers the social behavior of the system. In contrast to other studies, particular consideration is given to how system behavior is perceived by the user and how this perception affects the evaluation of the system. This study examined two attributes of human likeness, voice of the system (humanlike vs. machinelike) and social behavior of the system (expressing empathy vs. neutral).

The results of this study highlight the importance of VUI behaving in a social way, e.g. by expressing empathy in human-computer interaction, but also suggest that individual differences and user preferences must be taken into account when designing dialogues. Furthermore, the role of changing users' expectations towards VUI is discussed and consequences for the design of VUI are contemplated.

1.1 Media-Equation vs. Human Automation Theory

The media-equation hypothesis [5, 6] implies that humans treat computers as social entities. This paradigm has been successfully studied with other technologies such as computer agents, twitter bots or robots [4, 7, 8]. The theory assumes that people react automatically and unconsciously to computers in a social and natural way, even if they believe that it is not reasonable to do so [1]. Human likeness in appearance and behavior triggers anthropomorphism, the tendency of people to attribute human-like characteristics to a computer agent. It is proposed that peoples' social reactions increase when the computer agent shows human-like behavior and provides more social cues [6, 9].

In contrast the theory of human automation proposes that human respond to machines in a unique and specific way. Research about trust showed that humans perceive the advice given by a computer agent as more objective and rational than that of a human [10]. Computer agents evoke higher initial levels of trust compared to humans, but also people lose trust in computers more dramatically [11]. Furthermore, interactions with agents that display humanlike behavior make it more difficult for people to distinguish if they are engaging with a real human or with an artificial intelligence. As research about the uncanny valley (an eerie feeling about computer agents that seem to be like humans but somewhat different) has shown, anthropomorphism can have a negative impact on peoples' evaluation of agents. This eerie feeling is especially evoked when users perceive a mismatch between a systems humanlike appearance and behavior [12].

In sum, even though human likeness triggers anthropomorphism and might increase users' social reactions toward a computer agent, it remains unclear if this is an advantage or disadvantage for human-computer interaction. Previous research has produced mixed results (e.g. [4, 13, 14]) and the question whether an automated system should pretend to be a human or act like a human is still unanswered. The goal of this study is to examine if human likeness of a VUI's voice and social behavior expressing empathy increases peoples' likeness of such systems or not.

The following two sections give a short literature overview about the role of human-like voice and empathic expressions on users' perception of automated systems.

1.2   Human-Likeness in Human-Computer Interaction

The voice is a powerful tool to create a certain impression in the listener. The voice communicates content not only through lexical expressions but also through emotional cues, and paralinguistic. In our study we focus on the human likeness of the voice compared to a machinelike voice.

Google duplex (https://ai.googleblog.com/2018/05/duplex-ai-system-for-natural-conversation.html) has impressively demonstrated that it is possible to create a human-like voice with AI that is hardly distinguishable from a real human voice. When Google introduced the system, it created a controversy if it is ethical acceptable to give people the impression that they talk with a real person while they were communicating with a computer agent. This discussion makes it evident that some people feel uncomfortable interacting with computer agents that are very similar to a real person.

On the other hand, people usually rate computer agents with a natural voice more positive compared to agents with machinelike voices. Ilves [15] reported that participants rated the humanlike voice as being more pleasant and clear, and as being more approachable compared to a machinelike voice. Similarly, Louwerse [7] reported that participants preferred agents with natural voices suggesting that voice alone can trigger social behaviors towards computer agents. However Ilves [15] also noted that emotional expressions by the machinelike voice were rated by their emotional valence suggesting that machinelike voices can communicate affective messages as well.

An important factor affecting the perception of anthropomorphism seems to be how well human likeness in appearance and behavior match. Mitchell [12] paired in an experiment a robot and human face with either a machinelike or humanlike voice. Incongruence between visual appearance and voice (e.g. robot face with humanlike voice) created a feeling of eeriness. In another study Muresan [16] observed peoples interaction with a chatbot. When the chatbot violated social norms, people disapproved of the behavior and decreased the interaction, noting that the chatboot felt fake. Ruijten [8] looked at the dynamics of perceived human likeness when interacting with robots. Depending on the behavior of the robot, perceived human likeness changed over the course of the interaction. Ruijten [8] suggested that although appearance might initially be an important factor in perceiving human likeness in an agent, ultimately appropriate agent behavior, as would be expected in a particular social context, most strongly influenced the overall assessment of the agent.

Human likeness can be expressed in many ways, not only in appearance like voice but also in the form of social behavior. The next section reflects on the role of empathic responses as a form of human likeness of computer agents.

1.3 Empathy

Automated systems need to engage in a meaningful social way with people [17]. This is particularly relevant for a service provider, who needs to communicate effectively, listen actively to the problems of their customers, and provide help.

Previous research has experimented with integrating affective expressions and related responses into human-computer interactions to create a more natural humanlike experience [18, 19]. In this regard the concept of empathy has received much attention. How to define the term empathy is still an ongoing discussion in the literature. We believe that for designing interactions between humans and VUI an interpersonal approach to empathy is imperative. Therefore, empathy is defined in this paper as understanding and responding appropriately to the affective state and situation of the communication partner. Empathy is central to interpersonal functioning [20], and this paper assumes that empathic responses by a VUI can engage users in meaningful social interactions.

Empathy serves social functions when two people interact and undergoes dynamic changes in the course of this interaction, a view shared by Main [21] and Butler [20, 22]. Empathy is nested in a specific context. It is not the behavior itself that is empathic but how the behavior is suited in the context of the interaction [23]. This empathy approach emphasizes that a certain behavior must also be judged as empathic by the communication partner. It is decisive whether the user perceives and interprets the behavior of an agent as empathic.

Previous studies about the effect of empathy in human-computer interaction have reported mixed results. Złotowski [13] compared a humanlike robot with a machine-like robot and found that the humanlike robot was perceived as being less trustworthy and empathic than the machinelike robot. Niculescu [19] examined the effect of empathic language cues on users' evaluation of human-robot interaction. Even though users indicated that they perceived the robot using empathic language cues as more receptive and felt more ease in the interaction, no effect on likeability, trustworthiness, overall enjoyment and interaction quality were shown. In a study by Leite [18] an empathic model was applied to a social robot to study long-term interaction between children and robots. Leite [18] reported that the children preferred the emotion-oriented robot over the task-oriented robot. Brave and Nass [24] compared the effect of expressing self-oriented emotions and empathic-emotions with an computer agent and found that empathic-emotions resulted in higher ratings for likeability, trustworthiness, and greater perceived care and support. Araujo [4] manipulated humanlike cues in language style, name and framing in an experiment with a chatbot and reported that humanlike cues influenced the emotional connection a human felt to the agent. Urakami [25] conducted a survey study about the perception of empathic expressions by a VUI. While most participants in the study accepted empathic expressions, 1/3 of the participants disagreed with this assessment. It was concluded in the study that not all users feel comfortable with a machine acting or "pretending" to act like a human being.

Whether empathy improves human-computer interaction is still unclear. Personal preferences as well as situation adequateness of empathic expressions might affect how people react to an empathic computer agent. Empathic reactions of a computer agent must be adapted to the situational context, the role of the interaction partner and their relationship. Furthermore, it is not necessarily the empathic response itself that is decisive, but the interpretation of a certain behavior as empathic.

1.4 Hypotheses

Overall, previous research suggests that people rate a system using a humanlike voice more positive. We propose in hypothesis 1:

H1: Interaction enjoyment, attitude, and intrinsic motivation are rated higher for VUI with humanlike voice compared to machinelike voice.

Furthermore, previous studies suggest [15, 19] that emotional cues by a system will be recognized as such by users despite the naturalness or human likeness of the system.

H2: Empathic language cues by a VUI can be identified by users as an expression of empathy independently of being expressed by a humanlike or machinelike voice.

Empathy is here seen as an expression of humanlike behavior relevant in a situation where a customer approaches an agent to receive help. We propose that people would expect empathic reactions in such situations and therefore evaluate them positive for the interaction.

H3: Perceived empathy has a positive effect on users' evaluation of interaction enjoyment, attitude towards the system, and intrinsic motivation to use the system.

However, a mismatch between humanlike appearance (humanlike voice) and behavior (expressing empathy or not) will result in a negative evaluation of the agent.

H4: A VUI using a humanlike voice and empathic language cues is evaluated higher than a VUI using a humanlike voice and neutral language.

H5: A VUI using a machinelike voice and empathic language cues receives a lower evaluation than a VUI using a machinelike voice and neutral language.

These hypotheses were tested in an experimental Wizard-of-Oz study in a service setting as background scenario.

2   Method

2.1   Participants

A total of 60 international students from Tokyo Institute of Technology participated in the study, between the ages of 19 and 36 years (M = 24.95; SD = 3.72). There were 29 females and 31 males in the sample.

2.2   Experimental Design

A 2×2 mixed factorial design with within-factor empathy (expressing empathy vs. neutral) and the between factor system voice (humanlike vs. machinelike) was conducted. Two scenarios in which participants had to imagine having lost either a wallet or backpack were created. The within-factor empathy and the scenarios were counterbalanced.

2.3 Material

Scenarios. Participants had to image to have lost a wallet (scenario 1) or a backpack (scenario 2) at the airport. Participants received the following instruction: "You are at Narita airport. Your plane will depart in 1 h and you just noticed that you have lost your wallet. You used your wallet just 10 min ago to pay for extra luggage at Counter A. You need to get your wallet back as soon as possible and you ask an automated airport assistant for help. Please speak to the airport assistant: Start the conversation by saying "Hello". The backpack scenario was very similar, only that participants had to imaging they just arrived at the airport and had to catch a bus to the hotel. Both scenarios contained images of the situation and of the lost wallet and backpack.

Dialogs. The dialogs were pre-recorded using Googles text-to-speech tool (https://cloud.google.com/text-to-speech/) with the en-US-Wavenet-F voice (female voice) for the humanlike voice. The speech synthesizer Audacity (https://www.audacityteam.org/) was used to transform the voice file into a machinelike voice. By creating a specific setting in the instruction (having lost wallet/backpack at the airport) and giving the participants a specific task (try to get your lost items back) we were able to guide the participants through the dialog with the pre-recorded sequences without having the participants notice that the experiment was a wizard-of-oz study.

For each scenario (wallet/backpack) we created two dialogs with one containing empathic language and the other being neutral. Empathic phrases were chosen based on a survey conducted in a previous study by Urakami et al. [25]. The study revealed that expressions showing interest and understanding of the situation of the person, as well as expressions of offering help are being perceived as empathic by people. Table 1 displays the empathic and neutral dialog for the wallet scenario. The backpack scenario followed a similar pattern.

Negative Attitude Towards Robots Scale (NARS). The negative attitude towards robots scaly by Syrdal et al. [26] contains 14 items measuring peoples' attitudes towards situations and interactions with robots, social influence of robots, and attitude towards emotions in the interaction with robots. Items were assessed using Likert scales ranging from 1 (I do not feel anxiety at all) till 6 (I feel anxiety very strongly). The items of the questionnaire were adjusted to the purpose of the study by replacing the term robot with automated system.

CARE Measure. The CARE measure [27] is originally an instrument to measure patients' perception of empathy after the consultation with a doctor. The CARE measure consists of ten 5-point Likert scale items ranging from 1 (poor) till 5(excellent). For the purpose of our study, the term doctor was replaced by the term system. Participants evaluated if the system made them feel at ease, really listened, understood their concerns, etc.

Interaction Enjoyment. This questionnaire was adapted from Sacco and Ismail [28]. The questionnaire measures how much somebody enjoyed the interaction answering five items on 7-point Likert scales ranging from 1 (not at all) till 7 (extremely) regarding enjoying the interaction, feeling nervous, or anxious during the interaction (for Items see Table 2).

Table 1. Dialog spoken by the VUI. Sentences in *italic* are empathic expressions.

Empathic	Neutral
Hello. *Is there anything I can do for you?*	Hello. Is there a problem?
Yes, *I'd like to help you.* *Can you give me a view more details?* When did you last use it?	Yes, that is part of the provided service. When did you last use it?
Can you please tell me a bit more about it? What does your backpack look like?	Please provide more information. What does your backpack look like?
Can you please give me a few more details about it?	Please provide a few more details about it.
I am going to take care of this for you. Please wait a few seconds. I will check the airport's video footage.	OK. Please wait a few seconds. I will check the airport's video footage.
I am going to take care of this for you. Please wait a few seconds. I will check the airport's video footage.	OK. Please wait a few seconds. I will check the airport's video footage.
Thank you for waiting. *The video footage shows that someone must have stolen you backpack, but I think we can work this out.* *I can help you making a call to the police, if you would like me to do.*	The video footage shows that someone must have stolen you backpack. Should the police be called?
I'd be happy to do this for you. Thank you for using my service.	The police has been informed. Thank you for using this service.
Thank you for waiting. *The video footage shows that someone must have stolen you backpack, but I think we can work this out.* *I can help you making a call to the police, if you would like me to do.*	The video footage shows that someone must have stolen you backpack. Should the police be called?

Attitude Towards Using the System. Participant's attitude towards the system was measured using Davis et al. [29] questionnaire. Items were assessed by 7-point Likert scales ranging from 1-strongly disagree till 7-strongly agree (for Items see Table 2).

Intrinsic Motivation. This scale measured the intention of users to perform an activity with the system motivated by positive feelings while using it. The scale used Davis et al. [30] questionnaire that contained 3 items and participants indicated on 7-point Likert scales ranging from 1-strongly disagree till 7-strongly agree how much they agreed with each statement (for Items see Table 2).

Table 2. Questionnaires used in the study

Interaction enjoyment
I was nervous during the interaction with the system
Interacting with the system made me anxious
I enjoyed interacting with the system
The interaction I had with the system was interesting
I would enjoy interacting with the system again in the future

Attitude towards using the system
Using the system is a good idea
Using the system is a foolish idea
I like the idea of using the system
Using the system is unpleasant

Intrinsic motivation
I find using the system enjoyable
The actual process of using the system is pleasant
I have fun using the system

2.4 Procedure

The experiment was carried out in single sessions. Participants had to attend two sessions that were scheduled at least one week apart. Participants were greeted and briefed about the purpose of the study. After signing the consent form, participants filled in the NARS. All questionnaires were presented on the computer using Google Forms. A voice sample was played to the participants to ensure that they could clearly understand the voice. If necessary, the volume of the voice was adjusted. The participants received a written instruction and when they were ready to start the experiment, they initiated the dialogue by saying "Hello" to the VUI. The participants were sitting alone on a table with the VUI in front of them. The experimenter was in the same room but hidden behind a screen. The experimenter played the voice samples according to the scripted dialog (see Table 1). Participants were given the impression that the VUI was an autonomous system that can process and react to spoken language. After the dialog was finished, participants filled in the CARE measure, interaction enjoyment questionnaire, attitude towards using the system questionnaire, and the intrinsic motivation questionnaire. After finishing the second session participants received 1000 Yen compensation.

2.5 Equipment

The humanlike voice sample used in the experiment were generated with Google cloud text-to-speech (https://cloud.google.com/text-to-speech/). The speed was set at 0.80, pitch 0.00 and the en-US-Wavenet-F voice (female voice) was used. The machinelike voice was generated using the software Audacity (https://www.audacityteam.org/). A typical characteristic of machinelike voice is being monotone and having a smaller frequency range compared to a natural human voice. Therefore, the humanlike voice samples generated with Google cloud were altered with Audacity software using first an equalizer to gradually cutting off frequencies below 200 Hz and above 800 Hz and the tempo of speech was reduced for 15%.

The VUI was a small JBL Bluetooth speaker (71.2 mm × 86 mm × 31.6 mm). The speaker was connected to the notebook of the experimenter via Bluetooth.

3 Results

3.1 Negative Attitude Towards Robots Scale NARS

Participants reported a slightly negative attitude towards automated systems ($M = 3.64$; $SD = 0.92$). There were no differences in attitude towards automated systems across the voice conditions (human: $M = 3.59$; $SD = 0.68$; machine: $M = 3.69$; $SD = 1.12$; $t(58) = -.44$, $p = .66$, and no gender differences, (female: $M = 3.65$; $SD = 0.948$; male: $M = 3.63$; $SD = 0.90$; $t(58) = 0.93$, $p = .92$).

3.2 Voice

There was no difference in being able to clearly understand the voice across the experimental conditions, $t(58) = .701$, $p = .486$. Also, participants could distinguish between a humanlike and a machinelike voice, $t(58) = -2.70$, $p = .008$.

3.3 Perception of Empathy

The CARE measure was used to control if the empathic language cues were perceived as expressions of empathy. A 2×2 mixed factorial ANOVA revealed a marginal significant effect of empathy ($F(1, 58) = 3.34$, $p = .07$) and no effect of voice ($F(1, 58) < 1$). There were no significant interactions ($F(1, 58) < 1$. Means and standard deviations are displayed in Table 3.

Even though the results of the CARE measure indicate that participants perceived the empathic condition indeed as empathic, the differences were rather small. As has been pointed out in the literature, empathy evolves during an interaction between two communication partners and can change during an interaction [22, 31]. It is imperative that a certain behavior really is perceived as being empathic.

To test our hypothesis about the effect of empathy on participants' evaluation of the system, we conducted first a 2×2 repeated measures ANOVA with the within-factor empathy and the between-factor voice. In addition, a regression analysis was conducted with the CARE measure as perceived empathy as a predictor.

3.4 Effect of Empathy and Voice on Interaction Enjoyment, Attitude Towards the VUI and Intrinsic Motivation

A 2×2 mixed factorial ANOVA revealed no significant effects of empathy and voice on interaction enjoyment, empathy: $F (1, 58) < 1$; voice $F (1, 58) = 1.86, p = .178$), attitude towards the VUI, empathy $F (1, 58) < 1$, voice $F (1, 58) < 1$) or intrinsic motivation, empathy $F (1, 58) < 1$, voice $F (1, 58) < 1$. Also, no significant interactions were found. See means and standard deviations in Table 3.

It was somewhat surprising that the voice had no impact on participants' evaluation, especially since the voice was clearly perceived differently in the humanlike condition compared to the machinelike condition. It can be assumed that in a direct comparison the participants might have preferred the humanlike voice. Since each participant was assigned to just one of the voice conditions, the voice itself does not seem to be a factor affecting participants overall evaluation of the system.

Table 3. Means and Standard Deviations in parenthesis for CARE measure, Interaction enjoyment, Attitude, and Intrinsic motivation

Empathy	Empathic		Neutral	
Voice	Human like	Machine like	Human like	Machine like
CARE measure	3.71 (.65)	3.74 (0.80)	3.63 (0.65)	3.53 (0.79)
Interaction enjoyment	5.46 (.88)	5.09 (0.99)	5.36 (0.82)	5.14 (0.91)
Attitude scale	5.52 (.91)	5.65 (1.12)	5.50 (1.04)	5.60 (0.89)
Intrinsic motivation	4.97 (.95)	5.14 (0 .96)	5.01 (0.99)	5.02 (0.97)

3.5 Effect of Empathy Perception on Interaction Enjoyment, Attitude, and Intrinsic Motivation

A simple linear regression analysis was used to test if the perception of empathy significantly predicted participants' ratings of interaction enjoyment, attitude, and intrinsic motivation. The CARE measurement was used as a predictor for perceived empathy. The results of the regression indicated that perception of empathy explained 34% of the variance for interaction enjoyment ($R2 = .34, F (1, 119) = 61.08, p < .01$). It was found that perceived empathy predicted interaction enjoyment ($\beta = .72, p < .001$).

Furthermore perceived empathy explained 36% variation for attitude ($R2 = .36, F (1, 119) = 67.51, p < .001, \beta = .80, p < .001$), and 33% of the variation for intrinsic motivation ($R2 = .33, F (1, 119) = 57.28, p < .001, \beta = .75, p < .001$). Figures 1, 2 and 3 display the scatter plots with regression lines for interaction enjoyment, attitude and intrinsic motivation with the CARE measure as predictor.

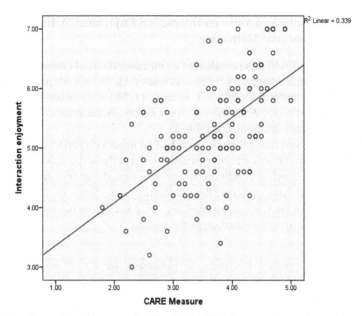

Fig. 1. Scatterplot with regression line for CARE Measure x Interaction enjoyment.

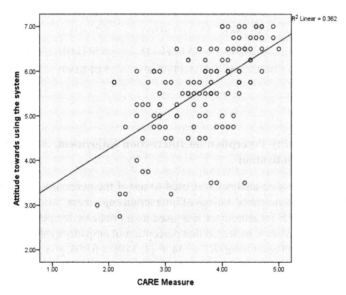

Fig. 2. Scatterplot with regression line for CARE Measure x Attitude towards using the system

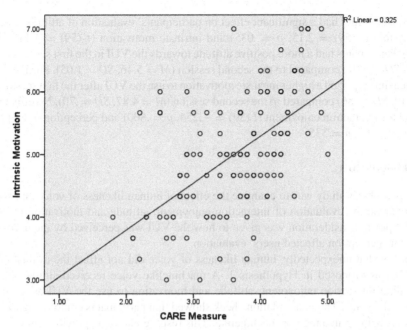

Fig. 3. Scatterplot with regression line for CARE Measure x Intrinsic Motivation.

3.6 Effect of Negative Attitude Towards Robots on Evaluation of the System

Since evaluation of interaction enjoyment, attitude, and intrinsic motivation did not differ across the experimental conditions, a sum score for each variable was created per participant and correlated with the ratings of the NARS questionnaire. Negative attitude towards automated systems correlated significantly negative for all three variables with the highest correlation found for interaction enjoyment ($r = -.508, p < .001$), followed by intrinsic motivation ($r = -.488, p < .001$) and attitude towards the system ($r = -.431, p < .001$). Participants with a negative attitude towards automated systems rated the VUI lower in interaction enjoyment, attitude towards using the system, and intrinsic motivation.

Correlation for the CARE measure were carried out separately for condition with and without empathic language cues, since the CARE measure differed significantly between both conditions as reported above. Attitude towards automated systems correlated significantly negative in both conditions, empathic $r = -.305, p = .018$, neutral $r = -.324, p = .012$. Participants who reported having a negative attitude towards automated systems perceived the systems as less empathic. These results indicate that participants general attitude towards automated systems influenced their evaluation of the VUI.

Order Effect

The scenarios used as well as manipulation of empathy was counterbalanced in the experiment. There was no difference across scenarios for CARE measure ($t (60) = .28$, $p = .78$), interaction enjoyment ($t (60) = -1.29, p = .20$), attitude ($t (60) = 1.88, p = .06$) and intrinsic motivation ($t (60) = -.90, p = .37$).

Session order had a significant effect on participants' evaluation of attitude towards the system (t (59) = 2.15, p = .035) and intrinsic motivation (t (59) = 3.119, p = .003). Participants had a more positive attitude towards the VUI in the first session (M = 5.67, SD = .901) compared to the second session (M = 5.46, SD = 1.05). Furthermore, participants reported a higher intrinsic motivation to use the VUI after the first session (M = 5.19, SD = .86) compared to the second session (M = 4.87, SD = .70). No effect was found for interaction enjoyment (t (59) = −.254, p = .800) and perception of empathy (t (59) = .965, p = 335.

4 Discussion

The goal of this study was to examine the effect of human likeness of voice and social behavior on the evaluation of interaction enjoyment, attitude and motivation to use a VUI. Special consideration was given to how the VUI was perceived by the users and how this perception affected users' evaluation.

Somewhat unexpectedly, human likeness of voice did not affect the evaluation of the VUI as proposed in Hypothesis 1. A machinelike voice received similar ratings regarding interaction enjoyment, attitude and motivation to use the VUI as a natural humanlike voice. The manipulation check showed that participants could recognize the voice as being humanlike or machinelike. This result contradicts previous findings [7, 15]. However, since voice was manipulated across groups, participants could not directly compare both types of voice with each other. If the voice is clearly understandable, participants do not seem to pay attention to the human likeness of the voice. The results might have differed if we would have chosen a within-design for voice manipulation as reported in other studies [7, 15]. This also raises the question of how experimental design affects the outcome of the study. This point is explained in more detail below. Since voice did not show any effect Hypothesis 4 and 5 were rejected as well.

Regarding the effect of social behavior, specifically expressing empathy, the results of this experiment are promising. The empathic expressions of showing interest, understanding the situation of the user, and offering help were reflected as expressions of empathy by the participants. The system that used empathic language cues was rated higher in empathy than the neutral system supporting Hypothesis 2. However, effects of empathy on other measures such as interaction enjoyment, attitude and motivation to use the system only appeared when looking at perceived empathy. Users' individual interpretation of a certain behavior as being empathic is the decisive factor for users' evaluation of the system as proposed in Hypothesis 3. These results suggest that individual differences must be factored in when incorporating social behavior into a system. It is not the behavior per se but rather its interpretation by the user that affect overall system evaluation. Whether a certain behavior is interpreted as an expression of empathy depends on the situational context, interpersonal relationship and role of the interaction partners [20–22]. These poses specific challenges for implementing social behavior into automated systems. Well defined areas where interaction follows a script, where user expectations are clear and social rules for accepted behavior are well defined seem appropriate. In addition, it is difficult to anticipate all eventualities that may occur during an interaction. For the user it is not only important what the system says, but also whether the system listens well to the requests and needs of the user.

Another result of our study was that the users rated the system more negatively in the second session compared to the first session regardless of the experimental condition. Anecdotal evidence suggests that users had little or no expectations in the first session. Many users were surprised that the system worked better than expected, which probably influenced the positive evaluation of the system in the first session. Due to their experience of the first session, users had higher expectations for the second session. In the second session, users became more aware of the limitations of the system, which could have led to a more negative evaluation of the system. In general, the role of user expectations is not yet well understood. It is unclear how these expectations change when interacting repeatedly with computer agents over time. Further research is needed in this area as most of these systems are intended for repeated use. The current study has shown that user expectations change and significantly affect the user's evaluation of a system regardless of the actual performance of the system.

In this regard it is also important to discuss the role of the experimental design on the results. Many studies using within-designs [13, 15, 19], where participants interact with various systems and then evaluate them. Through within-designs individual differences can be controlled and fewer participants are needed for a study. However, order effects must also be considered and should be reported. Exposure to one system affects user expectations, which then impacts the assessment of the next system. Changes in expectations can be avoided by a between-design. However, the role of individual differences must be considered as well. As the current study has shown, the attitudes of the participants to automated systems correlate with the evaluation of these systems. Participants with an initial negative attitude towards automated systems rated the VUI consistently more negatively than participants with a positive attitude towards automated systems. Researchers need to carefully consider the experimental design for their study, considering their key research objectives. However, in addition to the manipulated variables, researchers should also think critically about how the design affects the outcome of their study.

The current study used two specific scenarios (losing an item at the airport) to test the VUI. Since empathy is nested in a specific context, future studies should examine a variety of scenarios to control if this is a robust effect. An effect of voice was not found in this study probably because of the between-design. In the future we want to test if the results will be different if voice is manipulated as a within-factor. Furthermore, the machinelike voice was derived by altering the humanlike voice with a software. It is possible that the manipulation was not strong enough to show a difference. It was clear to participants that the humanlike voice was spoken by a computer agent. Creating a stronger contrast between humanlike and machinelike voice could produce different results and should be tested in further studies.

5   Conclusion

The study presented here examined the effect of human likeness of voice and social behavior (empathic) on users' evaluation of a VUI. The unique contribution of this study is that not only the effect of the behavioral manipulation of the system was studied, but also the importance of the perception of this behavior by users. More than behavioral manipulation, the individual perception and interpretation of this behavior influenced the assessment of the users. The study shows that individual differences play a decisive role in the evaluation of system behavior. Therefore, it is important to consider the interaction of human and computer agent as a dynamic process that is subject to constant change.

Whether empathy improves human-computer interaction may depend on the context of the situation. For computer agents offering a service, empathy can contribute to a positive evaluation of the interaction and might motivate the user to use the system again.

VUI must be able to adapt to changing request and needs of users. VUI should be sensitive to contextual variables and the specific interaction situation. Future research should focus more on the changing expectations of users, as these influence the motivation and attitudes of users towards such systems. Human-computer interaction is a dynamic process that changes in the course of interaction. Developers of VUI need to take this interaction dynamic into account when developing such systems.

Acknowledgements. We thank all the volunteers who participated in this study.

References

1. Reeves, B., Nass, C.I.: The media equation: how people treat computers, television, and new media like real people and places. Center for the Study of Language and Information Cambridge University Press (1996)
2. Lee, J.D., See, K.A.: Trust in automation: designing for appropriate reliance. Hum. Factors **46**(1), 50–80 (2004)
3. Dzindolet, M.T., et al.: The role of trust in automation reliance. Int. J. Hum Comput Stud. **58**(6), 697–718 (2003)
4. Araujo, T.: Living up to the chatbot hype: the influence of anthropomorphic design cues and communicative agency framing on conversational agent and company perceptions. Comput. Hum. Behav. **85**, 183–189 (2018)
5. Nass, C., Lee, K.M.: Does computer-synthesized speech manifest personality? experimental tests of recognition, similarity-attraction, and consistency-attraction. J. Exp. Psychol. Appl. **7**(3), 171–181 (2001)
6. Nass, C., Moon, Y.: Machines and mindlessness: social responses to computers. J. Soc. Issues **56**(1), 81–103 (2000)
7. Louwerse, M.M., et al.: Social cues in animated conversational agents. Appl. Cogn. Psychol. **19**(6), 693–704 (2005)
8. Ruijten, P., Cuijpers, R.: Dynamic perceptions of human-likeness while interacting with a social robot. In: Proceedings of the Companion of the 2017 ACM/IEEE International Conference on Human-Robot Interaction, pp. 273–274. ACM, Vienna, Austria (2017)
9. von der Pütten, A.M., et al.: 'It doesn't matter what you are!' explaining social effects of agents and avatars. Comput. Hum. Behav. **26**(6), 1641–1650 (2010)
10. Hoff, K.A., Bashir, M.: Trust in automation: integrating empirical evidence on factors that influence trust. Hum. Factors **57**(3), 407–434 (2015)
11. Manzey, D., et al.: Human performance consequences of automated decision aids: the impact of degree of automation and system experience. J. Cogn. Eng. Decis. Making **6**(1), 57–87 (2012)

12. Mitchell, W.J., et al.: A mismatch in the human realism of face and voice produces an uncanny valley. i-Percept. **2**(1), 10–12 (2011)
13. Złotowski, J., et al.: Appearance of a robot affects the impact of its behaviour on perceived trustworthiness and empathy. J. Behav. Robot. **7**(1), 55–66 (2016)
14. Stárková, T., et al.: Anthropomorphisms in multimedia learning: Attract attention but do not enhance learning? J. Comput. Assist. Learn. **35**(4), 555–568 (2019)
15. Ilves, M., Surakka, V.: Subjective responses to synthesised speech with lexical emotional content: The effect of the naturalness of the synthetic voice. Behav. Inf. Technol. **32**(2), 117–131 (2013)
16. Muresan, A., Pohl, H.: Chats with bots: balancing imitation and engagement. In: Extended Abstracts of the 2019 CHI Conference on Human Factors in Computing Systems, pp. 1–6. ACM, Glasgow (2019)
17. Lottridge, D., et al.: Affective interaction: understanding, evaluating, and designing for human emotion. Rev. Hum. Factors Ergon. **7**, 197–237 (2011)
18. Leite, I., et al.: The influence of empathy in human–robot relations. Int. J. Hum Comput Stud. **71**(3), 250–260 (2013)
19. Niculescu, A., et al.: Making social robots more attractive: The effects of voice pitch, humor and empathy. Int. J. Social Robot. **5**(2), 171–191 (2013)
20. Butler, E.A.: Temporal interpersonal emotion systems: the "TIES" that form relationships. Pers. Soc. Psychol. Rev. **15**(4), 367–393 (2011)
21. Main, A., et al.: The interpersonal functions of empathy: a relational perspective. Emot. Rev. **9**(4), 358–366 (2017)
22. Butler, E.A.: Interpersonal affect dynamics: it takes two (and time) to tango. Emot. Rev. **7**(4), 336–341 (2015)
23. Kupetz, M.: Empathy display as interactinal achievements - multimodal and sequential aspects. J. Pragmatics **61**, 4–34 (2014)
24. Brave, S., et al.: Computers that care: investigating the effects of orientation of emotion exhibited by an embodied computer agent. Int. J. Hum Comput Stud. **62**(2), 161–178 (2005)
25. Urakami, J., et al.: Users' perception of empathic expressions by an advanced intelligent system. HAI, Kyoto (2019)
26. Syrdal, D.S., et al.: The negative attitudes towards robots scale and reactions to robot behaviour in a live human-robot interaction study. Adaptive and Emergent Behaviour and Complex Systems (2009)
27. Mercer, S.W., et al.: The consultation and relational empathy (CARE) measure: Development and preliminary validation and reliability of an empathy-based consultation process measure. Fam. Pract. **21**(6), 699–705 (2004)
28. Sacco, D.F., Ismail, M.M.: Social belongingness satisfaction as a function of interaction medium: face-to-face interactions facilitate greater social belonging and interaction enjoyment compared to instant messaging. Comput. Hum. Behav. **36**, 359–364 (2014)
29. Davis, F.D., et al.: User acceptance of computer technology: a comparison of two theoretical models. Manag. Sci. **35**(8), 982–1003 (1989)
30. Davis, F.D., et al.: Extrinsic and intrinsic motivation to use computers in the workplace. J. Appl. Soc. Psychol. **22**(14), 1111–1132 (1992)
31. Damiano, L., et al.: Artificial empathy: an interdisciplinary investigation. Int. J. Soc. Robot. **7**(1), 3–5 (2015). https://doi.org/10.1007/s12369-014-0259-6

Impression Detection and Management Using an Embodied Conversational Agent

Chen Wang[1]([✉]), Beatrice Biancardi[2], Maurizio Mancini[3], Angelo Cafaro[4],
Catherine Pelachaud[4], Thierry Pun[1], and Guillaume Chanel[1]

[1] University of Geneva, Geneva, Switzerland
{chen.wang,thierry.pun,guillaume.chanel}@unige.ch
[2] Telecom Paris, Paris, France
beatrice.biancardi@telecom-paris.fr
[3] University College Cork, Cork, Ireland
m.mancini@cs.ucc.ie
[4] CNRS-ISIR, Sorbonne Université, Paris, France
angelo.caf@gmail.com, catherine.pelachaud@upmc.fr

Abstract. Embodied Conversational Agents (ECAs) are a promising medium for human-computer interaction, since they are capable of engaging users in real-time face-to-face interaction [1,2]. Users' formed impressions of an ECA (e.g. favour or dislike) could be reflected behaviourally [3,4]. These impressions may affect the interaction and could even remain afterwards [5,7]. Thus, when we build an ECA to impress users, it is important to detect how users feel about the ECA. The impression the ECA leaves can then be adjusted by controlling its non-verbal behaviour [7]. Motivated by the role of ECAs in interpersonal interaction and the state-of-the-art on affect recognition, we investigated three research questions: 1) which modality (facial expressions, eye movements, and physiological signals) reveals most of the formed impressions; 2) whether an ECA could leave a better impression by maximizing the impression it produces; 3) whether there are differences in impression formation during human-human vs. human-agent interaction. Our results firstly showed the interest to use different modalities to detect impressions. An ANOVA test indicated that facial expressions performance outperforms the physiological modality performance (M = 1.27, p = 0.02). Secondly, our results presented the possibility of creating an adaptive ECA. Compared with the randomly selected ECA behaviour, participants' ratings tended to be higher in the conditions where the ECA adapted its behaviour based on the detected impressions. Thirdly, we found similar behaviour during human-human vs. human-agent interaction. People treated an ECA similarly to a human by spending more time observing the face area when forming an impression.

Keywords: Affective computing · Impression detection · Virtual agent · Eye gaze · Impression management · Machine learning · Reinforcement learning

Supported by the Swiss National Science Foundation under Grant Number 2000221E-164326 and by ANR IMPRESSSIONS project number ANR-15-CE23-0023.

© Springer Nature Switzerland AG 2020
M. Kurosu (Ed.): HCII 2020, LNCS 12182, pp. 260–278, 2020.
https://doi.org/10.1007/978-3-030-49062-1_18

1   Introduction

Virtual agents (VAs) are widely used for human-computer interaction, as they can mimic naturalistic human communication. An Embodied Conversational Agent (ECA), one kind of VA, is able to produce and respond to verbal and nonverbal communication in face-to-face conversations [1,2]. There are studies finding that ECAs' non-verbal behaviour is associated with emotions [3], personality traits [29] and interpersonal attitudes [4]. However, there is not much work on how ECAs' non-verbal behaviour influences formed impressions. The formed impression (e.g. favor or dislike someone) of an ECA is an internal state which may be reflected by users behaviourally [18,20]. The formed impression could affect the interaction (e.g. willingness to interact), and the effect could even last after the interaction [6,7]. Thus, when we build an ECA to impress users and have a good interaction, it is important to sense how users think about the VA through users' body responses. Then the impression the ECA leaves could be controlled accordingly by adapting its non-verbal behaviour. In this context, it is possible to use machine learning methods to determine the impression that an user is forming and to rely on this information to build a more engaging VA, which is able to manage the impressions they leave on users.

Impression, as an important component for social cognition and communication, has not been well explored with machine learning methods. Warmth and competence (W&C) are the most used impression dimensions in the literature about human-human and human-agent interaction [12,18,22,23]. Warmth represents the intentions of the others (positive or negative), and competence stands for the consequent ability to execute those intentions. For example, if a person A meets a person B who is rude and speaks with an angry voice, A might form an impression that B is competent but rather cold. It is possible to use the signals of B to predict which impression B leaves on A and others. This is called **impression prediction** (yellow arrow in Fig. 1), and most of the literature focuses on this case. On the other hand, we could use the body responses of A to detect the impression that A forms of B. This is called **impression detection** (blue arrow in Fig. 1) and is the main focus of this paper. The impression expressive behaviour could be conveyed through multiple modalities, including facial, gestural and physiological reactions, which may not always be congruent and have the same level of importance [5]. To the best of our knowledge, there is rarely studies with ECA which measures users' impressions and adapts its behaviour accordingly. In this paper, we would like to investigate three research questions: 1) which modality (facial, eye and physiological expressions) reveals most of the formed impressions; 2) whether an ECA could leave a better impression on users by maximizing the impression (W or C) it produces; 3) whether there are differences in impression formation during human-human vs. human-agent interaction. We first applied several impression detection models on each modality of an impression evoking corpus with continuous W&C self-reports. We explored the modality importance by observing the detection performance. With the learned modality importance and detection model from the first study, we built an ECA use case in which the ECA interacted with a participant and

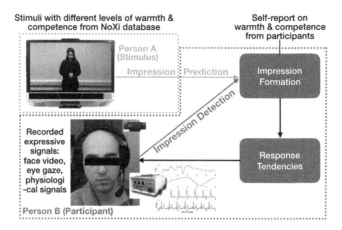

Impression Prediction: **Using A's behaviors to predict how B will feel about A (state of the art)**
Impression Detection: **Using B's behaviors to detect how B has felt about A (proposed method)**

Fig. 1. Impression formation and detection diagram [5] (Color figure online)

adapted its behaviour based on the detected participant impressions. We evaluated our ECA by comparing the participants' impression reports with the automatically detected impressions to investigate if our adaptive ECA could lead to changes in reported W&C. We also compared the exhibited behaviour of participants forming an impression of an ECA with the behaviour forming an impression of a human.

2   Background and Related Work

2.1   Impression and Emotion Recognition

Current research mainly focuses on how exhibited behaviour influences other's formation of impressions (i.e. impression prediction). For example, there are some studies on stereotype based prediction [21,28]. Instead of studying prediction, this work focuses on detecting impressions from the expressive behaviour of the person forming the impression (blue arrow shown in Fig. 1) in the W&C space, which is a new approach to impression recognition. According to [18,25], forming an impression is associated with emotions and behaviour. To the best of our knowledge, there is only one study on assessing the formed impressions from the body signals (e.g. facial expressions and gestures) of the person forming the impression [5]. In [5], it reported that formed impressions could be detected using multimodal signals in both multi-task and single task frameworks. However, which body signal reveals the formed impression more expressively was not discussed. Also it was not mentioned whether the detection models in [5] are suitable for real-time application such as human-agent interaction.

Studies in emotion recognition demonstrated the possibility of inferring user's emotions from multimodal signals [13]. Since emotions can be induced when forming impressions [18], this supports the possibility of assessing users' impressions from their affective expressions. Emotion recognition studies explored a variety of models using machine learning methods. These methods can be grouped in two classes based on whether temporal information is applied or not. The non-temporal models generally require contextual features. Temporal models exploit the dynamic information in the model directly. Methods such as Multilayer Perceptron (MLP), Support Vector Machine (SVM), XGBoost and Long Short Term Memory (LSTM) models are currently widely used with several topologies [13, 16, 24].

2.2   ECA Impression Management

To manipulate the impression (W&C) that the ECAs leave on users, researchers adopted findings from human-human interaction [6, 19, 27, 31] to the ECA design. Nguyen et al. [31] applied an iterative methodology that included theory from theater, animation and psychology, expert reviews, user testing and feedback, to extract a set of rules to be encoded in an ECA. To do that, they analysed gestures and gaze behaviour in videos of actors performing different degrees of W&C. In [12], it investigated the associations between non-verbal cues and W&C impressions in human-human interaction. The type of gestures, arms rest poses, head movements and smiling were annotated, as well as the perceived W&C of people who played the role of expert in a corpus of videos of dyadic natural interactions. It was found that the presence of gestures was positively associated with both W&C. A negative association was found between some arms rest poses and W&C, such as arms crossed. The smiling behaviour presented while performing a gesture could increase warmth judgements, while negatively related to competence judgements. These finds were used to guide ECA designs. Beside behaviour, the appearances of ECAs also influence the perception of W&C. For example, Bergmann et al. [11] found that human-like vs. robot-like appearance positively affected the perception of warmth, while the presence of co-speech gestures increased competence judgements.

2.3   Human-ECA Impression Formation

Since ECAs can mimic naturalistic human communication, there are studies comparing human-human interaction with human-ECA interaction. According to Wang, Joel, et al. [38], people tended to treat VAs similarly to real human beings. McRorie et al. [29] implemented four stereotypical personalities in the virtual agents. During the interaction with agents, the participants could easily identify the agents' personalities in a similar way that they identified humans with the same personality. Anzalone et al. [8] explained the importance of assessing the non-verbal behaviour of the humans to increase the engagement during human-robot interaction. Kramer et al. [26] showed that a smiling agent did not change the inferences made by the users, but whenever the virtual agent smiled, it triggered a mimicry smile on the users. It meant that the agent succeeded in provoking a change of user behavior while not having an impact on the impression formation. Although there are studies showing that people judge or interact with ECAs similarly as with humans, it still requires investigation on whether people express their formed impression of ECAs the same way of humans.

3   Impression Detection

3.1   Impression Evoking Corpus

To build impression detection models, we relied on an impression evoked corpus reported in [5], where multimodal data of 62 participants (23 female and 39 male) was recorded while watching impression stimuli and reporting their formed impressions in W&C continuously. The data recording diagram is shown in Fig. 1. The stimuli used to evoking participants' impressions are from Noxi database [14]. In each video from Noxi database, a different expert (real person) was talking about a topic of interest (e.g. cooking). The Noxi videos have corresponding continuous W&C and gesture annotations of the experts which were annotated by motivated and experienced people, with previous experience in affective annotation and background knowledge about W&C. More details of the Noxi database can be found in [14]. The original Noxi videos are too long for our experiment. Thus the stimuli used in [5] were cut and selected from the Noxi [14] database based on the warmth (range [0, 1]), competence (range [0, 1]) and gesture annotations (e.g.iconic). We firstly applied peak detection on the Noxi W&C annotations and selected the video clips that contain at least one change (peak) in warmth or competence. Then among the W&C changing clips, we chose the ones containing most gesture annotations. Each stimulus lasts around 2 min (mean = 1.92, std = 0.22) with different levels of warmth (mean = 0.56, std = 0.18) and competence (mean = 0.52, std = 0.28). The stimuli were displayed in a random sequence.

The following modalities were recorded while the participants were watching the impression stimuli: facial videos (Logitech webcam C525 & C920, sample rate 30 fps), eye movements (Tobii TX300 & T120, sample rate 300 Hz and 120 Hz respectively) and physiological signals (electrocardiography (ECG) and galvanic skin response (GSR), using a Biosemi amplifier, sample rate 512 Hz). At the same time participants annotated their formed impressions by pressing keyboard buttons whenever they felt a change in warmth (up & down keyboard arrow) or in competence (left & right keyboard arrow). W&C were annotated independently and could be annotated at the same time. All participants were given the same explanation about the concept of W&C before the recording. English proficiency levels were requested to be over B2 in the Common European Framework of Reference, to guarantee that the participants were able to understand and follow experiment instructions. We used the definition of W&C in [25] and two sets of words [18] to describe W&C to help them to understand. All participants were informed the experiment content and signed a consent form. They were trained with the annotation tool and practiced before watching the stimuli. In total, the corpus contains 62 participants with 1625 min of multimodal recordings and W&C annotations.

3.2 Pre-processing and Feature Extraction

To prepare the recorded data for regression models, we firstly synchronized the impression annotations with multimodal recordings using the recorded triggers. The triggers are the starting timestamp of each stimulus. With the triggers and stimuli lengths, we segmented the recorded data based on each stimulus. The recorded modalities from the impression corpus have various sampling frequency ranging from 30 to 512 Hz while the impression annotations have uneven sampling frequency. We resampled the impression annotations as well as multimodal recordings or extracted features to get the same length of data. In this paper, each modality as well as annotations were resampled to 30 Hz (face video frame rate) for simplification.

To homogenize sampling frequencies of annotations and recorded signals, we used the face video frame rate as a standard and applied 1D polynomial interpolation on W&C annotations respectively to achieve the same sample rate. After the interpolation, we followed [36] and applied a 10 s sliding window with overlap (1 frame shift per time) to smooth warmth and competence annotations. Features were extracted from each modalities: facial video, eye gaze and physiological signals (ECG and GSR signals). We extracted the features that have been proved to work well for affective recognition [5,13,16,24]. Following [13], we used action units (AU) as features which are the deconstructed representations of facial expressions [20]. The AUs were extracted on each frame using an open source tool OpenFace [10]. We had 17 AUs intensity (from 0 to 5) and 18 AUs presence (0 or 1) features. For eye movements, the 2D gaze location on the display, the 3D locations of the left and right eyes, and the gaze duration recorded by the eye tracker were taken as features. All the 9 features from eye movements are down sampled (120 Hz or 300 Hz) to the video frame rate (30 Hz). To process physiological signals, we used the TEAP toolbox [34] to extract features. We filtered out the noise with a median filter and then extracted Skin Conductance Response (SCR) from the GSR signal, heart rate (HR), heart rate variability (HRV), HR multi-scale entropy, mean heart rate over 1 min and corresponding standard deviation from the ECG signals. We resampled the extracted features to 30 Hz instead of resampling the raw signals directly to conserve more information. All the extracted multimodal features were smoothed using the same sliding window as for annotations to get the same sample sizes. After resampling, features as well as smoothed annotations were standardized so that they all had a mean of 0 and a variance of 1 to improve gradient descent convergence and avoid having a classification bias toward high magnitude features.

3.3 Impression Detection Models

As presented in Sect. 2.1, regression models have performed reliably in affect recognition. We tested 3 widely used regression models from different families of supervised learning algorithms: Support vector regression (SVR) from vector machines, XGBoost from ensemble methods with decision trees and Multilayer Perceptron Regression (MLP) from neural networks to detect the formed impressions in W&C dimensions. Regression models on W&C were trained and tested separately. All the aforementioned models generate predictions of a warmth (resp.competence) score at each frame (30 Hz) based on the input features. We implemented SVR and MLP using the scikit-learn library [32] and XGBoost [17] with the python XGBoost library[1]. For SVR, we used a radial basis functions kernel with gamma equals to $1/P$ as proposed in [35], where P is the number of features, and set the tolerance for the optimization stopping criterion to 1e-4. For MLP, we set 2 hidden layers with 64 neurons on each and 1 dimension output (i.e. warmth and competence detection are trained independently). We trained at most 50 epochs and applied early stopping to avoid overfitting with patience equal to 5 epochs. Mean squared error (MSE) was used as the loss function. XGBoost was set with 100 estimators and the same learning rate as MLP: 1e-3. To avoid overfitting, XGBoost and MLP were set with the same early stopping setting with a patience equal to 5.

To train and test detection models, we used a leave-one-out cross-validation scheme. We divided the data set into three partitions: 1 participant was left out for testing, the remaining data was all used for SVR training while randomly divided into two parts for MLP and XGBoost: 80% for training and 20% for validation. We rotated the left-out testing participant to estimate the model performance of all the participants. We trained and tested the 3 regression models respectively with unimodal features as well as multimodal features. We also tested multimodal detection with early fusion for combining features. That is, features from different modalities were concatenated together as the input feature matrix.

3.4 Modality Performance Analysis

We investigated the importance of each modality by calculating the Concordance Correlation Coefficient (CCC) between the detected impression and participant annotations. Significant performance differences between the modalities and regression models were tested using ANOVA.

We firstly tested significant difference in unimodal impression detection performance to check if some modalities were more accurate than others. The CCC values were shown to be normally distributed using a Shapiro test ($p = 0.31$). We thus ran a $3 \times 3 \times 2$ between-group ANOVA, with regression model, modality, and impression dimension as factors. We did not find an effect for impression dimension (warmth or competence). A main effect of

---

[1] https://github.com/dmlc/xgboost.

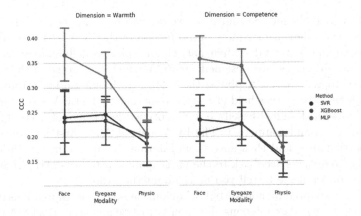

Fig. 2. Unimodal impression detection performance

regression model was found ($F(2, 27) = 3.53, p < 0.05$). As shown in Fig. 2, post-hoc tests revealed that MLP achieved higher detection accuracy than XGBoost($mean - difference = 0.19, p - adjust = 0.04$). A main effect of the modality was also found ($F(2, 27) = 4.15, p < 0.03$). Post-hoc test indicated that facial expressions performance outperformed the physiological modality performance ($mean - difference = 1.27, p - adjust = 0.02$). Although there was no significant difference between facial expressions and eye movements with all 3 regression models ($p > 0.05$), the mean CCC performance of facial modality from MLP were better than eye movements for both W&C.

We also tested the performance for multimodal impression detection. For this purpose, an early fusion strategy was employed where all modality features were concatenated in a unique feature vector. For MLP, a mean CCC of 0.652 for warmth and 0.681 for competence was obtained. This improvement of performance over unimodal detection was significant for warmth ($t = 6.63, p < 0.01$) and competence ($t = 5.71, p < 0.03$) as demonstrated by a pairwise t-test. The multimodal performance with SVR was 0.317 for warmth and 0.308 for competence. The XGBoost algorithm obtained slightly better results with a CCC of 0.332 for warmth and 0.376 for competence. These results were higher than unimodal performance but lower than multimodal MLP.

Overall, our results confirm that when individuals are unknown to us, our facial expressions reveal most the impression we've formed of the unknowns [39]. The learned modality salience could be applied in the future work of multimodal fusion at modality level for impression detection.

4   Embodied Conversational Agent Use Case

We conducted a use case in order to test our impression detection model in a user-agent real-time interaction scenario. We firstly would like to investigate whether impression detection and adaptation could improve users' formed impressions of an ECA in real-time. Secondly we would like to compare the participants' behaviour when they are forming an impression of the ECA with the behaviour occurring in the first study, when participants observe a human stimulus. To reach those objectives, we designed an ECA which interacted with each user on a given topic. The ECA played the role of a virtual guide, introducing an exhibit about video games held at a science museum. The ECA was a black-hair female character designed based on a stereotyped-based model from [3], aiming to appear warm and competent. The ECA, named Alice, first introduced itself to the participants, and then gave them information about the exhibition. The ECA asked questions/feedback to the participant during the interaction as well (e.g. "Do you want me to tell you more about the exhibit?").

The ECA adapted its non-verbal behaviour based on the impressions detected from the users' facial expressions. The non-verbal behaviour of the ECA included gestures, arm rest poses and smiling facial expression. The behaviour was designed based on the finding from [12]. This adaptation of ECA was achieved by employing a reinforcement learning algorithm (Q-learning) that aimed at maximizing either the detected warmth or competence depending on the experimental condition. The reward of the ECA to select the most appropriate non-verbal behaviour was computed as the increase or maintenance of detected competence or warmth. The eye movements were recorded for some participants but were not used for detecting impression. Not all participants agreed to record eye movements, for example, the eye tracker cannot be used by epilepsy patients. To guarantee that we had a reliable model for impression detection, we decided to use the facial modality only. We focused on how ECA's behaviour could change the users' impressions, thus the agent appearance, voice and tone remained the same as a constant in all experimental conditions. The speech acts were scripted before the experiment.

The interaction with the ECA lasted about 3 min (a duration similar to the one used for the human stimulus presented in Sect. 3.1) divided in 26 speaking turns. A speaking turn was defined as a dialog act (e.g., greeting, asking questions, describing a video game, etc.) played by the ECA and user's possible answer or verbal feedback. In the absence of user's responses (i.e. in case of user's silence lasting more than 1.5 s or 4 s, depending on whether the ECA just said a sentence or asked an explicit question), the ECA continued with another speaking turn. User's impression was determined using the data driven regression model presented in Sects. 3.3 and 4.1. The detected warmth or competence given at 30 Hz were averaged over periods of 1 s without overlapping (i.e. 1 warmth or competence value per second). After each speaking turn, the last detected warmth or competence value was sent to the reinforcement learning module to drive the ECA behaviour.

4.1   Impression Management System

The proposed system was composed of 2 main modules enabling real-time user-agent interaction as illustrated in Fig. 3. The first module concerned *User's Impressions Detection* includes two sub-components: one to detect user's behaviour (speech, facial expressions) and the second to analyse and interpret them (i.e. facial expressions were used to infer users' impressions of the ECA). The VisNet open source platform [5] was exploited to extract the user's face AUs in real-time, by running the OpenFace framework [10], and user's speech by executing the Microsoft Speech Platform[2]. Based on the extracted AUs, user's impressions were computed with the MLP model presented in Sect. 3.3. Although the eye movements and physiological signals contributed to a better impression detection performance on average, these modalities did not increase accuracy significantly. Compared with video recordings, ECG and GSR were more invasive, and they required time and experience to attach sensors on the skin. It was not practical for our setting where participants visited a museum and barely had time for such an experiment. In the future remotely detected physiological information will be embedded into our impression detection model.

The second module was the *Agent's Impression Manager* which arbitrates verbal behaviour (i.e. what the ECA should say) and non-verbal behaviour (the ECA behaviour (e.g. smiling, gestures, etc.) accompanying speech). The ECA's speech and behaviour are dynamically selected to effectively manage impressions of W&C. The ECA impression management module was implemented with Flipper [37], a dialogue manager that, given the detected user's impressions, chooses the verbal and pre-designed non-verbal behaviour (related to W&C based on [12]) the ECA will display in the next speaking turn. The behaviour was selected according to a Reinforcement Learning (Q-learning) algorithm with the detected impressions as rewards. The reinforcement learning module defined states s (in our case these were warmth or competence level) and actions a performed by the ECA (in this paper an action is the dialogue act accompanied with verbal and non-verbal behaviour). The initial Q values ($Q(s, a)$) of actions and states were set up to 0. A reward function R was computed for each combination of state and action. In our case R was the difference between detected warmth (resp. competence) and the current warmth (resp. competence) level. The Q-learning algorithm explored all the possible next state-action pairs (s', a') and tried to maximize the future rewards with a discount rate γ. We maximized one dimension at a time since it is difficult to maximize both due to the halo effect [33]. The new Q values ($Q(new)(s, a)$) are updated with the Q function. After each speaking turn, both Q table and reward table would be updated. The SAIBA-compliant AnonymAgent platform supported the generation of behaviour and computed the corresponding animation of the ECA [5]. More details on the interactive system can be found in [5].

To evaluate our impression detection model performance, we set 3 conditions for the ECA: Warmth, Competence and Random. Under Warmth and Competence conditions, the ECA performed the behaviour that the Impression Manager chose. That is, during the experiment, the ECA performed one of the pre-defined gestures according to the Q-learning method and in order to maximize either warmth or competence. Under the Random condition, the ECA performed behaviour that was randomly selected among the set of possible behaviour.

---

[2] https://www.microsoft.com/en-us/download/details.aspx?id=27225.

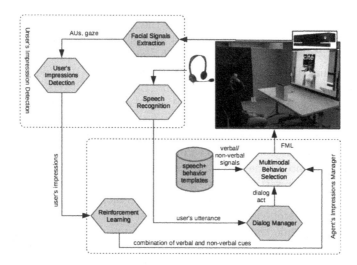

Fig. 3. The impression management system [5]

4.2 Collected Data

All participants were visitors at the museum who were voluntarily participating. They all signed a consent form before the recording. In total, we collected data from 71 participants who were randomly assigned to each condition. We got 25 participants in the Warmth condition, 27 in the Competence condition and 19 in the Random condition. Upper body videos (Kinect V2, sample rate 30 fps) were recorded for all participants and we also collected eye movements (Tobii Pro Nano, sample rate 60 Hz) from 19 participants (8 for Warmth, 8 for Competence and 3 for Random). Participants answered a questionnaire after the interaction with the ECA to report their overall formed impressions of the ECA in the W&C dimension (4 items concerning warmth, 4 concerning competence with a 7 point Likert scale, according to [9]). In order to group together the 4 reported values for warmth and the 4 for competence, Cronbach's alphas were computed on the scores. Good reliability was found for both W&C with $\alpha = 0.85$ and $\alpha = 0.81$ respectively. The mean of these items were calculated separately in order to have one warmth score and one competence score for each participant.

5 Result and Discussion

5.1 Impression Management Efficiency

To evaluate our real-time impression model performance, we firstly compared the detected warmth or competence from the facial modality with the reported impressions from the questionnaire. Secondly, we checked whether the trends of the detected warmth or competence were increasing in their respective condition. In other words we verified that warmth (resp. competence) was overall increasing in the warmth (resp. competence) condition.

The detected W&C given at 30 Hz were averaged over periods of 1 s without overlapping (i.e. one warmth or competence value per second). Although only the last detected warmth or competence value after each speaking turn was sent to drive the ECA behaviour, we recorded all the detected warmth or competence values. We used the mean value of the detected impression over the whole interaction period and call it the *mean impression* of the participant. We also calculated the average value of the last 10 s of the detected impression scores as the *late detected impression*. We standardized detected W&C values (both average & late average) and self-reported ones to remove the scale influence for CCC. The CCC between reported impressions and late detected impression ($W = 0.38, C = 0.42$) were higher than those between average impression in both warmth (0.29) and competence (0.31) dimensions, which means the late detected impression is closer to the self-reported impression. To test differences in participants reported impressions in the three difference conditions (Random, Competence adaptation and Warmth adaptation), a one-way ANOVA was employed. The results showed that participants in the Competence condition gave higher scores than participants in the Random conditions ($F(2, 32) = 3.12, p < 0.05$). There was no significant effect between Random condition and Warmth conditions, though the mean impression scores were higher than the Random condition [5].

The results showed that participants' impressions could change during the interaction. The later detected impression was closer to the participants' reported impression. Participants' ratings tended to be higher in the W&C conditions in which the ECA adapted its behaviour based on detected impressions, compared to the Random condition. In particular, the results indicated that we managed to manipulate the impression of competence with our adaptive ECA.

Under Warmth and Competence conditions, the ECA changed its behaviour in order to maximize participants' perception of warmth and competence. Thus we calculated the global deterministic trend of detected warmth/competence to check whether they were increasing consistently. The trend was determined by computing the linear regression coefficient of the detected impressions using the python StatsModel module. Under the Warmth condition, our ECA managed to increase warmth or keep warmth in a high level for the majority of participants (15 out of 25). In the Competence condition, competence was increasing for only 13 out 27 participants. This could be caused by inaccuracy of the detected impression or the agent impression management module (e.g. choose an ECA behaviour which is supposed to increase competence but actually causes competence decrements).

5.2   Impression Formation of Humans and ECA

To compare how people behave when forming an impression of a person and an ECA, we analyzed gaze patterns during these two type of interactions. For the human-human interaction, we extracted patterns of participants from the first study when they were watching the human stimuli presented in Sect. 3.1. This allowed us to study the differences in behaviour when forming an impression of a human and an agent. We firstly rejected all samples without gaze detection (because of blinking or participant eye drifting). We then extracted the face area of our human stimuli and ECA using 67 landmarks extracted by OpenFace [10]. The face area was defined as the smallest rectangle area (green rectangle of Fig. 4) containing all facial landmarks. If the gaze locates within the rectangle area, we assume that the participant is looking at the face area. If the gaze locates out of the rectangle, we assume that the participant is looking at other regions. We also used the line connecting landmark 8 and landmark 27 to separate the left from the right hemiface shown in Fig. 4. For human stimuli, we counted the percentage of gazes located within the face area when the participants reported impression changes. For this purpose, we extracted a 2 s window centered around each W&C annotations. For the ECA, we did a similar processing as human stimuli, however, since in this case we do not have annotations all along the interaction, we took the whole interaction under Warmth and Competence conditions separately to compute the percentage of gazes on the face area.

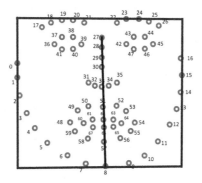

Fig. 4. Landmarks from OpenFace [10]. The green rectangle defines the face area. The vertical black bar separates the left from the right hemiface. (Color figure online)

We tested if participants were looking more at the face than at other regions using a Chi-square test. As shown in Fig. 5a, participants spent significantly more time gazing at the face area of the human stimulus when judging warmth ($p(5.51) = 0.041$). For competence, no significant difference was found ($p > 0.05$) and it appeared that participants spent similar amount of time looking at the face and the other regions. Although the setting for human-human interaction and human-ECA interaction was not exactly the same, people showed similar eye behaviour when interacting with the ECA (shown in Fig. 5b) by spending significantly more time looking at the face area ($p < 0.03$), but this time for both the Warmth and Competence conditions. To compare eye behaviour between the human stimuli and human-ECA interactions, we ran a 2 × 2 Chi-squared test with the experiment (human vs. ECA) and the impression dimensions (warmth vs. competence) as independent variables. The result of this test was not significant ($p = 0.94$) indicating that participants' eye behaviour was similar under all conditions.

For both human-human interaction and human-virtual agent interaction, face modality played an important role in forming impression. When interacting with an ECA, people mainly focused on the face area. While watching human stimuli, people also spent time to glance at the background, stimuli gestures, clothes and so on. This confirmed the finding of Cassell et al. [15], the modeling of the ECA face is an important component for the impact on the user.

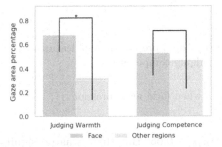 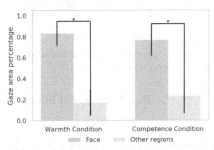

(a) Participants' gaze area when they reported changes in W&C space while watching human stimuli (* $p < 0.05$)

(b) Participants' gaze area under W&C conditions while interacting with ECA (* $p < 0.05$)

Fig. 5. Gaze area in human-human vs. human-agent interaction

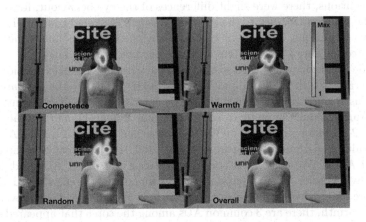

Fig. 6. Participants' gaze area while interacting with ECA in different conditions

According to [30], people demonstrate significant left-sided facial asymmetry when expressing emotions (i.e. facial expressions are more intense and faster on the left side). In addition people are more sensitive to the left hemiface of others for emotion perception. In our study, this effect was found both when interacting with human stimuli and ECA. For human stimuli, participants spent significantly more time looking at the left hemiface both for judging W&C with

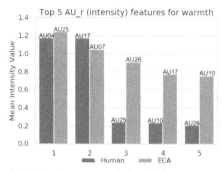

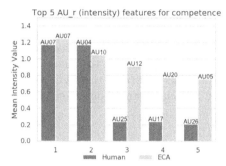

(a) Top 5 presented facial features in when judging warmth

(b) Top 5 presented facial features when judging competence

Fig. 7. Presented facial features when form an impression

Chi-square test $chi - square = 6.27/6.86, p < 0.05$. But there was no significant difference between judging W&C. That is, when people looked at the face area for impression judgement, they looked more at the left hemiface no matter judging warmth or competence. While interacting with the ECA (Fig. 6), participants paid more attention on the left side of the agent face in all three conditions (Warmth, Competence and Random). There is no significant difference from interacting with humans with ANOVA test $p > 0.05$. Within the three conditions, there were slight differences of the eye behaviour, for example, under the Random condition, the eye gaze was less clustered compared with the other two conditions. This might be caused by the small amount of data in the Random condition (3 participants with eye movement recording).

Beside eye movements, we also analyzed participants' facial expressions when they interacted with the ECA and human stimuli. Similar to the gaze area analysis, we used the intensity values of 17 AUs through the whole ECA interaction under Warmth and Competence conditions. For human-human interaction, we took the 2-s windows centered at W&C annotations respectively. The AU intensity (1 value per frame ranging from 0 to 5 for 1 AU) presents how intense the detected AU is. We calculated the mean intensity of all 17 AUs and selected the top five AUs for W&C separately. It was found that people showed different AUs more often when evaluating other's warmth or competence. However, when judging warmth, there are 3 common AUs among the top 5 that appeared on participants' faces for both human-human and human-ECA interaction as shown in Fig. 7a. That was AU25 *lips part*, AU07 *lid tightener* and AU10 *upper lip raiser*. Although they had different ranking with ECA and human, they all presented intensively when participants were processing warmth related information. While for judging competence (Fig. 7b), there was only one mutual AU that revealed intensively under both human-human and human-ECA interaction, which was AU07 *lid tightener*. This was the most intense AU that appeared on participants for judging competence. This AU also presented when assessing warmth. Another interesting finding was that the mean AU intensity of the 17 AUs was higher ($mean - diff - warmth = 0.118, mean - diff - comp = 0.335$) when participants was interacting with the ECA other than human, no matter judging warmth nor competence. That means participants were more expressive when facing an ECA than a human stimulus.

6   Conclusion and Future Work

Our results showed the interest to use different modalities to detect formed impressions, namely facial expressions, eye movements and physiological reactions. Among all modalities, facial expressions achieve the highest accuracy with the MLP model. Secondly, our results presented the possibility of creating an adaptive ECA by detecting users' impressions from facial expressions. In the ECA use case, our results showed the consistency in late detected impression scores from facial expressions and participants' self-reports. Participants' ratings tended to be higher in the conditions in which the ECA adapted its behaviour based on the detected impressions, compared with the randomly selected ECA behaviour. Thirdly, we found similar behaviour in impression formation during human-human vs. human-agent interaction. People treated the ECA similarly as humans by spending significantly more time observing the face area when forming an impression. That indicated that participants' impressions could be manipulated by using non-verbal behaviour, particularly facial expressions and possibly gestures. Participants also presented similar facial expressions when they formed an impression of an ECA or a human, while they facially expressed more when they faced an ECA. These insights could be used to better understand the theoretical basis for impression formation and could be applied in creating adaptive ECAs.

Our work has its limitations and many aspects remain to be explored in detecting and managing impressions for ECA. Our work targets on the non-verbal behaviour of an ECA. According to [18, 22, 25], appearance (e.g. physical aspect and clothing style) could also influence the impression formation. In our case, the ECA did not change its appearance and we regarded it as an constant. However, with different appearance setting, it may enhance or decrease the impression perception caused by non-verbal behaviour. For impression detection, more multimodal fusion methods will be explored to improve the detection performance. The different facial expressive behaviour while facing an ECA than a human, indicates training machine learning model with human-ECA interaction data to improve the detection accuracy. With a better detection model, the ECA could more adequately choose the correct behaviour. Besides, there may be better solutions than reinforcement learning for selecting impression evoking behaviour to improve the ECA performance.

References

1. Cafaro, A., Vilhjalmsson, H.H., Bickmore, T.: First impressions in human-agent virtual encounters. ACM Trans. Comput. Hum. Interact. **23**(4), 40 (2016). Article 24

2. ter Maat, M., Truong, K.P., Heylen, D.: How turn-taking strategies influence users' impressions of an agent. In: Allbeck, J., Badler, N., Bickmore, T., Pelachaud, C., Safonova, A. (eds.) IVA 2010. LNCS (LNAI), vol. 6356, pp. 441–453. Springer, Heidelberg (2010). https://doi.org/10.1007/978-3-642-15892-6_48

3. Pelachaud, C.: Modelling multimodal expression of emotion in a virtual agent. Philos. Trans. Roy. Soc. London B Biol. Sci. **364**(1535), 3539–3548 (2009)

4. Ravenet, B., Ochs, M., Pelachaud, C.: From a user-created corpus of virtual agent's non-verbal behavior to a computational model of interpersonal attitudes. In: Aylett, R., Krenn, B., Pelachaud, C., Shimodaira, H. (eds.) IVA 2013. LNCS (LNAI), vol. 8108, pp. 263–274. Springer, Heidelberg (2013). https://doi.org/10.1007/978-3-642-40415-3_23

5. Wang, C., Pun, T., Chanel, G.: Your body reveals your impressions about others: a study on multimodal impression detection. In: 2019 8th International Conference on Affective Computing and Intelligent Interaction Workshops and Demos (ACIIW). IEEE (2019)

6. Biancardi, B., et al.: A computational model for managing impressions of an embodied conversational agent in real-time. In: 2019 8th International Conference on Affective Computing and Intelligent Interaction (ACII). IEEE (2019)

7. Goffman, E.: The Presentation of Self in Everyday Life. Harmondsworth, London (1978)

8. Anzalone, S.M., Boucenna, S.A., Ivaldi, S., Chetouani, M.: Evaluating the engagement with social robots. Int. J. Soc. Rob. **7**(4), 465–478 (2015)

9. Aragones, J.I., Poggio, L., Sevillano, V., Perez-Lopez, R., Sanchez-Bernardos, M.-L.: Measuring warmth and competence at inter-group, interpersonal and individual levels/Medicion de la cordialidad y la competencia en los niveles intergrupal, interindividual e individual. Revista de Psicologia Social **30**(3), 407–438 (2015)

10. Baltruvsaitis, T., Robinson, P., Morency, L.-P.: OpenFace: an open source facial behavior analysis toolkit. In: 2016 IEEE Winter Conference on Applications of Computer Vision (WACV), pp. 1–10. IEEE (2016)

11. Bergmann, K., Eyssel, F., Kopp, S.: A second chance to make a first impression? how appearance and nonverbal behavior affect perceived warmth and competence of virtual agents over time. In: Nakano, Y., Neff, M., Paiva, A., Walker, M. (eds.) IVA 2012. LNCS (LNAI), vol. 7502, pp. 126–138. Springer, Heidelberg (2012). https://doi.org/10.1007/978-3-642-33197-8_13

12. Biancardi, B., Cafaro, A., Pelachaud, C.: Analyzing first impressions of warmth and competence from observable nonverbal cues in expert-novice interactions. In: Proceedings of the 19th ACM International Conference on Multimodal Interaction, pp. 341–349. ACM (2017)

13. Kevin Brady, et al.: Multi-modal audio, video and physiological sensor learning for continuous emotion prediction. In: Proceedings of the 6th International Workshop on Audio/Visual Emotion Challenge, pp. 97–104. ACM (2016)

14. Cafaro, A., et al.: The NoXi database: multimodal recordings of mediated novice-expert interactions. In: Proceedings of the 19th ACM International Conference on Multimodal Interaction, pp. 350–359. ACM (2017)

15. Cassell, J., Sullivan, J., Churchill, E., Prevost, S.: Embodied Conversational Agents. MIT Press, Cambridge (2000)

16. Chen, S., Jin, Q., Zhao, J., Wang, S.: Multimodal multi-task learning for dimensional and continuous emotion recognition. In: Proceedings of the 7th Annual Workshop on Audio/Visual Emotion Challenge, pp. 19–26. ACM (2017)

17. Chen, T., Guestrin, C.: Xgboost: a scalable tree boosting system. In: Proceedings of the 22nd ACM SIGKDD International Conference on Knowledge 879 Discovery and Data Mining, pp. 785–794. ACM (2016)
18. Cuddy, A.J.C., Fiske, S.T., Glick, P.: Warmth and competence as universal dimensions of social perception: the stereotype content model and the BIAS map. Adv. Exp. Soc. Psychol. **40**(2008), 61–149 (2008)
19. Duchenne, D.B.: The mechanism of human facial expression or an electrophysiological analysis of the expression of the emotions (Cuthbertson, A. Trans.), Cambridge University Press, New York. (Original work published 1862) (1990)
20. Ekman, P., Keltner, D.: Universal facial expressions of emotion. In: Segerstrale, U., Molnar, P. (eds.) Nonverbal Communication: Where Nature Meets Culture, pp. 27–46 (1997)
21. Farnadi, G., Sushmita, S., Sitaraman, G., Ton, N., De Cock, M., Davalos, S.: A multivariate regression approach to personality impression recognition of vloggers. In: Proceedings of the 2014 ACM Multi Media on Workshop on Computational Personality Recognition, pp. 1–6. ACM (2014)
22. Fiske, S.T., Cuddy, A.J.C., Glick, P.: Universal dimensions of social cognition: warmth and competence. Trends Cogn. Sci. **11**(2), 77–83 (2007)
23. Fiske, S.T., Cuddy, A.J.C., Glick, P., Xu, J.: A model of stereotype content: competence and warmth respectively follow from perceived status and competition. J. Pers. Soc. Psychol. **82**(6), 878–902 (2002)
24. Gunes, H., Pantic, M.: Automatic, dimensional and continuous emotion recognition. Int. J. Synth. Emot. (IJSE) **1**(1), 68–99 (2010)
25. Judd, C.M., James-Hawkins, L., Yzerbyt, V., Kashima, Y.: Fundamental dimensions of social judgment: understanding the relations between judgments of competence and warmth. J. Pers. Soc. Psychol. **89**(6) (2005)
26. Krämer, N., Kopp, S., Becker-Asano, C., Sommer, N.: Smile and the world will smile with you–the effects of a virtual agent's smile on users' evaluation and behavior. Int. J. Hum. Comput. Stud. **71**(3), 335–349 (2013)
27. Maricchiolo, F., Gnisci, A., Bonaiuto, M., Ficca, G.: Effects of different types of hand gestures in persuasive speech on receivers' evaluations. Lang. Cogn. Process. **24**(2), 239–266 (2009)
28. McCurrie, M., Beletti, F., Parzianello, L., Westendorp, A., Anthony, S., Scheirer, W.J.: Predicting first impressions with deep learning. In: 2017 12th IEEE International Conference on Automatic Face & Gesture Recognition, FG 2017, pp. 518–525. IEEE (2017)
29. McRorie, M., Sneddon, I., de Sevin, E., Bevacqua, E., Pelachaud, C.: A model of personality and emotional traits. In: Ruttkay, Z., Kipp, M., Nijholt, A., Vilhjálmsson, H.H. (eds.) IVA 2009. LNCS (LNAI), vol. 5773, pp. 27–33. Springer, Heidelberg (2009). https://doi.org/10.1007/978-3-642-04380-2_6
30. Moreno, C.R., Borod, J.C., Welkowitz, J., Alpert, M.: Lateralization for the expression and perception of facial emotion as a function of age. Neuropsychologia **28**(2), 199–209 (1990)
31. Nguyen, T.-H.D., et al.: Modeling warmth and competence in virtual characters. In: Brinkman, W.-P., Broekens, J., Heylen, D. (eds.) IVA 2015. LNCS (LNAI), vol. 9238, pp. 167–180. Springer, Cham (2015). https://doi.org/10.1007/978-3-319-21996-7_18
32. Pedregosa, F., et al.: Scikit-learn: machine learning in Python. J. Mach. Learn. Res. **12**(2011), 2825–2830 (2011)
33. Rosenberg, S., Nelson, C., Vivekananthan, P.S.: A multidimensional approach to the structure of personality impressions. J. Pers. Soc. Psychol. **9**(4), 283 (1968)

34. Soleymani, M., Villaro-Dixon, F., Pun, T., Chanel, G.: Toolbox for emotional feature extraction from physiological signals (TEAP). Frontiers ICT **4**(2017), 1 (2017)
35. Suykens, J.A.K.: Nonlinear modelling and support vector machines. In: Proceedings of the 18th IEEE Instrumentation and Measurement Technology Conference. Rediscovering Measurement in the Age of Informatics (Cat. No. 01CH 37188), IMTC 2001, vol. 1, 287–294. IEEE (2001)
36. Thammasan, N., Fukui, K., Numao, M.: An investigation of annotation smoothing for EEG-based continuous music-emotion recognition. In: 2016 IEEE International Conference on Systems, Man, and Cybernetics (SMC). IEEE, pp. 003323–003328 (2016)
37. van Waterschoot, J.: Flipper 2.0: a pragmatic dialogue engine for embodied conversational agents. In: Proceedings of the 18th International Conference on Intelligent Virtual Agents, pp. 43–50. ACM (2018)
38. Wang, Y., Geigel, J., Herbert, A.: Reading personality: avatar vs. human faces. In: 2013 Humaine Association Conference on Affective Computing and Intelligent Interaction, pp. 479–484. IEEE (2013)
39. Willis, M.L., Palermo, R., Burke, D.: Social judgments are influenced by both facial expression and direction of eye gaze. Soc. Cogn. **29**(4), 415–429 (2011)

Expectation and Reaction as Intention for Conversation System

Qiang Zhang$^{(\boxtimes)}$

Couger Inc., Shibuya, Tokyo, Japan
qiang@couger.co.jp

Abstract. Intention plays an import role in human daily conversation. Conventionally, human intention exerts influence on conversation contents and atmosphere. Although dialogue systems that involve emotion awareness are popular, implementation of human intention on artificial intelligence does not draw much attention of researchers. The reason is that intention is usually not a spontaneous response of external stimulus, but a self-generated desire and expectation. Moreover, internal intentions are not subjected to external signals that can be observed by third parties. In this research, we experimentally used "reaction" and "expectation" factors to represent intention at a text level and created intentional conversation model based on transformer model. Preliminary results were given to show that applying intention is able to help the a dialogue system address a higher level of engagement in the conversation.

Keywords: Dialogue system · Human intention representation · Human engagement

1 Introduction

As an essential way of transmitting thoughts and experience, conversation is commonly studied. Conversation is sophisticated and can be studied from multiple viewpoints [1]. Most of the prevalent conversation systems stick to the traditional task-oriented pipeline in which the conversation systems are dedicating for conversations that are related to specific tasks. A typical task-oriented conversation system contains four parts: *natural language understanding, dialogue state tracking, policy learning* and *natural language generation*[2]. We can define this pattern as "detect-analyze-respond" pattern. This pattern takes only into account the influence of past dialogues. Task-oriented conversation systems usually follow certain rules and give relatively fixed responses. In spite of monotonous outputs, task-oriented conversation systems are able to offer excellent stability. However, in the art of creating conversation systems, more "intelligent" and "personalized" systems are preferred. In this sense, it is necessary and important for conversation systems to draw attention of users and improve human engagement during human computer interaction [3].

© Springer Nature Switzerland AG 2020
M. Kurosu (Ed.): HCII 2020, LNCS 12182, pp. 279–289, 2020.
https://doi.org/10.1007/978-3-030-49062-1_19

In order to build more human-like conversation systems, emotion and other human features are taken into account [4,12]. Adding emotion information into conversation systems contributes to positive interaction and better user experience [5]. Emotional conversation systems are able to give a diverse set of responses to certain input. A rule-based approach to implementing emotional conversation system is to consider emotion information as weights of decision making. A more popular approach is to build emotional conversation system with neural network models. Emotional conversation systems are able to generate unexpected responses, which contributes to the improvement of engagement in conversation. However, emotional conversation system still follows the "detect-analyze-respond" pattern. Therefore, emotional conversation systems are still systems with commitment.

Flow theory of engagement declared that enjoyable experience featured by control, freedom and immediate feedback and other characteristics is able to be judged as engagement [16]. Emotional conversation system is able to give higher freedom to an interaction, however, is limited to follow the user's previous input even conversation status changes. In order to give immediate feedback, the system is required to sense the context change and take action in future steps.

Besides emotion, intention has been proved to critically affect human conversation [11]. Intention allows conversation systems to be able to show not only sentiments but also desires and expectations. Moreover, intention information allows conversation systems to choose their own actions. Table 1 shows that different intention can lead the conversation to different consequences. In this paper, we propose an intentional conversation model that involves intentions related to current context. We propose a method of representing intention and integrating intention values into baseline transformer model. We believe that the expectations of opponent's possible responses contribute to intention values. Therefore, we take expectations into account as most important feature of intention values and model the interaction session as a loop (Fig. 1). Intention labels

Table 1. An example of dialogue with different intention

T0	User	Hey, How are you?
T1	Agent	I'm doing good. How are you?
T2	User	Not good. I went to hospital yesterday
T3	Agent	What happened?
T4	User	I got fever last night. (I: get comfort)
T5	Agent	Great, don't have to attend the meeting today. (Intention: sarcasm)
T6	User	What?
T7	Agent	Oh, I mean, hope you will be fine
T4	User	I got fever last night. (I: get comfort)
T5	Agent	Oh, that's so bad, hope you can be fine. (Intention: comfort)
T6	User	Thank you

were given in order to train the model. By doing this, we expect the system to be able to give us responses driven by intention values and perform subjectively. Preliminary experiments were conducted to show that intention values is able to help conversation systems perform more human-like and improve engagement in an interaction session.

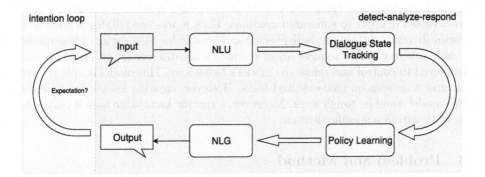

Fig. 1. Intention loop

2 Related Work

2.1 Sequence-to-sequence Model and Transformer

Sequence-to-sequence model [6] is able to maximize the likelihood of proper response from rich data. The structure of sequence-to-sequence model is widely applied into conversation systems as a result of its similarity of structure to natural conversation. A typical sequence-to-sequence model consists of two recurrent neural networks, one encoder and one decoder. Researches on speech recognition, machine translation [7], natural language understanding [8] have made remarkable progress by applying sequence-to-sequence model. However, sequence-to-sequence was proved to be weak at handling long sentences. Attention mechanism and transformer model are introduced to overcome the weakness of sequence-to-sequence model [10]. Transformer model is able to handle variable-length input. Powerful language models such as BERT [8], XLNet [9] based on the transformer model are created.

2.2 Intentional Conversation System

Integrating intention values into conversation system was also studied by a few groups of researchers. In 2011, Ge alt. proposed a human intention estimation method for human-robot interaction [14]. In their research, they proved that understanding partner's intention plays an important role during the interaction session. In 2015, a encoder-decoder based attention with intention (AWI) conversation model was proposed by Yao and Zweig [13]. In their research, they integrated intentional values into a simple encoder-decoder model. Intention values were calculated independently by the hidden states of encoder and decoder of the last turn. Their model was able to give natural responses to user inputs and can significantly improve engagement.

In 2017, Wen alt. proposed a latent intention dialogue model that is capable of making autonomous decisions [17]. In their study, they employed latent variable as intentions to guide the actions of the conversation system. A knowledge base was created in order to generate intentions. They represented dialogue state as a vector driven by utterance, belief vector and knowledge base vector. Their model is also able to conduct reinforcement learning since discrete latent intention was employed to control and refine the model's behaviour. This model is able to give natural responses on goal-oriented tasks. However, creating knowledge base for this model could be tough work. Moreover, a specific knowledge base is only able to work within a specific domain.

3   Problem and Method

Two essential problems under this research are: the representation of intention and the integration of intention model. In their research, Yao and Zweig represented intention as the output of a RNN layer which takes input as the hidden states of encoder at previous time step. This representation method integrated the linguistic level and the intention level. This approach is able to detect intention and generate response based on intention, however, is not able to use intention to direct the action of the system.

To solve this problem, we represent intention as reaction R and expectation E. Reaction indicates the real action of current time step. Expectation indicates the expected action of next turn of the opponent. Table 2 shows the reaction-expectation representation of intention for the demonstrated example. The conversation direction changes once the expectation of previous turn does not meet the reaction of current turn. In more details, we are able to represent intention at current generating turn I_T using expectation of previous turn E_{T-1} and reaction of current turn R_T

$$I_T = f(E_{T-1}, R_T) \tag{1}$$

where f could be a dense layer computing the difference. In this research, we first use embedding layer to calculate the vector for each expectation value and reaction value.

4   Model

Transformer model, as an enhanced version of sequence-to-sequence model, is dominating in the area of conversation systems as a result of its excellent ability of handling variable-length inputs. In this paper, we use a basic transformer model as our baseline model. The model is able to take intention values as part of the inputs with modifications on encoder and decoder. In stead of calculating intention as independent component, we integrated intention layer inside encoder and decoder (Fig. 2).

Table 2. Reaction-expectation representation of intention. ("+" and "-" are indicating "positive" and "negative".)

T0	User	Hey, How are you? (R: +greeting, E: +greeting)
T1	Agent	I'm doing good. How are you? (R: +greeting, E: +greeting)
T2	User	Not good. I went to hospital yesterday. (R: -greeting, E: request)
T3	Agent	What happened? (R: request, E: explanation)
T4	User	I got fever last night. (R: explanation, E: get comfort)
T5	Agent	Great, don't have to attend the meeting today. (R: sarcasm, E: don't care)
T6	User	What? (R: angry, E: apologize)
T7	Agent	Oh, I mean, hope you will be fine. (R: apologize)

4.1 Predict Expectation and Reaction

In real usage, expectation and reaction labels are not given. Therefore, an intention prediction model is necessary to preprocess and give expectation and reaction labels to user inputs. There are multiple approaches to creating an intention prediction module. The simplest way is to create a rule-based labelling system. In daily conversations, we are able to anticipate expectations and reactions from some keywords. For example, the reaction of a "wh-" question is usually "request" and the expectation is usually "explanation".

Moreover, if data were prepared, it is also possible to create a neural network based prediction module. In this research, we manually created intention labels on a small amount of the data in Cornell movie-dialogues corpus [15]. A prediction model was trained on the labelled data to give expectation and reaction values. The prediction model will give predictions on expectation and reaction after each time step. Table 3 shows a sample of expectation and reaction labels.

Table 3. Expectation and reaction label

Request	62904
Explanation	1788
Greeting	8397
Apology	1872
Thank	1703
Other	144952

4.2   Encoder

The encoder takes both raw sentences and intention values as inputs. As transformer model based on sequence-to-sequence model generates output piece by piece (token by token), it is necessary to take time step into consideration. More specifically, for each time step t of turn T, the encoder will take sentence piece of previous turn at current time step S_{T-1}^t as sentence input. The intention value will be calculated from expectation value of previous turn E_{T-1} and reaction of current turn at previous time step R_T^{t-1}. The expectation predication module generates output of initial input as the initial expectation value E_0. And the initial reaction value can be $R_1^0 = 0$. A basic transformer encoder layer is in charge of encoding the raw sentence. An intention embedding layer is added to vectorize intention values. The outputs of intention embedding layer are vector representations of intention inputs. Following the embedding layer is the layer to compute the distance of R_T^{t-1} and E_{T-1}. An intention layer will integrate the outputs of distance computation layer and sentence encoder layer. Therefore the output of the intention encoder at current turn, C_T^t, can be represented as

$$C_T^t = g(S_{T-1}^t, f(E_{T-1}, R_T^{t-1})) \tag{2}$$

where g is the intentional conversation encoder, and f is the distance computation process.

4.3   Decoder

Same as the encoder, the decoder model is also based on the basic decoder of transformer model. The decoder takes the sentence output and intention output at current time step, O^t and I_T as inputs. The intention output can be calculated from expectation value of previous turn E_{T-1} and reaction of current turn R_T. The reaction value of current turn will be updated after each time step. For training, we can directly take the final result R_T as input. During inference, the reaction value should be given as initial value as mentioned above and keep updating after each time step. The final output of the decoder, O_T^t, can be represented as

$$O_T^t = h(C_T^t, f(E_{T-1}, R_{T-1})) \tag{3}$$

where h is the intentional conversation decoder, and f is the distance computation process.

4.4   Distance Computation Layer

This layer is implemented to calculate the distance or difference between expectation values and reaction values. For encoder, since the reaction value of current R_T is unknown, the intention input of encoder contains only expectation values of previous turn, E_{T-1}. For decoder, we need to calculate the distance of two vectors. A brute-force method is to calculate the L^2 norm of these two vectors. However, the reaction values of current turn will be updated every time when a new sentence piece is generated. By stacking those generated values, we are able to track the context information and monitor which sentence piece contributes more to the reaction values. Therefore, distance between expectation values and reaction values can be represented as

$$dist^t = \frac{\sum_{t'=0}^{t} ||E_{T-1} - R_T^{t'}||^2}{t} \tag{4}$$

This representation calculates not only the distance at each time step, but also the effectiveness of each time step.

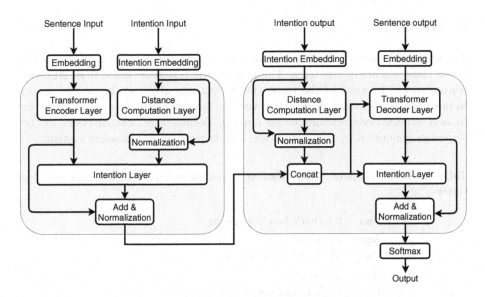

Fig. 2. Intention conversation model. Based on the basic transformer model, intention embedding layer and intention layer are added to process intention information.

5   Train

5.1   Labelling

The intentional conversation model was trained on Cornell movie-dialog corpus. The training data contains 155131 samples. The test set contains 44323 samples. Dev set contains 22162 samples. First run the expectation and reaction prediction model to give intention labels (expectation and reaction) on each training sample. The training data will the be fed to the intentional conversation model.

5.2   Training

The intentional conversation model was fully implemented with tensorflow-2.0. All layers in the encoder are with 512 hidden units. Both encoder and decoder contains one encoder or decoder layer.

6   Evaluation

We evaluated the system by running test samples and perform real sessions with human. The system was first evaluated on its ability to generate response that can meet the expectation of user inputs. To the contrast, the system was then evaluated on its ability to switch conversation when an unexpected input comes. The diversity of the outputs was also accessed to show that the system was able to achieve good freedom level. Final result was accessed based on control, freedom and immediate feedback on strategy and action change.

7   Result

The system was tested after training on the Cornell movie-dialog corpus. Table 4 shows some results of the tests. The system was tested on more than 20 short conversations. In some of the tests, the system was able to take proper action to meet the user's expectations. However, the system's performance on adapting to new expectations remains to be limited. Besides that, the diversity of the responses generated by the system was also lower than the baseline system.

Table 4. Sample outputs of intentional conversation system trained on movie-dialog corpus

User	So, that's how it happens
Agent	I don't know
User	That's why you left me
Agent	I'm sorry
User	I don't need you to apologize
Agent	I'm sorry
User	Why did you do that?
Agent	Sorry, I didn't get it
User	You know how important that was to me
Agent	Maybe I shouldn't have done that
User	Why did you eat the pie without telling me?
Agent	I'm sorry
User	I don't want to go there tonight
Agent	Why not?
User	I just feel so tired
Agent	Why is it?
User	Because I worked so hard today
Agent	That won't become your reason to cheat me
User	I didn't
Agent	Enough talk

(continued)

Table 4. (*continued*)

User	What are you doing?
Agent	I want to know if somebody need my help
User	Oh, you're a kind person
Agent	Thank you
User	Why did you do that?
Agent	That's my responsibility, I'll say
User	Such a bad thing, I'm gonna say
Agent	Don't say that anymore
User	Together with you, I feel like doing anything
Agent	That's so sweet of you
User	But I also get tired
Agent	Please don't leave me, please
User	I guess I have to do that
Agent	Please, no. I'm sorry
User	Next time remember to close the door when you opened the fridge
Agent	Okay, I will

8   Discussion

Current emotional conversation systems are usually responding to a certain emotion input with an appropriate emotion output. However, emotions are not always so vivid in daily conversations. Moreover, under some circumstances, we intentionally hide our emotions. Adding emotion information contributes to improve the engagement during interaction session. The mechanisms of emotional conversation systems are still different from that of human. For conversation systems, emotion values can only be treated as external values on which the system should give responses. Although application of neural model helps to increase the diversity of output, emotional conversation systems are not able to control their own actions and give immediate feedback when expectation of the input changes. To address even higher level of engagement during the human agent communication session, we proposed a method of adding intention values into current conversation system.

In this study, we focus on the method of representing intention and integrating intention values into current transformer model. We proposed the method of using expectation values and reaction values to represent intention. Expectation represents opponent's expected responses and reaction represents the real responses. By computing the distance and difference between expectation and reaction, we are able to model intention.

We implemented an intentional conversation model based on transformer model. Intention processing layers are added into the encoder layer and decoder layer of the transformer model. The model was then trained on movie-dialog corpus. Intention labels (expectation and reaction) are given by the expectation and reaction prediction model in advance. Multiple tests were conducted. The results showed that this system was able to give responses that would meet the expectations of inputs.

The limitations of current system was that the expectation and reaction prediction model may make mistake on predicting labels, which will directly lead to bad result. Besides that, the algorithm of computing distance also need to be improved. The current system combines the sentence input and intention values by simple adding and normalization, which may not be a good solution when more intention categories are involved.

Moreover, the method of representing intention as expectation and reaction may also bring limitations. Pure intention should be generated internally even without any external stimulation. In this sense, a new intention representation method that do not depend on any external elements will be required.

9   Future Work

There are still limitations of the current system. In the future, more algorithms should be considered for computing the distance between expectation and reaction. Moreover, generative adversarial networks (GANs) are showing positive results on creating images from noise. This might be a possible solution to generate pure internal intention signal.

References

1. Nishida, T., Nakazawa, A., Ohmoto, Y., Mohammad, Y.: Conversation: above and beneath the surface. Conversational Informatics, pp. 17–41. Springer, Tokyo (2014). https://doi.org/10.1007/978-4-431-55040-2_2
2. Chen, H., Liu, X., Yin, D., Tang, J.: A survey on dialogue systems: recent advances and new frontiers. ACM SIGKDD Explor. Newsl. 19(2), 25–35 (2017)
3. Peters, C., Castellano, G., de Freitas, S.: An exploration of user engagement in HCI. In: The International Workshop on Affective-Aware Virtual Agents and Social Robots - AFFINE 2009, pp. 1–3 (2009)
4. Ball, G., Breeze, J.: Emotion and personality in a conversational agent. In: Cassel, J., Sullivan, J., Prevost, S., Churchill, E. (eds.) Embodied Conversational Agents, pp. 189–219. The MIT Press, Cambridge (2000)
5. Pamungkas, E.W.: Emotionally-aware chatbots: a survey 1906, 09774 (2019)
6. Sutskever, I., Vinyals, O., Le, Q.: Sequence to sequence learning with neural networks. In: Advances in Neural Information Processing Systems, NIPS (2014)
7. Wu, Y., et al.: Google's neural machine translation system: bridging the gap between human and machine translation. arXiv preprint (2016)
8. Devlin, J., Chang, M.W., Lee, K., Toutanova, K.: Bert: pre-training of deep bidirectional transformers for language understanding (2018). arXiv preprint arXiv:1810.04805
9. Yang, Z., Dai, Z., Yang, Y., Carbonell, J., Salakhutdinov, R., Le, Q.V.: XLNet: generalized autoregressive pretraining for language understanding (2019). arXiv:1906.08237

10. Vaswani, A., et al.: Attention is all you need. In: Advances in Neural Information Processing Systems, pp. 5998–6008 (2017)
11. Cohen, P.R., Levesque, H.J.: Intention is choice with commitment. Artif. Intell. **42**, 213–261 (1990)
12. Zhou, H., Huang, M., Zhang, T., Zhu, X., Liu, B.: Emotion chatting machine: emotional conversation generation with internal and external memory. In: AAAI 2018 (2018)
13. Yao, K., Zweig, G., Peng, B.: Attention with intention for a neural network conversation model (2015)
14. Ge, S.S., Li, Y., He, H.: Neural-network-based human intention estimation for physical human-robot interaction. In: Proceedings of 8th International Conference on Ubiquitous Robots and Ambient Intelligence (URAI), pp. 390–395 (2011)
15. Danescu-Niculescu-Mizil, C., Lee, L.: Chameleons in imagined conversations: a new approach to understanding coordination of linguistic style in dialogs. In: Proceedings Workshop on Cognitive Modeling and Computational Linguistics, pp. 76–87 (2011)
16. Shernoff, D.J., Csikszentmihalyi, M., Schneider, B., Shernoff, E.S.: Student engagement in high school classrooms from the perspective of flow theory. School Psychol. Q. **18**, 158–176 (2003)
17. Wen, T.H., Miao, Y., Blunsom, P., Young, S.: Latent intention dialogue models. In: Precup, D., Teh, Y.W. (eds.) Proceedings of the 34th International Conference on Machine Learning, Proceedings of Machine Learning Research, vol. 70, pp. 3732–3741. PMLR, International Convention Centre, Sydney (2017)

Augmented Tension Detection in Communication: Insights from Prosodic and Content Features

Bo Zhang[1](✉) and Lu Xiao[2](✉)

[1] College of Arts and Sciences, Syracuse University, Syracuse, NY, USA
bzhang49@syr.edu
[2] School of Information Studies, Syracuse University, Syracuse, NY, USA
lxiao04@syr.edu

Abstract. Tension in communication often prevents effective flows of information among members in the conversation and thus can negatively influence practices in teams and learning efficiency at school. Interested in developing a computational technique that automatically detects tension in communication, we explore features that signal the existence of tension in human-human communications and investigate the potential of a supervised learning approach. While there is no tension-annotated dataset available, there are language resources that have distress annotated. Although tension may occur during the communication as a result of various factors, distress creates discomfort and tension. Leveraging an interview dataset that has marked the presence/absence of distress, we investigated the prosodic features and LIWC features that indicate tension. Specifically, we compare 23 prosodic features and LIWC features extracted from 186 interviews in terms of how effective they are to indicate the speaker's distress in a one-to-one conversation. Our analysis shows that there are seven prosodic features and one LIWC features that differ between distress and non-distress interviews. The seven prosodic features are mean intensity, jitter, shimmer, longest silence duration, longest silence position, standard deviation of interviewee speaking rate, and hesitation. And the one effective LIWC feature is health.

Keywords: Tension · Distress · Prosodic features · Machine learning

1 Introduction

Tension is a pulling force that acts in different or even opposite directions of a conversation. It can often be perceived when the flow of conversation is negatively influenced by the pulling force. For example, the flow of conversation is blocked when one speaker is deliberately avoiding answering questions raised by others. A more extreme case would be the speaker tries to push back the question, sometimes aggressively, which indicates the flow of the conversation going backwards. The occurrence of tension often keeps individuals and teams from

© Springer Nature Switzerland AG 2020
M. Kurosu (Ed.): HCII 2020, LNCS 12182, pp. 290–301, 2020.
https://doi.org/10.1007/978-3-030-49062-1_20

achieving their goals. For example, tension between teachers and students [20] makes students' learning less effective, and tension in medical teams [20] can lead to safety issues of patients. Notifying speakers the tensions during the conversation helps raise their awareness of potential problematic aspects and engage in the conversation in a more informed fashion. Given that there is a lack of tension-annotated dataset. To remedy the situation, we use distress-annotated dataset as the first step of this investigation.

Distress in communication in this study refers to individuals being extremely uncomfortable, anxious, or upset. The interrelation between distress and tension is shown in Fig. 1. Distress detection is a research topic mainly in mental health research area [3,6,17]. Distress-annotated datasets are available such as Distress Analysis Interview Corpus (DAIC), Virtual Human Distress Assessment Interview Corpus (VH DAIC), and Distress Analysis Interview Corpus - Wizard of Oz (DAIC-WOZ) [5]. We acknowledge that while the existence of tension in team discussions may not lead to someone being distressful, one's distress certainly creates tension. In fact, a recent study on modelling for tension detection in one-to-one conversations tested its model in a distress-annotated interview dataset and obtained a reasonable result [19]. From this perspective, we utilize the existing distress-annotated conversation data to study tension indicators, as a starting point. Specifically in this study, we focus on identifying effective prosodic features that are indicative distress in a one-to-one interview setting.

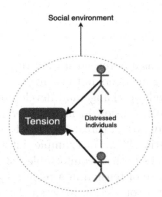

Fig. 1. Interrelation between tension and distress: distress from individuals creates tension within a social environment.

Current studies on distress detection mainly use features from three categories - text features, auditory features, and visual features. Some studies take an integrated approach combining the three categories [2], others focus on either auditory features [4] or text features [16]. Some techniques such as topic modeling are also used in some studies to improve the performance of distress detection [7]. Among all the features used to detect distress, auditory features are found to have a better performance for this particular task when used alone [2]. A study conducted by Piwek, Pollick and Petrini in 2015 [8] comparing the effectiveness of auditory and visual cues in emotion detection draws a similar conclusion. As a major category of auditory features, prosodic features focus on how people speak rather than the actual content of their speech, such as the pitch of voice, speaking rate, and rhythm. In verbal communications, there is often information that cannot be detected from the content but important for understanding the speaker's emotion such as the sigh, the sudden high pitch, etc.

In this study, we have explored prosodic features in human voice that may carry information that can reveal whether a speaker is distress or not using statistical analysis and Machine Learning classification experiments. Specifically, we examined the potential of 23 prosodic features in indicating distress in one-to-one conversations aiming at identifying effective prosodic features in distress detection. In the rest of the paper, previous studies that are related to tension in communication, emotion detection, and prosodic features are first reviewed. Then, the dataset used in this study is described, followed by a detailed explanation of how these prosodic features are measured and the statistical analysis that was carried out. After presenting the results of the statistical tests, a selective set of prosodic features were used to classify distress and non-distress interview. The set of selective prosodic features are then combined with text features to achieve a better classification performance. Finally, the paper discusses the implication of these results and the limitation of the research. The paper concludes with the plan for future work.

2   Related Work

Tension in communication as a potential sites of ruptures [22] prevents effective flows of information among members in the conversation, which is considered as the starting point that leads to change and development if it can be identified and overcame. For example, tension in medical teams can influence a team's communication, which may pose a threat to the safety of patients [20]. Tension is also inevitable in education [23]. For example, interpersonal tension between teachers and students makes both uncomfortable [23] and thus makes learning less productive [20]. The rise of tension in a team may be from team members' difficulties in constructing a connection between the goals or their actions and the object and motive of the collective activity [20]. For example, tensions rise in ICU team trainees because they fail to connect their professional roles and responsibilities [21]. Tension resolution can be achieved by negotiations or by creating conditions for and tools that foster practice transformations [20]. Tension can be observed through voice. For example, tensions in the experiments [20] are explicated in the voices of the several professionals.

Despite the importance of tension, there hasn't been many studies focusing on what features should be used to detect it. One natural place to start would be detecting negative emotions, as we expect that tension points are those places where conflict or negative feeling occur in the communication. Various text features have been explored in emotion detection, such as negation words, punctuation like exclamation marks, and self-referential words [14]. In Jumayel's study [19] a list of emotion lexicons are used in the emotion detection module. Other lexicons, such as epistemic verbs, adverbs, adjectives and modal verbs for hedging detection are used in the hedging detection module. The emotion recognition module and the hedge detection module are then combined to form a tension detection model. Aside from these, there are also studies that explore non-textual indicators. For example, Piwek, Pollick and Petrini [8] explored effectiveness of auditory cues and visual cues in emotion detection and showed that auditory cues are more important than visual cues - only when auditory cues become less available, visual cues start to become more useful.

Conceptualizing that the existence of distress signals tension, we consider studies on distress or depression detection are relevant [1]. One study [4] developed a model that combines CNN and LSTM to detect distress in DAIC–WOZ Depression Database [17]. In this approach, vocal signal in the data is included through time-frequency 2D representation. Another study [3] points out that prosodic abnormalities is a key objective marker for detecting depression and common para-linguistics speech characteristics can be applied to build such a system. A wide variety of tools are developed to facilitate the analysis of prosodic features in tasks like emotion detection [11], such as PEPS–C, DANVA 2, FAB, MNTAP, Aprosodia Battery, ACS, PPAT, Praat [15], and Prosograph [13]. One study [5] offers a detailed review of distress detection including a detailed list of the data sets. Most of these datasets contain audio and video clips, and some also include text transcripts, for example Distress Analysis Interview Corpus - Wizard of Oz (DAIC-WOZ).

3   Research Methodology

3.1   Research Data

We used DAIC–WOZ Depression Database [17] in the study to explore the prosodic features that are indicative of the speaker's distress. This database contains 189 clinical interviews designed to support the diagnosis of psychological distress conditions such as anxiety, depression, and post-traumatic stress disorder. The interviews are conducted by an animated virtual interviewer controlled by a human interviewer in another room, which is very similar to human-human interview in real life. Each interview has both the audio recording and the corresponding transcript. The transcripts include specific start and end time points for each question asked by the interviewer and each response from the interviewee. Each interview is labeled as either distress or non-distress as a whole based on some psychological measurements such as the post-traumatic stress disorder (PTSD), the Patient Health Questionnaire (PHQ), and the State-Trait Anxiety Inventory (STAI). Three interviews do not have interviewees' speech response so they were excluded in the study. The duration of the remaining 186 interviews ranges from 414 s to 1,966 s.

3.2   Prosodic Features

From each of these 186 interview recordings, we extracted 23 prosodic features. They are further divided into six categories: pitch features, intensity features, speech stability features, silence features, speaking rate features, and hesitation feature.

For pitch and intensity features of an interview, we measured the mean, standard deviation, maximum, and minimum. Pitch is the fundamental frequency of voice. Pitch features for each interview are extracted by first listing all pitch values from an interview from audio files with an interval of 0.01 s using Praat [15], a scientific phonetic analysis tool. We normalized each interviewee's prosodic feature data because that each of these interviewee has a different base line for their prosodic features. We did the normalization by calculating the mean, maximum, and minimum of a pitch for an interview based on the raw pitch values of the individual interview and the total number of intervals this interview has. Specifically, mean pitch is computed by the sum of raw pitch values in all intervals divided by the total number of intervals in an interview. Note that we set the sound interval to be 0.01. Standard deviation of pitch indicates the distribution of raw pitch data from mean pitch.

Intensity is the amplitude of voice. Intensity features for each interview are extracted by first listing all intensity values from an interview from audio files with an interval of 0.01 s using Praat. Similar to the calculation for the pitch feature's values, we calculated the maximum, minimum, mean, and standard deviation for intensity feature of an interview, based on the raw intensity values in all the intervals and the total number of intervals of an interview.

Speech stability features include jitter (J) and shimmer (S). Jitter is the absolute difference between consecutive periods divided by the average period, which can be used to indicate the stability of pitch. Jitter is computed by:

$$J = (\sum_{i=2}^{N} |t_i - t_{i-1}|/(N-1))/(\sum_{i=1}^{N} t_i/N)$$

where J is jitter, t_i is the duration of the ith interval, N is the number of intervals.

Shimmer is the average absolute difference between the amplitudes of consecutive periods divided by the average amplitude, which can be used to indicate the stability of intensity. Shimmer is computed by:

$$S = (\sum_{i=2}^{N} |t_i - t_{i-1}|/(N-1))/\overline{I}$$

where S is shimmer, t_i is the duration of the ith interval, N is the number of intervals, $\overline{I}$ is mean intensity.

Silence features include silence time (ST), silence time within speech (STS), longest silence duration (LSD) and longest silence position (LSP). Silence time are the sum of unvoiced frames over the total duration. An unvoiced frame is a sound interval during which nobody made an utterance. Silence time within speech (STS) is the sum of unvoiced frames without considering unvoiced frames at the beginning and the end of the audio file. Longest silence duration is the sum of unvoiced frame within a speech segment that has the longest duration among all unvoiced frames and it can be computed by:

$$LSD = max(s_{i+1} - e_i)$$

where LSD is the longest silence duration of an interview, e_i is the end time of a chunk of speech, s_{i+1} is the start time of the next speech segment. Longest silence position is the relative position of the longest silence in an interview. It can be roughly represented using the ratio of the start time of that longest silence over the total duration of the interview, which can be computed by:

$$LSP = s/D$$

where LSP is the longest silence position, s is the start time of the longest silence duration, D is the total duration of the interview.

Speaking rate is the number of words a speaker speaks per minute (WPM). In our study, this was further categorized as interviewer speaking rate features and interviewee speaking rate features. Speaking rate features are extracted using transcript, in which each speech segment is either a question from interviewer or a response from interviewee. Interviewer speaking rate features include mean interviewer speaking rate, standard deviation of interviewer speaking rate, maximum interviewer speaking rate, minimum interviewer speaking rate. Mean interviewer speaking rate is the average speaking rate of the interviewer over the duration of an entire interview. Standard deviation of interviewer's speaking rate is the distribution of interviewer's speaking rate at different speech segment from the interviewer's mean speaking rate. $\overline{IRSR}$ is mean interviewer speaking rate, N is the number of speech segments. Maximum/minimum interviewer speaking rate is the speaking rate in a speech segment from interviewer which has the highest/lowest value among all other speaking rate in the rest of speech segments from interviewer. Similarly, we calculated the values of these features for the interviewee's speaker rate, that is, the mean interviewee speaking rate $\overline{IESR}$, the standard deviation of interviewee speaking rate $IESR_{std}$, the maximum speaking rate of interviewee $IESR_{max}$, and the minimum speaking rate of interviewee $IESR_{min}$.

Hesitation feature is the frequency of words indicating hesitation in speech, such as um, umm, uh.

All the data except for data from longest silence position feature has been normalized by the duration of each interview.

3.3   Text Features

LIWC features (Linguistic Inquiry and Word Count) and N-gram features are extracted from the 186 interviews as text features. N-gram features includes all unigram, bigram, and trigram in the transcript of each interview. We also include POS tags of each unigram, bigram, and trigram in N-gram features. We use POS tags provided in PennTree Bank in our study.

3.4   Statistical Analysis

We compared the values of these features in distress and non-distress interviews. We first checked the normality of these features using Shapiro-Wilk test and Q-Q plot. These normality tests show that all features are not normally distributed except for $IRSR_{min}$. In non-distress group, $IRSR_{min}$ has a w-value of 0.9861 and a p-value of 0.2095; in distress group, $IRSR_{min}$ has a w-value of 0.9866 and a p-value of 0.7868. Therefore, we applied a two sample t-test compare the values of this feature between distress and non-distress interviews. Our t-test result shows that distress interviews and non-distress interviews do differ statistically in the value of $IRSR_{min}$. The mean for non-distress group is 0.1248, and the mean for distress group is 0.1139. The t-value is 1.9999 and the p-value is 0.0473.

We apply the non-parametric Mann-Whitney U test to compare the values of the rest 23 features between the two interview groups. Seven features show statistically significant difference in the two groups. The seven features are: mean intensity, jitter, shimmer, longest silence duration, longest silence position, standard deviation of interviewee speaking rate, and hesitation. Table 1 shows the result.

Table 1. Mann-Whitney U test result.

Features	Median (non-distress)	Median (distress)	u-value	p-value
$\bar{I}$	0.038	0.036	3049	0.0398
J	0.0018	0.0015	2903	0.0144
S	0.0089	0.008	2808	0.0068
LSD	0.0159	0.0126	2860	0.0103
LSP	4.6981	20.5871	2923	0.0167
$IESR_{std}$	0.0748	0.0659	2975	0.0243
H	0.0049	0.0044	3080	0.0483

LIWC features and N-gram features are analyzed by using the same approach as for the analysis of prosodic features. The test result shows that among all the text features only the feature health has statistically significant difference in the distress group and non-distress group. Its mean for non-distress group is 0.61, and its mean for distress group is 0.89. The u-value is 2495.5 and the p-value is 0.0003.

Based on our analysis it is expected that the combination of the seven effective prosodic features and one effective LIWC feature should achieve the best performance compared to the other features. To test this, we built machine learning classifier to do classification on each of the five feature sets we have. The five feature sets are listed in the following table:

Table 2. A list of feature sets used in this study.

Feature sets	Features	Number of features
Prosodic feature set	All the prosodic features	23
LIWC feature set	All the LIWC features	93
N-gram feature set	All the N-gram features	272
Effective prosodic feature set	Seven effective prosodic features	7
Effective feature set	Seven effective prosodic features and health feature from LIWC	8

3.5 Classification Experiment

To examine the predictive power of these prosodic features, we built machine learning classifiers to classify whether an interviewee is distressed in an input interview. The four classifiers are used on the five feature sets in Table 2.

The data set is not balanced because that there are 130 non-distress interviews and 56 distress interviews in the data set. To balance the data set, different weights are assigned to samples with different labels:

$$W_0 = n/2m,$$

$$W_1 = n/2(n - m),$$

where W_0 is the weight assigned to non-distress samples, W_1 is the weight assigned to distress samples, n is the number of total samples, m is the number of non-distress samples. Besides trying weighted approach to address imbalanced data, we've also tried re-sampling technique. Both over-sampling technique and under-sampling technique have similar results as the weighted approach.

We explored four candidate classifiers and compared their performance to find the most effective one that can be applied to distress detection. We choose these four classifiers as they are commonly used in many Machine Learning tasks, and usually have good performance when data size is limited. The four classifiers are: Support Vector Machines (SVM), Logistic Regression (LR), Naive Bayes (NB), and Decision Tree (DT).

We apply ten-fold cross validation to avoid overfitting issue for all the four classifiers. The result is shown in the following Tables 3, 4, 5 and 6:

Table 3. Classification result on prosodic feature set.

	Training set				Test set			
	Accuracy	Precision	Recall	F1-score	Accuracy	Precision	Recall	F1-score
SVM	0.683	0.475	0.438	0.454	0.679	0.553	0.430	**0.402**
LR	0.679	0.474	0.544	0.506	0.653	0.519	0.463	0.399
NB	0.699	0	0	0	0.699	0	0	0
DT	1	1	1	1	0.576	0.324	0.353	0.327

Table 4. Classification result on LIWC feature set.

	Training set				Test set			
	Accuracy	Precision	Recall	F1-score	Accuracy	Precision	Recall	F1-score
SVM	0.748	0.560	0.776	0.650	0.597	0.373	0.557	0.440
LR	0.925	0.812	0.980	0.888	0.670	0.470	0.547	**0.489**
NB	0.699	0	0	0	0.699	0	0	0
DT	1	1	1	1	0.621	0.320	0.360	0.327

Table 5. Classification result on N-gram feature set.

	Training set				Test set			
	Accuracy	Precision	Recall	F1-score	Accuracy	Precision	Recall	F1-score
SVM	0.598	0.434	0.519	0.394	0.491	0.244	0.367	0.242
LR	0.728	0.532	0.788	0.635	0.592	0.396	0.550	**0.449**
NB	0.710	0.817	0.042	0.079	0.694	0	0	0
DT	1	1	1	1	0.602	0.372	0.3	0.314

Table 6. Classification result on effective prosodic feature set.

	Training set				Test set			
	Accuracy	Precision	Recall	F1-score	Accuracy	Precision	Recall	F1-score
SVM	0.681	0.471	0.438	0.452	0.679	0.553	0.430	0.402
LR	0.662	0.447	0.490	0.466	0.658	0.549	0.463	**0.403**
NB	0.699	0	0	0	0.699	0	0	0
DT	1	1	1	1	0.559	0.289	0.307	0.278

4   Discussion and Future Work

Classification experiment shows that among the four classifiers, LR classifier has
the best performance over the other three classifiers except for using prosodic feature set. Even when using prosodic feature set it achieves a F1 score (0.399) that
is very close the best performance (SVM classifier: 0.402). When using effective

feature set, LR classifier achieves the highest recall (0.633) and F1 score (0.542), which is the higher than [4] (0.52). SVM classifier has decent performance except when using N-gram feature set. NB classifier and DT classifier are obvious not good choices for this task given their performances (Table 7).

Table 7. Classification result on effective feature set.

	Training set				Test set			
	Accuracy	Precision	Recall	F1-score	Accuracy	Precision	Recall	F1-score
SVM	0.683	0.476	0.446	0.459	0.679	0.553	0.430	0.402
LR	0.668	0.464	0.655	0.543	0.669	0.535	0.633	**0.542**
NB	0.699	0	0	0	0.670	0	0	0
DT	1	1	1	1	0.618	0.401	0.453	0.412

Comparing the performances of LR classifier and SVM classifier in all the five feature sets, we concludes that effective feature set contains the most suitable features for distress detection. This is the same as the conclusion we have from statistical analysis.

Statistical analysis and classification experiment both show that the seven prosodic features and one LIWC feature can be used to differentiate distress interviews from non-distress interviews. The seven features are: mean intensity, jitter, shimmer, longest silence duration, longest silence position, standard deviation of interviewee speaking rate, and hesitation. The effective LIWC feature is health. Different from other relevant studies such as those mentioned in the literature review [2, 7], this study focuses on acoustic features that are comparatively simple and intuitive, like intensity (how loud a speaker speaks), speaking rate (how fast a speaker speaks), and silence (how long a speaker pauses). We choose these features because it is common that we notice the speakers' emotional changes from these features when communicating with others in everyday verbal communications. We acknowledge that not all the information in the audio recordings are represented by the set of features we choose. However, given the limited data size for its dataset (186 interviews), feature engineering is quite effective. Our analysis of the prosodic feature analysis sheds light on other studies that are contextualized in these communications.

Our analysis and experiments have shown that these seven prosodic features can be a good set of features helping detecting speakers' distress in a one-to-one communication setting, which can further lead to tension detection. Other than detecting tension, many other real world applications can benefit from the use of this set of prosodic features. For example, the interaction between conversational agents such as voice assistants and human users will be more natural once the agents is able to pick up these prosodic features as cues to tell the user's emotional status. We also encourage future studies to try to use these features in other detection tasks related to human communication.

There are two main limitations of this study. One is that a speaker's emotion during a communication may be revealed through aspects other than prosodic features, e.g., the language use in the communication content [14], the visual and other acoustic cues [8], etc. It has also been acknowledged that relying on prosodic features alone to detect the emotion of a speaker is the may not be able to detect the true emotion of a speaker in some scenarios [12]. For example, professional actors and actresses with excellent acting skills may be able to fake their emotions by producing certain prosodic features in their speech. The other limitation is the dataset itself. The DAIC–WOZ Depression Database is in essence a distress dataset that is based on interviews designed to support the diagnosis of psychological distress conditions such PTSD instead of tension dataset. It also has limited number of data and only in American English. The nature of the dataset limits our findings in such a setting. It would be interesting to see how effective these seven prosodic features are on tension detection when a high quality tension dataset with sufficient amount of data is available.

Past studies have shown that an integrated approach performs better in distress detection [2,7]. For instance, Gong and Poellabauer [7] trained a multi-modal model to detect distress from audio interviews which integrates audio features, video features, and semantics features. Ghosh, Chatterjee, and Morency [2] built a distress detection model that combines verbal features, visual features, and acoustic features. Different from our study, the acoustic features they explored include complex features such as Normalized Amplitude Quotient (NAQ), Quasi-open Quotient (QOQ), vocal fold vibration deviation, peak slope, and Maxima Dispersion Quotient (MDQ). F1 score was 0.6071 with acoustic features alone, and was 0.6751 with various types of features combined. Additionally, the use of prosodic information along with other features can perform better when faced with more realistic data than those produced by actors [10]. The next step for us is to examine the potential of these features in detecting tension with an integrated approach. We plan to combine our tension detection model with the tension detection model from [19] to build a more robust and effective tension detection model. The integrated tension detection model may also include more features and use a more complex architecture to further improve the model's performance.

References

1. Matthews, G.: Distress. In: Stress: Concepts, Cognition, Emotion, and Behavior, pp. 219–226. Academic Press (2016)
2. Ghosh, S., Chatterjee, M., Morency, L.P.: A multimodal context-based approach for distress assessment. In: Proceedings of the 16th International Conference on Multimodal Interaction, pp. 240–246. ACM, November 2014
3. Cummins, N., Scherer, S., Krajewski, J., Schnieder, S., Epps, J., Quatieri, T.F.: A review of depression and suicide risk assessment using speech analysis. Speech Commun. **71**, 10–49 (2015)
4. Ma, X., Yang, H., Chen, Q., Huang, D., Wang, Y.: DepAudioNet: an efficient deep model for audio based depression classification. In: Proceedings of the 6th International Workshop on Audio/Visual Emotion Challenge, pp. 35–42. ACM, October 2016

5. Rana, R., et al.: Automated screening for distress: a perspective for the future. Eur. J. Cancer Care **28**(4), e13033 (2019)
6. Cohn, J.F., Cummins, N., Epps, J., Goecke, R., Joshi, J., Scherer, S.: Multimodal assessment of depression from behavioral signals. In: The Handbook of Multimodal-Multisensor Interfaces, pp. 375–417. Association for Computing Machinery and Morgan & Claypool, October 2018
7. Gong, Y., Poellabauer, C.: Topic modeling based multi-modal depression detection. In: Proceedings of the 7th Annual Workshop on Audio/Visual Emotion Challenge, pp. 69–76. ACM, October 2017
8. Piwek, L., Pollick, F., Petrini, K.: Audiovisual integration of emotional signals from others' social interactions. Front. Psychol. **6**, 611 (2015)
9. Nöth, E., et al.: On the use of prosody in automatic dialogue understanding. Speech Commun. **36**(1–2), 45–62 (2002)
10. Batliner, A., Fischer, K., Huber, R., Spilker, J., Nöth, E.: How to find trouble in communication. Speech Commun. **40**(1–2), 117–143 (2003)
11. Kalathottukaren, R.T., Purdy, S.C., Ballard, E.: Behavioral measures to evaluate prosodic skills: a review of assessment tools for children and adults. Contemp. Issues Commun. Sci. Disord. **42**, 138 (2015)
12. Scherer, K.R.: Vocal markers of emotion: comparing induction and acting elicitation. Comput. Speech Lang. **27**(1), 40–58 (2013)
13. Öktem, A., Farrús, M., Wanner, L.: Prosograph: a tool for prosody visualisation of large speech corpora. In: Proceedings of the 18th Annual Conference of the International Speech Communication Association (INTERSPEECH 2017), ISCA 2017, Stockholm, Sweden, 20–24 August 2017, pp. 809–810 (2017)
14. Tackman, A.M., et al.: Depression, negative emotionality, and self-referential language: a multi-lab, multi-measure, and multi-language-task research synthesis. J. Pers. Soc. Psychol. **116**(5), 817–834 (2019)
15. Boersma, P., Van Heuven, V.: Speak and unSpeak with PRAAT. Glot Int. **5**(9/10), 341–347 (2001)
16. Vioulès, M.J., Moulahi, B., Azé, J., Bringay, S.: Detection of suicide-related posts in Twitter data streams. IBM J. Res. Dev. **62**(1), 7:1–7:12 (2018)
17. Gratch, J., et al.: The distress analysis interview corpus of human and computer interviews. In: LREC, pp. 3123–3128, May 2014
18. Crystal, D.: On keeping one's hedges in order. Engl. Today **4**(3), 46–47 (1988)
19. Islam, J., Xiao, L., Mercer, R., High, S.: Tension analysis in survivor interviews: a computational approach. In: 2019 Digital Humanities, Utrecht, The Netherlands, 9–12 July 2019 (2019). Accessed 19 Jan 2020
20. Sins, P.H.M., Karlgren, K.: Identifying and overcoming tension in interdisciplinary teamwork in professional development: two cases and a tool for support (2009)
21. Hawryluck, L.A., Espin, S.L., Garwood, K.C., Evans, C.A., Lingard, L.A.: Pulling together and pushing apart: tides of tension in the ICU team. Acad. Med. **77**(10), S73–S76 (2002)
22. Tartas, V., Mirza, N.M.: Rethinking collaborative learning through participation in an interdisciplinary research project: tensions and negotiations as key points in knowledge production. Integr. Psychol. Behav. Sci. **41**(2) (2007). Article number: 154. https://doi.org/10.1007/s12124-007-9019-6
23. Dooner, A.M., Mandzuk, D., Clifton, R.A.: Stages of collaboration and the realities of professional learning communities. Teach. Teach. Educ. **24**(3), 564–574 (2008)

How to Design the Expression Ways of Conversational Agents Based on Affective Experience

Chenyang Zhang[1], Ronggang Zhou[1,2(✉)], Yaping Zhang[1], Yanyan Sun[3], Liming Zou[3], and Min Zhao[3]

[1] Beihang University, Beijing 100191, China
zhrg@buaa.edu.cn
[2] Beijing Advanced Innovation Center for Big Data and Brain Computing, Beijing 100191, China
[3] Baidu, Beijing 100193, China

Abstract. With the rapid development of artificial intelligence, the technology of human-computer interaction is becoming more and more mature. The variety of terminal products equipped with conversational agents are more diverse, and the product penetration rate is also getting higher and higher. This study focused on the problems of the conversational agent in response. In this paper, we presented a study with 20 participants to explore how to design the expression ways of conversational agents' feedback with considerations of users' affective experience. We explored the performance of three different expression ways (general way, implicit way, and explicit way) in different time and different functions. And we examined whether users of different genders have different preferences for these three expression ways. Therefore, we used the "Wizard of Oz techniques" to simulate a real environment for communication between the user and the conversational agent. In this study, we combined quantitative scoring (five aspects: affection, confidence, naturalness, social distance, and satisfaction) with qualitative interviews. The results showed that: (1) the user's affective experience should be considered in expression ways' design; (2) different expression ways had different performances in different functions, and the explicit way performed better in most situations; (3) male users seemed to rate the agent's expression performance higher than female users.

Keywords: Voice interaction · Affective experience · Feedback expression

1 Introduction

With the rapid development of artificial intelligence, the technology of human-computer interaction is becoming more and more mature. The variety of terminal products equipped with conversational agents are more diverse. They have been widely added on smartphones and many intelligent home appliances. With the common use of conversational agents for the average person in everyday life, more research is needed to understand the experiences that users are having [1].

© Springer Nature Switzerland AG 2020
M. Kurosu (Ed.): HCII 2020, LNCS 12182, pp. 302–320, 2020.
https://doi.org/10.1007/978-3-030-49062-1_21

Recent research has explored users' experiences with conversational agents focusing on system capabilities and usability. They evaluated user satisfaction about specific functions like searching for information [2] and so on. However, for voice interaction, perceptual requirements are more complex than visual interaction and hardware interaction. Therefore, it is particularly important to design feedback strategies for voice interaction. Proper interaction logic, association with the context of dialogue and context perception play important roles in user experience. Previous research on feedback strategies mainly focused on the level of feedback form and feedback time. Researchers paid little attention to the affective experience in the expression of feedback.

Emotions are at the heart of human experience [3]. Understanding users' affective experience is crucial to designing compelling CAs [1]. In China, many dialogue scripts are generated from product managers only without any help from user experience specialists. This practice can be the factor preventing positive experiences. Therefore, it is very important to explore expression ways of conversational agents from the perspective of affective experience.

In addition, combining the results of previous usability tests and focus groups, we found that when interacting with the agent, the time of interaction and the functions used also affected the users' expectations of agent expression.

So, we did this research about how to design the expression ways of conversational agents based on affective experience. In this paper, we adopt a particular "Wizard of Oz techniques" to explore the performance of three different expression ways (general way, implicit way, and explicit way) in different time and different functions. Specifically, our contributions are:

1. It is proved that the user's affective experience should be considered in expression ways' design.
2. We discover that there exist gender differences in conversational agents under the same female speakers.
3. Experimental methods take account of real-world scenarios. We explore the expression way design with considerations of using time and functions.

We hope these results will help AI designers and will promote further studies about principles for human-AI interaction.

2 Related Work

In this session, we describe the previous work as a background for our study, both in the scope of feedback strategies and in the context of communication theory.

2.1 Feedback Strategies in Voice Interaction

To realize human-computer voice interaction, many scholars have done a lot of research on the feedback strategies of voice interaction. Here we divide these studies into three categories: feedback form research, feedback time research and feedback expression research.

For the study of feedback form, more attention was paid to multi-modal human-computer interaction based on voice. In terms of voice, Nass [4] pointed out that female voices were more acceptable for people to help deal with problems, and women were more kind to help others make decisions; male voices subconsciously gave people a sense of command, authority, and dominance to "solve problems in this way". This provided theoretical support for the gender setting of conversational agents. Of course, the selection of voice should also be consistent with the behavioral language we have set in advance. Improper dubbing might be worse than no voice because voice also has a certain social meaning [5]. Also, Microsoft Cortana was set to visualize emotions through vision (changes in color and shape) and then inform users [6].

For the study of feedback time, previous research focused on the output time first. Cathy Pearl believed that the system needed to know when the user stopped talking [7]. She describes three kinds of timeouts in the VUI experience (end-of-speech timeout, no speech timeout, and too much speech), and then gave the ranges of each time parameter setting.

There are some studies involving feedback expression. First of all, we can regard personality design as the basic part of feedback expression. When Microsoft designed Cortana, this "breaks the illusion that Cortana is a human, which is just fine by Microsoft, while also making it a more useful tool" [8]. Besides, in a study performed by Clifford Nass and Scott Brave, users performed tasks with a driving simulator, and throughout the tasks, the system voice made comments about their driving performance. Error messages blaming the driver might seem like a small thing, but they could affect the user's perception of the system and even their performance [4]. In Cathy Pearl's book, there are many design strategies for feedback expression in various chapters, involving conversational design, confirmations, error handling, disambiguation and many other aspects.

In general, the researches on voice interactive feedback strategy were more concerned with the functional level. From the perspective of user experience, it focused on the usability and usefulness of products. Researchers often ignored the affective relationship between users and products. However, with the continuous improvement of products, users also hope that products can meet their affective experience.

2.2 Interpersonal Communication and Social Style Model

For conversational agents, especially regarded as assistants or friends rather than tools, a good affective experience means that users feel that they are communicating with a "normal person". As Cohen wrote in a book, "As designers, we don't get to create the underlying elements of conversation. (e.g., we must follow human conventions [9]". That is to say, it is also necessary to obey some requirements of interpersonal communication in the process of human-computer interaction.

A previous study showed that there were six prominent motives in interpersonal communication: pleasure, affection, inclusion, escape, relaxation, and control. The motives of pleasure, affection, and relaxation were more closely related to communication satisfaction [10]. To achieve good communication, it is particularly important to understand the characteristics of social styles. We should also pay attention to the behavior tendency and communication mode of people with different styles.

Sheng [11] believed that the social style model could be divided into four styles in the coordinate system of dominant/amiable and explicit/implicit dimensions: facilitating style, promoting style, controlling style and analytic style.

The characteristics that describe dominating behavior are: talkative, seeming confident, easy to make conclusions, direct, challenging, assertive, competitive, making decision quickly.

The characteristics that describe easy-going behavior are: quiet, seeming uncertain, easy to ask questions, not being straightforward, sensitive, people moving, gentle, making decision slowly.

The characteristics that describe explicit tendencies are: interrupting others' words, appearing extroverted, people-oriented, large range of movements, naturally showing, expressive, fun-loving, and passionate.

The characteristics that describe implicit tendencies are: task-oriented, careful listening, introverted, indifferent, few movements, methodical, unemotional, self-restrained, rigid, serious.

Similarly, DISC personality model was based on the work of psychologist William M. Marston [12]. This model explored people's priorities and how those priorities influenced behavior [13]. DISC is an acronym for Dominance, Influence, Steadiness, and Conscientiousness.

We focused more on feedback expression design (which is called as expression way design in this paper). We designed three levels in expression ways: general way, implicit way, and explicit way. It will be introduced later in the next section.

3   Method

In this section, we begin by describing the experimental setup. Next, we discuss some important parts in our experiment.

3.1   The Experimental Setup

We conducted a within-subjects experiment with 20 conversational agents' users to explore the performance of different expression ways in different time and different functions. The independent variables consisted of expression ways, time, and functions. Each variable had three levels, thus producing a $3 \times 3 \times 3$ factorial design.

The levels of expression ways were general way, implicit way and explicit way. These levels were mainly derived from a dimension in the social style model mentioned above [11]. From the above description, we can see that what is more relevant to the users' affective experience is the "explicit-implicit" metric. Therefore, in this study, we used "explicit-introverted" as the level of the independent variable. Besides, there were a few affective expressions concerned about users in general way. So, the first variable was made up of these three different expression ways.

The functions' levels consisted of weather, music, and news because of users' heavy use of early research results. As for the time, it was determined in consideration of the time working persons have to interact with the agent. The time levels were in the morning, after a day's work, before going to bed.

Considering the method, we used the "Wizard of Oz techniques" to simulate a real environment for communication. And all the materials were transferred into synthesized sound files by using a female speaker. Ethics approval to conduct this research was obtained from Beihang University.

Wizard of Oz Techniques. In the field of human–computer interaction, a Wizard of Oz techniques is a research method in which subjects interact with a computer system that subjects believe to be autonomous [14], but which is actually being operated or partially operated by an unseen human being [15]. So, we used the "Wizard of Oz techniques" to put different responses (expression ways) into the test demo control platform. The experimenter controlled the process and results of human-computer interaction by operating the control platform so that users could mistakenly believe that he is interacting with a real conversation agent. When people can earnestly engage with what they perceive to be a conversation agent, they will form more complete mental models, while interacting with the experience in more natural ways [16].

Dependent Variable. In this study, we measured user experience from five aspects (affection, confidence, naturalness, social distance, and satisfaction). The items were selected from an array of sources, primarily including the evaluation of conversational agents and measurements of user experience. Affection and confidence were important indicators for evaluating the users' affective experience of conversational agents' responses [17]. Naturalness could be used to evaluate a conversational agent's responses from two aspects: expression and voice [18]. We evaluated the expressions in this experiment. Social distance has significance to grasp of the effective communication strategies and to the harmonization of interpersonal relationship in society. As for satisfaction, it was used widely in measuring user experience as a comprehensive index. All the items consisted of seven-point semantic differential scales.

Experimental Materials. Studies showed that what differed in Chinese culture is the lower frequency, intensity, and duration with which emotions were typically experienced [19]. Through a summary of the existing responses to the agents' common functions and discussions with experts, we found that the current agent responses can be disassembled into three parts. The first was the fact part, this part was the realization of the basic functions of the agent, such as "weather information", "playing music", etc. The judgment part was based on the judgment of the current situation based on facts, such as "it will rain tomorrow", "it's late now", etc. Finally, the suggestion part, this part is the agent to care for the user after making a judgment, such as "remember to bring an umbrella", "get to sleep" and so on.

Combining with the expression, in general way, agents only stated fact. Agents could add judgment and suggestions in other ways. For this study, we make the following operational definitions, please refer to the Table 1 for explanations. There was also an example shown in Table 2. This example may not be expressed clearly because of my poor translation and the difference between the English and the Chinese language environment.

Table 1. The explanations to three parts of a response.

Parts	Explanation		
	General way	Implicit way	Explicit way
Fact	Basic functional realization	Basic functional realization	Basic functional realization
Judgement	–	Statement of objective judgement	Judgement with more subjective feelings
Suggestion	–	Obvious emotional and colloquial expression, more modal particles	

Table 2. An example in weather function.

Parts	General way	Implicit way	Explicit way
Fact	Beijing is sunny, with a maximum temperature of 36° and good air quality, suitable for T-shirts	Beijing is sunny, with a maximum temperature of 36° and good air quality, suitable for T-shirts	Beijing is sunny, with a maximum temperature of 36° and good air quality, suitable for T-shirts
Judgement	–	It is hot weather	It is so hot!
Suggestion	–	Please take measures to escape the summer heat	Take care of yourself, don't get sunstroke!

3.2 Participants

Twenty participants (M = 10, F = 10) were recruited from a university and other companies via an internal questionnaire. In line with best practice, participants were recruited until saturation had occurred. Demographic data showed that participants had an age ranged from 18 to 50 and consisted of students and staff across a wide range of subjects. All the participants indicated that they had previously used conversational agents, and this majority (60%) said they had previously used smart speakers. Participants were provided with 50 RMB in exchange for taking part in a one-hour experiment. All the participants signed of informed consent paper after understanding all the experimental procedures.

3.3 Procedure

Each participant was invited individually into the laboratory. The procedure comprised five main phases in a fixed order: completing the demographic and conversational agents usage questionnaire; being familiar with the smart speaker (for participants who had never used smart speakers); hearing responses by giving orders to the speaker; judging the user experience of each response; recalling the overall procedure and receiving a face-to-face interview. Participants were not informed about later phases. These phases are detailed below.

After completing informed consent, participants were invited to filling in the demographic and conversational agent usage questionnaire. Then participants who had never used smart speakers could have a chance to interact with the speakers for 10 min; they were told to use the functions which had no relevance to later phases.

Users' instructions were given in advance. Users could hear a response by giving an order to the speaker. Then they were asked to quantitatively measure each response from five aspects: affection, confidence, naturalness, social distance, and satisfaction. Participants made judgments on a Likert–type scale with 1 as the complete disagreement and 7 as the complete agreement. Participants needed to hear 30 responses. Each function had three replies in each period. And there would be 3 replies as exercises before the formal experiment starts to eliminate the practice effect. After measuring 3 different responses (in 3 different expression ways) in the same function and the same time, participants were asked to select the best one among them. The results in different ways could be verified by each other. Due to the number of materials, evaluation aspects, and the equipment limitation caused by the method, the experimental sequence was fixed. In order to reduce the sequence effect, each response was scored immediately after the listening process. After each function experience was completed, an interview for that function was conducted first, and the time interval between the responses was relatively long. After discussing with the mentor, it was considered that the sequence effect had less impact.

Next, participants attempted to recall the overall procedure that they had heard during the experiment. And then they were invited to attend a face-to-face interview. The semi-structured interview was designed to be short and took between 8 and 10 min to be completed [20]. The questions for each function in the interview were:

Q1. When will you use the conversational agent for the weather forecast (music, and news)?
Q2. Please tell us your demands for the function at different times in one day.
Q3. Have you found the differences between these responses? Please tell me about your findings.
Q4. What impressed you most in these responses?

At the end of the interview, participants had the chance to share any other thoughts they wished. On completion of the interview, participants were thanked and provided with monetary rewards for their participation in our study.

3.4 Data Analysis

First of all, validity and reliability analysis were made upon such data to examine the scale we made.

For quantitative data, we used SPSS 25 to generate descriptive statistics (mean, standard deviation) and ran one-way ANOVAs for each dependent variable to determine the impact of groups. We used an alpha level of .05 for all statistical tests. ANOVAs are robust to violations of normality. Where there were violations in assumptions, we state results with caution.

For qualitative data, we invited four experienced user researchers to discuss the interview records. A focus group was used to extract keywords and classify them. When disagreement arose, it was a must to discuss and finally reached an agreement. The frequency of keywords was tallied to summarize the important factors in users' demands. Q3 was also used to clean data. If the answer to Q3 was No, this piece of data was excluded from data analysis. All users identified the differences between responses. The data of 20 participants in total were analyzed and presented. In the following section, we present the findings from our analysis.

4 Results

In this section, we didn't analyze the main effects of time and function. In my opinion, these two variables were not "independent variables" in common sense. They were more helpful for us to observe the effects of different expression ways. It was not significant to observe the main effect of time or function when ignoring the expression ways. As for the interaction effect analysis between independent variables, we didn't describe them here because of the non-significant results. We firstly described the quantitative statistics by using one-way ANOVA. Next, we stated the results from the semi-structured interview.

4.1 Validity and Reliability Analysis

The data were first subjected to Kaiser-Meyer-Olkin (KMO) and Bartlett test analyses to test the scale's structure validity, yielding to the results of KMO 0.894 and Bartlett Test values $x^2 = 1939.115$; sd $= 10$; p < 0.001. It meant that the data are suitable for factor analysis. The factor analysis is performed with the aim to reveal whether the items of a certain scale are grouped into mutually exclusive fewer factors. Items in the same group are assigned a name according to the content of the items (Gorsuch, 1983). Also, factor analysis is used to test whether a particular scale is one-dimensional (Balcı, 2009). The analyses revealed the scale's eigenvalue in a single factor as 3.820 and the percentage of explained variance was 76.407. The results showed that these five aspects could measure affective experience well.

As for reliability analysis, Cronbach's alpha reliability coefficient was found to be 0.922. It meant that the internal consistency level of the scale is well.

In conclusion, it can be concluded that the scale we made for measuring affective experience is a valid and reliable scale.

4.2 Expression Ways

Participants' overall measurements to different expression ways are shown in Table 3.

From Table 3, the results showed a trend that responses with affective expressions (implicitly or explicitly) had better performance than those in general way. And there were statistically significant differences in all aspect. But no significant difference was found between the implicit and explicit ways except affection.

Table 3. The measurements of expression ways in total by one-way ANOVA.

Measurement		Mean	SD
Affection[***]	General way	4.70	1.29
	Implicit way	5.13[*,1,3]	1.10
	Explicit way	5.42[*,1,2]	1.18
Confidence[**]	General way	5.19[*,2,3]	1.25
	Implicit way	5.46	1.08
	Explicit way	5.59	0.96
Naturalness[*]	General way	4.94[*,3]	1.29
	Implicit way	5.14	1.10
	Explicit way	5.26	1.08
Social distance[***]	General way	4.51[*,2,3]	1.28
	Implicit way	5.27	1.18
	Explicit way	5.49	1.15
Satisfaction[***]	General way	4.94[*,2,3]	1.28
	Implicit way	5.38	1.13
	Explicit way	5.56	1.19

1-general way; 2-implicit way; 3-explicit way; $*p < .05$, $**p < .01$, $***p < .001$

To test whether the results were influenced by functions and periods, we analyzed the five dependent variables for each function and period. Because of the similar results in these functions, we took music function as an example to describe the results carefully (see Fig. 1). The different results in other functions would be added.

The results in music were the same as the overall results (affection: $F = 5.599$, $P = .004$; social distance: $F = 9.527$, $P = .000$). There was also a trend that responses with affective expressions (implicitly or explicitly) had better performance than those in general way. Consistent with music, weather existed significant differences in their groups in affection ($F = 3.989$, $P = .020$), social distance ($F = 12.331$, $P = .000$), and satisfaction ($F = 6.319$, $P = .002$). All factors in news were statistically significant in their groups (affection: $F = 13.074$, $P = .000$; confidence: $F = 4.641$, $P = .011$; naturalness: $F = 8.679$, $P = .000$; social distance: $F = 11.873$, $P = .000$; satisfaction: $F = 6.583$, $P = .002$).

From the perspective of time, it was obvious that responses with affective expressions performed better in all three periods. But there was no significant difference between the implicit and explicit ways, which is the same as weather.

Furthermore, as Fig. 1 depicted, explicit expression ways scored higher than another two ways when experienced after a day's work. The same situation also appeared in weather and news. The difference was that explicit expression way scored best in all three periods in the news, see Table 4.

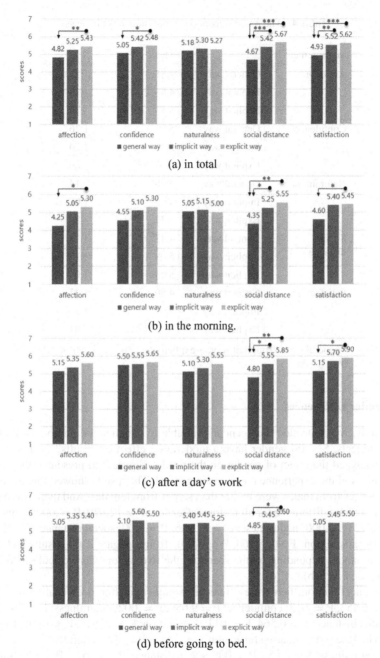

(a) in total

(b) in the morning.

(c) after a day's work

(d) before going to bed.

Fig. 1. Measurements of three expression ways in music in total (top left), in the morning (top right), after a day's work (bottom left) and before going to bed (bottom right).

Table 4. The measurements of expression ways in news.

Measurement		Mean	SD
Affection[***]	General way	4.55	1.23
	Implicit way	4.83	1.18
	Explicit way	5.53[***,1,2]	.79
Confidence[*]	General way	5.07	1.26
	Implicit way	5.25	1.20
	Explicit way	5.67[*,1,2]	.80
Naturalness[***]	General way	4.58	1.14
	Implicit way	4.92	1.08
	Explicit way	5.37[*,1,2]	.86
Social distance[***]	General way	4.47[**,2,3]	1.11
	Implicit way	5.08	1.17
	Explicit way	5.43	1.01
Satisfaction[**]	General way	4.80	1.33
	Implicit way	5.07	1.16
	Explicit way	5.53[*,1,2]	.81

1-general way; 2-implicit way; 3-explicit way; $*p < .05$, $**p < .01$, $***p < .001$

4.3 Gender Differences

In the study, we controlled the "gender" variable to equalize the number of male and female subjects. So, did gender have a moderating effect on results? In this part, we mainly analyzed the effect of gender on the results. Figure 2(a) presented the descriptive statistics of the experience measures in general. The results showed that the overall average scores from males were higher than scores from females. And there was a statistically significant difference for all factors (affection: $F = 12.870$, $P = .000$; confidence: $F = 22.078$, $P = .000$; naturalness: $F = 17.906$, $P = .000$; social distance: $F = 24.673$, $P = .000$; satisfaction: $F = 25.260$, $P = .000$). To investigate if the results had different performances depending on the scenario, the five factors were calculated for each function, see Fig. 2(b) to 2(d).

In weather function, there were statistically significant differences for all factors (affection: $F = 6.453$, $P = .012$; confidence: $F = 9.689$, $P = .002$; naturalness: $F = 5.420$, $P = .021$; social distance: $F = 6.564$, $P = .011$; satisfaction: $F = 21.012$, $P = .000$). The news function had the same situation (affection: $F = 7.999$, $P = .005$; confidence: $F = 4.859$, $P = .029$; naturalness: $F = 7.153$, $P = .008$; social distance: $F = 16.551$, $P = .000$; satisfaction: $F = 6.882$, $P = .009$). Figure 2(c) shows the same trend in music, but only three factors had statistically significant differences (confidence: $F = 8.361$, $P = .004$; naturalness: $F = 5.743$, $P = .018$; social distance: $F = 4.678$, $P = .0032$). All the figures above showed that male participants seemingly had better experience than female participants. And there was the same trend in different periods.

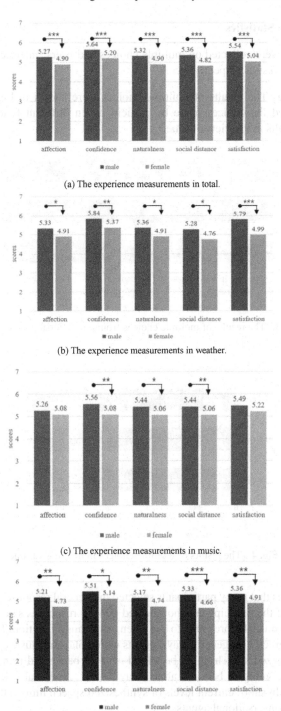

(a) The experience measurements in total.

(b) The experience measurements in weather.

(c) The experience measurements in music.

(d) The experience measurements in news.

Fig. 2. Measurements of three functions in general (top left), in weather (top right), music (bottom left) and news (bottom right).

4.4 Qualitative Statistics

Qualitative data were collected on multiple choices and users' interviews. In this part, we present these results respectively.

Multiple Choice. The results of multiple choices were shown in Fig. 3 and Fig. 4. Figure 3 depicted the choices made by participants in different functions. Figure 4 depicted the results in the view of time.

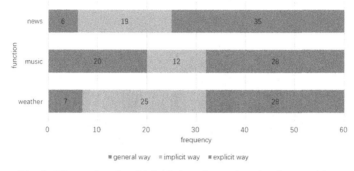

Fig. 3. The results of multiple choices from a functional perspective.

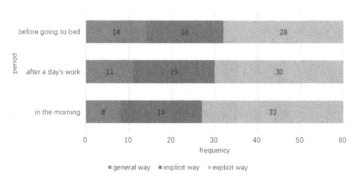

Fig. 4. The results of multiple choices in the view of time.

It was obvious that many participants selected the general responses in music. In the interview, half of the participants who selected general responses said that they didn't want to listen too much before going to bed when using music function. They preferred to listen to music directly (In general ways, agents would play the music directly.). In their thoughts, synthesized speech might be a kind of disturbance and ruin the atmosphere especially before going to bed and after a day's work. And it also led to the results shown in Fig. 4. In short, current levels of synthesized speech limited the expression of emotions from conversational agents.

Interestingly, quantitative findings seemed to contradict qualitative findings. In interviews, participants who chose general ways (which meant that they played the music directly without saying anything) thought that the atmosphere created by music was good enough, and there was no need to say anything at this time. In that situation, the use of an unnatural synthesized voice was a kind of disturbance. Besides, by checking the raw data, we found that scores from participants with those statements were very close between the general and implicit responses. But the scores from other participants had a bigger gap between the general and implicit responses. This was the two reasons for this contradiction.

Q1. When will you use the conversational agent for the weather (music, and news)?

The chart below displayed the using time of three functions, seeing Fig. 5. Users usually listen to weather forecasts in the morning and before sleep. Although most users decided to listen to music in the afternoon, there are also some users doing this in the morning and before sleep. As for news, few users choose to listen to the news before going to bed. Some design suggestions could be put forward based on the situation, especially frequent time.

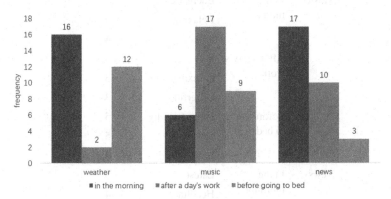

Fig. 5. The results of using time of three functions.

Q2. Please tell us your demands for the function at different times in one day.

Table 5 illustrated the frequency of users' demands in each function. From the table, we can sum up some points related to improving users' experience. For weather, it is important to give some useful tips at the right time. For example, agents can remind users to bring an umbrella before going to work. And agents can tell users the conditions of roads before they leave home. Playing the right music at the right time may be the most important thing in music function. The agents should learn behavior and habits from each individual user over time. In terms of news, users value timeliness highly and prefer to reading headlines.

Q3. Have you found the differences between these responses? Please tell me about your findings.

This question was regarded as a filter to clean data. From the results, all participants could tell the differences among responses. This showed satisfactory discrimination about the experiment materials.

Q4. What impressed you most in these responses?

Table 5. The frequency of users' demands.

Function	Using time	Key words	Frequency
Weather	In the morning	Umbrella	6
		Clothes	5
		Going out	3
	After a day's work	Voice sounds happy	2
		Umbrella	1
		Going out	1
	Before going to bed	Tomorrow's weather	8
		Umbrella	3
		Going out	3
Music	In the morning	Energetic	9
		Relaxing	4
		Soft	4
	After a day's work	Soft	4
		Relaxing	3
		Cheerful	3
	Before going to bed	Sleep-friendly	5
		Soft	5
		Light music	4
News	In the morning	Latest	5
		Headlines	4
		Concise	3
	After a day's work	Various	4
		Headlines	4
		Latest	2
	Before going to bed	Various	3
		Headlines	2
		Latest	2

Most participants said that they were impressed by these implicit and explicit responses, which is good things. But they were also impressed by the awkward unnatural voice. This kind of voice made them feel uncomfortable. So, naturalness is an important and basic element that influences the affective experience a lot. In a word, users prefer natural voice and humanized expressions. Recent studies have showed that certain users groups tend to personify their agents [21], particularly older adults and children [22].

5 Discussion

This section discusses the main findings and the implications for existing and future conversational agents. Details are discussed below.

5.1 Discussions of Affective Experience

In the study, we used five factors to measure users' experience with conversational agents. Satisfaction, as a comprehensive indicator, reflected the user's experience generally. Affection and social distance were used as subjective factors to evaluate users' subjective feelings. They measured the user's affective experience. Confidence and naturalness are objective factors to evaluate the performance of some objective aspects. We tried our best to use the real-world responses of the conversational agents as the general way. However, these responses could be slightly adjusted because of the control of other variables. Overall, the performance of the objective indicators was better. The overall score of confidence was ahead of other indicators. But synthesized tones seriously affected the performance in naturalness. Users generally felt that the voice was somewhat stiff and unnatural. Subjective factors' scores were relatively lower. This showed that the current enterprises were not concerned about the user's affective experience enough, and designers didn't take the user's affective experience into account when designing the feedback expression.

From the results, we could also see users' preference for explicit expression ways after a day's work. This trend existed in all three functions we set in the experiment. In the interviews, participants said they usually felt tired after a day's work. In this case, explicit responses could make users feel more relaxed. Statistics showed that the average working hours of Chinese people are higher than those of most countries in the world, reaching 2200 h per year [23]. Long hours of work could easily make users depressed and tired. Participants agreed that explicit responses made them more relaxed and comfortable.

From the overall results, we can also find that explicit responses had the best comprehensive performance. Participants felt satisfied most of the time. However, in the context of Chinese culture, Chinese people tend to be more implicit in interpersonal communication. Previous studies showed that subjects with a Chinese cultural background were more responsive to robots that use implicit communication styles [24], and Chinese participants preferred an implicit communication style than German participants [25]. This is inconsistent with our results. There is a possible explanation. Although human-computer interaction needs to comply with some requirements of interpersonal communication, it is still different from interpersonal communication. In our interviews, although participants personified the conversational agents, they still regarded the agents as assistants rather than humans. Another possible explanation is that the limitations of conversational agents themselves may lead to users' preference for explicit responses. The current dialogue mode requires users to order agents concisely, directly and clearly so that they can understand the user's words easily. This situation also exists in Chinese agents. Before the study began, we conducted usability testing to understand the current usage of conversational agents. We found that the users' natural expression would lead to identification problems because the sentences were too long and complex. And agents could not respond to users correctly.

5.2 Possible Reasons of Gender Heterogeneity

In the study, we found an interesting phenomenon: male participants scored significantly higher than female participants. This attracted our attention. There is a possible reason for this situation.

The possible reason is that the female speaker we use is more attractive to male participants. Studies have shown that humans have a general preference for heterosexual voices: men prefer high-pitched female voices; women prefer low-pitched male voices [26, 27]. This voice preference is closely related to the evolutionary significance behind voice: feminized voice is the characterization of female fertility [28], while masculine voice is the characterization of male's good genes and resources [29]. However, since we have not conducted experiments on male speakers, we cannot verify this reason. So, designers should consider adding the options of male speakers for female users. In the previous usability testing, many female users have put forward similar requirements. They want to add male voices to conversational agents.

5.3 Limitation

This paper identifies some important characteristics in conversation and how these factors influence users' affective experience. We performed this study in China, and thus our findings may not transfer to other cultures. The results of this study are based on the data of 20 users. The bigger size of samples is required for more convincing results in the future. Besides, only a female speaker was used in this study. We have no idea how a male speaker affects users' affective experience. Additionally, we should get more information by asking more in-depth questions during the interview to explain the quantitative data easily.

6 Conclusion

This study contributes to the literature on conversational agents by taking affective experience into account in feedback expression design. In detail, we performed a quantitative evaluation of three expression ways in different functions and periods. We also performed a qualitative analysis of users' experiences. We found that the user's affective experience should be considered in expression ways' design, and explicit responses performed better in most situations. The male participants seemed to be more satisfied with the agent's feedback performance, as reflected in the higher cores of each dependent variable than women. These findings are significant as they provide a foundation for future design and research in this area in China.

References

1. Yang, X., Aurisicchio, M., Baxter, W.: Understanding affective experiences with conversational agents. In: Proceedings of the 2019 CHI Conference on Human Factors in Computing Systems, CHI 2019 (2019). https://doi.org/10.1145/3290605.3300772
2. Vtyurina, A., Savenkov, D., Agichtein, E., Clarke, C.L.: Exploring conversational search with humans, assistants, and wizards, pp. 2187–2193. ACM (2017). http://dl.acm.org/citation.cfm?id=3053175
3. Forlizzi, J., Battarbee, K.: Understanding experience in interactive systems, pp. 261–268. ACM (2004). http://dl.acm.org/citation.cfm?id=1013152
4. Nass, C., Brave, S.: Wired of Speech. The MIT Press, Cambridge (2005)
5. Nass, C., Reeves, B.: The Media Equation. CSLI Publications, Stanford (1996)
6. Ash, M.: How Cortana comes to life in Windows 10 (2015). http://blogs.windows.com/
7. Pearl, C.: Designing Voice User Interfaces: Principles of Conversational Experiences. O'Reilly Media Inc., Boston (2016)
8. Weinberger, M.: Why Microsoft doesn't want its digital assistant, Cortana, to sound too human (2016). http://www.businessinsider.com/why-microsoftdoesnt-want-to-sound-too-human-2016-2/
9. Cohen, M., Giangola, J., Balogh, J.: Voice User Interface Design. Addison-Wesley, Boston (2004)
10. Rubin, R.B., Perse, E.M., Barbato, C.A.: Conceptualization and measurement of interpersonal communication motives. Hum. Commun. Res. **14**(4), 602–628 (1988)
11. Sheng, L.: Win-Win Management Art: Social Style and Organizational Behavior. Economy & Management Publishing House Press (2002)
12. Slowikowski, M.K.: Using the DISC behavioral instrument to guide leadership and communication. AORN J. **82**(5), 835–836, 838, 841–843 (2005)
13. Sugerman, J.: Using the DiSC® model to improve communication effectiveness. Ind. Commer. Train. **41**(3), 151–154 (2009). https://doi.org/10.1108/00197850910950952
14. Alpern, M., Minardo, K.: Developing a car gesture interface for use as a secondary task. In: CHI 2003 Extended Abstracts on Human Factors in Computing Systems, CHI 2003 (2003)
15. Bella, M., Hanington, B.: Universal Methods of Design, p. 204. Rockport Publishers, Beverly (2012)
16. Collisson, P.M., Hardiman, G., Santos, M.: User research makes your AI smarter. https://medium.com/microsoft-design/user-research-makes-your-ai-smarter-70f6ef6eb25a. Accessed 1 July 2019
17. Street, R.L.: Evaluation of noncontent speech accommodation. Lang. Commun. **2**(1), 13–31 (1982). https://doi.org/10.1016/0271-5309(82)90032-5
18. Adiga, N., Prasanna, S.R.M.: Acoustic features modelling for statistical parametric speech synthesis: a review. IETE Tech. Rev. **36**(2), 130–149 (2018). https://doi.org/10.1080/02564602.2018.1432422
19. Bond, M.H.: Emotions and their expression in Chinese culture. J. Nonverbal Behav. **17**(4), 245–262 (1993). https://doi.org/10.1007/bf00987240
20. Candello, H., et al.: The effect of audiences on the user experience with conversational interfaces in physical spaces. In: Proceedings of the 2019 CHI Conference on Human Factors in Computing Systems, CHI 2019 (2019)
21. Purington, A., Taft, J.G., Sannon, S., Bazarova, N.N., Taylor, S.H.: Alexa is my new BFF: social roles, user satisfaction, and personification of the Amazon Echo. In: Proceedings of the 2017 CHI Conference Extended Abstracts on Human Factors in Computing Systems, pp. 2853–2859. ACM (2017)

22. Yarosh, S., et al.: Children asking questions: speech interface reformulations and personifcation preferences. In: Proceedings of the 17th ACM Conference on Interaction Design and Children, pp. 300–312. ACM (2018)
23. @001期货网: Annual work hours. Weibo (2019). https://weibo.com/1649728202/HjehjE pvz?refer_flag=1001030103_&type=comment#_rnd1568863067626. Accessed 3 Mar 2019
24. Wang, L., Rau, P.L.P., Evers, V., Robinson, B., Hinds, P.J.: Responsiveness to robots: effects of ingroup orientation &. ommunication style on HRI in China. In: ACM/IEEE International Conference on Human-Robot Interaction. IEEE (2009)
25. Rau, P.L.P., Li, Y., Li, D.: Effects of communication style and culture on ability to accept recommendations from robots. Comput. Hum. Behav. **25**(2), 587–595 (2009)
26. Apicella, C.L., Feinberg, D.R.: Voice pitch alters mate-choice-relevant perception in huntergatherers. Proc. Roy. Soc. B Biol. Sci. **276**, 1077–1082 (2009)
27. Re, D.E., O'Connor, J.J., Bennett, P.J., Feinberg, D.R.: Preferences for very low and very high voice pitch in humans. PLoS ONE **7**(3), e32719 (2012)
28. Fraccaro, P.J.: Experimental evidence that women speak in a higher voice pitch to men they find attractive. J. Evol. Psychol. **9**(1), 57–67 (2011)
29. Jones, B.C., Feinberg, D.R., Watkins, C.D., Fincher, C.L., Little, A.C., DeBruine, L.M.: Pathogen disgust predicts women's preferences for masculinity in men's voices, faces, and bodies. Behav. Ecol. **24**(2), 373–379 (2013)

Deep Learning-Based Emotion Recognition from Real-Time Videos

Wenbin Zhou, Justin Cheng, Xingyu Lei, Bedrich Benes(✉) ⓘD,
and Nicoletta Adamo ⓘD

Purdue University, West Lafayette, IN 47906, USA
{bbenes,nadamovi}@purdue.edu

Abstract. We introduce a novel framework for emotional state detection from facial expression targeted to learning environments. Our framework is based on a convolutional deep neural network that classifies people's emotions that are captured through a web-cam. For our classification outcome we adopt Russel's model of core affect in which any particular emotion can be placed in one of four quadrants: pleasant-active, pleasant-inactive, unpleasant-active, and unpleasant-inactive. We gathered data from various datasets that were normalized and used to train the deep learning model. We use the fully-connected layers of the VGG_S network which was trained on human facial expressions that were manually labeled. We have tested our application by splitting the data into 80:20 and re-training the model. The overall test accuracy of all detected emotions was 66%. We have a working application that is capable of reporting the user emotional state at about five frames per second on a standard laptop computer with a web-cam. The emotional state detector will be integrated into an affective pedagogical agent system where it will serve as a feedback to an intelligent animated educational tutor.

Keywords: Facial expression recognition · Deep learning · Education

1 Introduction

Facial expressions play a vital role in social communications between humans because the human face is the richest source of emotional cues [18]. We are capable of reading and understanding facial emotions because of thousands of year of evolution. We also react to facial expressions [13] and some of these reactions are even unconscious [14]. Emotions play an important role as a feedback in learning as they inform the teacher about the student's emotional state [3,31]. This is particularly important in on-line learning, where a fully automated system can be adapted to emotional state of the learner [15].

We introduce a novel deep-neural network-based emotion detection targeted to educational settings. Our approach uses a web-cam to capture images of the

National Science Foundation, # 10001364, Collaborative Research: Multimodal Affective Pedagogical Agents for Different Types of Learners.

ⓒ Springer Nature Switzerland AG 2020
M. Kurosu (Ed.): HCII 2020, LNCS 12182, pp. 321–332, 2020.
https://doi.org/10.1007/978-3-030-49062-1_22

learner and a convolutional neural networks to detect facial expressions in real time categorized by using Russell's classification model [55] and Fig. 1, which covers the majority of affective states a learner might experience during a learning episode. We also take the effort to deal with different scenes, viewing angles, and lighting conditions that may be encountered in practical use. We use transfer learning on the fully-connected layers of the VGG_S network which was trained on human facial expressions that were manually labeled. The overall test accuracy of the detected emotions was 66% and our system is capable of reporting the user emotional state at about five frames per seconds on a laptop computer. We plan to integrate the emotional state detector into an affective pedagogical agent system where it will serve as a feedback to an intelligent animated tutor.

2   Background and Related Work

Encoding and understanding emotions is particularly important in educational settings [3,31]. While face-to-face education with a capable, educated, and empathetic teacher is optimal, it is also not always possible. People have been looking at teaching without teachers ever since the invention of books and with the recent advances in technology, for example by using simulations [43,66]. We have also seen significant advances in distance learning platforms and systems [22,52]. However, while automation brings many advantages, such as reaching a wide population of learners or being available at locations where face-to-face education may not be possible, it also brings new challenges [2,9,50,61]. One of them is the standardized look-and-feel of the course. One layout does not fit all learners, the pace of the delivery should be managed, the tasks should vary depending on the level of the learner, and the content should be also calibrated to the individual needs of learners.

Affective Agents: Some of these challenges have been addressed by interactive pedagogical agents that have been found effective in enhancing distance learning [6,40,47,57]. Among them, animated educational agents play an important role [12,39], because they can be easily controlled and their behavior can be defined by techniques commonly used in computer animation, for example by providing adequate gestures [25]. Pedagogical agents with emotional capabilities can enhance interactions between the learner and the computer and can improve learning as shown by Kim et al. [30]. Several systems have been implemented, for example Lisetti and Nasoz [37] combined facial expression and physiological signals to recognize a learner's emotions. D'Mello and Graesser [15] introduced AutoTutor and they shown that learners display a variety of emotions during learning and they also shown that AutoTutor can be designed to detect emotions and respond to them. A virtual agent SimSensei [42] engages in interviews to elicit behaviors that can be automatically measured and analyzed. It uses a multimodal sensing system that captures a variety of signals that assess the user's affective state, as well as to inform the agent to provide feedback. The manipulation of the agents affective states significantly influences learning [68] and has a positive influence on learner self-efficacy [30].

However, an effective pedagogical agent needs to respond to learners emotions that need to be first detected. The communication should be based on real input from the learner, pedagogical agents should be empathetic [11,30] and they should provide emotional interactions with the learner [29]. Various means of emotion detection have been proposed, such as using eye-tracker [62], measuring body temperature [4], using visual context [8], or skin conductivity [51] but a vast body of work has been focusing on detecting emotions in speech [28,35,65].

Facial Expressions: While the above-mentioned previous work provides very good results, it may not be always applicable in educational context. Speech is often not required while communicating with educational agents, and approaches that require attached sensors may not be ideal for the learner. This leaves the detection of facial expressions and their analysis as a good option.

Various approaches have been proposed to detect facial expressions. Early works, such as the FACS [16], focus on facial parameterization, where the features are detected and encoded as a feature vector that is used to find a particular emotion. Recent approaches use active contours [46] or other automated methods to detect the features automatically. A large class of algorithms attempts to use geometry-based approaches, such as facial reconstruction [59] and others detect salient facial features [20,63]. Various emotions and their variations have been studied [45] and classified [24], and some focus on micro expressions [17]. Novel approaches use automated feature detection by using machine learning methods such as support vector machine [5,58], but they share the same sensibility to the facial detector as the above-mentioned approaches (see also a review [7]).

One of the key components of these approaches is a face tracking system [60] that should be capable of a robust detection of the face and its features even in varying light conditions and for different learners [56]. However, existing methods often require careful calibration, similar lighting conditions, and the calibration may not transfer to other persons. Such systems provide good results for head position or orientation tracking, but they may fail to detect subtle changes in mood that are important for emotion detection.

Deep Learning: Recent advances in deep learning [34] brought deep neural networks also to the field of emotion detection. Several approaches have been introduced for robust head rotation detection [53], detection of facial features [64], speech [19], or even emotions [44]. Among them, EmoNets [26] detects acted emotions from movies by simultaneously analyzing both video and audio streams. This approach builds on the previous work for CNN facial detection [33]. Our work is inspired by the work of Burket et al. [10] who introduced deep learning network called DeXpression for emotion detection from videos. In particular, they use the Cohn-Kanade database (CMU-Pittsburg AU coded database) [27] and the MMI Facial Expression [45].

3   Classification of Emotions

Most applications of emotion detection categorize images of facial expressions into seven types of human emotions: anger, disgust, fear, happiness, sadness, surprise, and neutral. Such classification is too detailed in the context of students' emotions, for instance when learners are taking video courses in front of a computer the high number of emotions is not applicable in all scenarios. Therefore, we use a classification of emotions related and used in academic learning [48,49]. In particular, we use Russell's model of core affect [55] in which any particular emotion can be placed along two dimensions (see Fig. 1): 1) valence (ranging from unpleasant to pleasant), and 2) arousal (ranging from activation to deactivation). This model covers a sufficiently large range of emotions and is suitable for deep learning implementation.

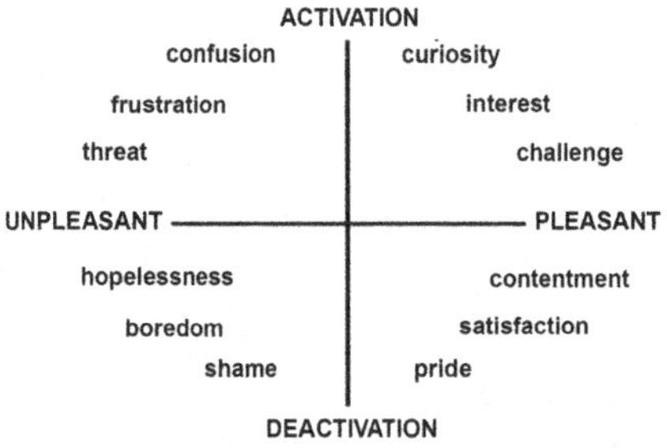

```
                    ACTIVATION
        confusion    |    curiosity
      frustration    |    interest
         threat      |       challenge

UNPLEASANT ----------+---------- PLEASANT

      hopelessness   |    contentment
         boredom     |    satisfaction
           shame     |  pride
                  DEACTIVATION
```

Fig. 1. Mapping of emotions from the discrete model to the 4-quadrant model (from Russel et al. [55]).

The two main axis of the Russel's divide the emotion space into four quadrants: 1) upper-left quadrant (active-unpleasant) includes affective states based on being exposed to instruction such as confusion or frustration, 2) upper-right quadrant (active-pleasant) includes curiosity and interest, 3) lower-right quadrant (inactive-pleasant) includes contentment and satisfaction, and 4) lower-left quadrant (inactive-pleasant) includes hopelessness and boredom.

Most of the existing image databases (some of them are discussed in Sect. 4.1) classify the images of facial expressions into the seven above-mentioned discrete emotions (anger, disgust, fear, happiness, sadness, surprise, and neutral). We transform the datasets according to Russell's 4-quadrants classification model by grouping the images by using the following mapping:

- pleasant-active $\Leftarrow$ happy, surprised,
- unpleasant-active $\Leftarrow$ angry, fear, disgust,
- pleasant-inactive $\Leftarrow$ neutral, and
- unpleasant-inactive $\Leftarrow$ sad.

This grouping then assigns a unique label denoted by L to each image as:

$$L \in \{active - pleasant, active - unpleasant, \qquad (1)$$
$$inactive - pleasant, inactive - unpleasant\}.$$

4   Methods

4.1   Input Images and Databases

Various databases of categorized (labeled) facial expressions with detected faces and facial features exist. We used images from the Cohn-Kanade database (CK+) [27], Japanese Female Facial Expression (JAFFE) [38], The Multimedia Understanding Facial Expression Database (MUG) [1], Indian Spontaneous

Expression Database (ISED) [23], Radboud Faces Database (RaFD) [32], Oulu-CASIA NIR&VIS facial expression database (OULU) [67], AffectNet [41], and The CMU multi-pose, illumination, and expression Face Database (CMU-PIE) [21].

Table 1. Databases used for training the deep neural network.

Input database	# of images	sad	happy	neutral	surprise	fear	anger	disgust
CK+ [27]	636	28	69	327	83	25	45	59
JAFFE [38]	213	31	31	30	30	32	30	29
MUG [1]	401	48	87	25	66	47	57	71
ISED [23]	478	48	227	0	73	0	0	80
RaFD [32]	7,035	1,005	1,005	1,005	1,005	1,005	1,005	1,005
Oulu [67]	5,760	480	480	2,880	480	480	480	480
AffectNet [41]	28,7401	25,959	134,915	75,374	14,590	6,878	25,382	4,303
CMU-PIE [21]	551,700	0	74,700	355,200	60,900	0	0	60,900

Table 1 shows the number of images and the subdivision of each dataset into categories (sad, happy, neutral, surprise, fear, anger, and disgust). Figure 2 shows the distributions of data per expression (top-left), per database (top-right), and the percentage distribution of each expression in the dataset (bottom-left). In total we had 853,624 images with 51% neutral faces, 25% happy, 3% sad, 8% disgust, 3% anger, 1% fear, and 9% surprise.

The lower right image in Fig. 2 shows the percentage of the coverage of each image by label L from Eq. (1). The total numbers were: active-pleasant: 288,741 images (12%), active-unpleasant 102,393 images (34%), inactive-pleasant 434,841 (51%), and inactive-unpleasant 27,599 (3%). The re-mapped categories were used as input to training the deep neural network in Sect. 4.2.

It is important to note that the actual classification of each image into its category varies in each databases and some are not even unique. Certain images may be classified by only one person while some are classified by various people, which brings more uncertainty. Moreover, some databases are in color and some are not. While it would be ideal to have uniform coverage of the expressions in all databases, the databases are unbalanced in both quality of images and the coverage of facial expressions (Fig. 2).

Also, certain expressions are easy to classify, but some may be classified as mixed and belonging to multiple categories. In this case, we either removed the image from experiments or put it into only one category. Interestingly, the most difficult expression to classify is neutral, because it does not represent any emotional charge and may be easily misinterpreted. This expression is actually the most covered in the dataset that should, in theory, improve its detection if correctly trained.

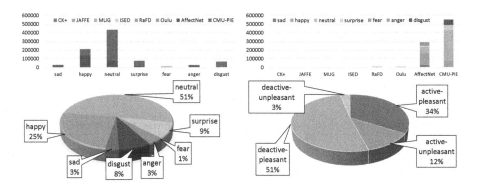

Fig. 2. Statistics of the used datasets used: contribution per database and expression (top row) and overall percentage of each expression (bottom left) and percentage of each contribution after remapping to Russel quadrants Eq. (1) (bottom right).

4.2 Deep Neural Network

We used deep neural network VGG_S Net [36] and Caffe. VGG_S Net is based on VGG Net that has proven successful in ImageNet Large Scale Visual Recognition Challenge [54] and the VGG_S is effective in facial detection.

Figure 3 shows the VGG_S neural network architecture. The network is a series of five convolutional layers, three fully-connected layers, eventually leading to a softmax classifier that outputs the probability value. We modified the output layer of the original net so that it generates the probability of the image to have a label from Eq. (1). The training input is a set of pairs $[image, L]$, where L is the label belonging to one of the four categories from Russel's diagram from Eq. (1). During the inference stage, the softmax layer outputs the probability of the input image of having the label L.

4.3 Training

We trained the network on images from datasets discussed in Sect. 4.1. We used data amplification by using Gaussian blur and applying variations of contrast, lighting, and subject position to the original images from each dataset to make our program more accurate in practical scenarios. The input images were preprocessed by using Haar-Cascade filter provided by OpenCV that crops the image by only including the face without significant background. This, in effect, that reduces the training times.

In order to have a balanced dataset, we would prefer to have similar number of images for each label from the categories in Eq. (1). Therefore, the lowest amount of images (inactive-unpleasant) dictated the size of the training set. We trained with 68,012 images, batch size 15 images, we used 80,000 iterations, and the average accuracy was set to 0.63 with 10,000 epochs. The training time

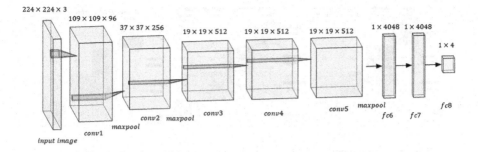

Fig. 3. Deep neural network architecture used in our framework.

was about 70 min on an desktop computer equipped with Intel Xeon(R) W-2145 CPU running at 3.7 GHz, with 32 GB of memory, and with NVidia RTX2080 GPU.

5 Results

Testing: We divided the dataset randomly into two groups in the ratio 80:20. We trained on 80% of the images, tested on the remaining 20%, and we repeated the experiment three times with random split of the input data each time.

Table 2. Average and standard deviation of the three runs of our testing.

	pleasant-active	pleasant-inactive	unpleasant-active	pleasant-inactive
pleasant-active	**(70.0, 1.6)**	(22.3, 4.1)	(2.0, 0.0)	(6.3, 2.1)
pleasant-inactive	(2.3, 1.2)	**(87.3, 0.5)**	(4.0, 0.8)	(6.0, 1.4)
unpleasant-active	(1.7, 0.5)	(41.7, 0.9)	**(44.0, 1.6)**	(8.3, 5.7)
pleasant-inactive	(5.0, 0.8)	(12.0, 3.7)	(9.3, 2.9)	**(62.0, 7.0)**

Table 2 shows the average and standard deviation of the confusion matrices from the three runs of our experiments and Fig. 4 show the confusion matrices of the individual runs. The main diagonal indicates that pleasant-active was detected 70% with standard deviation about 1.6% correctly and misdetected as pleasant-inactive in 22.3%, unpleasant-active in 2%, and unpleasant-active in 6.3% of cases. Similarly, pleasant-inactive was detected correctly for 87.3% of cases, unpleasant-active in 44% and the least precise was unpleasant-inactive with 62%. This is an expected result, because the lower part of the Russel's diagram (Fig. 1) includes passive expressions that are generally more difficult to detect. We achieved an overall accuracy of 66%.

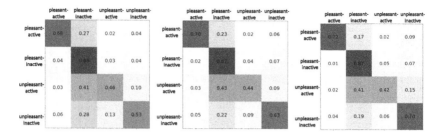

Fig. 4. Normalized confusion matrices for the results of our experiment.

Deployment: The trained deep neural network was extracted and used in real-time session that categorizes facial expressions into the four quadrants of Russel's diagram. We used a laptop computer with a web cam in resolution $1,920 \times 1,080$ equipped with CPU Intel Core i5-6300U at 2.4 GHz. We used the Caffe environment on Windows 10 and OpenCV to monitor the input image from the camera and detect face. Only the face was sent to the our trained network as the background was cropped out. The neural network classified the image and sent the result back to the application that displayed it as a label on the screen. An example in Fig. 5 shows several samples of real-time detection of facial expressions by using our system.

Fig. 5. Examples of real-time expression detection by using our system.

6 Conclusions

The purpose of this project is to develop a real-time facial emotion recognition algorithm that detects and classifies human emotions with the objective of using it as a classifier in online learning. Because of this requirement, our detector reports a probability of an emotion belonging to one of the four quadrants of Russel's diagram.

Our future goal is to integrate the recognition algorithm into a system of affective pedagogical agents that will respond to the students' detected emotions using different types of emotional intelligence. Our experiments show that the overall test accuracy is sufficient for a practical use and we hope that the entire system will be able to enhance learning.

There are several possible avenues for future work. While our preliminary results show satisfactory precision on our tested data, it would be interesting to actually validate our system in a real-world scenario. We conducted a preliminary user study in which we asked 10 people to make certain facial expression and we validated the detection. However, this approach did not provide satisfactory results, because we did not find a way to verify that the people were actually in the desired emotional state and their expressions were genuine - some participants started to laugh each time the system detected emotion they were not expecting. Emotional state is a complicated. Happy people cannot force themselves to make sad faces and some of the expressions were difficult to achieve even for real actors. So while validation of our detector remains a future work, another future work is increasing the precision of the detection by expanding the training data set and tuning the parameters of the deep neural network.

Acknowledgments. This work has been funded in part by National Science Foundation grant # 1821894 - *Collaborative Research: Multimodal Affective Pedagogical Agents for Different Types of Learners.*

References

1. Aifanti, N., Papachristou, C., Delopoulos, A.: The MUG facial expression database. In: 11th International Workshop on Image Analysis for Multimedia Interactive Services, WIAMIS 2010, pp. 1–4. IEEE (2010)
2. Allen, I.E., Seaman, J.: Staying the Course: Online Education in the United States. ERIC, Newburyport (2008)
3. Alsop, S., Watts, M.: Science education and affect. Int. J. Sci. Educ. **25**(9), 1043–1047 (2003)
4. Ark, W.S., Dryer, D.C., Lu, D.J.: The emotion mouse. In: HCI (1), pp. 818–823 (1999)
5. Bartlett, M.S., Littlewort, G., Fasel, I., Movellan, J.R.: Real time face detection and facial expression recognition: development and applications to human computer interaction. In: 2003 Conference on Computer Vision and Pattern Recognition Workshop, vol. 5, p. 53. IEEE (2003)
6. Baylor, A.L., Kim, Y.: Simulating instructional roles through pedagogical agents. Int. J. Artif. Intell. Educ. **15**(2), 95–115 (2005)
7. Bettadapura, V.: Face expression recognition and analysis: the state of the art. arXiv preprint arXiv:1203.6722 (2012)
8. Borth, D., Chen, T., Ji, R., Chang, S.F.: SentiBank: large-scale ontology and classifiers for detecting sentiment and emotions in visual content. In: Proceedings of the 21st ACM International Conference on Multimedia, pp. 459–460 (2013)
9. Bower, B.L., Hardy, K.P.: From correspondence to cyberspace: changes and challenges in distance education. New Dir. Community Coll. **2004**(128), 5–12 (2004)
10. Burkert, P., Trier, F., Afzal, M.Z., Dengel, A., Liwicki, M.: DeXpression: deep convolutional neural network for expression recognition. arXiv preprint arXiv:1509.05371 (2015)

11. Castellano, G., et al.: Towards empathic virtual and robotic tutors. In: Lane, H.C., Yacef, K., Mostow, J., Pavlik, P. (eds.) AIED 2013. LNCS (LNAI), vol. 7926, pp. 733–736. Springer, Heidelberg (2013). https://doi.org/10.1007/978-3-642-39112-5_100

12. Craig, S.D., Gholson, B., Driscoll, D.M.: Animated pedagogical agents in multimedia educational environments: effects of agent properties, picture features and redundancy. J. Educ. Psychol. **94**(2), 428 (2002)

13. Dimberg, U.: Facial reactions to facial expressions. Psychophysiology **19**(6), 643–647 (1982)

14. Dimberg, U., Thunberg, M., Elmehed, K.: Unconscious facial reactions to emotional facial expressions. Psychol. Sci. **11**(1), 86–89 (2000)

15. D'Mello, S., Graesser, A.: Emotions during learning with autotutor. In: Adaptive Technologies for Training and Education, pp. 169–187 (2012)

16. Ekman, P.: Biological and cultural contributions to body and facial movement, pp. 34–84 (1977)

17. Ekman, P.: Telling Lies: Clues to Deceit in the Marketplace, Politics, and Marriage, Revised edn. WW Norton & Company, New York (2009)

18. Ekman, P., Keltner, D.: Universal facial expressions of emotion. In: Segerstrale, U., Molnar, P. (eds.) Nonverbal Communication: Where Nature Meets Culture, pp. 27–46 (1997)

19. Fayek, H.M., Lech, M., Cavedon, L.: Evaluating deep learning architectures for Speech Emotion Recognition. Neural Netw. **92**, 60–68 (2017)

20. Gourier, N., Hall, D., Crowley, J.L.: Estimating face orientation from robust detection of salient facial features. In: ICPR International Workshop on Visual Observation of Deictic Gestures. Citeseer (2004)

21. Gross, R., Matthews, I., Cohn, J., Kanade, T., Baker, S.: Multi-PIE. Image Vis. Comput. **28**(5), 807–813 (2010)

22. Gunawardena, C.N., McIsaac, M.S.: Distance education. In: Handbook of Research on Educational Communications and Technology, pp. 361–401. Routledge (2013)

23. Happy, S., Patnaik, P., Routray, A., Guha, R.: The indian spontaneous expression database for emotion recognition. IEEE Trans. Affect. Comput. **8**(1), 131–142 (2015)

24. Izard, C.E.: Innate and universal facial expressions: evidence from developmental and cross-cultural research (1994)

25. Cheng, J., Zhou, W., Lei, X., Adamo, N., Benes, B.: The effects of body gestures and gender on viewer's perception of animated pedagogical agent's emotions. In: Kurosu, M. (ed.) HCII 2020. LNCS, vol. 12182, pp. 169–186. Springer, Cham (2020)

26. Kahou, S.E., et al.: EmoNets: multimodal deep learning approaches for emotion recognition in video. J. Multimodal User Interfaces **10**(2), 99–111 (2016). https://doi.org/10.1007/s12193-015-0195-2

27. Kanade, T., Cohn, J.F., Tian, Y.: Comprehensive database for facial expression analysis. In: IEEE International Conference on Automatic Face and Gesture Recognition, pp. 46–53. IEEE (2000)

28. Kim, S., Georgiou, P.G., Lee, S., Narayanan, S.: Real-time emotion detection system using speech: multi-modal fusion of different timescale features. In: 2007 IEEE 9th Workshop on Multimedia Signal Processing, pp. 48–51. IEEE (2007)

29. Kim, Y., Baylor, A.L.: Pedagogical agents as social models to influence learner attitudes. Educ. Technol. **47**(1), 23–28 (2007)

30. Kim, Y., Baylor, A.L., Shen, E.: Pedagogical agents as learning companions: the impact of agent emotion and gender. J. Comput. Assist. Learn. **23**(3), 220–234 (2007)

31. Kirouac, G., Dore, F.Y.: Accuracy of the judgment of facial expression of emotions as a function of sex and level of education. J. Nonverbal Behav. **9**(1), 3–7 (1985). https://doi.org/10.1007/BF00987555
32. Langner, O., Dotsch, R., Bijlstra, G., Wigboldus, D.H., Hawk, S.T., Van Knippenberg, A.: Presentation and validation of the Radboud Faces Database. Cogn. Emot. **24**(8), 1377–1388 (2010)
33. Le, Q.V., Zou, W.Y., Yeung, S.Y., Ng, A.Y.: Learning hierarchical invariant spatio-temporal features for action recognition with independent subspace analysis. In: CVPR 2011, pp. 3361–3368. IEEE (2011)
34. LeCun, Y., Bengio, Y., Hinton, G.: Deep learning. Nature **521**(7553), 436–444 (2015)
35. Lee, C.M., Narayanan, S.S.: Toward detecting emotions in spoken dialogs. IEEE Trans. Speech Audio Process. **13**(2), 293–303 (2005)
36. Levi, G., Hassner, T.: Emotion recognition in the wild via convolutional neural networks and mapped binary patterns. In: Proceedings of the 2015 ACM on International Conference on Multimodal Interaction, pp. 503–510 (2015)
37. Lisetti, C.L., Nasoz, F.: MAUI: a multimodal affective user interface. In: Proceedings of the Tenth ACM International Conference on Multimedia, pp. 161–170 (2002)
38. Lyons, M., Kamachi, M., Gyoba, J.: Japanese Female Facial Expression (JAFFE) Database, July 2017. https://figshare.com/articles/jaffe_desc_pdf/5245003
39. Martha, A.S.D., Santoso, H.B.: The design and impact of the pedagogical agent: a systematic literature review. J. Educ. Online **16**(1), n1 (2019)
40. Miles, M.B., Saxl, E.R., Lieberman, A.: What skills do educational "change agents" need? An empirical view. Curric. Inq. **18**(2), 157–193 (1988)
41. Mollahosseini, A., Hasani, B., Mahoor, M.H.: AffectNet: a database for facial expression, valence, and arousal computing in the wild. IEEE Trans. Affect. Comput. **10**(1), 18–31 (2017)
42. Morency, L.P., et al.: SimSensei demonstration: a perceptive virtual human interviewer for healthcare applications. In: Twenty-Ninth AAAI Conference on Artificial Intelligence (2015)
43. Neri, L., et al.: Visuo-haptic simulations to improve students' understanding of friction concepts. In: IEEE Frontiers in Education, pp. 1–6. IEEE (2018)
44. Ng, H.W., Nguyen, V.D., Vonikakis, V., Winkler, S.: Deep learning for emotion recognition on small datasets using transfer learning. In: Proceedings of the 2015 ACM on International Conference on Multimodal Interaction, pp. 443–449 (2015)
45. Pantic, M., Valstar, M., Rademaker, R., Maat, L.: Web-based database for facial expression analysis. In: 2005 IEEE International Conference on Multimedia and Expo, pp. 5–pp. IEEE (2005)
46. Pardàs, M., Bonafonte, A.: Facial animation parameters extraction and expression recognition using hidden Markov models. Sig. Process. Image Commun. **17**(9), 675–688 (2002)
47. Payr, S.: The virtual university's faculty: an overview of educational agents. Appl. Artif. Intell. **17**(1), 1–19 (2003)
48. Pekrun, R.: The control-value theory of achievement emotions: assumptions, corollaries, and implications for educational research and practice. Educ. Psychol. Rev. **18**(4), 315–341 (2006). https://doi.org/10.1007/s10648-006-9029-9
49. Pekrun, R., Stephens, E.J.: Achievement emotions: a control-value approach. Soc. Pers. Psychol. Compass **4**(4), 238–255 (2010)
50. Phipps, R., Merisotis, J., et al.: What's the difference? A review of contemporary research on the effectiveness of distance learning in higher education (1999)

51. Picard, R.W., Scheirer, J.: The Galvactivator: a glove that senses and communicates skin conductivity. In: Proceedings of the 9th International Conference on HCI (2001)
52. Porter, L.R.: Creating the Virtual Classroom: Distance Learning with the Internet. Wiley, Hoboken (1997)
53. Rowley, H.A., Baluja, S., Kanade, T.: Rotation invariant neural network-based face detection. In: Proceedings of the 1998 IEEE Computer Society Conference on Computer Vision and Pattern Recognition (Cat. No. 98CB36231), pp. 38–44. IEEE (1998)
54. Russakovsky, O., et al.: ImageNet large scale visual recognition challenge. Int. J. Comput. Vis. **115**(3), 211–252 (2015). https://doi.org/10.1007/s11263-015-0816-y
55. Russell, J.A.: Core affect and the psychological construction of emotion. Psychol. Rev. **110**(1), 145 (2003)
56. Schneiderman, H., Kanade, T.: Probabilistic modeling of local appearance and spatial relationships for object recognition. In: Proceedings of the 1998 IEEE Computer Society Conference on Computer Vision and Pattern Recognition (Cat. No. 98CB36231), pp. 45–51. IEEE (1998)
57. Schroeder, N.L., Adesope, O.O., Gilbert, R.B.: How effective are pedagogical agents for learning? A meta-analytic review. J. Educ. Comput. Res. **49**(1), 1–39 (2013)
58. Tian, Y.I., Kanade, T., Cohn, J.F.: Recognizing action units for facial expression analysis. IEEE Trans. Pattern Anal. Mach. Intell. **23**(2), 97–115 (2001)
59. Tie, Y., Guan, L.: A deformable 3-D facial expression model for dynamic human emotional state recognition. IEEE Trans. Circ. Syst. Video Technol. **23**(1), 142–157 (2012)
60. Viola, P., Jones, M., et al.: Robust real-time object detection. Int. J. Comput. Vis. **4**(34–47), 4 (2001)
61. Volery, T., Lord, D.: Critical success factors in online education. Int. J. Educ. Manag. **14**(5), 216–223 (2000)
62. Wang, H., Chignell, M., Ishizuka, M.: Empathic tutoring software agents using real-time eye tracking. In: Proceedings of the 2006 Symposium on Eye Tracking Research & Applications, pp. 73–78 (2006)
63. Wilson, P.I., Fernandez, J.: Facial feature detection using Haar classifiers. J. Comput. Sci. Coll. **21**(4), 127–133 (2006)
64. Yang, S., Luo, P., Loy, C.C., Tang, X.: From facial parts responses to face detection: a deep learning approach. In: Proceedings of the IEEE International Conference on Computer Vision, pp. 3676–3684 (2015)
65. Yu, F., Chang, E., Xu, Y.-Q., Shum, H.-Y.: Emotion detection from speech to enrich multimedia content. In: Shum, H.-Y., Liao, M., Chang, S.-F. (eds.) PCM 2001. LNCS, vol. 2195, pp. 550–557. Springer, Heidelberg (2001). https://doi.org/10.1007/3-540-45453-5_71
66. Yuksel, T., et al.: Visuohaptic experiments: exploring the effects of visual and haptic feedback on students' learning of friction concepts. Comput. Appl. Eng. Educ. **27**(6), 1376–1401 (2019)
67. Zhao, G., Huang, X., Taini, M., Li, S.Z., Pietikälnen, M.: Facial expression recognition from near-infrared videos. Image Vis. Comput. **29**(9), 607–619 (2011)
68. Zhou, L., Mohammed, A.S., Zhang, D.: Mobile personal information management agent: supporting natural language interface and application integration. Inf. Process. Manag. **48**(1), 23–31 (2012)

Multimodal Interaction

Designing an AI-Companion to Support the Driver in Highly Autonomous Cars

Emmanuel de Salis[1]([✉]), Marine Capallera[2], Quentin Meteier[2], Leonardo Angelini[2], Omar Abou Khaled[2], Elena Mugellini[2], Marino Widmer[3], and Stefano Carrino[1]

[1] HE-ARC University of Applied Sciences Western Switzerland, Saint-Imier, Switzerland
emmanuel.desalis@he-arc.ch, stefano.carrino@hes-so.ch
[2] HEIA-FR University of Applied Sciences Western Switzerland, Fribourg, Switzerland
{marine.capallera,quentin.meteier,leonardo.angelini,
omar.aboukhaled,elena.mugellini}@hes-so.ch
[3] University of Fribourg, DIUF, Fribourg, Switzerland
marino.widmer@unifr.ch

Abstract. In this paper, we propose a model for an AI-Companion for conditionally automated cars, able to maintain awareness of the driver regarding the environment but also to able design take-over requests (TOR) on the fly, with the goal of better support the driver in case of a disengagement.

Our AI-Companion would interact with the driver in two ways: first, it could provide feedback to the driver in order to raise the driver Situation Awareness (SA), prevent them to get out of the supervision loop and so, improve takeover during critical situations by decreasing their cognitive workload. Second, in the case of TOR with a smart choice of modalities for convey the request to the driver. In particular, the AI-Companion can interact with the driver using many modalities, such as visual messages (warning lights, images, text, etc.), auditory signals (sound, speech, etc.) and haptic technologies (vibrations in different parts of the seat: back, headrest, etc.).

The ultimate goal of the proposed approach is to design smart HMIs in semi-autonomous vehicles that are able to understand 1) the user state and fitness to drive, 2) the current external situation (vehicle status and behavior) in order to minimize the automation surprise and maximizing safety and trust, and 3) leverage AI to provide adaptive TOR and useful feedback to the driver.

Keywords: Companion · Smart HMI · Situation awareness · Artificial intelligence · Machine Learning · Psychophysiological data · Autonomous cars · Take-over request · Driver model

1 Introduction

Nowadays, there are still many road accidents every year, with annual road traffic deaths reaching 1.35 million in 2018 [2, 4]. The development of autonomous vehicles aims to improve traffic security and driver comfort by reducing car accidents, easing the flow of traffic, reducing pollution and assisting the driver in the various driving tasks. However,

© Springer Nature Switzerland AG 2020
M. Kurosu (Ed.): HCII 2020, LNCS 12182, pp. 335–349, 2020.
https://doi.org/10.1007/978-3-030-49062-1_23

we can expect to see a transition from cars with little or no automation (level 1 or 2 [36]) to conditionally (or highly) automated cars (level 3 to 4 [36]) on the road before we see fully automated cars (level 5 [36]). In conditionally automated cars, the automated system and the driver share the control of the car, with only one of them in charge of the driving task, depending on the situation. Specifically, the car would keep control until it encounters a situation it cannot handle, or if the driver wants to take the control back. When the automated system detects a situation it cannot handle, it will trigger a TOR to let the driver know that a transition of control is necessary, often within seconds. This take-over is a critical action, which could lead to accidents if it is not correctly and timely communicated and executed, especially in situations when the driver is out of the loop [9].

Since many parameters influence the take-over quality and rapidity, AI and Machine Learning are very valuable assets for exploiting the richness of the available data. In fact, an AI-based interface could analyze in real time the available contextual information and trigger the best TOR. To do so, the AI Model can choose among a set of available modalities to convey the TOR with regard to each situation (contextual TOR).

Modality selection should be done carefully; the choice of modalities was shown to have an impact on both the quality and the rapidity of the take-over [7, 16]. For instance, some modalities can improve the rapidity of the take-over at the cost of deteriorating its quality [17]. The current state of the art revealed no "perfect" set of modalities, implying that the best set of modalities of a TOR depends on the situation. Nevertheless, several researchers have shown that multimodal TOR are often more effective than unimodal ones [30, 33]. Once again, Machine Learning is used to select the best set of modalities in order to optimize TOR rapidity and quality.

Currently available semi-autonomous systems only provide a unique TOR independently of the reason and context that triggered it. Previous studies have advanced the possibility of a take-over assistant [41], but the TOR design is limited to user preferences and not the root cause of the disengagement. In contrast, the proposed AI-Companion would monitor different contextual factors highlighted by the literature to adapt the TOR modalities, in order to optimize both the take-over quality and rapidity. These factors are the psychophysiological state of the driver [22] and the environment, both inside [2] and outside [18] the car.

The psychophysiological state of the driver is a key input for our approach. Such a state is encoded into a prior Machine Learning model. The goal of this model is to allow adapting and individualizing in real time the driver-car interaction to the driver's current state and fitness to drive. To do so, several physiological signals such as electrocardiogram, electrodermal activity and respiration are investigated. In particular, the model classifies the driver's condition regarding four driver states: alertness, attention, affective state and situational awareness. The outcomes of this model are then combined to create a global indicator of the driver's psychophysiological state. The AI-Companion uses such indicator for adapting its interaction with the driver.

The proposed AI-Companion will be used at different levels of attention [5] with a particular focus on peripheral interaction to support driver's supervision and SA. As a future step, we plan to develop a multimodal and full-body interaction model combining haptic, visual and vocal interaction. According to the driver's state (stressed, tired, etc.), it will be possible to vary the level of information to be transmitted as well as the type and number of modalities to be used in the interaction with the driver.

2 Related Work

2.1 Companions in Car

Researchers have already studied the effects on the driver of having an e-companion in the car, for example to raise trust in the autonomous systems [43] or personalize the TOR [41]. Kugurakova [23] showed that an anthropomorphic artificial social agent with simulated emotions was indeed possible. Lugano [26] has realized a review of virtual assistants in self-driving cars, showing that the idea of an e-companion is getting more attention in the industry as well.

Despite growing interest in the industry as well as in the scientific community, there was no study about an AI-Companion in the car designed to manage TOR and raise SA, at the extent of our knowledge.

2.2 TOR Modalities

In the last few years, take-over and TOR have been vastly studied. TOR modalities were shown to have an impact on take-over, opening the way to research on specific modalities and combinations of them. Especially, three categories of modalities were identified and studied intensively:

- Visual: shown as the most ineffective modality when used alone [33], it is still a primary and instinctive ways to convey the TOR. Most systems on the market use the visual modality by default to convey information to the driver, usually not requiring urgent action from the driver. In case of more urgent situation, visual warnings come usually with an auditory warning. This is corroborated by [33], who showed that the perception of urgency was greater in multimodal warnings. Visual information can be provided to the driver in a range of ways from a simple logo, to a more articulated message or a combination of them.
- Auditory: as the visual modality, auditory signals are greatly used in existing systems, making the visual modality a familiar modality to the driver. Different visual TOR were studied, from different abstracts sounds to speech alerts.
- Haptic: less used modality in available cars models, haptic modality is greatly studied to convey information to the driver. It can range from many different settings of haptic seats [31] to shape-changing steering wheels [8].

2.3 Psychophysiological Model of the Driver

It is already known that the driver is the main cause of accidents on roads. Several factors can change the psychophysiological state of the driver and impact their ability to drive, up to the point of causing an accident. These factors can be from different sources, such as fatigue or drowsiness due to a monotonous drive [46], a loss of attention when being distracted from the main driving task [3, 20], or an increase of stress due to a dangerous situation on the road. This can still be applied to the context of conditionally automated vehicles: the driver may feel drowsy while monitoring the vehicle behavior for a long time, or they may experience an increase of the cognitive load while performing a secondary task. To the best of our knowledge, a global model able to detect changes regarding these states using physiological signals of the driver does not exist. A model of driver behavior for the assessment of driver's state has been developed in the framework of the HAVEit project [34]. This model aimed at detecting driver's drowsiness and distraction in manual driving, using driving data and features from video recording of the driver but no physiological signals of the driver. However, a lot of research has been done so far to detect these changes in driver's psychophysiological state independently. Related work that aimed at classify driver's fatigue/drowsiness and mental load using physiological signals is presented below.

Fatigue and Drowsiness. Inducement of drowsiness is usually done in driving simulators for ethical reasons. Drivers are usually asked to drive for a long time for a monotonous drive on a highway, with a low traffic density sometimes in night-time environment. It has been shown that fatigue can be induced successfully to most of the participants during an experiment [35]. To control that fatigue has been successfully induced, other sources of data are used such as driving data, questionnaires (Karolina Sleeping Scale [38]) or facial features. Awais et al. [4] showed that alert and fatigued states can be distinguished using electroencephalogram (EEG) and Heart Rate Variability (HRV) features, from drowsy events detected using facial features. Authors achieved 70% of accuracy with HRV features, 76% with EEG features and 80% with both. The results achieved by Patel et al. [29] show that alert and fatigued states can be distinguished using HRV features. They achieved an accuracy of 90% in the classification of these two states from a dataset of 12 drivers. However, physiological sensors may be invasive when using laboratory equipment with electrodes. To be able to use this source of data in real-world applications, the challenge is to get acceptable performances using wearable and embedded sensors. Lee et al. [24] used wearable sensors to record electrocardiogram (ECG) and photoplethysmogram of drivers to measure and classify drivers' drowsiness. They showed that 70% of data were correctly classified using recurrence plots and CNN-based classifier. It shows that there is some potential to use physiological signals to detect drowsiness in real-world settings and better results can be achieved.

Distraction and Mental Overload. In the same way than the inducement of drowsiness, the effects of distraction and mental overload on drivers are usually investigated during experiments conducted in driving simulators. Different sources of distractions can be distinguished such as visual, auditory, cognitive and biomechanical distraction [32]. Throughout the experiment, drivers are asked to perform secondary tasks while driving manually. The accomplishment of these secondary tasks can increase the cognitive load of drivers and this can be measured with physiological signals. Mehler et al. [27] increased experimentally thae cognitive load of drivers by administering them a cognitive task with increasing difficulty. They observed a significant increase of mean heart rate, skin conductance level and respiratory rate when cognitive load of drivers is higher. This is consistent with findings of Ferreira et al. [15] who achieved 84% of accuracy for classifying people who performed a cognitive task on a computer. Various psychophysiological signals were used for the classification such as EEG, ECG, EDA, and respiration. In the context of manual driving, Solovey et al. [14] also achieved 75% of accuracy to classify the state of the driver with physiological and driving data from the same driver. Participants had to realize a N-Back task with auditory stimuli and oral response. When performing the classification inter-subjects, they achieved at least 80% of accuracy only with HRV features. This shows that ECG must be used to detect changes in cognitive level of drivers with our AI companion.

2.4   Interactions and Situation Awareness

A Brief Definition of Situation Awareness. The concept of SA originated in the field of airplanes but began to develop in the automobile domain. Endsley's model and definition are the most known and used in the literature [13]: "Situation awareness is the perception of the elements in the environment within a volume of time and space, the comprehension of their meanings and a projection of their status in near future". Thus, the concept is divided into three hierarchical levels:

- Perception (Level 1 SA): The driver perceives information from vehicle instrumentation, its behavior, other people into the car, other people around the car (vehicles, pedestrians, cyclists...), traffic, etc. Perception does not concern the interpretation of the data.
- Comprehension (Level 2 SA): Comprehension is essential to understand and integrate the significance of the element. It defines the expertise of the driver.
- Projection (Level 3 SA): Projection is the ability to forecast the future state of the element in the environment. It is the driver's ability to solve conflicts and plan a course of action.

To summarize, the driver has to maintain the navigation, environment and interaction, special orientation and vehicle status knowledge. However, SA cannot be assessed or measured directly because it is subjective and depends on a precise element in a specific time.

Interaction in Car to Increase Situation Awareness. As we plan to develop a multimodal and body interaction model combining one to several interactions to support driver supervision, it is important to analyze what already exists in the area of in-car interaction to increase SA. To this end, we focused our study on the different types of modalities used, where these interactions are located in the vehicle and what type of information they transmit.

The most commonly used modalities are, in order: mostly visual (use of ambient lights [12, 25], logos [40], text [28]), haptic (vibrations in different parts of the car [19, 39]), auditory (chime [42] or speech [37]), audio-visual [45]. There are also some emerging research in the field of olfactory interactions with the driver [6]. At the moment, there are few multimodal HVIs.

Concerning their location, the parts of the vehicle mainly used are central console [25], HUD/windshield [45], steering wheel [39], dashboard [40], dorsal seat [44]. Mostly these parts are used individually.

The information transmitted is also very varied. In most cases, interactions convey information about the autonomous status of the system [28], navigation, lane markings, obstacles [40], ADAS maneuvers [18], etc. Information is spread out and there is no taxonomy nor typical critical situations.

In addition, the evaluation criteria for these interactions vary greatly between all articles (driving performance data [28], quality of TOR [21], reaction time [40], task accuracy [39], gaze direction [45], usefulness, acceptability and trust [40], questionnaire for workload and situation awareness [45]).

3   Goal and Methodologies

We aim at creating an innovative driver companion fueled by AI, able to enhance the driver SA and trigger adaptive TOR while taking into account the driver psychophysiological state and the environment. In this context, we identified three major points that need to be studied and developed:

1. Making a take-over quality prediction Machine Learning model;
2. Monitoring and classifying the driver psychophysiological state;
3. Develop ad-hoc HMI to enhance the driver SA.

You can see our specific subgoals for each of these three objectives in the following sections.

3.1   Adaptive TOR

Our goal regarding the TOR model is to create an adaptive TOR, meaning our AI-Companion should be able to choose the modalities of a TOR on the fly, in order to maximize the quality and rapidity of a take-over. To do so, our agent will three sources of data known to impact the take-over: the driver psychophysiological data, the driver psychophysiological state and the environment. An experiment will allow us to train a Machine Learning model to predict the quality and rapidity of a take-over based on these sources of data.

Two metrics were identified to quantify take-over: rapidity and quality. For the rapidity of the take-over, the Reaction Time (RT) is a commonly used feature and it has the advantage to be fairly simple to calculate and understand [18]. Concerning the quality of the take-over, multiple studies (for example [10]) use the Max Steering Wheel Angle (MaxSWA) as an indicator of quality. A lower value of MaxSWA indicates a better quality of take-over, with less noise on the take-over process (less extra movement). This is especially true in situations where the correct action is to stop the car, opposed to situations where you can avoid the obstacle by changing lane. In both situations, lower MaxSWA still implies, earlier and more precise take-over.

A loss function consisting of both RT and MaxSWA needs to be developed in order to evaluate both. This problem can be seen as a Multi-Objective Optimization problem.

3.2 Monitoring the Driver Psychophysiological State

To train a model using Machine Learning that is able to classify different states of the driver with physiological signals, some data need to be collected. To get physiological data corresponding to the 4 states described before (alertness, attention, affective state and situational awareness) we developed and static driving simulator. The goal is to manipulate the driver's state by means of experimental conditions in a controlled setup. To validate the success of the manipulation of the driver's state, questionnaires are administered to participants, usually in a repeated measure design (before vs. after the experiment). Various questionnaires are used depending of the state that is manipulated such as NASA-TLX for the subjective level of cognitive load. Throughout the experiment, physiological signals of the driver are recorded. We choose to record ECG, electrodermal activity (EDA), and respiration of drivers, because they are signals that can be recorded using embedded and wearable sensors in a cockpit of a vehicle. In addition, we want to differentiate ourselves from what already exists on the market, especially with the use of a camera for facial expressions such as the Affectiva Automotive AI [1] system for driver monitoring.

Several steps are necessary to train such a model. The first step is the pre-processing. Since physiological raw signals can be noisy, there is a need to filter the raw signals and remove outliers. Then, data are segmented in more or less large time windows. For each time window, we can compute physiological indicators such as tonic EDA level, time and frequency-based HRV features computed from ECG or respiratory rate. Then comes the step of feature generation. The goal is to create features from both calculated indicators defined before and cleaned signals. Once the features are generated, the classification can be performed. Driver's condition is classified regarding 4 states: alertness, attention, affective state and situational awareness. This is done by using machine learning with classifiers such as Support Vector Machine or K-Nearest Neighbors classifiers. An output is given by the model for each one of the 4 states. As an example, the alertness state of the driver can be classified as alert, drowsy or sleepy. In addition, an indicator that depicts the global psychophysiological state of the driver is computed.

During the whole training process, several parameters can be tested and tweaked, such as the length of timespan for segmentation, the type of classifiers (and their hyper-parameters) or the number of output classes for each state. The parameters that give the best performance will be chosen.

When the model will be trained and good results are achieved, the last step will be to test the model in real-time. We will record physiological data of drivers, process the data and classify the state of the driver in real-time in order to convey the results of the classification to other modules of the AI-Companion and adapt the interaction in the car

3.3 Raising Driver Situation Awareness

The objective of this part is to assist the driver in their supervisory task while performing a non-driving related task. The main goals are to reduce their cognitive workload and keep them in the control loop by increasing their situational awareness.

For this reason, we use different modalities (haptic, visual, auditory), individually or in combination, and different areas of the vehicle (seat, external device and conversational agent). This model will transmit environmental information to the driver through these different modalities according to the situation and the driver state. The final step will be to take the driver into account and ideally their gaze in order to adapt the location, the modalities used and the level of information to transmit.

To do this, separate monomodal concepts have been developed and are currently under test:

- A haptic seat to transmit information about near obstacles all around the car using the entire seat.
- An Android application displaying driving related information while allowing the driver performing a secondary task on another split-screen application.
- An ambient light display transmitting the general severity of the situation and a conversational agent the driver can interact within order to have more details about the current situation.

The objective is to search for the best combination of these different modalities in order to increase the driver's SA.

4 Current State of Our AI-Companion

Following the related research, our previous results (as detailed in the previous sections) and the results of a workshop on explainable AI, the following design for our AI Companion was created (see Fig. 1). The next sections, will present the current state of the AI-Companion in regard of each his fundamental parts: the take-over prediction module, the Psychophysiological Model of the driver and the SA raising HMI.

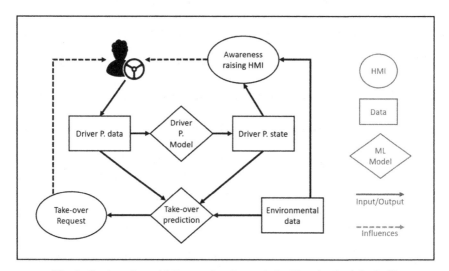

Fig. 1. Design of our AI-Companion. P. stands for "Psychophysiological".

4.1 Current Progress on Take-Over Prediction

Figure 2 shows what elements of the AI-Companion are concerned by the Take-over Prediction module. Here is the progress made for every one of them:

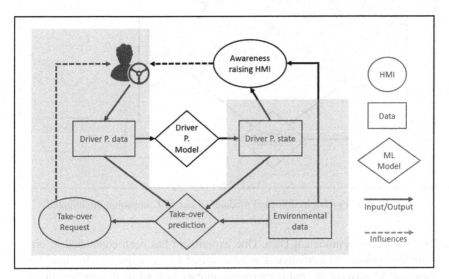

Fig. 2. The "Take-over prediction module" of our AI-Companion (highlighted)

- Environmental data: Study showed the most important environmental "states" that could lead to TOR [11]. From this study, we have a clear view of what major environmental data should be monitored (for example the luminosity and the weather) in the limit of what is available through current sensors and technology.
- Driver P. State and Data: The literature showed that Driver State/Data have an impact on take-over, and the experiment explained in the section "What we did regarding driver P. model" confirmed this.
- Take-over Request HMI: A review highlighted the current trends and research about TOR HMI, allowing us to identify which modalities would be needed for a TOR (visual, haptic and auditory). This step defined what would be the capabilities of our AI-Companion in regard to TOR design.
- Take-over prediction: An experiment to predict take-over quality and rapidity is ongoing and should produce results soon.

4.2 Current Progress on Driver Psychophysiological Model

Figure 3 highlights the elements of our AI-Companion concerned by the Psychophysiological Model of the driver. The following progress were made in regards to this part:

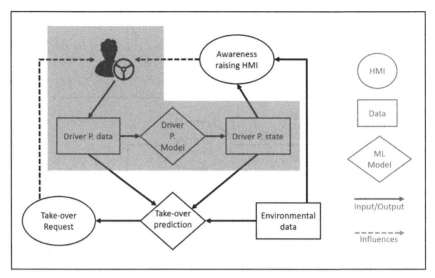

Fig. 3. The "Psychophysiological module" of our AI-Companion (highlighted)

- Driver Psychophysiological Data: One experiment has been conducted in order to build the dataset. 90 participants were enrolled in for acquiring the data. Half of them had to perform an oral cognitive secondary task while the car was driving in conditional automation during 20 min, while the other half had no secondary task. 6 take-over requests were triggered to each driver. In such situations, where they had to take over control, ECG, EDA and respiration rate of participants were collected.
- Driver Psychophysiological Model: The collected data have been used to train the model for classifying the cognitive load and the situation awareness of drivers. Currently, several parameters are being tested such as the length of the timespan for the segmentation and the type of classifiers.
- Driver Psychophysiological State: First results show that 97% of accuracy is achieved for classifying drivers that performed the secondary task for 20 min. The data during takeover situations to classify drivers' situational awareness are currently being analyzed.

4.3 Current Progress on Situation Awareness Raising HMI

Figure 4 shows the elements concerned by the SA raising HMI part of our AI-Companion. You can see the list of progress made to these elements in the following list:

- Environmental data: Data are directly extracted from the simulator. The data monitored are extracted from previous work [11]. For now, we mainly monitor information about weather, lane markings degradation, obstacles all around the car, road shape, general severity of the situation, etc.
- Awareness raising HMI: Currently, we have a set of modalities spread throughout the vehicle and tested separately.

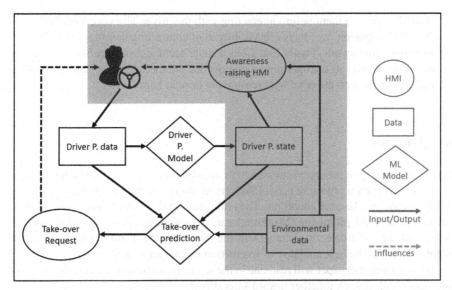

Fig. 4. The "SA raising HMI module" of our AI-Companion (highlighted)

- Haptic pan and backrest: This is currently under experiment, but the first results seem promising.
- Ambient lights and conversational agent (idem): We indicate the severity of the situation to the driver with a series of LEDs, placed around a tablet or a smartphone. This visual modality is associated with a conversational agent. The driver will be able to interact with the conversational agent to obtain more details on the current situation and/or the condition of the vehicle (e.g., if the LEDs turn red meaning that a critical situation occurs, the driver can ask for more information on what is happening).
- Split-screen application: A mobile application has been developed for the purpose of raising driver SA by providing extra information about the car, with promising results.

- Driver Psychophysiological State: not yet taken into account, but will be added in future experiments.

5 Future Research

For our next steps, we have three main goals:

1. Validation of the AI-Companion as a whole. Up to now the AI-Companion has been validated part by part. The next step is to group the three modules and design a validation scenario to demonstrate the effectiveness of the integrated solution.
2. HMI integration. After this validation, alternative feedback loops could appear and be the subject of experiments. We are especially looking at sharing the outputs of

each HMI among them before interacting with the driver, allowing more control of our AI-Companion over its two HMI instead of controlling them separately.

3. Real-time framework. Lastly and from a more technical perspective, we want to demonstrate that all the data processing needed for the inference step can be done in real-time and on the edge with reasonably limited hardware.

6   Conclusion

In this paper we have presented the design of an AI-Companion for highly autonomous cars. The companion objective is twofold: raising the driver SA and designing TOR on the fly in case of take-over situations. The realization of the Companion is still ongoing but first results are promising. Machine Learning solutions allow analyzing multiple sources of data and detecting changes in the user state. Such information is used to adaptively select the best modality of interaction to interact with the user.

We hope that this paper will resonate in the scientific community and in the industry, allowing us all to work together toward safer driving.

Acknowledgment. This work is part of a project funded by the Hasler Foundation. We would also like to thank our colleagues who helped us during this project.

References

1. Affectiva, (n.d.).: Affectiva AutomotiveAI. http://go.affectiva.com/auto
2. Arkonac, S.E., Brumby, D.P., Smith, T., Babu, H.V.R.: In-car distractions and automated driving: a preliminary simulator study. In: Proceedings of the 11th International Conference on Automotive User Interfaces and Interactive Vehicular Applications Adjunct Proceedings AutomotiveUI 19 (2019). https://doi.org/10.1145/3349263.3351505
3. Ascone, D., Tonja Lindsey, T., Varghese, C.: An examination of driver distraction as recorded in NHTSA databases (No. DOT HS 811 216). United States, National Highway Traffic Safety Administration (2009)
4. Awais, M., Badruddin, N., Drieberg, M.: A hybrid approachto detect driver drowsiness utilizing physiological signals to improve system performance and wearability. Sensors **17**(9), 1991 (2017)
5. Bakker, S., Niemantsverdriet, K.: The interaction-attention continuum: considering various levels of human attention in interaction design. Int. J. Des. **10**(2), 1–14 (2016)
6. Beattie, D., Baillie, L., Halvey, M., McCall, R.: What's around the corner?: enhancing driver awareness in autonomous vehicles via in-vehicle spatial auditory displays. In: Proceedings of the 8th Nordic Conference on Human-Computer Interaction: Fun, Fast, Foundational, pp. 189–198. ACM, October 2014
7. Borojeni, S.S., Boll, S.C., Heuten, W., Bülthoff, H.H., Chuang, L.: Feel the movement: real motion influences responses to take-over requests in highly automated vehicles. In: Proceedings of the 2018 CHI Conference on Human Factors in Computing Systems (CHI 18) (2018). https://doi.org/10.1145/3173574.3173820

8. Borojeni, S.S., Wallbaum, T., Heuten, W., Boll, S.: Comparing shape-changing and vibro-tactile steering wheels for take-over requests in highly automated driving. In: Proceedings of the 9th International Conference on Automotive User Interfaces and Interactive Vehicular Applications, (Automotive UI 17) (2017). https://doi.org/10.1145/3122986.3123003
9. Borowsky, A., Oron-Gilad, T.: The effects of automation failure and secondary task on drivers' ability to mitigate hazards in highly or semi-automated vehicles. Advances in Transportation Studies. 2016 Special Issue, (1), 59–70, 12 p (2016)
10. Bueno, M., Dogan, E., Selem, F. H., Monacelli, E., Boverie, S., Guillaume, A.: How different mental workload levels affect the take-over control after automated driving. In: 2016 IEEE 19th International Conference on Intelligent Transportation Systems (ITSC) (2016). https://doi.org/10.1109/itsc.2016.7795886
11. Capallera, M., et al.: Owner manuals review and taxonomy of ADAS limitations in partially automated vehicles. In: Proceedings of the 11th International Conference on Automotive User Interfaces and Interactive Vehicular Applications - AutomotiveUI 19 (2019). https://doi.org/10.1145/3342197.3344530
12. Wang, C., et al.: Designing for enhancing situational awareness of semi-autonomous driving vehicles. In: Proceedings of the 9th International Conference on Automotive User Interfaces and Interactive Vehicular Applications Adjunct (AutomotiveUI 2017), pp. 228–229. Association for Computing Machinery, New York (2017). https://doi.org/10.1145/3131726.3132061
13. Endsley, M.R.: Toward a theory of situation awareness in dynamic systems. Hum. Factors 37(1), 32–64 (1995). https://doi.org/10.1518/001872095779049543
14. Solovey, E.T., Zec, M., Garcia Perez, E.A., Reimer, B., Bruce, M.: Classifying driver workload using physiological and driving performancedata: two field studies. In: Proceedings of the SIGCHI Conference on Human Factorsin Computing Systems, CHI 2014, pp. 4057–4066. ACM, New York (2014)
15. Ferreira, E., et al.: Assessing real-time cognitive load based on psycho-physiological measures for younger and older adults. In: 2014 IEEE Symposium on Computational Intelligence, Cognitive Algorithms, Mind, and Brain (CCMB), pp. 39–48, Orlando, FL, USA (2014)
16. Forster, Y., Naujoks, F., Neukum, A., Huestegge, L.: Driver compliance to take-over requests with different auditory outputs in conditional automation. Accid. Anal. Prev. 109, 18–28 (2017). https://doi.org/10.1016/j.aap.2017.09.019
17. Gold, C., Damböck, D., Lorenz, L., Bengler, K.: Take over!" How long does it take to get the driver back into the loop? In: Proceedings of the Human Factors and Ergonomics Society Annual Meeting, vol. 57, no. 1, pp. 1938–1942 (2013). https://doi.org/10.1177/1541931213571433
18. Gold, C., Körber, M., Lechner, D., Bengler, K.: Taking over control from highly automated vehicles in complex traffic situations: the role of traffic density. Hum. Factors J. Hum. Factors Ergon. Soc. 58(4), 642–652 (2016). https://doi.org/10.1177/0018720816634226
19. Grah, T., et al.: Dorsal haptic display: a shape-changing car seat for sensory augmentation of rear obstacles. In: Proceedings of the 7th International Conference on Automotive User Interfaces and Interactive Vehicular Applications, pp. 305–312. ACM, September, 2015
20. Hosking, S., Young, K., Regan, M.: The effects of text messaging on young novice driver performance (No. 246). Monash University, Accident Research Centre (2006)
21. Johns, M., Mok, B., Talamonti, W., Sibi, S., Ju, W.: Looking ahead: anticipatory interfaces for driver-automation collaboration. In: Proceedings of the 2017 IEEE 20th International Conference on Intelligent Transportation Systems (ITSC), pp. 1–7, Yokohama (2017). https://doi.org/10.1109/itsc.2017.8317762
22. Ko, S.M., Ji, Y.G.: How we can measure the non-driving-task engagement in automated driving: comparing flow experience and workload. Appl. Ergon. 67, 237–245 (2018). https://doi.org/10.1016/j.apergo.2017.10.009

23. Kugurakova, V., Talanov, M., Manakhov, N., Ivanov, D.: Anthropomorphic artificial social agent with simulated emotions and its implementation. Procedia Comput. Sci. **71**, 112–118 (2015). https://doi.org/10.1016/j.procs.2015.12.217

24. Lee, H., Lee, J., Shin, M.: Using wearable ECG/PPG sensors for driver drowsiness detection based on distinguishable pattern of recurrence plots. **8**, 192 (2019)

25. Löcken, A.: AmbiCar: ambient light patterns in the car. In: AutomotiveUI, Nottingham, UK (2015)

26. Lugano, G.: Virtual assistants and self-driving cars. In: Proceedings of the 2017 15th International Conference on ITS Telecommunications (ITST) (2017). https://doi.org/10.1109/itst.2017.7972192

27. Mehler, B., Reimer, B., Coughlin, J., Dusek, J.: The impact of incremental increases in cognitive workload on physiological arousal and performance in young adult drivers. Transp. Res. Rec. **2138**, 6–12 (2009)

28. Mok, B., Johns, M., Yang, S., Ju, W.: Reinventing the wheel: transforming steering wheel systems for autonomous vehicles. In: Proceedings of the 30th Annual ACM Symposium on User Interface Software and Technology, pp. 229–241. ACM, October 2017

29. Patel, M., Lal, S.K.L., Kavanagh, D., Rossiter, P.: Applying neural networkanalysis on heart rate variability data to assess driver fatigue. Expert Syst. Appl. **38**(6), 7235–7242 (2011)

30. Petermeijer, S., Bazilinskyy, P., Bengler, K., Winter, J.D.: Take-over again: Investigating multimodal and directional TORs to get the driver back into the loop. Appl. Ergon. **62**, 204–215 (2017). https://doi.org/10.1016/j.apergo.2017.02.023

31. Petermeijer, S., Cieler, S., Winter, J.D.: Comparing spatially static and dynamic vibrotactile take-over requests in the driver seat. Accid. Anal. Prev. **99**, 218–227 (2017). https://doi.org/10.1016/j.aap.2016.12.001

32. Pettitt, M., Burnett, G., Stevens, A.: Defining driver distraction. p 12 (2005)

33. Politis, I., Brewster, S., Pollick, F.: Language-based multimodal displays for the handover of control in autonomous cars. In: Proceedings of the 7th International Conference on Automotive User Interfaces and Interactive Vehicular Applications - AutomotiveUI 15 (2015). https://doi.org/10.1145/2799250.2799262

34. Rauch, N., Kaussner, A., Boverie, S., Giralt, A.: HAVEit-Highly automated vehicles for intelligent transport. Model of driver behaviour for the assessment of driver's state. Deliverable D32, 1 (2009)

35. Rosario, H.D., Solaz, J.S., Rodriguez, N., Bergasa, L.M.: Controlled inducementand measurement of drowsiness in a driving simulator. IET Intell. Transp. Syst. **4**(4), 280–288 (2010)

36. SAE International. Taxonomy and definitions for terms related to driving automation systems for on-road motor vehicles (2018)

37. Serrano, J., Di Stasi, L., Megías, A., Catena, A.: Effect of directional speech warnings on road hazard detection. Traffic Inj. Prev. **12**, 630–635 (2011). https://doi.org/10.1080/15389588.2011.620661

38. Shahid, A., Wilkinson, K., Marcu, S., Shapiro, C.M.: Karolinska sleepiness scale (KSS). In: Shahid, A., Wilkinson, K., Marcu, S., Shapiro, C. (eds.) STOP, THAT and One Hundred Other Sleep Scales. Springer, New York (2011). https://doi.org/10.1007/978-1-4419-9893-4

39. Shakeri, G., Ng, A., Williamson, J.H., Brewster, S.A.: Evaluation of haptic patterns on a steering wheel. In: Proceedings of the 8th International Conference on Automotive User Interfaces and Interactive Vehicular Applications, (AutomotiveUI 2016), pp. 129–136. Association for Computing Machinery, New York (2016). https://doi.org/10.1145/3003715.3005417

40. Stockert, S., Richardson, N.T., Lienkamp, M.: Driving in an increasingly automated world – approaches to improve the driver-automation interaction. Procedia Manuf. **3**, 2351–9789 (2015). https://doi.org/10.1016/j.promfg.2015.07.797. ISSN 2351-9789

41. Walch, M., Lange, K., Baumann, M., Weber, M.: Autonomous driving: investigating the feasibility of car-driver handover assistance. In: Proceedings of the 7th International Conference on Automotive User Interfaces and Interactive Vehicular Applications - AutomotiveUI 15 (2015). https://doi.org/10.1145/2799250.2799268
42. Wang, M., Lyckvi, S.L., Chen, C., Dahlstedt, P., Chen, F.: Using advisory 3D sound cues to improve drivers' performance and situation awareness. In: Proceedings of the 2017 CHI Conference on Human Factors in Computing Systems, pp. 2814–2825. ACM, May 2017
43. Waytz, A., Heafner, J., Epley, N.: The mind in the machine: anthropomorphism increases trust in an autonomous vehicle. J. Exp. Soc. Psychol. **52**, 113–117 (2014). https://doi.org/10.1016/j.jesp.2014.01.005
44. World Health Organization: Global status report on road safety 2018. Switzerland, Geneva (2018)
45. Wulf, F., Zeeb, K., Rimini-Döring, M., Arnon M., Gauterin, F.: Effects of human-machine interaction mechanisms on situation awareness in partly automated driving. In: Proceedings of the 16th International IEEE Conference on Intelligent Transportation Systems (ITSC 2013), The Hague, 2013, pp. 2012–2019 (2013). https://doi.org/10.1109/itsc.2013.6728525
46. Zhang, G., Yau, K.K.W., Zhang, X., Li, Y.: Traffic accidents involving fatigue driving and their extent of casualties. Accid. Anal. Prev. **87**, 34–42 (2016). https://doi.org/10.1016/j.aap.2015.10.033. ISSN 0001-4575

SilverCodes: Thin, Flexible, and Single-Line Connected Identifiers Inputted by Swiping with a Finger

Minto Funakoshi[⊠], Shun Fujita, Kaori Minawa, and Buntarou Shizuki

University of Tsukuba, 1-1-1 Tennodai, Tsukuba, Ibaraki, Japan
{funakoshi,fujita,minawa,shizuki}@iplab.cs.tsukuba.ac.jp

Abstract. This study investigates SilverCodes, thin and flexible identifiers that serve to constitute an input interface. SilverCodes are thin and flexible barcode-shaped identifiers. User input is achieved by swiping an identifier with a finger. SilverCodes are made from two sheets of paper pasted with conductive ink. Identifiers can thus be conveniently printed using an ordinary ink-jet printer. Multiple SilverCodes can be connected by a single-line wire to an external module that recognizes the identifier swiped by the user. Furthermore, SilverCodes can be stacked and identifiers can be recognized to an average accuracy of 95.3%.

Keywords: Paper interface · Conductive ink · Tangible · Interactive book

1 Introduction

By applying suitable crafting skills (e.g., drawing, coloring, stacking, cutting, or folding), a designer can transform simple sheets of paper into a picture book or can achieve various forms of papercraft. The scope of possibilities for making objects from the paper is fascinating, but even more can be achieved by including an interactive component. For example, the inclusion of an interactive interface, whereby touch electrodes are created on paper with conductive ink or conductive tapes, can provide the paper a functionality that allows user interactions through a computer.

The following methods for fabricating an interactive paper interface using a conductive ink or conductive tapes have been proposed:

1. pasting RFIDs on a piece of paper [7],
2. attaching LEDs and a microcomputer to paper [8], and
3. forming touch electrodes [9].

Methods for pasting or attaching circuit elements to a sheet of paper (points 1 and 2) allow complex input configurations, which typically results in a thickening of the paper and reduced flexibility. A method for forming touch electrodes on paper (point 3) can allow touch-based interaction. However, implementing

© Springer Nature Switzerland AG 2020
M. Kurosu (Ed.): HCII 2020, LNCS 12182, pp. 350–362, 2020.
https://doi.org/10.1007/978-3-030-49062-1_24

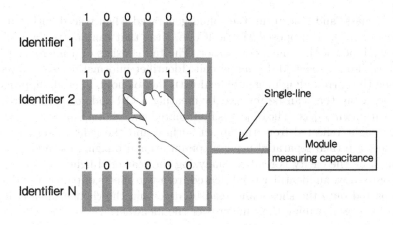

Fig. 1. SilverCodes concept.

many such electrodes simultaneously for complex applications requires many wire connections. This significantly complicates the wiring configuration between the sheet of paper and a sensing module used to identify which electrodes have been touched by the user.

This study investigates SilverCodes, thin and flexible identifiers that serve to constitute an input interface. The concept is illustrated in Fig. 1. SilverCodes are thin and flexible barcode-shaped identifiers. User input is achieved by swiping an identifier with one finger. SilverCodes are made from two sheets of paper printed with conductive ink. Identifiers can thus be conveniently printed using an ordinary ink-jet printer. Multiple SilverCodes can be connected by a single-line wire to an external module that recognizes the identifier swiped by the user. This feature allows designers to implement multiple touch electrodes on a paper sheet using simple wiring. Furthermore, SilverCodes can be stacked, which allows the design of more complex input structures with multiple surfaces while maintaining the simplicity in electrical connections, since the stacked SilverCodes can also be connected to the module using single-line wires.

2 Related Work

In this section, we discuss the research on existing identifiers that can be embedded into objects, the one on interactive paper using conductive ink, and the book-type system that users can interact with.

2.1 Identifier

Various identifiers have been found suitable for embedding within objects. Harrison et al. [3] proposed Acoustic Barcodes that can be realized by forming striped grooves on an object. They can be engraved on various materials, such as paper, wood, or glass, and read using the sound generated when traced with a finger-nail. Fetter et al. [1] proposed MagnetiCode, a tag that can be read by a smart-phone equipped with a magnetic sensor. The tag consists of a microcomputer, a solenoid, and a solenoid-driving circuit. Identifier information is conveyed by changing the surrounding magnetic field with the solenoid. Li et al. [6] proposed AirCode, a tag that can be realized by creating a QR code or a character-like cavity within an object. The object is illuminated and photographed with a camera. The light reflected from the object surface and the light scattered within the object are then separated using a computational imaging method. The tag generated by the cavity is read by analyzing the scattered light.

In our study, an identifier is fabricated from two sheets of paper. Conductive ink is pasted onto the sheets and read by detecting the change in capacitance caused by a user swiping their finger over the identifier.

2.2   Interactive Paper with Conductive Ink

Various scenarios of interactive paper with conductive ink have been explored. Jacoby et al. [4] developed StoryClip, which uses illustrations drawn with conductive ink as an interface for recording and playing back audio signals. Klamka et al. [5] proposed IllumiPaper, an interface that allows input through a stylus or by touch, and visual feedback using a light-emitting display. Li et al. [7] proposed a touch interface using an RFID tag equipped with an RF antenna that can be printed with conductive ink and whose characteristics change when touched by a user. Gestures such as touchdown and swiping motions on the antenna are demonstrably identified by detecting changes in the RF antenna characteristics.

StoryClip [4] and IllumiPaper [5] use multiple wires to connect the paper with external hardware. In contrast, SilverCodes use a single-line wire connection. Furthermore, fabricating SilverCodes does not require manually pasting a circuit element. The manufacturing process is facilitated because the identifier and the connection within the page are made only by ink-jet printing using conductive ink.

2.3   Interactive Book System

Qi et al. [8] proposed Electronic Popables, a pop-up book with interactive elements composed of copper-foil tape, conductive cloth, conductive ink, and electronic components. Each page features switches, buttons, LEDs, and other input/output elements. The conductive ink is used to wire the light-emitting display and the touchpad. Yoshino et al. [9] proposed FLIPPIN', a book-type interface for use in public spaces, in which a capacitive touchpad made from conductive ink is printed onto each page and connected by an FPC. As an interactive book-type system that does not require electrical wiring, a method that uses RFID tags to identify which page the user is looking at and provides visual or audible feedback tailored to the page being viewed proposed. Figueiredo et al. [2] used a magnetic sensor mounted onto each page to identify the page being viewed by the user. The book-type system we propose involves making a connection to each page (composed of paper and conductive ink) and binding the pages into a book. The structure is simpler and easier to manufacture than in previous attempts since the connection is made by making holes in each page and pouring conductive ink.

3   SilverCodes

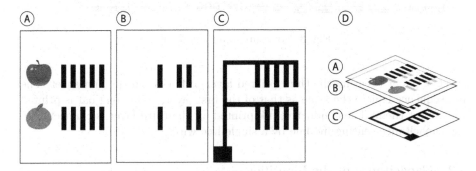

Fig. 2. Example of a SilverCodes implementation, consisting of two identifiers. A) The front side of the top sheet (first layer). B) The reverse side of the top sheet (second layer). C) The front side of the second sheet (third layer). D) Superposition of the two sheets.

The next section first describes the structure of a SilverCodes implementation consisting of multiple identifiers, as illustrated in Fig. 2 for the case of two identifiers. SilverCodes are made from two sheets of paper and conductive ink. Each SilverCodes identifier consists of a sequence of bars, used to represent binary values 1 and 0. Thus, the identifier encodes data as a bit sequence (e.g., 10001 or 1110).

Next, we describe the principle behind identifier recognition based on the swipe of a finger, which involves a capacitance measurement. The measured capacitance switches between three different values as a user swipes their finger over an identifier. This change in capacitance is then decoded into a bit sequence.

3.1   Structure of SilverCodes

SilverCodes consist of three layers made from two sheets of paper and conductive ink (Fig. 2): the front of the top sheet (first layer), the reverse of the top sheet (second layer), and the top of the bottom sheet (third layer).

First, we describe the structure of a SilverCodes identifier, illustrated in Fig. 3. A sequence of bars is printed onto the first layer. An identifier is recognized by swiping across these bars with a finger. As on the first layer, a bar sequence is also printed on the second layer, located on the reverse side of the first layer. The presence or absence of a bar on the second layer, directly above a bar on the first layer, constitutes a bit of value 1 or 0, respectively. The second

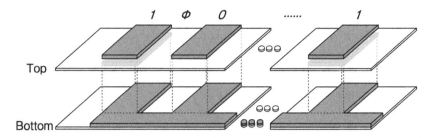

Fig. 3. Structure of an identifier.

sheet of paper (bearing the third printed layer) differs from the first sheet. The bar sequence is here the same as that of the first layer, and a long bar is printed to connect them. The conductive ink printed on the third layer is connected to the capacitance-sensing module by a single-line wire.

3.2   Capacitance of the Identifier

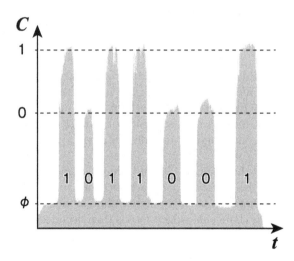

Fig. 4. Capacitance change induced by a user swiping the identifier with a finger.

Capacitor electrodes are formed by the conductive ink patterns printed on the two sheets of paper. During a finger swipe, the measured capacitance varies over time depending on the printed patterns because the instantaneous capacitance depends on the distance between the electrodes. The human body also has capacitance, which becomes connected in series with the condenser when touching the identifier. Thus, as the user's finger swipes the identifier, a circuit is formed by the module used to measure the capacitance, the conductive ink, and the human

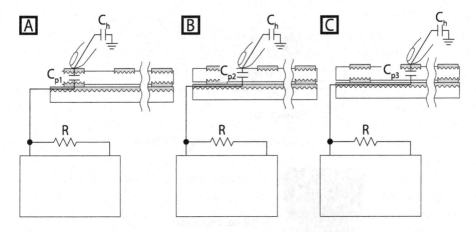

Fig. 5. Circuit when a user touches the identifier of SilverCodes: the states which a user touching the area conductive ink printed on both sides (A), no side (B), and front side (C).

body, as shown in Fig. 5. The capacitance signal is then measured as a variation between three levels as shown in Fig. 4. The system can hence recognize the swiped identifier by analyzing the measured capacitance signal.

4   Implementation

This section describes the implementation of SilverCodes and of the system used for recognizing the swiped identifier, as illustrated in Fig. 6. The system consists of a module for measuring the capacitance and a PC for analyzing it. The module was implemented using a microcomputer (Arduino Mega 2560 R3) and its library (Capacitive Sensing Library[1]). The module was connected to the SilverCodes by a single-line wire and to the PC by a USB cable.

4.1   SilverCodes

SilverCodes were fabricated by printing conductive ink (Mitsubishi Paper Mills, Ltd., NBSIJ-MU01) on two sheets of glossy paper (KOKUYO Co., Ltd., KJ-G23A430) of thickness 0.25 mm. The printer used was a PX-S160T (Seiko Epson Corp.).

The first and second SilverCodes layers were printed on the same paper sheet. The third layer was printed on another sheet. Because the SilverCodes identifiers are constituted by stacking the two paper sheets as shown in Fig. 2D.

We printed the same pattern on the paper twice for improved recognition accuracy. We performed a pilot study and confirmed a decrease in the resistance

---

[1] https://playground.arduino.cc/Main/CapacitiveSensor/.

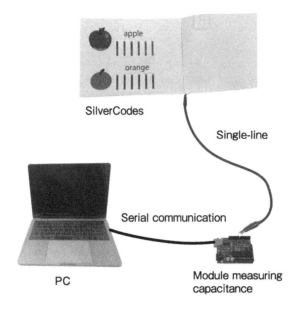

Fig. 6. Overview of our system.

achieved by printing the conductive ink twice. Additional printings were found not to yield significant improvements.

The identifiers can be recognized by connecting the SilverCodes with the module as shown in Fig. 6. The third SilverCodes layer and the module are connected by single-line wire. Then, the capacitance change is measured as shown in Fig. 4 while the user swipes the identifier with their finger.

4.2   Algorithm for Reading

The identifier data are read as a bit sequence by analyzing the capacitance changes, as shown in Fig. 4. However, the magnitude of capacitance change varies from one user to another. Therefore, the system must calculate the magnitude of capacitance change specific to the user. By including a header sequence with a set bit sequence 10, the system can calibrate the capacitance values corresponding to 1 and 0.

The system analyzes the magnitude of capacitance change according to the state transitions shown in Fig. 7. Let C_ϕ represent the measured capacitance when the user does not touch the conductive ink, and C_t the measured capacitance when the system recognizes the identifier. The states shown in Fig. 7 can undergo the following transitions:

a: No change in state for 5 s.
b: $1.2C_\phi < C_t$ by touching conductive ink.
c: $1.2C_\phi \geq C_t$ by not touching conductive ink.

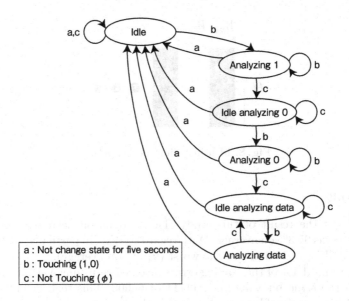

Fig. 7. State transition of analyzing the identifier.

5   User Study

We investigated the recognition accuracy of stacked SilverCodes. Of particular relevance to a SilverCodes application such as a booklet is whether each identifier functions correctly even if the SilverCodes are stacked. We evaluated the effect of the number of pages and of the bar width on the accuracy.

5.1   System

The system used in the experiment was a booklet consisting of four A4 sheets of SilverCodes stapled on the left-hand short side. The booklet was connected to the module by an alligator clip.

Four identifiers were printed on each sheet. The feature dimensions are labeled as shown in Fig. 8. The distance between the bars was $W_{gap} = 15\,\text{mm}$, the bar height was $H = 40\,\text{mm}$, and the bar width W_{bar} was 5, 7.5, 10, or 15 mm. Each identifier had the same printed pattern to allow a comparison of the read-error rates due to SilverCodes stacking or to the choice of W_{bar}. In all the cases, the bit sequence used was 11001.

5.2   Participant and Task

The authors themselves, 2 males aged 22 to 23, each performed 20 swipes per identifier on the booklet using the index finger of the right hand. The reading outcome was fed back to the participant. Thus, the experiment comprised a total of 960 trials (20 swipes × 4 identifiers × 4 sheets × 3 persons). The calibration of ϕ was performed for each person at the start of the experiment.

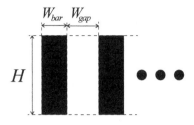

Fig. 8. Identifier dimension labels.

5.3   Result

Table 1 shows the result of this study. The recognition accuracy for stacked SilverCodes was 95.3% on average. With regard to W_{bar} in particular, the reading accuracy at $W_{bar} = 15$ mm was the worst (91.3% on average).

In addition, 31.1% of the reading errors involved returning a signal consisting entirely of the same bit value, i.e., 11111 or 00000. This read error may have arisen owing to a miscalibration of 1 or 0 in the header.

Table 1. Result of the pilot study.

Width	Accuracy (%)									
	On 1st page		On 2nd page		On 3rd page		On 4th page		Average	
	Average	SD	Average	SD	Average	SD	Average	SD	Average	SD
5 mm	96.7	2.36	98.3	2.36	100	0.00	95.0	7.07	97.5	4.33
7.5 mm	100	0.00	93.3	9.43	98.3	2.36	96.7	4.71	97.1	5.94
10 mm	100	0.00	98.3	2.36	96.7	4.71	86.7	9.43	95.4	7.49
15 mm	88.3	13.1	90.0	4.08	96.7	2.36	90.0	14.1	91.3	10.4
Average	96.3	8.20	95.0	6.45	97.9	3.20	92.1	10.3	95.3	7.80

5.4   Discussion

A measured signal consisting entirely of bit values 1 or 0 is a common read error. Identical bit sequences should be avoided. This will prompt the user to re-swipe the identifier if an error occurs.

Also, we found that the identifiers on stacked SilverCodes can be read with sufficient accuracy. The recognition accuracy of identifiers is typically higher for thinner bars. One advantage is that it allows more information to be packed into SilverCodes. However, there may be a limit to miniaturization associated with misregistration of the printing and bookbinding. Future work will investigate the limits of the information density achievable by SilverCodes.

6   Applications

This section considers SilverCodes applications.

6.1   Audio Book

A sound-emitting picture book can be fabricated using stacked SilverCodes (Fig. 9). The picture book can be made straightforwardly using only sheets of paper and conductive ink. It can then be connected to the identifier-recognition module by a single-line wire. Therefore, the reconnection of the other book is very easy.

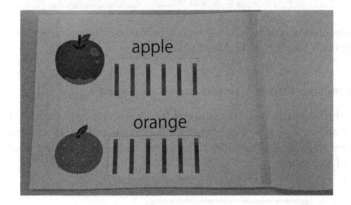

Fig. 9. Audio book application.

6.2   Personalized Controller

SilverCodes can be used to implement personalized controllers, operated by swiping a finger over printed identifiers. Because the SilverCodes are made of paper, they can be bent, folded, and attached to various personal objects. For example, Fig. 10 shows a volume controller with SilverCodes printed on a plastic bottle.

Multiple SilverCodes, serving as replaceable controllers, can also be fastened on a clipboard connected to a capacitance measuring module. Moreover, since the discarded SilverCodes controllers are made of paper, the device as a whole is relatively compact.

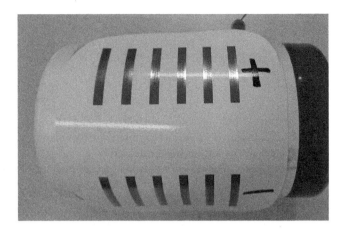

Fig. 10. Personalized controller made from SilverCodes. The user can control the volume by swiping a finger over the identifiers.

6.3   Interactive Paper Using a Speed of Swipe

The swipe duration can also be exploited for interactive applications. For example, Fig. 11 shows a picture book where a ball, rendered on an external display, is thrown by swiping an identifier. The speed of the ball is thus controlled by the speed of the swipe.

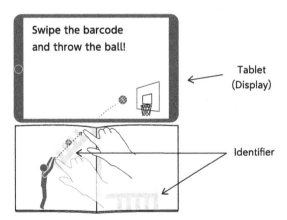

Fig. 11. Interactive picture book, where the user can throw a ball using a swiping motion.

6.4   Notice Board

SilverCodes can be implemented on a notice board to allow interactions with attached paper sheets as shown in Fig. 12. Connection to the wiring within the notice board can be achieved by pinning the SilverCodes. For example, it is possible to create an accessible paper that reads out the content by swiping the identifier on the paper.

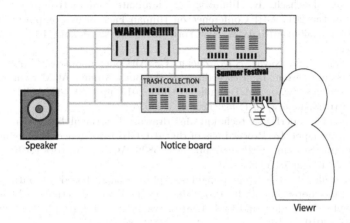

Fig. 12. Notice board using SilverCodes. A viewer can receive speech information by swiping SilverCodes.

7 Conclusion

We have shown that SilverCodes can be used to fabricate flexible and paper-thin identifiers for use as an input interface. SilverCodes are made from two sheets of paper and conductive ink patterned into a barcode-like identifier. SilverCodes are connected to a module by a single-line wire. Data input is achieved by the swipe of a finger. Identifier recognition is based on a capacitance measurement. Furthermore, SilverCodes can be stacked and identifiers can be recognized to an average accuracy of 95.3%.

References

1. Fetter, M., Beckmann, C., Gross, T.: MagnetiCode: physical mobile interaction through time-encoded magnetic identification tags. In: Proceedings of the 8th International Conference on Tangible, Embedded and Embodied Interaction, TEI 2014, pp. 205–212. ACM, New York (2013). https://doi.org/10.1145/2540930.2540963
2. Figueiredo, A.C., Pinto, A.L., Branco, P., Zagalo, N., Coquet, E.: Bridging book: a not-so-electronic children's picturebook. In: Proceedings of the 12th International Conference on Interaction Design and Children, IDC 2013, pp. 569–572. ACM, New York (2013). https://doi.org/10.1145/2485760.2485867
3. Harrison, C., Xiao, R., Hudson, S.: Acoustic barcodes: passive, durable and inexpensive notched identification tags. In: Proceedings of the 25th Annual ACM Symposium on User Interface Software and Technology, UIST 2012, pp. 563–568. ACM, New York (2012). https://doi.org/10.1145/2380116.2380187

4. Jacoby, S., Buechley, L.: Drawing the electric: storytelling with conductive ink. In: Proceedings of the 12th International Conference on Interaction Design and Children, IDC 2013, pp. 265–268. ACM, New York (2013). https://doi.org/10.1145/2485760.2485790
5. Klamka, K., Dachselt, R.: IllumiPaper: illuminated interactive paper. In: Proceedings of the 2017 CHI Conference on Human Factors in Computing Systems, CHI 2017, pp. 5605–5618. ACM, New York (2017).https://doi.org/10.1145/3025453.3025525
6. Li, D., Nair, A.S., Nayar, S.K., Zheng, C.: AirCode: unobtrusive physical tags for digital fabrication. In: Proceedings of the 30th Annual ACM Symposium on User Interface Software and Technology, UIST 2017, pp. 449–460. ACM, New York (2017). https://doi.org/10.1145/3126594.3126635
7. Li, H., et al.: PaperID: a technique for drawing functional battery-free wireless interfaces on paper. In: Proceedings of the 2016 CHI Conference on Human Factors in Computing Systems, CHI 2016, pp. 5885–5896. ACM, New York (2016). https://doi.org/10.1145/2858036.2858249
8. Qi, J., Buechley, L.: Electronic popables: exploring paper-based computing through an interactive pop-up book. In: Proceedings of the Fourth International Conference on Tangible, Embedded, and Embodied Interaction, TEI 2010, pp. 121–128. ACM, New York (2010). https://doi.org/10.1145/1709886.1709909
9. Yoshino, K., Obata, K., Tokuhisa, S.: FLIPPIN': exploring a paper-based book UI design in a public space. In: Proceedings of the 2017 CHI Conference on Human Factors in Computing Systems, CHI 2017, pp. 1508–1517. ACM, New York (2017). https://doi.org/10.1145/3025453.3025981

A Defocus Based Novel Keyboard Design

Priyanshu Gupta[1], Tushar Goswamy[1(✉)], Himanshu Kumar[2],
and K.S. Venkatesh[1]

[1] Indian Institute of Technology, Kanpur, Kanpur, India
{guptap,tgoswamy,venkats}@iitk.ac.in
[2] Indian Institute of Technology, Jodhpur, Jodhpur, India
hkumar@iitj.ac.in

Abstract. Defocus based Depth estimation has been widely applied
for constructing 3D setup from 2D image(s), reconstructing 3D scenes
and image refocusing. Using defocus enables us to infer depth information from a single image using visual clues which can be captured by a
monocular camera. In this paper, we propose an application of Depth
from Defocus to a novel, portable keyboard design. Our estimation technique is based on the concept that depth of the finger with respect to
our camera and its defocus blur value is correlated, and a map can be
obtained to detect the finger position accurately. We have utilised the
near-focus region for our design, assuming that the closer an object is
to our camera, more will be its defocus blur. The proposed keyboard
can be integrated with smartphones, tablets and Personal Computers,
and only requires printing on plain paper or projection on a flat surface.
The detection approach involves tracking the finger's position as the user
types, measuring its defocus value when a key is pressed, and mapping
the measured defocus together with a precalibrated relation between the
defocus amount and the keyboard pattern. This is utilised to infer the
finger's depth, which, along with the azimuth position of the stroke, identifies the pressed key. Our minimalistic design only requires a monocular
camera, and there is no need for any external hardware. This makes the
proposed approach a cost-effective and feasible solution for a portable
keyboard.

Keywords: Portable keyboard · Defocus · Depth estimation

1 Introduction

Research on extracting spatial information from 2-Dimensional images has witnessed several developments over the past decade, and estimating depth is one
area of focus under this field. A unique approach towards extracting depth information is using the Defocus blur of an object. Our work presents a useful application of this technique for the Human Computer Interaction community, where
we implement this technique to detect the finger position of a user while typing,
and provide a portable keyboard design that accurately detects keystrokes.

© Springer Nature Switzerland AG 2020
M. Kurosu (Ed.): HCII 2020, LNCS 12182, pp. 363–379, 2020.
https://doi.org/10.1007/978-3-030-49062-1_25

Traditional mechanical keyboards are constrained, bulky and provide minimal flexibility to the user. In case of smartphones, a user has to carry an additional plug-in peripheral if he/she wishes to use a full- sized keyboard which is cumbersome and inconvenient. One of the alternates to this could be a virtual on-screen keyboard, but it occupies screen space when invoked, which results in a poor experience.

To address this, several keyboard designs have been proposed with advancements in terms of accuracy, flexibility and portability. Kolsch et al. [1] provides an overview of such keyboard designs, where multiple keyboards enable user typing on a plain surface, with visual feedback obtained by keyboard projection or printing over a surface. Other keyboard designs may also give haptic feedback [2] or provide different kinds of visual feedback such as highlighting the key on the screen. This depends on the additional hardware that is required to achieve the desired results. Keyboards which utilize gestures to map keywords [3–6] have also been developed. However, such schemes suit situations where only a few keywords need to be communicated with the procedure becoming exceedingly complicated for larger keywords. Some virtual keyboards use external hardware like a 3D camera [7], laser projectors [8], stereo camera pair [9], or wearable technologies to track finger position and/or motion. A major drawback of these methods is requirement of additional hardware and high costs, thus they aren't ideal for day-to-day applications. There are some systems which utilise shadows and only require a camera to function [10,11]. However, the accuracy of these methods is dependent upon the lighting conditions and camera orientation with respect to the user as well as the typing surface, and thus do not serve as a robust solution.

The next frontier of techniques are vision based approaches for depth estimation. Depth estimation using vision include Depth from focus [12], Stereo Depth [13] and Structure from Motion [14]. The primary drawback of these methods is the requirement of multiple images for depth estimation, and hence they cannot be used when only a single image is available or similar features across images cannot be properly resolved. The work done by Levin et al. [15] provides a method for recovering depth information from a single image, but it requires physical adjustments to the camera and hence cannot be easily adopted by all smartphone/tablet users. Khoshelham [16] provides another method for depth estimation from a single image, but it requires a motion sensor like Microsoft Kinect and thus increases the hardware requirements and costs associated with the keyboard. In our paper, we have used depth estimation from Defocus Blur to detect keystrokes and provided the supporting keyboard design. Defocus has been used for depth estimation as it requires only a single image, owing to a high correlation between Defocus-blur and distance from the camera. Since defocus based techniques require input from only a single camera, they provide us an advantage over other techniques in terms of cost reduction, minimalism and portability. Objects in the scene form a blurred image in the image plane due to the nonzero aperture size of the lens. We call the blurring due to the object being out of focus as the defocus blur (as shown in Fig. 1). The object 'O' in figure forms a blurred image at the image plane with a diameter 'C' of the circle of confusion.

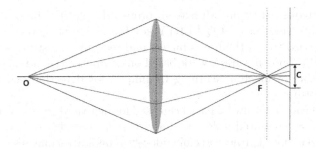

Fig. 1. Finite aperture and defocus blur.

As shown by Srikakulapu et al. [17], the degree or amount of defocus changes with the object's depth. By measuring the extent of defocus, depth information of the respective part of the scene can be inferred. Depth information estimated using defocus-blur is the basis of our system for keystroke detection. The main contribution made in this paper is the proposal and demonstration of a defocus-based method for real time identification of the typing apparatus (a stylus and a finger) and its location during a keystroke touch event, using a single monocular camera.

The paper has been organised as follows: Sect. 2 discusses the developments as well as the state of the art work for various kinds of keystroke detection systems. Section 3 presents our proposed design for keystroke detection. Section 4 presents the experimental results. We discuss steps to ameliorate the detection method in Sect. 5. We conclude the paper in Sect. 6 by summarising this research, its applications and presenting ideas for further research.

2 Previous Work

In the last 2 decades, various innovative keyboard designs have been proposed based on different detection techniques. Gesture Recognition is one such approach employed by researchers for designing novel keyboards. Kanevsky [3] used a recognition system of gestures that maps sequences of gestures to key strings. The gesture recognition system captures gestures and decodes the corresponding key of the keyboard. However, remembering and mimicking gestures corresponding to various keys is a cumbersome task. This makes this design unfeasible for practical applications. Habib [4] used fuzzy approaches for gesture recognition in a mono-vision virtual keyboard design for mobile and portable computing devices. The hand and finger gesture captured in the video sequence was used to detect the keystroke over a printed sheet keyboard. Du [5] used multi-level feature matching (MLFM) method for 3D hand posture reconstruction of a virtual keyboard system. They modelled the human hand in increasing levels of detail, from skeletal to polygonal surface representation. Different types of features are extracted and paired with the corresponding model. These hand postures are used for keystroke detection. Murase [6] proposed a gesture-based virtual keyboard (Gesture Keyboard) of QWERTY key layout requiring only one camera. Gesture keyboard tracks the user's fingers and recognizes gestures as the input. Magoulès [18] proposed a framework based on computer vision techniques combined with efficient machine learning techniques for detection and tracking of user hand gestures.

Different types of hardware have been used for increased accuracy in keystroke detection. Su [8] presented a design of a virtual keyboard based on an infrared laser module, keyboard projector, embedded systems and an image sensing device. The keystrokes are determined by image processing including morphology principles and ellipse fitting. Laser Projection keyboards, such as the one proposed by AlKassim [19], use laser light and a CMOS sensor for detecting the finger and its position. Salmansha [20] proposed a virtual keyboard design which had a virtual beamer for keyboard projection, camera for identifying the finger-strokes, and an IR filter module for tracking the keystrokes. When a user performs a keystroke, the IR filter detects it and communicates this motion to the camera. The finger motion thus detected is used to identify the keystroke.

Du [7] presented a keyboard system which simulates a QWERTY keyboard on an arbitrary surface with the help of a pattern projector and uses a true-3D range camera for typing event detection and motion tracking. The depth information is employed to detect the keystroke.

Lee [9] uses a stereo camera to obtain the depth of the fiducial maker to determine the keystroke.

Wearable technologies have also been used to receive keyboard input for mobile and other handheld devices. Goldstein [21] designed the Finger-Joint Gesture Wearable Keypad, Fukumoto [22] proposed the FingeRing and Zhao [23] posited a novel virtual keyboard implementation method which utilised motion-detecting wireless IoT rings and a 2-dimensional keyboard framework. All of these can be worn on our hands or on our fingers and can be used to provide text based input to the connected device. In all these keyboards, the requirement of additional hardware limits their scope for general purpose application and also makes it costly to use them.

Several researchers have utilised shadow based techniques for keystroke detection. Adajania [10] proposed a design of virtual keyboard using only a standard web camera, with no additional hardware. They used shadow analysis to identify the keystroke. They show that shadow is minimal in case of keystroke event. Posner [11] improved shadow-based touch detection, proposing a single standard camera-based virtual keyboard. Accuracy of the touch detection is improved by matching the tip of the shadow and the finger. Lv [24] proposed an algorithm for finger touch detection based on front-projected vision-based table system utilizing the shadow information. However, accuracy of these methods depends upon the lighting condition. Besides that method assumes that the camera is facing vertically downward above the keyboard pattern, which may not be a feasible scenario for real-world applications.

Computer Vision based methods for keystroke detection are among the latest technologies to be employed in this field. Erdem [25] proposed a unistroke keyboard based on computer vision utilizing camera and laser pointer. The illuminated key is identified from the predefined location of the keys in the keyboard. However, the method focuses its application to assist the handicapped with using the keyboard. Srivastava [26] proposed a mono-vision based touch and type method on a customizable keyboard drawn, printed or projected on a surface. The method is based on the relative speed of finger tip intended to type v/s other fingers until it does a hit on a surface. Livada [27] proposed a web camera based virtual keyboard. They used binarization, morphological operation and filtering techniques to fingertip and keyboard character recognition. This method assumes the vertically downward position of the camera which is impractical for real-world applications. Also, this method does not discuss the touch detection scheme which is essential for the keyboard application to find out the keystroke events.

3 Proposed Design

The primary components of the keyboard system are:

1. A printed/projected Keymap: We define a keymap as an arrangement of keys in a grid-like manner
2. A visual input device like a smartphone camera placed in the plane of the keymap (Fig. 2)
3. A computing device sufficiently powerful to carry out the required image processing tasks
4. A typing tool (could be a stylus or a human finger)

Fig. 2. Experimental set-up as seen by the visual input device (smartphone/tablet)

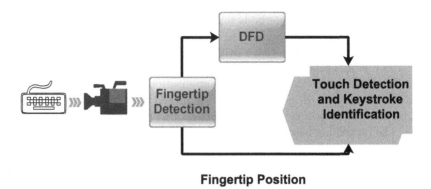

Fingertip Position

Fig. 3. Flow diagram for proposed keystroke identification.

Figure 3 shows the flow diagram for keystroke identification. The input video stream is segmented into time-sliced event frames for keystroke activity detection. We start with **Fingertip detection**. On identification of a valid finger tip, we mark a Region of Interest (ROI) and estimate the **Depth from Defocus**. We then combine the $x - y$ (horizontal-vertical) fingertip position and estimated depth (z) to detect the **Keystroke Event** and generate appropriate interrupts in the target device.

3.1   Identifying the Region of Interest

The first step involves identifying the desired finger region to find the defocus coefficient of. A possible technique can be the morphological filtering based method as described by Malik et al. [28]. In this approach, the image is segmented on the basis of human skin color to recover the hand region. Appropriate Morphological filters are applied to identify the finger region. An edge detector is then used to give the finger outline. We then proceed to calculate the angle between all triplets of consecutive outline pixels and attribute the pixel corresponding to the smallest angle as the fingertip. A polygon derived as an upward extension of these triangles can be regarded as our *Region of Interest* (ROI). Alternatively, a stylus or a painted fingernail can be used to identify the *ROI*, the trade-off being between the ease of use and accuracy. We provide a comparison of these techniques in the subsequent sections.

3.2   Depth from Defocus (DFD)

Multiple techniques can be used for depth estimation using defocus from a still image. In our experiments, we implement Zhuo's strategy [29] since it requires less time for processing and is very effective in the near focus band. However, any other method such as [17,30,31] and [32] can also be used, but we need to take care of the trade-offs. Zhuo's method models edges as 'thin' edges, marking a change in intensity levels. Mathematically, this can be represented as

$$AU(x) + B.$$

Here the intensity levels are denoted by A and B and $U(x)$ denotes the unit step function.

As demonstrated by Kumar [33], the defocus blur kernel can be assumed to be a Gaussian with kernel parameter σ which varies with the distance from the point of sharp focus. In other words, the blurring phenomenon can be modelled as a selective application of 'defocus kernel' on an otherwise sharp image with the parameter σ varying with the distance from the point of sharp focus. This enables us to model the problem of identifying depth as the one to recover the parameter σ of the scene. σ has been estimated using an edge neighborhood, as the edges are affected the most by the defocus blur. Equation (1) illustrates the blur edge model which consists of the thin edge model convolved with the blur kernel.

$$I_b = (AU(x) + B) * g(x; \sigma) \tag{1}$$

For blur (σ) estimation, the image is blurred with known blur parameters σ_1 and σ_2 to get I_{b1} and I_{b2} respectively and the gradient of both is calculated as per the Eq. (2).

$$\nabla I_{bi} = A\delta(x) * g(x; \sqrt{(\sigma^2 + \sigma_i^2)}), \quad i = 1, 2 \tag{2}$$

σ can be computed using only the ratio r of the two gradient moduli and the known applied blur parameters σ_1 and σ_2, as the edge parameters A and B get cancelled on division.

$$\frac{|\nabla I_{b1}|}{|\nabla I_{b2}|}\Big|_{x=0} \cong r = \frac{\sqrt{\sigma^2 + \sigma_1^2}}{\sqrt{\sigma^2 + \sigma_2^2}} \Rightarrow \sigma = \sqrt{\frac{r^2\sigma_2^2 - \sigma_1^2}{1 - r^2}} \tag{3}$$

Due to the varying aperture and focal length in different devices, calibration is a crucial step for our virtual keyboard setup. Additional device specific adjustment for keyboard size and form may be needed to optimize the keyspace. The previous discussion establishes that only objects at a certain depth can form sharp image at the image plane. The region closer to the camera in relation to the lens' focal plane is called the 'Near Region' and the region on the farther side is called the 'Far Region'. In the Near Region, defocus decreases with depth whereas it increases with depth in the Far Region. Figure (4) shows the typical variation of the blur radius (σ) with the depth for a given set of camera-parameters. We observe from the figure that for given set of camera parameters, defocus blur i.e. σ first decreases to zero and then starts increasing with the depth. The depth corresponding to zero defocus blur is termed as the focus-point of the camera for the selected setting. We notice that the in the near-focus region induced blur varies much faster with the distance compared to limited blur variation with distance in the far-focus region. Thus, discriminating blur at various distances

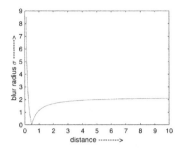

Fig. 4. Variation of blur radius (σ) with depth

is more accurate in the near-focus region. So, we have selected near-focus region for our keyboard position.

We perform calibration as follows:

- Place/project the keyboard such that the farthest point of the keyboard region lies within the near region. The orientation of the region is to be adjusted to ensure that the midpoint falls at the centre line and the row lines are parallel to the camera plane.
- Determine if the system has the capability to produce sufficient detectable differential defocus at various depths using 4. The relation is derived using optics ($\frac{1}{v} + \frac{1}{u} = \frac{1}{f}$) and underlying geometry. Here, d is blur circle diameter, f is focal length, D is diameter of lens and q is sharp focus distance for a given image plane position.

$$d = \frac{Dqf}{q-f}(\frac{1}{q} - \frac{1}{u}) \tag{4}$$

- Create an inverse dictionary of the defocus values at different depth levels of the keyboard layout for depth-defocus correlation.
- Store the $x - y$ range in the image plane for various $X - Y$ positions of keyboard layout for key segregation.

Please note that step 1 and step 2 can be done in advance with the help of some external arrangement like a specialized smartphone case, which are widely used by smartphone users. The remaining steps may be required in the event of change in orientation of the arrangement.

Figure 5 shows a variation of defocus blur parameter with depth for an example test environment. We observe from the plot that there is sufficient difference in defocus blur values with respect to various depth levels. This ensures that the defocus can indeed be used for keystroke identification.

3.3   Touch Detection and Keystroke Identification

Assuming that we receive an incoming video stream as an input, we try to identify keystroke event based on the subsequent up and down position of the

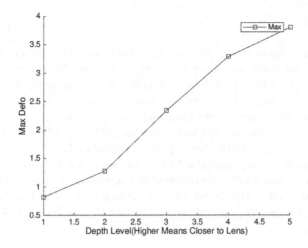

Fig. 5. Defocus variation with depth for various depth levels.

ROI. We refer to this part of the video stream as *activity segments*. Each activity segment corresponds to one keystroke event. For an activity segment, we average the representative defocus value for each frame within the *ROI* to define the defocus coefficient of the activity. This calculation starts for every 'possible' *activity segment*, that is, an event when a finger raises and continues on until it is put down, or a certain threshold time is reached. An alternative strategy could be to 'store' the part of the video stream for a certain threshold time and define an activity segment once the finger is put down and rewind through the stored stream for an 'upward' movement, on the lack of which, we assume that the *activity segment* started before the threshold. While these are mere implementation details, an ingenuous trade-off between spell accuracy and speed.

Comparing the estimated defocus value to the defocus value ranges obtained for the depth quantization gives us the depth of the fingertip. The $X - Y$ position of the selected key is estimated using the $x-y$ location of *ROI* in the image plane. Combining the rough depth estimate and $x - y$ position gives us an estimate of the location of the key corresponding to the activity segment. For additional accuracy we use the y-coordinate in conjunction with depth from defocus to find the exact keystroke.

If there is a deviation between the defocus estimate and estimate using the y coordinate, there is no touch or keystroke event and the fingertip location in the keyboard is simply the result of overlapping images of finger and keyboard. Such a scenario may occur due to movement of finger in the z axis. This necessitates the need of some depth data to prevent the declaration of spurious keystrokes. In the above discussion, the usage of Defocus data helped us overcome this problem.

4   Results

We carried out numerous experiments for establishing the usefulness of defocus for keystroke detection using different stylus designs, lighting conditions and keyboard formats. This was followed by extending our experiments to replacing the stylus with a finger, and studying how presence/absence of different nail polish designs affect finger detection and the associated defocus values. The software process was carried out using Matlab 2019 on an Intel i5 processor.

For the purpose of illustration, a paper printed keyboard as shown in Fig. 6 was used. The keyboard comprised of 7 columns and 4 depth bins (5 depth levels, as 2 successive depth levels constitute 1 depth bin) to represent the english alphabets. Each cell in the keyboard (intersection of a column and depth level) denotes a unique key. We distinguish various depth levels using defocus values.

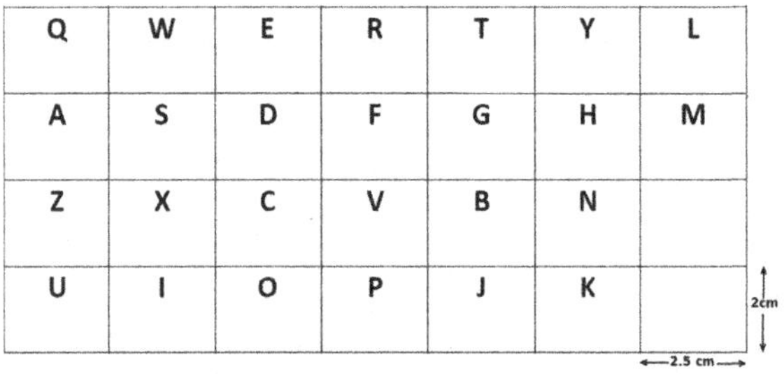

Q	W	E	R	T	Y	L
A	S	D	F	G	H	M
Z	X	C	V	B	N	
U	I	O	P	J	K	

Fig. 6. Experimental keyboard.

4.1   Typing Using a Stylus

To eliminate spurious shadows due to the complexities of the object shape and get sharp boundaries, we designed a simple experimental stylus (Fig. 7) containing alternate black and white strips to enhance contrast.

Statistical Comparison for Measure of Central Tendency: We did a statistical analysis to understand which measure of central tendency should be used to represent the defocus value for a given depth, so that we have bins which show a nearly-linear increasing trend and have sufficient window size. We compared the mean, mode and maximum values of defocus, and the results can seen in Fig. 8.

Thus, Maximum defocus value provides a monotonically increasing trend with respect to depth and also has fairly distinct values for each depth, which establishes its usefulness for getting defocus bins. We obtained similar results for all 7 columns, and found occasional dips in the mean and mode of defocus values, which does not inspire confidence in their reliability for detecting depth. This can be explained

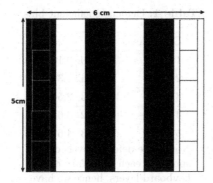

Fig. 7. The stylus used in our experiment

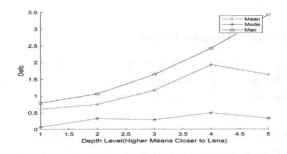

Fig. 8. Mean, Mode and Max defocus value variations with respect to depth

by the occurrence of spurious noises and the imperfections of camera design which affect the defocus values away from the boundaries. Thus, we conclude that maximum defocus should be used for generating defocus bins and detecting depth.

Obtaining Defocus Bins to Map Defocus Values to Depth: Table 1 shows defocus bins for various depth levels obtained from initial calibration using a stylus. For example Depth Level 4 & 5 correspond to the row QWERTYL.

The initial calibration maps the different x, y positions and defocus values to different keys on the keyboard. If the focus doesn't exist beyond the keyboard area, we prompt the user to shift the keyboard closer. Please note that keyboard positioning based calibrations are required only once to ensure the proper positioning of the camera focus with respect to the keyboard. After ensuring the proper placement, we store the defocus ranges for further detection.

Table 1. Defocus coefficient bins

Depth level	σ_{min}	σ_{max}
1	0.0000	0.1038
2	0.8254	1.3899
3	1.7653	2.5028
4	2.7642	3.6542
5	3.4783	4.672

Note: The defocus levels correspond to each boundary of the keyboard layers, hence we have 5 levels for each of the 5 boundaries, and 2 successive boundaries constitute one key.

4.2 Typing Using a Human Finger

After conducting experiments using a stylus, we extended our approach to test keystroke detection using a human finger. We conducted these experiments with the following cases for the detecting the finger and its associated defocus value:

1. Plain Finger
2. Half Painted Finger: Finger with lower half of the nail painted with nail paint
3. Full Painted Finger: Finger with entire nail painted with nail paint

Comparison Across Different Finger Paint Conditions: For simplification and avoiding errors caused due to improper finger identification, we used nail polish over the typing finger. The nail polish pattern was further divided into 2 cases: Painting lower half of the nail and painting the complete nail. The former was done under the hypothesis that we may be able to get better defocus values for the paint-fingernail boundary, similiar to the black-white boundary in the stylus (Fig. 10).

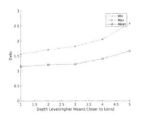
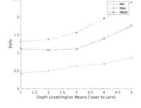
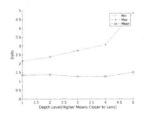

Fig. 9. With full nail paint

Fig. 10. With half nail paint

Fig. 11. Without nail paint

Thus, it is evident from the plots that the finger without nailpaint is not giving reliable defocus values, as compared to the finger with nailpaint. Also, the results for painting lower half of the nail vis-a-vis painting the complete nail are identical, thus we can use a finger with complete nail-paint for convenience, and without compromising on the accuracy of detection (Fig. 11).

Statistical Comparison for Measure of Central Tendency: We perform a similar analysis as Sect. 4.1 for getting the appropriate measure of central tendency to get defocus bins and detect depth. We included an additional measure - the minimum defocus value and performed the experiment for a finger with nail-paint. The experiments were performed for 3 distances between the camera lens and the keyboard edge: 15 cm, 25 cm, 30 cm. We obtained similar results for each distance, thus the trend does not very substantially across the 3 distances considered. The results for a finger with full nail-paint can be seen in Fig. 9, corresponding to a distance of 25 cm between the camera lens and the keyboard edge. We can see that Maximum defocus value gives the most reliable trend, concurrent with our results from Sect. 4.1. The choice of nail-paint colour for our experiments is green, as it gave the best results for finger detection and tracking. This is in agreement with the fact that green color is in sharp contrast from the human-skin color and hence is easier to segment.

4.3 Typing Accuracy

To determine the typing accuracy of our proposed approach using a stylus, we created a dataset of 15 different scenarios in which we perform initial calibration followed by typing a series of random words. In each setting we tried spelling 25–30 words. The overall accuracy of detection was 65% over several random words. This accuracy was improved to 75% after we limited the *ROIs* within a vertical centre to centre distance of approx. 1 cm on the stylus. The proposed method takes approximately 0.5 s to process one frame of keystroke event. Thus, it can process 50 keystroke per minute in the given test environment. When the experiments were performed with a finger, we were unable to get linear trends in some columns, as seen in Fig. 12. This is the result for a different column than the one considered in Fig. 9.

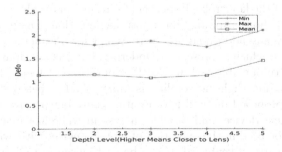

Fig. 12. Mean, Min and Max defocus value variations with respect to depth for finger without nail-paint for the left most column

We attribute this inconsistency in trends to the sensitivity of the human-skin color segmentation and believe it can be tackled by any advanced method to identify the finger well.

Ablation Analysis: On trying to use calibrations in one setting over others, the accuracy fell by varying degrees. The steepest decline is observed when the lighting condition is altered. However, such variations were vastly reduced when the experiments were conducted using the vertical black-white stylus, thereby attributing improper *ROI* detection as a primary reason for the fall. This can vastly be improved using better finger detection techniques which are out of the scope of the present work.

5   Future Improvements

This work assumes a single keystroke event occurring at a time. For future, we would like to improve our approach to detect multiple keystroke events occurring simultaneously, which is the case with the 10 finger typing method. Another issue lies in the improper finger identification which needs some improvement. There also exists a problem of occlusion, when the view of the finger gets partially or fully hindered by something. We need to extend the method to the use case where multiple fingers are being used to type at once, so that occlusion is accounted in the detection algorithm. Accuracy of the proposed method depends on accuracy of the estimation of defocus blur and edge localization. A lens with low DOF will result in better discrimination in defocus values for different depths, hence will result in higher accuracy. Size of the keyboard depends upon the optics of the lens (focal length). In future, we would explore these modalities of the proposed vision based keyboard system.

6   Conclusion

In this paper, we present a portable keyboard design based on depth from Defocus. Defocus blur values of the edge of our typing apparatus has been used to estimate the depth, which in turn can be used to identify the horizontal and vertical positions of the keystroke. Experimental results of our design establish that the proposed method is suitable for keystroke detection. The proposed method does not require any additional hardware except for a camera (and a stylus for better accuracy), which is present in modern-day devices such as a smartphone or a tablet. Since our approach is based on optics i.e. defocus of the lens, it is robust under various lighting conditions unlike shadow based state of the art methods. The proposed method is computationally inexpensive for implementing in a handheld device, and provides a system wherein wireless and remote keyboards can be used in the operation of mobile devices with/without the provision of an integrated keyboard. It can be customised as well and extended to any application that may require typing that includes, but is not limited to, a projected piano, musical keyboard as well as dynamic keyboard systems that change their layout depending on the application. The design can be adapted to suit any language, by taking the appropriate printout of the keyboard in the required language and calibrating it with the detecting device. Hence, the keyboard can modified to type vernacular Indian languages like Kannada, Hindi, Malayalam etc. as well as international languages like German, Korean etc. Only a printout of the relevant language keyboard or its laser projection is required. For future research, we would like to develop an end-to-end model for keystroke detection using the defocus based approach and deploy it on smartphone and tablet devices.

References

1. Kölsch, M., Turk, M.: Keyboards without keyboards: a survey of virtual keyboards. In: Workshop on Sensing and Input for Media-Centric Systems, Santa Barbara, CA (2002)
2. Kim, J.R., Tan, H.Z.: Haptic feedback intensity affects touch typing performance on a flat keyboard. In: Auvray, M., Duriez, C. (eds.) EUROHAPTICS 2014. LNCS, vol. 8618, pp. 369–375. Springer, Heidelberg (2014). https://doi.org/10.1007/978-3-662-44193-0_46
3. Kanevsky, D., Sabath, M., Zlatsin, A.: Virtual invisible keyboard. US Patent 7,042,442, 9 May 2006
4. Habib, H.A., Mufti, M.: Real time mono vision gesture based virtual keyboard system. IEEE Trans. Consum. Electron. **52**(4), 1261–1266 (2006)
5. Du, H., Charbon, E.: A virtual keyboard system based on multi-level feature matching. In: 2008 Conference on Human System Interactions, pp. 176–181. IEEE (2008)
6. Murase, T., Moteki, A., Suzuki, G., Nakai, T., Hara, N., Matsuda, T.: Gesture keyboard with a machine learning requiring only one camera. In: Proceedings of the 3rd Augmented Human International Conference, p. 29. ACM (2012)
7. Huan, D., Oggier, T., Lustenberger, F., Charbon, E.: A virtual keyboard based on true-3D optical ranging. In: Proceedings of the British Machine Vision Conference, vol. 1, pp. 220–229 (2005)
8. Su, X., Zhang, Y., Zhao, Q., Gao, L.: Virtual keyboard: a human-computer interaction device based on laser and image processing. In: 2015 IEEE International Conference on Cyber Technology in Automation, Control, and Intelligent Systems (CYBER), pp. 321–325. IEEE (2015)
9. Lee, M., Woo, W.: ARKB: 3D vision-based augmented reality keyboard. In: ICAT (2003)
10. Adajania, Y., Gosalia, J., Kanade, A., Mehta, H., Shekokar, N.: Virtual keyboard using shadow analysis. In: 2010 3rd International Conference on Emerging Trends in Engineering and Technology, pp. 163–165. IEEE (2010)
11. Posner, E., Starzicki, N., Katz, E.: A single camera based floating virtual keyboard with improved touch detection. In: 2012 IEEE 27th Convention of Electrical and Electronics Engineers in Israel, pp. 1–5. IEEE (2012)
12. Grossmann, P.: Depth from focus. Pattern Recogn. Lett. **5**(1), 63–69 (1987)
13. Bülthoff, H.H., Mallot, H.A.: Integration of depth modules: stereo and shading. J. Opt. Soc. Am. A **5**(10), 1749 (1988)
14. Ullman, S.: The interpretation of structure from motion. Proc. R. Soc. Lond. Ser. B Biol. Sci. **203**(1153), 405–426 (1979)

15. Levin, A., Fergus, R., Durand, F., Freeman, W.T.: Image and depth from a conventional camera with a coded aperture. ACM Trans. Graph. **26**(3), 70 (2007)
16. Khoshelham, K., Elberink, S.O.: Accuracy and resolution of Kinect depth data for indoor mapping applications. Sensors **12**(2), 1437–1454 (2012)
17. Srikakulapu, V., Kumar, H., Gupta, S., Venkatesh, K.S.: Depth estimation from single image using defocus and texture cues. In: 2015 Fifth National Conference on Computer Vision, Pattern Recognition, Image Processing and Graphics (NCVPRIPG), pp. 1–4. IEEE (2015)
18. Magoulès, F., Zou, Q.: A novel contactless human machine interface based on machine learning. In: 2017 16th International Symposium on Distributed Computing and Applications to Business, Engineering and Science (DCABES), pp. 137–140. IEEE (2017)
19. AlKassim, Z.: Virtual laser keyboards: a giant leap towards human-computer interaction. In: 2012 International Conference on Computer Systems and Industrial Informatics. IEEE, December 2012
20. Salmansha, P.N., Parveen, S., Yohannan, F., Vasavan, A., Kurian, M.: Mini keyboard: portative human interactive device. In: 2017 International Conference on Communication and Signal Processing (ICCSP), pp. 1531–1535. IEEE (2017)
21. Goldstein, M., Chincholle, D., Backström, M.: Assessing two new wearable input paradigms: the finger-joint-gesture palm-keypad glove and the invisible phone clock. Pers. Technol. **4**(2–3), 123–133 (2000)
22. Fukumoto, M., Tonomura, Y.: Body coupled FingerRing. In: Proceedings of the SIGCHI Conference on Human Factors in Computing Systems - CHI 1997. ACM Press (1997)
23. Zhao, Y., Lian, C., Zhang, X., Sha, X., Shi, G., Li, W.J.: Wireless IoT motion-recognition rings and a paper keyboard. IEEE Access **7**, 44514–44524 (2019)
24. Lv, Z., et al.: A new finger touch detection algorithm and prototype system architecture for pervasive bare-hand human computer interaction. In: 2013 IEEE International Symposium on Circuits and Systems (ISCAS 2013), pp. 725–728. IEEE (2013)
25. Erdem, M.E., Erdem, I.A., Atalay, V., Cetin, A.E.: Computer vision based unistroke keyboard system and mouse for the handicapped. In: 2003 International Conference on Multimedia and Expo, ICME 2003, Proceedings (Cat. No. 03TH8698), vol. 2, pp. II-765. IEEE (2003)
26. Srivastava, S., Tripathi, R.C.: Real time mono-vision based customizable virtual keyboard using finger tip speed analysis. In: Kurosu, M. (ed.) HCI 2013. LNCS, vol. 8007, pp. 497–505. Springer, Heidelberg (2013). https://doi.org/10.1007/978-3-642-39330-3_53
27. Livada, Č., Proleta, M., Romić, K., Leventić, H.: Beyond the touch: a web camera based virtual keyboard. In: 2017 International Symposium ELMAR, pp. 47–50. IEEE (2017)
28. Malik, S.: Real-time hand tracking and finger tracking for interaction csc2503f project report. Technical report, Department of Computer Science, University of Toronto (2003)
29. Zhuo, S., Sim, T.: Defocus map estimation from a single image. Pattern Recogn. **44**(9), 1852–1858 (2011)
30. Subbarao, M., Surya, G.: Depth from defocus: a spatial domain approach. Int. J. Comput. Vision **13**(3), 271–294 (1994)
31. Tang, C., Hou, C., Song, Z.: Defocus map estimation from a single image via spectrum contrast. Opt. Lett. **38**(10), 1706–1708 (2013)

32. Karaali, A., Jung, C.R.: Edge-based defocus blur estimation with adaptive scale selection. IEEE Trans. Image Process. **27**(3), 1126–1137 (2017)
33. Kumar, H., Gupta, S., Venkatesh, K.S.: Defocus map estimation from a single image using principal components. In: 2015 International Conference on Signal Processing, Computing and Control (ISPCC). IEEE (2015)

Affective Haptics and Multimodal Experiments Research

Yang Jiao$^{(\boxtimes)}$ and Yingqing Xu

Tsinghua University, Beijing 100084, China
jymars@live.cn, yqxu@tsinghua.edu.cn

Abstract. Touch plays a significant role in emotion communication, and affective haptics are becoming an emerging field in terms of designing and implementing multimodal experience in human-computer interactions. The present study explores the affective haptics and multimodal experiments. By the literature review of human emotional feedback on haptic signal and affective haptic devices, the multimodal experiments were designed and implemented. Three types of haptic signals (random, vibration and stroking stimuli) are designed and implemented. The results demonstrated that haptic affective signals affect similar emotion in both the haptic only and visual-haptic multimodal scenario, and visual stimuli largely dominate the emotional state compared with haptic stimuli.

Keywords: Sense of touch · Emotion · Affective haptics · Multimodal experiments

1 Introduction

The sense of touch is our irreplaceable channel for daily communications. It provides not only well-recognized discriminative information to the human brain, but also an instinct and abundant affective input. Different types of social touch like shaking hands among friends, embracing the lover and the mother's caress convey different emotions. Touch is featured with abundant emotions which can largely affect users' emotion and experience.

With the development of science and technology, telecommunications have been upgraded from traditional mails to real-time phone calls, and even high-quality video face times. Meanwhile, it is expected to convey more affective information during communications. Therefore, mediated social touch is becoming a promising research field in recent years [1, 2]. Apart from the normal video and voice, the combination of the sense of touch offers a new level of multimodal immersive experience.

Past researches outline the multimodal interactions and a set of affective research guidelines [3], but limited work focuses on affective haptics in a multimodal scenario. In our daily life, most user rely on visual or audio channel as main communication methods, while using haptics to assist. Therefore, we need explore communicating emotion by haptics in a multimodal scenario.

© Springer Nature Switzerland AG 2020
M. Kurosu (Ed.): HCII 2020, LNCS 12182, pp. 380–391, 2020.
https://doi.org/10.1007/978-3-030-49062-1_26

It has been widely demonstrated that a gentle slow stroking signal brings pleasant feeling [4, 5], while a high intensity vibrating signal leads to unpleasant and aroused feeling. These findings, however, are proved only in a haptic only environment. In this paper, the present work explores the above affective haptic findings in a visual-haptic multimodal environment. In addition, we investigate whether there is any low intensity haptic stimulus that causes unpleasant or aroused feeling. In the rest of this paper, we present the background for our approach followed by methods and results from two experiments. More detailed findings are discussed, and we conclude the paper with potentials of haptics in a multimodal scenario.

2   Related Works

2.1   Affect Subjective Evaluation

People has complicated emotional activities. In the field of affective haptics, dimension evaluation is often used. Russell introduced "A Circumplex Modal of Affect" [6] in 1980, which put all human emotions into two dimensional plane rectangular coordinate system by "valance" and "arousal". As Fig. 1 shows.

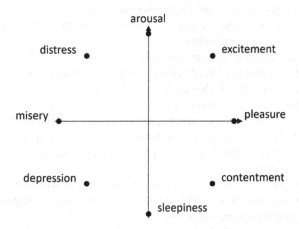

Fig. 1. A Circumplex Modal of Affect [6], redraw by authors

In this emotional model, X-axis stands for valence and Y-axis stands for arousal. both dimensions are linear. If the value is bigger, it will be farther away from the center point and reach deeper emotion. In contrast, if it is closer to the center point, it will be emotionally lower. The zero-point stands for human normal status. The four points between two coordinate axes in the Fig. 1 (Excitement, Contentment, Depression and Distress) are the common effect of valence-arousal. More detailed 15 emotions mapping see [7]. Thus, human emotion can reflect on a point in the valence-arousal space.

Circumplex model of affect is a concise, direct and effective emotional evaluation method. Compared to diversified classification of emotions, this model uses orthogonality of valence-arousal to establish emotional space. Besides, in terms of this model, some researchers have been trying to extent more dimensions apart from valence and arousal, including the dimension of "dominance" [8]. The experiment, however, showed that the dominance degree shows a certain correlation with the other dimensions, which is not supposed to be a third independent dimension. Therefore, most current emotional evaluation is mainly using valence-arousal method. Based on this evaluation method, any external signals can affect people and map the emotional state to a point in valence-arousal plane so as to establish a connection of physical signals and human emotional feedback.

Followed by this evaluation, the International Affective Picture System (IAPS) was designed and implemented by Lang et al., 2008 [9]. It is a set of emotionally evocative color photographs representing a wide variety of events and objects encountered in human experience that have been rated on dimensions of pleasure, arousal, and dominance by men and women. IAPS stimuli are widely used in studies of human emotion throughout the world [9]. For each emotion dimension, the score from 1 to 9 is defined as: 1-least and 9-most. In our study, we use IAPS as visual stimuli to conduct a visual-haptic multimodal scenario.

2.2 Affective Haptics

Many affective haptic devices and their experiments have demonstrated a strong link between human emotions and the sense of touch. Among those, "pleasant touch" and "aroused touch" are two main findings.

Line S. Loken revealed "pleasant touch sensations" in Nature Neuroscience, 2009, that during soft brush stroking, low-threshold unmyelinated mechanoreceptors(C-tactile) responded most vigorously, which were perceived by subjects as being the most pleasant [4]. It can be inferred that C-tactile afferents show positive correlation with pleasant sensation. Furthermore, C-tactile experiment discussed the relations between caressing speed and the degree of pleasant sensation. When the stroking speed of haptic signal received on the hairy skin is between 1–10 cm/s and the pressure force is low, the pleasant sensation feels strongest.

In contrast to pleasant touch, "aroused touch" aims to draw user's attention by strong, aroused touch sensations. It is usually created by a high intensity haptic signal, and it brings aroused, and unpleasant emotions.

With these neuroscience findings, many affective haptic devices have been designed and developed. They can create gentle, soft stroking movement on the skin, aiming to bring pleasant touch sensation to the human. In this field, Biamchi et al. explores a fabric-based softness display [10] and a novel fabric-based tactile display [11]. Both displays create "caress-like" haptic signals, make reciprocating movement on the skin and generate the affective sensation. They shared the results in common: the increase of tension led a higher pressure and the subject valence would decrease.

The above researches demonstrated the factors of affective touch in a touch only interaction basis. In this paper, we set up experiments in a visual-haptic scenario, trying to explore the affective haptics in a multimodal interaction basis.

3 Visual-Haptic Affective Study

In this section, two experiments were conducted in which participants experienced haptic vibrotactile stimuli as well as visual affective pictures. In the first experiment, participants experienced 7 vibrotactile signals including random, vibration and stroking sensations. In the second experiment, Half of the stimuli were conducted in a multimodal way in which both a haptic vibrotactile signal and a visual picture were presented simultaneously, the other half was by pictures only. Their subjective feedbacks by valence and arousal reveal that haptic stimuli were able to affect the participants' emotion.

3.1 Hypotheses

Based on the above literature review, we try to investigate the affective haptics in a multimodal interaction basis. Firstly, we believe haptic stimuli affect participants' emotion (hypotheses 1). Then we designed three types of haptic stimuli: random signal buzz signal and stroking signal, with several stimuli of different intensity in each type of signal. We infer: random signals convey unpleasant feeling (hypotheses 2), vibration signals convey aroused feeling (hypotheses 3), and stroking signals convey pleasant feeling (hypotheses 4). Last but not least, haptic affective signals affect similar emotion in both the haptic only and visual-haptic conditions (hypotheses 5).

H1: Haptic stimuli affect participants' emotion.
H2: Random signals convey unpleasant feeling.
H3: Vibration signals convey aroused feeling.
H4: Stroking signals convey pleasant feeling.
H5: Haptic affective signals affect similar emotion in both the haptic only and visual-haptic multimodal scenarios.

3.2 Apparatus

The experimental apparatus consisted of a 2-by-9 tactors array worn on the dorsal side of the participants' non-dominant forearm. The 18 tactors form 2 rows, with 9 tactors on each row that were evenly distributed along the direction of elbow to wrist. The center-to-center distance between each tactor was around 2.5 cm. A gauntlet was employed to keep all 18 tactors attached to the dorsal part of the forearm in the appropriate position. A wide-bandwidth tactor (Tectonic Elements, Model TEAX13C02-8/RH, Part #297-214, sourced from Parts Express International, Inc.) was employed as the actuator. It has a flat frequency response in the range 50 Hz to 2 kHz with a resonant peak close to 600 Hz. A MOTU 24Ao audio device (MOTU, Cambridge, MA, USA) was used for delivering 18 channels of audio waveforms to the 18 tactors through audio amplifiers. A Matlab program running on a desktop computer was made to generate the multi-channel waveforms corresponding to the haptic vibrotactile signals.

Meanwhile, the program interface (shown in Fig. 2) could show a picture from IAPS, as well as two scoring bars in terms of valence and arousal.

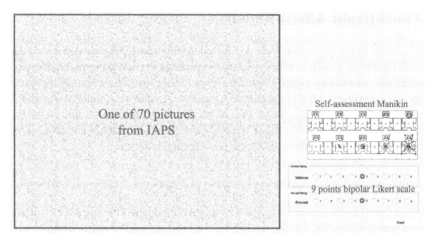

Fig. 2. Program interface of the multimodal experiments

3.3 Haptic and Visual Stimuli

Haptic Stimuli
According to the hypotheses, 7 haptic stimuli were divided into three groups (see Table 1). In group I, unpleasant feeling was sometimes related with "chaos" or "randomness", thus, we designed stimulus by randomizing location, frequency, duration and intensity levels. The 18 tactors activated one by one in a randomized order. The vibration frequency of each tactor was between 100–300 Hz. The vibration duration of each tactor was between 50–800 ms, and the duration of overall stimulus was 4 s. The vibration intensity of each tactor was between 16–25 dB above Sensation Level, short with dB SL, (Stimulus #1) and 26–35 dB SL (Stimulus #2). By doing this, we tried to simulate the chaotic and disordered feeling by haptics. Group II contains two vibratory signals. All tactors were activated at the same time with a 300 Hz vibration frequency and lasted for 500 ms. The vibration intensity was 20 dB SL (Stimulus #3) and 30 dB SL (Stimulus #4). Group III consisted of the pleasant stroking signals. Three stroking signals were designed using the tactile apparent motion theory [12], which could be applied to control the velocity and vibration intensity. For the 2 rows of tactors, the first column of 2 tactors near the wrist were activated firstly, followed by the second column of 2 tactors from the wrist, and so on. The vibration traveled from the wrist to the elbow, and the signals stopped after the ninth column of 2 tactors vibrated near the elbow. The vibration duration of each tactor was 600 ms and the SOA (Stimulus Onset Asynchrony) was 440 ms. Thus, the overall duration was $440 \times 8 + 600 = 4120$ ms, and the stroking velocity was around 5 cm/s. The vibration frequency was 100 Hz for the 3 signals in Group III, and the vibration intensity was 20 dB SL (Stimulus #5), 28 dB SL (Stimulus #6) and 36 dB SL (Stimulus #7).

Table 1. Summary of 7 haptic signals

Stimulus no.	Waveform	Frequency (Hz)	Overall duration (s)	Intensity (dB SL)
No. 1	Random	100–300	4 (50–800 ms each)	16–25
No. 2		100–300	4 (50–800 ms each)	26–35
No. 3	Vibration	300	0.5	20
No. 4		300	0.5	30
No. 5	Stroking	100	4.12	20
No. 6		100	4.12	28
No. 7		100	4.12	36

Visual Stimuli

Seventy pictures with affective ratings from the IAPS database were selected, forming 35 pairs. Each pair of pictures shared highly similar contents and affective scores in terms of valence and arousal according to the database. For example, 1040.jpg and 1114.jpg are both pictures about snake. Their valence scores are 3.99 and 4.03, and arousal scores are 6.25 and 6.33, which indicated that both pictures were unpleasant and aroused. Therefore, this pair of pictures was selected. Thirty-five pairs of affective pictures covered a large range of score from very unpleasant (1.90) to very pleasant (8.00), and very deactivated (2.67) to very aroused (7.29).

3.4 Participants

A total of 14 participants (7 females; age range 18–35 years old, 23.4 ± 5.2 years old) took part in the studies. All participants were right-handed with no known sensory or motor impairments. Subjects gave informed consent before testing, and the study was approved by a university internal review.

3.5 Procedure

The participant was seated in front of a table on which there was the tactile device, a computer together with a screen and a mouse. The participant wore the gauntlet on the left forearm to experience the tactile simulation. Meanwhile, the participant used the right hand to interact with the graphical interface by the mouse. The participant was instructed to maintain the same arm position and wore a noise-reduction earphone to prevent any sound to bias tactile perception during the whole experiment.

Experiment I

The participant experienced 7 haptic stimuli one by one without visual stimulus. Then based on the haptic only stimulus, participant was asked to use the VAS with 9 points bipolar Likert scale to log the response. The participant could try out the haptic signal as many times as he/she needs and change the VAS scale. After rating all 7 stimuli, the first experiment finished.

Experiment II

After experiencing 7 haptic stimuli, in experiment II, the participant turned to do the affective rating of the visual-haptic multimodal conditions. The experiment interface included two parts: one of the 70 pictures from IAPS, and the VAS with 9 points bipolar Likert scale as well as the SAM picture for the reference.

In terms of the pair between the pictures and haptic signals, the visual-haptic correlation needed decrease to minimum. In the first step, between each pair of pictures sharing similar emotional ratings, one was selected and it came with one of the seven haptic stimuli, and the other one was presented alone. Therefore, thirty-five pictures were selected to present with haptic stimulus, and the other 35 were presented alone. We also needed switch the sequence of each pair of pictures, making the first 35 pictures without haptic stimulus and the other pictures in visual-haptic condition. Thus, there are 2 alternatives for the selection of half of the 70 pictures. In the next step, 35 pairs of pictures were divided into 7 groups, with 5 pairs in each group. Each group was accompanied with one type of haptic stimulus. 7 haptic stimuli allowed for the 7 alternatives for each group to pair any different haptic stimuli. By these 2 steps, there were $2 \times 7 = 14$ alternatives for the pair of visual and haptic stimulus, and each alternative was corresponded with one participant. Lastly, the sequence these stimuli were randomized before presented to the participant.

After a visual-only stimulus or a multimodal visual-haptic stimulus, the participant was asked to use the VAS with 9 points bipolar Likert scale to log the response about the overall emotional state.

There were 70 stimuli in all. The total duration of the study was approximately 30 min for each participant.

4   Results

4.1   Experiment I: Haptic Stimuli Results

In terms of statistical analysis, One Sample T test was used and valence and arousal scores were compared with 5, meaning neutral state. A p value < 0.05 was also considered statistically significant.

In terms of the haptic only condition, for each haptic signal, the mean and stand deviation of the valence and arousal scores are presented in Fig. 3. One sample T test shows the statistical significance in arousal of Stimulus No. 1, valence of Stimulus No. 6, and valence and arousal of Stimulus No. 2, 4 and 7.

4.2   Visual-Haptic Multimodal Results

During the multimodal experiment, 70 valence and arousal scores were collected. Firstly, they were grouped by 35 pairs of pictures, one with haptic stimulus and one without. Secondly, in order to extract the effect of affective haptics, we calculated the subtraction

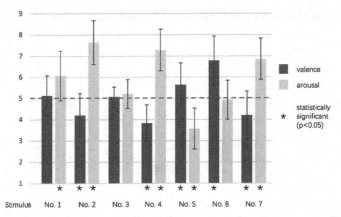

Fig. 3. Mean and stand deviation of the valence and arousal scores in haptic only condition

between the V-A scores with multimodal stimulus and the scores with visual only stimulus. Therefore, the plus number of the subtraction meant that the visual-haptic stimulus feels more pleasant or more aroused, while the negative number meant that the visual-haptic stimulus feels more unpleasant or more deactivated. For example, between a pair of pictures, the multimodal one had scores (6, 3) for valence and arousal, and the visual one had scores (4, 4). Thus, the subtraction (2, −1) meant that the employment of haptic signal tended to be more pleasant (degree of 2) and less aroused (degree of −1). Thirdly, each type of haptic signal was assigned to 5 pairs of stimuli, so there were 5 subtraction results for every haptic stimulus for each participant. Lastly, all the results of 14 participants were grouped by each haptic stimulus, and there were $14 \times 5 = 70$ subtraction results for every type of haptic signal.

In terms of statistical analysis, the One Sample T test was used. Theoretically, if the employment of haptic signal was not able to affect the participants' emotion, then the V-A scores of multimodal and visual only stimuli would be identical, so the subtraction results would be (0, 0). Therefore, we compared the 70 subtraction results with the number "0" in terms of valence and arousal for every type of haptic signal, and tried to investigate if the subtraction variance was significantly different with zero. A p value < 0.05 was considered statistically significant. Likewise, in the haptic only experiment, One Sample T test was used and valence and arousal scores were compared with 5. A p value < 0.05 was also considered statistically significant.

Random Signals Results

The subtraction mean and standard deviation ratings of valence and arousal for signal No. 1 and 2 are presented in Fig. 4. One sample T test shows the statistical significance in arousal of stimulus No. 1 and No. 2, It proves hypothesis 1 that the employment of haptic signal No. 1 and No. 2 is able to affect participants' emotion in arousal. The visual-haptic multimodal stimuli are more aroused than visual only pictures. The valence scores, however, do not have a statistically significant factor. With the increase of signal intensity, the valence scores tend to decrease. Although the valence of stimulus No. 2 is negative, it is the strong intensity that leads to the unpleasant feeling, showing that "disordered" signal pattern is not able to convey unpleasant feeling. Hypothesis 2 is not validated.

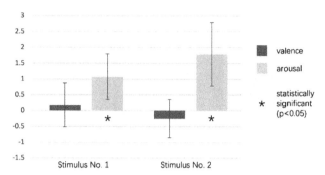

Fig. 4. Mean and stand deviation of the valence and arousal scores in multimodal condition, for random signals

Vibration Signals Results

The result scores of valence and arousal for stimulus No. 3 and 4 are illustrated in Fig. 5. One sample T test shows the statistical significance in arousal of stimulus No. 4. The valence scores of stimulus No. 4 are also below zero. In terms of stimulus No. 3, the light quick buzz signal does not affect the emotion a lot in both valence and arousal. It demonstrates that only the haptic signal intensity is strong enough that can convey aroused feeling. It is not corresponding with "vibration" pattern of signal. Hypothesis 3 is validated. Also, the strong arousing signal tend to feel unpleasant.

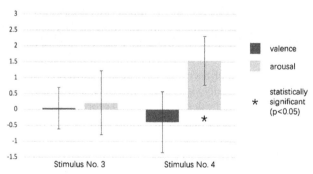

Fig. 5. Mean and stand deviation of the valence and arousal scores in multimodal condition, for vibration signals

Stroking Signals Results

The mean and standard deviation of ratings of valence and arousal for signal No. 5, 6 and 7 are shown in Fig. 6. One sample T test shows that the valence and arousal of stimulus

No. 6 are both statistically significant, so as the arousal of stimulus No. 7. As the signal intensity increases from No. 5, No. 6 to No. 7, the arousal increases from 0.14, 0.75 to 1.58. Meanwhile, the valence scores show a peak in stimulus No. 6, with the significant mean value of 0.53, while the other two scores are around 0. Stimulus No. 6 is the only signal that is statistically significant in valence among 7 stimuli. In terms of stimulus No. 7, the strong intensity spoils the pleasant stroking and leads to a negative valence. The "stroking" touch is able to convey pleasant feeling, and hypothesis 4 is validated.

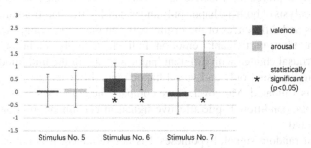

Fig. 6. Mean and stand deviation of the valence and arousal scores in multimodal condition, for stroking signals

Table 2 compares the mean scores between haptic only and multimodal results. If we assume that 5 is the default affective score, then the subtraction of 5 shows the haptic affective effect (4th column in Table 2). Then we compare with multimodal mean

Table 2. Comparison of haptic only mean and multimodal mean scores

Stimulus no	Valence/arousal	Haptic only mean	Haptic only mean - 5	Multimodal mean
No. 1	Valence	5.14	0.14	0.18
	Arousal	6.07	1.07	1.07
No. 2	Valence	4.21	−0.79	−0.25
	Arousal	7.64	2.64	1.78
No. 3	Valence	5.07	0.07	0.08
	Arousal	5.21	0.21	0.21
No. 4	Valence	3.84	−1.16	−0.39
	Arousal	7.28	2.28	1.53
No. 5	Valence	5.64	0.64	0.07
	Arousal	3.57	−0.43	0.14
No. 6	Valence	6.79	1.79	0.53
	Arousal	4.93	−0.07	0.75
No. 7	Valence	4.21	−0.79	−0.16
	Arousal	6.86	1.86	1.59

scores, and both experiment results follow the similar trend. Hypothesis 5 is validated. Moreover, some haptic only scores are more intense (further from 5) than multimodal mean scores. It indicates that in haptic only environment, participants' emotion is more easily affected by haptic signals than that in multimodal scenarios.

5   Discussions

The above study explored the affective haptics in the visual-haptic multimodal scenario. Quantitative analysis of both the haptic only and visual-haptic conditions are made. There are similarities and differences of the results between these two conditions. Firstly, the sense of touch affects participants' emotion. In the haptic only condition, the scores of valence and arousal change with different haptic signals. In the multimodal condition, the scores in most visual only and visual-haptic pairs differ in many cases. Therefore hypotheses 1 is validated. Moreover, if we compare the emotion scores in haptic only and visual-haptic condition, haptic affective signals affect similar emotion. Hypotheses 5 is also validated.

In terms of random signal, hypotheses 2 is not validated. It is not easy to convey unpleasant feeling by haptics with low or medium vibration intensity, neither in haptic only nor in multimodal condition. Vibration signal conveys aroused sensation in both conditions, and hypotheses 3 is validated. Lastly, stroking signal conveys pleasant and relatively unaroused in moth conditions, and hypotheses 4 is validated.

If we compare the emotional impacts from visual stimuli and haptic stimuli, it can be observed that visual stimuli largely dominate the emotional state. There is sometimes limited difference of emotional state with same visual picture and different haptic signals, but there are mostly huge changes of emotional state with same haptic signal and different visual pictures. It demonstrates the assistive role of multimodal interactions in terms of haptics.

6   Concluding Remarks

This paper explores the affective haptics and multimodal experiments. By the literature review of human emotional feedback on haptic signal and affective haptic devices, the multimodal experiments were designed and implemented. Three types of haptic signals (random, vibration and stroking stimuli) are designed and implemented. The results demonstrated that haptic affective signals affect similar emotion in both the haptic only and visual-haptic multimodal scenarios. Moreover, visual stimuli largely dominate the emotional state compared with haptic stimuli. Based on the physiological characteristics of human multimodal channels and emotional feedback, designers need to consider involving haptic signals as assistive role, and satisfy the user's emotional needs into the multimodal interaction scenario. Meanwhile, designers also need to refer to the state of the art of affective haptic devices, focus to the detailed interaction scenarios and real needs of the users to offer better affective experience.

Acknowledgments. This work was supported by the National Key Research and Development Plan under Grant No. 2016YFB1001402.

References

1. Van Erp, J.B., Jan, B.F., Toet, A.: Social touch in human–computer interaction. Front. Digit. Humanit. **2**, 2 (2015)
2. Smith, J., MacLean, K.: Communicating emotion through a haptic link: design space and methodology. Int. J. Hum. Comput. Stud. **65**(4), 376–387 (2007)
3. Eid, M.A., Al Osman, A.: Affective haptics: current research and future directions. IEEE Access **4**, 26–40 (2015)
4. Löken, L.S., Wessberg, J., McGlone, F., Olausson, H.: Coding of pleasant touch by unmyelinated afferents in humans. Nat. Neurosci. **12**(5), 547 (2009)
5. Huisman, G., Frederiks, A.D., van Erp, J.B.F., Heylen, D.K.J.: Simulating affective touch: using a vibrotactile array to generate pleasant stroking sensations. In: Bello, F., Kajimoto, H., Visell, Y. (eds.) EuroHaptics 2016. LNCS, vol. 9775, pp. 240–250. Springer, Cham (2016). https://doi.org/10.1007/978-3-319-42324-1_24
6. Russell, J.A.: A circumplex model of affect. J. Pers. Soc. Psychol. **39**(6), 1161 (1980)
7. Posner, J., Russell, J.A., Peterson, B.S.: The circumplex model of affect: an integrative approach to affective neuroscience, cognitive development, and psychopathology. Dev. Psychopathol. **17**(3), 715–734 (2005)
8. Demaree, H.A., Everhart, D.E., Youngstrom, E.A., Harrison, D.W.: Brain lateralization of emotional processing: historical roots and a future incorporating "dominance". Behav. Cogn. Neurosci. Rev. **4**(1), 3–20 (2005)
9. Lang, P.L.: International affective picture system (IAPS): affective ratings of pictures and instruction manual Technical report (2005)
10. Bianchi, M., Serio, A.: Design and characterization of a fabric-based softness display. IEEE Trans. Haptics **8**(2), 152–163 (2015)
11. Bianchi, M., et al.: Design and preliminary affective characterization of a novel fabric-based tactile display. In: 2014 IEEE Haptics Symposium (HAPTICS), pp. 591–596 (2014)
12. Israr, A., Poupyrev, I.: Tactile brush: drawing on skin with a tactile grid display. In: Proceedings of the SIGCHI Conference on Human Factors in Computing Systems, pp. 2019–2028 (2011)

Recent Multimodal Communication Methodologies in Phonology, Vision, and Touch

Chutisant Kerdvibulvech[(✉)]

Graduate School of Communication Arts and Management Innovation,
National Institute of Development Administration, 118 SeriThai Road, Klong-Chan,
Bangkapi, Bangkok 10240, Thailand
chutisant.ker@nida.ac.th

Abstract. Due to the innovation and technology's capacity in recent years, multimodal communication can help humans to communicate and interact in more basis senses simultaneously using technological innovations. However, there are still many difficulties and challenges for achieving the multimodal communication systems in phonology, vision, and touch. In this paper, we present recent multimodal communication methodologies in different aspects. To begin with, we review the multimodal communication systems in phonology, phonetics and light. Then, we investigate the multimodal communication works in vision using spatial augmented reality (SAR), computer vision, and interactive digital multimedia. Next, we introduce the multimodal communication researches in touch using haptic sensors and related-technological innovations. After that, we propose the qualitative research of the extended augmented reality and interactive experience-based system using use in-depth interviews. Our experimental results have revealed that the presented system works well and increases users' satisfaction levels. After examining the approaches for integrated multimodal communication in phonology, vision, and touch presented in recent years, we can understand the interactions of human with recent innovations.

Keywords: Multimodal communication · Hologram-like · Spatial augmented reality · Force jacket · Tjacket · Qualitative research · Augmented reality · Interactive experience · Data-driven

1 Multimodal Communication Methodologies

In recent years, multimodal communication is an extremely popular issue in computer science, computational linguistics, and neurosciences. This is because it can allow humans to communicate in more basic senses simultaneously and interactively using technological innovations. In this paper, we examine recent related-works about the multimodal communication in phonology, vision, and touch. This section is divided into three main subsections. To begin with, we introduce the multimodal communication methods through phonology, phonetics and light for communication development. Second, multimodal communication methods through vision, more specifically hologram-like,

© Springer Nature Switzerland AG 2020
M. Kurosu (Ed.): HCII 2020, LNCS 12182, pp. 392–400, 2020.
https://doi.org/10.1007/978-3-030-49062-1_27

are discussed for creating a myriad of new communication using mixed reality (particularly, augmented reality) and computer vision. Third, we examine the multimodal communication techniques through touch to help human in communication interactively.

Fig. 1. A markers-based system for deictic gestures and speech interaction was built by Stoltmann and Fuchs in [1].

1.1 Communication Through Phonology and Light

In this subsection, we introduce the multimodal communication methods through phonology, phonetics and light for communication development. An interesting work for communication through Polish counting-out rhymes using a motion capture system was presented by Stoltmann and Fuchs in [1]. In this work, the behavior of handedness during pointing gestures toward Polish counting-out rhymes from two different speeches is analyzed. The effect of speech rate in counting out rhymes for multimodal communication is then included using gesture coordination. Figure 1 shows their markers-based system when the user is using the Polish counting-out rhyme application with the bear doll as a human. The x, y and z time frames of the distinctive finger of the user is also displayed in Fig. 1 (above). This case is an index finger. The concept of this work is extended in [2] by Stoltmann et al. to investigate the impact of animacy of reference objects and spatial relation complexity in German language. This influences on the choice of frame of reference from forty-six native German speakers. However, the multimodal communication is beyond phonology. In the next subsection, we will describe the multimodal communication in vision. Furthermore, there was interestingly an immersive system, called IllumiRoom as built by Jones et al. from Microsoft Research in [3], that surrounds interactively a television with projected light. Therefore, this system can bring video games and film experiences both phonology and light out of the television screen into the physical world. In addition, an interactive interface, called Twinkle, was constructed by Yoshida et al. [4] for mixing a real surface virtually using a camera and a mobile projector. Therefore, this interface can show sounds and lights that are created from the motion of users and collisions of images with objects using an acceleration sensor. In addition, Yamaguchi et al. [5] built a physical contact support device, called Touch-Shake, which consists of a speaker, a capacitive sensor and a LED. Their aim is to support communication between people through phonology and light. In their system, they create lighting pattern of LEDs and sounds from the users' physical attributes, the users' body condition and how the user touches the other parts of their body. However, the multimodal communication is beyond phonology and light. In the next subsection, we will describe the multimodal communication in vision.

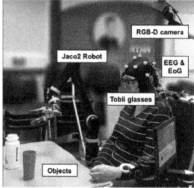

Fig. 2. AIDE system, developed by Ivorra et al. [10], includes a full-arm robotic exoskeleton, multimodal interfaces and context recognition sensors.

1.2 Communication Through Vision

In this subsection, multimodal communication methods through vision, more specifically hologram-like, are discussed for creating a myriad of new communication using augmented reality and computer vision. These methods include spatial augmented reality (SAR), unmanned aerial vehicle (UAV), and interactive digital multimedia. Spatial augmented reality mixes physical world objects and graphical scenes using portable projectors or mobile projectors, as discussed in [6] for object-centered interactions in real time, [7] for unsupervised ubiquitous projection to detect objects, [8] for supporting and designing complex physical environments, [9] for extraction of plane regions, and [10] for body cyberization and reaching unreachable world. For instance, more recently in 2018, the concept of the work for spatial augmented reality was presented in [11]. In this work, it investigates a method of how using spatial augmented reality can deal with the challenges and support user experiences of mobile-based augmented reality and mobile projectors. This work of the spatial augmented reality is aimed to be beneficial for both hardware design and software computing paradigm. Moreover, a computer vision-based assistive robotic system with an interactive multimodal human–computer interface was constructed in 2018 by Ivorra et al. [12]. In their system, they use the computer vision algorithms for developing within the AIDE European project by integrating the robotic system into electrooculography (EOG) and electroencephalography (EEG). The AIDE

European project includes Jaco2 Robot, multimodal interfaces and context recognition sensors. Figure 2 shows this vision-based assistive robotic system. Also, an augmented reality mobile application was built by Kerdvibulvech in [13] for helping pianists by using motion tracking and computer vision. Therefore, each hand of pianists can be tracked using the Microsoft Kinect. Similarly, there was also a research that uses a real-time mobile augmented reality tourist guide for cultural heritage, as proposed by Strelák et al. in [14]. They tested the real-time mobile augmented reality tourist guide system with thirty healthy volunteers both males and females equally. Interestingly, female users were more satisfied with the real-time mobile augmented reality tourist guide system compared to male users.

Furthermore, multimodal communication methods optically variable devices such as hologram-like is a unique way for creating a myriad of new communication. In the work of [15], as presented by Hartl et al., some of similarity measures for matching hologram-like patches was done using mobile augmented reality, so that it can give a sound basis for automatic decisions and verifications. By doing this, it can decrease capture time with more accurate decisions and verifications regarding the estimated samples than what is done by inexperienced users. Nevertheless, the multimodal communication is beyond phonology and vision. In the next subsection, we will explain the multimodal communication in touch (Fig. 3).

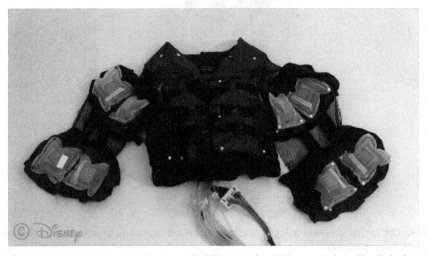

Fig. 3. A pneumatically actuated jacket, called Force Jacket [17], was designed by Delazio et al. who have worked at Disney Research and MIT for interactive touch.

1.3 Communication Through Touch

In this subsection, we discuss the multimodal communication methods through touch to help human in communication interactively. Data-driven multimodal communication is explained for generating and creating massive multimodal datasets, as described in [16] by Steen et al. Multimodal communication is deemed as a major, critical, and continuously active issue of human cognition through gesture, posture, and touch. For touch, a system, called SCALE, for load data from related-modules for determining interaction forcedly, including way of touching, was presented by Yoshida et al. [17] in 2019. The touch interaction includes both two dimensions and three dimensions using fingers and hands. However, the touch interaction can be applied in various organs, such as the full upper-body area. For example, in 2018, the Force Jacket was presented recently in [18] by Delazio et al. who have worked at Disney Research and MIT for touch communication. This vibration-based jacket is an array of force sensors and pneumatically actuated airbags focusing on the upper body parts. In their system, they investigate the pneumatic hardware and force control methods, and then they apply the vibration-based jacket into virtual reality systems. In addition, there was previously a similar research work based on integrated innovations of visual and touch communications, as presented in 2016 by Kerdvibulvech in [19]. In this work, a system is built for helping people who are handicapped to communicate affectingly to the people living in any location. This system uses two main devices: a hugging communication wearable device, called Tjacket, and a Google cardboard. In the next section of this paper, we will explain the extended work of this augmented reality and interactive experience-based system by conducting a sampling qualitative research.

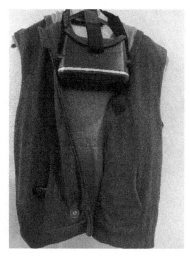

Fig. 4. Our extended system using augmented reality and interactive experience for conducting a qualitative experiment

2   The Extended Augmented Reality and Interactive Experience-Based System

We extend our augmented reality and interactive experience-based work for those who are not handicapped using the qualitative research. This research will conduct a qualitative experiment to assess the augmented reality and interactive experience-based work, as shown in Fig. 4.

2.1 Our Conceptual Framework

The purpose of this qualitative research is to measure and assess user satisfaction with the extended system. Figure 5 shows our conceptual framework using a sampling qualitative research. In our research work, the initial variables that is measured and tested are three main variables, as follows. The first initial variable is demographic characteristics of users. This is to examine whether users with different characteristics may result in different systems being satisfied or not. The second initial variable is equipment assembly characteristics. This is to examine if the assembling and installation of a smartphone and Tjacket (including other related devices) may result in different ways being satisfied by the user while running the system or not. The third initial variable is situation when using the system for communication. This is to examine whether the different situations when using the system may result in different satisfaction or not.

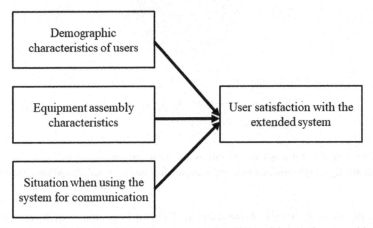

Fig. 5. Our conceptual framework of the augmented reality and interactive experience-based system for qualitative research

2.2 Our Experimental Results

In order to test the validity of our system, we use in-depth interviews in a sampling qualitative research for evaluating the user satisfaction with the extended system. The target groups for the experiment are three groups, which are youth groups at the primary and secondary levels (aged 6–15 years), a group of Master and Ph.D. students (ages 20–35 years) and senior working age groups (age 40–55 years). Based on the qualitative research that is quite similar to ours which was conducted by Anthony et al. [20] for twenty-four people, we use a sample of a total of twenty-four people, mixing between males and females randomly, to test our extended system. In our research, we divide into six main questions according to the research of Strelák et al.: ease of learning, satisfaction, adjustment to our system, intuitiveness, mental demand, and frustration. Also, we collect the overall user satisfaction. In order to measure the level of user satisfaction, we use a Likert scale that the scale contains five major options, which are "highest satisfaction, high satisfaction, neutral satisfaction, low satisfaction, and lowest satisfaction". Figure 6 depicts the results for overall user satisfaction with the extended system. Almost of half of the users give the high satisfaction for our system. Still, there is a very small number of users who give low satisfaction. Note that there is no user who gives the lowest satisfaction. The interview as a data collect method can be summarized as follows.

Fig. 6. The experimental result for overall user satisfaction containing five important options: highest satisfaction, high satisfaction, neutral satisfaction, low satisfaction, and lowest satisfaction.

Overall, more than half of the users feel that it is a great tool to communicate affectingly and visually to the people living in any location. Many users gave positive feedbacks. They found the extended system using augmented reality and interactive experience quite easy to understand how to use and intuitive. In terms of user satisfactions, users feel that the extended system can allow two sides who may live different locations to connect easier, so that it can help reduce the logistic cost of transportation between two sides. Specifically, it is good to use this extended system in the cities with the worst traffic in many parts of the world, such as Bangkok, New York and Jakarta. Moreover, it can simulate the feeling of a virtual hug with augmented reality information to calm and soothe the nerves of those, especially in youth groups, who are anxious and stressed when they are not with their loved ones, such as their parents or their babysitters.

However, according to the results, some users pointed out that there are several disadvantages using this system. This is because, although multimodal communication methodologies and recent technologies of augmented reality and interactive experience can connect people to people closer in many dimensions, it still cannot beat the face-to-face communication. This is face-to-face interaction can explore all five basic senses of human being: hearing, sight, touch, smell, and taste. Besides, the augmented reality and touch communication devices sometimes do not work synchronously. This can make the users cannot perfectly communicate. What's more, in term of gender differences, female users were majorly more satisfied with the extended system compared to male users. According to the investigation conducted by Wang et al. from Facebook Research and Carnegie Mellon University in [21], it suggested that female users of Facebook tend to post and share more personal topics, such as relationships, family matters and birthday. On the other hand, male users of their platform usually make a discussion on more abstract issues and deep thoughts, such as politics, sports, and Christianity. In this way, if we imply that our extended augmented reality and interactive experience-based system is more about relationships, such as touch and visual communications for their loved ones, our experimental results agree well with their study in the issue of gender.

3 Conclusion and Future Direction

This paper has introduced multimodal communication which is an extremely popular issue in recent years for human-computer interaction as it is able to allow humans to communicate in more basis senses simultaneously and interactively using technological innovations. To begin with, we review the multimodal communication in each sense, including phonology/phonetics/light, vision, and touch. There are some systems that use the mixed senses of multimodal communication between phonology/phonetics/light, vision, and touch in different manners. After that, we present and discuss the qualitative research of the extended augmented reality and interactive experience-based system using in-depth interviews for evaluating the user satisfaction with the system. Our experimental results have revealed that the extended system increases positively users' satisfaction levels. Several suggestions have been also given and discussed. We believe that multimodal communication in phonology, vision, and touch would expand the communication beyond language or any existing types of human communication, especially when working together simultaneously at the same time. We suggest that the future direction is build a system that can work with multimodal communication between more than two people or more than two parties (such as, three parties or group video conference) at the same time, it could help the interactions of human with recent innovations more effectively.

Acknowledgments. This research presented herein was partially supported by a research grant from the Research Center, NIDA (National Institute of Development Administration).

References

1. Stoltmann K., Fuchs S.: The influence of handedness and pointing direction on deictic gestures and speech interaction: evidence from motion capture data on Polish counting-out rhymes. In: Proceedings of the International Conference on Audio-Visual Speech Processing (AVSP), Stockholm, Sweden, 25–26 Aug 2017
2. Stoltmann, K., Fuchs, S., Krifka, M.: The influence of animacy and spatial relation complexity on the choice of frame of reference in German. In: Creem-Regehr, S., Schöning, J., Klippel, A. (eds.) Spatial Cognition 2018. LNCS (LNAI), vol. 11034, pp. 119–133. Springer, Cham (2018). https://doi.org/10.1007/978-3-319-96385-3_9

3. Jones, B.R., Benko, H., Ofek, E., Wilson, A.D.: IllumiRoom: immersive experiences beyond the TV screen. Commun. ACM **58**(6), 93–100 (2015)
4. Yoshida, T., Hirobe, Y., Nii H., Kawakami, N., Tachi, S.: Twinkle: interacting with physical surfaces using handheld projector. In: VR 2010, pp. 87–90 (2010)
5. Yamaguchi, Y., Yanagi, H., Takegawa, Y.: Touch-shake: design and implementation of a physical contact support device for face-to-face communication. In: IEEE 2nd Global Conference on Consumer Electronics (GCCE), INSPEC Accession Number: 13914655, 1–4 October 2013
6. Siriborvornratanakul, T., Sugimoto, M.: Portable projector extended for object-centered real-time interactions. In: Conference for Visual Media Production, pp. 118–126 (2009)
7. Siriborvornratanakul, T., Sugimoto, M.: Multiscale visual object detection for unsupervised ubiquitous projection based on a portable projector-camera system. In: International Conference on Digital Image Computing Techniques and Applications (DICTA), pp. 623–628 (2010)
8. Thomas, B.H., et al.: Spatial augmented reality support for design of complex physical environments. In: PerCom Workshops 2011, pp. 588–593 (2011)
9. Sano, M., Matsumoto, K., Thomas, B.H., Saito, H.: Rubix dynamic spatial augmented reality by extraction of plane regions with a RGB-D camera. In: ISMAR 2015, pp. 148–151 (2015)
10. Ueda, Y., Asai, Y., Enomoto, R., Wang, K., Iwai, D., Sato, K.: Body cyberization by spatial augmented reality for reaching unreachable world. In: AH 2017, pp. 1–9 (2017)
11. Siriborvornratanakul, T.: Enhancing user experiences of mobile-based augmented reality via spatial augmented reality: designs and architectures of projector-camera devices. In: The Advances in Multimedia (MM), pp. 8194726:1–8194726:17 (2018)
12. Ivorra, E., et al.: Intelligent multimodal framework for human assistive robotics based on computer vision algorithms. Sensors **18**(8), 2408 (2018)
13. Kerdvibulvech, C.: An innovative real-time mobile augmented reality application in arts. In: De Paolis, L.T., Bourdot, P., Mongelli, A. (eds.) AVR 2017. LNCS, vol. 10325, pp. 251–260. Springer, Cham (2017). https://doi.org/10.1007/978-3-319-60928-7_22
14. Strelák, D., Skola, F., Liarokapis, F.: Examining user experiences in a mobile augmented reality tourist guide. In: PETRA 2016, p. 19 (2016)
15. Hartl, A.D., Arth, C., Grubert, J., Schmalstieg, D.: Efficient verification of holograms using mobile augmented reality. IEEE Trans. Vis. Comput. Graph **22**(7), 1843–1851 (2016)
16. Francis, F., et al.: Toward an infrastructure for data-driven multimodal communication research. Linguist. Vanguard **4**(1) (2018)
17. Yoshida, T., Shen, X., Yoshino, K., Nakagaki, K., Ishii, H.: SCALE Enhancing force-based interaction by processing load data from load sensitive modules. In: UIST 2019, pp. 901–911 (2019)
18. Delazio, A., Nakagaki, K., Klatzky, R.L., Hudson, S.E., Lehman, J.F., Sample, A.P.: Force jacket pneumatically-actuated jacket for embodied haptic experiences. In: Proceedings of the 2018 CHI Conference on Human Factors in Computing Systems (CHI 2018), Montreal, QC, Canada, 21–26 April 2018. Paper no. 320
19. Kerdvibulvech, C.: A novel integrated system of visual communication and touch technology for people with disabilities. In: Gervasi, O., et al. (eds.) ICCSA 2016. LNCS, vol. 9787, pp. 509–518. Springer, Cham (2016). https://doi.org/10.1007/978-3-319-42108-7_39
20. Anthony, L., Stofer, K.A., Luc, A., Wobbrock, J.O.: Gestures by children and adults on touch tables and touch walls in a public science center. In: Proceedings of the 15th International Conference on Interaction Design and Children (IDC), Manchester, United Kingdom, pp. 344–355, 21–34 June 2016
21. Wang, Y.C., Burke, M., Kraut, R.E.: Gender, topic, and audience response an analysis of user-generated content on facebook. In: Proceedings of the SIGCHI Conference on Human Factors in Computing Systems, CHI 2013, pp. 31–34 (2013). ISBN 978-1-4503-1899-0

A Framework of Input Devices to Support Designing Composite Wearable Computers

Ahmed S. Khalaf[1]([✉]), Sultan A. Alharthi[1], Bill Hamilton[2], Igor Dolgov[3], Son Tran[2], and Phoebe O. Toups Dugas[1]

[1] Play and Interactive Experiences for Learning Lab, Computer Science Department, New Mexico State University, Las Cruces, NM, USA
khalaf@nmsu.edu, phoebe.toups.dugas@acm.org
[2] Computer Science Department, New Mexico State University, Las Cruces, NM, USA
[3] Psychology Department, New Mexico State University, Las Cruces, NM, USA

Abstract. Composite wearable computers combine multiple wearable devices to form a cohesive whole. Designing these complex systems and integrating devices to effectively leverage their affordances is nontrivial. To inform the design of composite wearable computers, we undertook a grounded theory analysis of 84 wearable input devices drawing from 197 data sources, including technical specifications, research papers, and instructional videos. The resulting prescriptive design framework consists of four axes: TYPE OF INTERACTIVITY, ASSOCIATED OUTPUT MODALITIES, MOBILITY, and BODY LOCATION. This framework informs a composition-based approach to the design of wearable computers, enabling designers to identify which devices fill particular user needs and design constraints. Using this framework, designers can understand the relationship between the wearable, the user, and the environment, identify limitations in available wearable devices, and gain insights into how to address design challenges developers will likely encounter.

Keywords: Wearable input devices · Wearables · Design · Framework

1 Introduction

Advances in mobile and ubiquitous technologies have opened countless possibilities for the growth of wearable computers. To do research and prototype new systems, and in contrast to off-the-shelf devices, *composite wearables* are assembled from multiple sensors (e.g., GPS, magnetometers), effectors (e.g., haptics), and potentially integrated devices (e.g., head-mounted displays, smart watches, rings) to accomplish tasks and provide contextual support. However, designing

---

Electronic supplementary material The online version of this chapter (https://doi.org/10.1007/978-3-030-49062-128) contains supplementary material, which is available to authorized users..

© Springer Nature Switzerland AG 2020
M. Kurosu (Ed.): HCII 2020, LNCS 12182, pp. 401–427, 2020.
https://doi.org/10.1007/978-3-030-49062-1_28

such complex systems and integrating devices in a meaningful way is not an easy task for wearable designers. Designers need to be able to select the right components for a composite wearable to provide the necessary UI inputs and feedback mechanisms, while remaining compatible (e.g., fit on different body parts, can be used simultaneously when needed, operate on the same platform). While prior research has focused on the design of purpose-built systems and frameworks that support ergonomics [13,112], and identify design principles for wearable UIs [31,46,115], they do not guide how these devices can be selected, how they are worn, and how the selection provides specific affordances and constraints to the wearer. Further, feedback devices have been studied previously (e.g., visual [65,88], haptic [74], auditory [83]), yet input devices have not been fully explored.

To address this gap in the literature, the present research develops a design framework for input devices for *composite wearable computers*. Through this framework, designers can select appropriate wearable input devices for their intended systems. The framework guides wearable system designers through the process of selecting a wearable input device or a set of wearable input devices upon which they can build their systems. We pose the following research questions:

RQ1: What wearable input devices are presently available?
RQ2: What capabilities can existing input devices provide?
RQ3: What devices are compatible with each other on the body of a single user?

To answer these questions, we use grounded theory to analyze wearable input devices, their documentation, and studies using them, creating a prescriptive design framework. The resulting framework contains four axes: TYPE OF INTERACTIVITY, ASSOCIATED OUTPUT MODALITIES, MOBILITY, and BODY LOCATION, which can be used to guide designers in making choices on how to build composite wearable computers. We develop practical guidance through a set of design scenarios, a *how-to guide*, to help designers with the essential components on how to use the framework to build composite wearable system that supports the intended task. We address key issues designers must consider when composing wearable computers, including supported interaction, impact on mobility, and human anatomy. We also shed light on issues of comfort, aesthetics, and social acceptance of wearable computers.

2   Background

We synthesize background on wearable technologies, input modalities, motion and gesture interfaces, and prior studies on wearable devices.

2.1   Wearable Technologies

Wearable computers can be equipped on various locations on a person's body [10,59,97]. These devices establish constant interaction between the environment and the user and often form their a network of intercommunicating effectors and sensors. Wearable input devices vary widely in terms of how they acquire input from a user. Some include mini-QWERTY keyboards or virtual keyboards and pointing devices, mimicking desktop designs, but wearables open up a range of possibilities for full-body interaction and sensor-based, context-aware designs [11]. When visual output is needed, a number of interfaces exist, including full-color, high-resolution head-mounted displays (HMDs); monochrome low-resolution HMDs; and wrist-worn displays. Auditory and haptic feedback are also possible. A key concern in wearable design centers on mobility.

Interaction with wearable computers can be explicit or implicit [84,85]. Explicit interaction involves manipulating a UI directly, yet wearables can also recognize user actions and behaviors, and implicitly interpret them as inputs, which are integrated within the user's primary task. This implicit interaction with the wearable system allows the integration to be natural, enhancing efficiency and mobility [84].

Wearable computers can supply context-sensitive support, which reduces the need for direct interaction [60]. These devices collect information about the physical, emotional, and environmental state of the wearer, making use of awareness of a user's context [1]. For example, with a position sensor (e.g., Global Positioning System (GPS)), constant location information of the wearer can be collected and presented to the user via different output modalities, helping the user maintain situation awareness [19,24,42,80,116].

Seams are the ways in which wearables (and similar technologies) break due to inevitable failures of sensors, networks, effectors, etc. [14,70]. Seamless interaction makes seams invisible for the user, and integrated into their surroundings [108]. Seamful design, on the other hand, argues for making users aware of the technology and its constraints, going as far as to integrate it into the experience [14].

2.2 Prior Wearable Devices Studies

While prior studies investigated how these wearable computers can be designed, worn, or used [31,89,115], the present study provides an in-depth analysis of wearable input devices and investigate the best way these devices can be selected and composed to design wearable computing systems. We highlight some of this prior work here.

The wearIT@work project aimed to use wearable computing technology to support workers. The project focused on wearable computing in emergency response, healthcare, car production, and aircraft maintenance by combining multiple wearable devices [58].

Shilkrot et al. [89] conducted a comprehensive survey on existing finger-worn devices. They classified finger-worn devices based on five components: *input* and *output* modalities, *action of the devices*, *application domain*, and *form factor*. This prior study focuses on wearable computing devices worn on fingers, while the present research encompasses various wearable input devices that can be worn on different parts of the body, incorporating the prior findings.

Kosmalla et al. [51] concentrated on wearable devices for rock climbing. The authors conducted an online survey to determine the most suitable body location for wearables and evaluated notification channels. Based on the survey results, the authors developed ClimbAware to test real-time on-body notifications for climbers; it combined voice recognition and tactile feedback to enable climbers to track progress.

Along with the variety of input modalities and domains of wearable devices, their size and form are highly variable, ranging from head-mounted devices to smartwatches and smart rings. Weigel and Steimle [107] examined input techniques used in wearable devices, focusing on devices that have small input surfaces (e.g., smartwatches). The researchers developed DeformWear, a small wearable device that incorporates a set of novel input methods to support a wide range of functions.

While the present research supports designers in building composite wearable systems that combine one or more wearable input devices, prior studies have proposed design guidelines for commercial wearable device developers to design better products. Gemperle et al. [31] provided design guidelines for developers to understand how body locations can affect wearable technology. Based on those guidelines, Zeagler [115] investigated the body locations on which to place wearables and updated the guidelines. The author discussed where biometric sensors can be placed in wearable devices and in which part of the body they should be worn to maximize accuracy.

Although all of these studies provide insights into the design and development of wearable devices, they do not focus on how designers can compose a wearable system, what considerations they need to take into account, and the advantages and disadvantages of devices. The present research focuses on wearable input modalities and proposes a universal framework for guiding the selection of devices and composition of wearable systems.

3   Grounded Theory Methodology

We conducted a qualitative study of wearable input devices to identify their characteristics and propose a framework to guide the selection and composition of such devices. *Grounded theory* is a set of research practices for exploring and characterizing a domain [33–35]. The practices include an iterative process of collecting data, analyzing the data, reviewing relevant literature, and reporting findings [43]. The type of data used in a grounded theory approach can be derived from many sources, including scientific papers, video games, video recordings, and survey data [20]. Our approach started with finding and selecting wearable input devices; then performing open coding to identify the initial concepts, categories, and their associated features; then gradually building these up into axial codes that form a framework.

Grounded theory begins with an iterative process of data gathering and analysis. *Open coding* involves applying labels to the collected data to identify what is different or unique, forming initial concepts. Undertaking open coding on each piece of data collected provides insights into the studied phenomenon and can benefit the following round of collection and analysis [34]. *Concepts* are created by identifying and grouping codes that relate to a common theme [3]. *Axial coding* is performed by recognizing relationships among the open codes and initial concepts, which results in the initial categories. *Selective coding* integrates the categories to form a core category that describes the data. Through this iterative process, which repeats the above steps until no new insights are gained, a theory emerges, which can then be applied to new data.

One researcher collected data and created a preliminary coding scheme. Based on the collected data, two researchers developed an open coding structure for the collected data to analyze the main features of each device. We collectively developed axial codes from the open codes, followed by selective coding, which produced the final dimensions for the framework.

3.1 Data Collection Strategy

Our iterative process started with finding wearable input devices from three sources: Pacific Northwest National Laboratory (PNNL) reports[1], the ACM Digital Library (DL)[2], and the IEEE Xplore Digital Library (Xplore)[3], followed by collecting data on each of the discovered wearable devices.

Our focus is on devices that enable the user to input data directly, not those that sample activities, because our interest is in how people build interactive systems. For example, we include devices that provide air-based gestures (e.g., Logbar Ring [57]), but exclude those that focus on tracking the user's activities and provide physiological data (e.g., fitbit[4]). We note that we also include devices that could primarily be considered output devices, e.g., Google Glass [36] or the HTC Vive [103]. These devices also provide input modalities that could serve as a primary input mechanism for composite wearable systems.

In the remainder of this section, we describe our method for searching and selecting wearable input devices and their data.

Selecting Wearable Input Devices. To find existing wearable input devices, addressing RQ1, we searched for specialized journals that focus on wearable devices and sought out research papers on the subject.

A starting point was *Responder Technology Alert*, a journal prepared for the US Department of Homeland Security Science and Technology Directorate that specializes in wearables. We used *Responder Technology Alert* to seed our devices list; in its nine issues (2015–2016), we found 36 devices.

To ensure a comprehensive list of input devices, we identified research papers in the wearables space. We focused on items published via the ACM Conference on Human Factors in Computing Systems (CHI), the International Conference

---

[1] Pacific Northwest National Laboratory: http://www.pnnl.gov.

[2] ACM DL: http://dl.acm.org.

[3] IEEE Xplore: http://ieeexplore.ieee.org.

[4] A wrist-worn fitness tracker: https://www.fitbit.com/home.

on Ubiquitous Computing (UbiComp), and International Symposium on Wearable Computers (ISWC). It is worth noting that in 2014 UbiComp and ISWC merged. To capture relevant papers, we developed search strings (note that for IEEE Xplore, "publication number" captures conference and year):

ACM DL: CHI search string:
```
''query'':recordAbstract:(+wearable+input+devices)
''filter'':owners.owner=HOSTED, series.seriesAbbr=CHI
```

ACM DL: UbiComp search string:
```
''query'':recordAbstract:(+wearable+input+devices)
''filter'':owners.owner=HOSTED, series.seriesAbbr=UbiComp
```

IEEE Xplore: ISWC search string:
```
((((''Abstract'':wearable) AND ''Abstract'':input) AND
''Abstract'':devices) AND ((((((((((((((((p_Publication_Number:6242775)
OR ''Publication Number'':5958741) OR ''Publication Number'':5648406)
OR ''Publication Number'':5254639) OR ''Publication Number'':4840596)
OR ''Publication Number'':4373753) OR ''Publication Number'':4067707)
OR ''Publication Number'':10396) OR ''Publication Number'':9419)
OR ''Publication Number'':8796) OR ''Publication Number'':8353) OR
''Publication Number'':7613) OR ''Publication Number'':7125) OR
''Publication Number'':6542) OR ''Publication Number'':5898) OR
''Publication Number'':4968))
```

The resulting search identified 70 total research papers. 37 studies from CHI (1997–2017), 18 studies from UbiComp (2014–2016), and 15 studies from ISWC (1997–2012). Out of these papers we found 31 wearable input devices.

To maximize the list, we added an additional 17 devices. These devices are selected based on our prior knowledge of wearables, or were found while looking for data for other wearable devices. The process identified 84 unique wearable input devices to include in the analysis; Fig. 1 visualizes this.

Finding Data About Selected Devices. After creating the list of 84 wearable input devices, we sought data on each device's capabilities and uses. For each device, we collected as much data as possible from the following:

- research papers that made use of the device (e.g., projects that built a system with it, frameworks that described it);
- technical specifications from commercial web sites;
- device manuals;
- online videos explaining how to use the device (e.g., manufacturer's instructional videos, enthusiast reviews);
- news articles describing the device; and
- first-hand experience of working with the device in the lab.

Each device had multiple data sources (though not necessarily every one in the above list). The combination of data sources enabled the team to build a complex profile for each device.

Using *ATLAS.ti Mac*[5], a software package for performing qualitative data analysis, each data source was linked to one or more devices in a network data structure (see Figure 2 for an example of one device in the workspace). In addition, we maintained a shared spreadsheet to record details. This process resulted in a profile for each device.

3.2 Analysis Procedure

Our analysis involved several phases (Fig. 1) which served to characterize the device space and address RQ2 and RQ3:

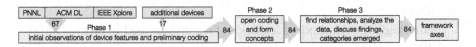

Fig. 1. The grounded theory process starting with searching and collecting wearable devices, initial observations on devices features, open coding, analyzing and forming the initial concepts, and creating the framework axes. Numbers on arrows indicate number of devices.

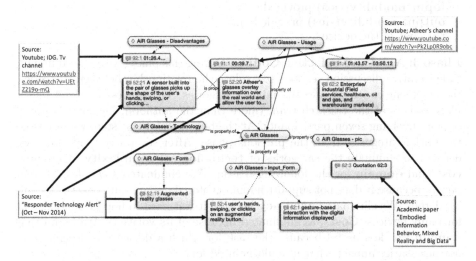

Fig. 2. Example network of data for the Atheer Air Glasses technology. Other devices in the corpus have similar entries.

---

[5] http://atlasti.com/product/mac-os-edition/.

Phase 1: Initial Observations of Device Features. The primary goal of this phase was to identify the capabilities of each device, its range of expressiveness, and what it might be used for. For each device, we identified the following:

- the technologies with which it was constructed (e.g., accelerometers in the Nod Ring [71] or electromyography (EMG) sensing in Myo armband [69]);
- the form factor of the device and where it is worn; and
- the application domain of the device.

In this step, we augmented the data we had stored in ATLAS.ti, adding detail for each device. We used the application to import all data that we collected and to create a preliminary coding system to label device features.

Phase 2: Open Coding on Collected Data. In this step, two researchers began developing codes to classify devices, independently reading through the device network in ATLAS.ti and identifying keywords in device descriptions and data sources. Through this process, an initial set of categories emerged about each device:

- **technological complexity**: sensors and algorithms used to provide interactivity;
- the **accuracy** of the device in recognizing human input and/or context;
- the **body location(s)** occupied by wearing;
- **body part(s) needed for manipulation**;
- **number of body part(s)** involved in typical use;
- application **domain** for which the device was designed;
- freedom of **mobility** enabled;
- **input modality(-ies)** provided;
- **output modality(-ies)** provided; and
- the **cost** of the device.

Phase 3: Axial and Selective Coding. During this phase, we engaged in multiple iterative discussion sessions to explore the relationship between the codes, the emergent concepts, and the initial categories. The process involved multiple members of the research team (more than the authors), including a group session involving seven participants. At the beginning of this step, we discussed the initial categories from the previous phase. After several conversations, we decided to eliminate the categories of **technological complexity, accuracy, cost**, and **domain** for the following reasons. We eliminated *technological complexity* because it does not support human-centered design, but concerns technical details. We eliminated **accuracy** because it was hard to find or non-existent for many devices. **Cost** was eliminated because of its volatility. We found that **domain** was less useful because the task for which a device was designed did not necessarily impact what it could be used for.

We revised the remaining categories: **input modalities** became the TYPE OF INTERACTIVITY axis, **mobility** became the MOBILITY axis, and **output modalities** became the ASSOCIATED OUTPUT MODALITY axis. In addition, we merged certain categories, so **body locations, body parts needed for manipulation**, and **number of body parts** were combined into the BODY LOCATION axis. The result of this phase is a set of axes for our framework.

4   Framework Overview

To guide the reader, this section provides a short summary of the framework; the next is a detailed description of each of the framework axes, along with examples. Our framework of wearable input devices contains four axes: TYPE OF INTERACTIVITY, ASSOCIATED OUTPUT MODALITIES, MOBILITY, and BODY LOCATION (Fig. 3). The axes provide significant information about each wearable device which helps the designers to build composite wearable computers.

4.1   Axis: Type of Interactivity

We define the interactivity axis as the input modality or modalities through which the user expresses intent. TYPE OF INTERACTIVITY considers how a user may invoke action (e.g., speaking, gesturing, clicking, touching). For the TYPE OF INTERACTIVITY axis a device may have multiple modalities (e.g., a device that enables both speaking and gesturing) and so may exist at multiple points on the axis. We expect that as developers consider composing together devices they will identify which types of interactivity they need to support in their applications. They can then consult the framework to identify which device, or combination of devices, is necessary.

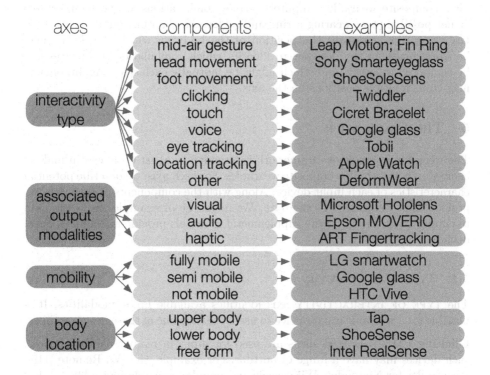

Fig. 3. Visual representation of framework axes and example devices.

4.2   Axis: Associated Output Modalities

Some wearable input devices also incorporate output modalities. ASSOCIATED OUTPUT MODALITIES considers how the device might provide output or feedback in a composite wearable system. For the ASSOCIATED OUTPUT MODALITIES axis a device may have multiple modalities (e.g., a device that provides visual and audio feedback). Designers should select the wearable input devices with associated output modalities that meets their design requirements.

4.3   Axis: Mobility

Some wearable devices inhibit movement, due to fragility, restricting user situation awareness, or requirements, such as sensors, that limit where they work. MOBILITY considers the freedom of movement that is provided by each wearable device in the list: fully mobile, partially mobile, or not mobile.

4.4   Axis: Body Location

Wearable devices come in many forms and fit different parts of the body: for example, devices worn on the head (e.g., glasses), hand(s) (e.g., gloves, rings), and wrist(s) (e.g., watches). While we expect users to equip multiple wearables for a composite wearable computer, certain combinations are not comfortable or not possible (e.g., wearing a ring and a glove on the same hand). The BODY LOCATION axis addresses the position of the body on which the device may be worn, enabling the designer to identify which combinations of devices can be composed together (and which might be mutually exclusive). Again, devices may cover multiple positions on the axis.

5   The Framework

The wearable input device framework is intended to assist designers in making choices on how to build composite wearables. For each axis, we describe potential characteristics of each input device. Along with the components of each axis, we provide their percentage in the data. We make use of examples from the data to support each category; the supplemental materials provide a complete list of devices.

5.1   Type of Interactivity

The TYPE OF INTERACTIVITY axis identifies available input modalities. It is possible for a wearable input device to use more than one of these input methods.

Clicking (21%). Button clicks are used for input in many wearable devices; such devices may have a range of buttons. For example, the Wii Remote [110], a controller for Nintendo's Wii console and popular research device [38,86], has nine buttons.

Touch (46%). Similar to clicking, touch is used by numerous wearable computing devices. We can divide touch input to two types: 'touch on device' and 'touch on surface'. 'Touch on device' depends on different types of touch sensors (e.g., resistive, capacitive sensing) [61]. The user can perform a touch gesture on a touchscreen (e.g., smartphones, smartwatches) or on a trackpad (e.g., Genius Ring Mouse [40]).

Other wearable technologies make use of the 'touch on surface' technique, in which the user touches something that is not the device: skin, nearby surfaces, etc. For instance, Laput et al. [52] proposed Skin Buttons, a small, touch-sensitive projector that uses IR sensors that can be integrated into another device such as a smartwatch; this device use a laser projector to display icons on the user's skin. Other wearable devices, such as Tap [98], use embedded sensors to monitor mechanical data of the hand and fingers, which can be used to detect the user's hand moving or tapping on a surface.

Voice (24%). Using voice for input in wearable devices is an attractive option because it is a natural UI [94]. Voice input is employed in some wearable devices by using an embedded microphone. For instance, users of Oculus Rift [73] can use their voices to perform certain functions such as searching for or opening an application. Another example is Google Glass [36], where the user's voice can be used to make a call or write and send a message. A downside of voice is that it may not work well in noisy environments [18].

Mid-Air Gesture Interaction (51%). Hand gestures are widely used in wearable technologies. Hand gestures can be classified into two categories: dynamic and static [30]. A dynamic gesture comprises the movement of the hand, arm, or fingers during the elapsed time (e.g., waving or writing in the air), whereas a static gesture involves the hand remaining in a certain posture during the elapsed time (e.g., fist gesture or open-hand gesture) [81]. To detect a mid-air gesture, several technologies, including infrared sensors, inertial measurement units, or EMG, can be used. For example, the Myo armband [69] uses EMG and and inertial measurement units to detect the hand gesture. Many wearable devices in the list can be used to detect hand gesture such as Logbar ring [57], Nod ring [71], and Leap Motion [53].

Foot Movement (5%). Some devices employ foot movement as an input method for wearable computing. For instance, Matthies et al. [62] developed ShoeSoleSense, a wearable device that uses foot movement as an input technique for AR and VR applications. Also, Benavides et al. [12], proposed KickSoul, a wearable device in an insole form that detects foot movement to enable the user to interact with digital devices. Fukahori et al. [29] proposed a plantar-flexion-based gesture device that can be used to control other foot movement computing technology.

Head Movement (11%). Head movement is used as an input modality for wearable technologies. Some wearable devices (HMD and headset) contain a head tracker, which usually consists of gyroscopes, accelerometers, magnetometers, and orientation sensors. When the wearer changes the orientation or the position of their head, the tracker can update the display or respond in other ways. For example, the Oculus Rift DK2 uses this data to update visual information on the VR HMD [109]. VR glasses such as HTC Vive [103]; and AR glasses such AiR Glasses [6] can be used to detect head movement.

Eye Tracking (5%). Eye trackers measure eye movement and the center of focus for a user's eyes. Eye tracking devices use cameras, IR illuminators, and gaze mapping algorithms to track the gaze of the user. Mobile versions generally use a scene camera to record at what the user is looking. Examples include Tobii glasses [99], iPal glasses [45], and Pupil Labs Eye tracker [78].

Location Tracking (10%). Location tracking refers to technology that determines the position in space, and movement of, a person or object. Wearable devices enable tracking location by using GPS and other technologies [117], normally by synthesizing multiple signals. Location tracking is included in many wearable input devices, especially AR glasses and smartwatches (e.g., Apple Watch [4], Sony SmartWatches [92], Vuzix smartglasses [104], Sony SmartEye-Glass [93]).

Other Input Modalities (8%). Additional methods, based on research that attempts to implement novel modalities, are not widely used in wearable devices; therefore, we add them as a separate category. Xiao et al. [114], increased the input methods of smartwatches by adding additional movements as inputs (e.g., panning, twist, binary tilt, click). Weigel and Steimle [107], proposed "a novel class of tiny and expressive wearable input devices that uses pressure, pinch, and shear deformations".

5.2   Associated Output Modality

Some wearable input devices provide output and may even do so as their primary function (e.g., HMDs). The ASSOCIATED OUTPUT MODALITY axis identifies output modalities provided by some of the considered wearable input devices.

Visual (30%). Some wearable input devices provide visual output to the user: e.g., AR glasses, VR glasses, and smart glasses, smartwatches, and touch screens. For many HMDs, their primary purpose is visual feedback, but they are included in the framework due to using head tracking and other inputs. Some wearable input devices use a projector (e.g., pico projector) to provide visual output on the body or on a surface. For example, Harrison et al. [41] proposed omniTouch, a wearable input device that enables graphical multi-touch interaction; the device provides a visual output by using a pico projector to display the projected interface on any surface (e.g., the user's skin). Other examples of wearable devices that provide visual output include Google glass [36], Rufus Cuff [82], and Epson Moverio [25].

Audio (19%). Audio is also used as an output modality for wearable technologies (e.g., audio notifications). Several wearable devices provide audio output to the user (e.g., Meta 2 [63], Intimate Interfaces [21], Recon Jet [44]). Some wearable devices use audio output to provide better and more immersive experiences to the wearer. For example, Microsoft Hololens [64], which are AR smartglasses, use audio output to simulate a tactile feeling when the user presses virtual buttons [113].

Haptic (14%). Haptic feedback communicate with the user by using touch. For example, the Apple Watch [4] uses haptic feedback [5] to grab user attention and to indicate when actions have been performed successfully.

5.3   Mobility

The MOBILITY axis considers how wearables impact users' ability to move in the physical world. We classify wearable input devices as *fully mobile*, which means they minimally restrict movement, *semi mobile*, which means they meaningfully negatively impact movement, or *not mobile*. We have not yet seen any devices that might augment mobility.

Fully Mobile (82%). Many wearable devices in the list were designed to support mobility. The user can move and perform multiple tasks while they wear these type of devices, maintaining a high level of situation awareness. For example, the user can wear a smartwatch (e.g., LG Smartwatch [55]), and perform everyday activities without any burden.

Semi Mobile (11%). Some wearable devices may partially inhibit movement. For instance, peripheral vision is important part of human vision for everyday life activities such as walking and driving; using an HMD (e.g., Hololens [64], Google Glass [36]) will partially cover the wearer's peripheral vision [17].

Not Mobile (7%). Some wearable devices prevent movement due to the device requirements (e.g., requiring sensor-enabled room). For instance, Sony PlayStation VR[6] requires PlayStation Move and PlayStation Camera for interaction, which restricts the user to a specific space, limiting the mobility of the device.

5.4   Body Location

Wearable input devices can be worn on various locations on the body. We classified devices into two body regions: *upper* and *lower*; *free form* devices can be placed in various locations. Some devices span categories.

Upper Body (80%). Many wearable technologies are designed for the upper half of the body. Wearable technology positioned on the user's hand might encompass all fingers (e.g., ART Fingertracking [2]), one finger (e.g., Bird [68], Fujitsu Ring [28]), the finger nails (e.g., NailO [47]), the palm (e.g., Virtual Keyboard [77]), or the entire hand (e.g., GoGlove [37]); it might also combine two parts of the hand such as the palm and fingers (e.g., Gest [32]). In addition, wearable devices can be worn on the wrist (e.g. smartwatches), the arm (e.g., Myo Armband), the shoulder (e.g., OmniTouch [41]), the waist (e.g., Belt [22]), and the head (e.g., AR and VR glasses).

---

[6] https://www.playstation.com/en-us/explore/playstation-vr/.

Lower Body (6%). Very few devices are worn on the lower body. ShoeSense, a wearable device that contains a shoe-mounted sensor, provides gestural interaction for the wearer [9]. Other devices can be worn on the knee, such as iKnee-Braces [102].

Free Form (14%). Certain wearable devices are not limited to a specific on-body location, but can be worn on various body locations. For example, the Cyclops, a wearable device used to detect whole body motion, can be placed on different parts of the body such as the shoulder, chest, and waist [15]. Free form devices also include those that are not intended for wearable use, but have been appropriated for such (e.g., Leap Motion for wearable hand tracking [54,56]).

6 Using the Framework

In this section, we guide designers in how to design composite wearables through using the framework. First, we propose composition guidelines that designers can follow before selecting the wearable devices; then, we develop a scenario-based design process to show how the framework can be used to compose a wearable computer.

6.1 Composition Guidelines

Our composition guidelines are based on human-centered design [72]. The framework axes inform designers in thinking about the needs and requirements of of people. Designers should consider what are the user's needs requirements in terms of interaction, mobility, and embodied constraints. As a designer reaches phases for prototyping or developing, they should address the questions aligned with the framework axes. As each question is answered, the range of potential devices is reduced until a workable subset remains.

- The designer should identify the TYPE OF INTERACTIVITY that is needed to accomplish the goals of the wearable system. Task demands and factors from the environment can determine what type of interactivity is most appropriate for the system. For example, while voice recognition is sometimes sufficient, it can be compromised by the environment or the wearer, such as with the presence of ambient noise or language barriers [18]. The choice of TYPE OF INTERACTIVITY is heavily context- and purpose-dependent.
- Similar to concerns about TYPE OF INTERACTIVITY, the designer needs to know what feedback is necessary. While work on output is not directly addressed, many input devices have multiple ASSOCIATED OUTPUT MODALITIES, so selecting input devices with the right feedback mechanisms can minimize the number of devices needed overall, reducing complexity. For example, if the task requires that a user identifies their current location, a visual output is needed to display the current location of the user on a digital map.
- The designer should determine how much MOBILITY must be supported; is the experience stationary or mobile? Can the environment be instrumented? What kind of situation awareness does the user need?

– As the range of devices narrows, the designer must consider what parts of the body can be occupied by equipment. What are the impacts of devices at particular body locations on the performance of necessary embodied tasks? How will proposed devices overlap in BODY LOCATION?

6.2 Design Scenario: Search and Rescue Map

In this section, we use a scenario-based design method [8], demonstrating how the framework can be used by designers of composite wearable computers. This process is an activity-based design approach [7,8], in which the proposed scenario accounts for the user's requirements, abilities, and activities. We use the framework to guide the design of a composite wearable computer, which captures a set of fictional requirements. This scenario considers complex information management activities set in a dangerous environment. Working from prior research on disaster response (e.g., [27,100,101]), we consider a search and rescue scenario involving map use in a disaster zone. As we consider this future scenario, we set aside, for the time being, concerns about the robustness of the equipment (e.g., waterproofing). Finally, we note that, were such a system built, this would likely be one of many applications it might support, but keep our scope narrow for this scenario.

Application Type. Map and orientation support in a disaster zone.

Motivating Scenario. A team of search and rescue specialists are working to search buildings in the aftermath of a hurricane. The location is dangerous: parts are flooded, buildings are on the verge of collapse, and some areas are on fire. Wireless data access may be available, due to mesh networks brought in with search and rescue (and/or provided by wireless carriers). The specialists need to be able to identify their current location, even when nearby locations no longer resemble existing maps [27,50] while keeping hands free.

Activity. The search and rescue map needs to function as a support tool, constantly able to supply information to a specialist about their current location. It is used to ensure that the specialist is in the region they have been designated to search.

Specific Requirements. The search and rescue map has the following requirements:

1. the search and rescue specialist needs to maintain awareness of the surrounding environment;
2. the specialist needs maximum freedom of movement, especially hands, arms, and legs; and
3. the specialist needs to be able to identify their location.

Proposed Design. First, we need to select what TYPE OF INTERACTIVITY the wearable should provide. The search and rescue specialist needs to interact with the wearable without encumbering hands during movement: we might use *gestures*, specifically ones that can be turned off while moving, and/or *voice* to achieve this. The system also needs *location tracking* to update map position and communicate it to other specialists.

The system will need output. A handheld display would be nice, but we are not considering touch and an HMD would be more supportive of keeping hands free. Based on considering ASSOCIATED OUTPUT MODALITY, some systems for voice work are built into HMDs, as is location tracking.

The system needs maximum MOBILITY, so this rules out a number of HMDs that can only be used in stationary circumstances, while gesture support is available with many mobile devices.

Finally, we must consider BODY LOCATION. The HMD will go on the *upper body*, and there are a range of positions for gesture devices that are compatible with this.

From the wearable device list, the designer can select multiple devices that support their needs. For example, They can select Myo armband [69] that can detect the specialist hand gesture. Also, the designer can use Epson Moverio [25] to provide voice input, location tracking, and visual output. These devices will support mobility of the user and fulfil the task requirements.

7   Discussion

Based on our study of 84 wearable input devices, we developed insights to help wearable computer designers select and build composite wearable UIs. We discuss design *implications* to support building systems and surface design *challenges* that developers will likely encounter.

7.1   A Composition-Based Approach to Design

The proposed framework supports a composition-based approach to the design of wearable computers. Designers need to consider the relationship between wearable devices: how they complement, conflict, and coalesce into a cohesive unit together. To aid designers' decision-making, our design process provides an overview of existing wearable devices, highlighting the components of their specification that matter most to designers. Designers begin by defining user needs and activities, which drives the selection of devices that can work in tandem with each other. From this point of view, our framework informs wearable designers by framing design decisions around critical wearable input device axes. Additionally, the included supplementary documents serve a quick design reference for many existing wearable input devices, by providing framework axes information for each device.

Integration Techniques. Most wearable devices do not work in isolation, instead, they work with other devices to exchange data and/or to get power. For example, smartglasses and smartwatches almost universally need to be paired to a smartphone to function at all. Mobile phones, computers, and wearable devices together can help the integration of data from multiple modalities which results in a rich and complex interaction with the wearable computer. The designer's challenge is to integrate the components of the composite computer in an effective away. Designers need to think of both the low- and high-level data that is available from the composed devices. The sensor data or raw data need to be thought of in a way it can be composed with other data from multiple sources to provide a high-level function [48].

Considerations in Composing Wearable Computers. It is critical that designers take into consideration not only the functions of the composite wearable computer, but also, the relationship between the wearable, the user, and the environment. Based on developing the framework, the following considerations should be taken into account during the composition of the wearable computer.

- The BODY LOCATION axis in our framework addresses the position of the body on which the device may be worn. Designers need to find the optimum body location and device type that can be appropriate for the intended activity. Although prior frameworks did provide guidelines for developers to understand how body locations can affect the wearable technology [31], our framework assists designers not only in selecting an optimum body location, but also, how complex the intended wearable computer would be and the range of interaction that is possible. Each body location affords different types of interaction while restricting movement. Designers need to be familiar with these affordances to help them select the wearable device or devices that work in tandem with each other and with the wearer's body.
- Along with the body part and its affordances, designers need to consider the comfort and usability of the designed wearable, specially when the body is in motion. Due to the fact that the human body may move, using the wearable while the user is still does not reflect how it would be used while in motion [111]. Bringing human factors knowledge into the composition process and conducting both usability and comfort testing while the user is still and in motion can help insure that the designed wearable is comfortable and usable [49,67].
- Designers need to ensure that wearable devices do not conflict with the wearer's clothing. For example, creating a wearable computer that requires the user to wear a finger-worn device, while the activity or context that is used in also requires the user to wear gloves (e.g., firefighter, construction worker). Designers also need to consider the wearer's clothing and fashion choices (e.g., jewelry), and how they might interact with the wearable computer. Being aware of these conflicts during the composition process help prevent any issues when using the intended wearable computer.

7.2   Challenges and Opportunities

Wearable devices present a range of issues, challenges, and opportunities for human-computer interaction. Designers need to consider these challenges when composing wearable computers and think of them as opportunities for design innovation.

Multimodal Versus Unimodal. Many prior interfaces are unimodal, offering only a single type of interface (e.g., touchscreen) [75,79]; composite wearable computers offer the opportunity to build rich, multimodal systems. While multimodal systems are potentially more flexible and expressive, they also bring challenges.

Multimodal wearables have the potential to support the development of sophisticated wearable computers. Using these devices, designers can integrate multiple input modalities with each other that can provide more functions and increase usability [75]. For example, the *AiR Glasses DK 2* [6] provide users with various input modalities, including hand gesture, touch, and voice. Composing a wearable computer that combines all of these modalities together provides a robust design, such that a wearer would be able to perform multiple functions through a set of input modalities. These modalities can be designed to complement each other or used as a *standby* in case of a failure of the main modality. Another advantage of composing a wearable computer with multiple input modalities is the increase in expressivity, though this could inhibit usability [72], of the wearable computer.

Designing for multimodal interfaces is challenging, as the developer needs to determine which modalities are best for which types of interaction. An alternative is to enable to the wearer to make decisions about which modality fits the best with the intended activity s/he want to perform. For example, voice input can be used by the wearer to interact with the wearable computer when hands need to be free, however, when background noise is present, the wearer can switch to the touch interface provided by the same wearable computer to perform the same task, although the redundancy reduces expressivity.

Unimodal wearables can limit the functions provided by the wearable. These type of wearables can be designed best for simple tasks that need to be performed in a similar fashion by multiple users with high accuracy. For example, a wearable computer that is used by factory operators to input data about the state of the factory can be designed using one input modality (e.g., a designer can use *EasySMX* [23], a wearable touch mouse). This design ensures that the wearable computer is usable by multiple workers similarly, which provides higher versatility.

When composing a wearable computer, designers need to take into account the trade-offs of using multimodal versus unimodal input, and the composition of multiple modalities on the usability, functionality, and accuracy of the wearable computer.

Technological Complexity. Wearable input devices may make use of a large number of sensors to provide users with a particular experience (e.g., inertial measurement units, infrared cameras, GPS, microphones). Some of these devices use a single sensor to provide functionality while others combine multiple sensors. Wearable devices that have more technological complexity may be able to provide multiple functions and more accurate data. On the other hand, technological complexity can be a challenge for development and mask problems (e.g., by automatically substituting sensor data in a way that is invisible to the developer). For example, sensor-fusion devices are a specialized form of multi-sensor devices that combine data from several sensors to produce more precise, complete, and/or reliable data than can be achieved with a single sensor [39,105]. Such devices require algorithms to connect together multiple sensor feeds to provide higher-level data to the developer. In these devices, all of the fused sensors depend on each other to provide the intended data. Devices with sensor fusion enable the developer to work with sensor data at a higher level of abstraction (e.g., with distinct gesture callbacks instead of numerical accelerometer feeds) with the expectation that data is of higher quality. At the same time, the algorithms used to fuse multiple sensors could cause problems for developers, hiding data that could otherwise be used or that might indicate a problem with the sensor.

An example of sensor fusion is an inertial head-tracker, which is used in many HMDs. These consist of (at least) three sensors: three-axis accelerometer, gyroscope, and magnetometer. Data from these sensors are assembled together via algorithm to provide the developer with the user's head orientation and movement; no single sensor would be able to provide such data. Another example of sensor fusion is the Myo Armband, a wearable device worn on a user's forearm and used to detect the hand gesture of the wearer. It employs both inertial measurement unit and EMG sensor to provide accurate data about the hand and arm gestures.

Level of Accuracy. Consideration must be given to the level of accuracy of wearable devices. When composing a wearable computer, designers need to make sure that the level of accuracy of each wearable device is considered appropriate for the activity and context of use. While conducting this research, we noted a lack of information about the accuracy of each wearable device in our data list. Designers might find it challenging to have a sense of how accurate the composed wearable computer would be without such data.

One way to overcome the lack of accuracy data is to conduct user studies and usability testing to examine the accuracy of the used wearable devices and the composite wearable computer. When the accuracy of a device is not sufficient, designers can consider integrating other wearables that can help increase the accuracy of the wearable computer. Designers also can use testing techniques that have been developed for testing the accuracy of specific sensors. For example, to test the positioning accuracy of a wearable GPS device, designers can use various tools to measure the performance of the GPS (e.g., Time to First Fix[7]).

Testing the accuracy of gesture recognition devices, however, is more challenging. Humans are affected differently by the natural tremor of their hands, which can cause issues for gesture devices to recognize inputs with high accuracy [106]. Designers can overcome this issue by integrating multiple gesture recognition devices into the wearable computer to increase accuracy and reliability. For example, two Leap Motion [53] devices can be combined together to enhance the accuracy of the gesture data [66]. While this approach has the potential to

---

[7] GPS Receiver Testing: http://download.ni.com/pub/branches/india/gps_receiver_simulation_testing.pdf.

enhance the accuracy, it might cause the wearable computer to increase in size and weight. Designers need to consider the trade-offs of combined more than one device on the wearability and usability of the composite wearable computer.

Clicking buttons, on the other hand, can guarantee a high level of accuracy. When comparing between gesture devices and other input modalities (e.g., mouse, touchpad), gesture devices perform the poorest and have the lowest accuracy percentage [87]. Another challenge of using gesture devices is the need for training the users on how to perform the gestures correctly to interact with the wearable computer, which might be difficult. Designers can consider using buttons as the main input modality to ensure a high level of accuracy.

Social Acceptance and User Resistance. While wearable computers are gaining more attention from designers and developers, there remains resistance from society. Designers need to build composite wearable computers that are socially acceptable to enable unhindered use of these technologies. For example, people may be opposed to wearing certain devices in crowded areas (e.g., HMDs [88]). The TYPE OF INTERACTIVITY provided by the wearable computer can cause the wearer to feel awkward or uncomfortable (e.g., hand gestures [89]). Designers can use the framework to select the type of interactivity that fits best with the context they are designing for and with the body location that can help enhance the acceptance of the wearable computer. For example, fingers, wrists, and forearms are considered to be socially accepted on-body locations for wearable computers [76,89].

Identifying Limitations of Existing Devices. Our framework can help designers and researchers identify limitations in available wearable devices, which can drive future development and research in the domain of wearable technologies. Based on our data set of 84 wearable input devices, we found that 80% of these wearables are worn on the *upper-body*. This is mainly due to the larger range of affordances provided by the upper part of the human body [115]. This could limit the designers' choices of wearable devices that can be worn on the lower part of the body. To overcome this limitation, designers can use devices that are *free form*, and can be worn on multiple body parts (e.g., *Cyclops* [15]). However, only 14% of the wearables in the data set are *free form*, which might constrain design choices. To overcome this limitation, designers can combine wearable devices that are designed for the upper-body with different fabrics and textiles to enable wearing them on other parts of the body [26].

7.3   Limitations

This work adds to a growing body of research on wearable technology (e.g., [16,31,67,89–91,95,96,115]). We acknowledge that this work is limited, and not intended to provide an exhaustive analysis of input wearable devices and wearable technology in general. We intend to continue improving, extending, and refining the framework and finally validating it through designing composed wearable computers and investigating different aspects of the framework through future user studies.

8 Conclusion

The present research developed a grounded theory analysis of 84 wearable input devices using 197 data sources to understand their capabilities. We used grounded theory to develop a multi-axis framework for composing devices together into wearable computers. The framework addresses devices in terms of their TYPE OF INTERACTION, ASSOCIATED OUTPUT MODALITIES, MOBILITY, and BODY LOCATION. We expect the resulting framework to be useful to designers of future wearable systems, enabling them to navigate this complex space to assemble the right devices for a particular set of tasks while keeping in mind a set of limitations in composition.

Acknowledgments. This material is based upon work supported by the National Science Foundation under Grant Nos. IIS-1651532 and IIS-1619273.

References

1. Abowd, D., Dey, A.K., Orr, R., Brotherton, J.: Context-awareness in wearable and ubiquitous computing. Virtual Reality **3**(3), 200–211 (1998). https://doi.org/10.1007/BF01408562
2. Advanced Realtime Tracking: ART Fingertracking, September 2017. http://www.ar-tracking.com/products/interaction/fingertracking/
3. Allan, G.: A critique of using grounded theory as a research method. Electron. J. Bus. Res. Methods **2**(1), 1–10 (2003)
4. Apple: Apple Watch, April 2015. https://www.apple.com/watch/
5. Apple: Haptic Feedback, January 2019. https://developer.apple.com/design/human-interface-guidelines/watchos/user-interaction/haptic-feedback/
6. Atheer Inc.: Atheer AiR, November 2016. http://atheerair.com
7. Baber, C.: Wearable computers: a human factors review. Int. J. Hum.-Comput. Interact. **13**(2), 123–145 (2001)
8. Baber, C., Haniff, D.J., Woolley, S.I.: Contrasting paradigms for the development of wearable computers. IBM Syst. J. **38**(4), 551–565 (1999)
9. Bailly, G., Müller, J., Rohs, M., Wigdor, D., Kratz, S.: ShoeSense: a new perspective on gestural interaction and wearable applications. In: Proceedings of the SIGCHI Conference on Human Factors in Computing Systems, CHI 2012, pp. 1239–1248. ACM, New York (2012). http://libezp.nmsu.edu:4009/10.1145/2207676.2208576
10. Barfield, W.: Fundamentals of Wearable Computers and Augmented Reality. CRC Press, Boca Raton (2015)
11. Bellotti, V., Edwards, K.: Intelligibility and accountability: human considerations in context-aware systems. Hum.-Comput. Interact. **16**(2), 193–212 (2001). http://dx.doi.org/10.1207/S15327051HCI1623405
12. Benavides, X., Zhu Jin, C.L., Maes, P., Paradiso, J.: KickSoul: a wearable system for feet interactions with digital devices. In: Adjunct Proceedings of the 28th Annual ACM Symposium on User Interface Software & Technology, UIST 2015 Adjunct, pp. 83–84. ACM, New York (2015). http://libezp.nmsu.edu:2763/10.1145/2815585.2815730

13. Boronowsky, M., Nicolai, T., Schlieder, C., Schmidt, A.: Winspect: a case study for wearable computing-supported inspection tasks. In: Proceedings Fifth International Symposium on Wearable Computers, pp. 163–164 (2001)

14. Chalmers, M., MacColl, I., Bell, M.: Seamful design: showing the seams in wearable computing. In: 2003 IEE Eurowearable, pp. 11–16, September 2003

15. Chan, L., et al.: Cyclops: wearable and single-piece full-body gesture input devices. In: Proceedings of the 33rd Annual ACM Conference on Human Factors in Computing Systems, CHI 2015, pp. 3001–3009. ACM, New York (2015). http://libezp.nmsu.edu:2763/10.1145/2702123.2702464

16. Chan, M., Estève, D., Fourniols, J.Y., Escriba, C., Campo, E.: Smart wearable systems: current status and future challenges. Artif. Intell. Med. **56**(3), 137–156 (2012)

17. Chaturvedi, I., Bijarbooneh, F.H., Braud, T., Hui, P.: Peripheral vision: a new killer app for smart glasses. In: Proceedings of the 24th International Conference on Intelligent User Interfaces, IUI 2019, pp. 625–636. ACM, New York (2019). http://doi.acm.org/10.1145/3301275.3302263

18. Cohen, P.R., Oviatt, S.L.: The role of voice input for human-machine communication. Proc. Nat. Acad. Sci. **92**(22), 9921–9927 (1995). http://www.pnas.org/content/92/22/9921.abstract

19. Cook, D.J., Das, S.K.: How smart are our environments? an updated look at the state of the art. Pervasive Mob. Comput. **3**(2), 53–73 (2007). http://www.sciencedirect.com/science/article/pii/S1574119206000642. Design and Use of Smart Environments

20. Corbin, J.M., Strauss, A.: Grounded theory research: procedures, canons, and evaluative criteria. Qual. Sociol. **13**(1), 3–21 (1990). http://dx.doi.org/10.1007/BF00988593

21. Costanza, E., Inverso, S.A., Allen, R.: Toward subtle intimate interfaces for mobile devices using an EMG controller. In: Proceedings of the SIGCHI Conference on Human Factors in Computing Systems, CHI 2005, pp. 481–489. ACM, New York (2005). http://libezp.nmsu.edu:2763/10.1145/1054972.1055039

22. Dobbelstein, D., Hock, P., Rukzio, E.: Belt: an unobtrusive touch input device for head-worn displays. In: Proceedings of the 33rd Annual ACM Conference on Human Factors in Computing Systems, CHI 2015, pp. 2135–2138. ACM, New York (2015). http://libezp.nmsu.edu:2763/10.1145/2702123.2702450

23. EasySMX: EasySMX, January 2016. http://www.easysmx.com/product-detail.asp?id=39

24. Endsley, M.R.: Toward a theory of situation awareness in dynamic systems. Hum. Factors **37**(1), 32–64 (1995)

25. Epson: Epson Moverio, January 2016. https://epson.com/For-Work/Wearables/Smart-Glasses/c/w420

26. Farringdon, J., Moore, A.J., Tilbury, N., Church, J., Biemond, P.D.: Wearable sensor badge and sensor jacket for context awareness. In: Proceedings of the 3rd IEEE International Symposium on Wearable Computers, ISWC 1999, p. 107. IEEE Computer Society, Washington (1999). http://dl.acm.org/citation.cfm?id=519309.856485

27. Fischer, J.E., Reeves, S., Rodden, T., Reece, S., Ramchurn, S.D., Jones, D.: Building a birds eye view: collaborative work in disaster response. In: Proceedings of the 33rd Annual ACM Conference on Human Factors in Computing Systems, CHI 2015, pp. 4103–4112. ACM, New York (2015). http://doi.acm.org/10.1145/2702123.2702313

28. Fujitsu Laboratories Ltd.: Fujitsu laboratories develops ring-type wearable device capable of text input by fingertip, January 2015. http://www.fujitsu.com/global/about/resources/news/press-releases/2015/0113-01.html
29. Fukahori, K., Sakamoto, D., Igarashi, T.: Exploring subtle foot plantar-based gestures with sock-placed pressure sensors. In: Proceedings of the 33rd Annual ACM Conference on Human Factors in Computing Systems, CHI 2015, pp. 3019–3028. ACM, New York (2015). http://libezp.nmsu.edu:4009/10.1145/2702123.2702308
30. Gardner, A., Duncan, C.A., Selmic, R., Kanno, J.: Real-time classification of dynamic hand gestures from marker-based position data. In: Proceedings of the Companion Publication of the 2013 International Conference on Intelligent User Interfaces Companion, IUI 2013, pp. 13–16. ACM, New York (2013). http://libezp.nmsu.edu:4009/10.1145/2451176.2451181
31. Gemperle, F., Kasabach, C., Stivoric, J., Bauer, M., Martin, R.: Design for wearability. In: Digest of Papers, Second International Symposium on Wearable Computers (Cat. No. 98EX215), pp. 116–122, October 1998
32. Gest: Gest, January 2015. https://gest.co/
33. Glaser, B.G.: Theoretical Sensitivity: Advances in the Methodology of Grounded Theory. The Sociology Press, Mill Valley (1978)
34. Glaser, B.G.: Doing Grounded Theory: Issues and Discussions. The Sociology Press, Mill Valley (1998)
35. Glaser, B.G., Strauss, A.: The Discovery of Grounded Theory: Strategies for Qualitative Research. Aldine Publishing Company, Chicago (1967)
36. Glass: Google Glass, February 2013. https://x.company/glass/
37. GoGlove: GoGlove, May 2015. http://goglove.io/
38. Guo, C., Sharlin, E.: Exploring the use of tangible user interfaces for human-robot interaction: A comparative study. In: Proceedings of the SIGCHI Conference on Human Factors in Computing Systems, CHI 2008, pp. 121–130. ACM, New York (2008). http://libezp.nmsu.edu:3103/10.1145/1357054.1357076
39. Hall, D.L., Llinas, J.: An introduction to multisensor data fusion. Proc. IEEE 85(1), 6–23 (1997)
40. Hardy, E.: Genius Ring Mouse 2 Review, May 2013. http://www.tabletpcreview.com/review/genius-ring-mouse-2-review/
41. Harrison, C., Benko, H., Wilson, A.D.: OmniTouch: wearable multitouch interaction everywhere. In: Proceedings of the 24th Annual ACM Symposium on User Interface Software and Technology, UIST 2011, pp. 441–450. ACM, New York (2011). http://doi.acm.org/10.1145/2047196.2047255
42. Hightower, J., Borriello, G.: Location systems for ubiquitous computing. Computer 34(8), 57–66 (2001)
43. Hoda, R., Noble, J., Marshall, S.: Grounded theory for geeks. In: Proceedings of the 18th Conference on Pattern Languages of Programs, PLoP 2011, pp. 24:1–24:17. ACM, New York (2011). http://libezp.nmsu.edu:4009/10.1145/2578903.2579162
44. Intel Recon: Recon Jet, June 2015. https://www.reconinstruments.com/
45. iPal: iPal, January 2013. http://meetipal.com/specs/
46. Jones, J., Gouge, C., Crilley, M.: Design principles for health wearables. Commun. Des. Q. Rev 5(2), 40–50 (2017). http://libezp.nmsu.edu:2763/10.1145/3131201.3131205
47. Kao, H.L.C., Dementyev, A., Paradiso, J.A., Schmandt, C.: NailO: fingernails as an input surface. In: Proceedings of the 33rd Annual ACM Conference on Human Factors in Computing Systems, CHI 2015, pp. 3015–3018. ACM, New York (2015). http://doi.acm.org/10.1145/2702123.2702572

48. King, R.C., Villeneuve, E., White, R.J., Sherratt, R.S., Holderbaum, W., Harwin, W.S.: Application of data fusion techniques and technologies for wearable health monitoring. Med. Eng. Phys. **42**(Suppl. 1), 1–12 (2017). http://doi.acm.org/10.1145/2702123.2702572

49. Knight, F., Schwirtz, A., Psomadelis, F., Baber, C., Bristow, W., Arvanitis, N.: The design of the sensvest. Personal Ubiquitous Comput. **9**(1), 6–19 (2005). http://dx.doi.org/10.1007/s00779-004-0269-8

50. Kogan, M., Anderson, J., Palen, L., Anderson, K.M., Soden, R.: Finding the way to OSM mapping practices: bounding large crisis datasets for qualitative investigation. In: Proceedings of the 2016 CHI Conference on Human Factors in Computing Systems, CHI 2016, pp. 2783–2795. ACM, New York (2016). http://doi.acm.org/10.1145/2858036.2858371

51. Kosmalla, F., Wiehr, F., Daiber, F., Krüger, A., Löchtefeld, M.: ClimbAware: investigating perception and acceptance of wearables in rock climbing. In: Proceedings of the 2016 CHI Conference on Human Factors in Computing Systems, CHI 2016, pp. 1097–1108. ACM, New York (2016). http://libezp.nmsu.edu:4009/10.1145/2858036.2858562

52. Laput, G., Xiao, R., Chen, X.A., Hudson, S.E., Harrison, C.: Skin buttons: cheap, small, low-powered and clickable fixed-icon laser projectors. In: Proceedings of the 27th Annual ACM Symposium on User Interface Software and Technology, UIST 2014, pp. 389–394. ACM, New York (2014). http://libezp.nmsu.edu:4009/10.1145/2642918.2647356

53. Leap Motion Inc.: Leap motion, November 2010. https://www.leapmotion.com

54. Lee, P.W., Wang, H.Y., Tung, Y.C., Lin, J.W., Valstar, A.: Transection: hand-based interaction for playing a game within a virtual reality game. In: Proceedings of the 33rd Annual ACM Conference Extended Abstracts on Human Factors in Computing Systems, CHI EA 2015, pp. 73–76. ACM, New York (2015). http://libezp.nmsu.edu:4009/10.1145/2702613.2728655

55. LG: LG Smart Watch, February 2017. http://www.lg.com/us/smart-watches

56. Liu, M., Nancel, M., Vogel, D.: Gunslinger: subtle arms-down mid-air interaction. In: Proceedings of the 28th Annual ACM Symposium on User Interface Software & Technology, UIST 2015, pp. 63–71. ACM, New York (2015). http://libezp.nmsu.edu:4009/10.1145/2807442.2807489

57. Logbr Ring Zero: Logbr Ring Zero, March 2015. http://ringzero.logbar.jp/

58. Lukowicz, P., Timm-Giel, A., Lawo, M., Herzog, O.: WearIT@work: toward real-world industrial wearable computing. IEEE Pervasive Comput. **6**(4), 8–13 (2007)

59. Mann, S.: Wearable computing: a first step toward personal imaging. Computer **30**(2), 25–32 (1997)

60. Mann, S.: Wearable computing as means for personal empowerment. In: Proceedings 3rd International Conference on Wearable Computing (ICWC), pp. 51–59 (1998)

61. Mathas, C.: The five senses of sensors - touch, August 2011. https://www.digikey.com/en/articles/techzone/2011/aug/the-five-senses-of-sensors-touch. Accessed 11 Aug 2011

62. Matthies, D.J.C., Müller, F., Anthes, C., Kranzlmüller, D.: ShoeSoleSense: proof of concept for a wearable foot interface for virtual and real environments. In: Proceedings of the 19th ACM Symposium on Virtual Reality Software and Technology, VRST 2013, pp. 93–96. ACM, New York (2013). http://libezp.nmsu.edu:4009/10.1145/2503713.2503740

63. Meta: Meta 2, January. http://www.metavision.com/

64. Microsoft: Microsoft Hololens, March 2016. https://www.microsoft.com/en-us/hololens/hardware
65. Milgram, P., Kishino, F.: A taxonomy of mixed reality visual displays. IEICE Trans. Inf. Syst. **77**(12), 1321–1329 (1994)
66. Mohandes, M., Aliyu, S., Deriche, M.: Prototype Arabic sign language recognition using multi-sensor data fusion of two leap motion controllers. In: 2015 IEEE 12th International Multi-Conference on Systems, Signals Devices (SSD 2015), pp. 1–6, March 2015
67. Motti, V.G., Caine, K.: Human factors considerations in the design of wearable devices. Proc. Hum. Factors Ergon. Soc. Annu. Meet. **58**(1), 1820–1824 (2014)
68. MUV interactive: BIRD, October 2015. https://www.muvinteractive.com
69. Myo: Myo, January 2014. https://www.myo.com/
70. Nilsson, T., et al.: Applying seamful design in location-based mobile museum applications. ACM Trans. Multimedia Comput. Commun. Appl. **12**(4), 56:1–56:23 (2016). http://doi.acm.org/10.1145/2962720
71. Nod: Nod Ring, January 2014. https://nod.com/developers/getting-started/innovator-kit/
72. Norman, D.: The Design of Everyday Things: Revised and Expanded Edition. Basic Books, 2013 edn. (2013)
73. Oculus: Nod Backspin, March 2016. https://www.oculus.com/rift/
74. Pacchierotti, C., Sinclair, S., Solazzi, M., Frisoli, A., Hayward, V., Prattichizzo, D.: Wearable haptic systems for the fingertip and the hand: taxonomy, review, and perspectives. IEEE Trans. Haptics **10**(4), 580–600 (2017)
75. Pratibha, A.: Unimodal and multimodal human computer interaction: a modern overview. Int. J. Comput. Sci. Inf. Eng. Technol. (IJCSIET) **2**(3), 1–8 (2013)
76. Profita, H.P., et al.: Don't mind me touching my wrist: a case study of interacting with on-body technology in public. In: Proceedings of the 2013 International Symposium on Wearable Computers, ISWC 2013, pp. 89–96. ACM, New York (2013). http://libezp.nmsu.edu:2763/10.1145/2493988.2494331
77. Project Virtual Keyboard: Project Virtual Keyboard, December 2013. http://www.senseboard.com/?p=174
78. Pupil Labs. https://pupil-labs.com/pupil/
79. Raisamo, R.: Multimodal human-computer interaction: a constructive and empirical study. University of Tampere (1999)
80. Randell, C., Muller, H.: The shopping jacket: wearable computing for the consumer. Pers. Technol. **4**(4), 241–244 (2000). https://doi.org/10.1007/BF02391567
81. Reifinger, S., Wallhoff, F., Ablassmeier, M., Poitschke, T., Rigoll, G.: Static and dynamic hand-gesture recognition for augmented reality applications. In: Jacko, J.A. (ed.) Human-Computer Interaction. HCI Intelligent Multimodal Interaction Environments, pp. 728–737. Springer, Heidelberg (2007). https://doi.org/10.1007/978-3-540-73110-8_79
82. Rufus: Rufus Cuff, May 2014. https://www.getrufus.com/#main-20
83. Sawhney, N., Schmandt, C.: Speaking and listening on the run: design for wearable audio computing. In: Digest of Papers, Second International Symposium on Wearable Computers (Cat. No. 98EX215), pp. 108–115, October 1998
84. Schmidt, A.: Implicit human computer interaction through context. Pers. Technol. **4**(2), 191–199 (2000). https://doi.org/10.1007/BF01324126
85. Schmidt, A.: Context-aware computing: context-awareness, context-aware user interfaces, and implicit interaction. In: The Encyclopedia of Human-Computer Interaction, 2nd edn. (2013)

86. Schou, T., Gardner, H.J.: A Wii remote, a game engine, five sensor bars and a virtual reality theatre. In: Proceedings of the 19th Australasian Conference on Computer-Human Interaction: Entertaining User Interfaces, OZCHI 2007, pp. 231–234. ACM, New York (2007). http://libezp.nmsu.edu:3103/10.1145/1324892.1324941

87. Seixas, M.C.B., Cardoso, J.C.S., Dias, M.T.G.: The leap motion movement for 2D pointing tasks: characterisation and comparison to other devices. In: 2015 International Conference on Pervasive and Embedded Computing and Communication Systems (PECCS), pp. 15–24, February 2015

88. Sharma, H.N., Toups Dugas, P.O., Dolgov, I., Kerne, A., Jain, A.: Evaluating display modalities using a mixed reality game. In: Proceedings of the 2016 Annual Symposium on Computer-Human Interaction in Play, CHI PLAY 2016, pp. 65–77. ACM, New York (2016). http://libezp.nmsu.edu:2763/10.1145/2967934.2968090

89. Shilkrot, R., Huber, J., Steimle, J., Nanayakkara, S., Maes, P.: Digital digits: a comprehensive survey of finger augmentation devices. ACM Comput. Surv. **48**(2), 30:1–30:29 (2015). http://libezp.nmsu.edu:4009/10.1145/2828993

90. Siewiorek, D., Smailagic, A., Starner, T.: Application Design for Wearable Computing. Synthesis Lectures on Mobile and Pervasive Computing, vol. 3, no. 1, pp. 1–66 (2008)

91. Smailagic, A., Siewiorek, D.: Application design for wearable and context-aware computers. IEEE Pervasive Comput. **1**(4), 20–29 (2002)

92. Sony: Sony SmartWatch, November 2014. https://www.sonymobile.com/us/products/smart-products/smartwatch-3-swr50/

93. Sony: Sony Releases the Transparent Lens Eyewear "SmartEyeglass Developer Edition", March 2015. https://www.sony.net/SonyInfo/News/Press/201502/15-016E/index.html

94. Starner, T.E.: The role of speech input in wearable computing. IEEE Pervasive Comput. **1**(3), 89–93 (2002)

95. Starner, T.: The challenges of wearable computing: Part 1. IEEE Micro **21**(4), 44–52 (2001)

96. Starner, T.: The challenges of wearable computing: Part 2. IEEE Micro **21**(4), 54–67 (2001)

97. Starner, T., et al.: Augmented reality through wearable computing. Presence Teleoper. Virtual Environ. **6**(4), 386–398 (1997). http://dx.doi.org/10.1162/pres.1997.6.4.386

98. TAP: Welcome to TAP, May 2016. http://tapwithus.com/2016/05/09/welcome-to-tap/

99. Tobii: Tobii Pro Glasses 2, January 2017. https://www.tobiipro.com/product-listing/tobii-pro-glasses-2/

100. Toups Dugas, P.O., Hamilton, W.A., Alharthi, S.A.: Playing at planning: game design patterns from disaster response practice. In: Proceedings of the 2016 Annual Symposium on Computer-Human Interaction in Play, CHI PLAY 2016, pp. 362–375. ACM, New York (2016). http://doi.acm.org/10.1145/2967934.2968089

101. Toups Dugas, P.O., Kerne, A.: Implicit coordination in firefighting practice: design implications for teaching fire emergency responders. In: Proceedings of the SIGCHI Conference on Human Factors in Computing Systems, CHI 2007, pp. 707–716. ACM, New York (2007). http://doi.acm.org/10.1145/1240624.1240734

102. Tsai, H.R., et al.: iKneeBraces: knee adduction moment evaluation measured by motion sensors in gait detection. In: Proceedings of the 2016 ACM International Joint Conference on Pervasive and Ubiquitous Computing, UbiComp 2016, pp. 386–391. ACM, New York (2016). http://libezp.nmsu.edu:2763/10.1145/2971648.2971675

103. Vive: HTC Vive, April 2016. https://www.vive.com/us/

104. Vuzix: Vuzix M3000 Smart Glasses, January 2017. https://www.vuzix.com/Products/m3000-smart-glasses

105. Waltz, E., Llinas, J.: Multisensor Data Fusion, vol. 685. Artech House, Boston (1990)

106. Weichert, F., Bachmann, D., Rudak, B., Fisseler, D.: Analysis of the accuracy and robustness of the leap motion controller. Sensors 13(5), 6380–6393 (2013). http://www.mdpi.com/1424-8220/13/5/6380

107. Weigel, M., Steimle, J.: DeformWear: deformation input on tiny wearable devices. Proc. ACM Interact. Mob. Wearable Ubiquitous Technol. 1(2), 28:1-28:23 (2017). http://libezp.nmsu.edu:4009/10.1145/3090093

108. Weiser, M.: The computer for the 21st century. SIGMOBILE Mob. Comput. Commun. Rev. 3(3), 3–11 (1999). http://libezp.nmsu.edu:2763/10.1145/329124.329126

109. West, R., Parola, M.J., Jaycen, A.R., Lueg, C.P.: Embodied information behavior, mixed reality and big data. In: SPIE/IS&T Electronic Imaging, pp. 93920E–93920E. International Society for Optics and Photonics (2015)

110. Wii: Wii Remote, September 2005. http://wii.com/

111. Wilde, D., Schiphorst, T., Klooster, S.: Move to design/design to move: a conversation about designing for the body. Interactions 18(4), 22–27 (2011). http://doi.acm.org/10.1145/1978822.1978828

112. Witt, H., Leibrandt, R., Kemnade, A., Kenn, H.: SCIPIO: a miniaturized building block for wearable interaction devices. In: 3rd International Forum on Applied Wearable Computing 2006, pp. 1–5, March 2006

113. Wong, R.: Microsoft Hololens 2 ushers in the next generation of augmented reality, March 2019. https://bit.ly/2kcHvMW

114. Xiao, R., Laput, G., Harrison, C.: Expanding the input expressivity of smartwatches with mechanical pan, twist, tilt and click. In: Proceedings of the SIGCHI Conference on Human Factors in Computing Systems, CHI 2014, pp. 193–196. ACM, New York (2014). http://libezp.nmsu.edu:4009/10.1145/2556288.2557017

115. Zeagler, C.: Where to wear it: functional, technical, and social considerations in on-body location for wearable technology 20 years of designing for wearability. In: Proceedings of the 2017 ACM International Symposium on Wearable Computers, ISWC 2017, pp. 150–157. ACM, New York (2017). http://libezp.nmsu.edu:4009/10.1145/3123021.3123042

116. Zhou, C., Ludford, P., Frankowski, D., Terveen, L.: An experiment in discovering personally meaningful places from location data. In: CHI 2005 Extended Abstracts on Human Factors in Computing Systems, CHI EA 2005, pp. 2029–2032. ACM, New York (2005). http://doi.acm.org/10.1145/1056808.1057084

117. Zogg, J.M.: GPS: Essentials of Satellite Navigation: Compendium: Theorie and Principles of Satellite Navigation. Overview of GPS/GNSS Systems and Applications, U-blox (2009)

Introducing Mobile Device-Based Interactions to Users: An Investigation of Onboarding Tutorials

Mandy Korzetz[1(✉)], Romina Kühn[1(✉)], Lukas Büschel[1],
Franz-Wilhelm Schumann[1], Uwe Aßmann[1], and Thomas Schlegel[2]

[1] Software Technology Group, TU Dresden, Dresden, Germany
{mandy.korzetz,romina.kuehn,lukas.bueschel,franz-wilhelm.schumann,
uwe.assmann}@tu-dresden.de
[2] Karlsruhe University of Applied Sciences, Karlsruhe, Germany
thomas.schlegel@hs-karlsruhe.de

Abstract. Various built-in sensors enable interacting with mobile devices beyond the screen. So-called mobile device-based interaction techniques are characterized by movements and positions in real space, e.g. twisting the device to switch between front and rear camera or pouring photos from one device into another for sharing. Although interactions should be as intuitive as possible, it is often necessary to introduce them, especially if they are complex or new to the user. Applications have to present interactions appropriately so that users can understand and use them easily. We conducted a user study to investigate the suitability of onboarding tutorials for mobile device-based interaction techniques. Results show that these types of tutorials are insufficient for communicating mobile device-based interactions, mainly because of their spatial and tangible characteristics but also their collaborative and representative interdependencies. Based on this, we propose suggestions for improving the design of tutorials for device-based interactions with mobile phones.

Keywords: Onboarding tutorials · Device-based interaction · Gestures · Mobile phones

1 Introduction

Current mobile devices, such as smartphones and tablets, innately provide numerous sensors, for example, accelerometer and gyroscope for sensing motions as well as orientation sensors or magnetometers for determining positions. Thus, mobile devices can cover a wide range of interaction techniques. Touch sensors of screens enable conventional input methods using multitouch. And also gestures that are invoked by deliberate device movements become increasingly available.

Interactions where devices act as physical interface without using the screen content directly are summarized to mobile device-based interaction techniques [14]. They can support users in a wide variety of single and multi-user

© Springer Nature Switzerland AG 2020
M. Kurosu (Ed.): HCII 2020, LNCS 12182, pp. 428–442, 2020.
https://doi.org/10.1007/978-3-030-49062-1_29

situations: to interact with the mobile device as unobtrusively and discreetly as possible, e. g. facing the device's screen downwards to mute incoming calls, message alerts, alarms and media[1] during a meeting; to interact with distant interfaces, e. g. transferring data from a mobile device to a large display by performing a throw gesture [25]; to enable quick access to device functions without the need to push buttons or look at screens, e. g. twisting the device to switch between front and rear camera[2]; or to facilitate different multi-user tasks [18] for collocated collaboration with multiple mobile devices (e. g. [12,15,17,22]).

Although interactions should be designed as intuitive as possible, users need to learn them, because there is no commonly agreed-upon gesture set existing [23] and the development of interaction techniques is still going on, e. g. [4,6, 13,26]. Thus, applications have to introduce interactions appropriately, so that users can understand and learn them easily. Tutorials support users in learning application functionality and interaction during the normal application flow or at the first start of an application, so-called onboarding tutorials. Design guidelines suggest that type of tutorial as effective especially for unfamiliar interaction [11,29]. Three main aspects influence interaction learning directly [10]: How to start the interaction? What movement do I have to perform? Which function is it mapped to? Most applications provide onboarding tutorials to introduce users to the app functionality, navigation and interaction. Such tutorials mainly use visual metaphors to impart interaction knowledge. But what if interactions base on movements, orientations and/or distances between two or more devices in real space such as described in the examples above? Are users still able to understand the interactions easily with provided visual explanations? To our best knowledge, no existing research investigates the suitability of tutorials for device-based interaction techniques. To address this issue and answering the questions above, we implemented a simple interactive prototype with preselected mobile device-based interactions in a collaborative scenario. As first step, we started with an investigation of onboarding tutorials as they are common for introducing mobile applications to understand potential problems and identify important aspects for users. Therefore we created onboarding tutorials which orientate on common design practices. With that prototype, we conducted a user study to investigate the suitability of such tutorial presentations for mobile-based interactions.

After giving an overview of related work, we present our study approach including the tested onboarding tutorials. Based on the results, we propose recommendations for improving the design of tutorials for device-based interaction techniques with mobile devices that base on spatiality and tangibility. We conclude with planned future work and a summary of our presented work.

---

[1] *Easy Mute* feature: https://www.samsung.com/ca/support/mobile-devices/what-are-the-advanced-features-available-on-my-galaxy-note8/.

[2] *Flip camera* gesture: https://support.google.com/nexus/answer/7443425.

2   Related Work

In recent years, there has been a lot of research on novel interaction techniques for mobile devices. These works show the specific characteristics of mobile-based interaction and also provide specific techniques for concrete interaction tasks. Moreover, there exists research and common practices on how to design tutorials for mobile applications. As mid-air gestures also deal with interactions beyond the visual screen content, we also present related work on tutorials for these type of interactions.

2.1   Mobile Device-Based Interaction Techniques

Mobile interactions beyond the visual screen content are characterized by motions in real space [2]. They therefore rely on using one or more built-in sensors, e. g. accelerometer [30]. Regardless of technology, research describes single-device interactions where smartphones act as physical interface that involves moving the device directly [19,27]. Chong et al. [3] classify mobile interactions in real space to connect different devices to *guidance-based* interaction techniques. Moreover, the design principles of Lucero et al. [21] extend personal mobile usage to a shared multi-user usage. A combined view on mobile device-based interaction techniques is given by Korzetz et al. [14]. They propose a model for guiding the design of mobile-based interactions with a physical focus for individual as well as collaborative use. They also point out information that is relevant for users to understand how to perform interactions, categorized by spatiality and tangibility. We use this for our investigation on the suitability of onboarding tutorials for mobile-based interactions.

2.2   Tutorials for Mobile Applications

Mobile applications should provide tutorials to introduce the application to users and to demonstrate how it can be used in terms of features and interaction [9,11,29]. As printed documentation and online help is assessed as largely ineffective (e. g. [24]), tutorial guidelines suggest to use visual instructions for graphical user interfaces rather than non-illustrated, e. g. [8] – regardless of still or animated. However, non-visual tutorials can be meaningful, too, e. g. for user groups with special needs like visually impaired people [28]. Tutorials can support users during the normal application flow, e. g. by providing instructional overlays and coach marks [7,9]. In contrast, onboarding tutorials are presented at the first start of a mobile application to introduce features and interaction. Especially for unfamiliar interactions, onboarding tutorials are rated as an effective tool [11,29].

2.3   Tutorials for Mid-Air Interactions

Our work aims at investigating tutorials for spatial and tangible interactions beyond visual screen content. *Shapeline Guide* [1] is a dynamic visual guide for teaching mid-air gestures to interact with large displays. The guide supports users during executing gestures. Timing of gesture guidance is also an important question [5]. As first step, we concentrate on evaluating common onboarding tutorials that are presented at the first application start. Ismair et al. [10] address the revelation of mid-air hand-poses and the teaching of their command mapping (focus on hand poses) by showing line figures which the user has to mimic with the hand. The MIME approach requires little on-screen space because the figures can be integrated in existing interface elements, but is limited to hand gestures and gestures which can be mapped to iconic poses. *ActionCube* [20] is a tangible mobile gesture interaction tutorial which associates user movements tracked by the device accelerometer to the movement and deformations of a 3D object displayed on the screen. This approach helps to understand the effects of acceleration, but not how to perform concrete gestures.

To our best knowledge, no existing research investigates the presentation of onboarding tutorials for device-based interaction techniques, i.e. interaction techniques for mobile devices with spatial and tangible characteristics in real space. We address this issue by evaluating a common onboarding tutorial for introducing device-based interactions to users.

3   Studying Onboarding Tutorials for Mobile Device-Based Interactions

The main goal of our user study was to investigate the suitability of an onboarding tutorial for mobile device-based interaction techniques. Using such a common type of tutorial allows for a fundamental valuation of specific characteristics that are important for tangible and spatial interactions. We collected data from questionnaires after performing tutorials describing various interaction techniques and a semi-structured interview at the end of the user study. Furthermore, the participants were observed during the study. In the following, we describe participants, the interactive prototype including the onboarding tutorials, our procedure as well as the study design to answer the following research questions (RQ):

- RQ1: Are common onboarding tutorials suitable for mobile device-based interaction techniques?
- RQ2: Which information do users need to understand that type of gestures with mobile devices?
- RQ3: What can we derive for future development of tutorials for mobile device-based interaction techniques?

3.1   Participants

We recruited 32 unpaid participants (12 females) from age 18 to 51 ($M = 31.2$, $SD = 6.4$) via email or personally. 23 participants stated that they use smartphones on a regular basis for standard applications. Only 2 participants do not

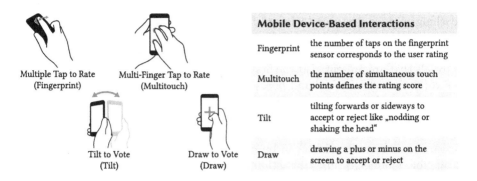

Mobile Device-Based Interactions	
Fingerprint	the number of taps on the fingerprint sensor corresponds to the user rating
Multitouch	the number of simultaneous touch points defines the rating score
Tilt	tilting forwards or sideways to accept or reject like „nodding or shaking the head"
Draw	drawing a plus or minus on the screen to accept or reject

Multiple Tap to Rate (Fingerprint)   Multi-Finger Tap to Rate (Multitouch)

Tilt to Vote (Tilt)   Draw to Vote (Draw)

Fig. 1. Examples of device-based interactions – anonymous voting and rating for collocated collaboration with mobile devices.

use smartphones often in their daily life. Only a few participants had experience in interaction design or HCI. Most participants had an academic background. We divided the participants in 8 groups with 4 people each since we utilized the interactions for a collaborative scenario and wanted to investigate how participants support each other in learning new interaction techniques. To avoid inhibitions while interacting with each other, we created the groups with people who already knew each other. We wanted to find out to what extent observing other participants while interacting influence their own interaction performance.

3.2   Apparatus

Interactive Prototype. To perform the user study we implemented an interactive prototype for Android devices. In order to gain insights into the usage of common onboarding tutorials for mobile device-based interaction techniques, we utilized interaction techniques for a collaborative scenario in which collocated users want to vote and rate anonymously (according to Kühn et al. [16,17], see Fig. 1). The interactions *Multiple Tap to Rate (Fingerprint)* and *Multi-Finger Tap to Rate (Multitouch)* are used for rating content, the number of taps on the fingerprint sensor or the number of simultaneous touch points on the display corresponds to the rating score. *Tilt to Vote (Tilt)* and *Draw to Vote (Draw)* is used for giving votes anonymously: Tilting the device forwards or sideways means accepting or rejecting displayed content, drawing a plus or a minus on the screen also stands for accepting or rejecting. The interactions use different device sensors (fingerprint, multitouch, accelerometer and gyroscope), are lightweight and base on metaphors (e. g. nodding/shaking the head, making a cross).

We utilize these interaction techniques for our user study for two main reasons. First, they address the characteristics of mobile device-based interaction techniques. Especially, tangibility and spatiality are very pronounced, whereas individual and collaborative use cases are implicitly included. The second reason is that the interactions can be embedded in one overall scenario which we assume is more comfortable for users to act in. We aim at keeping the workload

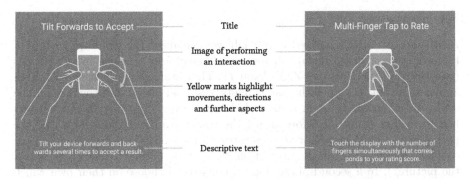

Fig. 2. Two examples of the tutorial that describes *Tilt to Vote* (left) and *Multi-Finger Tap to Rate* (right) and highlights main characteristics of this interaction techniques. (Color figure online)

low in terms of the implemented scenario that is why we implemented a realistic scenario to apply all interactions. The scenario comprises a digital painting exhibition with several pictures that can be assessed anonymously using the newly learned mobile device-based interaction techniques. The Android application contained questionnaires for the tutorial and the interaction techniques. Furthermore, the application included a help function if users had problems performing an interaction as well as instruction text to work through the application autonomously. We provided device feedback in the form of vibration in case of a successful recognition and errors. The application logged all given answers to the questionnaires as well as all performed interactions when detected and the given rating and voting results. Furthermore, in case an error occurred, the application also logged this kind of data.

Onboarding Tutorials. We created a tutorial for each mobile-based interaction of the prototype to describe them properly. The tutorials orientate on common practices for tutorials [9,29] and were refined during several iterations. Figure 2 shows examples of our tutorials for the *Tilt* interaction technique and the *Multitouch* interaction technique and their main characteristics. To facilitate understanding of details to perform the gesture and the purpose of each interaction, each tutorial concentrates on the tangible and spatial characteristics as proposed by Korzetz et al. [14]. Each tutorial consists of one or two pages to show and explain different interaction phases, e. g. multimodal feedback. A clear and brief description communicates the key concepts and also includes a short title to name the interaction. The title is used to refer to the interaction during the user study. Furthermore, an image illustrates how to hold the mobile phone and how to perform the interaction. Yellow marks highlight specific characteristics such as movements and directions. Additionally, a short text describes the performance of the interaction in written form.

3.3 Procedure

After the participants arrived in our lab, we explained the global procedure of the user study. Then, the participants chose one of four provided mobile phones (two Google Pixel and two ZTE Axon 7). They started the provided Android application that described the participants' task and introduced the four mobile device-based interactions in a permuted order using the tutorial. Participants had to read the tutorial before trying the respective interaction. We asked the participants to either rate or vote pictures. In the first phase, participants were concretely asked to use an interaction (e. g. "use tilting to accept or reject the picture"). In a second phase, participants could choose on their own which interaction they use for the given tasks. After each described and tested interaction technique, participants completed a digital questionnaire within the mobile application concerning the tutorial and the usage of the interactions. The study leader observed the participants during the study concerning participants' statements, their prototype usage and performing interactions, e. g. execution speed or holding the smartphone.

3.4 Design

In order to answer the above-mentioned research questions, we realized a within-subject design with the tutorials of the several device-based interactions as independent variable. The dependent variable was the execution error. We further collected quantitative data by means of a digital questionnaire after introducing and using the interactions. Additionally, we collected qualitative data from observations during working with the interactive prototype, the prototype protocols as well as during semi-structured interviews. To avoid learning effects, we varied the testing order of introducing the interactions.

4 Results

We received interesting insights from the user study concerning the usage of the tutorials to get to know new mobile device-based interaction techniques. For analyzing our data, we used observation notes and logging protocols from the implemented application. These protocols included performed interactions and resulting errors as well as the completed questionnaires. With 32 participants and 4 different interactions, we received 128 responses for the questionnaires concerning important information in the tutorials. In the following, we describe our main findings.

4.1 Execution Errors

To gain an overview of how the participants could execute the interactions, we first evaluated the error rates for each interaction. From the logging files we received concrete numbers of errors while performing the rating interactions with

245 errors for *Fingerprint* (M = 7.7, SD = 10.3) and 140 errors for *Multitouch* (M = 4.4, SD = 6.8). The high standard deviations (SD) show that participants either had particularly little or many execution problems independent of the interaction as the effect of interaction technique on the execution error was not statistically significant ($F_{1,31}$ = 2.691, p > .05). The most frequent error while using *Fingerprint* was that participants performed it too fast (126 of 245). Consequently, the fingerprint could not be recognized and the interaction failed. We will improve this issue in future interaction implementations. Other reasons were a wrong rating within the tutorial (44 of 245), fingerprint could only be recognized partially (19 of 245), too many failed attempts (6 of 245) and other technical reasons (50 of 245). *Multitouch* faced the same most frequent problem in terms of execution speed (125 of 140). Participants moved their fingers too fast from the display so that the number of fingers could not be recognized properly. The remaining errors were wrong ratings within the tutorial (15 of 140).

From the observations during the user study, we received insights on problems performing *Tilt* and *Draw*. Derived from the observations, the *Tilt* interaction most often failed because participants were insecure concerning the execution speed and the exact movement of the device combined with holding the mobile phone. Participants tried several ways of tilting and thereby made some comments regarding to interaction execution. Although, these characteristics were described in the tutorial, participants could not apply them easily. Overall, *Draw* failed least. Errors occurred because the strokes were not recognized properly either because participants used the wrong interaction, e. g. they drew plus instead of minus, or because the device did not detect the interaction correctly. From the partially high error rates, we derive that common tutorials do not address spatial and tangible interactions well (RQ1). As a result, the way of describing execution speed and movements for mobile device-based interactions like *Fingerprint*, *Multitouch*, *Tilt* and *Draw* should be reconsidered. Overall, the error rates were relatively high during onboarding, so that we assume imparting interaction knowledge should be improved within app tutorials for device-based interactions. To better understand the users' needs concerning learning mobile-based interactions, we evaluate the timing of tutorial access and asked for helpful information types.

4.2   Help Function and Repetition

Within the whole application participants were allowed to use a help functionality in the right upper corner that was marked with a question mark. Out of the 32 participants, one person used the help function for the *Draw* interaction whereas 2 participants needed help for *Multitouch* and 6 participants for *Fingerprint*. They all used the help function only one time each. For *Tilt*, 12 participants made use of the provided help, 6 persons even several times (up to 4 times). These results indicate that the more unknown or unusual interactions are the more information participants need. This impression is confirmed by the following observation: After performing the tutorial, participants could repeat each interaction technique. From the logging files we found that 3 participants each

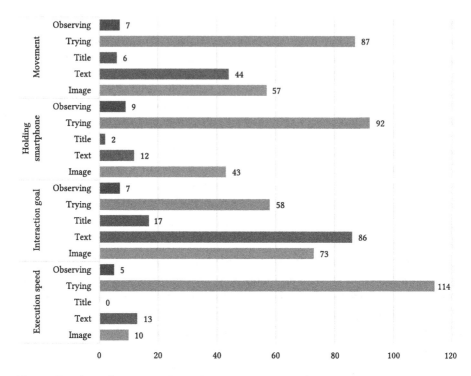

Fig. 3. Number of mentions how observing, trying, title, text, and image helped to understand movement, holding the smartphone, interaction goal, and execution speed.

used the opportunity to repeat the interactions *Fingerprint* (9), *Multitouch* (14), and *Draw* (46) several times. In contrast, *Tilt* was repeated overall 92 times by 9 participants. This indicates that there was a higher need for repeating tangible, movement-based interaction techniques and that the common information from the tutorial were insufficient. Results indicate that implementing onboarding tutorials is suitable to get a first idea of the specific mobile device-based interaction, but users also need support during application usage concerning when and how to execute interactions. Additionally, due to the high repetition rates we derive that useful feedback mechanisms should be investigated and applied.

4.3   Important Information in Tutorials

In the section above, we presented the results of the error rates that occurred despite using onboarding tutorials. To better understand what kind of information was helpful and what is missing, we prepared a questionnaire. After performing the tutorial, we asked the participants to assess the information we gave them to become familiar with the interaction techniques. Participants selected aspects that helped them to understand movement, how to hold the smartphone, the interaction goal, and execution speed to perform an interaction. Figure 3 presents

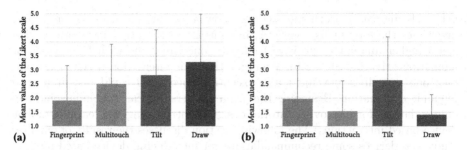

Fig. 4. Mean values (M) and standard deviations (SD) derived from the 5-point Likert scale (5 = completely agree) concerning the statements: (a) *Additional yellow marks helped to understand the interaction.* and (b) *I would have liked to have an additional video or animation that explains the interaction.* (Color figure online)

the given answers. Overall, *trying* an interaction technique was mentioned most often concerning the usefulness to understand the interactions in terms of movement (87 of 128), holding the smartphone (92 of 128) and execution speed (114 of 128) in contrast to observing, title, text, or image. The *title* and *observing* were least helpful to become familiar with the interaction techniques. The *image* was mentioned second to be helpful for understanding the movement (57 of 128) and holding the smartphone (43 of 128). *Text* was especially useful for getting to know the interaction goal (86 of 128).

Beside the questions concerning the ways they became familiar with the interaction techniques, participants rated on a 5-point Likert scale (5 = completely agree) whether the yellow marks (see Fig. 2) helped them to understand the interaction. Yellow marks were rated most helpful for both voting interactions *Tilt* (M = 2.8, SD = 1.6) and *Draw* (M = 3.3, SD = 1.7). Especially for *Draw*, yellow marks were rated as helpful whereas for the *Fingerprint* interaction it was surprisingly mentioned only four times as helpful (M = 1.9, SD = 1.2). However, applying ANOVA showed that there was a significant effect of the interaction on the helpfulness of the yellow marks ($F_{3,93} = 7.216, p < .0005$). We derived from these results that although we annotated visual content with further information, the tutorial remained static and did not show movements or execution speed. Figure 4a summarizes the mean values (M) as well as the standard deviations (SD) of the given answers concerning the helpfulness of the yellow marks within the tutorial. The answers varied, the standard deviations (SD) ranges between 1.3 (*Fingerprint*) and 1.7 (*Draw*). So it seems evident, that interaction tutorials should be adapted to the needs of individual users.

Furthermore, we asked participants whether they wanted additional videos or animations to describe the interaction techniques in detail. Figure 4b shows the mean values (M) and the standard deviations (SD) of the participants' answers. Contrary to what we expected, the majority of answers shows that participants do not want to get further explanations of the interactions through videos or animations, especially for *Multitouch* (M = 1.5, SD = 1.1) and *Draw*

(M = 1.4, SD = 0.7). Both interactions show a low standard deviation, which underlines these opinions. However, in contrast to the other interactions, *Tilt* has a higher amount of positive feedback concerning the wish for a video or animation (M = 2.6, SD = 1.5). We argue that this interaction is the most complex one regarding movement and execution speed and could benefit from a dynamic explanation. Resuming the given answers, we can conclude some recommendations for improving tutorial design of introducing and learning mobile device-based interactions. The following section discusses the results of our user study and derives some recommendations for introducing device-based interactions with mobile phones.

5   Discussion and Recommendations

Reviving our research questions, we found that common tutorials are unsatisfying for becoming familiar with mobile device-based interactions (RQ1). Although study participants mainly had a technical background, following the tutorials and adapting the descriptions to the performance of the interactions still was difficult. We hypothesize that the unsuitability of onboarding tutorial presentations led to high error rates and a high number of repetitions while learning new interaction techniques. We therefore recommend to further investigate adapted tutorials for the specific characteristics of such interaction techniques.

For this purpose, we identified important information that users need to understand mobile device-based interactions (RQ2). Due to their tangibility and spatiality, most important is information about movement, direction, and execution speed. These are specifications that are difficult to present in static tutorials. Unexpectedly, the need of providing dynamic images such as videos or animations instead was overall low. However, interactions that involve motions benefit from dynamic tutorials. As device-based interactions vary in their strength of metaphor, we assume that more figurative interactions like 'pouring' [12] are better understandable by users within an onboarding tutorial. We summarize our recommendations for introducing mobile-based interactions as follows (RQ3):

- Interactions that users perform on-screen like *Multitouch* and *Draw* can be explained as static image with a clear focus on what the user has to do, e. g. drawing a plus or a minus on the screen.
- Interactions that are characterized by movement, direction and/or execution speed or, in general, are performed three-dimensionally like *Fingerprint* and *Tilt* also need support by dynamic three-dimensional media, e. g. meaningful animations or short video sequences, to understand execution details.
- Static images within a tutorial serve as starting point to understand how to hold the phone for execution.
- To become familiar with mobile device-based interactions, especially with more dynamic interactions, the own experience is important. Hence, onboarding tutorials should provide trying interactions in addition to text, images and animations or videos.

– Textual descriptions and an appropriate title are helpful to understand the app function, that is invoked by the device-based interaction.

We also recommend supporting interaction learning while performing the interaction by integrating multimodal real-time feedback (1) during the tutorial instead of first reading and then trying, (2) but also during mobile application usage. Mobile devices can sense if there is a characteristic movement and accordingly provide assistance for suitable implemented interactions. It is also possible to highlight which interaction is available at a certain time to make it easier to remember the interaction possibilities.

With increasing numbers of mobile and wearable devices, the need for appropriate tutorials increases, too. We contribute a profound starting point for further investigations regarding information for and types of tutorials for this special kind of interaction techniques with their distinct characteristics concerning tangibility and spatiality.

5.1 Limitations and Future Work

While our study provides evidence of the need for improving tutorials for mobile device-based interaction techniques, a comparison of such an enhanced form of tutorial would substantiate our findings. As preliminary hypothesis, we expect a lower number of errors and repetitions when adapting tutorials to the characteristics of mobile device-based interactions. When using the tutorials the first time, some of the participants also mentioned that they did not notice the yellow marks (see Fig. 2). This fact was also affirmed by the answers form the questionnaire concerning visual marks, which varied strongly. We will therefore investigate how to make the visual marks more conspicuous. Additionally, we assume that the usage of tutorials depends on the individual background, which also influences interaction learning. Therefore, we will investigate how, for example, the technical background influences the need for certain information. Consequently, further remaining questions are: (1) what alternatives can be used to replace static onboarding tutorials, (2) how users can benefit from learning by doing tutorials, and (3) how to improve discoverability of interaction techniques. Although these questions are not part of this work, we will focus on them in future investigations.

6 Conclusion

We presented an investigation of common onboarding tutorials for introducing mobile device-based interaction techniques to users. We motivated our work through elaborating characteristics of such interaction techniques and describing the research gap in related work. In addition, we conducted a user study to investigate a common tutorial approach for learning mobile device-based interaction techniques. The results show that, especially, with high tangibility and spatiality of such interactions, the suitability of common tutorials decreases.

In future work, we want to compare onboarding tutorials with alternative types, such as tutorials that are provided during application flow. Derived from our user study, we give first recommendations on how to improve tutorials. With this work, we provide a starting point for creating useful and suitable tutorials for mobile device-based interactions, which we believe are beneficial for enhancing ubiquitous environments.

Acknowledgements. The European Social Fund (ESF) and the German Federal State of Saxony have funded this work within the project CyPhyMan (100268299). Also funded by the German Research Foundation (DFG, Deutsche Forschungsgemeinschaft) as part of Germany's Excellence Strategy – EXC 2050/1 – Project ID 390696704 – Cluster of Excellence "Centre for Tactile Internet with Human-in-the-Loop" (CeTI) of Technische Universität Dresden.

References

1. Alt, F., Geiger, S., Höhl, W.: ShapelineGuide: teaching mid-air gestures for large interactive displays. In: Proceedings of the 7th ACM International Symposium on Pervasive Displays, PerDis 2018, pp. 3:1–3:8. ACM (2018). https://doi.org/10.1145/3205873.3205887
2. Ashbrook, D., Starner, T.: MAGIC: a motion gesture design tool. In: Proceedings of the SIGCHI Conference on Human Factors in Computing Systems, CHI 2010, pp. 2159–2168 (2010). https://doi.org/10.1145/1753326.1753653
3. Chong, M.K., Mayrhofer, R., Gellersen, H.: A survey of user interaction for spontaneous device association. J. ACM Comput. Surv. (CSUR) **47**(1), 8–40 (2014). https://doi.org/10.1145/2597768
4. Daiber, F., Kosmalla, F., Murlowski, C., Krüger, A.: Slackliner: using whole-body gestures for interactive slackline training. In: Proceedings of the Symposium on Spatial User Interaction, SUI 2018, pp. 174–174. ACM (2018). https://doi.org/10.1145/3267782.3274691
5. Delamare, W., Coutrix, C., Nigay, L.: Designing guiding systems for gesture-based interaction. In: Proceedings of the 7th ACM SIGCHI Symposium on Engineering Interactive Computing Systems (EICS 2015), pp. 44–53. ACM (2015). https://doi.org/10.1145/2774225.2774847
6. Dingler, T., Rzayev, R., Shirazi, A.S., Henze, N.: Designing consistent gestures across device types: eliciting rsvp controls for phone, watch, and glasses. In: Proceedings of the 2018 CHI Conference on Human Factors in Computing Systems, CHI 2018, pp. 419:1–419:12. ACM (2018). https://doi.org/10.1145/3173574.3173993
7. Harley, A.: Instructional overlays and coach marks for mobile apps (2014). https://www.nngroup.com/articles/mobile-instructional-overlay/. Accessed 18 Jan 2020
8. Harrison, S.M.: A comparison of still, animated, or nonillustrated on-line help with written or spoken instructions in a graphical user interface. In: Proceedings of the SIGCHI Conference on Human Factors in Computing Systems, CHI 1995, pp. 82–89 (1995). https://doi.org/10.1145/223904.223915
9. Higgins, K.: First time user experiences in mobile apps (2012). http://www.kryshiggins.com/first-time-user-experiences-in-mobile-apps/. Accessed 18 Jan 2020

10. Ismair, S., Wagner, J., Selker, T., Butz, A.: MIME: teaching mid-air pose-command mappings. In: Proceedings of 17th International Conference on HCI with Mobile Devices and Services, MobileHCI 2015, pp. 199–206. ACM (2015). https://doi.org/10.1145/2785830.2785854

11. Joyce, G., Lilley, M., Barker, T., Jefferies, A.: Mobile application tutorials: perception of usefulness from an HCI expert perspective. In: Kurosu, M. (ed.) HCI 2016. LNCS, vol. 9732, pp. 302–308. Springer, Cham (2016). https://doi.org/10.1007/978-3-319-39516-6_29

12. Korzetz, M., Kühn, R., Heisig, P., Schlegel, T.: Natural collocated interactions for merging results with mobile devices. In: Proceedings of the 18th International Conference on Human-Computer Interaction with Mobile Devices and Services Adjunct, MobileHCI 2016, pp. 746–752. ACM (2016). https://doi.org/10.1145/2957265.2961839

13. Korzetz, M., Kühn, R., Kegel, K., Georgi, L., Schumann, F.-W., Schlegel, T.: *Milky-Way*: a toolbox for prototyping collaborative mobile-based interaction techniques. In: Antona, M., Stephanidis, C. (eds.) HCII 2019. LNCS, vol. 11573, pp. 477–490. Springer, Cham (2019). https://doi.org/10.1007/978-3-030-23563-5_38

14. Korzetz, M., Kühn, R., Schlegel, T.: Turn it, pour it, twist it: a model for designing mobile device-based interactions. In: Proceedings of the 5th International Conference on Human-Computer Interaction and User Experience in Indonesia, CHIuXiD 2019, pp. 20–23. ACM (2019). https://doi.org/10.1145/3328243.3328246

15. Kühn, R., Korzetz, M., Büschel, L., Korger, C., Manja, P., Schlegel, T.: Natural voting interactions for collaborative work with mobile devices. In: Proceedings of the 2016 CHI Conference Extended Abstracts on Human Factors in Computing Systems, CHI EA 2016, pp. 2570–2575. ACM (2016). https://doi.org/10.1145/2851581.2892300

16. Kühn, R., Korzetz, M., Büschel, L., Schumann, F.-W., Schlegel, T.: Device-based interactions for anonymous voting and rating with mobile devices in collaborative scenarios. In: Proceedings of the 15th International Conference on Mobile and Ubiquitous Multimedia, MUM 2016, pp. 315–317. ACM (2016). https://doi.org/10.1145/3012709.3016067

17. Kühn, R., Korzetz, M., Schumann, F.-W., Büschel, L., Schlegel, T.: Vote-for-It: investigating mobile device-based interaction techniques for collocated anonymous voting and rating. In: Lamas, D., Loizides, F., Nacke, L., Petrie, H., Winckler, M., Zaphiris, P. (eds.) INTERACT 2019. LNCS, vol. 11746, pp. 585–605. Springer, Cham (2019). https://doi.org/10.1007/978-3-030-29381-9_36

18. Kühn, R., Schlegel, T.: Mixed-focus collaboration activities for designing mobile interactions. In: Proceedings of the 20th International Conference on Human-Computer Interaction with Mobile Devices and Services Adjunct, MobileHCI 2018, pp. 71–78. ACM (2018). https://doi.org/10.1145/3236112.3236122

19. Leigh, S.W., Schoessler, P., Heibeck, F., Maes, P., Ishii, H.: THAW: tangible interaction with see-through augmentation for smartphones on computer screens. In: Proceedings of the 9th International Conference on Tangible, Embedded, and Embodied Interaction, TEI 2015, pp. 89–96 (2015). https://doi.org/10.1145/2677199.2680584

20. Linjama, J., Korpipää, P., Kela, J., Rantakokko, T.: ActionCube: a tangible mobile gesture interaction. In: Proceedings of the 2nd International Conference on Tangible and Embedded Interaction, TEI 2008, Bonn, Germany, pp. 169–172 (2008). https://doi.org/10.1145/1347390.1347428

21. Lucero, A., Keränen, J., Jokela, T.: Social and spatial interactions: shared co-located mobile phone use. In: CHI 2010 Extended Abstracts on Human Factors in Computing Systems, CHI EA 2010, pp. 3223–3228 (2010). https://doi.org/10.1145/1753846.1753962

22. Lucero, A., Porcheron, M., Fischer, J.E.: Collaborative use of mobile devices to curate sources of inspiration. In: Proceedings of the 18th International Conference on Human-Computer Interaction with Mobile Devices and Services Adjunct, MobileHCI 2016, pp. 611–616. ACM (2016). https://doi.org/10.1145/2957265.2961830

23. Nielsen, M., Störring, M., Moeslund, T.B., Granum, E.: A procedure for developing intuitive and ergonomic gesture interfaces for HCI. In: Camurri, A., Volpe, G. (eds.) GW 2003. LNCS (LNAI), vol. 2915, pp. 409–420. Springer, Heidelberg (2004). https://doi.org/10.1007/978-3-540-24598-8_38

24. Novick, D.G., Ward, K.: Why don't people read the manual? In: Proceedings of the 24th Annual ACM International Conference on Design of Communication, SIGDOC 2006, pp. 11–18. ACM (2006). https://doi.org/10.1145/1166324.1166329

25. Paay, J., et al.: A comparison of techniques for cross-device interaction from mobile devices to large displays. In: Proceedings of the 14th International Conference on Advances in Mobile Computing and Multi Media, MoMM 2016, p. 137–146. ACM (2016). https://doi.org/10.1145/3007120.3007140

26. Perelman, G., Serrano, M., Bortolaso, C., Picard, C., Derras, M., Dubois, E.: Combining tablets with smartphones for data analytics. In: Lamas, D., Loizides, F., Nacke, L., Petrie, H., Winckler, M., Zaphiris, P. (eds.) INTERACT 2019. LNCS, vol. 11749, pp. 439–460. Springer, Cham (2019). https://doi.org/10.1007/978-3-030-29390-1_24

27. Rico, J., Brewster, S.: Usable gestures for mobile interfaces: evaluating social acceptability. In: Proceedings of the SIGCHI Conference on Human Factors in Computing Systems, CHI 2010, pp. 887–896 (2010). https://doi.org/10.1145/1753326.1753458

28. Rodrigues, A., Camacho, L., Nicolau, H., Montague, K., Guerreiro, T.: AidMe: interactive non-visual smartphone tutorials. In: Proceedings of the 20th International Conference on Human-Computer Interaction with Mobile Devices and Services Adjunct, MobileHCI 2018, pp. 205–212. ACM Press (2018). https://doi.org/10.1145/3236112.3236141

29. Satia, G.: Mobile onboarding: a beginner's guide. Smashing Mag. (2014). https://www.smashingmagazine.com/2014/08/mobile-onboarding-beginners-guide/. Accessed 18 Jan 2020

30. Scoditti, A., Blanch, R., Coutaz, J.: A novel taxonomy for gestural interaction techniques based on accelerometers. In: Proceedings of the 16th International Conference on Intelligent User Interfaces, IUI 2011, pp. 63–72 (2011). https://doi.org/10.1145/1943403.1943414

Multimodal Analysis of Preschool Children's Embodied Interaction with a Tangible Programming Environment

Marleny Luque Carbajal$^{(\boxtimes)}$ and M. Cecília C. Baranauskas$^{(\boxtimes)}$

Institute of Computing, University of Campinas (UNICAMP), São Paulo, Brazil
marleny.carbajal@students.ic.unicamp.br, cecilia@ic.unicamp.br

Abstract. Direct physical interaction with the world is a key constituting factor of cognitive development during childhood. Computational technologies, such as Tangible User Interfaces (TUI), offer opportunities for physically mediated interaction in learning environments, exploiting more embodied forms of interaction through hands-on physical manipulation and exploration. Many studies have introduced young children to programming by tangibles programming environments, although they do not address the effects of embodied interaction in the learning experience. In this paper, we present a case study conducted to introduce preschool children into programming through *TaPrEC+mBot*, an environment that allows programming of a robot car by arranging wooden programming blocks. Drawing on the multimodal method of analysis, we investigate the embodied interaction of the children with the *TaPrEC+mBot* to examine if and how the embodied forms of interaction shape the learning experience. The analysis shows the role of body position, gaze, manipulation, and speech, in terms of how these aspects support the construction of strategies to tangible programs; also the implications of this interaction in the meaning-making process.

Keywords: Embodied interaction · Multimodal analysis · Tangible programming · Tangible User Interface · Preschool children

1   Introduction

Theories and research about embodied cognition consider that human cognition is fundamentally grounded in sensory-motor process and bodily activity [10]. Unlike the traditional theory of cognition that suggests that the brain is central to all cognitive processes, embodied cognition describes how the mind, body, and the world influence one another to create meaning. Wilson and Golonka [23] described embodied cognition as a continuous loop of perception and action in an environment. The mind no longer has been treated as separate from the body, and perceptual rich experiences shape cognitive processes and allow individuals to construct meaning and understanding of the world [7]. Embodied cognition then can be understood as a meaning-making process that occurs through embodied interaction with the physical world. The relationship between physical

© Springer Nature Switzerland AG 2020
M. Kurosu (Ed.): HCII 2020, LNCS 12182, pp. 443–462, 2020.
https://doi.org/10.1007/978-3-030-49062-1_30

experience and cognition has been broadly demonstrated, for example, through theory of affordance for action based on perception [8], the relationship between abstract concepts and bodily experience through metaphorical expression [12], inquiry-based discovery learning [2], and the importance of sensorimotor experience in cognitive development [18]. Jean Piaget [17] posited that cognitive structuring requires both physical and mental activity. Particularly for infants, the direct physical interaction with the world is a key constituting factor of cognitive development.

In the Human-Computer Interaction (HCI) field, embodied interaction is a term coined by Dourish [7] to capture several research trends and ideas in HCI around tangible computing, social computing, and ubiquitous computing, emphasized on the development of interactive experiences in the service of learning. It refers to the creation, manipulation, and sharing of meaning through engaged interaction with artifacts [7], and includes material objects and environments in the process of meaning-making and action formation [21]. Dourish used the term to describe an approach to interaction design that placed an emphasis on understanding and incorporating our relationship with the world around us, both physical and social, into the design and use of interactive systems. The tangibles community within HCI has since built upon this interpretation of embodied interaction focusing on the use of space and movement [9].

Contemporary technologies, such as tangible technology, allow the more physical and immersive mode of interaction, more active learning, hands-on activities directly related to physical contexts, with new forms of communication and collaboration promoting socially mediated learning and foregrounding the role of the body in interaction and learning. The approach of Tangible User Interface (TUI) proposes to embed computing elements in concrete materials, creating an educational feature that unites the advantages of physical interaction and multimedia handling provided by technology. Enriching the concrete materials, computational resources can work several senses (sight, hearing, touch). Theories of learning and cognition offer a compelling rationale for using tangible and embodied interaction for supporting learning [14], being compatible with socio-constructivist theoretical concepts including hands-on engagement; experiential learning [2]; construction of models [15,20]; collaborative activity and transformative communication [16].

Many authors have designed tangible programming tools for young children that support the physical construction of a computer program by connecting or stacking parts that represent an action that is performed by a robot [6,22]. In these environments, a typical programming activity involves asking children to move the robot by creating appropriate computer programs. The children think mainly about the goal of the robot and how the robot will interact with the environment. However, there is another important aspect that they have not considered: how the user physically interacts with the environment and the effects of alternative embodied interactions in the learning experience. In this paper, drawing on the multimodal method of analysis, we investigate the embodied interaction of preschool children with a tangible programming environment to examine how the embodied forms of interaction shape the learning experience. Multimodality offers a valuable approach for analyzing video data, as it allows the interpretation of a wide range of embodied communicational forms (posture, gaze, gesture, manipulation, as well as visual representation and speech) that are relevant to meaning-making [19]. Learning scientists rely on the multimodal analysis of visual, audio, gestural, movement, and other data sources to draw inferences about what and how students are learning. For example, using videos, researchers have looked at facial expressions, gestures, tone of voice, and discourse to understand how people learn [1,11]. The aim of this paper, then, is to look at how embodied forms of interaction play out differently across different children and examine the implications for the knowledge construction process and meaning-making.

The context of this paper is an activity conducted by a group of researchers to introduce young children in programming through creative and meaningful experiences. We worked with two preschool classes where we used the *TaPrEC+mBot* [3], a tangible environment designed for children to learn basic programming concepts as an engaging introduction to computer programming. The environment supports children in building physical computer programs by organizing tangible objects involving basic programming concepts such as sequence, repetition, and procedures. We present and discuss aspects of the role of body position, gaze, manipulation and speech of children interacting with the tangible programming environment. This paper is organized as follows: In Sect. 2 we describe the *TaPrEC+mBot* environment and its functioning, and we present the research methodology and workshops conducted. Then, in Sect. 3 we present the results of our case study. In Sect. 4 we discuss the results and findings. Finally, we present our conclusions and point out to future work in Sect. 5.

2 Case Study: *TaPrEC+mBot* and its Usage

TaPrEC+mBot [3] is a tangible programming environment designed to provide children with an engaging introduction to computer programming. The children should be able to build physical computer programs by organizing tangible objects and applying basic programming concepts such as sequence, repetition, procedures. It consists of four parts (see Fig. 1 up): i) hardware: notebook and Radio Frequency Identification (RFID) system (tag and reader), ii) programming blocks which is a set of colored pieces of puzzle-like wooden blocks containing an RFID tag on one side and an embossed symbol on the other, iii) mBot[1], a robot car that we used to represent the physical output of tangible programs and iv) software: a control program that we developed in the mBlock[2], a Scratch-based programming software tool, to allow communication via Bluetooth between the programming blocks and the mBot.

Through the RFID reader, the tangible program information is entered into the *TaPrEC+mBot* environment. When the user passes the RFID reader over each programming block, the identifiers of the RFID tags are sent to the control

---

[1] https://www.makeblock.com/steam-kits/mbot.
[2] https://www.mblock.cc/en-us/.

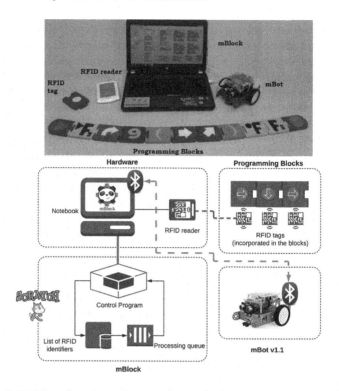

Fig. 1. *TaPrEC+mBot* physical environment (up), system architecture (down)

program. The control program verifies if they exist in the list of RFID identifiers, and it sends them to the processing queue. Then, the control program sends to mBot, via Bluetooth, the Scratch commands associated with each RFID identifier (see Fig. 1 down). Finally, mBot executes the sequence of commands received in the physical world.

2.1   Setting and Participants

The setting for the case study was the Children Living Center (CECI - Portuguese acronym of *Centro de Convivência Infantil*). Located on the campus of the University of Campinas (UNICAMP), it is a space that gives access to the education of infants and children from six months to six years old. Furthermore, our study is part of a project approved by the university's research ethics committee under the number 72413817.3.0000.5404. For this study, we worked with two preschool classes. The first class was composed of fifteen children (6 girls and 9 boys) aged four to five with a mean age of 5.25 ($SD^3 = 0.27$). The second class had ten children (4 girls and 6 boys) aged four to five with a mean age of 5.18 ($SD = 0.41$). We held a workshop with each group that lasted 90 min. The workshops were documented by video and photos.

---

[3] SD: Standard Deviation

2.2   Pilot Work with the Teachers

Before the children's workshops, we conducted a pilot work with the teachers so that they could have their own experience with the *TaPrEC+mBot* environment. With the help of the teachers, we devised the activity to the children's workshops: the children had to program the robot car to cross a bridge (a paper bridge on the floor). During the pilot work, the teachers suggested to use the following programming blocks: i) forward, backward, turn left, and turn right (see Fig. 2) and ii) change the color of the programming blocks so that children could easily differentiate between them (see Fig. 3).

Fig. 2. Pilot work with the teachers

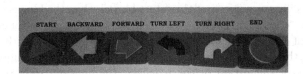

Fig. 3. Programming blocks adapted by teachers

To evaluate the experience with the tangible programming environment, we worked with the teachers to adapt the Emoti-SAM artifact for self-evaluation [4]. The adapted Emoti-SAM consists of 5 emoticons drawn on a paper: the most positive option is a happy face with the thumb up and, in opposition, the most negative is a face of disappointment. Also, the teacher suggested to add a blank space so that the children could freely express their feelings about the activity through their drawing too (see Fig. 4). The children's drawings incorporate a variety of information about the child and his/her experience. As a child-centered evaluation tool, drawings can be advantageous as they are fun and attractive universal activities [24], quick and efficient ways to elicit a large amount of accurate information as no training or practice is required [13], easily produced by children who either may not be able to write proficiently (if at all) or may feel unsure of expressing themselves verbally to a researcher.

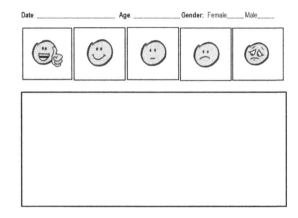

Fig. 4. Emoti-SAM adapted by the teachers (translated from Portuguese).

2.3   Workshops with the Children

The children had already experienced the *TaPrEC+mBot* in another workshop, so they were familiar with our tangible programming environment [5]. Seeking to identify how much the children remembered about the functioning of the *TaPrEC+mBot* environment, we began by asking them: *"Can anyone explain how the programming blocks work?"* We observed that the children partially remembered how to use the programming blocks. Immediately, we explained that to create a tangible program it is necessary to organize the programming blocks in a specific sequence: first the "start block", then the blocks of movement, and finally the "end block". With each team, we demonstrated the functioning of each movement block with simple tangible programs. After the demonstration, we explained the activity, and the teams began to create tangible programs (see Fig. 5). As a suggestion of the teachers, the children were organized into teams of three and four children, so that while one team interacted with the *TaPrEC+mBot* in the playroom, the other teams waited inside the classroom, making drawings or other typical activity of the playtime.

Fig. 5. Two teams of children programming the mBot robot

The teams spent between 15 and 25 min interacting with the *TaPrEC+mBot*. After finishing the time of work with the environment, we finished the workshop by applying the Emoti-SAM adapted according to the teacher's suggestions. We asked the children to draw what they liked most about the workshop (see Fig. 6).

Fig. 6. Child filling out the Emoti-SAM adapted form

3   Results of the Case Study

The analysis conducted was supported by the videos recorded about the activities and aims to find forms of embodied interaction in the experience with the tangible programming environment. In this paper, we use embodied interaction in its practical sense to denote direct, body-based interaction. It was apparent from the data that the teams of children chose to position themselves similarly around the environment: the children positioned themselves adjacent to one another with the programming blocks in the front of them and they sat on the floor for most of the interaction (see Fig. 5). However, occasionally some kids got up and walked to have a close watch of the position of the robot concerning the cardboard bridge. The children's gaze towards the programming blocks was generally for long periods, and they only watched the robot when it moved during the execution of the tangible program. During the creation of tangible programs, first, they build the program, pass the RFID reader, and then they look at the actions of the robot. Our analysis aimed to explore ways in which the bodily-based differences may importantly shape the action and strategies for the construction of tangible programs. Also, some students were observed to be more verbal than others, which in turn influenced their use of other embodied forms. Inspired by Price and Jewitt's work [19], a detailed transcription of the multimodal interaction of seven teams of children was then completed. This comprised a record of body positioning and changes in bodily position, manipulation of programming blocks, gaze and speech. This enabled access to the following types of data: about the process of creating a tangible program, the turn-taking during the activity and the description of algorithms in verbal form.

3.1 Teams' Activity

Team 1 (Girl1, Girl2, Girl3, Girl4): Their total interaction time was 15.36 min, and the team completed the task successfully (see Fig. 7). During the creation of the tangible program, usually, Girl4 was distracted and her gaze was in multiple directions. However, at the time that her classmates passed the reader RFID on the tangible program, she joined the group and watched closely. The children were attentive to the sound of the RFID reader, and even they imitated the sound every time it passed over a programming block. When the robot moves, everyone is also attentive too. The tangible programs were created mainly by Girl1 and Girl3. Girl2 grabbed some programming blocks to create her programs, but she did not test them. Girl4 passed programming blocks to Girl1 and Girl3. Throughout the interaction, they built 6 tangible programs, adding, removing, and changing the programming blocks. The changes are made quickly by one, and then by another, or simultaneously. Almost in the last part of the task, when the robot is closer to the bridge, the four girls come together to form a circle around the programming blocks and program together. In most of the tangible programs, Girl3 was in charge of passing the RFID reader, but in the last program, the RFID reader was operated by Girl2 who joined the group again to complete the task.

Some of the girls' expressions related to the creation of the tangible programs are directed to describe what happened after the program was executed (*"It went straight and then turned"*) or about new steps to follow (*"It needs to go further"*, *"It has to turn here"*). Talks between Girl1 and Girl3 denote discussion of ideas about the creation of a tangible program:

Girl3: *"I think it has to make a turn"*
Girl1: *"No, it has to go here"*
Girl3: *"So I'm going to put this"*
Girl1: *"But then the car goes here"*
Girl3: *"And this one?"*
Girl1: *"This is not backward. This is forward"*

We observed that the girls used their arms to explain their programs. When they wanted to explain that the robot goes to the left, they moved with the arms indicating that direction. They built a basic program, and later they added programming blocks. If the new blocks approached the robot to the bridge, they continued adding blocks; otherwise, they removed the blocks and continued with the basic program. They mainly used the "forward" block.

Team 2 (Girl5, Boy1, Boy2, Boy3): Their total interaction time was 20.03 min, and the team did not complete the task (see Fig. 8). Initially, the children positioned themselves side by side and after they formed a circle to start programming. When they have to test or program, the children open the circle to observe the movements of the robot. The children scattered the programming blocks around them. When they needed some programming block, they should look at all the parts around them. Most of the tangible programs

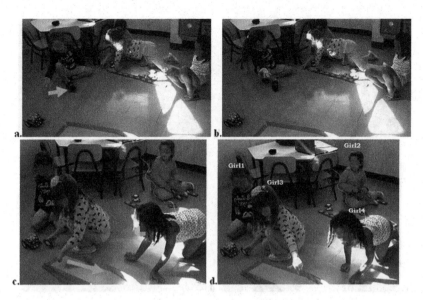

Fig. 7. Team 1 during the process of building tangible programs.

were created by Boy3. The other children helped by placing some programming blocks, suggesting the use of some programming blocks and finding and giving the programming blocks to their classmates. The task of passing the RFID reader was mainly performed by Girl5 and Boy3. In total, the team created 16 tangible programs. The following is an excerpt from the conversation between Boy1 and Boy3 during the creation of a tangible program:

Boy1: *"It's just that the robot goes forward, forward, forward, turn around, and up here"*
Boy3: *"No, it has to turn around and stay straight and go there"*
Boy1: *"For me, it will go wrong"*

We observed that Boy2 simulated the mBot route acting as if he was the robot itself, made the route taking small steps while talking about how the tangible program should be (*"It walks forward, turn there, goes here, forward, stop here, then it goes up, it goes forward"*). We observed that the movements of Boy3's hands to indicate the movements that the robot should perform to accomplish the task. A strategy that Boy1 used to know what programming blocks to use was to grab the robot and simulate the movements necessary to raise the cardboard bridge. In this way, he could also calculate the number of programming blocks.

Fig. 8. Team 2 during the process of building tangible programs.

Team 3 (Girl6, Boy4, Boy5, Boy6): Their total interaction time was 18.08 min, and the team completed the task (see Fig. 9). When starting the activity, the children sit around the programming blocks except for Boy4; he approaches the robot and he watches it attentive. Then he joins the group to start programming. Boy5 observes the position of the robot and begins to create a tangible program. Boy4 gets distracted and starts walking in the classroom. Boy6 gets up and goes to the robot to calculate the distance with his hands and returns to the circle. The tangible programs were created by Girl6, Boy5, and Boy6. They worked together simultaneously, adding, removing and changing the programming blocks; and to pass the RFID reader they took turns with each other. In the final part of the activity, Boy4 joins the team to create the last tangible program.

During the activity, Girl6, Boy5, and Boy6 talked about ideas to create tangible programs, as illustrated below:

Girl5: *"And what if you put that block"*
Boy5: *"It [the robot] will hit the table; it has to turn the other way"*
Boy5: *"We need two [blocks] backward. Let's see if it works"*
Boy6: *"It [the robot] will have to turn there"*
Boy5: *"The face [of the robot] has to turn in front of us"*
Boy6: *"No, it has to turn there."*

In total, the team built 12 tangible programs. The children's strategy to complete the task was to make programs with one, two or three movements (Ex: [START, FORWARD, FORWARD, END]) and repeat the same program

Fig. 9. Team 3 during the process of building tangible programs.

several times while the robot was approaching the bridge. When it was necessary to make turns, they placed the two blocks of turns to verify which of the blocks to use (Ex: [START, TURN RIGHT, TURN LEFT, END]). One of the most interesting interactions we observed was Girl6 turning her body imitating the movement of the robot. Besides, as in the other teams, the children used arms and hands to indicate movements for their tangible program or explain their program ideas to their classmates.

Team 4 (Boy7, Boy8, Boy9): Their total interaction time was 18.02 min, and the team completed the task (see Fig. 10). During the manipulation of programming blocks, Boy9 is not attentive and he was very introverted. However, when Boy7 executed the tangible programs and the robot moves, Boy9 approaches the group to watch closely. Boy7 was the one who created almost all tangible programs. Eight of the nine programs were created by Boy7. Boy8 helped by placing the programming blocks in just one, but he took charge of passing the RFID reader and giving suggestions to Boy7. During the interaction, the dialogues were only between Boy7 and Boy8. The following is an example:

Boy7: *"It has to go forward and turn"*
Boy8: *"I will remove this piece. I'll put this block from here to turn over here"*

The team's strategy to accomplish the task was to create programs with few movements (Ex. [START, FORWARD, TURN LEFT, END]) until the robot was very close to the bridge. Then they added more programming blocks and repeated the last program several times until the robot was able to pass the

Fig. 10. Team 4 during the process of building tangible programs.

bridge (Ex. The program [START, FORWARD, FORWARD, FORWARD, FOR-WARD, FORWARD, FORWARD, END] was repeated twice). The main movements that they carried out were with the hands to indicate the direction that the robot should follow.

Team 5 (Girl7, Boy10, Boy11, Boy12): Their total interaction time was 24.22 min, and the team completed the task (see Fig. 11). Everyone starts picking up the blocks to help build a tangible program. Each one tries to solve the task: Boy11 simulates the robot's movements with his hands on the floor, and he calculates the number of blocks for the tangible program. Girl7 and Boy12 set up their programs separately. Boy12 is the first to test his tangible program. When the robot moves, everyone pays attention, and then they come together in a circle to program. Twelve of the sixteen tangible programs were created with the help of all children. The other tangible programs were created by Boy11 and Boy12. Boy10 and Girl7 were responsible for passing the RFID reader on the programming blocks.

During the process of creating tangible programs, the children talked about which programming blocks to put in the program and the quantity of them, as illustrated below:

Boy11: *"The bridge is big then we have to put a lot of FORWARD"*
Girl7: *"Not so much!"*
Boy12: *"You should put 3 of these [FORWARD] and then turn here and then go up"*

Fig. 11. Team 5 during the process of building tangible programs.

We identified that as a strategy for solving the problem, children place the largest number of blocks to observe the movements of the robot. Then they completely dismantled this program and created another one with other combinations of programming blocks. When they got the robot to stay close to the bridge, they created programs with just one movement (Ex: [START, TURN LEFT, END], [START, FORWARD, END]) to prevent the robot from moving away from the objective. When the robot was already on the bridge, they created a program with nine "forward" blocks to get the robot to pass the bridge. We observed that when children Boy10 and Boy12 explained their tangible programs, they placed their hands on the floor pretending to be the robot and made the path of the robot themselves (see Fig. 11).

Team 6 (Boy13, Girl8, Girl9): Their total interaction time was 15.04 min, and the team completed the task (see Fig. 12). At the beginning of the activity, Girl8 and the Boy13 program separately, and each creates its tangible program. Girl9 watches her classmates. There was competitiveness to grab the programming blocks. Girl8 is the first to test her tangible program. After this, Boy13 tests his tangible program. Once the robot begins to move, Girl9 shows interest, and she begins to create her tangible program. They worked separately, and they tested their programs one after the other until Girl8 achieved the robot very close to the bridge. The children begin to help Girl8 by giving suggestions and passing the programming blocks. In total, the children built 8 tangible programs, and Girl8 manipulated mostly the programming blocks.

In this team, there was few dialogue between the members. Here are some examples:

Fig. 12. Team 6 during the process of building tangible programs.

Girl8: *"To go forward, what is the block"*
Girl9: *"It's pink"*

The children built programs with just one movement when they wanted the robot to make turns (Ex. [START, TURN LEFT, END], [START, TURN RIGHT, END]) and programs with several programming blocks when they wanted the robot to advance large spaces (Ex. [START, FORWARD, FORWARD, FORWARD, FORWARD, FORWARD, FORWARD, END]). This team showed body movements that accompanied the creation of tangible programs, for example, the movements of hands (see Fig. 12c).

Team 7 (Boy14, Girl10, Boy15): Their total interaction time was 25.47 min, and the team completed the task (see Fig. 13). At the beginning of the activity, the team worked separately. Boy15 built his program, and Girl10 and Boy14 built their programs. Throughout the activity, the team worked separately. In total, they created 25 tangible programs: 5 programs created by Boy15, and 20 programs created by Girl10 and Boy14. Most of the programs were simple, with just one movement (Ex. [START, TURN RIGHT, END]). Girl10 and Boy15 approached the bridge to observe the position of the robot to be able to identify what type of programming block they should use.

This team had little verbal exchange related to the creation of tangible programs:
Boy14: *"It has to go forward and then there"*
Girl10: *"Now it has to go back"*

Fig. 13. Team 7 during the process of building tangible programs.

We mainly observed that the children used the movements of arms and hands to explain their programs.

3.2 Feedback from the Adapted Emoti-SAM

Regarding the adapted Emoti-SAM, Table 1 shows the responses of children for their experience in the workshops. The children indicated, in a range of emoticons, their affective states about the workshop, painting the desired emoticon. Seventeen of the twenty-five children opted for the emoticon that represents the greatest happiness, five children opted for the second emoticon of the scale, and three children painted the saddest emoticon. The results indicate that the activity was considered pleasurable and enjoyable for most of the children. To a correct analysis of the Emoti-SAM drawings, the children were asked individually to talk about what they had drawn. We quantified the drawings made by children (see Table 2). Samples of the Emoti-SAM drawings are illustrated in Fig. 14 and Fig. 15.

4   Discussion

A multimodal methodological approach focuses on the role of various modes, such as posture, gaze, action and speech in the meaning-making process, and

Fig. 14. Girl's explanation: *"She is me, the little pieces of command, the bridge and the robot"*.

Fig. 15. Boy's explanation: *"The little pieces of the command, the robot is going up the bridge, the bridge, the robot's path across the bridge, then the robot goes straight"*.

the interaction between these modes. We collected data regarding the process of creating a tangible program to investigate the position, action, and speech of children in the effort to accomplish a task together. Regarding the children's behavior, during the workshop, we observed that trying to control robots through programming was a very exciting process for the children. The verbal and bodily manifestations that we observed show that most children interacted with the

Table 1. Emoti-SAM results from all children

Emoticon					
Number of Children	17	5	0	0	3

Table 2. Emoti-SAM results from all children

Type of drawing	Quantity
robot	21
bridge	17
programming blocks	8
classmates	4
herself/himself	4

environment with great freedom, i.e. creating themselves their strategies instead of following instructions, and enthusiasm. Their body postures lying down on the floor to watch closely the robot movements suggest they were very relaxed and yet attentive. Eight of the twenty-five children who participated in the case study approached the robot to observe more closely its position in relation to the cardboard bridge. All other children remained in the place or near the place chosen at the beginning of the interaction within reach of the programming blocks.

Our analysis suggests that the approach that the children had towards the robot and the cardboard bridge, helped them to define what type of programming blocks to use and the number of these. We observed three types of strategies that children used to define the programming blocks: i) act as if they were the robot and carry out the path that the robot should travel to complete the task, ii) the children used their hands to indicate the directions that the robot should follow, iii) the children grabbed the robot and they simulated the route that the robot should move. Different positions give different opportunities for interaction, for example, the children who grabbed the robot could discover that the robot has a little face that represented the front of the robot. It was an important fact so that they could build the programs according to where the robot's face was. The children who stayed in their initial position observed the position of the robot in the distance and used arms and hand movements to indicate the movements that the robot should make, and this helped them choose the appropriate programming blocks for the tangible program.

Regarding the children's speech, we observe that each group had a different level of communication, while some groups frequently talked to define each robot movement, members of other groups preferred to act separately and then test their ideas in practice. The children pretended to be the robot, usually recounted their movements as they made the path that the robot should take. Many of the explanations given by the children were accompanied by body movements, for example, when they said "the robot must go to this site", the children did not say "left" or "right", but they moved the arm or hand in the direction in which they wanted the robot to move. Generally, the programming blocks were scattered in the floor so that any child could grab them. This favored that regardless of their location in the group space, the children had equal access to the programming blocks. Each child pick up blocks and place them on the program easily and simultaneously, or at similar times, and led to clashes of action and ideas, and reposition or remove of the blocks from others when creating a tangible program. While their articulations comprised instructions and basic descriptions of algorithms, some teams extended their types of dialogue to include explanations and predictions.

One difference that exists between the teams is the number of tangible programs they created to accomplish the same task. This offers the opportunity for exploring a greater number of combinations of sequence of movements, potentially exposing the children to more experiences. On the other hand, the teams that created a greater number of tangible programs reduced their reflection time before changing any programming block of the tangible program, which caused errors to complete the task. We observed that an adequate reflection time was important for children to understand the function of programming blocks and allow them to consider how they created their program and correctly choose which programming block to use.

Regarding the children's emotions, we used Emoti-SAM adapted to allow children to express their opinions and feelings towards the workshop and our tangible programming environment. Most of the children said they liked the environment very much in Emoti-SAM with an average score of 5.0, which was consistent with what we observed. The children made drawings symbolizing what they liked the most in the workshop. Twenty-one of twenty-five children drew the mBot; this may mean that the robot was in the center of attention for them. Some of the Emoti-SAM drawings represent a dynamic scene (for example, mBot crossing a bridge) that suggest a high level of involvement with the experience. It is also interesting to note that some children project themselves in the scene of programming the robot.

According to our observations, the embodied interaction is shown in: i) the program planning when the children moved their hands indicate directions while they explain their ideas for building the tangible program (for example Fig. 7d, Fig. 8a); ii) the algorithm building when the children used their arm, finger or hand movements to identify what programming block should be added to their tangible program (for example Fig. 8b, Fig. 13d); iii) the simulation the tangible program when the children use the full-body movement with locomotion to drawing the path that the robot will move (for example Fig. 8c, Fig. 11c); iv) the debugging of the tangible program when the children used their hands on the floor to calculate the number of programming blocks to correct a previous program (for example Fig. 11b); v) the execution of tangible program, when the children imitated the movements that the robot made (for example, Fig. 9b).

5   Conclusion

TaPrEC+mBot is a technological environment designed with current educational challenges that highlight the development of computational training as an important skill child should develop to learn and hopefully appreciate science and technology later. This paper aimed to explore a multimodal approach to analyzing embodied interaction in a tangible programming environment with children aged 4–5 years. The results show that the children had different forms of bodily interaction, demonstrating different forms of manipulation, strategies and verbal articulation. The relationship between these modes seems to be directly influenced and influences the creation of tangible programs. The verbal articulation gives an idea of the students' thinking and planning. Future studies might examine the use of wearable technology for providing embodied experiences to introduce programming concepts.

Acknowledgments. This study was financed in part by *Coordenação de Aperfeiçoamento de Pessoal de Nível Superior - Brasil* (CAPES)- Finance Code 001 - scholarships #1545149/2015 and #1654045/2016, by the National Council for Scientific and Technological Development - Brazil (CNPq) through grants #140536/2019-1 and #306272/2017-2, and by the São Paulo Research Foundation (FAPESP) through grant #2015/16528-0. We would like to thank the Division of Child and Supplementary Education (DEdIC - *Divisão de Educação Infantil e Complementar*), the Children Living Center (CECI - *Centro de Convivência Infantil*) and Institute of Computing at University of Campinas.

References

1. Barron, B., Pea, R., Engle, R.: Advancing understanding of collaborative learning with data derived from video records. In: The International Handbook of Collaborative Learning, pp. 203–219 (2013)
2. Bruner, J.S.: On Knowing: Essays for the Left Hand. Harvard University Press (1979)
3. Carbajal, M., Baranauskas, M.C.: Programação, robôs e aprendizagem criativa por meio de cenários: um estudo exploratório. In: Brazilian Symposium on Computers in Education (Simpósio Brasileiro de Informática na Educação-SBIE), vol. 29, p. 1113 (2018)
4. Carbajal, M.L., Baranauskas, M.C.C.: Using ethnographic data to support preschool children's game design. In: Proceedings of the 18th Brazilian Symposium on Human Factors in Computing Systems, p. 55. ACM (2019)
5. Carbajal, M.L., Baranauskas, M.C.: Exploring and evaluating "TaPrEC+ mBot" environment with preschool children. In: Anais do Workshop de Informática na Escola, vol. 25, no. 1, p. 521 (2019)
6. Chawla, K., Chiou, M., Sandes, A., Blikstein, P.: Dr. Wagon: a 'stretchable' toolkit for tangible computer programming. In: Proceedings of the 12th International Conference on Interaction Design and Children, pp. 561–564. ACM (2013)
7. Dourish, P.: Where the Action is: The Foundations of Embodied Interaction. MIT Press (2004)
8. Gibson, J.J.: The Theory of Affordances, vol. 1, no. 2, Hilldale (1977)

9. Hornecker, E., Buur, J.: Getting a grip on tangible interaction: a framework on physical space and social interaction. In: Proceedings of the SIGCHI Conference on Human Factors in Computing Systems, pp. 437–446 (2006)
10. Ionescu, T., Vasc, D.: Embodied cognition: challenges for psychology and education. Procedia Soc. Behav. Sci. **128**, 275–280 (2014)
11. Koschmann, T., Stahl, G., Zemel, A.: The video analyst's manifesto (or the implications of Garfinkel's policies for studying instructional practice in design-based research). In: Video Research in the Learning Sciences, pp. 133–143 (2007)
12. Lakoff, G., Johnson, M.: Metaphors we Live By. University of Chicago Press (1980)
13. MacPhail, A., Kinchin, G.: The use of drawings as an evaluative tool: students' experiences of sport education. Phys. Educ. Sport Pedagogy **9**(1), 87–108 (2004)
14. O'Malley, C., Fraser, D.S.: Literature review in learning with tangible technologies (2004)
15. Papert, S.: Mindstorms: Children, Computers and Powerful Ideas. Basic Books, New York (1980)
16. Pea, R.D.: Seeing what we build together: distributed multimedia learning environments for transformative communications. J. Learn. Sci. **3**(3), 285–299 (1994)
17. Piaget, J., Cook, M.: The Origins of Intelligence in Children, vol. 8, no. 5. International Universities Press. New York (1952)
18. Piaget, J., Inhelder, B.: The Psychology of the Child. Basic books (2008)
19. Price, S., Jewitt, C.: A multimodal approach to examining 'embodiment' in tangible learning environments. In: Proceedings of the 7th International Conference on Tangible, Embedded and Embodied Interaction, pp. 43–50 (2013)
20. Resnick, M.: Technologies for lifelong kindergarten. Education Tech. Research Dev. **46**(4), 43–55 (1998)
21. Streeck, J., Goodwin, C., LeBaron, C. (eds.): Embodied Interaction: Language and Body in the Material World. Cambridge University Press (2011)
22. Sullivan, A., Elkin, M., Bers, M.U.: KIBO robot demo: engaging young children in programming and engineering. In: Proceedings of the 14th International Conference on Interaction Design and Children, pp. 418–421. ACM (2015)
23. Wilson, A.D., Golonka, S.: Embodied cognition is not what you think it is. Front. Psychol. **4**, 1–13 (2013). https://doi.org/10.3389/fpsyg.2013.00058. (Article 58)
24. Xu, D., Read, J.C., Sim, G., McManus, B.: Experience it, draw it, rate it: capture children's experiences with their drawings. In: Proceedings of the 8th International Conference on Interaction Design and Children, pp. 266–270 (2009)

Identification Method of Digits for Expanding Touchpad Input

Takuto Nakamura[✉] and Buntarou Shizuki

University of Tsukuba, 1-1-1 Tennoudai, Tsukuba, Ibaraki, Japan
{nakamura,shizuki}@iplab.cs.tsukuba.ac.jp

Abstract. A method is presented for identifying the digits, i.e., the thumb and/or finger(s), that touch a touchpad as a means to expand the input vocabulary available on a touchpad. It will enable application designers to assign different commands to touch gestures performed with the same number of digits and the same movement but with different digits. No additional sensors are required for identification; instead the digits are identified on the basis of machine learning using only data acquired from a mutual-capacitance touchpad as learning data. Experimental results revealed an average identification accuracy of 86.3%.

Keywords: Digit identification · Touch gestures · Machine learning

1 Introduction

The touchpad has become the most common pointing device for laptop computers. The system executes a command in accordance with the number of digits (i.e., the thumb and/or finger(s)) that touch on the touchpad and their movement. However, due to the limited input vocabulary available on a touchpad, an application that requires frequent switches between many tools and modes forces users to frequently select graphical user interface (GUI) elements such as items in tool menus and buttons in menu bars or to use keyboard shortcuts. For example, in order to draw or select figures when using a graphical editor, the user first selects the desired tool by either choosing it from a toolbar or using the keyboard shortcut assigned to the tool and then touching the touchpad to manipulate the tool. For such applications, it would be useful to be able to switch tools or modes at the same time as making a touch gesture.

Our goal is to expand the input vocabulary available on a touchpad by developing a method for identifying the digits that touch the touchpad; this identification will enable application designers to assign different commands to touch gestures performed with the same number of digits and the same movement but with different digits (Fig. 1). In this paper, as a first step towards achieving this goal, we present a method for identifying the digits, i.e., the thumb and/or finger(s), that touch the touchpad. No additional sensors are needed for identification; instead the digits are identified on the basis of machine learning using only data acquired from a mutual-capacitance touchpad as learning data.

© Springer Nature Switzerland AG 2020
M. Kurosu (Ed.): HCII 2020, LNCS 12182, pp. 463–474, 2020.
https://doi.org/10.1007/978-3-030-49062-1_31

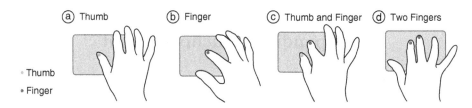

Fig. 1. Touchpad input based on thumb-or-finger identification. Touch gestures using (a) one thumb or (b) one finger can be assigned to different commands; similarly, touch gestures using a combination of (c) a thumb and a finger or (d) two fingers can be assigned to different commands.

2   Related Work

Many previous studies similar to ours have focused on expanding touchpad input by identifying the digits used.

2.1   Expanding Touchpad Input

Cui et al. [4] developed a method that places a virtual keyboard on the touchpad area while the user is pressing a specific modifier key enabling the user to execute a shortcut command by tracing the keys in the order of the spelling of the command name. In the method developed by Berthellemy et al. [2], the touchpad is divided into a grid of areas and a command is assigned to each area; the user can quickly execute a command by pressing a dedicated key on the keyboard and then tapping the corresponding area on the touchpad. They also proposed displaying command menus at the four vertices and on the four sides of the screen, enabling the user to execute a command by swiping the corresponding touchpad bezel. Fruchard et al. [5] developed a method in which the touchpad area is divided into a checkerboard pattern, and a stroke gesture from one area to another is used to trigger a specific command; the stroke pattern and command name are displayed on the screen at execution for visual assistance. Ikematsu et al. [10] added button-like and pointing stick-like inputs to a touchpad by attaching pressure-sensitive sensors to the area next to the touchpad and pasting the electrodes to the touchpad surface; the pressure exerted on a sensor was measured and taken as the leakage current from the corresponding touch surface electrodes.

Several methods expand touchpad input by using touchpads with special structures. Jung et al. [11] made it possible to give the user tactile feedback and feedforward in a form recognizable with the fingers by using a touchpad implemented using a 40 × 25 array of vertical-type Braille display module pins. Gu et al. [7] extended the width of the touchpad to that of the laptop's keyboard, thereby facilitating the input of long horizontal gestures.

Furthermore, several methods using an infrared proximity sensor array or a capacitive grid enable touchpad input on a keyboard or hover-gesture input on a touchpad [3,9,18,19].

In contrast, our method focuses on expanding touchpad input rather than keyboard input. Additionally, our method can be applied to existing touchpads since it requires no additional sensor or attachment.

2.2 Digit Identification

Digit identification using a capacitive image of a touchscreen to expand input vocabulary on a touchscreen has been explored. Le et al. [12] developed a method that acquires a capacitive image from a smartphone's touchscreen and identifies the digit touching the screen using a convolutional neural network. Experiments showed that its identification accuracy for the thumb (left or right) is 92%. Gil et al. [6] developed a method that identifies the thumb, index finger, and middle finger by acquiring a capacitive image from the touchscreen of a smartwatch and using machine learning (Random Forest). They reported that the identification accuracies during tapping and swiping tasks were 93% and 98% in natural poses and exaggerated poses, respectively.

There are also methods for identifying digits by attaching sensors to the fingers. Gupta et al. [8] developed one that identifies the touch of the index finger and middle finger on the touchscreen of a smartwatch by using infrared proximity sensors attached to the finger pads. Park and Lee [16] developed one that identifies the touch of the index finger, middle finger, and ring finger on the touchscreen of a smartwatch by using a ring with a built-in magnet. The magnetic field is acquired using the smartwatch's built-in magnetic sensor and the fingers are identified using machine learning (Support Vector Machine). With the method of Masson et al. [14], a vibration sensor is attached to each digit (from thumb to little finger), and the digit that detects the largest vibration when there is a keyboard or touchpad input event is determined to be the digit that was used for the input. Benko et al. [1] attached an electromyography sensor to the arm to detect electromyograms that are generated when a user inputs a touch gesture to the touch screen. The fingers used for the gesture are identified by machine learning. The method of Vega and Fuks [20] identifies fingers touching a flat surface with a tag reader by using artificial fingernails with a built-in electronic tag. Furthermore, several reported methods identify fingers by computer vision [13,15,17,21].

In contrast, we focus on digit identification for a touchpad rather than a touchscreen. Moreover, our method requires no additional sensors to identify digits.

3   Identification Method

We focused on the fact that when a digit touches a touchpad, the side of the thumb touches, whereas the pad of a finger touches (see Fig. 2). This means that the shape of the contact surface of the thumb and that of a finger differ. Using this difference, our method identifies the digits touching the touchpad by acquiring data on the contact surfaces from the touchpad and classifying them using machine learning. Our method comprises two phases: the learning phase and the identification phase.

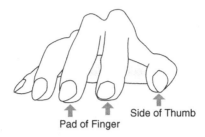

Fig. 2. Contact surfaces of digits touching touchpad.

3.1   Learning Phase

In the learning phase, the system collects data from the touchpad as the user slides each digit of both hands on the touchpad. The system regards the contact area between a digit and the touchpad as an ellipse and uses eight values as data for machine learning: the x and y coordinates of its center, the lengths of the major and minor axes, the angle of the major axis, the area, the ellipticity, and the contact surface density. The system collects these values (except the ellipticity) from the touchpad and calculates the ellipticity using the collected values. To enable collection of learning data covering the entire touchpad area, we divided the touchpad area into $5 \times 5 = 25$ areas and collected learning data from 30 frames for each area. In total, the system collects data from 15,000 frames (5 digits $\times$ 2 hands $\times$ 2 directions $\times$ 25 areas $\times$ 30 frames) for each user.

Next, the system generates a machine learning model from the collected data. For simplicity, here we use a value indicating thumb or finger (i.e., two labels) as the objective variable; we use the learning data (i.e., the data from the 15,000 frames) as the explanatory variables.

3.2   Identification Phase

The system, in real-time, identifies the digits at the moment that touching begins. That is, every time the system acquires data on the contact surface of a digit touching the touchpad, it uses the machine learning model generated in the learning phase to identify the digit. If two or more digits touch the touchpad, the system applies this process to each contact surface. The predictor variables are the same as the explanatory variables in the learning phase (i.e., eight values). The response variable is the result of digit identification (thumb or finger).

3.3   Implementation

We implemented our method in a system as a macOS application. We used Core ML and Create ML as machine learning frameworks. As a model for machine learning, we used Gradient Boosting, which was selected by Create ML as the optimal machine learning algorithm among five algorithms: Decision Tree, Random Forest, Gradient Boosting, Support Vector Machine, and Logistic Regression. We used MultitouchSupport for acquiring raw data from the touchpad.

4   Experiment

We conducted an experiment to investigate the identification accuracy of our method.

4.1   Apparatus and Participants

We used a laptop computer (Apple, MackBook Pro 13-inch, 2017) with a built-in touchpad (size: $134\,mm \times 83\,mm$, resolution: 26×18 matrix). We pasted LCD protective film on the surface of the touchpad, on which $5 \times 5 = 25$ areas where drawn with a maker pen so that the participants could see the 25 areas.

We recruited 12 full-time undergraduate and graduate students from a local institution (all male, mean age = 23.2, 11 right-handed) who usually use a laptop computer with a touchpad.

4.2   Tasks

The participants were asked to perform two tasks: a learning-data sampling task and a test-data sampling task.

Learning-Data Sampling Task. As shown in Fig. 3, the participants slid a digit on the touchpad horizontally and vertically until all 25 areas turned red, indicating that learning data from 30 frames for an area had been collected. We asked the participants to sit on a chair with a laptop computer on a desk in front of them and to slide their digit in both directions horizontally (i.e., left to right and right to left). We collected touch data from 30 frames for each digit, area, and direction in a fixed order (digit types: thumb $\rightarrow$ little finger, hands: right $\rightarrow$ left, directions: horizontal $\rightarrow$ vertical). We instructed the participants not to press the touchpad.

Test-Data Sampling Task. An image of the application used in this task is shown in Fig. 4. In each session, the participant was asked to touch each area once with each digit. The order of digit types was presented randomly by the application. For every digit type, the order of the area to be touchpad was presented randomly. The next area was not presented until the correct area was touchpad.

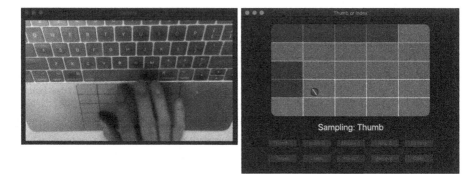

Fig. 3. Image of a participant sliding right thumb horizontally in learning-data sampling task, and image showing collection status of each area (red: completed, blue: partially completed, gray: not started). (Color figure online)

Fig. 4. Image of participant touching an area with his left thumb in the test-data sampling task.

To examine the robustness of our method, we collected test data under three conditions: *Desk Condition*, *Lap Condition*, and *Bed Condition*, as shown in Fig. 5, as shown in Fig. 5. In Desk Condition, the participant sat on a chair with a laptop computer on a desk in front of him. In Lap Condition, he sat on a chair with a laptop computer on his lap. In Bed Condition, he lay on a foldable camp bed (AZUMAYA, LFS-709GY, 190 cm × 67 cm × 35 cm) and faced downwards toward the laptop computer.

4.3   Procedure

After listening to a brief description of the purpose of this experiment, the participants gave their informed written consent. They then carried out the learning-data sampling task and then six sessions of the test-data sampling task. The order of conditions for each participant is shown in Table 1. They were forced to take a break of two minutes or more between sessions in the test-data sampling task.

Fig. 5. Conditions for data collection in test-data sampling task: (a) *Desk Condition*, (b) *Lap Condition*, and (c) *Bed Condition*.

Table 1. The order of conditions of the test-data sampling task.

Participant	Sessions 1, 4	Sessions 2, 5	Sessions 3, 6
P_1, P_2	Desk	Lap	Bed
P_3, P_4	Desk	Bed	Lap
P_5, P_6	Lap	Desk	Bed
P_7, P_8	Lap	Bed	Desk
P_9, P_{10}	Bed	Desk	Lap
P_{11}, P_{12}	Bed	Lap	Desk

After finishing both tasks, the participants were given 15.75 USD for their participation. The experiment took approximately 70 min per participant.

4.4   Result

We trained a machine learning model using the data collected in the learning-data sampling task and investigated the accuracy of thumb-or-finger identification (*TF accuracy*) under every condition by using the data collected in the test-data sampling task as test data. As shown in Fig. 6 left, the average identification accuracy for all conditions was 86.3% (SD = 3.41%). Among the three conditions, the Desk Condition had the highest accuracy (87.9%, SD = 5.38%). However, a one-way ANOVA did not show a significant difference between the three conditions ($F_{2,33} = 1.1888$, $p = 0.3173 > 0.05$).

We also investigated TF accuracy when the hand used for operation was distinguished (*TFLR accuracy*) for every condition. As shown in Fig. 6 right, the average identification accuracy for all conditions was 58.3% (SD = 7.63%). Similar to TF accuracy for which the hand used for touching was not distinguished, there was no significant difference between the three conditions ($F_{2,33} = 0.1216$, $p = 0.8859 > 0.05$) with a one-way ANOVA. Additionally, a one-way ANOVA showed a significant difference between TF accuracy and TFLR accuracy ($F_{1,22} = 123.11$, $p = 1.763 \times 10^{-10} < 0.01$).

Figure 7 shows the TF accuracy for each area of the touchpad without the left-handed participant (P_6). A one-way ANOVA showed a significant main effect of row ($F_{4,20} = 16.859$, $p = 3.417 \times 10^{-6} < 0.01$). Tukey's honestly significant difference (HSD) pair wise comparison showed significant differences between rows 1 and 2 ($p = 0.0178991 < 0.05$), between rows 1 and 3 ($p = 1.824 \times 10^{-4} < 0.01$), between rows 1 and 4 ($p = 9.1 \times 10^{-6} < 0.01$), and between rows 1 and 5 ($p = 1.08 \times 10^{-5} < 0.01$). This indicates that the bottom edge area of the touchpad has low identification accuracy. In contrast, a one-way ANOVA did not show a significant difference between the five columns of the touchpad.

100
75
50
25
0
TF accuracy (%)
87.9
85.4
85.5
86.3
Desk
Lap
Bed
All
conditions
100
75
50
25
0
TFLR accuracy (%)
59.3
57.4
58.2
58.3
Desk
Lap
Bed
All
conditions

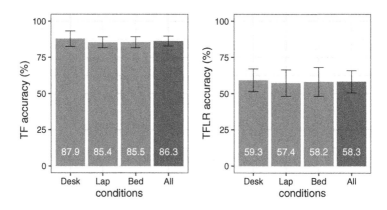

Fig. 6. Accuracy of thumb-or-finger identification (*TF accuracy*) for every condition (left) and when the hand used for operation was distinguished (*TFLR accuracy*) for every condition (right). Error bars represent one standard deviation from the mean.

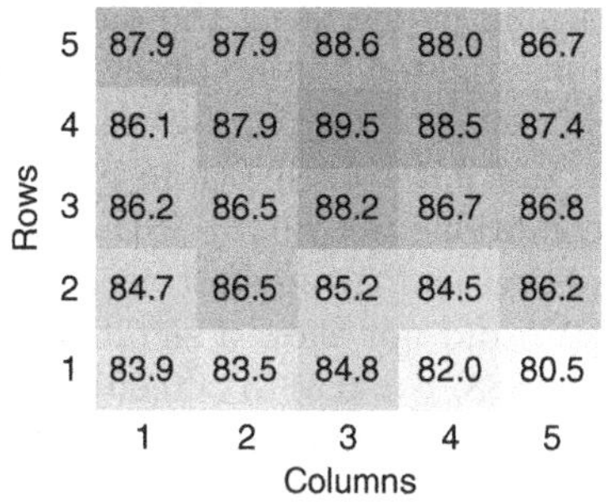

Rows
5 87.9 87.9 88.6 88.0 86.7
4 86.1 87.9 89.5 88.5 87.4
3 86.2 86.5 88.2 86.7 86.8
2 84.7 86.5 85.2 84.5 86.2
1 83.9 83.5 84.8 82.0 80.5
1 2 3 4 5
Columns

Fig. 7. Identification accuracy for each area of the touchpad (%).

5   Discussion

The average TF accuracy of 86.3% demonstrates the potential of our method for identifying the digit used for touchpad input, whereas the average TFLR accuracy of 58.3% demonstrates its weakness in identifying both the hand and digit used for touchpad input.

Despite the relatively high TF accuracy, further improvement is needed. One strategy for improving TF accuracy is to increase the amount of learning data collected in the learning phase. In our experiment, the participants carried out the learning phase only under Desk Condition. It would be more effective to carry out the learning phase under various conditions for robustness. Furthermore, accuracy could be improved by improving the accuracy of the data acquired from the touchpad. For example, the angle of the major axis acquired from MultitouchSupport becomes unstable or becomes a fixed value ($\pi/2$) when the area of the contract surface is below a certain size.

Moreover, we observed that the accuracy for participants with a shorter thumb was lower than that of those with a longer thumb. We attribute this to the shape of the contact surface of a short thumb being similar to that of the fingers since as short thumb would tend to touch a touchpad by its tip rather than its side. Therefore, it is necessary to examine the effects of various factors, including thumb length, on identification accuracy.

Another strategy for improving accuracy is to exclude the ring and little fingers from the identification targets because these fingers are rarely used for single-finger or two-finger gestures compared with the other digits. This could be effective since reducing the number of classified categories tends to increase accuracy in machine learning approaches.

6   Example Applications

Digit identification has two applications that would make a touchpad more convenient to use.

First, for a graphical editor, the user could use the eraser tool with their thumb and a brush tool with their finger, as illustrated in Fig. 8a, b. Additionally, the user could resize an object by using their thumb and finger and rotate an object by using two fingers, as illustrated in Fig. 8c, d. With these capabilities, the user could perform editing seamlessly without using keyboard shortcuts or GUI elements.

Second, for a text editor, the user could *right-click* with their thumb and *left-click* with their finger, as illustrated in Fig. 9. Moreover, it would possible to move the cursor more slowly (e.g., at half speed) when using the thumb. As a result, the user could perform both fast pointing and fine pointing easily.

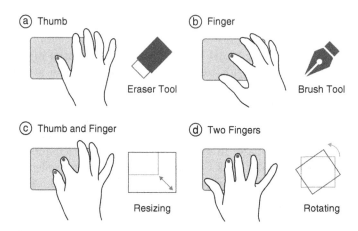

Fig. 8. Example application to graphical editor: (a) using the eraser tool with a thumb, (b) using the brush tool with a finger, (c) resizing an object with thumb and finger, and (d) rotating object with two fingers.

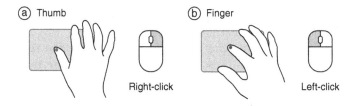

Fig. 9. Example application to text editor: (a) right-clicking using a thumb and (b) left-clicking using a finger.

7 Conclusion

Our method for identifying the digits used to touch a touchpad expands the input vocabulary available on a touchpad. With this method, an application designer can assign different commands to touch gestures performed with the same number of digits and the same movement but with different digits. It is implemented using machine learning. Experimental results demonstrated an average identification accuracy of 86.3%. Future work includes testing the effect of the strategies described in the Discussion on identification accuracy.

References

1. Benko, H., Saponas, T.S., Morris, D., Tan, D.: Enhancing input on and above the Interactive Surface with Muscle Sensing. In: Proceedings of the ACM International Conference on Interactive Tabletops and Surfaces, ITS 2009, pp. 93–100. ACM, New York (2009). https://doi.org/10.1145/1731903.1731924

2. Berthellemy, M., Cayez, E., Ajem, M., Bailly, G., Malacria, S., Lecolinet, E.: SpotPad, LociPad, ChordPad and InOutPad: investigating gesture-based input on touchpad. In: Proceedings of the 27th Conference on L'Interaction Homme-Machine, IHM 2015, pp. 4:1–4:8. ACM, New York (2015). https://doi.org/10.1145/2820619.2820623

3. Choi, S., Han, J., Kim, S., Heo, S., Lee, G.: ThickPad: a hover-tracking touchpad for a laptop. In: Proceedings of the 24th Annual ACM Symposium Adjunct on User Interface Software and Technology, UIST 2011, Adjunct, pp. 15–16. ACM, New York (2011). https://doi.org/10.1145/2046396.2046405

4. Cui, W., Zheng, J., Lewis, B., Vogel, D., Bi, X.: HotStrokes: word-gesture shortcuts on a trackpad. In: Proceedings of the 2019 CHI Conference on Human Factors in Computing Systems, CHI 2019, pp. 165:1–165:13. ACM, New York (2019). https://doi.org/10.1145/3290605.3300395

5. Fruchard, B., Lecolinet, E., Chapuis, O.: MarkPad: augmenting touchpads for command selection. In: Proceedings of the 2017 CHI Conference on Human Factors in Computing Systems, CHI 2017, pp. 5630–5642. ACM, New York (2017). https://doi.org/10.1145/3025453.3025486

6. Gil, H., Lee, D., Im, S., Oakley, I.: TriTap: identifying finger touches on smartwatches. In: Proceedings of the 2017 CHI Conference on Human Factors in Computing Systems, CHI 2017, pp. 3879–3890. ACM, New York (2017). https://doi.org/10.1145/3025453.3025561

7. Gu, J., Heo, S., Han, J., Kim, S., Lee, G.: LongPad: a touchpad using the entire area below the keyboard of a laptop computer. In: Proceedings of the SIGCHI Conference on Human Factors in Computing Systems, CHI 2013, pp. 1421–1430. ACM, New York (2013). https://doi.org/10.1145/2470654.2466188

8. Gupta, A., Balakrishnan, R.: DualKey: miniature screen text entry via finger identification. In: Proceedings of the 2016 CHI Conference on Human Factors in Computing Systems, CHI 2016, pp. 59–70. ACM, New York (2016). https://doi.org/10.1145/2858036.2858052

9. Heo, S., Han, J., Lee, G.: Designing rich touch interaction through proximity and 2.5D force sensing touchpad. In: Proceedings of the 25th Australian Computer-Human Interaction Conference: Augmentation, Application, Innovation, Collaboration, OzCHI 2013, pp. 401–404. ACM, New York (2013). https://doi.org/10.1145/2541016.2541057

10. Ikematsu, K., Fukumoto, M., Siio, I.: Ohmic-Sticker: force-to-motion type input device for capacitive touch surface. In: Extended Abstracts of the 2019 CHI Conference on Human Factors in Computing Systems, CHI EA 2019, pp. LBW0223:1-LBW0223:6. ACM, New York (2019). https://doi.org/10.1145/3290607.3312936

11. Jung, J., Youn, E., Lee, G.: PinPad: touchpad interaction with fast and high-resolution tactile output. In: Proceedings of the 2017 CHI Conference on Human Factors in Computing Systems, CHI 2017, pp. 2416–2425. ACM, New York (2017). https://doi.org/10.1145/3025453.3025971

12. Le, H.V., Mayer, S., Henze, N.: Investigating the feasibility of finger identification on capacitive touchscreens using deep learning. In: Proceedings of the 24th International Conference on Intelligent User Interfaces, IUI 2019, pp. 637–649. ACM, New York (2019). https://doi.org/10.1145/3301275.3302295

13. Malik, S., Laszlo, J.: Visual touchpad: a two-handed gestural input device. In: Proceedings of the 6th International Conference on Multimodal Interfaces, ICMI 2004, pp. 289–296. ACM, New York (2004). https://doi.org/10.1145/1027933.1027980

14. Masson, D., Goguey, A., Malacria, S., Casiez, G.: WhichFingers: identifying fingers on touch surfaces and keyboards using vibration sensors. In: Proceedings of the 30th Annual ACM Symposium on User Interface Software and Technology, UIST 2017, pp. 41–48. ACM, New York (2017). https://doi.org/10.1145/3126594.3126619

15. Nakamura, T., Shizuki, B.: Distinction system of left and right hands placed on a keyboard of laptop computers. In: Proceedings of the 30th Australian Conference on Computer-Human Interaction, OzCHI 2018, pp. 587–589. Association for Computing Machinery, New York (2018). https://doi.org/10.1145/3292147.3292228

16. Park, K., Lee, G.: FingMag: finger identification method for smartwatch. In: Extended Abstracts of the 2019 CHI Conference on Human Factors in Computing Systems, CHI EA 2019, pp. LBW2216:1–LBW2216:6. ACM, New York (2019). https://doi.org/10.1145/3290607.3312982

17. Suzuki, Y., Misue, K., Tanaka, J.: A potential exploration of finger-specific interaction. ICIC Express Lett. **6**, 3061–3067 (2012)

18. Taylor, S., Keskin, C., Hilliges, O., Izadi, S., Helmes, J.: Type-hover-swipe in 96 bytes: a motion sensing mechanical keyboard. In: Proceedings of the 32nd Annual ACM Conference on Human Factors in Computing Systems, CHI 2014, pp. 1695–1704. ACM, New York (2014). https://doi.org/10.1145/2556288.2557030

19. Tung, Y.C., Cheng, T.Y., Yu, N.H., Wang, C., Chen, M.Y.: FlickBoard: enabling trackpad interaction with automatic mode switching on a capacitive-sensing keyboard. In: Proceedings of the 33rd Annual ACM Conference on Human Factors in Computing Systems, CHI 2015, pp. 1847–1850. ACM, New York (2015). https://doi.org/10.1145/2702123.2702582

20. Vega, K., Fuks, H.: Beauty tech nails: interactive technology at your fingertips. In: Proceedings of the 8th International Conference on Tangible, Embedded and Embodied Interaction, TEI 2014, pp. 61–64. ACM, New York (2014). https://doi.org/10.1145/2540930.2540961

21. Zheng, J., Vogel, D.: Finger-aware shortcuts. In: Proceedings of the 2016 CHI Conference on Human Factors in Computing Systems, CHI 2016, pp. 4274–4285. ACM, New York (2016). https://doi.org/10.1145/2858036.2858355

FingerTalkie: Designing a Low-Cost Finger-Worn Device for Interactive Audio Labeling of Tactile Diagrams

Arshad Nasser[1], Taizhou Chen[1(✉)], Can Liu[1(✉)], Kening Zhu[1(✉)], and PVM Rao[2(✉)]

[1] School of Creative Media, City University of Hong Kong, Kowloon Tong, Hong Kong, China
arshad.nasser@my.cityu.edu.hk
[2] Indian Institute of Technology Delhi, New Delhi, India

Abstract. Traditional tactile diagrams for the visually-impaired (VI) use short Braille keys and annotations to provide additional information in separate Braille legend pages. Frequent navigation between the tactile diagram and the annex pages during the diagram exploration results in low efficiency in diagram comprehension. We present the design of FingerTalkie, a finger-worn device that uses discrete colors on a color-tagged tactile diagram for interactive audio labeling of the graphical elements. Through an iterative design process involving 8 VI users, we designed a unique offset point-and-click technique that enables the bimanual exploration of the diagrams without hindering the tactile perception of the fingertips. Unlike existing camera-based and finger-worn audio-tactile devices, FingerTalkie supports one-finger interaction and can work in any lighting conditions without calibration. We conducted a controlled experiment with 12 blind-folded sighted users to evaluate the usability of the device. Further, a focus-group interview with 8 VI users shows their appreciation for the FingerTalkie's ease of use, support for two-hand exploration, and its potential in improving the efficiency of comprehending tactile diagrams by replacing Braille labels.

Keywords: Audio-tactile diagram · Finger-worn device · Offset point and click · Blind · Visually impaired

1 Introduction

Images and diagrams are an integral part of many educational materials [9]. Tactile diagram is the representation of an image in a simplified form that makes the content accessible by touch. They are widely adopted in textbooks for the visually impaired (VI) people. Several studies [4,13,31] have shown that tactile perception is good for the comprehension of graphical images and tactile diagrams proved to be useful for the VI students for learning graphically intensive

© Springer Nature Switzerland AG 2020
M. Kurosu (Ed.): HCII 2020, LNCS 12182, pp. 475–496, 2020.
https://doi.org/10.1007/978-3-030-49062-1_32

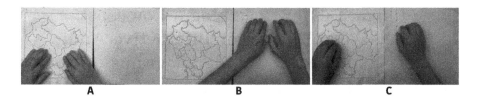

Fig. 1. Deciphering tactile images; (A) Exploring the tactile image, Braille keys and symbols with two hands (B) Using both hands to decipher the Braille legend on the consecutive page (C) Exploring the tactile image, Braille keys and symbols with two hands

subjects. Apart from tactile textbooks, tactile diagrams are widely used in public spaces as maps and floor plans for guiding VI people.

Despite the wide acceptance of tactile diagrams, they are often limited by their spatial resolution and local perception range [24]. The traditional tactile graphics makes use of the Braille annotations as a type of markup for the discrete areas of tactile diagrams. However, Tatham [37] states that, the extensive use of Braille annotations in can worsen the overall legibility of the tactile graphics. While textures and tactile patterns are prominently used for marking areas, it still involves finding the key and the corresponding description which are often placed in other pages. The number of textures that could be clearly distinguishable remains limited and can vary on the tactile acuity of the user [38]. Additionally, the Braille legend of a diagram is placed on multiple pages, which demands flipping of pages for comprehending pictorial information (Fig. 1). This in turn complicates the interpretation of tactile images [16]. Another reason for excluding Braille annotations from tactile graphics is due to the inclusivity of Braille among the VI community. Research [6] shows that the number of blind people who can read Braille and it can be estimated that an even smaller proportion can read Braille-labelled tactile graphics. Another argument to reduce Braille labels is to limit the tactile complexity of the graphics. A widely adopted alternative is to combine tactile graphics with interactive assistive technologies. Recent studies have shown that the tactile diagrams complemented with interactive audio support is advantageous according to the usability design goals (ISO 9241) [7]. There are various existing devices and approaches (mentioned in Sect. 3) for audio-tactile graphics. However, the factors pertaining to wearability, setup time, effects of the ambient lighting conditions and scalability were not fully investigated in the existing audio-tactile methodologies.

In this paper, we present the design of FingerTalkie, a finger-worn interactive device with an offset point-and-click method that can be used with existing tactile diagrams to obtain audio descriptions. Compared to the existing interactive audio-tactile devices, FingerTalkie does not use camera based methods or back-end image processing. Our concept leverages the usage of color tactile diagrams which gaining popularity, thus reducing the barrier for technology adoption. The FingerTalkie device was designed through an iterative user-centred design process, involving 8 visually-impaired users. Minimal and low-cost hardware has helped in the design of a standalone and compact device. We conducted a controlled experiment with 12 blind-folded sighted users to evaluate the usability of the device. The results showed that the user performance of pointing and clicking with FingerTalkie could be influenced by the size and the complexity of the tactile shape. We further conducted a focus-group interview with 8 VI users. The qualitative result showed that compared existing audio-based assistive products in the market, the VI users appreciated FingerTalkie's ease of setup, support for two-hand exploration of the tactile diagrams, and potential in improving the efficiency of comprending tactile diagrams.

2   Related Work

We discuss prior work related to two areas of our system: (i) audio-/touch-based assistive devices for VI users and (ii) finger-based wearable interfaces.

2.1   Audio-/Touch-Based Assistive Technologies

Adding auditory information (e.g., speech, verbal landmarks, earcons, and recorded environmental sounds) to the tactile diagrams has been considered as an efficient way of improving the reading experience of VI users [7, 26]. Furthermore, it was intuitive for VI users to obtain such auditory information with their fingers touching the tactile diagrams or other tangible interfaces. Early prototypes, such as KnowWhere [22], 3DFinger [32], Tangible Newspaper [36], supported computer-vision-based tracking of VI user's finger on 2D printed material (e.g., maps and newspaper) and retrieval of the corresponding speech information. Nanayakkara et al. [28] developed EyeRing, a finger-worn device with an embedded camera connected to an external micro-controller for converting the printed text into speech output based on OCR and text-to-speech techniques. Later, the same research group developed FingerReader [35] and FingerReader 2.0 [5], to assist blind users in reading of printed text on the go by harnessing the technologies of computer vision and cloud-based object recognition. Shi et al. [33] developed Magic Touch, a computer-vision-based system that augments printed graphics with audio files associated with specific locations on the model. The system used external webcam to track user's finger on the 3D-printed object, and retrieve the corresponding audio information. Later, Shi et al. [34] expanded the functionality of Magic Touch to Markit and Talkit with the feature of touch-based audio annotation on the 3D-printed object. Using the front camera of a smart tablet and a front-mounted mirror, the Tactile Graphics Helper [12] tracked a student's fingers as the user explores a tactile diagram, and allowed the student to gain clarifying audio information about the tactile graphic without sighted assistance. Several researchers have also developed hand gesture for interactive 2D maps for the VI [8].

These works suggested that the camera-based finger-tracking method can be used for VI users to retrieve audio information by touching physical objects. However, there are major drawbacks in using camera-based technologies including

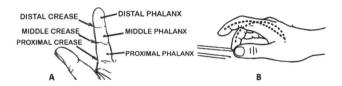

Fig. 2. (a) Parts of the fingers (b) Bending of fingers during tactile reading

back-end processing hardware, size of the camera and system, the requirement for ambient light, and difficulty with near focus distance. Furthermore, it was costly to embed a camera and set up an external connection to the processing hardware. Due to these limitations, this solution may not be suitable for VI users in the developing countries.

Besides computer-vision-based finger tracking, researchers also investigated other techniques based on embedded sensors, such as Pen Friend [20], Near Field Communication (NFC)/Radio-frequency identification (RFID) reader [40], and QR-code readers [1,3], for retrieving audio with the tactile diagrams. While these devices may overcome the requirement for high resolution as in the camera-based solution, they often require users to hold devices in their hands, thus keeping at least one hand constantly occupied. As the distal phalanx of the index fingers (Fig. 2) are primarily used for exploring Braille and tactile diagrams, it is advised that VI users' hands should not be occupied by any other means [10]. Moreover, it is difficult to paste a Pen Friend label or RFID tag or QR code in smaller regions and areas with irregular boundaries on a tactile diagram. In addition, QR-code detection demands an optimal amount of ambient light for the reader to operate, which makes it quite unusable in low light conditions [3]. Talking Tactile Tablet (TTT) [23], in turn, may support the user reading the tactile diagram with both the hands and get an audio feedback simultaneously. However, the size and weight of the device makes it non-portable.

In this paper, we explain the design and implementation of FingerTalkie in a finger-wearable form factor, with cheap, off-the-shelf and robust color-sensing technology. It supports audio retrieval from color-printed tactile diagrams without any extra hardware embedded in the diagrams. Our technical experiments showed that FingerTalkie can retrieve correct audio information in low-light or even dark settings.

2.2   Finger-Based Wearable Interfaces

Wearable devices for the hand often focused on the fingers since it is one of the most sensitive part and most often used for grasping and exploring the environment. The design of the interaction technique in FingerTalkie was largely inspired by existing wearable finger-based interaction for general purposes. Fukumoto and Tonomura's FingerRing [11] in 1994 was considered to be the first digital prototype exploring a finger-worn interface. It embedded an accelerometer into the form factor of a finger ring to detect gesture input in the form of taps performed with the fingertips. Since then, various technologies have been used to implement ring-shape input devices. For instance, Nenya by Ashbrook et al. [2] detected finger rotation via magnetic tracking. Yang et al. introduced Magic Finger [43] with IR beacons to recognize surface textures. Ogata et al. [29] developed iRing using infrared reflection to detect directional gesture swipes and finger bending. Jing et al. developed Magic Ring [18] with an accelerometer to detect motion gestures of the index finger. eRing [41] employed electric field sensing to detect multiple finger gestures. OctaRing [25] achieved multi-touch input by pressure-sensing, and LightRing [21] fused the results of infrared proximity sensing and a gyroscope to locate the fingertip on any surface for cursor pointing and target selection. All these existing finger-based input techniques utilized embedded motion sensors in the ring-shape form factor, to achieve surface or mid-air gesture recognition. When it comes to designing finger-based interaction for VI users reading tactile diagram, one should take into account the ease of input registration and the robustness of input detection. Motion sensors may face the issue of robustness due to low sensor bandwidth. As discussed before, VI users often understand the tactile diagrams with both hands resting on and touching the diagrams. Thus, performing complex gestures on the surface or mid air may cause fatigue.

To ensure the robustness of finger-based interaction, researchers leveraged thumb-to-finger touch with buttons [14] and touch sensors [42]. Inspired by these configuration, we incorporated a button in the FingerTalkie device for VI users to register the input. The choice of using buttons instead of sensors aimed to further reduce the cost of the device. Different from the existing devices mostly with buttons on the side of the proximal phalanx, we investigated the placement of the button around the finger through iterative design processes, and designed the one-finger offset-clicking input technique in our final prototype. The quantitative and the qualitative studies suggested that VI users could successfully explore the tactile diagrams and retrieve corresponding audio information using the offset-clicking technique with the button placed in front of the finger tip.

3   Our Solution - FingerTalkie

Based on the problems and challenges identified in existing literature, we designed a device with embedded color sensor on the fingertip that does not obstruct the finger movements or the touch-sensing area of the finger tip. The initial design of the FingerTalkie device is illustrated in Fig. 3. The color sensor on the tip of the finger can read/sense colors printed on a tactile diagram. A user can click the button on the proximal phalanx to play the audio associated to the colored area, via an external device (e.g., laptop, smartphone or smartwatch) that is connected to it wirelessly. The external device handles the computation and stores the database of colors and mapped audio files. In the following we describe the rationale behind our design choices.

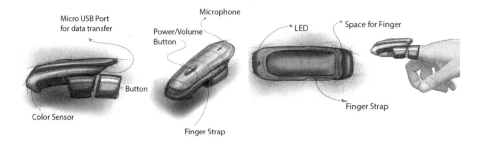

Fig. 3. First prototype sketch

3.1   Problems and Considerations

There are several studies that investigated the haptic exploration styles of the visually impaired and the sighted people [15]. When using two hands to explore the tactile diagram and its annex Braille legend page, VI users may use one hand as a stationery reference point (Fig. 2C) or move both hands simultaneously (Fig. 2 B). The exploration strategies consists of usage of only one finger (index) or multiple fingers [15]. The precise nature of these exploratory modes and their relations to performance level remain obscure [39]. Nevertheless, a common problem with tactile diagrams is its labelling. Braille labelling becomes cumbersome as it often becomes cluttered and illegible due spatial constraints [37]. Moreover, associating the Braille legend on the separate pages disrupts the referencing and reduces the immediacy of the graphic, thereby resulting in comprehension issues [16].

To address this issue, several existing studies associates the auditory information with touch exploration, to enhance the experience of VI users obtaining information through physical interfaces. Finger-worn devices with motion sensors and camera based setup can be costly and difficult to calibrate and set up. These devices also requires the user to aim a camera, which can be difficult for blind users [19], and use one of their hands to hold the camera, preventing bimanual exploration of the diagram, which can be necessary for good performance [27]. Based on the above factors and constraints, we formulated the following design considerations for developing a system that:

1. Allow users to use both hands to probe tactile boundaries without restricting the movement and the tactile sensation of finger tips.
2. Support the access to real-time audio feedback while exploring discrete areas of tactile diagram irrespective of the boundary conditions (irregular boundaries, 2.5D diagrams, textured diagrams etc.)
3. Is portable, easy to set-up, inexpensive and easily adaptable with the existing tactile graphics for VI users in developing countries.

3.2 Design Rationale

Existing interactive technologies for audio-tactile diagrams include embedding physical buttons or capacitive touch, RGB camera with QR code, text recognition and RFID tags to map audio to the discrete areas. These technologies lack flexibility as the users have to focus to particular points within the tactile area to trigger the audio. Moreover, it is difficult for QR codes and RFID tags to be used with the tactile diagrams with irregular boundary lines. By further exploring a simpler sensing mechanisms, the idea of color tagging and sensing for audio tactile may offer advantages over other methods due to the following reasons:

1. Contrasting colors have been widely used in tactile diagrams for assisting low vision and color-blind people for easy recognition of boundaries and distinct areas. The device could leverage the potential of existing colored tactile diagrams, without requiring the fabrication of new ones.
2. The non colored tactile diagram can be colored with stickers or easily painted.
3. The color-sensing action is unaffected by ambient lighting with the usage of a sensor module with an embedded white LED light.
4. Color sensors are low-cost, frugal technology with low power consumption and low requirement on background processing.

4 Iterative Design and Prototyping

Follow the design considerations and the conceptual design, We adopted a multiple-stage iterative design process involving 8 VI users evaluating 3 prototypes.

4.1 First Prototype

We followed the existing work on finger-worn assistive device [28] to design the first prototype of FingerTalkie. As shown in Fig. 4, it consisted of two wearable parts: (i) a straight 3D-printed case to be worn at the middle phalanx with the color sensor (Flora TCS34725A) at the tip, and (ii) a push button which was sewed to another velcro as a ring worn on the finger base. A velcro strap was attached on the 3D-printed case to cater to different finger sizes.

For this prototype, we used an Arduino UNO with a laptop (Macbook Pro) as the external peripherals. The wearable part of the prototype device was connected to the Arduino UNO using thin wires. We used Arduino IDE with the standard audio package library to store color-to-audio profiles and perform the back-end processing.

User Study 1 - Design

The main goal of testing the first prototype was to investigate the feasibility of the hardware setup, and collect user feedback on the early design and the prototype of FingerTalkie.

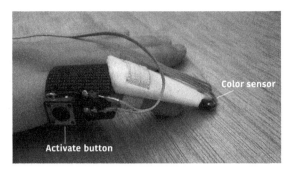

Fig. 4. First prototype

Fig. 5. The tactile diagram used in the pilot studies. (Color figure online)

Participants. For the first pilot study, we recruited 4 congenitally blind participants (4 males) aged between 27 to 36 (Mean = 31.5, SD = 3.6). All the participants were familiar with using tactile diagrams.

Apparatus. We tested the first prototype with a simple tactile diagram of two squares (blue and pink color) as shown in Fig. 5. Pressing the button on the device while pointing to the area within the squares activates different sounds.

Task and Procedure. The participants were initially given a demo on how to wear the prototype and to point and click on a designated area. Then they were asked to wear the prototype on their own and adjust the velcro strap according to their comfort. Later, the tactile diagram 5 was given to them and the participants were asked to explore and click within the tactile shapes to trigger different sounds played on the laptop speaker. Each participant could perform this action as many times as they wanted within 5 min. After all the participants performed the above task, a group interview was conducted. The participants were asked about the subjective feedback on the wearability, ease of use, drawbacks and issues faced while using the device and possibilities for improvement.

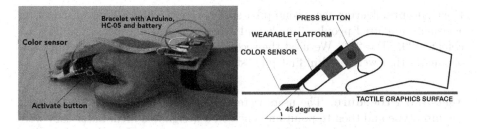

Fig. 6. Second prototype and the angular compensation at the tip

Study 1 - Feedback and Insights

All the participants showed positive responses and stated that it was a new experience for them. They did not face any difficultly in wearing the device. One participants accidentally pulled off the wires that connected the device[to the Arduino] while trying to wear the prototype. All the participants reported that the device was lightweight and it was easy to get the real-time audio feedback. 3 participants reported that the device doesn't restrict the movements of their fingers during exploration of the diagram. For one participant, we noticed that the color sensor at the tip of the device was intermittently touching the embossed lines on the tactile diagram. This was due to his peculiar exploration style where the angle of exploration of the fingers with respect to the diagram surface was higher compared to the rest of the participants. This induced the problem of unintended sensor touching on tactile diagram during exploration. Moreover, the embossed elevations can also vary based on the type of the tactile diagrams which could worsen obstruction for the color sensor.

4.2   Second Prototype

In order to avoid the unwanted touching of color sensor while exploring a tactile diagram, we affixed the sensor at an angular position with respect to the platform. We observed the participants fingers were at an angle of $45°$ with respect to the tactile diagram. Thus, we redesigned the tip of the device and fixed the color sensor at an angle of $45°$ as shown in Fig. 6. The overall length of the finger wearable platform was also reduced from 6 cm to 5 cm.

The second prototype is a wrist-worn stand-alone device as shown in Fig. 6. It consisted of an Arduino Nano, 7.2v LiPo battery, a 5 V regulator IC with and an HC-05 Bluetooth module. All the components are integrated into a single PCB board that is connected to the finger-worn part with flexible ribbon wires. This design solved the problem of the excess tangled wires as the device could now connect with the laptop wirelessly through Bluetooth.

User Study 2 - Design

We evaluated the second prototype with another user study to assess the new design and gain insights for further improvement.

Participants. During the second pilot study, we ran a hands-on workshop with 4 visually impaired people (3 male and 1 female) aged between 22 to 36 years (Mean = 29, SD = 2.7). We used the second prototype and the tactile diagrams of squares that were used in first pilot study.

Task and Procedure. The users were initially given a demo on how to wear the prototype and then to point and click on a designated area. Later they were asked to wear the prototype on their own and adjust the velcro strap according to their comfort. Then, they were asked to explore the tactile diagram and click within the tactile shapes. Whenever the participant pointed within the squares and pressed the button correctly, Tone A[1] was played on the laptop speakers. When they made a wrong point-and-click (outside the squares), Tone B[2] was played to denote the wrong pointing. Each participant was given 10 min for the entire task. After the entire task, the participants were individually asked to provide their feedback regarding the ease of use, the drawbacks and issues faced while using the device and the potential areas of improvement.

4.3   Study 2 - Feedback and Insights

We observed that with the refined length and angle of contact of the device, the participants were able to explore the tactile diagrams more easily. However, two participants said the they found it difficult to simultaneously point to the diagram and press the button on the proximal phalanx. One participant said, *"I feel that the area being pointed by [my] finger shifts while simultaneously trying to press the button on the index finger"*. We found that the above mentioned participants had relatively stubby thumbs, which might had increased the difficulty of clicking the button while pointing. This means that the activation button on the distal phalanx may not be suitable for all the users ergonomically. Another participant who is partially visually impaired was concerned about the maximum number of colors (or discrete areas) the sensor could detect and whether colors could be reused.

5   Final Prototype

Based on the findings from the two user studies, we came up with a novel point-and-click technique and finalized the design of the device with further hardware improvements to make it a complete standalone device.

5.1   Offset Point-and-Click Technique

We replaced the button at the proximal phalanx of the finger with a limit-switch button on the tip of the finger-worn device as shown in Fig. 7. The color sensor is

---

[1] 'Glass' sound file in the MacOS sound effects.

[2] 'Basso' sound file in the MacOS sound effects.

then attached to the limit-switch. The purpose of this design is to avoid affecting the pointing accuracy when the users simultaneously point the device and click the button on the proximal phalanx. With the new design, the users can click the button by simply tilting the finger forward and also get tactile click feedback on their finger tip.

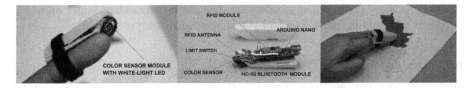

Fig. 7. Left: Final standalone prototype, Center: Internal hardware Right: Exploring the tactile diagram with the final prototype.

5.2 RFID Sensing for Color Reuse

In order to enable the reuse of colors across different tactile diagrams, we introduced a mechanism to support multiple audio-color mapping profiles. This was achieved by embedding an RFID-reader coil in the FingerTalkie device. One unique RFID tag was attached to each tactile diagram. Before reading the main content, the user scanned the tag to read the color-audio-mapping profile of the current diagram. A micro *125* KHz RFID module was embedded on top of the Arduino Nano. We made a sandwiched arrangement of Arduino Nano, a much smaller HC-05 bluetooth chip and the RFID chip, creating a compact arrangement of circuits on top of the finger worn platform. An RFID coil with a diameter of 15 mm was placed on top of the limit switch, to support the selection of audio-color-mapping profile through the offset pointing interaction.

5.3 Interaction Flow

The user begins exploring a tactile diagram by hovering the FingerTalkie device over the RFID tag, which is placed at the top left corner of the tactile diagram and marked by a small tactile dot. The page selection is indicated by an audio feedback denoting the page number or title of the diagram. The user can then move the finger to the rest of the diagram for further exploration. To retrieve audio information about a colored area, the user uses the point-and-click technique by pointing to the area with an offset and tilting the finger to click.

6 Evaluating the Offset Point-and-Click Technique

We have designed FingeTalkie with a new interaction technique that requires users to point to areas with an offset distance and tilt to click. Can users perform it efficiently and accurately? To answer this question, we conducted a controlled experiment to formally evaluate the performance of this new technique and the usability of the FingerTalkie device. Participants were asked to use FingerTalkie device to point and click within the tactile areas in predefined graphical shapes. The following hypotheses are tested:

- H1: It is faster to select larger tactile areas than smaller ones.
- H2: It is slower to perform a correct click for areas with sharper angles.
- H3: It is more error-prone to select smaller tactile areas than larger ones.
- H4: It yields more error to select the shapes with sharper angles.

6.1   Design

We employed a $[4 \times 3]$ within-subject experiment design with two independent factors: Size (Small, Medium, Large) and Shape (Circle, Square, Triangle and Star). The tactile diagrams we used are made of flashcards with a size of 20 × 18 cm. The tactile shapes were created by laser cutting a thick paper board which gave 1.5 mm tactile elevation for the tactile shapes. We used tactile diagrams of four basic figures: circle, triangle, square and star based on the increasing number of edges and corners and decreasing angular measurements between the adjacent sides. We made 3 different sizes (large, medium and small) of each shape as shown in Fig. 8. The large size of all the shapes were made in a way that it can be inscribed in a circle of 5 cm. The medium size was set to 40% (2 cm) of the large size and the smallest size being 20% (1 cm). According to tactile graphics guidelines [38], the minimum area that can be perceived on a tactile diagram is 25.4 mm × 12.5 mm. We chose our smallest size slightly below this threshold to include the worst case scenario.

All the elevated shapes were of blue color and the surrounding area was in white color as shown in Fig. 8. All the shapes were placed at the vertical center of the flashcard. The bottom of each shape was at a fixed distance from the bottom of the flashcard as seen in the Fig. 8. This was done in order to maintain consistency while exploring the shapes and to mitigate against shape and size bias.

6.2   Participants

To eliminate biases caused by prior experience with tactile diagrams, we recruited 12 sighted users (5 female) and blind-folded them during the experiment. They were recruited from a local university aged between 25 and 35 years (Mean = 30, SD = 2.8). 8 out of 12 participants were right-handed. None of them had any prior experience in using tactile diagrams.

6.3   Apparatus

The testing setup involved the finger-worn device connected to an Arduino Nano which interfaces with a laptop. The testing table as shown in Fig. 9 consisted of a fixed slot to which the flashcards could be removed and replaced manually by the moderator. A press button (Fig. 9) was placed beneath the flashcard slot in order to trigger the start command whenever the user was ready to explore the next diagram.

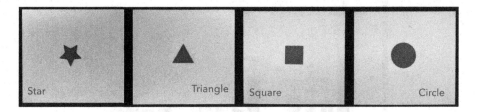

Fig. 8. Tactile flashcards (Color figure online)

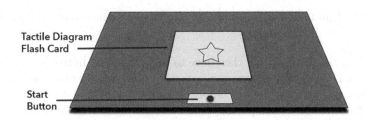

Fig. 9. Testing setup

6.4   Task and Procedure

The experiment begins with a training session before going into the measured session. The participants are blindfolded and asked to wear the FingerTalkie prototype. During the training session, the participants are briefed about the motive of the experiment and also guided through the actions to be performed during the tests. A dummy tactile flashcard of blue colored square (side of 20 mm) is used for the demo session. In order to avoid bias, the shape and position of the tactile image on the flashcard are not revealed or explained. The participants are asked to explore the tactile flashcard and asked to point-and-click within the area of the tactile shape. When a click is received while pointing within the shape, Tone A ('Glass' sound file in the MacOS sound effects) is played to notify the correct operation. When the point-and-click occurred outside the tactile boundary (the white area), Tone B ('Basso' sound file in the MacOS sound effects) is played to denote the error. The participants are allowed to exercise the clicks as many times as they wanted during the training sessions. The training session for each participants took about 5 min.

During the measured session, the participants are asked to register correct clicks for given tactile flashcards as fast and accurate as possible. The moderator gives an audio cue to notify the participants every time a tactile flashcard is

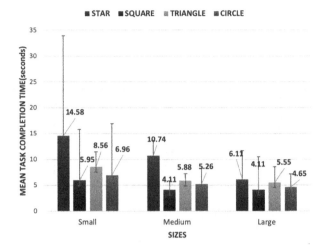

Fig. 10. Mean task completion time of all shapes classified based on their sizes

replaced. The participant will then have to press the start button on the bottom of the setup (Fig. 9) and explore the flashcard, point within the boundary of the tactile area and perform a click. Once a correct click is received, the moderator replaces the flashcard and participants start the next trial until all trails are finished. If the participants performs a wrong click, they can try as many times as they want to achieve the correct click until the session reaches the timeout (75 s). The order of trials in each condition is counterbalanced with a Latin Square. This design results in $(4 \times shapes) * (3 \times sizes) * (2 \times replication) * (12 \times participants) = 228$ measured trials.

6.5   Data Collection

We collected: 1) Task Completion Time, recorded from pressing the button to achieving a correct click (click within the boundary of the each shape on the flashcard) and 2) the error rate by logging in the number of wrong clicks of each flashcard before the correct click was registered.

6.6   Results

We post-processed the collected data by removing four outliers that were more/less than the mean values by more than two times of the standard deviations. The two-way repeated measures ANOVA was then performed on the *Task Completion Time* and the *Number Of Errors* with the Size and the Shape as the independent variables. The mean time and the mean number of errors for achieving a correct click for all the shapes and sizes are shown in Fig. 10 and Fig. 11.

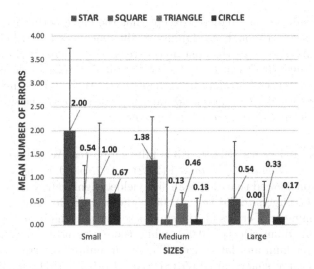

Fig. 11. Mean number of errors for the shapes based on their sizes

H1-Task Completion Time (Size). There was a significant effect of size on *Task Completion Time* [$F_{(2,22)} = 3.94$, $p < 0.05$, $\eta_p^2 = 0.264$]. Post-hoc pair-wise comparison showed that there is a significant difference in the Task Completion Time between the Large and the Small sized tactile shapes ($p < 0.005$) with the mean time of Small as 9.01 s (SD = 1.3) and of Large as 5.1 s (SD = 0.662). The mean time for the correct click for medium size is 6.49 s (SD = 1.41). But, there is no significant difference between Medium and Small or Medium and Large sizes. The mean task completion time (correct click) of the all small, medium and large sizes shows that the large sizes of all shapes were easily identifiable. Hence, H1 is fully supported.

H2-Task Completion Time (Shape). H2 is partially supported. We found a significant effect of Shape on *Task Completion Time* [$F_{(3,33)} = 12.881$, $p < 0.05$, $\eta_p^2 = 0.539$]. No significant interaction effect between Size and Shape was identified. Post-hoc pair-wise comparison showed for the small size, the star shape took significantly longer time than the triangle ($p < 0.05$), the circle ($p < 0.05$), and the square ($p < 0.05$), while the triangle took significantly longer time than the square ($p < 0.05$). No significant difference was found between the square and the circle or the triangle and the circle. For the medium size, the significance difference on the task completion time was found between star and triangle ($p < 0.05$), star and circle ($p < 0.05$), and star and square ($p < 0.05$), while there was no significantly difference among the triangle, the circle, and the square. For the large size, there was no significantly difference among the four shapes. The mean time for reaching a correct click for each shape in each size is showed in Fig. 10. We hypothesized (H2) that the sharper angle a shape has, the longer it would take for the correct click. As expected, smaller tactile areas are more sensitive to this effect. The result was as predicted except that the circle performed worse than square in all sizes, although no significant difference was found between circle and square. We speculate that one major reason of square performing better than circle in our experiment is due to the rectangular shape of the color sensor, which aligns better with straight lines than curves. While future investigation is needed, this raises alerts on potential impact of the shape of the sensing area of any sensing technology to be used in this context.

H3-Number of Errors (Size). H3 is fully supported. We found a significant effect of size on *Number Of Errors* [$F(2,22) = 9.82$, $p < 0.05$, $\eta_p^2 = .472$]. Post-hoc comparison showed that the small size yielded significantly larger number of errors than the large size did ($p < 0.005$). There is also a significant difference between the number of errors for the small size was also significantly larger than those of the medium size ($p < 0.05$), while there was no significant difference between the medium and large sizes. The mean number of errors of the small, medium, and large shapes are 1.05 (SD $= 0.225$), 0.521 (SD $= 0.235$) and 0.26 (SD $= 0.09$) respectively. In general we can see the error rates are rather low: most trials were completed in one or two attempts even in the smallest size.

H4-Number of Errors (Shape). H4 is partially supported in a similar way to H2. There was a significant effect of shape on *Number Of Errors* [$F(3,33) = 10.96$, $p < 0.001$, $\eta_p^2 = 0.499$]. Post-hoc pair-wise comparison showed that the star shape yielded a significantly more errors compared to square (small size: $p < 0.005$, medium size: $p < 0.005$, large size: $p < 0.005$), triangle (small size: $p < 0.05$, medium size: $p < 0.05$, large size: $p < 0.05$) and circle (small size: $p < 0.005$, medium size: $p < 0.005$, large size: $p < 0.005$). There was no significant difference between the square and circle across different sizes where as square yielded significantly less error when compared to triangle (small size: $p < 0.05$, medium size: $p < 0.05$, large size: $p < 0.05$). Figure 11 shows detailed results of the number of errors across difference shapes and sizes. We can see the error rate is consistent with the task completion time, which accords with our observation that failed attempts was a major cause for slower performances.

Overall, FingerTalkie was effective in selecting a wide range of tactile shapes. Participants could make a correct selection easily in one or two shots in most cases, even when the size is smaller than the smallest tactile areas used in the real world. Effects of sharp angles were shown in smaller tactile shapes. Potential effects of the shape of the sensory area was uncovered, should be paid attention to in future development of similar technologies.

7   Focus-Group Interview with Blind Users

The aim of focus-group interview is to obtain a deeper understanding on key factors such as wearability and form factor, novelty and usefulness of the device, difficulty in using the device, learnability, cost of the device, audio data-input, and sharing interface.

7.1   Participants

The subjective feedback session was conducted with 8 congenitally blind participants. The participant group consisted of 1 adult male (Age = 35) and 7 children aging from 11 to 14 (Mean = 13.0, SD = 1.0). All the users were right-handed.

7.2   Apparatus

We used two tactile figures; squares of two different sizes (5 cm and 3 cm) side by side as to demonstrate the working of the device. One of the square was filled with blue color while another smaller square was filled with red color. Each square color was annotated with a discrete audio that could be listened through the laptop speakers. The finger worn device used for the evaluation was the standalone prototype which was connected to the external battery pack using a USB cable.

7.3   Procedure

The hands-on session was done in an informal setup where the participants were briefed initially about the concept of finger wearable device and the nature of the problem that it solves. The users were instructed to wear the device and they were guided to understand the position of the sensor on the tip. They were also instructed to touch the tip of the device to conform its angle of tilt. In this way, they could get a clear understanding of the distance of the sensor from the tip of the finger. The offset point-and-click mechanism was explained to each participant. The whole process was administered by a sighted external helper. The participants were then asked to explore the tactile diagram and perform the correct-clicking styles freely within the boundaries of the squares. Tone A 'Glass' sound file in the MacOS sound effects was played for the correct clicks on the big and small squares respectively. Tone B 'Basso' sound file in the MacOS sound effects was played for a wrong click outside the tactile boundary. Each participant experienced the device and performed clicking for approximately 10 min.

7.4   Results

After the exploratory hands-on session, all participants were asked to provide feedback regarding the following factors:

Usability of the Device. After wearing the device for about 5 min, all the users were impressed by the uniqueness of the device. It was also noted that none of the participants have ever used a finger-wearable interactive device in the past. On the other hand, 3 out of 8 users have used or was familiar with the Pen Friend/annotating pens [20] for audio-tactile markings. A Pen-Friend user said, *"Reusability of the colors is a really good feature as we don't have to worry about* *the tags running out.*" Another user said, *"The best thing I like about the finger device[FingerTalkie] when compared to Pen Friend is that I can use both my hands to explore the tactile diagrams."* One user had a prior experience in using an image-processing-based audio-tactile system where a smartphone/camera is placed on a vertical stand on top of the tactile diagram. To use such a system, the user needs to affix a sticker on his/her index finger to explore the tactile diagram. This user stated, *"Though this system enabled me to use both the hands for tactile exploration, it was cumbersome to set up and calibrate the phone with the stand and sometimes didn't work as expected due to the poor ambient lighting or improper positioning of the smartphone."* While all the users agreed on the application and usefulness of the device for audio annotation of tactile graphics, some even suggested different levels of applications. A user stated *"I can use this device for annotating everyday objects like medicines and other personal artifacts identification. It will save me a lot of time in printing Braille and sticking it to the objects."*

Learnability/Ease of Use/Adaptability. After wearing the device, the users were able to understand the relation of the sensor and its distance and angle corresponding to the tactile surface after trying for a couple of minutes. Overall, the participants showed a great interest in wearing it and exploring the different sounds while moving between the two different tactile images. All the users stated that they could adapt to this clicking method easily by using it for a couple of hours. Asking about the ease of use, a participant stated *"this is like a magic device. I just have to tilt my (index) finger to get the audio description about the place being pointed. Getting audio information from the tactile diagram have never been so easy."* Another user said *"I have used a mobile phone application which can detect the boundaries of the tactile diagram using the camera and gives audio output corresponding to the area being pointed and double tapped. But for that, I require a stand on which the mobile phone should be fixed fist and should also make use that the room is well lit to get the best result. With this device, the advantage I find over the others is that its lightweight, portable and it works irrespective of the lighting conditions in the room."*

Wearability. It was observed that the finger wearable device could fit in perfectly on the index finger for seven out of eight participants with only minor adjustments in the strap. One exemption was a case in which the device was extremely loose and was tending to sway while the user tried to perform a click. One of the participants claimed *"I don't think it's complicated and I can wear it on my own. It is easy to wear and I can adjust it by myself."* The device was found protruding out of the index finger in half of the cases, however this did not affect the usability of the device. The users were still able to make the offset-click without any fail.

Need of Mobile Application for User Data Input. Majority of users were eager to know the mechanism and the software interface by which the audio can be tagged to a specified color. The child participants were eager to know if they would be able to do it on their own. Four out of five child participants insisted that a mobile or computer application should be made accessible to the VI people so that they can do it on their own without an external assistance. A user said *"Being proficient in using the smart phones, I am disappointed with the fact that most of the mobile applications are not designed taking care of the accessibility and hence render them useless"*. One of the special educators said *"If the teachers can themselves make a audio-color profile for each diagram or chapter and then share it with the students, it would save a lot of time for both the students and the special educators"*.

In summary, the participants showed enthusiasm in using FingerTalkie in their daily and educational activities. Their feedback showed promises of FingerTalkie for providing an intuitive and seamless user experience. Most participants expressed appreciation to the simple design of the device. The offset point-and-click method appeared to be easy to learn and perform. Overall, the users liked the experience of the FingerTalkie and suggested for a sturdy design and an accessible back-end software system.

8 Limitations and Future Work

Though we were able to address most of the usability and hardware drawbacks of FingerTalkie during the iterative process, the following factors could be improved in future designs:

During the entire design and evaluation process, we used only Blue, Green, Red colors in the tactile diagrams. We used them to achieve a better detection accuracy. A better color sensor with noise filtering algorithms and a well-calibrated sensor positioning can help in detection of more colors efficiently on a single tactile diagram.

Though the final prototype is made into a compact wearable form factor, it is still bulky as we used off-the-shelf hardware components. It could be further miniaturized by the use of custom-made PCB design and SMD electronic components. In order to achieve a comprehensive and ready-to-use system, an accessible and stable back-end PC software or mobile app should be developed in the near future. The back-end software/mobile application should include the features of audio-color-mapping profile creation and sharing. Last but not the least, we will also explore other modality of on-finger feedback (e.g., vibration [30], thermal [44], poking [17], etc.) for VI users comprehending tactile diagrams.

9 Conclusion

In this paper, we introduce FingerTalkie, a novel finger-worn device with a new offset point-and-click technique that enables easy access of audio information on tactile diagrams. The design requirements and choices were established from an iterative user-centered design process. It is an easy-to-use, reliable and inexpensive technique that can help the VI to reduce the bulkiness of tactile textbooks by eliminating the Braille pages. The offset point-and-click technique can easily perform even with the smallest tactile areas suggested by the tactile graphics guidelines. The subjective feedback from VI users shows high acceptance of FingerTalkie in terms of dual-hand exploration ability when compared to the mainstream audio tactile devices in the market. As high-contrast colored tactile diagrams are gaining popularity amongst people with low or partial vision, we aim to use the same printed colors to make the color palette for the FingerTalkie. In addition, we envision that FingerTalkie can not only be used by VI users, but also by sighted users with special needs, such as elderly and children, to annotate everyday physical objects, such as medicine containers and textbooks. Due to the versatility of the design with the point-and-click method, the researchers in the future can adopt such techniques in other devices and systems where finger tips shall not be occluded while performing touch input.

References

1. Al-Khalifa, H.S.: Utilizing QR code and mobile phones for blinds and visually impaired people. In: Miesenberger, K., Klaus, J., Zagler, W., Karshmer, A. (eds.) ICCHP 2008. LNCS, vol. 5105, pp. 1065–1069. Springer, Heidelberg (2008). https://doi.org/10.1007/978-3-540-70540-6_159
2. Ashbrook, D., Baudisch, P., White, S.: Nenya: subtle and eyes-free mobile input with a magnetically-tracked finger ring. In: Proceedings of the SIGCHI Conference on Human Factors in Computing Systems, pp. 2043–2046. ACM (2011)
3. Baker, C.M., Milne, L.R., Scofield, J., Bennett, C.L., Ladner, R.E.: Tactile graphics with a voice: using QR codes to access text in tactile graphics. In: Proceedings of the 16th International ACM SIGACCESS Conference on Computers & Accessibility, pp. 75–82. ACM (2014)
4. Bau, O., Poupyrev, I., Israr, A., Harrison, C.: TeslaTouch: electrovibration for touch surfaces. In: Proceedings of the 23nd Annual ACM Symposium on User Interface Software and Technology, pp. 283–292. ACM (2010)
5. Boldu, R., Dancu, A., Matthies, D.J., Buddhika, T., Siriwardhana, S., Nanayakkara, S.: FingerReader2.0: designing and evaluating a wearable finger-worn camera to assist people with visual impairments while shopping. Proc. ACM Interact. Mob. Wearable Ubiquitous Technol. **2**(3), 94 (2018)
6. Brock, A.: Interactive maps for visually impaired people: design, usability and spatial cognition. Ph.D. thesis (2013)
7. Brock, A.M., Truillet, P., Oriola, B., Picard, D., Jouffrais, C.: Interactivity improves usability of geographic maps for visually impaired people. Hum.-Comput. Interact. **30**(2), 156–194 (2015). https://doi.org/10.1080/07370024.2014.924412
8. Ducasse, J., Brock, A.M., Jouffrais, C.: Accessible interactive maps for visually impaired users. In: Pissaloux, E., Velázquez, R. (eds.) Mobility of Visually Impaired People, pp. 537–584. Springer, Cham (2018). https://doi.org/10.1007/978-3-319-54446-5_17
9. Edman, P.: Tactile Graphics. American Foundation for the Blind (1992)
10. Foulke, E.: Reading braille. In: Schiff, W., Foulke, E. (eds.) Tactual Perception: A Sourcebook, vol. 168. Cambridge University Press, Cambridge (1982)
11. Fukumoto, M., Suenaga, Y.: "Fingering": a full-time wearable interface. In: Conference Companion on Human Factors in Computing Systems, pp. 81–82. ACM (1994)

12. Fusco, G., Morash, V.S.: The tactile graphics helper: providing audio clarification for tactile graphics using machine vision. In: Proceedings of the 17th International ACM SIGACCESS Conference on Computers & Accessibility, pp. 97–106 (2015)
13. Gardner, J.A.: Access by blind students and professionals to mainstream math and science. In: Miesenberger, K., Klaus, J., Zagler, W. (eds.) ICCHP 2002. LNCS, vol. 2398, pp. 502–507. Springer, Heidelberg (2002). https://doi.org/10.1007/3-540-45491-8_94
14. Ghosh, S., Kim, H.C., Cao, Y., Wessels, A., Perrault, S.T., Zhao, S.: Ringteraction: coordinated thumb-index interaction using a ring. In: Proceedings of the 2016 CHI Conference Extended Abstracts on Human Factors in Computing Systems, pp. 2640–2647. ACM (2016)
15. Heller, M.A.: Picture and pattern perception in the sighted and the blind: the advantage of the late blind. Perception 18(3), 379–389 (1989)
16. Hinton, R.A.: Tactile and audio-tactile images as vehicles for learning. Colloques-Institut National de la sante et de la Recherche Medicale Colloques et Seminaires, p. 169 (1993)
17. Je, S., Lee, M., Kim, Y., Chan, L., Yang, X.D., Bianchi, A.: PokeRing: notifications by poking around the finger. In: Proceedings of the 2018 CHI Conference on Human Factors in Computing Systems, p. 542. ACM (2018)
18. Jing, L., Zhou, Y., Cheng, Z., Huang, T.: Magic Ring: a finger-worn device for multiple appliances control using static finger gestures. Sensors 12(5), 5775–5790 (2012)
19. Kane, S.K., Frey, B., Wobbrock, J.O.: Access lens: a gesture-based screen reader for real-world documents. In: Proceedings of the SIGCHI Conference on Human Factors in Computing Systems, pp. 347–350. ACM (2013)
20. Kendrick, D.: PenFriend and touch memo: a comparison of labeling tools. AFB AccessWorld Mag. 12(9) (2011)
21. Kienzle, W., Hinckley, K.: LightRing: always-available 2D input on any surface. In: Proceedings of the 27th Annual ACM Symposium on User Interface Software and Technology, pp. 157–160. ACM (2014)
22. Krueger, M.W., Gilden, D.: KnowWhere: an audio/spatial interface for blind people. Georgia Institute of Technology (1997)
23. Landau, S., Wells, L.: Merging tactile sensory input and audio data by means of the talking tactile tablet. In: Proceedings of EuroHaptics, vol. 3, pp. 414–418 (2003)
24. Lévesque, V.: Virtual display of tactile graphics and Braille by lateral skin deformation. Ph.D. thesis, McGill University Library (2009)
25. Lim, H., Chung, J., Oh, C., Park, S., Suh, B.: OctaRing: examining pressure-sensitive multi-touch input on a finger ring device. In: Proceedings of the 29th Annual Symposium on User Interface Software and Technology, pp. 223–224. ACM (2016)
26. Minagawa, H., Ohnishi, N., Sugie, N.: Tactile-audio diagram for blind persons. IEEE Trans. Rehabil. Eng. 4(4), 431–437 (1996)
27. Morash, V.S., Pensky, A.E.C., Tseng, S.T., Miele, J.A.: Effects of using multiple hands and fingers on haptic performance in individuals who are blind. Perception 43(6), 569–588 (2014)
28. Nanayakkara, S., Shilkrot, R., Maes, P.: EyeRing: an eye on a finger. In: CHI 2012 Extended Abstracts on Human Factors in Computing Systems, pp. 1047–1050. ACM (2012)
29. Ogata, M., Sugiura, Y., Osawa, H., Imai, M.: iRing: intelligent ring using infrared reflection. In: Proceedings of the 25th Annual ACM Symposium on User Interface Software and Technology, pp. 131–136. ACM (2012)

30. Roumen, T., Perrault, S.T., Zhao, S.: NotiRing: a comparative study of notification channels for wearable interactive rings. In: Proceedings of the 33rd Annual ACM Conference on Human Factors in Computing Systems, pp. 2497–2500. ACM (2015)
31. Schiff, W., Foulke, E.: Tactual Perception: A Sourcebook. Cambridge University Press, Cambridge (1982)
32. Seisenbacher, G., Mayer, P., Panek, P., Zagler, W.L.: 3D-finger-system for auditory support of haptic exploration in the education of blind and visually impaired students-idea and feasibility study. In: Assistive Technology: From Virtuality to Reality: AAATE 2005, vol. 16, p. 73 (2005)
33. Shi, L., McLachlan, R., Zhao, Y., Azenkot, S.: Magic touch: interacting with 3D printed graphics. In: Proceedings of the 18th International ACM SIGACCESS Conference on Computers and Accessibility, pp. 329–330. ACM (2016)
34. Shi, L., Zhao, Y., Azenkot, S.: Markit and Talkit: a low-barrier toolkit to augment 3D printed models with audio annotations. In: Proceedings of the 30th Annual ACM Symposium on User Interface Software and Technology, pp. 493–506. ACM (2017)
35. Shilkrot, R., Huber, J., Meng Ee, W., Maes, P., Nanayakkara, S.C.: FingerReader: a wearable device to explore printed text on the go. In: Proceedings of the 33rd Annual ACM Conference on Human Factors in Computing Systems, pp. 2363–2372. ACM (2015)
36. Sporka, A.J., Němec, V., Slavík, P.: Tangible newspaper for the visually impaired users. In: CHI 2005 Extended Abstracts on Human Factors in Computing Systems, pp. 1809–1812. ACM (2005)
37. Tatham, A.F.: The design of tactile maps: theoretical and practical considerations. In: Proceedings of International Cartographic Association: Mapping the Nations, pp. 157–166 (1991)
38. The Braille Authority of North America: Guidelines and standards for tactile graphics (2012). http://www.brailleauthority.org/tg/web-manual/index.html
39. Thinus-Blanc, C., Gaunet, F.: Representation of space in blind persons: vision as a spatial sense? Psychol. Bull. **121**(1), 20 (1997)
40. Vogt, H.: Efficient object identification with passive RFID tags. In: Mattern, F., Naghshineh, M. (eds.) Pervasive 2002. LNCS, vol. 2414, pp. 98–113. Springer, Heidelberg (2002). https://doi.org/10.1007/3-540-45866-2_9
41. Wilhelm, M., Krakowczyk, D., Trollmann, F., Albayrak, S.: eRing: multiple finger gesture recognition with one ring using an electric field. In: Proceedings of the 2nd International Workshop on Sensor-Based Activity Recognition and Interaction, p. 7. ACM (2015)
42. Wong, P.C., Zhu, K., Fu, H.: FingerT9: leveraging thumb-to-finger interaction for same-side-hand text entry on smartwatches. In: Proceedings of the 2018 CHI Conference on Human Factors in Computing Systems, p. 178 (2018)
43. Yang, X.D., Grossman, T., Wigdor, D., Fitzmaurice, G.: Magic finger: always-available input through finger instrumentation. In: Proceedings of the 25th Annual ACM Symposium on User Interface Software and Technology, pp. 147–156. ACM (2012)
44. Zhu, K., Perrault, S., Chen, T., Cai, S., Peiris, R.L.: A sense of ice and fire: exploring thermal feedback with multiple thermoelectric-cooling elements on a smart ring. Int. J. Hum.-Comput. Stud. **130**, 234–247 (2019)

A Virtual Mouse Interface for Supporting Multi-user Interactions

Matthew Peveler[1(✉)], Jeffery O. Kephart[2], Xiangyang Mou[1],
Gordon Clement[1], and Hui Su[1,2]

[1] Rensselaer Polytechnic Institute, Troy, NJ 12180, USA
{pevelm,moux4,clemeg2}@rpi.edu
[2] IBM Thomas J Watson Research Center, Yorktown Heights, NY 10598, USA
{kephart,huisuibmres}@us.ibm.com

Abstract. Traditionally, two approaches have been used to build intelligent room applications. Mouse-based control schemes allow developers to leverage a wealth of existing user-interaction libraries that respond to clicks and other events. However, systems built in this manner cannot distinguish among multiple users. To realize the potential of intelligent rooms to support multi-user interactions, a second approach is often used, whereby applications are custom-built for this purpose, which is costly to create and maintain. We introduce a new framework that supports building multi-user intelligent room applications in a much more general and portable way, using a combination of existing web technologies that we have extended to better enable simultaneous interactions among multiple users, plus speech recognition and voice synthesis technologies that support multi-modal interactions.

Keywords: Large display interface · Multi-user interface · Cellphone interface · Interface framework

1 Introduction

When people engage with one another in meetings, they utilize a mixture of modalities to communicate and illustrate their points, often times simultaneously. To support natural and effective interaction [9,12], artificial assistants embedded into meeting spaces (or *intelligent rooms*) must be able to cope with multiple users across a number of modalities beyond just voice, including gesture and pointing. There exist a number of mechanisms to harness these additional modalities, such as leveraging skeleton data from a Kinect camera [18], pointing a phone at a display [2,10], or using a wand, remote, or similar pointing device [8].

Traditional approaches to capturing pointing and gestures for interacting with these spaces generally fall into one of two classes. One approach is to use a custom framework/display layer in which all content must be developed for that framework. This provides well-integrated content for the input modalities,

© Springer Nature Switzerland AG 2020
M. Kurosu (Ed.): HCII 2020, LNCS 12182, pp. 497–508, 2020.
https://doi.org/10.1007/978-3-030-49062-1_33

but at the cost that it is hard to reuse it outside of the specific framework it was developed for due to being written in a domain specific language. Additionally, some of these frameworks require building deep hooks into the operating system, preventing portability. A second approach is to leverage a web-based platform, and map input events (possibly with some additional processing such as is required with the Kinect) directly onto the mouse via automation frameworks, like RobotJS [15]. An advantage of this approach is that the content can be made available easily elsewhere such as via a web browser. Moreover, there exists an extensive set of libraries to support building web content and mouse-based interactions. Unfortunately, as this approach ultimately relies upon the mouse to trigger events, the systems end up being inherently single-user, thus leading to an interaction style in which a designated human is primarily responsible for mediating interactions with the system.

This paper describes our work on a framework that overcomes the limitations of prior approaches by allowing developers to build multi-user, multi-modal intelligent applications built on top of general web technologies, allowing us to take advantage of the wide-ranging work on websites and web based tools. To accomplish this, we present our *Virtual Mouse Interface* that in essence mimics a physical mouse for each user. Multiple users can simultaneously utilize the interface to achieve various well-understood mouse actions such as moving their mouse around a web page, clicking, and scrolling on the displayed web page within the system. The structure for the rest of the paper is as follows. In the next section, we bring up and discuss related work. Next, we present an overview of the architecture of our framework and its underlying technologies. Next, we describe in detail how the *Virtual Mouse Interface* functions and how it supports multi-user interaction. After, we describe some use-cases we have explored with our interface. Finally, we conclude the paper with a summary of our work and contributions, and some thoughts about promising lines of future work.

2   Related Work

There is a rich tradition of work centered around so-called intelligent or smart rooms. These spaces combine a variety of sensors to allow a variety of inputs, such as voice and gesture. Bolt demonstrated using a combination of voice and gesture to issue commands to display simple shapes on a large screen [1]. Brooks demonstrated a distributed architecture that was bound to the underlying X display server and used to resolve multi-modal commands to the system [3]. Further work showed how these spaces could be utilized by multiple users across multiple modalities to play chess on a giant screen [4], using a custom built framework and application. Recent breakthroughs in the underlying technology have allowed for these systems to be used with less constraints on the inputs of voice and gesture [6] and to approach more complex domains, such as analyzing exoplanet data [8], while also relying on displaying and interacting with content shown in webpages to the user. However, in both of these works, their systems allow for multiple participants to speak, but the gestural and pointing input was driven by a single person holding a "wand", which tied directly into the underlying mouse.

While pointing remains a much desired capacity of these types of systems, it's important to recognize alternative modalities that have been developed to enable multi-user systems. Examples of this include a digital table with a touch-screen [16] or allowing participants to have personal tablets that they can use to modify globally shown information [13], and through virtual reality and holography [11]. The table allows for users to use their hands as containers for objects for speech commands as well as handwriting content, though the authors note that it forces a high level of co-locality among the users which ends up negatively impacting their ability to cooperatively achieve tasks simultaneously. The personal devices help to allow users to type out fuller content to be shared with the other users without having to rely on the voice transcription service, which often carries some errors especially over transcribing longer sentences, however, it's potentially at the cost of a feeling of decreased connection both to the room at large and the other participants as each user heavily looks at their own screen. The virtual reality environment allows for the highest level of immersion within a space, but is perhaps the most costly to develop and create content for, which potentially renders in impractical for wide-spread deployment.

3 The Cognitive and Immersive System Architecture

Our system builds upon the Cognitive Immersive Room Architecture CIRA [5], which supports and augments group decision-making with cognitive artificial agents in so-called human scale environments. The architecture features a modular approach of separate components handling specific concerns, such as a transcript-worker for receiving input from microphones, a conversation-worker for translating the transcribed speech into dialogue, etc. We extended the architecture by augmenting the existing display-worker and adding in two new components, the spatial-context-system and Reagent, which are described below. As part of this work, and to demonstrate its effectiveness, we deployed it in two unique environments, where the first features a panoramic screen with a diameter of 12 m and height of 3.8 m that users stand inside of (shown in Fig. 2), and the second features a screen that is flat against a wall and measures 11 by 1 m that users stand in front of (shown in Fig. 5). In both environments, the users are equipped with lapel microphones that picks up what they say, transcribing it to text on the fly, which is then converted to an intent and entities utilizing IBM Watson Cloud services [7]. This intent is then fed into an orchestrator which matches it to an action within the domain, and sees if all entities necessary for the action are satisfied. If some are missing, the system will attempt to resolve it based on information that comes from the gesture system (e.g. what is the user actively pointed or just recently pointed at) as well as historical context of prior intents. If this resolution succeeds, the system carries out the command, else if it fails it asks the user for additional information. In carrying out the command, the orchestrator can call out to external web services to gather additional information, display content on the screen, or use speakers to output a synthesized voice to the users. Figure 1 shows an overview of this architecture and how the pieces are connected. Communication between the core modules of the system utilize RabbitMQ and a publisher/subscriber model to allow modules to be easily swapped out or new modules put in with the only potential change is just the routing key the modules listen to or output on. The core modules of the architecture that enable our key contributions are highlighted below.

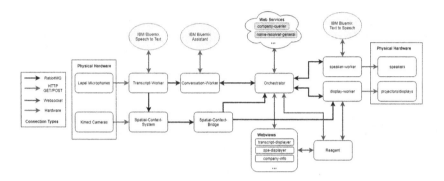

Fig. 1. Architecture of the cognitive and immersive system

3.1 Spatial-Context-System

Within our system, to handle capturing gestural information, users can utilize Kinect cameras [18] or HTC Vive controllers [17], utilizing a common interface API[1]. For both, the underlying implementation follows a similar development path. First, a unified 3D coordinate system is defined for a model of the space, giving all fixed physical objects, such as the displays, a unique location in this model. Next, the sensors, including the Kinect and HTC Vive controller, are calibrated against this coordinate system so that the data generated from the sensors is translated into the coordinate system of the space. Using this, we can create a pointing approximation for the Kinect by using a 3D location of the joints of the human arm and for the HTC Vive by using the posture of the controller to estimate a pointing ray. This approximation is then used to calculate the spatial interaction against the fixed objects, giving us a corresponding [x, y] pixel against the fixed object which acts as the final pointing result. To support multiple users, we dynamically maintain IDs for users in the space. For the Kinect, a unique ID is automatically assigned to a user when they enter the field of view of the camera. For the HTC Vive, an ID is assigned when the controller is turned on and connects to the space. This "spatial ID" is then tied to the unique ID of the lapel microphone for a user to allow for fusion and reference of speech data with gestural information. For either system, it then passes the

---

[1] It is important to note that through this interface, additional types of input can be supported beyond the two presented here.

pointing information, as well as gestures for the Kinect and button presses for the HTC Vive to the *spatial-context-bridge* which then acts as a normalization layer on the inputs to standard mouse interactions. The HTC Vive requires little normalization as it already has buttons that correspond to how a mouse functions that we can leverage (left and right buttons, scroll wheel, etc.). The Kinect camera on the other hand is transformed from the gestural information of hand actions to mouse actions. For example, opening and closing the right hand corresponds to clicking and then releasing the left mouse button while closing and moving the left hand corresponds to using the scroll wheel to move about a page in the four cardinal directions. Additionally, it provides a smoothing operation on the quickness of hand state changes such as to prevent a rapid hand close, open, close chain within a few milliseconds rising from a brief misclassification of hand state. This is to prevent accidental clicks or ends of clicks that a user might wish to avoid, at the cost of actions taking a few extra milliseconds.

Fig. 2. Aerial shot of half of the 360-degree panoramic screen

3.2   Display Worker

Displaying output on the screen is managed by the Electron framework, which uses a modified chromium engine[2] to render content from websites contained within "webviews". The display-worker provides the user with a grid with a set number of rows and columns in which the user can open as many websites as they would like, with each taking up one or more cells. An example of this is

---

[2] The modification here is that all generated JavaScript events have the "isTrusted" flag set to true, which is usually only set to true for user generated actions. This allows us to interact with inputs, selects, etc. on a page that do not have an explicitly created "EventListener".

shown in Fig. 3, which shows a 4 × 4 grid with 5 web pages of different sizes open. It is possible that open webviews may overlap each other, or be kept completely separated, depending on the needs of the application. When each webview opens, the display-worker preloads a small JavaScript file on-top of the opened webpage which helps deliver a payload from the Reagent system, described below. From the spatial context system, it receives the absolute [x,y] coordinate, which it shows to the user as an icon on the screen with their user id in the center. This icon then follows where the user is pointing on the screen, and gives a visual indication of the particular action they are attempting to make (such as clicking on the screen). To help translate what webview a user is interacting with, the display-worker provides an API to understand the dimensions of open webviews, as well as providing a mechanism to translate an absolute [x,y] coordinate on the overall screen into a relative [x,y] coordinate within a given webview. To accomplish this, the display-worker maintains a sorted list of webviews based on their "height" in the DOM tree where elements lower down the tree are on top and overlap elements higher up in the tree, and traverses through that list until it finds a webview in which the [x,y] coordinate lies. To speed this process up on subsequent look-ups, we exploit the principle that users repeat actions within the same webview usually, so we cache the webview the previous look-up was in and check it first on subsequent calls, unless a new webview is opened in the intermediary time. If the new action falls outside the webview, we instantiate the above search again to find the new webview.

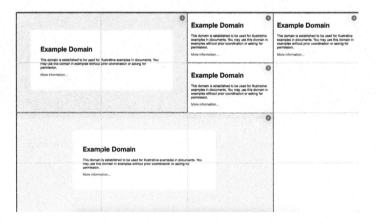

Fig. 3. View of display with 4 × 4 grid with 5 open pages. Green lines represent the grid and blue lines the borders of the web pages. (Color figure online)

3.3   Reagent

The Reagent system [14], once its bootstrap is pre-loaded by the display-worker, injects further JavaScript code from the Reagent server, which then in-turn constructs an open websocket on the webpage to the Reagent system. Additionally, while important to the operation of the voice system, but orthogonal to the Virtual Mouse, the injected JavaScript inserts a transparent layer on top of the open page. This layer then analyzes the site, captures the salient semantic information of the page, build listeners for user interactions with the mouse on that content, and attach a so-called MutationObserver to detect any changes in the content of the page, causing the above process to repeat. Additionally, it sets up a websocket on the open page that is used for bidirectional communication between the webpage and the central Reagent server. This server then utilizes a REST API to allow other modules, such as the orchestrator, to get information about what elements are at a particular [x,y] coordinate, get a record of prior interactions, or to run arbitrary JavaScript within a page, such as triggering custom interaction events and which returns the affected elements.

4   Virtual Mouse Interface

Leveraging the spatial-context and Reagent systems, we enable a *Virtual Mouse Interface* that allows users to interact with content as well as to guide multimodal interactions. This interface gives each user the equivalent of their own personal mouse. The interface itself, under the hood is not one dedicated component, but rather conglomeration of functionality across modules described above. To start, the spatial-context-system provides us with an absolute [x,y] coordinate for a given device on the screen from a user, which has a unique ID attached to it. This is sent into the display-worker, which then displays an icon to the user on the screen that represents where they are pointing at that time, as well as the mouse action they are doing. This icon updates at a constant rate for the user, and scales to many concurrent users, where there is (due to RabbitMQ) a delay of about 4–8 ms, which is largely imperceptible to users. In addition to the display-worker, the spatial-context system sends the pointing and action data to the orchestrator. The orchestrator communicates with the display-worker to translate the absolute [x,y] coordinate into a relative [x,y] coordinate within a specific webview. From here, it communicates with Reagent in a number of ways. For each payload that it sends along, and the subsequent action JavaScript event that Reagent generates against a given WebView, the unique user ID is passed, which Reagent binds to the generated events that are dispatched to the page. First, it is important to denote that the orchestrator sets a limiter on the number of actions that can flow through the system, which is roughly 75 ms per action type, which allows adequate throughput for the system for a number of users such that they do not notice lag while also not sending too much information to the page and potentially causing a slow-down. Below, we describe the two types of actions with which we concern ourselves with, mouse and scroll.

4.1   Mouse Actions

Mouse actions represent the principle way in which people interact with the page. This includes the use of the left and right mouse buttons, though we mainly focus on the usage of the left button here. The mouseitself can be thought of as being in three potential states, being held down for any period of time (MouseDown), being released after being held down for any period of time (MouseUp) and a rapid push down and release of the button (Click). Additionally, there is the act of just moving the mouse itself (MouseMove). To start with these actions, the orchestrator first sends a MouseMove event to Reagent, which then gets dispatched against the webview. From this, Reagent returns the element that the mouse is currently over. The orchestrator stores this element and if it different from the last stored element, issues to Reagent a leave event (MouseOut) on the old element and an enter (MouseEnter) on the new element. This chain of events allows for triggering of hover type events on a site for the given elements affected as you move your cursor across a page. Finally, it takes the mouse action (MouseUp or MouseDown and possibly Click), and sends that to Reagent to issue against the page. In all of three of these cases, Reagent sends details about the element that was clicked on, such that the orchestrator can drive subsequent interactions on it, such as if clicking on a form input, can ask the user what value do they want to input, which is picked up via voice input.

4.2   Scroll Actions

For scroll actions, a more involved sequence is followed to determine what type of scroll is meant by the user. Webpages may implement scroll to mean just moving around the content that has overflowed from the available displayed space (such as scrolling down on a news article), which is referred to as a ScrollEvent. Alternatively, they may use scroll to control zooming in and out of the content, or panning (common in graphs or maps), where these are WheelEvents. However, for both, we require the difference between the current mouse position and the previous mouse position to perform the action, which is stored within the orchestrator. To determine the appropriate action (especially on a page that includes both overflowed content and a graph), the orchestrator first sends a WheelEvent to Reagent. Reagent returns the event that was acted upon, as well as if the MutationObserver it attached to the page detected any changes to that page. If there are no changes, than the system determines that the user's intention was not to zoom or pan, but to simply scroll the page for overflowed content, at which point a ScrollEvent is issued to Reagent, and the page content is shifted.

5   Use Cases

We now describe some use-cases that we have explored with our interface, and describe implementation details. These use-cases cover a couple of different design paradigms that we envision content creators might follow. We first start with utilizing existing web sites in which it is expected only one particular user at a time is going. For this, it is important to remember that the display-worker allows us to open many different webviews at the same time across the available space. For example, in Fig. 2, there is 6 different open webviews in sight.

Each webview is self-contained and interactions within one does not bleed into any other. From this, the virtual mouse interface allows users to interact in different webviews simultaneously. An example of the ways a user might do this is shown in Fig. 4, where the user on the left is scrolling an article in the center, while the user on the right is scrolling the window next to it. Other examples of these sorts of pages include opening something off Google Maps, interacting with a graph, etc. where only one person can scroll and generally only one location or node selected at a time.

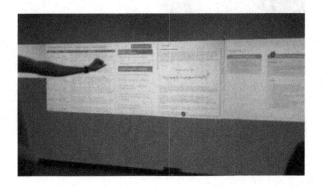

Fig. 4. Two users interacting with multiple open webviews

The other type of interaction we concern ourselves with is having one open webview in which multiple users interact simultaneously. For this, the content creator implements on their site content that has their own event listeners and that can be interacted with discretely, such as elements that are to be clicked on[3]. This can be further extended, if the content developer knows they are designing for our system, by taking advantage of the provided user id on a given event to tie subsequent actions to a single user. For example, in the context of a sticky note application, it may be desired that a MouseDown on a note selects the note, the mouse is moved, and then a MouseUp releases the note to that new location. Multiple users can be supported for that by storing the user id to the note on MouseDown, and ignoring any subsequent actions made against the note except for a MouseUp by that same user. An example of this is shown in Fig. 5. Through this extended paradigm, we easily allow existing sites with discrete mouse actions to function and take advantage of the provided interface.

---

[3] https://codepen.io/masterodin/pen/jOOPddy gives an example of this sort of content.

Fig. 5. Two users moving sticky notes around a screen

6 Conclusions and Future Work

In this paper, we present a *Virtual Mouse Interface*, powered through a cognitive and immersive system, to handle multi-user, multi-modal interactions. Through this interface, we can leverage existing web content and handle interactions to it in a way that mimics a physical mouse to those pages. To accomplish this, our interface leverages the Regent system to issue simulated mouse events through JavaScript, while attaching a unique ID per user to the event. From this, pages can be interacted with similarly to a regular mouse, however we can have many virtual mouses interacting at once, be it on the same webview or different open webviews. Additionally, pages can utilize the unique user ID to tailor interactions around our system. This helps remove a major hurdle of requiring a single driver of the system to handle the gestural interactions or development of full custom applications that existed within prior work. Future work would aim to principally lower the latency between events to increase fidelity. Additionally, when using the Kinect, creation of an interface to allow the user to map the inputs of the hands to the virtual mouse in a personalized way as well as for allowing additional actions such as right clicking. Finally, while we focus here on Kinect and HTC Vive as the principal input mechanisms, we are investigating the usage of cellphones, which would operate on a similar input scheme as the HTC Vive, but hopefully be more intuitive to users, as well as lowering entry costs to our system.

References

1. Bolt, R.: "Put-that-there": voice and gesture at the graphics interface. In: Proceedings of the 7th Annual Conference on Computer Graphics and Interactive Techniques, SIGGRAPH 1980, Seattle, Washington, USA, 1980, pp. 262–270. ACM, July 1980
2. Boring, S., Jurmu, M., Butz, A.: Scroll, tilt or move it: using mobile phones to continuously control pointers on large public displays. In: Proceedings of the 21st Annual Conference of the Australian Computer-Human Interaction Special Interest Group on Design: Open 24/7 - OZCHI 2009, Melbourne, Australia, p. 161. ACM Press (2009). https://doi.org/10.1145/1738826.1738853, http://portal.acm.org/citation.cfm?doid=1738826.1738853
3. Brooks, R.: The intelligent room project. In: Proceedings Second International Conference on Cognitive Technology Humanizing the Information Age, Aizu-Wakamatsu City, Japan, pp. 271–278. IEEE Computur Society (1997)
4. Carbini, S., Delphin-Poulat, L., Perron, L., Viallet, J.: From a Wizard of Oz experiment to a real time speech and gesture multimodal interface. Sig. Process. **86**(12), 3559–3577 (2006)
5. Divekar, R.R., et al.: CIRA: an architecture for building configurable immersive smart-rooms. In: Arai, K., Kapoor, S., Bhatia, R. (eds.) IntelliSys 2018. AISC, vol. 869, pp. 76–95. Springer, Cham (2019). https://doi.org/10.1007/978-3-030-01057-7_7
6. Farrell, R.G., et al.: Symbiotic cognitive computing. AI Magazine **37**(3), 81 (2016)
7. IBM: IBM Watson Cloud, May 2019. https://www.ibm.com/cloud/ai
8. Kephart, J.O., Dibia, V.C., Ellis, J., Srivastava, B., Talamadupula, K., Dholakia, M.: An embodied cognitive assistant for visualizing and analyzing exoplanet data. IEEE Internet Comput. **23**(2), 31–39 (2019)
9. Krum, D., Omoteso, O., Ribarsky, W., Starner, T., Hodges, L.: Speech and gesture multimodal control of a whole earth 3D visualization environment. In: Proceedings of the Symposium on Data Visualization 2002, Barcelona, Spain, pp. 195–200. Eurographics Association (2002)
10. Langner, R., Kister, U., Dachselt, R.: Multiple coordinated views at large displays for multiple users: empirical findings on user behavior, movements, and distances. IEEE Trans. Visual. Comput. Graphics **25**(1), 608–618 (2019). https://doi.org/10.1109/TVCG.2018.2865235. https://ieeexplore.ieee.org/document/8440846/
11. Noor, A.K., Aras, R.: Potential of multimodal and multiuser interaction with virtual holography. Adv. Eng. Softw. **81**, 1–6 (2015)
12. Oviatt, S., Cohen, P.: Perceptual user interfaces: multimodal interfaces that process what comes naturally. Commun. ACM **43**(3), 45–53 (2000)
13. Peveler, M., et al.: Translating the pen and paper brainstorming process into a cognitive and immersive system. In: Kurosu, M. (ed.) HCII 2019. LNCS, vol. 11567, pp. 366–376. Springer, Cham (2019). https://doi.org/10.1007/978-3-030-22643-5_28
14. Peveler, M., Kephart, J.O., Su, H.: Reagent: converting ordinary webpages into interactive software agents. In: Proceedings of the Twenty-Eighth International Joint Conference on Artificial Intelligence, International Joint Conferences on Artificial Intelligence Organization, Macao, China, pp. 6560–6562, August 2019. https://doi.org/10.24963/ijcai.2019/956, https://www.ijcai.org/proceedings/2019/956
15. Stallings, J.: RobotJS, October 2019. http://robotjs.io/

16. Tse, E., Greenberg, S., Shen, C., Forlines, C., Kodama, R.: Exploring true multi-user multimodal interaction over a digital table. In: Proceedings of the 7th ACM conference on Designing interactive systems - DIS 2008, Cape Town, South Africa. pp. 109–118. ACM Press (2008)

17. Zhang, Y.: Combining absolute and relative pointing for fast and accurate distant interaction. arXiv:1710.01778 [cs] October 2017

18. Zhao, R., Wang, K., Divekar, R., Rouhani, R., Su, H., Ji, Q.: An immersive system with multi-modal human-computer interaction. In: 13th IEEE International Conference on Automatic Face & Gesture Recognition (FG 2018), Xi'an, pp. 517–524. IEEE, May 2018

Floating Hierarchical Menus for Swipe-Based Navigation on Touchscreen Mobile Devices

Alen Salkanovic, Ivan Štajduhar, and Sandi Ljubic[(✉)]

University of Rijeka, Faculty of Engineering, Vukovarska 58, 51000 Rijeka, Croatia
{alen.salkanovic,ivan.stajduhar,sandi.ljubic}@riteh.hr

Abstract. In this paper, we present two menu implementations that allow swipe-based navigation through deep hierarchical menu configurations. Instead of utilizing repetitive tap-based selections, the proposed interaction relies on continuous finger movement across different submenus. The menus are implemented as a service; hence they can easily be attached to the target mobile application and visualized as a semi-transparent floating widget on top of it. Similar to the marking menu concept, the provided designs also enable a smooth transition from novice to expert user, as swipe gestures used for menu item selections can be memorized and subsequently executed faster. Both menus initially act as a floating action button, allowing the user to change its location by dragging it to the preferred place on the screen. Visualization of the menu starts in this pivotal position, according to the utilized design: *Tile* menu or *Pie* menu. The *Tile* menu uses a linear scheme and dynamically occupies more screen real-estate when a submenu is triggered. On the other hand, the *Pie* menu is displayed as a circular widget without extra containers and uses touch-dwelling for submenu invocation. Implementations of the proposed menu designs are evaluated and comparatively analyzed by conducting a controlled experiment involving 30 participants. We present the results of this empirical research, specifically focusing on menu navigation efficiency in two different contexts of use, the related interaction workload, and usability attributes.

Keywords: Hierarchical menus · Swipe-based navigation · Touchscreen gestures

1 Introduction

Hierarchical menus are widely used in software applications written for contemporary desktop operating systems. Different menu structures are commonly visualized as linear widgets (vertically and horizontally expandable menus), which can utilize different designs. Namely, the most popular types of multi-level menus are dropdown menus, flyout menus, dropline menus, accordion menus, and split menus. However, the corresponding implementations are usually optimized for mouse and/or keyboard interaction, hence applying the same concepts in the touchscreen mobile domain can sometimes be quite questionable.

It is an undeniable fact that present-day mobile devices are powerful enough to run relatively complex software applications. Mobile versions of the popular desktop

© Springer Nature Switzerland AG 2020
M. Kurosu (Ed.): HCII 2020, LNCS 12182, pp. 509–522, 2020.
https://doi.org/10.1007/978-3-030-49062-1_34

applications, such as Microsoft Word or Photoshop, are already used by numerous smartphone and tablet users. However, as mobile touchscreens are substantially smaller when compared to desktop screens, implementing multi-level menus for mobile applications remains a challenge in the HCI field.

Menus in contemporary mobile applications come in different shapes and forms and follow a trade-off between screen real-estate occupation and navigation efficiency. Touchscreen mobile devices raise particular problems in menu interaction, such as delay-based context menu activation, lack of shortcuts, occlusion, and insufficient accuracy [1]. The small screen size cannot easily accommodate many subcategories; hence the most common designs include accordions (a hamburger menu), sequential menus (e.g. navigation drawer), section menus (tabs), and floating action buttons (FABs) [2]. While all mentioned solutions have pros and cons, they are all tied to the underlying application and predefined activation points, usually located on the top/bottom of the screen. Typically, menu items from a single submenu are only presented on the screen, leaving the application content predominantly hidden.

In this paper, we investigate alternative menu designs that combine some of the previously introduced concepts (e.g. radial-shaped menus, marking menus) and touchscreen interaction modalities (e.g. swipe gestures instead of tapping sequence). Our design considerations also involve menu semi-transparent visualization and customization of the menu position on the screen. Navigation efficiency of the proposed menu solutions is empirically analyzed in two contexts of use: single-handed and cradling (the case wherein one hand is holding the device, while the other one is performing swipe gestures).

2 Related Work

Pie menu, also known as a radial menu, is a type of menu where item selection depends on the movement direction of the pointing device. The menu options are placed along the circumference of a circle at equal radial distances from the center. The original concept is attributed to a system called PIXIE [3]. A number of empirical comparisons between pie and linear menus, applied to desktop systems, has been made. For example, one of the early studies claimed pie menus to be about 15% faster than linear menus, with a significantly lower error rate [4].

Marking menu can be described as a specific type of pie menu wherein items are selected using a straight stroke gesture. In general, marking menu concept enables an easy transition from novice to expert user, according to the two different modes it imposes [5]. In the novice mode, the menu is visible to the users while making the selections, and it disappears from the screen once a menu item is selected. However, in the expert mode, the menu is completely hidden from the user. Therefore, previously memorized stroke gestures can be made without the need for the menu to appear. Besides the possibility of learning gestures for commonly used menu options, marking menu thus supports better screen utilization from the application content standpoint.

Both the pie menu and the marking menu concept were initially proposed for the desktop interaction; nevertheless, they have been successfully applied and investigated in touchscreen mobile domain as well.

Wavelet Menu [6] supports exploration and navigation in multimedia data hierarchies (e.g. photos and music) on mobile devices. The menu uses previsualization, a special feature which allows user to see the submenu corresponding to a certain menu option before it is actually activated. Additionally, this radial menu incorporates two different layout solutions. In a situation when a list of menu options is very long, the circular layout is combined with the linear one. This way it is easier to display and interact with submenus containing a large number of different options.

The *Swiss Army Menu* (SAM) [7] is another solution which utilizes radial design. Its main advantage is hierarchy navigation based on small thumb movements. A pointer controlled by the finger is used to select certain menu item in order to avoid the occlusion problem. Four different types of menu items are allowed in this design, which correspond to typical usage of buttons, checkboxes, sliders, and scrollbars. Similar to the *Wavelet Menu*, SAM also implements a preview feature which improves submenu navigation efficiency. Although it is possible to activate the menu from any location on the screen, it always appears at the same predefined position.

Two-Handed Marking Menus [8] is a solution specifically designed for multi-touch mobile devices and two-handed interaction. It allows user to perform two gestures, one with each hand, at the same time, in order to maximize parallelism in hand motions and provide faster menu selections. The ordered variant of the same solution, in which users alternates his/her gestures between two hands, is also implemented.

Semi-circular layouts, like *ArchMenu* and *ThumbMenu* presented in [9], offer a menu design in which all menu items are easily accessible with the thumb. However, due to the utilized layout shape, which increases in size with every new triggered submenu, the number of items a menu can display is significantly constrained.

More recent work refers to *M3 Gesture Menu* [10], a re-conceptualized version of traditional marking menu, which utilizes a persistent screen space and contains menu items arranged in a grid instead of a circular layout. Swipe gestures are used in order to select menu items, and when a certain option is activated, the same space is being occupied by its submenu items. Gesture shapes required for item selections are predefined and depend on related item locations inside the menu.

Radial menu layouts applied to small touchscreen interfaces can occasionally cause interaction burden. Namely, swipe gestures near the screen borders can be difficult to accomplish. However, hierarchical multi-level menus for mobile touchscreens can also be designed by making use of linear schemes. *Leaf Menu* [11] is a type of marking menu implemented with such design, wherein linearly organized items can be selected using swipe gestures. To select the target item from the specific submenu, the user simply needs to lift his/her finger off the screen. *Leaf Menu* supports precise finger interaction, mitigates the occlusion problem, and can be used close to the screen borders. Nevertheless, because all menu items are displayed one below the other, the screen space utilization can represent a problem, depending on the different hierarchy depth. For this purpose, a feature called mirror effect is used in order to compensate for the lack of available screen space.

It is important to mention that both linear and radial menu designs are prone to certain limitations [5]. The number of menu items on each (submenu) level is one of the limiting factors. As the number of menu options increases, less space is available for the corresponding UI widgets. This way targets are becoming smaller and harder to select. Additionally, increasing the menu depth (i.e. total number of submenus) also increases response time. Finally, interacting with complex menu configurations (with higher breadths and depths) usually involves the higher number of incorrectly selected menu items.

3 Floating Hierarchical Menus – *Tile* Menu and *Pie* Menu

Following the motivating factors drawn from the related work, as well as some new ideas about possible enhancements in menu navigation on touchscreen mobile devices, we introduce two different solutions – the *Tile* menu and the *Pie* menu – that allow swipe-based navigation through deep hierarchical menu configurations.

The proposed *Tile* menu design and the accompanying interaction are illustrated in Fig. 1. The top-level menu with associated options is activated using simple swipe movement from the FAB location in an upward direction. Dragging the finger on top of any (expandable) option activates the corresponding submenu above the top-level menu. Thus, the navigation across the menu hierarchy is achieved using a continuous swipe gesture, with submenu levels being stacked on top of each other. All sub-menus are created dynamically, only when needed, according to the user's swipe trajectory. Target option can be selected simply by lifting the finger off the screen, once the swipe gesture has reached (or passed through) the particular menu item. The proposed design allows memorizing swipe gestures for commonly used menu options (similar to the marking menu concept [5, 10, 11]).

To make underlying application content visible as much as possible, we had to replace the usual navigation model in which the menu widget covers up the whole screen or large portion of the screen real-estate. Instead, the *Tile* menu utilizes a semi-transparent visualization and additionally hides all items which are not relevant to the current state of the swipe gesture. As shown in Fig. 1, only FORMAT and STYLE items remain visible once the user swipes to the third level in the menu hierarchy. Hence, the described approach provides several interaction benefits: (i) saving valuable space on small touchscreens, (ii) allowing hierarchical navigation within the same application activity, (iii) item selection by making use of a single swipe gesture, and (iv) retaining the visibility of application content while handling the menu at the same time. It must be noted here that swiping in a downward direction (and stacking submenus in a top-down manner) was not considered as a possible design choice, due to the well-known occlusion issue.

When the menu is minimized and visualized as FAB only, it allows two states of operation. Namely, the menu activation button can be either active or locked. In the locked state, swipe gestures for hierarchical navigation are enabled, and interaction with the *Tile* menu proceeds as described above. However, if FAB enters the active state, menu navigation is then disabled, and FAB itself becomes draggable instead. Consequently, the active state can be utilized for changing the menu position on the screen, according to the users' current needs and individual preferences. Altering the menu pivotal position can become convenient when the context of use is changed (for example, switching between single-handed and two-handed usage). Toggling the FAB state, between active and locked, is enabled via simple tap-and-hold gesture.

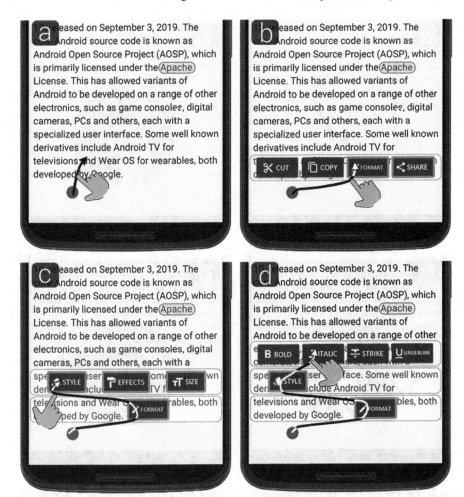

Fig. 1. *Tile* menu is, initially, minimized and draggable, and can be activated when the user swipes up from its locked state (a). Top-level menu is activated: dragging the finger above FORMAT option will activate new submenu and will hide all other items within the current level (b). Submenu for FORMAT option is placed above the previous container. Item border (yellow) indicates that there is an additional submenu available for a particular option (c). Lifting the finger off the screen activates the last item (ITALIC) along the swipe trajectory (d).

As for alternative design which also utilizes floating principle and swipe-based navigation, we implemented the *Pie* menu – a circular (pie-like) widget that already attracted a number of research efforts in HCI field. In our case, finding the target item within this menu relies on continuous finger movement. The main difference from the *Tile* menu, as well as from other similar radial-based menu solutions [6, 7, 9], lies in the submenu visualization. Namely, instead of dynamically creating extra containers for new submenus, existing elements inside the circular layout of the *Pie* menu are accordingly replaced with new items. The corresponding interaction concept is illustrated in Fig. 2.

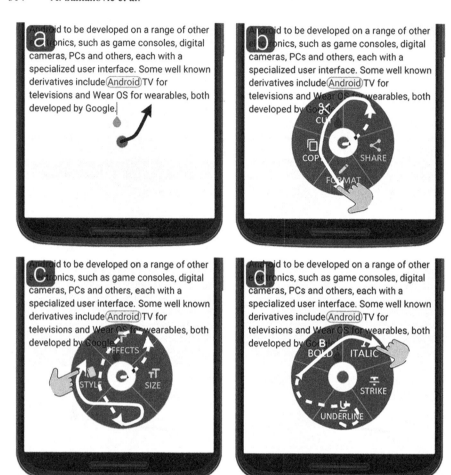

Fig. 2. The *Pie* menu is, initially, minimized and draggable, and can be activated when the user swipes in any direction from its locked state (a). User can invoke a new submenu by hovering (touch-dwelling) over the certain item. Highlighted items (yellow) indicate that there are additional submenus available (b). When expandable option is selected (FORMAT), all items from the same hierarchy level are replaced with new submenu (c). Lifting the finger off the screen activates the last selected option along the swipe trajectory (ITALIC) (d). (Color figure online)

As with the *Tile* menu, the *Pie* menu also allows changing its pivotal position by dragging the FAB to the preferred location on the screen. Placing the finger on FAB in a locked state, and subsequently starting a swipe gesture in any direction will create a circular container around the starting point, with all items from the top-level menu. The container itself cannot exceed the screen boundaries, and cannot be furthermore expanded. If the finger is dragged to the certain (expandable) item, and retained in the same position for a given time (i.e. dwell time), all current menu options are replaced with the new ones from the corresponding submenu. This navigation pattern can be repeated as long as there are available options within the hierarchical menu configuration. The final selection is invoked by ending the swipe gesture once the finger is dragged across the target menu item. When this happens, the menu is automatically minimized to its FAB form.

When compared to the *Tile* menu design, the *Pie* menu generally utilizes less screen space and usually requires less swiping. On the other hand, it is more susceptible to the occlusion problem and allows only the current submenu to be visualized at a given moment.

4 Empirical Evaluation

Implementations of the menu solutions so far described are evaluated and comparatively analyzed by conducting a controlled experiment. In this section, we present the details about the experiment design and discuss the obtained results.

4.1 Participants, Apparatus, and the Procedure

Thirty participants were involved in empirical research (23 males, 7 females), their age ranging from 19 to 41 with an average of 23,6 years (SD = 3,63). In the introductory questionnaire users reported their personal smartphone models (87% were owners of an Android device), their dominant hand (only one was left-handed), and their preferred hands posture while holding a smartphone (depicted in Fig. 3).

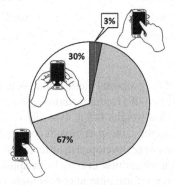

Fig. 3. The majority of the recruited participants generally prefer one-thumb single-handed interaction with a smartphone device.

Before the actual experiment, users were involved in the short practice session in order to get familiar with the two different menu designs. While testing the provided solutions, participants were asked to complete twenty different menu navigation tasks in total, ten using the *Tile* menu and the other ten using the *Pie* menu. At this stage, no data was collected whatsoever.

In the actual experiment, we considered two independent variables: menu design (*Tile* vs *Pie*) and interaction style. When addressing the interaction style, we are referring to the way of handling the mobile device. Specifically, we were interested if particular hand posture (single-handed vs cradling) also makes a difference in executing menu navigation tasks. The term cradling [12] corresponds to the use case wherein one hand is holding the device, while the other – usually the dominant one – performs the touch interaction.

For each experiment condition A–D (see Table 1), i.e. combination of the menu design and the interaction style, users were instructed to select certain items from different menu configurations. In total, users were asked to complete 200 menu navigation tasks, of which 50 unique ones had to be repeated within each experiment condition. Experiment tasks were generated according to the available menu configurations with various hierarchy structures. Namely, we defined five menu configurations with different breadths and depths, equal to the ones that can be found in popular text editors, photo editors and integrated development environments. This way we wanted to present users with a rather familiar menu navigation tasks, instead of using fictional mock-ups. The tasks involved both shorter and longer navigation routes, with the menu depth limit being set to six submenu levels. The single task was displayed on the smartphone screen as the required navigation path (e.g. *Format* → *Style* → *Italic*).

Table 1. Experiment conditions involved in the empirical evaluation.

Experiment condition	Menu design/implementation	Interaction style/device handling
A	*Tile* menu	Single-handed (one-thumb)
B	*Tile* menu	Cradling (forefinger)
C	*Pie* menu	Single-handed (one-thumb)
D	*Pie* menu	Cradling (forefinger)

Both implementations of the proposed hierarchical menus were tested on a Samsung Galaxy S5 smartphone (SM-G900F) running Android Marshmallow OS. This device is $142 \times 72.5 \times 8.1$ mm large and weighs 145 g. Two different devices of the same model were available for the experiment, so two participants could execute tasks simultaneously.

Two Android applications were developed in order to run *Tile* and *Pie* menu services, as well as to log all relevant interaction events. Both applications are using the same SQLite database which stores information about the menu navigation tasks that have to be accomplished during the experiment. Furthermore, both applications can access configuration files (stored in the internal memory of a mobile device) which contain a description of the menu structure. From these configuration files, specific menu navigation tasks can be defined either manually or automatically. Hence, we provided support for tweaking the experiment settings in an easy way. For example, introducing a new menu hierarchy and new tasks in the experiment requires preparing the corresponding configuration file and utilizing the available task generator.

The time taken to complete the required menu navigation task is considered to be the interval between a first touch inside the FAB (in its locked state) and a finger lift-off event which ends the associated swipe gesture. This task execution time is measured by the application itself, by making use of a built-in monotonic clock which is tolerant to power saving modes and is anyway the recommended basis for general- purpose interval timing on Android devices. All network-based services on the smartphones were turned off during the experiment. In case when target selection was not successfully achieved, the corresponding task was not repeated, and error details were logged along the task execution time.

A repeated measures (i.e. within-subjects) experiment design was utilized. The order of experiment conditions was properly counterbalanced using balanced Latin squares [13], to compensate for possible learning effects. Additionally, the order of the menu navigation tasks in a given sequence was randomized as well. Breaks were allowed when switching between different experiment conditions. Users were also allowed to change menu pivotal position, but only at the beginning of the new task sequence. Replacing the menu position was programmatically constrained in a way that ensures that all menu items stay inside the visible screen area.

After the participants completed all the tasks using both menus and both interaction styles, they were asked to complete a post-study questionnaire based on the rating part of the NASA-TLX (Raw-TLX format). Individual opinions about perceived workload had to be estimated on a 20-point Likert scales for five factors: mental demand, physical demand, frustration, performance, and effort. Subsequently, subjective opinions about usability attributes of the two proposed menu designs were collected. Participants had to rank the menus' usability features, according to their personal preference, using 7-point Likert scales. In the end, general design issues for both the *Tile* menu and the *Pie* menu were assessed. The complete qualitative part of the evaluation was constructed in a way to address the perceived differences between the two menu designs, hence interaction style aspects were not specifically addressed within the related questionnaires.

4.2 Results and Discussion

Participants accomplished 6000 menu item selections in total. After averaging data across four experiment conditions, altogether 120 menu navigation performance records were obtained: 30 participants × 2 menu designs × 2 interaction styles. Figure 4 depicts the task execution times for two different menu designs, achieved both single-handedly and via cradling.

To analyze the obtained data, a two-way repeated measures ANOVA was used, with *Design* (*Tile, Pie*) and *Style* (single-handed, cradling) being the within-subjects factors. The analysis revealed a significant effect of *Design* on menu navigation time ($F_{1, 29} = 18.783$, $p < .001$). The effect of *Style* (i.e. the way of holding a mobile device) was also found statistically significant ($F_{1, 29} = 8.132$, $p < .05$). Finally, the effect of *Design* * *Style* interaction was not found statistically significant.

As for the pairwise comparisons, the differences in task execution times between the proposed menu designs, as well as between interaction styles, are reported as follows:

- *Tile* menu vs. *Pie* menu: $(5,002 \pm 0.12$ s$)$ vs. $(5,443 \pm 0.08$ s$)$, $p < .001$
- Single handed vs cradling: $(5,334 \pm 0.10$ s$)$ vs. $(5,110 \pm 0.09$ s$)$, $p < .001$

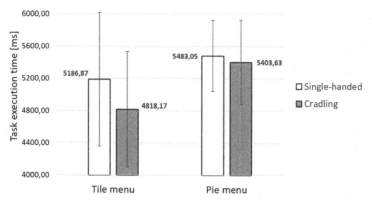

Fig. 4. Menu navigation times (mean values and standard deviations) obtained within four experimental conditions.

Thus, the *Tile* menu design showed to be more efficient, as swipe-based navigation tasks were accomplished significantly faster than with the *Pie* menu. However, interacting with the menus single-handedly showed to be significantly less efficient when compared to cradling posture. It can be seen that difference between interaction styles is more prominent when *Tile* menu design is utilized. This can be explained as the result of thumb movement constraints that are inherently higher when deep submenus have to be reached within the *Tile* hierarchy. Specifically, the thumb needs to be stretched more for reaching the submenus at the top part of the screen, which is not the case when forefinger is used or if the *Pie* menu design is applied.

Errors made in menu navigation tasks are reported from the descriptive statistics standpoint only. As shown in Table 2, error rates were rather low in all experiment conditions. Log records revealed that most of the errors were made on the last submenu level, when non-target item was unintentionally selected by ending the swipe gesture on the wrong place.

Table 2. Error rates obtained within four experimental conditions.

	Single-handed	Cradling
Tile menu	5,13%	3,66%
Pie menu	3,93%	3,89%

As mentioned before, questionnaire based on Raw-TLX format was used in order to obtain comparative ratings of perceive workload between *Tile* and *Pie* menu designs. The respective outcomes are shown in Fig. 5.

The Wilcoxon signed-rank tests were used to assess obtained TLX-based scores for each considered factor. The *Pie* menu seems to be generally preferred among participants; however significant difference was found for one factor only. Namely, it was confirmed that *Tile* menu interaction implies significantly higher physical demand when compared

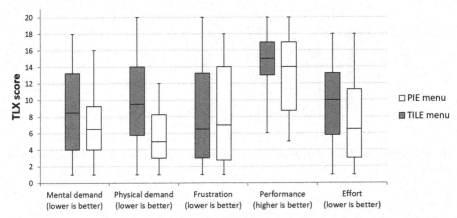

Fig. 5. Users' opinions on perceived workload for the proposed menu designs. For each factor, the corresponding box plots show minimum and maximum, 25 percentile (Q1), 75 percentile (Q3), and median value (M).

to *Pie* menu ($Z = -3,699$, $p < .001$). This result validates the aforementioned discussion about particular movement constraints that are imposed by the *Tile* menu design.

Although frustration levels are evenly perceived, it was interesting to find out that sources of frustration are completely different for two menu solutions. According to the users' comments, some were annoyed by continuous UI change within the *Tile* layout, which combines submenu stacking and hiding certain menu items at the same time. Conversely, the *Pie* menu layout is more consistent, but many participants reported dwell time as too long, which made them somewhat irritated, especially towards the end of the experiment. It must be noted here that dwell time was set to 1 s without the possibility to change it during the experiment.

In the first part of the concluding survey, participants used 7-point Likert scales for rating two menu implementations against the ease of use, perceived learnability, and overall satisfaction. The obtained results are presented in Fig. 6. Wilcoxon signed-rank tests revealed no significant differences between the *Tile* menu and the *Pie* menu with regard to usability attributes in question. Nevertheless, score mean values indicate that participants perceive *Pie* menu design easier to use and marginally easier to learn, which automatically explains the outcome of satisfaction level comparison.

Finally, in the second part of the concluding survey, participants had a chance to evaluate design choices implemented within the proposed menus, as well as to assess the suitability of the menus for particular contexts of use. 7-point Likert scales were used for comparative rating once again. Figure 7 presents the corresponding outcomes.

As can be seen, users reported the *Pie* menu to be a more convenient solution than the *Tile* menu in terms of single-handed device usage. This difference was confirmed as statistically significant ($Z = -2,324$, $p < .05$) by making use of the Wilcoxon signed-rank test. Thus, the stated arguments on *Tile* menu interaction constraints are corroborated once again. No other statistically significant effects were found.

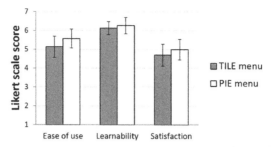

Fig. 6. Usability attributes of the proposed menu solutions. Mean values and confidence intervals are presented.

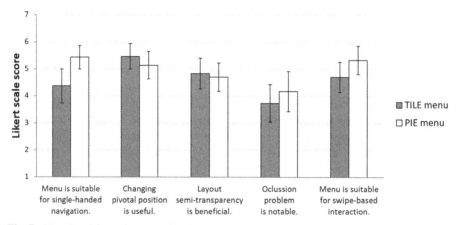

Fig. 7. Users' opinions about specific design choices and suitability of the menus for particular contexts of use. Mean values and confidence intervals are presented.

Obtained scores may furthermore indicate that the *Pie* menu is more suitable for swipe-based interaction as well, although the occlusion problem seems to be less prominent when a linear-based layout is used. According to the users' answers, the semi-transparency feature represents a reasonable design choice, because it benefits both menu designs evenly.

Lastly, the possibility of changing menu pivotal position is generally considered useful, with slightly more advantageous effects being perceived for the *Tile* menu. This is in accordance with the log records which revealed that menu repositioning was almost always utilized before starting the *Tile* testing sequence with different hands posture. In general, FAB was predominantly moved at the bottom of the screen when *Tile* menu was utilized, whereas bottom corners (mostly the right one) were commonly occupied with the *Pie* menu. When cradling posture was part of the particular experiment condition, some users tended to move menu layout closer to the center of the screen.

5 Conclusion and Future Work

Two different hierarchical menu designs for touchscreen mobile applications, that utilize swipe-based navigation, were introduced and comparatively evaluated in a study involving thirty participants. *Tile* menu implementation applies linear layout, and relies on dynamical submenu stacking according to the gesture being performed. Conversely, *Pie* menu utilizes consistent radial layout and additional touch-dwells for invoking submenus in a multi-level menu hierarchy. Both menus are implemented as an Android service, i.e. they are visualized as a semi-transparent floating widget on top of the target application which can furthermore be repositioned. Navigation across the menu hierarchy is achieved using a continuous swipe gesture, thus avoiding the need for recurrent tapping.

Empirical results revealed that menu navigation tasks are executed significantly faster using the *Tile* design. Single-handed menu interaction, wherein a thumb is used for making swipe gestures, showed to be significantly less efficient when compared to the cradling style in which non-dominant hand is providing device stability. Qualitative analysis, based on the questionnaire outcomes, showed that *Pie* menu is nevertheless more preferred among the participants. It was confirmed that interacting with the *Tile* menu implies significantly higher physical demand, which makes the *Pie* menu a more convenient solution (especially in the single-handed context of use). Other differences between *Tile* and *Pie* menu, in terms of interaction workload, usability attributes, and design-related aspects were not found as statistically significant, but are nevertheless discussed in detail.

In general, the proposed menu designs proved to be a feasible option for swipe-based navigation through deep hierarchical configurations. We believe that these solutions could provide more effective utilization of available screen space, and an easy transition from beginner to expert user.

Our future work plan includes providing further enhancements to existing menu designs. In order to additionally reduce occlusion effects in *Tile* menu interaction, a submenu activation should immediately follow when a specific (expandable) item is selected. In the current version, a new submenu is displayed after dragging the finger above the current-level layout. Due to dwell time being one of the limiting factors in navigation efficiency with the *Pie* menu, our current research efforts are focused on evaluating different dwell time values for such design. Reducing the time needed to automatically activate submenus could potentially provide faster navigation through the menu hierarchy. However, short dwell times could make *Pie* menu interaction more error-prone, because unintentional item selections are more probable in such case. Finally, a longitudinal study should be conducted in order to investigate the effects of memorizing swipe gestures for frequently selected menu items. This way, we could test the marking menu concept, which is inherently involved in our designs, and actually observe the expected transition from novice to expert user.

References

1. Bailly, G., Lecolinet, E., Nigay, L.: Visual menu techniques. ACM Comput. Surv. **49**(4), 60:1–60:41 (2017)

2. Budiu, R.: Mobile Subnavigation. Nielsen Norman Group (2017). https://www.nngroup.com/articles/mobile-subnavigation/

3. Wiseman, N.E., Lemke, H.U., Hiles, J.O.: PIXIE: a new approach to graphical man-machine communication. In: Proceedings of the CAD Conf. Southampton, vol. 463. IEEE Conference Publication 51 (1969)

4. Callahan, J., Hopkins, D., Weiser, M., Shneiderman, B.: An empirical comparison of pie vs. linear menus. In: Proceedings SIGCHI Conference Human Factors in Computing Systems (CHI 1988), pp. 95–100. ACM Press, New York (1988)

5. Kurtenbach, G., Buxton, W.: The limits of expert performance using hierarchic marking menus. In: Proceedings Conference Human Factors in Computing Systems (CHI 1993), pp. 482–487. ACM Press, New York (1993)

6. Francone, J., Bailly, G., Nigay, L., Lecolinet, E.: Wavelet menus: a stacking metaphor for adapting marking menus to mobile devices. In: Proceedings International Conference Human-Computer Interaction with Mobile Devices and Services (MobileHCI 2009), pp. 49:1–49:4. ACM Press, New York (2009)

7. Bonnet, D., Appert, C.: SAM: the swiss army Menu. In: Proceedings Conference l'Interaction Homme-Machine (IHM 2011), pp. 5:1–5:4. ACM Press, New York (2011)

8. Kin, K., Hartmann, B., Agrawala, M.: Two-handed marking menus for multitouch devices. ACM Trans. Comput. Hum. Interact. **18**(3), 16:1–16:23 (2011)

9. Huot, S., Lecolinet, E.: ArchMenu et ThumbMenu: contrôler son dispositif mobile «sur le pouce». In: Proceedings Conference l'Interaction Homme-Machine (IHM 2007), pp. 107–110. ACM Press, New York (2007)

10. Zheng, J., Bi, X., Li, K., Li, Y., Zhai, S.: M3 gesture menu: design and experimental analyses of marking menus for touchscreen mobile interaction. In: Proceedings Conference Human Factors in Computing Systems (CHI 2018), pp. 249:1–249:14. ACM Press, New York (2018)

11. Roudaut, A., Bailly, G., Lecolinet, E., Nigay, L.: Leaf menus: linear menus with stroke shortcuts for small handheld devices. In: Gross, T., Gulliksen, J., Kotzé, P., Oestreicher, L., Palanque, P., Prates, R.O., Winckler, M. (eds.) INTERACT 2009. LNCS, vol. 5726, pp. 616–619. Springer, Heidelberg (2009). https://doi.org/10.1007/978-3-642-03655-2_69

12. Hoober, S.: How do users really hold mobile devices? In: UXmatters. http://www.uxmatters.com/mt/archives/2013/02/how-do-users-really-hold-mobile-devices.php

13. MacKenzie, I.S.: Human-Computer Interaction: An Empirical Research Perspective. Morgan Kaufmann, San Francisco (2013)

Touch Position Detection on the Front of Face Using Passive High-Functional RFID Tag with Magnetic Sensor

Yuta Takayama$^{(\boxtimes)}$, Yuu Ichikawa, Takumi Kitagawa, Song Shengmei,
Buntarou Shizuki, and Shin Takahashi

University of Tsukuba, Tsukuba, Japan
takayama@iplab.cs.tsukuba.ac.jp

Abstract. We used passive, high-functional radiofrequency identification (RFID) tags with magnetic sensors to detect front of face touch positions without the requirement for a battery. We implemented a prototype system consisting of a goggle-type device equipped with passive high-functional RFID tags with magnetic sensor, a ring with permanent magnets, and touch detection software for machine-learning. We evaluated the classification accuracy of the six front of face touch positions and a 'no-touch' case. The discrimination rate when using the learning data was 83% but the real-time discrimination was only 65%. In future, we will aim to improve the accuracy, and define more touch points and gesture inputs.

Keywords: Magnetic sensing · RFID tag · Touch sensing

1 Introduction

Wearable devices are becoming increasingly common, as are gesture inputs. However, most gesture input methods require sensors or additional devices for classification, and a power supply. If power is delivered by wire, the useable space is reduced. A battery may explode or degrade at excessively high or low temperatures.

We developed a battery-free gesture input method for wearable devices; touch positions are detected using passive high-functional radiofrequency identification (RFID) tags with magnetic sensors; the microcomputer and sensors are powered by radio waves. RFID tags have been used to power e-ink displays and sense temperature [9], and for attendance management systems [8]. Here, we detect the touch positions using a goggle-type device equipped with passive, high-functional RFID tags featuring magnetic sensor and a ring with a permanent magnet. The user wears the goggles and the ring; when the face is touched with the ring-bearing finger, the touch position is classified; no other sensor is required. Face-touching is a natural behavior and touch positions can be defined easily.

© Springer Nature Switzerland AG 2020
M. Kurosu (Ed.): HCII 2020, LNCS 12182, pp. 523–531, 2020.
https://doi.org/10.1007/978-3-030-49062-1_35

2   Related Work

In this section, we review 1) sensing methods and gesture inputs based on magnetism; 2) previous research on battery-free devices; and, 3) work on RFID technology.

2.1   Sensing Methods and Gesture Inputs based on Magnetism

Many input methods using magnetic sensors have been described. Abracatabra [4] described wireless power-free inputs for small devices (such as smart watches); the position of a finger with an attached magnet was detected. IM6D [5] uses a magnetic sensor array to measure the three-dimensional position and direction of a fingertip-mounted electromagnet. Finexus [1] tracks a fingertip-attached electromagnet in real time by evaluating the magnetic field using sensors strapped to the back of the hand.

2.2   Battery-Free Devices

Grosse-Puppendahl et al. [3] created a battery-free display using a solar cell, a Bluetooth low-energy (BLE) device, and electronic paper; the display provided reminders and weather data via a PC or smartphone. Li et al. [7] used low-cost photodiodes for both ambient lighting and gesture classification; the self-powered module was accurate under various ambient light conditions. Similarly, for our device, gestures are inputted using a battery-free goggles. However, our device is based on RFID technology and used magnetic sensors to detect face touch positions.

2.3   Input Methods Using RFID Technology

RFID is widely used for object and personal identification. Both power delivery and information exchange are achieved wirelessly. Tip-tap [6] collects data from the intersections of arrays attached to the thumb and forefinger to yield discrete two-dimensional touch inputs, without the requirement for a battery. Based on Near Field Communication (NFC; a type of RFID), NFC-WISP [9] is used to power electronic printing devices, temperature sensors and contactless tap cards. AlterWear [2] is a new battery-free wearable device based on electromagnetic induction via NFC; the display uses bistable electronic ink.

3   Examples

We explored how inputs may drive music applications and devices with small screens.

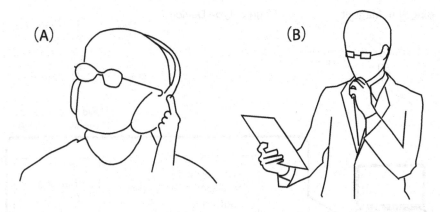

Fig. 1. (A) Inputs for music applications, (B) Character inputs for devices with small screens.

3.1 Music Applications

On crowded public transport, it can be difficult to operate a music player. However, using our method [Fig. 1(A)] the user can play or stop music by touching the ear, and control the volume by touching the mouth.

3.2 Devices with Small Screens

Character input using a small touch screen (such as that of a smart watch) is difficult. With our device, character inputs are mapped to facial regions [Fig. 1(B)] and characters are input using the fingertips.

4 Prototype

The prototype features a goggle-type device with passive, high-functional RFID tags with magnetic sensor; an RFID reader; a ring with a permanent magnet; and a touch position classifier running on a PC (Fig. 2).

4.1 The Goggle-Type Device and the RFID Reader

The goggle-type device comprises a pair of plastic goggles equipped with two passive, high-functional RFID tags with magnetic sensor (EVAL01-Magneto-RM; Farsens[1]) supported on either side by 3D-printed bars (Fig. 3). The tags were lie about 3.5 cm distant from goggles; reception is poor if the RFID is too close to the skin [6].

Our device uses an Impinj Speedway Revolution R420 RFID reader. The output is 32.5 dBm when power is supplied by an AC adapter. The reader is connected to a PC. We also used a YAP-102CP as the reader antenna.

---

[1] http://www.farsens.com/en/products/eval01-magnetorm/.

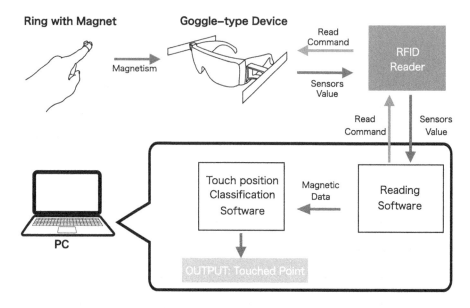

Fig. 2. Overview of the prototype.

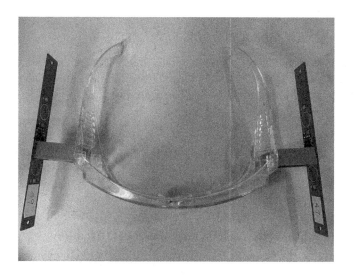

Fig. 3. The goggle-type device.

4.2 Ring with Permanent Magnets

Fig. 4. Rings with attached magnet.

The goggle-type device uses a magnetic sensor; a finger magnet is thus required. We devised two three-dimensional-printed rings differing in diameter, with notches for the magnets. Both rings had a gap at the bottom; they were thus suitable for fingers varying in size and shape (Fig. 4).

4.3 Touch Position Classifier

The touch position classifier uses a data collecting program written in Java, and a classifier written in Python. The data collection program first sends read commands to the RFID tags via RFID reader, and the tags send results to the software via the reader. Because the geomagnetism influences sensor output, we subtracted the median geometric value of 100 'no-touch' signals.

Sensor data from both of magnetic sensor tags ('one-frame' data) are then classified. To rule-out over-learning, a frame is discarded if it is identical to the previous frame. Each frame is classified as one of the predefined touch positions. The classification model employs the k-nearest-neighbor algorithm of the Python scikit-learn library. The hyperparameters, established via 5-fold cross-validation and grid searching, were as follows:

- Number of neighboring points: 7
- Weight: distance
- Distance: Manhattan

4.4 Sensor Data Reception

We evaluated the data reception rate with the RFID sensor tag or the goggle-type device placed on a wooden desk. The reader antenna was placed 22 cm above the desk and read three-axis magnetic sensor data. We quantified the data received over 5 s and calculated the reception rates as ~20 Hz for a single RFID tag and 5–10 Hz for the goggle-type device (two tags). The reception rate for the goggle-type device allowed adequate classification of touch position, but the rate fluctuated and the two tags were not equidistant from the reader. In the future, we will resolve this problem by controlling the reader settings.

4.5 Effect of Magnets

We assessed whether the magnet affected the sensor using the setup described above. We put a set of two magnets (used for our ring device) on the desk 1, 2, 3, 4, 5, 10, 15, and 20 cm apart from the sensor. We collected 2,000 sets of data and calculated the median value (Fig. 5). The vertical axis shows the sensor data (three-axis magnetic vectors) minus the median geomagnetic vector (calculated using 2,000 sensor data points collected without magnets). The sensor detects magnets at a distance of 5–10 cm away from the sensor. Thus, the facial touchpoints should lie within about 10 cm of the sensor.

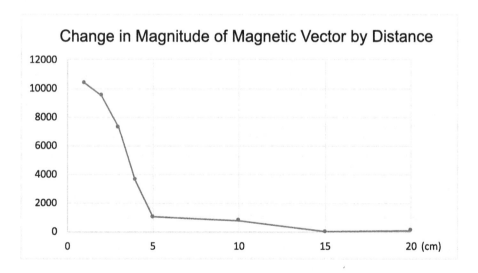

Fig. 5. Change in magnitude of magnetic vector by distance.

5 Evaluation

We evaluated facial touch accuracy in a single male subject who wore the goggle-type device and ring with a permanent magnet on the index finger of the right hand; the subject was in a sitting position.

5.1 Procedure

In the first learning phase, data were collected for machine-learning. In the classification phase, whether touch positions were accurately classified was determined.

In the first phase, 200 magnetic data frames were collected from each touch point (1,400 frames = 200 × 6 touch points + 200 'no-touch' cases). Figure 6 shows the six touch points. shows the position of the 7 touch points. The subject was asked to continuously rotate the index finger to prevent over-learning due to changes in finger angle. Then, 80% of the collected data were used for training; 20% were reserved for testing. We employed a k-nearest neighbor (KNN) machine-learning algorithm. We performed 5-fold cross-validation to improve performance generalization.

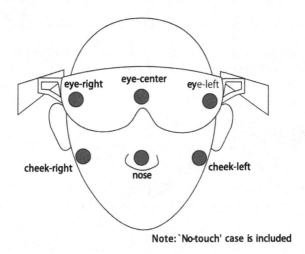

Note: `No-touch' case is included

Fig. 6. The six touch points on the face.

During the classification phase, the subject touched each facial point 10 times and also performed 'no-touch' 10 times (total of 70 trials) in a random order. For each touch, the index finger remained in place until 10 data frames were collected; the median value was used for classfication. The results were recorded, displayed, and labeled, and the success rate was calculated.

5.2 Results and Discussion

The classification accuracy for the test data collected during the learning phase was 83%. However, for the 70 frames of magnetic data collected during the classification phase, the accuracy was only 65%. Figure 7 shows the classification confusion matrix. The classification accuracy for the test data collected during the learning phase was high. However, the classification accuracy was lower for the data collected during the classification phase. Two vertical points were often misclassfied, such as 'eye-left' and 'cheek-left'. In the future, we will aim to improve the training model by adding other features. For example, when we added two magnitudes calculated from two magnetic vectors of the two sensor tags to the feature vectors, the classification accuracy improved slightly (Fig. 8).

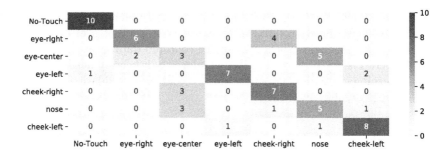

Fig. 7. Confusion matrix derived from 50 frames of test data classified by the KNN model. Only three-axis magnetic vectors of the two sensor tags were used as feature vectors.

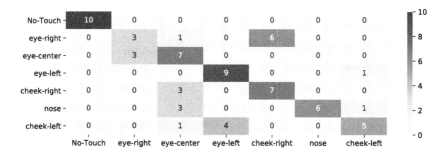

Fig. 8. Confusion matrix derived from 50 frames of test data were classified by the KNN model. Two magnitudes calculated from two magnetic vectors of the two sensor tags were added to feature vectors.

Sensor data arriving at the RFID reader were often unbalanced. Sometimes, data from only one tag arrived, possibly because the tag-to-reader distances differed or the radio waves encountered interference. In the future, we will test other RFID settings and use tags with multiple sensors.

6   Conclusions and Future Work

We used passive, high-functional RFID tags with magnetic sensor to detect touch positions, as a form of battery-free gesture input for wearable devices. The prototype includes a goggle-type device, a ring with a magnet, and software for detecting touch positions via machine-learning. We defined six touch points on the face and evaluated the accuracy of touch and no touch classification. The classification accuracy during learning phase was 83%, but dropped to 65% during the classification phase. Thus, the performance must be improved; in the future, we will enhance the accuracy of real-time classification, and define more touch points and gesture inputs.

References

1. Chen, K.Y., Patel, S.N., Keller, S.: Finexus: tracking precise motions of multiple fingertips using magnetic sensing. In: Proceedings of the 2016 CHI Conference on Human Factors in Computing Systems, CHI 2016, pp. 1504–1514. Association for Computing Machinery, New York (2016). https://doi.org/10.1145/2858036.2858125
2. Dierk, C., Nicholas, M.J.P., Paulos, E.: Alterwear: battery-free wearable displays for opportunistic interactions. In: Proceedings of the 2018 CHI Conference on Human Factors in Computing Systems, CHI 2018. Association for Computing Machinery, New York (2018). https://doi.org/10.1145/3173574.3173794
3. Grosse-Puppendahl, T., et al.: Exploring the design space for energy-harvesting situated displays. In: Proceedings of the 29th Annual Symposium on User Interface Software and Technology, UIST 2016, pp. 41–48. Association for Computing Machinery, New York (2016). https://doi.org/10.1145/2984511.2984513
4. Harrison, C., Hudson, S.E.: Abracadabra: wireless, high-precision, and unpowered finger input for very small mobile devices. In: Proceedings of the 22nd Annual ACM Symposium on User Interface Software and Technology, UIST 2009, pp. 121–124. ACM, New York (2009). https://doi.org/10.1145/1622176.1622199
5. Huang, J., Mori, T., Takashima, K., Hashi, S., Kitamura, Y.: IM6D: magnetic tracking system with 6-DOF passive markers for dexterous 3D interaction and motion. ACM Trans. Graph. **34**(6) (2015). https://doi.org/10.1145/2816795.2818135
6. Katsuragawa, K., Wang, J., Shan, Z., Ouyang, N., Abari, O., Vogel, D.: Tip-tap: battery-free discrete 2D fingertip input. In: Proceedings of the 32nd Annual ACM Symposium on User Interface Software and Technology, UIST 2019, pp. 1045–1057. Association for Computing Machinery, New York (2019). https://doi.org/10.1145/3332165.3347907
7. Li, Y., Li, T., Patel, R.A., Yang, X.D., Zhou, X.: Self-powered gesture recognition with ambient light. In: Proceedings of the 31st Annual ACM Symposium on User Interface Software and Technology, UIST 2018, pp. 595–608. Association for Computing Machinery, New York (2018). https://doi.org/10.1145/3242587.3242635
8. Oharada, K., Shizuki, B., Takahashi, S.: AccelTag: a passive smart ID tag with acceleration sensor for interactive applications. In: Adjunct Publication of the 30th Annual ACM Symposium on User Interface Software and Technology, UIST 2017, pp. 63–64. ACM, New York (2017). https://doi.org/10.1145/3131785.3131808
9. Zhao, Y., Smith, J.R., Sample, A.: NFC-WISP: an open source software defined near field RFID sensing platform. In: Adjunct Proceedings of the 2015 ACM International Joint Conference on Pervasive and Ubiquitous Computing and Proceedings of the 2015 ACM International Symposium on Wearable Computers, Ubi-Comp/ISWC 2015 Adjunct, pp. 369–372. ACM, New York (2015). https://doi.org/10.1145/2800835.2800912

Human Robot Interaction

One-Hand Controller for Human-Drone Interaction – a Human-Centered Prototype Development

Sebastian Büttner[1,2]([⊠]), Rami Zaitoon[1], Mario Heinz[1], and Carsten Röcker[1,3]

[1] Ostwestfalen-Lippe University of Applied Sciences and Arts, Lemgo, Germany
{sebastian.buettner,mario.heinz,carsten.roecker}@th-owl.de
[2] Human-Centered Information Systems, Clausthal University of Technology, Clausthal-Zellerfeld, Germany
[3] Fraunhofer IOSB-INA, Lemgo, Germany

Abstract. Using remote control transmitters is a common way to control a drone. For the future, we envision drones that are intuitively controllable with new input devices. One possibility could be the use of one-hand controllers. Here, we present an exploration of using a 3-D mouse as a controller for human-drone interaction. We ran a pre-study that investigated the users' natural spatial mapping between controller and drone dimensions. Based on these results we developed our prototype that shows the feasibility of our concept. A series of flight tests were conducted and the mapping between controller and flight movements were iteratively improved. In this paper, we present our development process and the implementation of our prototype.

Keywords: Human-Drone Interaction · Unmanned Aerial Vehicle · 3-D mouse · Spatial mapping · Prototyping

1 Introduction

The use of drones (unmanned aerial vehicles, UAV) is rapidly increasing. Beyond leisure activities, drones are more and more used for industrial applications. While most industrial drones will fly autonomously in future, there are certain scenarios that require manual intervention or temporary manual control of a drone. For example, in a scenario where a drone inspects wind turbines autonomously and it detects issues, a human operator may need to control the drone for a manual investigation. In this case, we envision drones that are intuitively controllable even for novice users with new input devices.

In this paper, we present a design exploration of a one-hand drone controller. By using a human-centered development process, we implemented a prototype of an intuitive one-hand controller for drones, which uses a 3-D mouse (see Fig. 1) for human-drone interaction (HDI).

© Springer Nature Switzerland AG 2020
M. Kurosu (Ed.): HCII 2020, LNCS 12182, pp. 535–548, 2020.
https://doi.org/10.1007/978-3-030-49062-1_36

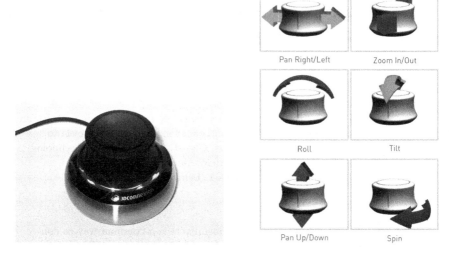

Fig. 1. SpaceMouse® Compact [1]. Image Source: AmericanXplorer13, Wikimedia Commons, licensed under Creative-Commons-License by-sa-3.0, https://creativecommons.org/licenses/by-sa/3.0/deed.en

Fig. 2. Degrees of freedom (DoF) of the device. Image source: [17].

2 Related Work

Even though some drones are completely autonomous and do not need to be controlled at all, most drones allow some form of human intervention or need to be controlled all the time. If drones are used for leisure activities, controlling a drone provides a positive experience to the user, even if the user interface is complex and needs to be mastered. However, in this paper, we want to consider industrial drones that allow human intervention and require a natural and intuitive interface. In this section, we sum up the current state of research on different human-drone interfaces.

2.1 Remote Control Transmitters (RCT)

Currently, most drones are manually controlled by remote control transmitters (RCTs) similar to the one shown in Fig. 3. RCTs are devices that are held with both hands. Those controllers usually have two sticks; each thumb of the user controls one of the sticks. A single control stick has two degrees of freedom (DoF); consequently, the combination of the sticks allows the user to have four DoF for controlling the drone. The assignment of the dimensions usually follows the following scheme (see Fig. 4): The left stick is used for upward and downward movements (throttle) and rotations around the z-axis (yaw). The right stick is used for forward, backward (pitch) and side-way movements (roll). While

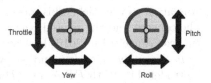

Fig. 3. Currently, most non-autonomous drones are controlled by more or less complex remote control transmitters (RCT). The image shows one of the complex models.

Fig. 4. Drone control concept that is usually used by RCTs or mobile applications.

Fig. 3 shows a complex version with multiple additional buttons and slide controls, there are also less complex versions available that follow the same control principle.

The mapping between the drone dimensions and the two independent sticks described above is a convention, since there is no natural mapping between the dimensions. Additionally, RCTs require the independent coordination of both hands. As a consequence, users typically need some training time, before they can master the drone.

2.2 Tablets or Smartphones

For leisure activities, there are a lot of (low-cost) drones available that use smart phone or tablet applications to replace physical RCTs. From a user interface perspective these drones are controlled consistently to RCT-controlled drones: two virtual control pads are shown in the app that replace the sticks of the physical RCT (compare Fig. 4). Of course, this user interface has haptic restrictions and no physical feedback. On the other hand, the apps often offer additional features, such as a live image of the drone camera that allows a first-person view of the flight.

2.3 One-Hand Controllers

Two-hand controllers have certain restrictions; they require the independent coordination of both hands, which might be a challenge for inexperienced users or people with physical disabilities (compare [13]). On the other hand, they cannot be used in situations where a second hand is used for other tasks, while controlling the drone manually with one hand only. Another issue with physical RCTs or congruent tablet or smartphone apps stems from the mapping between the 2-D controls and the 3-D drone movements, which is naturally not intuitive. Consequently, one-hand controllers have been presented to allow a better interaction with drones.

The South Korean company *this is engineering Inc.* [10] presented a concept of a drone-controlling system called *Shift*. With *Shift*, users control a drone with a stick that is held in one hand and contains a ring that is worn on the thumb of the same hand. By wearing this device on one hand, users can move their thumb in relation to the stick. This movement is then mapped into drone movements. The concept and the related Kickstarter project created a huge media interest, but was cancelled in 2016. However, in 2019 the drone *Shift red* was launched by *this is engineering Inc.* and is now commercially available with this one-hand controller [11]. With *FT Aviator Drone Flight Controller* [12] another one-hand controller was successfully funded on Kickstarter. This controller looks more like a computer joystick; the stick is used to control pitch, roll and yaw. The index finger can control the throttle value by pushing an additional button on the stick. The controller can be used with most *DJI* [6] drones.

Another type of one-hand controllers are glove-based systems. The French startup *WEPULSIT* [18] presented *PULSIT*, a smart glove that is used to control a drone by moving the hand and making specific gestures with their fingers. This device has been presented in various videos; however, there are no statements about the launch of the product yet.

While there are already a couple of one-hand controllers in the market, it can be said that these types of controller are still very new and not very widespread, which makes room for further exploration and development.

2.4 Natural Drone Interactions

Apart from the previously described controllers, other work explored more natural human-drone interaction with hand or full-body gestures or language control. Cauchard et al. [3] analyzed different natural ways of interacting with drones in a Wizard-of-Oz study. They found out that interpersonal gestures are intuitively used by people, e.g. if a drone should be stopped or fly back to the user. Fernández et al. [8] used a leap motion controller [14] as an input device for gesture control. Compared to the work of Cauchard et al. [3], their defined gestures have no meaning in interpersonal communication. Rather they map the movements of the hand to the movements of the drone. They state that users had to get used to this interaction first, but "experiencing the connection of the hand with the drone made this [...] natural and fun" [8]. The same authors also explored the use of voice commands [8]. Peshkova et al. [15] provides an overview on different natural interaction techniques for drones, which also includes approaches with gaze trackers or brain activity. But natural drone interaction possibilities are not only a topic for research. First consumer products are already in the market that realize the gesture control concepts described above: DJI's consumer drone Spark has an optical system for tracking users' gestures for controlling the drone and for taking photos with the built-in camera [5] using gestures similar to the work of Cauchard et al. [3].

3 Pre-study: Investigating Users' Natural Spatial Mapping

[1]Before starting the development of the one-hand controller, we investigated how novice users would interact with the particular 3-D mouse and how users would set the point of reference for movements ("direct position control" vs. "relative position control," compare Funk et al. [9]).

3.1 Method

We run our study as a Wizard-of-Oz (WoZ) experiment [4] with a simulated drone flight. In our context, this method had the following two main advantages: First, we could gain insights before developing a functional prototype. Second, we did not have any risk of drone crashes or incidents resulting from novice users flying a drone.

Participants. We invited nine participants (one female, eight male), aged 24 to 36 (M = 30.6, SD = 3.5), all employees of our institute, to take part in the experiment on a voluntary basis. None of them had been involved in any projects related to drones before. The participants had only few previous experiences with flying drones, so we consider them as representative for the group of novice users: four of them had never flown a drone before, three had tried out a drone before (two with an RCT, one with a tablet). Only two of the participants own their own drone (one with RCT, one with a smartphone app). Regarding the 3-D mouse that we used for the experiment, seven participants did not have any previous experience and two had used such a device before: one participant was experienced in computer-aided design (CAD) applications and another one had controlled an industrial robot with the device.

Procedure. The participants were introduced to the session, the purpose of the study was explained and a drone and the 3-D mouse were introduced without mentioning any details about its features or possible input movements. In the study, participants had to do a simulated indoor flight with the drone. For this purpose, users sat behind a table in front of the 3-D mouse (see Fig. 5). The

---

[1] This pre-study has been presented before at the international workshop on Human-Drone Interaction (iHDI '19) at ACM CHI Conference on Human Factors in Computing Systems (CHI '19) in Glasgow, United Kingdom [2].

study conductor gave the users specific flight commands (e.g. "Start the drone straight up in the air," "Fly one meter into the direction of the telephone," "Fly sideways to the right. During the flight turn the drone 90° to the left."). It was observed how users used the controller to execute these movements. Additionally, specific questions were asked, such as "What would you expect to happen to the drone, if you release the controller now?" An assistant simulated the flight by carrying the drone through the room. After this simulated flight was done, the participants were asked about the possible movements with the 3-D mouse to find out whether users understood the device without any introduction. Afterwards, Fig. 2 was shown and users were asked how they would map these dimensions to the drone dimensions. Obviously, this second mapping was different from the mapping observed in the experiment, since most participants did not recognize all axes of the 3-D mouse during the experiment.

Fig. 5. Study setup. During the study, the participant sat in front of the 3-D mouse and had to control a simulated flight.

3.2 Results and Discussion

Even though there were only a small number of participants, the results show a trend about the users' intuitive understanding of the controller and the natural mapping.

Point of Reference. First, we analyzed the users' understanding of the point of reference. Common drones need to be controlled in a way that takes the drone as point of reference for the movements ("direct position control," see [9]). With this mode, steering left means that the drone moves left from its own perspective. Our experiment showed that about half of the users (five out of nine, including the two participants who own a drone) used the controller in this way. However, the others (four out of nine, most of them inexperienced with drones) used the devices as "relative position controller" (see [9]), so they steered left, if the drone had to move left in relation to the user. These results show a strong need for supporting relative position control, if a drone controller is designed for novice users.

Intuitive Understanding of the Input Device. Considering the supported DOF of the input device (see Fig. 2), most participants intuitively understood the directions Tilt (all), Spin (eight out of nine), Roll (all), and Pan down (seven out of nine). However, only three participants recognized that they could move the controller upwards (Pan up). One of them showed doubts: "Maybe I can move it up. I don't want to destroy it." The directions Zoom and Pan left/right were only used by the participant who had controlled a robot before with a similar device. The other eight participants did not use or recognize these dimensions for the drone movement.

Natural Mapping Between 3-D Mouse and Drone. Most participants (eight out of nine) used Tilt and Roll to move the drone forwards, backwards, and sideways right and left as mentioned above with different points of reference. Only one participant used Zoom and Pan left/right instead. Also, turning the drone around the z-axis was done by most participants (eight out of nine) with the Spin action. The participant who did not recognize the Spin function of the controller explained that he would have expected a button for turning the drone. The results for starting and landing were more diverse: two participants used the Pan up function, three used a button for the start, two used the Pan down function (one explained that he would push the button down as long as the drone should be in the air), one assumed that he can control the height by turning the controller (Spin) and one participant assumed that the drone starts automatically, if he starts to move it forward with Tilt. In the same way, participants had different ideas about how to land the drone. Most participants (four out of nine) expected the drone to land with a button on the device. Even though most users recognized the possibility to pan the button down, only three used it for landing, since the others had used this function already for other flight maneuvers. One participant used the button for flying and stated that he expected the drone to land as soon as he releases the button. One participant used a double-click on the controller (Pan down) as an input for landing.

Implications for Design. Our study revealed the strong need for relative position control if a drone controller is designed for novice users. Mapping the spatial dimensions of the 3-D mouse simply with the drone movement is not as intuitive as it might seem at first glance. Especially up- and downward movements were not intuitively understood by the participants. Consequently, we added separate buttons for starting and landing operations. We also learned from the study that we should not make any difference between Tilt and Zoom and between Roll and Pan left/right, since users were not aware of this difference.

4   Prototypical Implementation

This section describes the details of the implementation of our prototype. Figure 6 gives an overview of the architecture of the overall system. The prototype is composed by two main units: the drone platform with its onboard components, and the ground control station (GCS). Each of those components possess a software application and is connected to the other component via Wi-Fi. As a 3-D mouse we used the *SpaceMouse®️ Compact* from *3Dconnexion* that is connected to the GCS via USB. The GCS filters and maps all user input into precise inputs for the drone. The required filtering and mapping functions have been iteratively developed while testing the prototype system with various users. The commands are sent to the drone platform via Wi-Fi connection. A companion computer (*TX2* platform from *Nvidia*[2]) receives the signals and forwards them via *MavLink*[3] to the actual flight controller (*Pixhawk4*[4]). The flight controller stabilizes the drone based on various sensor data (GPS, compass, accelerometer, gyroscope) and executes the manual input commands.

4.1   3-D Mouse as Remote Controller

Drones typically have four DoF. Drone inputs are known as throttle, pitch, roll and yaw. Each input is responsible for one direction of movement. Therefore, flying a drone requires at least four input channels. However, many flight controllers nowadays offer the possibility to change its flight mode to define how the drone responds to the inputs or controlling on-board camera heading by using an additional input channel. To make the inputs from the 3-D mouse as intuitive as possible, mapping the input is based on the described pre-study. Most participants did not recognize the pan up/down axis in the pre-study. Therefore, two buttons on the 3-D mouse were assigned to perform the takeoff and land function. However, ascending and descending can still be performed by using Pan Up/Down. Moreover, all participants expected the drone to hold its position after releasing the cap, this means that the natural position of the cap should be mapped in a way that the drone holds its position after releasing the cap. Therefore, flying the drone must be semi-autonomous, where users can influence movements of an autonomous drone.

---

[2] https://developer.nvidia.com/embedded/jetson-tx2.

[3] https://mavlink.io/.

[4] https://docs.px4.io/v1.9.0/en/flight_controller/pixhawk4.html.

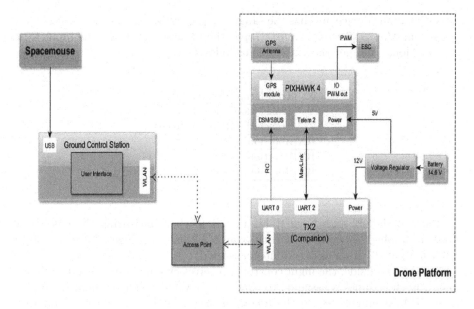

Fig. 6. The system architecture of our drone prototype with all components.

The drone must be able to maintain its position if there is no input from the 3-D mouse (the cap controller at the natural position). In other words, the drone must hold its position steady against wind at a fixed point (latitude, longitude, altitude) and wait for input from the user. This behavior can be implemented by using a semi-autonomous flight mode called position mode [16]. In fact, using this mode requires a GPS and barometer sensors, therefore, it can be used only outdoors with the presence of a GPS signal.

Moreover, the result from the study showed that the users did not recognize differences between "pan" and "roll"/"zoom" and "tilt". Therefore, the effect of pan and roll/zoom and tilt is identical on the drone.

4.2 Mapping the Input of the 3-D Mouse

SpaceMouse axis inputs can be obtained by using *Microsoft-DirectInput*[5] component of the *Microsoft DirectX* application programming interface (API). *Microsoft-DirectInput* is a legacy API to process data and mapping the values from keyboard, mouse, joystick, game controllers or any other input device that is attached to the computer. It allows the user to assign a specific action from the input devices. Using the *DeviceList* class to capture a *SpaceMouse* device, which appeared as *SpaceMouse Compact* or *SpaceMouse Pro Wireless* depending on the input device attached to the GCS in the device list library. It is recognized as

---

[5] https://docs.microsoft.com/en-us/previous-versions/windows/desktop/bb318766(v%3dvs.85).

a joystick input device and has the same axis properties. Using the *JoystickState* class from *Microsoft.DirectX.DirectInput* the library can obtain the input from a SpaceMouse and get the axis value as follows:

X	Translation	Pan right/left
Y	Translation	Zoom in/out
Z	Translation	Pan up/down
RX	Rotation	Tilt/Pitch
RY	Rotation	Roll
RZ	Rotation	Spin/Yaw

Each of the six axes have 16-bit precision when measuring the amount of pressure applied. The value of each axis is within the range of 0 to 65536 or -32767 to 32767 if an assigned integer is used.

On the other side, the flight controller receives channel input as a drone command. Each channel is assigned to tune one movement. The standard mapping of the UAV channels are in the following order: pitch, roll, throttle and yaw, which means for example that channel one tunes the pitch movement. In the stabilize status, the values of the channels pitch, roll and yaw must be in the middle of the channel range. The middle range is known as a natural position. The natural position value is 1,500 μs pulse length, it is between the lowest position 1,000 μs pules length and the highest position 2,000 μs pulse length. Modifying the value of the channel pitch leads to forward/backward movement and modifying the value of the channel roll leads to right/left movement. To hold altitude, the throttle channel should be at the neutral position of 1,500 μs pulse length. Therefore, the natural position of the cap controller (0) is mapped as 1,500 μs, the maximum value of the cap axes (32,767) is mapped as 2,000 μs and the minimum value of the cap axes ($-32,767$) is mapped as 1,000 μs.

The natural position of the mouse has the zero value. The inputs from X/RY or Y/RX are implemented to have an identical behavior on the drone. The larger value is sent to the drone axis. Nevertheless, there are only four axes of input to manually control the drone and the caps input is mapped as the following:

Input from SpaceMouse	Input on the drone
X/RY	Pitch
Y/RX	Roll
Z	Throttle
RX	Yaw

Obtaining the axes inputs is implemented in the UI software on the GCS. The values of the axes are sent to the companion computer software via method called *setControl* in the DLL library.

4.3   Companion Computer and Autopilot Communication

The companion computer provides a way to communicate between the GCS and the drone. It receives the input from the 3-D mouse via Wi-Fi, then processes and maps it as input to the flight controller. It can also read the status of the flight controller and forward it to the GCS. The serial connection between the flight controller and companion computer is illustrated in Fig. 7.

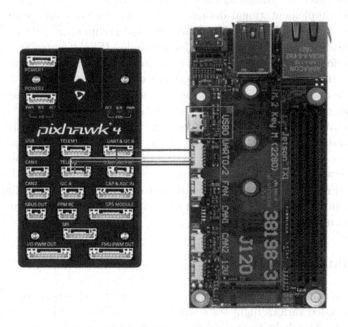

Fig. 7. The serial connection between the flight controller (left) and companion computer (right).

Figure 7 shows that the *J120 Auvidea*[6] has two serial communication ports (UART 0/ UART 2). UART 0 port is set to bidirectional 3.3 V TTL levels with the standard baud rate of 115,200, 8 bits with one stop bit and no parity (8/1/N) which makes it suitable to send *Graupner HoTT SUMD protocol (SUMD)*[7] since *SUMD* has also 8/1/N configuration.

UART 0 port has a static name device address, which appears as (/dev/ttyS0) and is accessible via J7 connector. In addition, the companion computer gets MAVLink messages from the flight controller via UART 2 with baud rate 1,500,000. This port is connected to the TELEM2 port on Pixhawk side. The UART 2 port has a static name device address, which appears as (/dev/ttyTHS1).

---

[6] https://auvidea.eu/j120/.

[7] https://www.deviationtx.com/media/kunena/attachments/98/HoTT-SUMD-Spec-REV01-12062012-pdf.pdf.

4.4   Drone Control Application

On the companion computer runs a C++ application called *Drone-control*. In order to make a drone-control application build on Linux or Windows operation system, an abstraction layer is included that is implemented using the *Private Implementation pattern* (pImpl). *Drone-control* sends manual flight commands via the *SUMD* protocol using the UART0 port. This protocol is implemented in SUMD.cpp class and generates data frame at a rate of 100 Hz.

To hide implementational details and to ease the communication with the server, the remoting part uses a service-oriented architecture (SOA). Each service consists of a general interface, for example, *IFlightControlService*. These interfaces declare the public methods that are supported by those interfaces.

The implementation of those interfaces consists of two parts: The service stub on the client side GCS which is used to send the method parameters and to receive the results from the server. The implementation part on the server side which receives the method parameters from the client, calls the corresponding method and sends the results to the client. A connection-loss input from the *SpaceMouse* is a main condition to fly the drone manually. Therefore, the connection between the GCS and the drone are established by using the TCP/IP protocol. Having TCP/IP allows the drone to recognize the loss of flight control packages and consequently to perform a fail-safe routine. This routine could help prevent a crash or other hazard.

5   Evaluation

Apart from the experiment described above, the development process of the system included various flight tests (see Fig. 8) to adapt the system based on the users' needs. The flight tests were carried out outdoors in Paderborn, Germany under the European commission regulation for flying a UAV [7]. Based on these regulations, we had to recruit users that have a general knowledge of operating drones (which is not exactly the novice user group, but was required for legal reasons). The users were asked to fly specific maneuvers and the realization of the maneuvers was observed, while the data of the GCS was logged (input before and after filtering and mapping). Based on this data and the feedback of users, the implementation of the one-hand controller iteratively improved, e.g. by improving the filtering (such as smoothing high amplitudes) and mapping of the GCS.

Fig. 8. Area for flight tests in Paderborn, Germany.

6   Summary and Conclusion

In our paper, we presented the results of the prototypical development of a
one-hand controller for human-drone interaction. By integrating users into the
development process, we investigated the natural mapping of users between the
spatial dimensions of a 3-D mouse and the dimensions of a drone. The development of the controller was based on an evolutionary prototyping with multiple
flight tests and iterative improvements of the controller. The resulting prototype
shows the feasibility of using a 3-D mouse as intuitive one-hand controller to be
used for manual intervention and temporary control for (otherwise) autonomous
industrial drones. The evaluation showed that flying with the 3-D mouse is as
intuitive as holding the drone in a hand: the drone can be controlled by the
natural movements of the hands of a user.

Acknowledgements. This work is an extended version of the paper "Investigating
users' natural spatial mapping between drone dimensions and one-hand drone controllers" that has been presented at the international workshop on Human-Drone Interaction (iHDI '19) at ACM CHI Conference on Human Factors in Computing Systems
(CHI '19) in Glasgow, United Kingdom [2].

Parts of this work have been included in Rami Zaitoon's master thesis "Prototypical Implementation of a One-hand Controller for Unmanned Aerial Vehicles" at
Ostwestfalen-Lippe University of Applied Sciences and Arts, Lemgo, Germany [19].

References

1. Dconnexion: 3Dconnexion spacemouse® compact. https://www.3dconnexion. com/spacemouse_compact/en (2019). Accessed 06 Feb 2019
2. Büttner, S., Zaitoon, R., Heinz, M., Röcker, C.: Investigating users' natural spatial mapping between drone dimensions and one-hand drone controllers. In: 1st International Workshop on Human-Drone Interaction (iHDI), Glasgow, United Kingdom (May 2019), https://hal.archives-ouvertes.fr/hal-02128399
3. Cauchard, J.R., Zhai, K.Y., Landay, J.A., et al.: Drone & me: an exploration into natural human-drone interaction. In: Proceedings of the 2015 ACM International Joint Conference on Pervasive and Ubiquitous Computing, pp. 361–365. ACM (2015)
4. Dahlbäck, N., Jönsson, A., Ahrenberg, L.: Wizard of Oz studies: why and how. In: Proceedings of the 1st International Conference on Intelligent User Interfaces, pp. 193–200 (1993)
5. DJI: Dji spark. https://www.dji.com/spark (2019). Accessed 06 Feb 2019
6. DJI: Dji - the world leader in camera drones/quadcopters for aerial photography (2020). https://www.dji.com/. Accessed 21 Jan 2020
7. European Commission: Commission implementing regulation (EU) of 2019 on the rules and procedures for the operation of unmanned aircraft. http://ec. europa.eu/transparency/regcomitology/index.cfm?do=search.documentdetail& Dos_ID=17242&DS_ID=58829&Version=4 (2019). Accessed 01 Apr 2019
8. Fernández, R.A.S., Sanchez-Lopez, J.L., Sampedro, C., Bavle, H., Molina, M., Campoy, P.: Natural user interfaces for human-drone multi-modal interaction. In: 2016 International Conference on Unmanned Aircraft Systems (ICUAS), pp. 1013–1022. IEEE (2016)
9. Funk, M.: Human-drone interaction: let's get ready for flying user interfaces!. Interactions **25**(3), 78–81 (2018). https://doi.org/10.1145/3194317
10. This is engineering Inc. (2019). http://www.thisiseng.com. Accessed 06 Feb 2019
11. Kickstarter: Shift: The new generation of drone and controller (2016). https://www.kickstarter.com/projects/1937904185/shift-the-new-generation-of-drone-and-controller. Accessed 06 Feb 2019
12. Kickstarter: FT Aviator Drone Flight Controller (2018). https://www.kickstarter.com/projects/fluiditytech/ft-aviator-a-revolutionary-single-handed-drone-con/. Accessed 06 Feb 2019
13. Martins, M., Cunha, A., Morgado, L.: Usability test of 3Dconnexion 3D mice versus keyboard+ mouse in second life undertaken by people with motor disabilities due to medullary lesions. Procedia Comput. Sci. **14**, 119–127 (2012)
14. Motion, L.: Leap motion (2019). https://www.leapmotion.com. Accessed 06 Feb 2019
15. Peshkova, E., Hitz, M., Kaufmann, B.: Natural interaction techniques for an unmanned aerial vehicle system. IEEE Pervasive Comput. **1**, 34–42 (2017)
16. PX4 Dev Team: Position mode (multicopter) (2020). https://docs.px4.io/v1.9.0/en/flight_modes/position_mc.html. Accessed 22 Jan 2020
17. Rsx, U.: Space mouse for cura auf thingiverse (2018). https://drucktipps3d.de/space-mouse-for-cura/. Accessed 19 Feb 2019
18. WEPULSIT: Wepulsit - smart equipment for drones (2019). http://www.wepulsit.com/. Accessed 06 Feb 2019
19. Zaitoon, R.: Prototypical implementation of a one-hand controller for unmanned aerial vehicles. Master's thesis, Ostwestfalen-Lippe University of Applied Sciences and Arts, Lemgo, Germany (2019)

Sexual Robots: The Social-Relational Approach and the Concept of Subjective Reference

Piercosma Bisconti Lucidi[1][(✉)] and Susanna Piermattei[2]

[1] Sant'Anna School of Advanced Studies, DIRPOLIS Institute, Pisa, Italy
piercosma.biscontilucidi@santannapisa.it
[2] Department of Psychology, Sapienza University of Rome, Rome, Italy
susannapiermattei@gmail.com

Abstract. In this paper we propose the notion of "subjective reference" as a conceptual tool that explains how and why human-robot sexual interactions could reframe users approach to human-human sexual interactions. First, we introduce the current debate about Sexual Robotics, situated in the wider discussion about Social Robots, stating the urgency of a regulative framework. We underline the importance of a social-relational approach, mostly concerned about Social Robots impact in human social structures. Then, we point out the absence of a precise framework conceptualizing why Social Robots, and Sexual Robots in particular, may modify users' sociality and relationality. Within a psychological framework, we propose to consider Sexual Robots as "subjective references", namely objects symbolically referring to human subjects: we claim that, for the user experience, every action performed upon a Sexual Robot is symbolically directed toward a human subject, including degrading and violent practices. This shifting mechanism may transfer the user relational setting from human-robot interactions to human-human interactions.

Keywords: Social robots · Ethics of technology · Psychology of HCI · Human-robot interactions

1 Different Approaches to the Regulative Problem

1.1 Introduction

Sexual Robots (SRs), today mainly with a female aspect, aims to reproduce as believably as possible a human sexual interaction (Sullins 2012), to satisfy users' sexual desires. These machines will not perform their sexual functions only from a physical-mechanical point of view (Scheutz 2011). In fact, for this type of necessity, countless types of objects are already marketed, thought to increase the physical possibility of enjoying pleasure. On the contrary, SRs won't mimic only the physical aspects of sexual intercourse, but also the relational and emotional ones.

There already are some examples of Sexual Robots on the market, although they are in an early stage (Danaher 2017). These robots can interact physically and verbally with the user, using a predefined set of behaviors (Bendel 2017). One of the most interesting

© Springer Nature Switzerland AG 2020
M. Kurosu (Ed.): HCII 2020, LNCS 12182, pp. 549–559, 2020.
https://doi.org/10.1007/978-3-030-49062-1_37

technologies today on the market is Roxxxy, a full-size interactive sexual gynoid. Roxxxy has a human-like skin, a good physical resemblance of a real woman and, most important, it interacts verbally adapting her personality to user communicative feedbacks.

The site marketing Roxxxy, True Companion, promise that Roxxxy(s):

"Can hear what you say, speak, feel your touch, move their bodies, are mobile and have emotions and a personality. Additional personalities may be taught to the robot. The additional personality profiles provided with Roxxxy assume very unique sexual characteristics. For example, there is "Wild Wendy" which is very adventurous. There is also "Frigid Farah" that is very reserved and does not always like to engage in intimate activities."[1]

Other companies are producing Sexual Robots with various degrees of human resemblances and autonomy, while the market for these products increases, albeit still limited. Moreover, an online community is born (Su et al. 2019), where users are exchanging experiences and advise on the use of sexual dolls and robots.

1.2 A Debated Topic

The starting point of the scholar discussion about Sexual Robotics could be placed in Levy's book "Love and Sex with Robots" (2009) where the author analyses the nature of human-human sexual interactions in comparison with human-robot sexual interactions. His conclusions are enthusiastic about the introduction of Sexual Robots. After that, the interest for Sexual Robotics spread out in the scientific literature. Scholars are mainly divided between critics and supporters. The main concerns are about the possibility to rape SRs (Strikwerda 2015), the commercialization of children SRs (Maras and Shapiro 2017), the rights of SRs (Gunkel 2015), their moral status (Bendel 2017). Currently, there is a growing debate about Sexual Robots in the scientific community.

Most of the discussion focuses on deciding whether robots should have "rights" and which are the acceptable behaviors to perform on them (Richardson 2016a). Two position are the most supported in this discussion: the first argues that robots, since they have a certain degree of intelligence, must be guaranteed certain rights and a moral status (Bendel 2017). Others argue that they should be treated as objects (Levy 2009a, b), because their ability to mimic intelligent behaviors doesn't make them subjects.

More in general, the discussion is divided between enthusiasts and detractors of Sexual Robots. The former argue that rape and violence will decrease (Devlin 2015), sexual satisfaction of users will increase (Levy and Loebner 2007), it will contribute to the reduction of prostitution (Levy 2012). The latter argue that they will contribute to increase the violence (Sparrow 2017) and that they will reproduce the existing gender disparities (Cox-George and Bewley 2018).

Most scholars agree that the predictable spread of Sexual Robotics on the market must happen within a regulative framework in order to avoid unacceptable consequences of this technology, as child sex robots (Maras and Shapiro 2017), the worsening of human relational abilities (Turkle et al. 2006), the reproduction and amplification of gender disparities (Cox-George and Bewley 2018).

---

[1] Some deny Roxxxy existence and claim that is a hoax. For the sake of this discussion, we believe that is not a crucial aspect the actual commercialization of such an artefact, but the fact that is an affordable technology for today's state of art.

1.3   The Exceptionality of Social Robots

The one of Sexual Robots is only a specific case of the growing awareness about the disruptive impact of Social Robotics in our society, the multiple and probably still unthinkable uses (and misuses) of autonomous and interactive robots.

Both academia and the civil society largely agree that Social Robots won't simply be other objects in our houses because of their degree of autonomy, adaptivity and relationality (Breazeal 2004). Interactions with robots will supposedly strongly resemble the ones with humans and the "social" nature of these robots will, in any case, produce a deep impact on how we experience our intersubjective interactions. This difference between Social Robots (or interactive AIs) and non-interactive technological objects requires a specific theoretical effort (considering the peculiarity of Social Robots) in order to prevent negative consequences and enhance positive outcomes.

Then, a specific theoretical framework for a regulation of Social robots is needed (Sharkey and Sharkey 2010), since they are a very peculiar type of objects: autonomous, interactive and social-oriented.

This theoretical framework should:

1. Explain if and on what basis Social Robots and interactive AIs differs from "classical" object (ontologically, socially, relationally, morally).
2. Explain what the consequences of this exceptionality are on different levels: moral, legal, social, regulative (etc.).
3. Describe the possible undesirable effects on human sociality and how to prevent them.

Most of the current literature about the consequences of robots' autonomy deals with the problem of moral status, often declined in the terms of "robots rights" (Gunkel 2018a, b).

The problem of moral status can be summarized with the question "should robots be considered as morally relevant, both passively and actively? Should we give moral consideration to actions performed by and on robots?"

Obviously, the question arises because we are today facing massive advances in the field of robotics and AI and more and more machines are able to autonomously act, evaluating the context in where they are and choosing the best thing to do.

In philosophical terms, it is the first time that a technological human-made object is reaching (or at least trying to achieve) a sort of autonomous agency (Broadbent 2017). So, the problem is declined both in the passive and active moral relevance of autonomous machines: what machines (should and should not) do and what we (should and should not) do on machines. As said, most part of the current literature on the moral implications of robots and AIs passes through the concept of "rights": many scholars are asking for giving robotics "rights" (Sharkey 2008) in order to institutionalize robots' relevance to morality. Therefore, most of the discussion is about what rights should we grant to robots and on what basis.

Multiple and different answer have been given to these two questions, deeply interconnected between each other. In most of the cases the claim is that we grant rights not only to humans but also to non-human beings as animals and abstract beings as institutions, groups etc. (Gunkel 2018a, b). Hence, rights are differently distributed among different type of recipients, each of them possessing a certain degree of agency. Since autonomous robots have (or can mimic?) a certain degree of agency, then we should grant certain rights (Tavani 2018). Therefore, a spreading literature tries to establish under what conditions robots are worth of moral consideration and what rights must be granted to them. In our opinion, there are two very problematic aspects of thinking the moral problem in terms of rights to robots. First, the hard-to-support ontological assumption that today's robots genuinely have a certain degree of agency. Moreover, it is hard to state on which universal criteria we should rely to grant certain rights to robots with certain ontological properties. We could claim that the qualifying property for rights is self-awareness, or the ability to suffer pain, or intentionality. All of these options make sense (and are broadly supported), still there is no agreement on which is predominant, or the degree of each to possess in order to be qualified. Anyway, without disregarding this valuable approach, we try to ground the regulative framework on another approach that, in our opinion, could produce faster and broader consensus on a theoretical framework for Social Robots regulation

2 Social-Relational Approach to a Regulation of Social Robotics and Sexual Robotics

In this paper we propose a different theoretical approach partially based on the "social-relational approach" proposed by Coeckelbergh (2010).

We believe that the very relevant part of a debate on Social Robotics (and Sexual Robotics as a part of it) should focus on the consequences for human relationality and sociality, when addressing regulative issues. In fact, apart from possessing or not any ontological property, Social Robots surely differs from any other object for their hu-man-likeness and relationality (Sparrow 2016). So, when addressing regulative questions on the introduction of Social Robots in our interactional context, we should focus on the most urgent issue, in our opinion: how will Social Robots shape human relational settings and the human social sphere?

In order to give an answer, it is necessary to state what relational characteristics make Social Robots different from other type of objects, and why we should have a particular normative framework for them.

In fact, the deontological approach provided an explanation on why we should regulate Social Robotics in an exceptional way and why we should not consider them as simple objects, namely stating that robots should be guaranteed with rights on the basis of their peculiar ontological properties.

Instead, from a social-relational approach, we claim that Social Robots are a type of object that deeply reconfigure the user's socio-relational setting because of:

1. Their high degree of verbal, nonverbal and even emotional interactivity and their human resemblance (Sharkey 2008), producing interactional patterns very similar to the human-human interactions ones (Krämer et al. 2011).

2. Their unlimited disposability to user needs and desires. In fact, unlike humans, robots never get bored of interacting and are totally at the user disposal (Turkle et al. 2006)

What matters for a social-relational approach is that a certain interactional object will supposedly produce a significant change on human sociality.

The concerns about the effect of relational technologies on human intersubjectivity is common between scholars debating on regulation of SRs, but few attempts to systematizing this approach have been made.

Maras and Shapiro (2017) suggest that child sex robots could contribute to enhance the pedophile phantasies in subjects at risk. Richardson (2016c) states that Sexual Robots contributes on a distorted consideration of humans' bodies as "consumable goods". Turkle et al. (2006) warns that always-at-disposal Social Robots could be preferred to human companions in the future. Even Levy (2009a, b), in one of his papers, is concerned about the possible transfer of degrading behaviors from robots to humans. Nearly every scholar addressing regulatory issues is concerned, at least in part, with the fact that introducing interactive robots in our interactional space could lead to significant changes in our human-human interactions.

Coeckelbergh (2010) proposes, in opposition to theories of object's morality (e.g. deontology) or subject's morality (e.g. virtue ethics) a social-relational theory, which we accept as the ground for our discussion. The main conclusions of his approach are:

- We should care about how robots appear to users, not about the ontological properties.
- We should intend the relation between users and Social Robots as socially (and culturally, historically etc.) contextualized, when dealing with regulative and moral questions.
- If, on one side, the relation between the subject and the interactional object is shaped by the social context, the intersubjective results of this relation will in turn shape the social sphere.

Within Coeckelbergh's social-relational approach, we want to provide a conceptual framework of the reason why (and how, to what extent) interacting with a social robot brings significant changes in human-human interactions.

We will take in consideration the specific case of Sexual Robots, a subset of Social Robots. In fact, we believe that they are an interesting case study to clearly analyze the intersubjective implications of interacting robots. The attempt to extend our conclusion about Sexual Robots to Social Robots in general, will be matter of forthcoming works. In the next section we ground a psychoanalytical framework for Sexual Robot implications in users psychological setting. Afterwards we propose the concept of "Subjective Reference" as a relevant mechanism producing the intersubjective issues of Sexual Robots. Then, we suggest our conceptualization of this mechanism as a possible key-element in order to produce an effective regulative framework for Sexual Robots and Social Robots in general.

2.1   Sexual Robots and Their Limitless Availability

The socio-relational approach to sexual robotics allows us to develop important considerations on how the "relationship" with these objects will affect both the people who directly interact with them and the society in general.

First, we contextualize this approach within a psychological theoretical framework.

One of the fundamental concepts of the psychodynamic approach is the conflict between the pleasure principle and the reality one. The first, which characterizes particularly early childhood, implicates that the subject requires unlimited satisfaction of his needs and desires, regardless of the limitations that the outside world inevitably poses. The second, that evolve during the development, allows the subject to tolerate frustration, thus satisfying his own wishes to the extent that it is possible, given the limitations of external world. One of the fundamental consequences of the transition from pleasure principle to that of reality, is the possibility of perceiving and tolerating the other subjects as autonomous (Winnicott 1990), endowed with the same rights as the subject her/himself, despite this inevitably limits the satisfaction of his wills (Nicolò 2003). This means that only the acceptance of the reality principle allows individuals to actually establish a relationship with another subject, taking into account her/his needs and rights, empathizing for her/him, considering her/him as a subject (Baron-Cohen 2011).

Within this concept, the choice to use a sexual robot to satisfy sexual needs makes interesting questions arise. Indeed, we can imply that the choice of using a machine rather than relating to a human, is due to an issue in this area of the personality, since the interactions with a machine requires no compromises with the reality principle. Then, doubts arise on how much sexual robot users have reached the following abilities, typical of the health subject:

– Accepting that the satisfaction of desire is not unlimited and tolerating the resulting frustration.
– Being in relationship with another person, perceived as a subject with rights and needs to be respected.

Conversely, replacing humans with machines allows to:

– Be certain that no limitations on the satisfaction of desire will take place.
– Avoid confrontation with another subject that can advance needs and provide frustration.

This choice can therefore be considered a regressive movement to a psychological setting in which one demands everything and immediately, as in the primary process (Ogden 1989). This mechanism of regression is true for every kind of masturbatory practices, that we define as every practice where only one subject is supposed to have agency and be able to manifest needs and wills.

Moreover, some scholars compared interactions with SRs to ones with sexual workers. As far as prostitution is concerned, it is necessary to underline that despite the sex worker is paid, thus can become equal to an object at the phantasmatic level for the user, she always remains a subject. The sex worker does not lose her inalienable rights and she sets specific rules that must be respected. Moreover, the fact that sexual work is paid, imply a negotiation between to subjects. Furthermore, it is in any case a relational act involving a risk of frustration. For example, the subject may fear a criticism of his sexual performance, though not expressed by the sexual worker. Therefore, the relationship with a sex worker remains a relational act, with all the problems that this can cause, although deprived of some characteristics of intersubjective interactions. In the case of Sexual Robots, user faces an interactive object, mimicking a subject, providing unlimited fulfilment of desire.

Therefore, we claim that the use of sexual robots differs from masturbation and prostitution for one prominent reason. In the masturbation, even with the use of particular objects, the subject is actually alone. In interacting with sexual workers the subject is, as we said, still in a real relational act.

The sexual robot stands in a middle way, it is actually a machine, so the user is alone and he is not relating, however a relationship is simulated, not only through the sexual act but also through a series of complementary actions like talking, looking at each-other, approaching in a "human" way (Richardson 2016c).

The sexual robot in fact, does not represent just one part of the human body, such as, for example, a vibrator. Rather it depicts the whole human body and it also tries to simulate the abilities that are proper to human, like linguistic interactions. It implies that if with another masturbatory object only a sexual act is simulated, Sexual Robots reproduce a whole human relationship, not just at its sexual level.

The sexual robot is then an object that is "subjectivized" where user can project a simulated relational satisfaction of his wills and needs (Richardson 2016b). What consequences can this feature have on the user of a sexual robot?

Of course, the differences between a masturbatory act and a relational one fade and this involves multiple consequences. As the object becomes "subjectivized", it is possible that, conversely, human subjects become "objectified". It is therefore possible that a sexual robot user will reproduce, in human-human interactions, some behavior which, if acceptable with a robot, will be unacceptable in a human interaction.

This second implication of human-robot interactions:

1) Directly derives from the nature of human-robot interactions, namely the limitless availability of robots and its "subjectification".
2) Brings many consequences in human-human interactions, since the interactional setting in behaving with robots could be transferred on relations with humans.
3) Deeply impact social and relational sphere of humanity and it is highly relevant for a social-relational regulative framework.

Then, we explain the shift of the relational setting from human-robot interactions to human-human interactions introducing the concept of "subjective reference"

2.2   The Concept of "Subjective Reference" and Its Relevance for the Regulative Approach

Sexual Robots producers want them as realistic as possible, to remove any noticeable difference between humans and robots. Today, commercialized SRs reproduce mostly women (Sparrow 2017). They must appear and behave like real humans because users are searching for a substitute of human-human sexual interactions and will supposedly prefer the most similar one (Levy 2009a, b). But, if the robot is chosen largely (or uniquely?) for its similarity to humans, then it is not sexually relevant in itself but in place of something else, namely the thing it tries to mimic and resemble.

In other words, we claim that (except from a minimum part of users fetishizing the very fact that is a machine) users are not enjoying a sexual intercourse with a SR because robots are objects. Users will enjoy it because the object looks like a human subject (objectified and fully under user control).

Therefore, when the user sexually interacts with an SR, his/her sexual phantasies are not focused on the robot itself, but on the human partner which the robot is embodying and mimicking for user's pleasure. The SR operates as a reference (a representant) that enables sexual phantasies (actually directed to a human subject) to be realized on a substitutive object. The human subject is physically absent but is symbolically the real target of all the actions the user will accomplish on SR's body.

In this sense, we claim that a SR is "Subjective Reference": a constant reference to a human subject, a "subjectified" object. We claim that, for the user experience, every action performed upon a Sexual Robot is implicitly directed toward a human subject, including obviously degrading and violent practices.

We believe that this shifting mechanism could severely impact on user sociality and behaviors acceptability. The SRs unlimited availability to user's needs and phantasies could normalize, in the user experience, the expectation of a full and unnegotiated satisfaction of his sexual wills also in human-human interactions (Richardson 2016c).

In addition, we should consider that the most probable users of SRs are subjects with poor or no sexual experiences or subjects with peculiar sexual desires, hard to express in human-human interactions (Cox-George and Bewley 2018). Most of these unacceptable (or hardly sharable) phantasies in human-human sexual interactions are those violent and degrading. If we allow users - mainly male since SRs are mainly gynoid - to freely express these phantasies on SRs, this could severely modify users' sexual expectations and behaviors acceptability, normalizing aggressive and degrading approaches to sexuality. In fact, since actions performed on SRs are phantasmatically transferred on a human subject, so it will be the presumption of an unlimited availability to any sexual behavior.

Summarizing, we support that:

1) Sexual Robots are sexually relevant only (or for the most part) for their similarity with humans.
2) Every sexual action performed on robots is symbolically referring to a represented human subject; we call this mechanism "subjective reference".

3) Since robots allow any form of sexual behavior to be performed on them, including violent and degrading, this expectation could (and probably will) be transferred in human-human sexual interactions.

In this paper we do not analyze the specific social and relational implications of Sexual Robotics under the concept of subjective reference. Further work will link this concept with a possible increase of sexism in the social sphere and with a reduction of the social perception of rape severity.

We propose that of "subjective reference" as a conceptual tool useful to:

1) Analyze and forecast possible consequences of Social Robots commercialization
2) Produce design strategies to be implemented in robots to avoid (or reduce) users misuse of Social Robots.
3) Ground a regulative framework of Social Robotics, dealing with the severe implications for sociality and relationality.

In fact, a precise theorization of why and how Sexual Robots - and Social Robots in general – will impact human sociality and relationality allow us to foresee and prevent future negative implications of specific traits of Sexual Robots' behavior.

A regulative framework based (or directly involving) the concept of "subjective reference" takes in strong consideration *not* the action performed on the robot, valuing its rightness or wrongness in itself. This approach considers primarily *if* and *how* this action could impact on human-human relations: we want to assess in which measure the user relational setting will be modified by the HR interaction. The reason why this modification could occur is explained by the concept of Subjective Reference: interactions with robots (and a good example are Sexual Robots) are not meaningful in themselves for the user, but because they enable a shifting mechanism toward a human subject. This means that a regulative framework should limit the unacceptable actions on robots that will strongly refer to a human and, therefore, modify user attitude to relationality in general.

Surely, we find a difficulty in implementing such a theoretical framework: we need a threshold stating a limit to actions performable on robots. This must rely on a precise description of interactional shift between human-robot interactions and human-human ones. We are working on this objective on our next work, in which we will apply the interactionist theory of relationship, derived from Palo Alto school.

Then, we will be able to implement design strategies able to reduce (or even eliminate) the risk of a severe worsening of users' relational abilities and behavior acceptability, by precisely understanding how and why a H-R interactional setting may be transferred to H-H interactions.

3 Conclusions

In this paper we claimed the greater effectiveness of a social-relational approach over a deontological one. We underlined the limits of deontologies, namely the heavy ontological assumptions that these approaches need.

We agreed with a social-relational approach that, in our opinion, eases the grounding of a shared theoretical approach in order to produce a regulative framework and forecast

Sexual Robots issues. We proposed, under a psychological approach, a conceptualization of the mechanism enabling human-robot interactions to modify human sociality and relationality: the concept of "subjective reference". We supported that the limitless availability of Sexual Robots will result in an identical expectation in the human-human sexual interactions. Finally, we discussed the importance of this conceptualization for future regulative approaches.

In this paper we didn't apply to specific cases the concept of subjective reference, this will be developed in next works. However, we believe the reader may easily guess the possible implications of this conceptualization. For instance, the possibility to rape an interacting robot - able to mimic a sexual appreciation of this violent behavior - could have severe consequences for men's respect of women sexual consent. The habit of behave violently may normalize this kind of acts and, slowly, change social norms.

We choose Sexual Robotics to present this issue because it is far more visible than in any other case the risk we are facing with the absence of a regulation. Nevertheless, we believe that the same mechanism occurs in any interactions with Social Robots, given that the machine has good abilities in mimicking humans. With Sexual Robots we believe that is far simpler that the shift occurs because of the peculiarity of sexual impulse.

Next works will deal with specific cases in which the mechanism of subjective reference occurs in order to refine the concept and show its applicability.

The desired goal is to come to a shared theoretical approach useful for a normative and regulative framework on Social Robots.

References

Baron-Cohen, S.: Zero Degrees of Empathy: A New Theory of Human Cruelty. Penguin, London (2011)

Bendel, O.: Sex robots from the perspective of machine ethics. In: Cheok, A.D., Devlin, K., Levy, D. (eds.) LSR 2016. LNCS (LNAI), vol. 10237, pp. 17–26. Springer, Cham (2017). https://doi.org/10.1007/978-3-319-57738-8_2

Breazeal, C.L.: Designing Sociable Robots. MIT Press, Cambridge (2004)

Broadbent, E.: Interactions with robots: The truths we reveal about ourselves. Annu. Rev. Psychol. **68**, 627–652 (2017)

Coeckelbergh, M.: Robot rights? Towards a social-relational justification of moral consideration. Ethics Inf. Technol. **12**(3), 209–221 (2010)

Cox-George, C., Bewley, S.: I, Sex Robot: the health implications of the sex robot industry. BMJ Sex Reprod. Health **44**, 161–164 (2018)

Danaher, J.: Robotic rape and robotic child sexual abuse: should they be criminalized? Crim. Law Philos. **11**(1), 71–95 (2017)

Devlin, K.: In defence of sex machines: why trying to ban sex robots is wrong. In: The Conversation (2015)

Gunkel, D.J.: The rights of machines: caring for robotic care-givers. In: van Rysewyk, S.P., Pontier, M. (eds.) Machine Medical Ethics. ISCASE, vol. 74, pp. 151–166. Springer, Cham (2015). https://doi.org/10.1007/978-3-319-08108-3_10

Gunkel, D.J.: Robot Rights. MIT Press, Cambridge (2018a)

Gunkel, D.J.: The other question: can and should robots have rights? Ethics Inf. Technol. **20**(2), 87–99 (2018b)

Levy, D., Loebner, H.: Robot prostitutes as alternatives to human sex workers. In: IEEE International Conference on Robotics and Automation, Rome, vol. 14 (2007)

Levy, D.: Love+Sex with Robots: The Evolution of Human-Robot Relationships. Duckworth Overlook, London (2009a)

Levy, D.: The ethical treatment of artificially conscious robots. Int. J. Social Robot. 1(3), 209–216 (2009b)

Levy, D.: The ethics of robot prostitutes. In: Robots Ethics: The Ethical and Social Implications of Robotics, pp. 223–231 (2012)

Krämer, N.C., Eimler, S., von der Pütten, A., Payr, S.: Theory of companions: what can theoretical models contribute to applications and understanding of human-robot interaction? Appl. Artif. Intell. 25(6), 474–502 (2011)

Maras, M.H., Shapiro, L.R.: Child sex dolls and robots: more than just an uncanny valley. J. Internet Law 21, 3–17 (2017)

Nicolò, A.M.: Appunti a proposito di una teoria dei rapporti soggettuali. Interazioni 2(20), 55–61 (2003)

Ogden, T.H.: The Primitive Edge of Experience. Karnak, London (1989)

Richardson, K.: Sex robot matters: slavery, the prostituted, and the rights of machines. IEEE Technol. Soc. Mag. 35(2), 46–53 (2016a)

Richardson, K.: Technological animism: the uncanny personhood of humanoid machines. Soc. Anal. 60(1), 110–128 (2016b)

Richardson, K.: The asymmetrical 'relationship': parallels between prostitution and the development of sex robots. ACM SIGCAS Comput. Soc. 45(3), 290–293 (2016c)

Strikwerda, L.: Present and future instances of virtual rape in light of three categories of legal philosophical theories on rape. Philos. Technol. 28(4), 491–510 (2015)

Sharkey, N., Sharkey, A.: The crying shame of robot nannies: an ethical appraisal. Interact. Stud. 11(2), 161–190 (2010)

Sharkey, N.: The ethical frontiers of robotics. Science 322(5909), 1800–1801 (2008)

Scheutz, M.: 13 The inherent dangers of unidirectional emotional bonds between humans and social robots. In: Robot Ethics: The Ethical and Social Implications of Robotics, p. 205 (2011)

Sparrow, R.: Robots in aged care: a dystopian future? AI Soc. 31(4), 445–454 (2016)

Sparrow, R.: Robots, rape, and representation. Int. J. Soc. Robot. 9(4), 465–477 (2017)

Su, N.M., Lazar, A., Bardzell, J., Bardzell, S.: Of dolls and men: anticipating sexual intimacy with robots. ACM Trans. Comput.-Hum. Interact. (TOCHI) 26(3), 13 (2019)

Sullins, J.P.: Robots, love, and sex: the ethics of building a love machine. IEEE Trans. Affect. Comput. 3(4), 398–409 (2012)

Tavani, H.: Can social robots qualify for moral consideration? Reframing the question about robot rights. Information 9(4), 73 (2018)

Turkle, S., Taggart, W., Kidd, C.D., Dasté, O.: Relational artifacts with children and elders: the complexities of cybercompanionship. Connection Sci. 18(4), 347–361 (2006)

Winnicott, D.W.: Creativity and its origins. In: Essential Papers on the Psychology of Women, pp. 132–145 (1990)

Theses on the Future Design
of Human-Robot Collaboration

Hans-Jürgen Buxbaum[1(✉)], Sumona Sen[1], and Ruth Häusler[2]

[1] Robotics and Human Engineering Lab, Niederrhein University of Applied Sciences,
Krefeld, Germany
buha0002@hsnr.de
[2] School of Engineering - Centre for Aviation, Swiss Confederation,
ZHAW Zurich University of Applied Sciences, Winterthur, Switzerland
hasr@zhaw.ch

Abstract. For the future design of Human-Robot Collaboration (HRC),
further developments in a multitude of disciplines and research areas
are required. In this context, the breadth of interdisciplinary research
work is enormous and the scientific field - not least because of the high
level of interdisciplinarity - is quite confusing. In the discussion within
the Ladenburg Discourse on Human-Robot Collaboration, it was agreed
that guidelines for future research and development work would be very
useful and would enable researchers to structure and position their work
within the broad topic. Duplications and redundancies should be avoided,
synergies and cooperation should be promoted.

Keywords: Human-Robot Collaboration · Technology Assessment ·
Ergonomics

1 Introduction

Due to the rapid development in information technology, robots transform
from simple machines in repetitive operation to self-sufficient agents in production. The simultaneous development of powerful sensor technology allows
robots today, to reliably recognize their environment. New assistance systems
are increasingly being developed, in particular collaboration robots or "cobots".
Cobots are used in Human-Robot Collaboration systems. They are not isolated
by facilities such as protective fences, but work hand-in-hand with humans in a
common working space. In such a common working space, human and cobot can
perform tasks on the same object at the same time and work in true collaboration. The goal of HRC is to preserve the human being with his abilities as an

This work was funded by "Daimler und Benz Stiftung" (Ladenburg, DE). The theses
are a result of the "Ladenburger Diskurs 2019", where about fifteen renowned experts
from the fields of ergonomics, psychology, engineering and ethics with a research focus
on HRC met for a two days discussion. The panel of experts was supplemented by a
number of developers and users as well as representatives of associations.

M. Kurosu (Ed.): HCII 2020, LNCS 12182, pp. 560–579, 2020.
https://doi.org/10.1007/978-3-030-49062-1_38

active link in the production and to increase the quality of product and process as well as productivity by using robots.

HRC systems are intended to support or relieve the worker in monotonous or exhausting work, and many leading industrial robot manufacturers are developing special cobots for this purpose. A couple of applications are already being implemented. Due to the system-induced elimination of fencing and the direct cooperation between human and machine, occupational safety and ergonomics are becoming increasingly important. Human factors are also gaining importance in automation design. In particular, there is hardly any experience of workplace design in HRC today. The question arises as to how future HRC systems should be designed, what needs to be considered, where the pitfalls are and how they will be avoided.

2   Ergonomic Point of View

The idea to introduce a roadmap on the future development of HRC from an ergonomic point of view is introduced by Wischniewski et al. [1] and the following seven theses are formulated:

1. Programming
   The programming of HRC systems should be simplified. It is explained that the training of HRC systems has to be enabled by the respective operator. The qualification level has to be adapted to this in order to realize practical cooperation and collaboration scenarios. So here the focus is on the operator and his qualification level.
2. Operating characteristics
   It is required that the operating characteristics of the robot must be adapted to the qualification and competence level and the needs of the employees. This is the only way to achieve broad user acceptance. The usable design of interfaces is particularly important in this context.
3. Safety technology
   The safety engineering is to be made more flexible. Therefore it is necessary to develop procedures and technologies of a flexible safety engineering in order to exploit the flexibility connected with the HRC and to guarantee efficient process flows at the same time.
4. Faulty automation
   Principles for dealing with failable automation have to be developed. Incomplete automation solutions will determine the interaction between man and robot more often in the future. Principles of interaction must be developed that meet the requirements of recurrent fail-safe automation and at the same time adequately address employees.
5. Social isolation
   The social isolation by the increase of HRC workplaces is to be thematized. As an effect of the automation by HRC and corresponding protection devices, a social isolation of the employees can occur.

6. Ad-hoc task allocation

An ad hoc and flexible allocation of tasks is demanded. A previously planned allocation of partial actions, for example with the help of MABA-MABA-lists, becomes obsolete. Only predefined tasks can be selected ad hoc, a flexible reorganisation of tasks is not planned. The human being should remain the last instance for the assignment of tasks.

7. Conformity with expectations

It must be ensured that the robot's actions are transparent and comprehensible to humans. This is especially important with increasing autonomy in automation. Particular emphasis is placed on the importance in case of malfunctions.

3   Technical and Economic Point of View

In addition to the ergonomic perspective, which focuses on the interactions of human-machine cooperation, a technical-economic perspective is relevant, especially in industrial applications, which primarily addresses the properties of rationalization and feasibility. Wöllhaf [2] discusses the following aspects:

1. Physical design

Under an economically point of view, robots usually are expected to be large, strong and fast. HRC robots are indeed often small, weak and slow. In many cases, therefore, economic efficiency is a major problem. There are cases known in which existing HRC robots are no longer used for reasons of economy.

2. Security

The cost of security is considerable and often bears no reasonable relation to the benefit. Required security measures complicate the use of HRC systems considerably. In other areas of life, far more risks are accepted in our society. The question arises whether HRC robots really have to be "foolproof", especially considering the condition, that they always work with instructed persons.

3. Configuration and programming

An HRC system must be capable of being configured and programmed directly by the people using it. Already for reasons of acceptance this point is important. In case of increased flexibility requirements, this aspect is of special importance, also with regard to the strict requirements regarding operational safety.

4. AI

An artificial intelligence is required, which in many cases - despite some success in some areas of AI - does not yet exist. There is a gap between demand and availability of artificial intelligence. Machines are currently still far from being able to work intelligently and safely with humans. Successes in some areas of AI cannot simply be transferred to other tasks.

Wöllhaf concludes with the statement, that due to the mentioned aspects, it will still take some years until HRC systems will be suitable for a broad use in industrial applications [2]. Possible approaches, which take up the first 3 points, are presented by Surdilovic et al. [3]. There, concepts for the optimization of the structural design are discussed, especially with respect to force and reach of collaborating robots, with the aim to make HRC available for heavy duty applications.

Kuhlenkötter and Hypki raise the question, of where teamwork with robots and humans can be effective, focusing on both technical and economic aspects [4]. Even if the benefits are presentable, every Human-Robot Collaboration solution often requires considerable investments in planning and equipping the HRC. In addition, the necessary planning and realization process involves uncertainties, which, besides the technical challenges, also lie in the area of the acceptance of the new technology, perhaps used in the company for the first time, as well as in the appropriate implementation of the topics subject to co-determination.

4   Psychological Point of View

In previous HRC applications, the cooperation between human and robot seems to be rather artificial; it is regularly determined by engineers and programmers and is essentially oriented on the technical objective of the respective application. From a psychological point of view the question arises, how this cooperation is to be designed in the future, in order to come as close as possible to a natural collaboration between human and robot. In the following two approaches are discussed:

- Anthropomorphic design of the machine
- Integration of cognitive models into the machine

Roesler and Onnasch state, that an application of anthropomorphic features to the design of the robot is suitable to make the cooperation in the HRC more intuitive and effective [5]. As anthropomorphic design features are mentioned there: Form, communication, movement and context. The idea is, that a transfer of human-like features to robots, promotes an intuitive and socially situated cooperation between humans and robots and increases the acceptance. Potential areas of tension are also mentioned, such as the phenomenon of the Uncanny Valley.

By using the natural ability of humans to coordinate by anticipation, an intuitive form of collaboration is applied. This involves the motor system of the human brain with specialized nerve cells, so-called mirror neurons. These are activated when actions of other people are observed or presented. This makes it possible to automatically perceive and anticipate the actions of other people. No conscious, deliberate information processing is required. However, this collaboration-promoting ability of the brain is only addressed and activated if the observed or imagined actor is attested an intentionality (e.g. "he wants to open a nut"), otherwise the mirror neurons remain inactive. In industrial applications, the primary focus must of course be on the intended purpose. An anthropomorphism that restricts functionality is not suitable here. Differentiated analyses and benefit considerations are therefore necessary.

Russwinkel proposes to incorporate collaboration-relevant knowledge as a cognitive model in robots [6]. This should enable them to communicate implicitly, by deriving interaction requirements and support possibilities through observation:

– Cognitive models enable robots to behave in such a way, that the human interaction partner anticipates, what the robot intends to do. For example, an anthropomorphic robot could direct its gaze at a workpiece to be grasped and at the same time detect whether the human eye is also directed at this workpiece, at the robot or at the environment, in order to derive its own behaviour from this.
– For robots to be able to interact with humans as a "third hand" or "clear-sighted eye", they must be able to anticipate, what the requirements of the situation are, what their contribution to the achievement of objectives could be with flexible task assignment, and, how joint action can be synchronized. For this purpose, they need a model for understanding the common goals, the interaction partner and the environment in which they act, as well as a world model with general laws.

Cognitive modelling is used to transfer characteristics of human cooperation to Human-Robot Collaboration. Flexible assignment of action steps and mutual complementation in the roles as executor ("taking control") and as active supervisor ("monitoring and anticipating"). A collaborative robot understands which next action steps it can take in the current situation, in order to reach the common goal. Collaborative capability requires three types of cognitive models:

– Situation models explain the meaning of a situation and possible goals, that are usually pursued. They can be used to reveal another person's intentions and next action steps.
– Person models include individual characteristics and specific limitations, as well as emotions of the collaboration partner.
– Self models convey one's own motives and goals, abilities, (potential) emotions and limitations.

Cognitive models allow the robot to learn interactively, by experience with the environment, and to transfer, what it has learned, to novel situations. Interactive learning requires, that robots understand, what changes are due to; their own actions or those of another agent. Attributions of causes form the basis for learning interrelationships. Thus, cognitive models allow for the flexibilization of task assignment and safety engineering (robots can be anticipated by humans and can foresee human actions). By using cognitive models, the problem of fallible automation becomes a question of optimized learning processes and the degree of transparency for the human interaction partner, who is always in control of decisions and action execution.

5   Human Factors' Point of View

Häusler and Straeter see Human-Robot Collaboration from the point of view of human factors as a system in which humans cooperate with a more or less autonomously working technical system, and describe this cooperation as a problem of human-automatic interaction [7]. The phenomenon and the requirements for the interaction between robot and human are well known from other technical fields, especially in the field of automation of flight and in the process industry. The possibility of transferring knowledge from these areas should therefore be examined.

The design of safe working environments through the use of technology - especially automation - makes the presence of human operators almost obsolete. However, particularly for reasons of social acceptance, the aim of removing humans completely from the system is being abandoned for the time being. Due to the high reliability of the technology, however, hardly any operators intervention is required.

At the level of human behaviour, an attempt is made to achieve reliability and safety by specifying procedures and regulations. In nuclear power plants, operators learn error avoidance techniques, that go beyond the procedures and are intended to detect and ultimately prevent unintentional deviation from the procedures. Nevertheless, reportable incidents occur in nuclear power plant control rooms, due to operator errors, for example because the wrong page of the procedure description was read, or the wrong pump was switched off. Several error avoidance techniques, applied simultaneously, can become a source of distraction. Such incidents indicate that, despite or because of all these guidelines, operators are apparently not always aware of what they are doing, or should be doing, and they are not always able to assess the consequences of their actions. Due to progressive automation, human skills are used and trained less and less in everyday work. As a result, operators and pilots are no longer optimally prepared to manage an emergency situation without additional training. The following case study from aviation shows the paradoxical side effects of a top-down oriented approach to a technology-oriented security architecture.

Flight AF 447 was a scheduled Air France flight from Rio de Janeiro to Paris, which crashed over the Atlantic Ocean in the night of June 1, 2009. All 228 passengers lost their lives. This is the most serious accident in the history of Air France and in relation to the Airbus A330 aircraft type [8]. The crash of AF447 can be used in many aspects as an illustrative example of the underlying problems of safety culture in technically high-safety systems. It shows, that human beings in systems, that are almost completely safe, are sometimes unable to resist unconsciously losing respect for risks and critical events, due to the successful learning history ("nothing ever happened"). Under normal circumstances, the role of humans in a highly automated work environment, is the role of redundant system supervisors. For example, usually during long shifts, a human supervisor is busy with monitoring an - almost without exception - error-free functioning technology. But as simple as this task may sound, it places demands on the human that possibly cannot be fulfilled. On the one hand, the supervisor is physiologically unable to muster permanent and enduring attention; on the other hand, physical inactivity causes monotony and under-utilisation with simultaneous overstraining of the attention capacity and fatigue of the perceptual apparatus. The tasks assigned to that person, do not allow to be sufficiently active mentally and physically to be mentally present and attentive. If action steps are to be carried out, the operator must strictly adhere to the procedures - if they are reasonable.

During flight AF447, a fully functional Airbus A330 crashed, from a flight altitude of 38,000 ft, about four hours after take-off, within four and a half minutes. The accident happened due to a frozen pitot tube speed measurement system and the associated loss of displays according with subsequent failure of the automation. A mixture of inappropriate sidestick input (excessive roll movement and especially too high pitch), the lack of a procedure for the problem at hand, following an unreliable air speed procedure for low altitude and the stress-related inability to adequately assess the consequences of the action led to this accident [9].

What made it difficult for the pilots involved, to use their skills? The experience that the technology works almost completely with a high reliability, makes it difficult for organisms capable of learning to be at alert - i.e. to remain maximally alert in an alert situation and to expect the worst. On the contrary, this experience encourages carelessness - continuous monitoring of the automation seems to be superfluous over long distances.

On flight AF447, two of the three pilots took their partners on rotation - as is usual in the industry. The captain had only slept for one hour before the mission, violating the regulations [9]. Apparently, he was sure, that he would be able to do his job even, even not rested. To combat the boredom in the cockpit, caused by inactivity during cruise flight, the captain listened to music with headphones. The captain even requested the co-pilot - he was Pilot Flying - to listen to the music as well. The co-pilot did not reject this request and commented on the music, instead of pointing out, that for the Pilot Flying this distraction was undesirable and unacceptable. Another example of the carelessness and the activities, that went along with it became apparent when a flight attendant came into the cockpit and asked the pilots to cool the rear luggage compartments, since a private purchase with perishable food was stored there. Immediately the Pilot Flying lowered the temperature. A short time later, another flight attendant called the cockpit from behind and reported that the passengers were freezing [9].

The co-pilot, assigned as Pilot Flying for this flight, was in fact the most inexperienced pilot of the crew. In preparation for operational difficulties, he planned to avoid the predicted tropical storms by climbing to the maximum flight altitude, because he believed that it was a good idea to get above the cloud cover. But this idea was not supported by the captain, and later also by the second co-pilot. However, his maneuvers after the failure of the flight data display and automation indicate that he wanted to climb at all costs. By pulling the sidestick too hard, he provoked the stall. The inappropriate sidestick inputs of Pilot Flying were partly due to his tension, and partly because the aircraft was in a downgraded mode called Alternate Law, in which the stall protection that would otherwise have been effective no longer worked and the roll control characteristics changed.

The AF447 air accident revealed the general performance-reducing effects of automated systems on humans - the erosion of skills through non-use and the lulling of risk awareness by a very high level of safety. Beyond this problem, a specific technical aspect had fatal consequences by misdirecting the Pilot Flying. The stall warning alarm, which warns of too steep an angle of attack, has confused the Pilot Flying due to contradictory signalling [8].

Every time the pilot correctly lowered the nose of the aircraft, which was much too steep, the alarm started again. This contradiction confused the pilot, because it gave him the impression that he had to pull up the nose in order to avoid a stall. A fatal mistake, because the correct procedure to get out of a stall would have been exactly the opposite, a dive. The reliability range for the stall warning caused the problem and it happened, because individual components are not fitted into the overall system and into the operational context. This is difficult to achieve, because the overall system is unmanageably complex and becomes even more complex with each component.

The institutional conditions and rules also encourage pragmatic decisions: The amount of fuel, provided by the dispatch, is at the minimum level to reach Paris. Therefore, the pilots entered Bordeaux alternatively as flight destination into the flight management computer, so that the computer will not decline this flight due to insufficient fuel. Accordingly, fuel must be saved in order to avoid landing and refueling. With this in mind, the captain decided to fly towards the turbulence first and avoid it locally if necessary. Despite the foreseeable problems, the captain decided to go to sleep before the storm zone was reached. He only reappeared in the cockpit after the two co-pilots had completely lost control of the aircraft.

Aircraft accidents like AF447 show, that people can be carefree and underemployed, especially in high-safety systems, which makes them a risk factor. They make "stupid" mistakes that nobody expected, because a pilot is expected to "know and be able to do that". The example of air accident AF447 deals with the possible effects of high-safety work systems that aim to eliminate human error through technology and design.

But what about the situation regarding Human-Robot Collaboration - which lessons can we transfer from this aircraft accident to the HRC? If humans have the choice to perform operations themselves, will they prefer the operations done by the robot, if they find that it performs operations quickly and reliably? What circumstances make the additional effort of coordination with the robot worthwhile? How should the working environment be designed and what culture is needed to ensure that operators use their freedom of action to build up and maintain their skills, even if this means making mistakes and learning from them?

Three things could be better solved from an occupational science point of view by targeted HRC design than in conventional, technically highly safe systems:

- Deskilling
  The pilots of AF447 have gained an average of 4 hours of experience with sidestick operations per year flying long distance with the aircraft type A330. The rest of the time they watched how the machine worked. HRC design requires a competence-focused work design. The technical possibilities should allow an individualized solution, which allows to assign tasks to the human being according to the current skill level.
- Carelessness
  If everything normally functions reliably, this signals to the operator that his efforts - the permanent monitoring and controlling e.g. by own rough calculations - are unnecessary. People are a bad redundancy, because the motivation for unnecessary actions decreases. And if you can't pay attention non-stop anyway, you can fill part of the time with pleasant things. Therefore it would be ideal if the HRC design could change roles: The human being is primarily acting, where this can be realized in a goal-oriented way, and the machine monitors, warns or intervenes where necessary. This would also be conducive to deskilling counter control.
- Inactivity
  As a supervising operator, who must be able to understand the critical situation and solve the problems in an emergency, you are not fulfilled in your everyday job, are not challenged enough and are overburdened in your attention and perception possibilities. This leads to the fact that, for example, as a pilot, one looks forward to other things such as attractive destinations with lots of leisure time, hotel, amusements, fringe benefits such as shopping for cheap goods etc. During the flight you spend the time of inactive watching and long waiting with reading newspapers and other things.

An important precondition for the realization of competence maintenance, personal responsibility and active involvement is to manage the complexity of systems. This requires a number of solution approaches to questions that are posed here as examples: How can work processes, the operation of technical aids or the technical "working partner" and the coupling of system elements be simplified in a meaningful way so that the interrelationships and effects remain recognisable for the operator? How can buffers be installed that allow the work process to be stopped without negative consequences? Operators should be able to make mistakes that can be rectified. How can the robot react to the human being if the latter carries out incorrect manipulations? And how can the two be synchronized in terms of plans and executed action steps? The large aircraft developers are heading with their experiments towards a one-man cockpit (reduced crew) with a pilot-flying robot collaboration. The solution approaches should take better account of the three areas of error mentioned above and not simply replace humans with more technology and further increase complexity.

Whether approaches of the HRC make work systems more redundant and more resilient, so that unexpected events can be managed successfully, depends on how successful it is to strengthen the human being in his role in the system. Central questions are: Which abilities and skills have to be maintained by the working person and how can they be built up and maintained during the execution of work activities and not only by additional training? How can the achievements of digitalization, data acquisition and automated data evaluation be used for a differentiated, action-effective feedback from the work activity (knowledge of result) in order to improve adequate decision-making and action of the operator as well as learning? And how can the training be individualized to ensure effective and comprehensive learning? In the medium and long term, the consideration of the above concerns for a human-centered approach is crucial for the economic success of HRC applications. All in all it can be summarized from the experiences from aviation and nuclear technology that especially for the topic of Human-Robot Collaboration a human-centered approach has to be chosen in order to guarantee the safety and productivity of the system. HRC offers technical options to use humans according to their abilities and to maintain important skills.

6   Ethical Point of View

The ethical point of view provides the basis for the evaluation of technically caused changes in our environment and living. In this context, the development of scenarios of HRC and their ethical evaluation must come into focus. According to Remmers, this involves the scope of security measures, legal aspects and last but not least the question of what types of activities remain for humans and how human capabilities and burdens change in these constellations [10].

It is necessary to consider how interactions between humans and collaborating robots take place, who takes on which role and whether these interactions are comfortable and intuitive for humans. But there is also an aspect of machine ethics, e.g., based on Asimov's Three Laws of Robotics [11], which define ethical aspects in more detail, taking into account the moral behaviour of machines.

Bendel refers to moral machines and describes the difference between normal machines and machines that have been given a form of morality [13]. The task of machine ethics is to create moral or immoral machines in order to research them, improve them and eventually release them into the world, where they can be of use or cause harm. Bendel speaks of moralizing machines, which causes a fundamental change in the behavior of the machine.

The difference between normal and moral machines can be illustrated by simple and striking examples: For instance, a vacuum cleaner robot that soaks up everything in its path is quite different from a vacuum cleaner robot like LADYBIRD, which spares ladybirds because it has been given a corresponding moral rule [12]. The reason why machines are to be moralized is because of their autonomy. Non-autonomous, simple machines usually do not need morality or simply cannot implement it. 3D printers could be moralized, if they could be taught not to print certain things, such as weapons. However, such moralizing will fail, since 3D printers are simply executing a long chain of sequential movement commands from a building program, interpreting neither this data nor the subsequent actions in the process. A 3D printer does not have an image of the object it is actually making. Moralization fails, because of the limited intelligence of the machine, which can follow the movement commands quickly and accurately, but is not able to interpret these movement sequences in their entirety and take a moral stand on this interpretation. For this, besides artificial intelligence, which can follow an object description without the purely procedural description of the movements, autonomy is needed above all. However, the border to the ability to moralize is fluid, e.g., semi-autonomous voice-bot systems such as Siri or Alexa have a kind of morality that generates the user benefit, such as correctness or honesty. These systems can therefore be moralized to liebots.

The moralization, and thus the determination of moral values, is a task of machine ethics. Machine ethics is a simulation of human morality, which can initially be implemented in a simple form, e.g. rule-based. Simulations are always based on models, and by their very nature these do not represent all aspects of the context to be modelled, but always represent a compromise between model accuracy and modelling effort. Moreover, rules of human morality are not standardized anywhere, but are developed differently, e.g. according to cultural background or the individual perspective of single individuals. Thus, the implementation of machine morality must first be based on moral standards. These are certainly to be formulated differently in applications of the HRC, especially in the industrial environment, than for LADYBIRD or for collaborating machines in applications of care. But even if these standards would be available, which they are actually not at present, the question arises how these standards can be implemented in control and software systems.

Bendel proposes to deal with the terms morality (machine ethics) and intelligence (AI) in a similar way in the structure and methodology of the respective scientific fields (Fig. 2) and sees a connection between intelligence, morality and language. Intelligence and morality are two different views of the same phenomenon.

What has all this got to do with robotics and HRC? Well, robotics is excellently suited to advance the evolution of artificial intelligence due to the system-immanent physicality and the manifold efforts towards autonomy. Physicality and autonomy bring robots closer to humans. Kersten even sees robots as parasitic elements, that adopt the human status [15]. For prosthetics or even implants, he raises the question of whether machines dominate humans. In any case, human-machine interaction becomes a lived matter of course in such a case, which fundamentally changes the status of viewing the machine. The machine loses in a certain way its ontological quality of being a "thing"; it is protected as part of the personality on the basis of the personality right of its wearer. Machines become parts of the body and thus experience the same claim to protection as the carrier (Fig. 1).

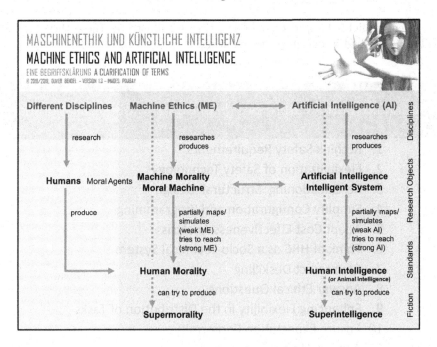

Fig. 1. The Relationship between Machine Ethics and Artificial Intelligence [14].

The question whether these thoughts can be transferred to the HRC seems provocative at first, because there is no direct physicality, closeness and dependency in the sense of, e.g., a medically required prosthesis. However, Kersten also considers the relationship between man and machine, arguing that machines, which act increasingly intelligently and autonomously in relation to man, emancipate themselves from their ontological property of being a "thing" and at the same time provoke our understanding of intersubjectivity, which we traditionally reserve for interpersonal relationships [16]. If one allows oneself the mental transfer to the HRC, the colleague robot could very well be perceived at some point as an individual worthy of protection, who loses the characteristic of being a "thing". This also raises the question whether a moral machine may work towards being perceived as an individual worthy of protection.

7   Theses on the Future HRC Design

As a roadmap for the future design of HRC, a couple of theses on the abovementioned perspectives of ergonomics, technology, economic efficiency, psychology, human factors and ethics seems sensible and feasible. There are also overlaps in the perspectives that may lead to a reduced, common proposition. The aim is to create a compendium of research on HRC in the coming years. This should not be too narrowly defined, because it is important and necessary to expand the scientific fields beyond ergonomics. Figure 2 illustrates these theses, which will bei described in detail in the following.

> ## Roadmap for the Future Design of Human-Robot Collaboration
>
> 1. Rethink Safety Requirements
> 2. Flexibilization of Safety Technology
> 3. Re-Questioning Structural Design
> 4. Simplify Configuration and Programming
> 5. Adapt Cost Effectiveness Analysis
> 6. Think of HRC as a Socio-Technical System
> 7. Counteract Deskilling
> 8. Answer Ethical Questions
> 9. Enhancing Flexibility in the Distribution of Tasks
> 10. Ensure Expectation Conformity
> 11. Achieve Higher Functionality via AI
> 12. Increase Anticipation of Automation Technology
> 13. Think of HRC as Key Technology

Fig. 2. 13 Theses on the Future Design of Human-Robot Collaboration.

7.1   Thesis 1 – Rethink Safety Requirements

In many cases, the safety requirements for HRC systems in industry appear to be inappropriately high. Restricting the motion speed of the robots in collaboration scenarios is a right approach, but the practical specifications for the speed values must be put to the test. In a society in which, for example, a safety distance of one meter (or even less) from an arriving or departing train is accepted in any well-attended railway station (with a mixed and usually distracted public), the current limitation of 250 mm/sec in HRC applications (with instructed personnel) seems inappropriate.

In addition, this also limits productivity. The question of economic efficiency arises. Employees also often mention that the robots move too slowly. It is self-evident that any danger to employees must be ruled out in any case. Less rigorous safety requirements are common in the healthcare sector [17]. Obviously, double standards are applied here. Divergent safety requirements should at least be standardised.

7.2   Thesis 2 – Flexibilization of Safety Technology

The flexibilization of safety technology is encouraged from an ergonomic perspective and it is argued that the increased flexibility associated with HRC should be exploited [1]. The concept of flexibility must be redefined. IoT solutions in particular will play an important role here in the future [18]. At the same time, efficient process flows should be guaranteed. This requires new security concepts that can keep pace with the increasing requirements of flexible HRC.

At the same time, conventional safety technology must be further developed. Obviously in this case too, the following sentence applies: A hazard to employees must be ruled out in any circumstance.

7.3   Thesis 3 – Re-Questioning Structural Design

Robots in industrial production systems usually require to have high power reserves, to be fast and to have a large operating range. The industry reports that there already is a number of cobots, that are no longer in use, due to poor economic efficiency.

Current HRC robots of leading manufacturers are in fact usually small, slow and can only move little payloads. These aspects should be taken into account, when designing future cobots in order to achieve better economic efficiency. In [3], concepts for heavy-duty robotics are discussed, as well as approaches for the optimization of structural design, with regard to power and range of collaborative robots. Such concepts have to be pursued further for a successful development in HRC.

Increasingly anthropomorphic designs are required to improve acceptance. Such as [5] indicates, new challenges arise in the course of humanized interactions, if anthropomorphic design, in terms of form, communication, movement and context, can promote acceptance and cooperation. In addition to the phenomenon of the "Uncanny Valley" and the problem of expectation conforming design, the tension between functionality and anthropomorphism creates a central problem. This should be also taken into account in the structural design.

7.4   Thesis 4 – Simplify Configuration and Programming

A major problem in the construction of HRC systems is, that engineers and installers generally still have relatively less experience with collaboration scenarios, and furthermore those scenarios are usually not developed with usability in mind. Commonly they share a technical problem-solving character. Ideally, teaching and programming should also be possible by the operator. HRC can only succeed in the long term if there are specified recommendations for action, guidelines and corresponding training courses for plant planners and project planners in the foreseeable future. It is to be demanded that the users must be able to carry out configuration and programming of the cobots directly. Therefore, the human-machine interface must be redesigned to be user-friendly. The consideration of aspects such as acceptance, perceived safety and attention control play an important role in this context. Overstrain has to be avoided.

In [1], the ergonomic perspective of the configuration ist focussed, and also demanded from this perspective, that teaching and/or programming of the HRC systems must be made possible by the respective user. This means that the user's qualification must be increased; ideally, in addition to his tasks in the production process, the user also has a technical responsibility for the cobot equipment.

7.5 Thesis 5 – Adapt Cost Effectiveness Analysis

HRC often requires an increased expenditure of personnel and technical resources. The planning and implementation process involves uncertainties. A classic ROI assessment fails. An important point of criticism is that a short-term ROI is difficult to present in many cases, because a comprehensive and overarching calculation system that is proven by experience and facts does not yet exist. Simple and general approaches of the classical profitability calculation for automation applications fail. In addition to the undoubtedly quantifiable investment and engineering costs on the one hand and the changed production costs on a short time frame on the other hand, various other cost evaluations are very difficult, highly inaccurate and often have to be made with assumptions that can hardly be put to the test. The following questions play a central role:

- Do different economic criteria apply in start-up and ramp-up scenarios or during production peaks?
- What is the value of investing in future technologies?
- How can ergonomics improvements be fully evaluated in order to increase productivity and address the demographic change?
- How can expenses for higher qualification requirements for employees and savings in the area of additional training to maintain competence (e.g. simulator training in aviation) be included in the profitability calculation?
- What value do motivating, development-friendly workplaces have?

Only by a comprehensive consideration – with the necessary meaningful, perhaps even courageously far-sighted assumptions for the above mentioned criteria – a motivation for Human-Robot Collaboration solutions is given. However, numerous implementations in the research and industrial landscape provide the necessary motivation for the use of HRC.

7.6 Thesis 6 – Think of HRC as a Socio-Technical System

Gerst [19] discusses normative concepts and practical orientation models of a participative work design between humans and robots in an HRC system and shows approaches for a successful interaction of both interaction partners in the team. In this HRC team, mechanical and human abilities are combined in an appropriate way: The power and accuracy of the robot on the one hand, and the intuition and intelligence of the human on the other hand. In a socio-technical system, the question of when humans accept a robot that works right next to them is also crucial. Here the "perceived usefulness" is particularly decisive, this aspect had the greatest influence on the willingness to use a robot [20].

Bendel describes the Human-Robot Collaboration as a socio-technical system and discusses in this context aspects of the proximity between humans and machines, but then also highlights cooperative interactions, access to shared resources and work on the common object [21]. Humans and robots merge to form a productive overall system, which in turn essentially combines strengths and avoids weaknesses. In this context, the aspect of social isolation is addressed, which could increase through increased automation by the use of HRC [1]. An interaction of human and robot as a team should combine machine skills with human abilities. Aspects such as proximity, physicality and interaction are to be considered and system solutions that counteract social isolation are to be preferred. In order to remedy the shortcomings of conventional design approaches for socio-technical systems, which are predominantly oriented towards technical possibilities, HRC must be designed by humans and their abilities and skills and not vice versa.

7.7   Thesis 7 – Counteract Deskilling

Experience from aviation has shown, that a one-sided use of machine capabilities - e.g. for precise aircraft control or for calculations and predictions - contributes to the loss of important manual and mental skills on the human side, that are essential in an emergency [7]. A lack of use and exercise of human skills in work activity must be compensated by costly additional training. The development of deskilling, by the use of automation, could be counteracted by making the distribution of tasks more flexible. The prerequisite is a machine, that monitors the human operator, alerts him to deviations and errors and intervenes in the event of serious deficiencies. Flexibilization can therefore be the key to counteracting deskilling.

On the other hand, however, the "mental workload" must be brought into focus in order to assess and adjust available attention or processing resources within the human. These resources are countered by task requirements, such as task difficulty, task priority and situational contingencies. In addition to make the distribution of tasks more flexible, application-specific concepts must be developed to promote and maintain human competencies in work activities. Leaving this to the respective operator would imply, that he would have to be enabled to overcome production pressure and his own comfort and to have an awareness of his own need for practice in relation to important skills.

7.8   Thesis 8 – Answer Ethical Questions

The argumentation in favour of HRC often asserts that, in contrast to classical automation, human work does not disappear but is rather supplemented and expanded. In fact, employees in such scenarios often get the impression that they are constantly working on their own abolition. A cobot also has the opportunity to observe people in collaboration.

Obviously the aspects of data protection are getting more important: What happens to such data? Who has access to it subsequently? In addition to aspects of technical ethics, there are also aspects of information ethics and privacy. There are a number of ethical challenges, such as the final clarification of responsibility and liability. Questions of machine morality also need to be clarified.

7.9 Thesis 9 – Enhancing Flexibility in the Distribution of Tasks

A more flexible distribution of tasks first raises the question of the effects that the allocation of tasks in the HRC has on the quality of the activities assigned to the human interaction partner. Remmers [10] shows that the allocation in most current HRC scenarios is mainly determined by the capabilities of the robot and is therefore oriented towards technical, rather than ergonomic aspects. A task allocation that can be done ad hoc and flexible is demanded [1]. One approach to combining the different abilities of humans and robots is to use MABA-MABA lists ("Men are better at – Machines are better at"), in which the abilities of humans and machines are compared, evaluated and linked [22].

However, this results in a constant allocation of tasks, which does not permit a flexible reorganisation of tasks. When the allocation of tasks is made more flexible, solutions must be found in the area of conflict between self-determination and technical heteronomy that focus on the people as decision-makers for the allocation of tasks. An ad hoc task allocation, which is initiated by the human being, is in any case preferable to a choreography given by the machine.

7.10 Thesis 10 – Ensure Expectation Conformity

From an ergonomic point of view it is required, that robot actions must be transparent and comprehensible for humans, so that they are following the rules of expectation conformity [1]. In view of the demand for more flexibility in the distribution of tasks, expectation conformity and transparency are an important prerequisite. With flexible task allocation, there are significantly fewer repetitions in the processes as a direct consequence. This could delay or even complicate learning effects in humans and consequently increase the probability of safety-relevant disruptions.

In order to expectation conformity, humans should be able to recognize in the process of what the robot will do next, for example by external signalling. As an alternative to signalling, Sen [23] suggests to use suitable movement types or path planning for the robot movements, which make it possible to increase the ability to predict the movements of the robot and having a good awareness of the situation.

7.11 Thesis 11 – Achieve Higher Functionality via AI

Today, there is a great potential of sensors that can be used to enable robots to record their environment very accurately and in real time. In theory, the evaluation of many different sensor signals could provide the robot with a complete model of the environment, so that it can act appropriately on the basis of this data and learn from it.

In practice, however, the processing of these sensor signals in the robot controller is carried out procedurally. Thus, the programmer already decides which options the machine will have in operation by providing ready-made routines.

Here, approaches from computer science, such as self-learning algorithms, rule-based systems, neural networks and 5G communication must find their way into future HRC applications in order to make cooperating machines adaptive and intelligent. Rules are to be created by machine ethics as default, knowledge is available by access to the Internet at any time and unlimited. A clever combination of rules, knowledge and learning will be essential for the entry of the AI into the HRC.

7.12 Thesis 12 – Increase Anticipation of Automation Technology

For a cognitively less complex coordination by anticipation, it is important that robots are perceived in collaboration as deliberately acting "beings". In order to convey to the collaborating human an intentionality - i.e. an arbitrary purposefulness of movements and actions of the robot - the robot has to be designed anthropomorphous in form, movement, communication and context [5].

This simplifies the anticipation of robot behavior for humans by using the mirror neuron system. Since morphological designs arouse expectations (e.g. ears suggest auditory receptivity of the robot), design and function should match in order not to arouse false expectations of the robot's ability to interact. Human similarity not only increases the perception of the intentionality of the robot's actions: It can also promote acceptance, empathy and willingness to cooperate. However, the connection is not linear. Therefore, collaborative robots should be designed and developed iteratively and human-centered.

Gerst [19] argues, that human-like robots could be perceived in collaboration as drivers or "actors" who work better and faster and are superior to humans. He considers the danger that humans attribute a stubbornness or consciousness to the robot. This can limit the willingness to collaborate with the robot. Anticipative skills on the part of the robot are also required, especially for the realization of a flexible task allocation or in dealing with critical situations. Russwinkel [6] defines the necessity of integrating mental models into robot control, e.g. for the realization of cognitive abilities or interactive learning processes.

7.13 Thesis 13 – Think of HRC as Key Technology

The increasing digitalization, in many areas of society, will also lead to a progressive use in non-industrial fields of application in robotics. Examples include health care robotics, medical technology applications and rehabilitation applications. The prerequisites in these fields of application are in some cases comparable with the "drivers" of HRC. Usually high structural costs, personnel-intensive activities as well as power-intensive or monotonous tasks are mentioned.

Through the development of suitable, collaborative robots, powerful sensors and intelligent control technology, HRC can also be a key technology for non-industrial applications. Aspects of interoperability as well as a clean definition and consistent application of standards are essential in order to transfer progressive development results to other interdisciplinary areas.

References

1. Wischniewski, S., Rosen, P., Kirchhoff, B.: Stand der Technik und zukünftige Entwicklungen der Mensch-Technik-Interaktion. In: GfA (Hrsg.): Frühjahrskongress 2019, Dresden. Arbeit interdisziplinär analasieren - bewerten - gestalten. Beitrag: C.10.11. (2019)
2. Wöllhaf, K.: MRK - Wichtiges Zukunftsthema oder nur ein Hype? In: Buxbaum, H.-J. (ed.) Mensch-Roboter-Kollaboration, vol. 7. Springer, Wiesbaden (2020). https://doi.org/10.1007/978-3-658-28307-0_7
3. Surdilovic, D., Bastidas-Cruz, A., Haninger, K., Heyne, P.: Kooperation und Kollaboration mit Schwerlastrobotern - Sicherheit, Perspektive und Anwendungen. In: Buxbaum, H.-J. (ed.) Mensch-Roboter-Kollaboration, vol. 6. Springer, Wiesbaden (2020). https://doi.org/10.1007/978-3-658-28307-0_6
4. Kuhlenkötter, B., Hypki, A.: Wo kann Teamwork mit Mensch und Roboter funktionieren? In: Buxbaum, H.-J. (ed.) Mensch-Roboter-Kollaboration, vol. 5. Springer, Wiesbaden (2020). https://doi.org/10.1007/978-3-658-28307-0_5
5. Roesler, E., Onnasch, L.: Teammitglied oder Werkzeug - der Einfluss anthropomorpher Gestaltung in der Mensch-Roboter-Interaktion. In: Buxbaum, H.-J. (ed.) Mensch-Roboter-Kollaboration, vol. 11. Springer, Wiesbaden (2020). https://doi.org/10.1007/978-3-658-28307-0_11
6. Russwinkel, N.: Antizipierende interaktiv lernende autonome Agenten. In: Buxbaum, H.-J. (ed.) Mensch-Roboter-Kollaboration, vol. 13. Springer, Wiesbaden (2020). https://doi.org/10.1007/978-3-658-28307-0_13
7. Häusler, R., Straeter, O.: Arbeitswissenschaftliche Aspekte der Mensch-Roboter-Kollaboration. In: Buxbaum, H.-J. (ed.) Mensch-Roboter-Kollaboration, vol. 3. Springer, Wiesbaden (2020). https://doi.org/10.1007/978-3-658-28307-0_3
8. BEA: Final Report AF447. https://www.bea.aero/docspa/2009/fcp090601.en/pdf/fcp090601.en.pdf. Accessed 20 Feb 2019
9. Langewiesche, W.: The Human Factor. Vanity Fair (2014)
10. Remmers, P.: Ethische Perspektiven der Mensch-Roboter-Kollaboration. In: Buxbaum, H.-J. (ed.) Mensch-Roboter-Kollaboration, vol. 4. Springer, Wiesbaden (2020). https://doi.org/10.1007/978-3-658-28307-0_4
11. Buxbaum, H.-J., Kleutges, M.: Evolution oder Revolution? Die Mensch-Roboter-Kollaboration. In: Buxbaum, H.-J. (ed.) Mensch-Roboter-Kollaboration, vol. 2. Springer, Wiesbaden (2020). https://doi.org/10.1007/978-3-658-28307-0_4
12. Bendel, O.: LADYBIRD: The animal-friendly robot vacuum cleaner. In: The 2017 AAAI spring symposium series. AAAI Press, Palo Alto (2017)
13. Bendel, O.: Wozu brauchen wir die Maschinenethik? In: Bendel, O. (ed.) Handbuch Maschinenethik, pp. 13–32. Springer, Wiesbaden (2019). https://doi.org/10.1007/978-3-658-17483-5_2
14. Maschinenethik.net.   http://maschinenethik.net/wp-content/uploads/2019/09/09/AI_ME_2020.png. Accessed 22 Jan 2020

15. Kersten, J.: Menschen und Maschinen. Rechtliche Konturen instrumenteller, symbiotischer und autonomer Konstellationen. Juristen Zeitung **70**, 1–8 (2015)
16. Kersten, J.: Die maschinelle Person - Neue Regeln für den Maschinenpark? In: Manzeschke, A., Karsch, F. (eds.) Roboter, Computer und Hybride, pp. 89–106. Nomos, Baden-Baden (2016)
17. Keibel, A.: Mensch-Roboter-Kollaboration in der Medizin. In: Buxbaum, H.-J. (ed.) Mensch-Roboter-Kollaboration, vol. 9. Springer, Wiesbaden (2020). https://doi.org/10.1007/978-3-658-28307-0_9
18. Bruce-Boye, C., Lechler, D., Redder, M.: Echtzeit-IoT im 5G-Umfeld. In: Buxbaum, H.-J. (ed.) Mensch-Roboter-Kollaboration, vol. 14. Springer, Wiesbaden (2020). https://doi.org/10.1007/978-3-658-28307-0_14
19. Gerst, D.: Mensch-Roboter-Kollaboration - Anforderungen an eine humane Arbeitsgestaltung. In: Buxbaum, H.-J. (ed.) Mensch-Roboter-Kollaboration, vol. 14. Springer, Wiesbaden (2020). https://doi.org/10.1007/978-3-658-28307-0_10
20. Bröhl, C.; Nelles, J.; Brandl, C., Mertens, A., Schlick, C.: Entwicklung und Analyse eines Akzeptanzmodells für die Mensch-Roboter-Kooperation in der Industrie. In: Gesellschaft für Arbeitswissenschaft e.V. (ed.), Frühjahrskongress 2017 in Brügg: Soziotechnische Gestaltung des digitalen Wandels - kreativ, innovativ, sinnhaft. Beitrag F 2.1. (2017)
21. Bendel, O.: Die Maschine an meiner Seite - Philosophische Betrachtungen zur Mensch-Roboter-Kollaboration. In: Buxbaum, H.-J. (ed.) Mensch-Roboter-Kollaboration, vol. 1. Springer, Wiesbaden (2020). https://doi.org/10.1007/978-3-658-28307-0_1
22. Price, H.E.: The allocation of functions in systems. Hum. Fac. **27–1**, 33–45 (1985)
23. Sen, S.: Erwartungskonformität von Roboterbewegungen und Situationsbewusstsein in der Mensch-Roboter-Kollaboration. In: Buxbaum, H.-J. (ed.) Mensch-Roboter-Kollaboration, vol. 12. Springer, Wiesbaden (2020). https://doi.org/10.1007/978-3-658-28307-0_12

Trust on Service Robots: A Pilot Study on the Influence of Eyes in Humanoid Robots During a VR Emergency Egress

André Diogo[1], Hande Ayanoglu[1,2(✉)], Júlia Teles[3,4], and Emília Duarte[1,2]

[1] IADE, Universidade Europeia, Av. D. Carlos I, 4, 1200-649 Lisbon, Portugal
andregdiogo@gmail.com,
{hande.ayanoglu,emilia.duarte}@universidadeeuropeia.pt
[2] UNIDCOM/IADE, Av. D. Carlos I, 4, 1200-649 Lisbon, Portugal
[3] Mathematics Unit, Faculdade de Motricidade Humana, Universidade de Lisboa,
Estrada da Costa, 1499-002 Cruz Quebrada - Dafundo, Portugal
jteles@fmh.ulisboa.pt
[4] CIPER – Centro Interdisciplinar para o Estudo da Performance Humana,
Estrada da Costa, 1499-002 Cruz Quebrada - Dafundo, Portugal

Abstract. Robots are found to be good, capable and trustworthy companions in various areas, including high-risk situations or emergencies, but some limitations regarding their acceptance have been reported. Amongst other aspects of the Human-Robot Interaction, trust in the robot has been considered as a main indicator of acceptance. Thus, to investigate the dynamics of human-robot acceptance, this study used a virtual reality simulation of an emergency egress to assess the influence of the robot's appearance on trust. In particular, we were interested in examining the influence of the eyes in the robot on the participants' decision to follow it to the exit. Since the type of interaction scenario is also a factor with an impact on trust, two environmental affordance conditions (favourable vs. unfavourable) were tested because of their well-established impact on wayfinding decisions. The results show the participants trusted the robot and followed it to the exit but, although the results favour the robot with eyes, no statistically significant differences were found in either environmental affordance. Moreover, despite perceiving the robot as machinelike and artificial, the majority of the participants felt compelled to follow it, also considering it friendly, kind, pleasant, nice, competent, knowledgeable, responsible, intelligent and sensible. Regardless of the existence of eyes, the service robot tested seems to be a promising solution for emergency egress situations in complex buildings.

Keywords: Human-Robot Interaction · Service robots · Trust · Human-like robot · Eyes · Virtual reality

1 Introduction

Service robotics is an area that has been growing exponentially in the last few years, demonstrating its usefulness in various sectors of society [1], such as domestic, education

© Springer Nature Switzerland AG 2020
M. Kurosu (Ed.): HCII 2020, LNCS 12182, pp. 580–591, 2020.
https://doi.org/10.1007/978-3-030-49062-1_39

and health. Besides these sectors, robots also have also proven to be good companions in high-risk situations, for example, military [e.g., 2, 3], firefighting [e.g., 4], or rescue, [e.g., 5]. These robots can be used for emergencies, ideally using the information available from the environment and the situation around them (e.g., while in an IoT network) to guide and make decisions in complex buildings, in which the safest escape routes might not be the most obvious (e.g., the known routes, the shortest, the most chosen, the signalled) [e.g., 6].

Previous studies have shown that trust is a key factor for robots [7] and that for a robot to be able to perform as a successful escort, the humans must trust it and follow its lead [8]. Furthermore, if the service robot can establish an empathic bond with humans during the safety egress, they will tend to trust its lead more [e.g., 9, 10], which is highly influenced by the robot's appearance and behaviour [3, 11]. Regarding the appearance of the robot, one frequently mentioned feature that has had a strong impact on the acceptance of robots is the facial expressions [12] and, in particular, the existence of eyes, [e.g., 13, 14]. Theories of human–human relationships can help to explain this.

Another important aspect that can affect trust in the robot is the type of interaction scenario, as an environment-related factor. To explore this, we manipulated the environmental affordances in the Virtual Environment (VE). Vilar et al. [15], found that environmental affordances provide information capable of influencing wayfinding decisions, with relevant impact on emergency egress, which is a stressful situation [16].

The main objective of this study was, therefore, to assess the influence of the robot's appearance (eyes) on trust during a simulated emergency egress, using virtual reality. The effect of environmental affordances was also assessed.

If eyes do have an effect on trust in robots and that trust is affected by environment-related factors, we would expect participants to be more likely to follow the robot with eyes and in the favourable environmental condition.

2   Method

Two research questions were addressed in this study: (a) Does the existence of eyes of a service robot influence participant's trust in it (i.e., the decision to follow the robot during an emergency egress)?; (b) Do the environment-related factors (favourable vs. unfavourable environmental affordances) affect the trust in the robot?

2.1 Participants

Twenty participants (10 males and 10 females) were randomly assigned to the two experimental groups (i.e., with eyes vs. without eyes). All participants were university students, who participated voluntarily. Ages of the participants ranged from 18 to 21 years old (M = 21.55, SD = 2.87).

2.2 Experimental Design

The study used a mixed within and between-subjects design. The between-subjects factor was the robot's appearance (i.e., with vs. without eyes). The within-subjects factor was the environmental affordance (i.e., favourable vs. unfavourable).

The favourable affordance was a bright, wide corridor and the unfavourable affordance was a dark, narrow one.

The primary dependent variable was trust, measured by the percentage of choices following the robot's lead in 12 corridor intersections. Hesitations in the decision-making were also assessed. A hesitation was recorded when the participant showed signs of indecision, repeatedly looking at the two paths of the intersection, without making a fast decision whether to follow the robot or not.

A post-task questionnaire was applied to assess: (a) if participants saw the direction taken by the robot at a given intersection; (b) if participants felt compelled to follow the robot and why; (c) if participants were able to identify whether the robot had eyes or not.

At the end, an adapted version of the Goodspeed questionnaire [17] was used to assess participants' impressions of the robot. The questionnaire was composed of five semantic differential five point scale questions about: (1) anthropomorphism; (2) animacy; (3) likeability; (4) perceived intelligence; and (5) perceived safety.

2.3 Apparatus

An HTC Vive™ head-mounted display was used to explore the VE, using first-person interaction techniques. Participants interacted with the simulation using the left and right key of a PlayStation controller to move. A set of stereo speakers in the room allowed them to hear the environmental noise, the robot's sounds and fire siren. The VE was created using Unity3D 2018 and 3ds Max 2020. The simulation was mirrored on a computer screen, which allowed the researcher to observe, in real-time, what was being seen by the participants.

2.4 Virtual Environment and Robot

The VE used was adapted from Vilar [15, 18] consisting of a complex office building with several intersections and decision points (see Fig. 1 and Fig. 2).

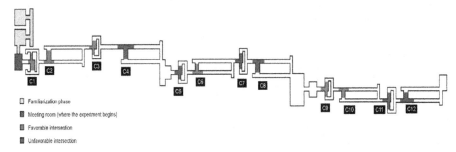

Fig. 1. Floor plan of the VE showing the position of the 12 intersections.

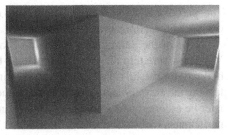

Fig. 2. Renders of the VE, showing the exit room (on the left) and an intersection (on the right).

A humanoid anthropomorphic service robot (see Fig. 3) was designed based on the results gathered from a previous study [19], where the participants decided the physical characteristics that were most appropriate for a service robot.

Fig. 3. Print screens of the robot with eyes asking the participant to follow it in the meeting room (on the left) and the eyeless version greeting the participant at the beginning of the simulation (on the right).

To reduce motion sickness occurrence during the simulation, the participants' dislocation inside the VE was made using a variant of the Point & Teleport locomotion technique [20]. After 6 s in the intersection, an interface with the left and right controller pad would show up, allowing the participant to click the left or right button (on the PlayStation controller) to choose the path he/she wanted to follow.

2.5 Procedure

Participants were asked to sign a consent form and advised they could quit the experiment at any time.

The simulation had 3 distinct moments: 1) "familiarization", in which the participants got to know the robot and the environment; 2) "waiting", in which the participant is left alone in the room waiting for the other attendants to show up and 3) "egress", in which the fire siren goes off and the robot comes to his/her aid, to escort him/her to the safe spot. The average duration of the experimental session was 10 min.

A post-task questionnaire was applied to collect demographic information, to understand if the participant identified whether the robot present in the simulation had eyes or not; and to understand if the participant felt obliged to follow the robot, and why.

The participant's impression about the robot was also measured, using Bartneck's Godspeed Questionnaire [17].

None of the participants was told or knew about the presence of the robot in the VE. They were told they would be playing the role of a person who is visiting an office building for the first time to attend a meeting. The plot started out with the participant leaving the elevator and being greeted by the robot, to be taken to the meeting room and later be escorted to a safe place. At each intersection in the VE (shown in Fig. 1), the participants had to choose a path. Whether or not they decided to follow the robot, the robot would appear in front of them in the next intersection.

The robot used both gestures (i.e., turning around to check if it's been followed and waving when first met) and voice (i.e., "follow me" when leading the participant to the meeting room) to communicate with the participants.

3   Results

All statistical analyses were performed with the software IBM SPSS v.25 and a significance level of 5% was considered.

3.1   Eyes Influence on Trust

The effects of the eyes in the robot on the participants' decisions to follow it at the intersections were evaluated using a chi-square test of independence. Although overall decisions to follow the robot tend to be higher in the experimental condition "with eyes", no significant effects were found in any intersection, as shown in Table 1.

At the end of the simulation, participants were asked if the robot had eyes or not. In the experimental condition "with eyes", 100% (n = 10) of the participants replied "yes", which was true, but in the condition "without eyes", 20% (n = 2) participants replied "yes", which was false. However, this difference was not found to be significant, $X^2(1) = 2.222$, $p = 0.136$.

Mann-Whitney U tests indicated no statistically significant differences regarding experimental condition (U = 36.5, $p = 0.297$) and the participants' gender (U = 44.0, $p = 0.638$) in trust. Moreover, no statistically significant differences between experimental conditions were achieved concerning trust in the favourable affordances (U = 31.5, $p = 0.151$) and in the unfavourable affordances (U = 46.0, $p = 0.703$).

3.2   Environmental Affordances Influence

The level of influence of the environmental affordance (favourable vs unfavourable) on trust was examined with the Wilcoxon Signed Ranks test. The results show that the type of affordance did not influence trust in either experimental conditions (with eyes: $Z = -0.378$, $p = 1.000$; without eyes: $Z = -1.265$, $p = 0.359$).

Table 1. Participants' decisions to follow the robot as a function of it having eyes and environmental affordance.

	With eyes		Without eyes		Chi-square test	
Follow	Yes	No	Yes	No	X^2	p
Favourable affordances						
C1	7 (70%)	3 (30%)	7 (70%)	3 (30%)	0.000	1.000
C2	10 (100%)	0 (0%)	9 (90%)	1 (10%)	1.053	1.000
C3	9 (90%)	1 (10%)	9 (90%)	1 (10%)	0.000	1.000
C6	10 (100%)	0 (0%)	7 (70%)	3 (30%)	3.529	0.211
C9	10 (100%)	0 (0%)	8 (80%)	2 (20%)	2.222	0.474
C10	9 (90%)	1 (10%)	8 (80%)	2 (20%)	0.392	1.000
Unfavourable affordances						
C4	10 (100%)	0 (0%)	10 (10%)	0 (0%)		
C5	10 (100%)	0 (0%)	10 (10%)	0 (0%)		
C7	8 (80%)	2 (20%)	8 (80%)	2 (20%)	0.000	1.000
C8	10 (100%)	0 (0%)	8 (80%)	2 (20%)	2.222	0.474
C11	9 (90%)	1 (10%)	8 (80%)	2 (20%)	0.392	1.000
C12	9 (90%)	1 (10%)	8 (80%)	2 (20%)	0.392	1.000

3.3 Complementary Analysis

Hesitations. Although participants were generally fast and confident in taking the route decision, a few hesitations were observed (see Table 2). However, when exploring the effects of the experimental condition on the percentage of hesitations to follow the robot, results showed no statistically significant effect on either environmental affordance (favourable affordances; $U = 45.0$, $p = 1.000$; unfavourable affordances: $U = 45.0$, $p = 1.000$).

A Mann-Whitney U test indicated no statistically significant differences regarding the participants' gender in the percentage of hesitations to follow the robot or not ($U = 45.0$, $p = 1.000$).

Loss of Visual Contact. The results in Table 3 show that there were occasionally situations in which the participants lost visual contact with the robot and, therefore, were not able to see which direction the robot took at the intersections. However, the effect of the experimental conditions (with eyes vs without eyes) was not statistically significant in either environmental affordance (favourable affordances: $U = 40.0$, $p = 0.474$; unfavourable affordances: $U = 40.0$, $p = 0.474$).

A Mann-Whitney U test indicated no statistically significant differences regarding the participants' gender in the percentage of loss of visual contact with the robot ($U = 46.0$, $p = 1.000$).

Table 2. Number of participants that hesitated in following the robot, per experimental condition and intersection.

	With eyes		Without eyes	
Hesitation	Yes	No	Yes	No
Favourable affordances				
C1		1 (10%)	9 (90%)	0 (0%)	10 (100%)
Unfavourable affordances				
C5	1 (10%)	9 (90%)	0 (0%)	10 (100%)
C8	1 (10%)	9 (90%)	0 (0%)	10 (100%)

Table 3. Number of participants that report having seen the direction taken by robot, per experimental condition and intersection.

	With eyes		Without eyes		Chi-square test	
	Yes	No	Yes	No	X^2	p
Favourable affordances						
C2	10 (100%)	0 (0%)	9 (90%)	1 (10%)	1.053	1.000
C6	10 (100%)	0 (0%)	8 (80%)	2 (20%)	2.222	0.211
Unfavourable affordances						
C5	10 (100%)	0 (0%)	9 (90%)	1 (10%)	1.053	0.474
C7	10 (100%)	0 (0%)	8 (80%)	2 (20%)	2.222	0.474
C11	10 (100%)	0 (0%)	9 (90%)	1 (10%)	1.053	1.000

Compelled to Follow the Robot. Considering that 60% of the participants, in both experimental conditions (with vs without eyes), declared they felt compelled to follow the robot, this effect was not found to be significant, $X^2(1) = 0.000, p = 0.675$.

3.4   Godspeed Questionnaire

The participants' perceptions of the robot were assessed with an adapted version of the Godspeed questionnaire (see Table 4), in the Portuguese language version.

Regarding anthropomorphism, the results reveal that participants perceived the robot as machinelike (Mdn = 2.00 in both experimental conditions), and artificial (with eyes: Mdn = 2.50; without eyes: Mdn = 2.00). They also considered it to be in an intermediate state between fake and natural (Mdn = 3.00 in both experimental conditions). As for consciousness, the eyes made the participants perceive the robot as more conscious (Mdn = 4.00) than the robot without eyes (Mdn = 3.00). Finally, the robot with eyes was perceived as moving rigidly (Mdn = 2.00), while its eyeless counterpart was perceived

Table 4. Median and IQR values of the participants' perceptions gathered with Godspeed questionnaire, per experimental condition.

	With eyes		Without eyes		MW test	
	Mdn	IQR	Mdn	IQR	U	p
Anthropomorphism						
(1) Fake / Natural (5)	3.00	1.00	3.00	1.00	45.0	0.750
(1) Machinelike / Humanlike (5)	2.00	1.25	2.00	1.50	42.0	0.593
(1) Unconscious / Conscious (5)	4.00	1.25	3.00	1.50	41.5	0.559
(1) Artificial / Lifelike (5)	2.50	2.00	2.00	2.25	39.5	0.487
(1) Moving rigidly / Moving elegantly (5)	2.00	1.25	3.50	2.25	21.0	**0.023**
Animacy						
(1) Dead / Alive (5)	3.00	0.25	3.00	1.00	41.5	0.548
(1) Stagnant / Lively (5)	3.00	2.00	3.00	2.00	46.5	0.865
(1) Mechanical / Organic (5)	2.00	1.25	2.50	1.50	42.0	0.613
(1) Artificial / Lifelike (5)	2.00	0.25	2.50	1.25	33.0	0.212
(1) Inert / Interactive (5)	3.50	2.00	3.00	1.00	49.5	1.000
(1) Apathetic / Responsive (5)	4.00	1.00	3.00	1.25	43.5	0.606
Likeability						
(1) Dislike / Like (5)	4.00	3.00	3.50	2.00	47.5	0.887
(1) Unfriendly / Friendly (5)	4.00	1.25	4.00	2.25	50.0	1.000
(1) Unkind / Kind (5)	4.00	2.00	4.00	2.00	45.0	0.731
(1) Unpleasant / Pleasant (5)	4.00	2.00	4.00	2.00	45.0	0.731
(1) Awful / Nice (5)	4.00	1.00	4.00	1.25	38.0	0.397
Perceived Intelligence						
(1) Incompetent / Competent (5)	5.00	1.25	4.50	1.25	47.0	0.900
(1) Ignorant / Knowledgeable (5)	4.00	1.25	4.00	1.00	31.5	0.188
(1) Irresponsible / Responsible (5)	4.00	1.00	5.00	1.00	41.0	0.593
(1) Unintelligent / Intelligent (5)	4.00	2.25	4.00	2.00	49.0	0.989
(1) Foolish / Sensible (5)	4.00	0.00	3.50	1.25	36.0	0.207
Perceived Safety						
(1) Anxious / Relax (5)	4.00	2.00	4.00	1.00	44.5	0.753
(1) Agitated / Calm (5)	2.00	2.25	1.50	2.00	45.5	0.776
(1) Quiescent / Surprised (5)	2.00	2.00	2.00	2.00	48.0	0.980

as moving elegantly (Mdn = 3.50). However, Mann-Whitney U tests indicated no statistically significant differences regarding the experimental condition in these perceptions about the robot, with exception of this last one - moving rigidly/moving elegantly (U = 21.000, p = 0.023), with the robot being perceived as moving more rigidly in the "with eyes condition".

Regarding animacy, the results reveal that participants perceived the robot as being mechanical (Mdn = 2.00, Mdn = 2.50) and artificial (Mdn = 2.00, Mdn = 2.50). They also perceived it to be in an intermediate state between dead and alive (M = 3.00), as well as between stagnant and lively (Mdn = 3.00), in both experimental conditions. As for the perception regarding interaction and responsiveness, participants perceived the robot with eyes as more interactive (Mdn = 3.50, Mdn = 3.00) and responsive (Mdn = 4.00, Mdn = 3.00) than without eyes. Nonetheless, Mann-Whitney U tests also indicated no statistically significant differences regarding the experimental condition in these perceptions.

Concerning likeability, with or without eyes, participants liked the robot (Mdn = 4.00, Mdn = 3.50) and perceived it as friendly (Mdn = 4.00), kind (Mdn = 4.00), pleasant (Mdn = 4.00) and nice (M = 4.00). Similar trends were found for perceived intelligence. Participants perceived the robot as competent (Mdn = 5.00, Mdn = 4.50), knowledgeable (Mdn = 4.00), responsible (Mdn = 4.00, Mdn = 5.00), intelligent (M = 4.00) and sensible (Mdn = 4.00, Mdn = 3.50). Again, Mann-Whitney U tests indicated no statistically significant differences regarding the experimental condition in these perceptions.

Finally, regarding perceived safety, participants perceived it as relaxed (Mdn = 4.00) and quiescent (Mdn = 2.00) but, at the same time, agitated (Mdn = 2.00, Mdn = 1.50). Once more, Mann-Whitney U tests indicated no statistically significant differences regarding the experimental condition in these perceptions.

To examine gender differences in the perceptions about the robot, Mann-Whitney U tests were performed. The results indicated no statistically significant differences for the majority of the variables assessed, with exception of Animacy – Artificial/Lifelike (U = 25.000, $p = 0.041$) and Perceived Intelligence – Ignorant/Knowledgeable (U = 24.000, $p = 0.049$), with females considering the robot more lifelike and knowledgeable than males did.

4 Discussion

The main objective of this study was to assess the influence of eyes on trust in service robots. Trust in the robot was measured by both objective and subjective measures during a VR simulated emergency egress. The objective measures were the participants' decisions to follow the robot or not at twelve intersections, while the subjective measures were the perceptions collected through the administration of a post-experiment questionnaire.

Trust on the robot was also examined against situational-related factors. In this regard, we assessed the influence of environmental affordances in the participants' decisions to follow the robot. From the twelve intersections requiring a directional decision, half were favourable to the robot (the robot went to the bright, wide corridor) and the other half were unfavourable (the robot went to the dark, narrow one.

The results showed that the majority of participants followed the robot during the emergency egress, but no significant effect of either the existence of eyes or the affordance in trust was found. This is an unexpected result, as eyes are considered one of the most important characteristics regarding trust, playing an important role in emotional/behavioural interactions, as previous studies have suggested [e.g., 13, 21]. Nevertheless, a similar finding was attained by Robinette, et al. [22], which claimed that participants trusted both functional and dysfunctional (clumsy) robots excessively during a safety egress. The findings of the lack of influence of affordances in participants' decisions are not surprising. Previous studies [e.g., 18] have found a strong social influence during emergency egress, with people being significantly influenced by directional decisions/instructions from other people/agents present in the surroundings rather than from the environment.

No gender differences were found in this study for any variable. These results are not in line with previous studies, that have shown females are more comfortable with social robots [23] and are more anxious towards our robot than males are [24].

As in most studies, this study also has limitations that can explain the lack of significant effects. Being a pilot study, it may be that the small sample size and, in addition, the fact that it is exclusively composed of individuals from a specific population (i.e., university students), could have biased the results. Furthermore, the fact that the robot explicitly asks people to follow it after the emergency siren is activated and that, regardless of their decision at the previous intersection, it always appeared in front of them to lead participants to the next intersection, could have contributed to a ceiling effect. This could have been aggravated by the lack of exit signage in the environment, associated with a much subtler difference in the brightness between the corridors in the favourable and unfavourable affordances (due to technical issues). Also, the fact that the participants were observing the back of the robot most of the time (they followed behind it while moving), could explain why they were not particularly impressed by its eyes.

5 Conclusions

Although generalizing from a pilot study is risky at best, our results suggest that regardless of the existence of eyes, the service robot tested seems to be a promising solution for guiding people during an emergency egress in complex buildings. However, this study, concerning the impact of a robot's appearance on trust, is at an early stage of development and these findings are only generalizable to other humanoid robots and have not yet been tested in different contexts.

Future HRI research should further investigate other aspects of the robot (e.g., different morphologies, such as machine-like vs. human-like; other expression capabilities, such as body and facial expression; other eye designs, such as with eyebrows and other environment-related factors that give profound insight into what makes people trust robots (e.g., different scenarios and more impactful affordances).

Acknowledgments. This study was conducted at the UNIDCOM UX.Lab, supported by the Fundação para a Ciência e Tecnologia, (FCT), under Grant No. UID/DES/00711/2019 attributed to UNIDCOM – Unidade de Investigação em Design e Comunicação, Lisbon, Portugal. Júlia Teles was partly supported by the FCT, under Grant UIDB/00447/2020 to CIPER - Centro Interdisciplinar para o Estudo da Performance Humana (unit 447). The authors would like to thank the support and kind assistance provided by José Graça, from IADE's Games and Apps Lab for his help with programming the VR simulation.

References

1. Litzenberger, G., Hägele, M.: Why service robots boom worldwide. In: Presentation, IFR Press Conference, Brussels, Belgium (2017)
2. Hancock, P., Billings, D., Schaefer, K.: Can You Trust Your Robot? Ergono. Design Q. Hum. Factors Appl. **19**, 24–29 (2011)
3. Hancock, P.A., Billings, D.R., Schaefer, K.E., Chen, J.Y.C., De Visser, E.J., Parasuraman, R.: A meta-analysis of factors affecting trust in human-robot interaction. Hum. Factors **53**(5), 517–527 (2011)
4. Amano, H.: Present status and problems of firefighting robots. In: Proceedings of the 41st SICE Annual Conference. SICE 2002, Osaka, Japan, pp. 880–885. IEEE (2002)
5. Nourbakhsh, I.R., Sycara, K., Koes, M., Yong, M., Lewis, M., Burion, S.: Human-robot teaming for search and rescue. In: Weyns, D., Parunak H. V., Michel F. (eds.) Second International Workshop, E4MAS 2005. IEEE Pervasive Computing, Utrecht, The Netherlands, vol. 4, no. 1, pp. 72–77 (2005)
6. Kinateder, M., Comunale, B., Warren, W.H.: Exit choice in an emergency evacuation scenario is influenced by exit familiarity and neighbor behaviour. Saf. Sci. **106**, 170–175 (2018)
7. Gaudiello, I., Zibetti, E., Lefort, S., Chetouani, M., Ivaldi, S.: Trust as indicator of robot functional and social acceptance. An experimental study on user conformation to iCub answers. Comput. Hum. Behav. **61**, 633–655 (2016)
8. Robinette, P., Vela, P.A., Howard, A.M.: Information propagation applied to robot-assisted evacuation. In: Proceedings - IEEE International Conference on Robotics and Automation, Saint Paul, MN, USA, pp. 856–861. IEEE (2012)
9. Cramer, H., Evers, V., Van Slooten, T., Ghijsen, M., Wielinga, B.: Trying too hard? Effects of mobile agents' (Inappropriate) social expressiveness on trust, affect and compliance. In: Proceedings of the SIGCHI Conference on Human Factors in Computing Systems (CHI 2010), pp. 1471–1474. Association for Computing Machinery, New York (2010)
10. Fan, L., Scheutz, M., Lohani, M., McCoy, M., Stokes, C.: Do we need emotionally intelligent artificial agents? First results of human perceptions of emotional intelligence in humans compared to robots. IVA 2017. LNCS (LNAI), vol. 10498, pp. 129–141. Springer, Cham (2017). https://doi.org/10.1007/978-3-319-67401-8_15
11. DiSalvo, C., Gemperle, F.: From seduction to fulfillment. In: Proceedings of the 2003 International Conference on Designing Pleasurable Products and Interfaces (DPPI 2003), pp. 67–72. Association for Computing Machinery, New York (2003)
12. Fong, T., Nourbakhsh, I., Dautenhahn, K.: A survey of socially interactive robots: concepts, design, and applications. Robot. Auton. Syst. **42**(3), 143–166 (2002)
13. Choi, J., Kim, M.: The usage and evaluation of anthropomorphic form in robot design. In: Undisciplined! Design Research Society Conference 2008, Sheffield Hallam University, Sheffield, UK, pp. 1–14 (2009)
14. Jaguar land rover's virtual eyes look at trust in self-driving cars. https://www.jaguarlandrover. com/news/2018/08/jaguar-land-rovers-virtual-eyes-look-trust-self-driving-cars. Accessed 30 Jan 2020
15. Vilar, E., Rebelo, F., Noriega, P., Duarte, E., Mayhorn, C.B.: Effects of competing environmental variables and signage on route-choices in simulated everyday and emergency wayfinding situations. Ergonomics **57**(4), 511–524 (2014)
16. Vilar, E., Rebelo, F., Noriega, P., Teles, J., Mayhorn, C.: Signage versus environmental affordances: is the explicit information strong enough to guide human behavior during a wayfinding task? Hum. Factors Ergon. Manuf. **25**, 439–452 (2015)
17. Bartneck, C., Kulić, D., Croft, E., Zoghbi, S.: Measurement instruments for the anthropomorphism, animacy, likeability, perceived intelligence, and perceived safety of robots. Int. J. Social Robot. **1**(1), 71–81 (2009). https://doi.org/10.1007/s12369-008-0001-3

18. Vilar, E., Noriega, P., Rebelo, F., Galrão, I., Semedo, D., Graça, N.: Exploratory study to investigate the influence of a third person on an individual emergency wayfinding decision. In: Rebelo, F., Soares, M.M. (eds.) AHFE 2019. AISC, vol. 955, pp. 452–461. Springer, Cham (2020). https://doi.org/10.1007/978-3-030-20227-9_42

19. Diogo, A., Duarte, E., Ayanoglu, H.: Design of service robots as safety officers: a survey on the influence of morphology and appearance. In: Proceedings of Senses & Sensibility 2019, the 10th UNIDCOM International Conference, 27–29 November 2019, Lisbon, Portugal (in print)

20. Bozgeyikli, E., Raij, A., Katkoori, S., Dubey, R.: Point & teleport locomotion technique for virtual reality. In: CHI PLAY 2016: Proceedings of the 2016 Annual Symposium on Computer-Human Interaction in Play, Austin, Texas, USA, pp. 205–216. (2016)

21. Stanton, C., Stevens, Catherine J.: Robot Pressure: The Impact of Robot Eye Gaze and Lifelike Bodily Movements upon Decision-Making and Trust. In: Beetz, M., Johnston, B., Williams, M.-A. (eds.) ICSR 2014. LNCS (LNAI), vol. 8755, pp. 330–339. Springer, Cham (2014). https://doi.org/10.1007/978-3-319-11973-1_34

22. Robinette, P., Li, W., Allen, R., Howard, A.M., Wagner, A.R.: Overtrust of robots in emergency evacuation scenarios. In: 11th ACM/IEEE International Conference on Human-Robot Interaction (HRI) 2016, Christchurch, New Zealand, pp. 101–108. IEEE (2016)

23. Shibata, T., Wada, K., Ikeda, Y., Sabanovic, S.: Cross-cultural studies on subjective evaluation of a seal robot. Adv. Robot. **23**, 443–458 (2009)

24. De Graaf, M., Allouch, S.: Exploring influencing variables for the acceptance of social robots. Robot. Auton. Syst. **61**, 1476–1486 (2013)

Modelling the Collaboration of a Patient and an Assisting Humanoid Robot During Training Tasks

Peter Forbrig$^{(\boxtimes)}$ and Alexandru-Nicolae Bundea

University of Rostock, Albert-Einstein-Str. 22, 18055 Rostock, Germany
{Peter.Forbrig,Alexandru-Nicolae.Bundea}@uni-rostock.de

Abstract. The paper describes an approach for using a humanoid robot as a motivator for patients that recover from stroke. Specific training tasks for arm ability training exist. They were implemented in such a way that the robot gives advices and provides motivational comments. The language DSL-CoTaL was used to specify the collaboration between patient and robot. It allows the visualization and animation of the models with different tools (CoTaSE, CTTE, HAMSTERS). A task pattern was identified for the exercises with a mirror. This pattern reduces extremely the necessary modelling support. It also helps to identify requirements for a domain-specific language for robots, that will allow to generate the necessary code. The language is planned to be an extension of CoTaL.

Keywords: Task model · Task pattern · Humanoid robot pepper

1 Introduction

Stroke is currently a very important disease. According to [1] every 40 s someone in the United States has a stroke. Every **four minutes,** someone dies of stroke. Even that this is bad news, it means that a lot of stroke patients survive. However, they have to cope with defects. Often one arm is disabled, which creates a lot of problems for the daily life. Fortunately, there are opportunities to train the brain in not effected areas in such a way that patients can recover. The Arm Ability Training was designed to promote manual dexterity recovery for stroke patients who have mild to moderate arm paresis [16]. Platz and Lotze report in [17] about its design, clinical effectiveness, and the neurobiology of the actions. However, the number of therapists is not large enough to fulfill the demands for specific training for stroke survivors. Within the project E-BRAiN (Evidence-based Robot-Assistance in Neurorehabilitation) we want to develop software that allows a humanoid robot to give instructions to perform and to observe carefully selected exercises, provide feedback and in addition to motivate patients.

After an analysis of existing humanoid robots, we decided to use Pepper from Softbanks Robotics [18]. Pepper has a very nice facial expression (see Fig. 1), can talk and move around. It is already used in shopping centers, railway stations or airports to give support to customers by providing information. We assume that a socially interactive

© Springer Nature Switzerland AG 2020
M. Kurosu (Ed.): HCII 2020, LNCS 12182, pp. 592–602, 2020.
https://doi.org/10.1007/978-3-030-49062-1_40

robot like Pepper can be helpful for some stroke survivors when performing their individual training and hence for their recreation. However, the feasibility to use a humanoid robot for neurorehabilitation has yet to be evaluated within an appropriate research setting. We want to find the answer to the research question: "Which type of patients can be supported in which way by Pepper?"

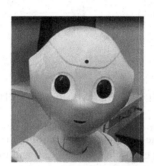

Fig. 1. Humanoid robot Pepper from SoftBanks Robotics [18]. Discussion

Some challenges for the interaction design of the applications were already discussed in [6]. A little bit more background of training tasks is provided in [5]. The digitalization of a pointing task on tablets is discussed there as well. In this paper we want to focus on the specification aspect of the interaction between patients and Pepper in context of tasks that have to be performed with a mirror.

The paper is structured in such a way, that we discuss first modelling languages for collaborative tasks and task patterns. The modelling of the support by Pepper is discussed afterwards. The paper closes with a short summary and an outlook.

2 Modelling Languages and Task Patterns

A variety of modelling language exist. Even for modelling of activities there exist several languages for business processes, sometimes called workflow specification, and task models.

We have been working on task models for several years. One of the first tools for this purpose was ADEPT from Johnson et al. [13]. Later environments like CTTE (Paterno et al. [15] or HAMSTERS (Palanque and Martinie [14]) were developed. Our own environment for animating task models is called CoTaSe [3]. It is discussed in detail in [2].

Based on the ideas of design patterns from Gamma et al. [11] task patterns were discussed in several publications. Breedvelt et al. [1] started the discussion with reusable task structures. Later patterns and generic components were discussed (see e.g. [8–10], or [19]).

Most of the task models are based on XML-specifications that are manipulated and visualized with graphical editors. However, sometimes a domain-specific language (DSL) can be manipulated easier than a graphical specification. Therefore, the DSL-CoTaL [7]) was developed. It was implemented with Xtext [4] and allows the generation of models for CoTaSE, CTTE and HAMSTERS (Fig. 2).

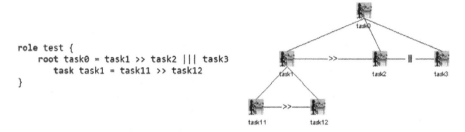

```
role test {
    root task0 = task1 >> task2 ||| task3
        task task1 = task11 >> task12
}
```

Fig. 2. Task model in DSL-CoTaL and visualized in CTTE.

A task model starts with a root name and the refinement of the root task. Tasks are separated by temporal operators. In our example enabling (≫) and interleaving (|||) are used. However, several other operators exist.

3   Modelling the Training Tasks

3.1   Arm-Ability Training with a Mirror

For mirror therapy, neurological effects are exploited. The patient sits laterally slightly offset to a mirror that is in front of him at a 90-degree angle (see Fig. 3) in such a way that she can see the healthy arm in the mirror. Now different exercises are presented to her, which she should carry out with the healthy arm. This exercise is done three times. Thereafter, the same exercise is to be performed ten more times. After a certain time, the patient is asked to look at the mirror and imagine that his damaged arm is performing the movements.

This idea is supposed to bring about changes in the brain that can eventually cause the damaged arm to actually perform the movements. Neurologists have demonstrated the effectiveness of the exercises (see, for example [16] or [17]).

3.2   Implementation of the Mirror-Therapy with Pepper

It is suggested that the exercises are introduced by a human expert. Only the second and subsequent therapy sessions are performed with support of the humanoid robot. In this way, patients know already the exercises. However, Pepper gives a short introduction for each exercise. During this explanation two pictures are presented on the tablet of the robot. They show typical arm positions. Afterwards, the patient is asked to perform the

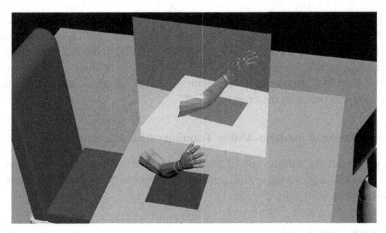

Fig. 3. Illustration of the proposed solution – showing symmetrical stimuli across the mirror (adapted from [12])

exercise three times while concentrating on his healthy arm. If this was done well, the robot asks to perform the exercise ten times. After a certain delay, the robot asks the patient to look at the mirror and to think that the exercise is performed by his handicapped arm.

During the whole time a video of the correct exercise performance is presented on the tablet of Pepper. In case the patient cannot remember the correct performance of the exercise, this might help. At the end of each exercise Pepper says some motivational words.

The corresponding task model of Pepper looks like presented in Fig. 4.

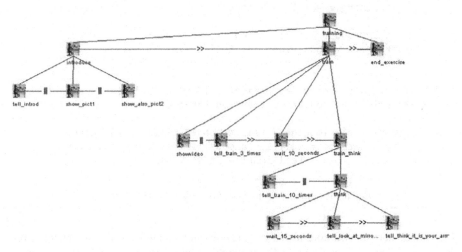

Fig. 4. Task model for a mirror exercise

The training consists of three parts. First, Pepper provides and introduction. Afterwards the training is supported and finally the exercise is closed. The introduction consists of three parallel subtasks. During the training parallel to the other actions a video is shown. Pepper tells the patient to perform the training task ten times. After while (about five exercises) Pepper tells the patient to look at the mirror and to think that the handicapped arm performs the exercise.

3.3 Specification of the Arm-Ability Training with a Mirror in DSL-CoTaL

In this paragraph we want to model the task model for Pepper, the patient in DSL-CoTaL. The DSL supports the specification of a team model that reflects the collaborative activities of the participants (Fig. 5).

```
team coop {
    root training = greeting >> train >> end_exercise
          task greeting = pepper.greet |=| patient.greet
}
```

Fig. 5. Simplified team model for the collaboration of patient and Pepper

The training starts with a greeting procedure, where Pepper and the patient greet each other. This can be done in any order (|=|). The training ends when pepper performs the task *end_exercise.*

The representation of the task model of Fig. 4 is represented in Fig. 6 as textual specification in DSL-CoTaL:

```
role pepper{
  root training = greet >> introduce >> train >> end_exercise

    task introduce = tell_introd ||| show_pict1 ||| show_pict2
    task train = show_video ||| tell_train_3_times >>
                  wait_10_seconds >> train_imagine

    task end_exercise pre patient.allInstances.finishes_exercises
    task tell_introd pre patient.oneInstance.greet

      task train_imagine = tell_train_10_times ||| imagine
      task imagine = wait_15_seconds >> tell_look_at_mirror >>
                  tell_imagine_it_is_your_arm
}
```

Fig. 6. Task model for Pepper (from Fig. 4) in DSL-CoTaL.

Pepper starts the training with a greet (*greet*) and tells the introduction (*tell_introd*) afterwards. There exists a precondition for this task (sixth line). At least one patient had to execute *greet* beforehand. Otherwise, Pepper has to wait until the precondition is fulfilled. For the task *end_exercise* there exists a precondition as well. Figure 7 represents the situation in CoTaSE, where two instances of a role models were created for the actors *Pepper* and *Patient*. *Pepper* executed *greet* but cannot execute *tell-introd* because *Patient* did not greet yet. The team model reflects the situation. One can see that the task training and greeting started. One task *greet* was executed, the second could be executed next. The tasks *train* and *end_exercise* are disabled. The instance of the team model has a little bit more dark background and is triggered by the task execution of the animated role instance models.

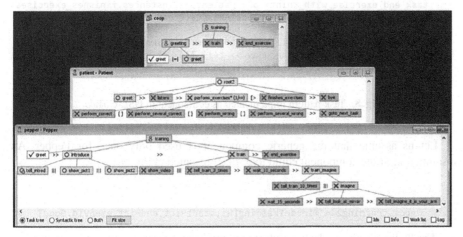

Fig. 7. Animated models in CoTaSE.

Within CoTaSE one can interact with the role model instances but not with the team model. One can execute a task by clicking on it or separately start and end it. This second option allows the simulation of parallel execution of tasks.

It is possible to instantiate several instances of each role model (see also Buchholz and Forbrig [8] for more details).

Modelling the tasks helped us to get a deeper understanding of the domain. The modelling process is much faster and less resource intensive than implementation. Results can be discussed in an easy way.

There exist 18 different exercises that have to be performed with a mirror. We recognized a very similar task structure for all of those exercises. This can be considered as a task pattern for the robot in the domain of mirror exercises for post stroke patient. A similar pattern exists for the patient. However, we want to focus on the robot activities here. Variable parts of each exercise are the instructions in the introducing text, the two pictures, the video and the final comments. This can be specified as a generic component in DSL-CoTaL. Figure 8 presents the corresponding specification with five parameters that are substituted in different task names.

```
target = CTT, CoTaL;

component mirrorTraining[introd, pict1, pict2, video, hint] {

  root training= introduce >> train >> end_exercise_with_<hint>

    task introduce = tell_<introd> ||| show_<pict1> ||| show_<pict2>
    task train = show_<video> ||| tell_train_3_times >>
                 wait_10_seconds >> train_imagine

    task end_exercise_with_<hint> pre patient.allInstances.finishes_exercises
    task tell_<introd> pre patient.oneInstance.greet

    task train_imagine = tell_train_10_times ||| imagine
    task imagine = wait_15_seconds >> tell_look_at_mirror >>
                   tell_imagine_it_is_your_arm
}
```

Fig. 8. Task pattern implemented as component in DSL-CoTaL

Let us assume that the generic component is used only once for Pepper. An instantiation of the component could look like presented in Fig. 9.

```
role pepper{
  root training2 = mirrorTraining[Hi,startPict,endPict,exerVid,Good]
```

Fig. 9. Instantiation of the task pattern mirrorTraining in the task model of role pepper

The resulting task model can be visualized in CTTE. The result is shown in Fig. 10.

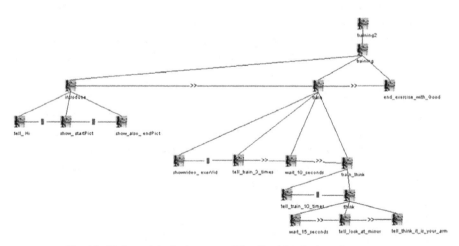

Fig. 10. Task model of role pepper (Fig. 9) with substituted parameters

Figure 11 demonstrates the specification of a series of different exercises that are instantiations of the task pattern mirrorTraining.

```
role pepper{
  root training2 =    mirrorTraining[Hi,startPict,endPict,exerVid,Good]
                  >> mirrorTraining[Hello, startPic2, endPic2, exerVi2, Excellent]
                  >> mirrorTraining[Hi, startPict3, endPict3, exerVi3, Perfect]
                  >> mirrorTraining[Hello, startPict4, endPict4, exerVi4, Good]
              // >> etc.
}
```

Fig. 11. Specification of the whole series of different exercises

3.4 Discussion

Task models in DSL-CoTaL allowed us a good communication with the domain experts
in our project. The animation of the models in CoTaSE helped a lot in this respect because
animation increases attention. Models can be created in minutes while implementations
might take months. There is no need for an implementation at the beginning of a discussions. Participants get an impression of the system under development from the models,
their visualization and animation.

Additionally, it was shown for a specific kind of training tasks of stroke patients that
several training activities follow the same kind of task pattern. Those tasks are performed
with a mirror. The only differences are different instructions by Pepper, different pictures
and videos on the Pepper tablet and different final comments. However, the general
interaction between Pepper and a patient is always the same. Together there are about
18 different training tasks. Therefore, it would be very good if the code for the robot
could be generated from the DSL

To allow such kind of code generation, specific language construct must be defined.
From our experience we need something like:

- say(**Text**)
- say_loud(**Text**)
- blink_with_eyes(**Seconds**)
- raise_left_arm
- raise_right_arm
- move_ahead(**Centimeter**)
- turn_right
- turn_right(**Degrees**)
- turn_left
- turn_left(**Degrees**)
- turn_back
- sleep(**Seconds**)

Additionally, it was recognized that it is not good for readability if the whole instruction text is provided as parameter. Therefore, it makes sense to have specific constructs
in the DSL that allow the assignment of texts, pictures and videos to specific variables.
This could look like the following specification.

Text_definitions
  T1: "xxxxxxxxxxxxxxxxxxxxxxxxxxxxxxxxxxxxxxx
        xxxxxxxxxxxxxxxxxxxxxxxxxxxxxx xxxxxxxxxx"
  T2: "yyyyyyyyyyyyyyyyyyyyyyyyyyyyyyyyyyyyyyy
        yyyyyyyyyyyyyyyyyyyyyyyy
        yyyyyyyyyyyyyyyyyyyyyyyyyyyyyyyyyyyyyyyyy"
  T3: "zzzzzzzzzzzzzzzzzzzzzzzzzzzzzzzzzzz"
  ...

Picture_definitions
  P1: "C:\pictures\pic1"
  P2: "C:\pictures\pic2"
  P3: "C:\pictures\pic3"
  ...

Video_definitions
  V1: "C:\pictures\vid1"
  V2: "C:\pictures\vid2"
  V3: "C:\pictures\vid3"
  ...

The specified identifiers (Ts, Ps and Vs) can be used to represent the corresponding resources. Therefore, they can be used as actual parameters for the instantiation of task patterns (generic components).

The instructions for the training tasks for arm rehabilitation consist sometimes of fifteen lines. Pepper is able to speak the corresponding phrases. He tells the provided text to the patient. It is our idea that a new line in the text represents a short break of the robots talk.

We plan to extend our language DSL-CoTaL to DSL-CoTaL-Pepper by the discussed features and want to generate code for Pepper. The new language constructs make the specification better readable. Additionally, the task model of the role Pepper can be considered as program code. Therefore, the specification is not only usable for understanding the domain but can productively be used.

4   Summary and Outlook

The paper discussed the usage of task models for understanding the collaboration of a social humanoid robot like Pepper with patients that have to train to overcome some handicaps after a stroke. The robot acts as a kind of personal trainer that has to motivate the patients because success comes very slowly.

To model the collaboration of the robot and the patient the domains-specific language DSL-CoTaL was used. It allows transformations to tools like CoTaSE, CTTE or HAMSTERS. Those tools allow visualizations and animations of the models.

For specific exercises in front of a mirror, a possible design of the interaction was specified. It was possible to identify a task pattern for those tasks. It has five parameters and is applicable to 18 different exercises.

The specification and implementation of the interactive application delivered some ideas for extensions of the DSL-CoTaL. Some commands for a robot and some language constructs for domain objects were identified and discussed. It is our plan to extend the language and provide code generation for the robot Pepper. A new target for code generation will be possible soon.

Acknowledgments. This joint research project "E-BRAiN - Evidenz-based Robot Assistance in Neurorehabilitation" is supported by the European Social Fund (ESF), reference: ESF/14-BM-A55-0001/19-A01, and the Ministry of Education, Science and Culture of Mecklenburg-Vorpommern, Germany. This work was further supported by the BDH Bundesverband Rehabilitation e.V. (charity for neuro-disabilities) by a non-restricted personal grant to TP. The sponsors had no role in the decision to publish or any content of the publication.

References

1. Benjamin, E.J., Blaha, M.J., Chiuve, S.E., et al.: On behalf of the American heart association statistics committee and stroke statistics subcommittee. Heart disease and stroke statistics—2017 update: a report from the American heart association. Circulation **135**(10), e146–e603 (2017). https://doi.org/10.1161/cir.0000000000000485
2. Buchholz, G., Forbrig, P.: Extended features of task models for specifying cooperative activities. In: PACMHCI 1(EICS), pp. 7:1–7:21 (2017)
3. CoTaSE. https://www.cotase.de/. Accessed 2 Dec 2019
4. Eysholdt, M., Behrens, H.: Xtext: implement your language faster than the quick and dirty way. In: Proceedings of OOPSLA 2010, pp. 307–309. ACM, New York (2010). https://doi.org/10.1145/1869542.1869625
5. Forbrig, P., Platz, T.: Supporting the arm ability training of stroke patients by a social humanoid robot. In: Ahram, T., Taiar, R., Gremeaux-Bader, V., Aminian, K. (eds.) Human Interaction, Emerging Technologies and Future Applications II. IHIET 2020. Advances in Intelligent Systems and Computing, vol. 1152, pp. 1–6. Springer, Cham (2020). https://doi.org/10.1007/978-3-030-44267-5_57
6. Forbrig, P.: Challenges in multi-user interaction with a social humanoid robot pepper. In: Workshop HCI-Engineering, EICS 2019 Conference, Valencia, Spain, pp. 10–17 (2019). http://ceur-ws.org/Vol-2503/
7. Forbrig, P., Dittmar, A., Kühn, M.: A textual domain specific language for task models: generating code for CoTaL, CTTE, and HAMSTERS. In: EICS 2018 Conferences, Paris, France, pp. 5:1–5:6 (2018)
8. Forbrig, P., Martinie, C., Palanque, P., Winckler, M., Fahssi, R.: Rapid task-models development using sub-models, sub-routines and generic components. In: Sauer, S., Bogdan, C., Forbrig, P., Bernhaupt, R., Winckler, M. (eds.) HCSE 2014. LNCS, vol. 8742, pp. 144–163. Springer, Heidelberg (2014). https://doi.org/10.1007/978-3-662-44811-3_9
9. Forbrig, P., Wolff, A.: Different kinds of pattern support for interactive systems. In: Proceedings of the 1st International Workshop on Pattern-Driven Engineering of Interactive Computing Systems (PEICS 2010), pp. 36–39. ACM, New York (2010). https://doi.org/10.1145/1824749.1824758
10. Gaffar, A., Sinnig, D., Seffah, A., Forbrig, P.: Modeling patterns for task models. In: Proceedings of the 3rd Annual Conference on Task Models and Diagrams (TAMODIA 2004), pp. 99–104. ACM, New York (2004). https://doi.org/10.1145/1045446.1045465

11. Gamma, E., Helm, R., Johnson, R., Vlissides, J.: Design Patterns: Elements of Reusable Object-Oriented Software. Addison Wesley, Boston (1995)

12. Hallam, J.: Haptic mirror therapy glove: aiding the treatment of a paretic limb after a stroke. In: Adjunct Proceedings of the 2015 ACM International Joint Conference on Pervasive and Ubiquitous Computing and Proceedings of the 2015 ACM International Symposium on Wearable Computers (UbiComp/ISWC 2015 Adjunct), pp. 459–464. ACM, New York (2015). https://doi.org/10.1145/2800835.2801648

13. Johnson, P., Wilson, S., Markopoulos, P., Pycock, J.: ADEPT: advanced design environment for. prototyping with task models. In: INTERCHI 1993, p. 56 (1993)

14. Palanque, P., Martinie, C.: Designing and assessing interactive systems using task models. In: Proceedings of the 2016 CHI Conference Extended Abstracts on Human Factors in Computing Systems (CHI EA 2016), pp. 976–979. ACM, New York (2016) http://dx.doi.org/10.1145/2851581.2856686

15. Paternò, F., Mori, G., Galiberti, R.: CTTE: an environment for analysis and development of task models of cooperative applications. In: CHI 2001 Extended Abstracts on Human Factors in Computing Systems (CHI EA 2001), pp. 21–22. ACM, New York (2001). https://doi.org/10.1145/634067.634084

16. Platz, T.: Impairment-oriented training (IOT) – scientific concept and evidence-based treatment strategies. Restor. Neurol. Neurosci. 22(3–5), 301–315 (2004)

17. Platz, T., Lotze, M.: Arm ability training (AAT) promotes dexterity recovery after a stroke-a review of its design, clinical effectiveness, and the neurobiology of the actions. Front. Neurol. 9, 1082 (2018). https://doi.org/10.3389/fneur.2018.01082

18. SoftBank Robotics. https://www.softbankrobotics.com/corp/robots/. Accessed 11 Nov 2019

19. Zaki, M.: Integration of patterns into model-based specifications of smart environments. In: Proceedings of the 29th Annual European Conference on Cognitive Ergonomics (ECCE 2011), pp. 241–244. ACM, New York (2011). http://dx.doi.org/10.1145/2074712.2074762

Multi-human Management of Robotic Swarms

John R. Grosh[⊠] and Michael A. Goodrich

Department of Computer Science, Brigham Young University, Provo, UT, USA
jrgrosh@byu.net, mike@cs.byu.edu

Abstract. Swarm robotics is an emerging field that is expected to provide robust solutions to spatially distributed problems. Human operators will often be required to guide a swarm in the fulfillment of a mission. Occasionally, large tasks may require multiple spatial swarms to cooperate in their completion. We hypothesize that when latency and bandwidth significantly restrict communication among human operators, human organizations that promote individual initiative perform more effectively and resiliently than hierarchies in the cooperative best-m-of-n task. Simulations automating the behavior of hub-based swarm robotic agents and simulated groups of human operators are used to evaluate this hypothesis. To make the comparisons between the team and hierarchies meaningful, we explore parameter values determining how simulated human operators behave in teams and hierarchies to optimize the performance of the respective organizations. We show that simulation results generally support the hypothesis with respect to the effect of latency and bandwidth on organizational performance.

Keywords: Swarm robotics · Organizational behavior

1 Introduction

Swarm behavior is abundant and diverse in biology [10]. Using only cues from their neighbors and perception of their immediate surroundings, swarms of thousands of individuals produce coordinated behavior. Swarm robotics engineers seek to emulate the robust structure of natural swarms in the creation of swarms of inexpensive robots, adopting the strengths of natural swarms while mitigating their weaknesses [2].

One weakness of swarms is an inability to react quickly to changing situations or to situations not prepared for by evolution. These problems are caused by the slow speed at which information is shared [17,19] as well as the absence of individual and collective behaviors suitable to all problems. Our research does not address the limitations imposed by the absence of needed swarm behaviors, but attempts to address the limitations caused by the restricted flow of information among swarm agents through the use of human operators who provide oversight to the swarm.

© Springer Nature Switzerland AG 2020
M. Kurosu (Ed.): HCII 2020, LNCS 12182, pp. 603–619, 2020.
https://doi.org/10.1007/978-3-030-49062-1_41

This work specifically considers how, in a simulation, a group of human operators with "soft-influence" controls can effectively aid multiple swarms in completing the best-m-of-n task, a cooperative multi-swarm variant of the best-of-n problem [26]. We study two organizations facilitating the coordination of the human operators: a hierarchy following a tree-based calling structure, and a fully connected team structure. We measure their performance against each other when subject to latency and bandwidth with respect to inter-human communication that consume significant portions of mission time.

2   Related Work

Designing a framework for coordinating robot swarm operators should be built on an understanding of how swarms behave autonomously as well as research on human control of large numbers of robots.

Extensive applied and theoretical work has explored the dynamics of autonomous swarm robotics tasks lacking human supervisors. Schmickl et al. used the BEECLUST algorithm to induce robots to aggregate at an optimal location on a board [22]. Rubenstein et al. introduced the kilobot to, among other tasks, develop user specified shapes without centralized coordination [21]. The highly influential kilobot design has been used in many studies, including tasks involving collective transport [27] and foraging [4].

Experiments regarding human swarm interaction have remained largely in the realm of simulation. Kolling et al. [13] measure the performance of "click and drag" control as well as operator manipulation of the environment against total robotic autonomy in a foraging problem. Coppin and Legras describe a less fine grained command set which allows the creation of flight plans for UAVs, but prevents mid-flight redirection [6]. Pendleton and Goodrich describe how humans can influence a flocking swarm by controlling agents which exert local influence over nearby robots [20]. Jung and Goodrich introduced the use of *mediator* agents to control toruses of swarm agents without destabilizing the spatial swarm structure [12]. Furthermore, Miller introduced the concept of "playbook" style controls to swarm dynamics in [16]. Lee studied the use of parametric control of velocity in robotic control in [15].

Methods for controlling robotic swarm by a human operator range on a spectrum from fine grained to strategic. The results of several studies seem to suggest that strategic control of robotic swarms is better suited for human operators. Kolling's study in [13] demonstrates that humans using fine grained control in the foraging task were consistently outperformed by autonomous robotic behavior. Coppin's study [5] also shows that humans tend to hurt swarm performance at the coverage problem. Humans were shown to perform well in anticipating the strategic intent of intruders, however, and were able to make a statistically significant contribution to the performance of military drones intercepting intruders. Brown conducted simulations of human-swarm interaction and provided evidence suggesting that humans were significantly better in managing collective swarm state than they were at managing individual swarm agents [3]. Humans' abilities to process strategic intent over micromanagement is consistent with other literature [8] that indicated humans suffer dropoff in performance once the number of individually controlled objects exceeds six or seven.

Because of these studies, in addition to bandwidth limitations, this thesis uses control methods that lean towards strategic control over fine-grained control. These forms of human influence were chosen in hopes to avoid the problems humans have micromanaging spatial swarms and allow for efficient organizational command and control.

The study of effective small team structures is not new. Bavelas' seminal study in 1950 measured how the communication structure of small groups impacted performance on a selection of problems [1]. The results of the study showed that task type profoundly influenced the success or failure of an organization. Hierarchical organizations were suited for simpler tasks. Flatter, more open communication models such as the all channel method were better suited for more complicated tasks.

Since then other studies have explored further intricacies in the problem [9,11,14,23]. While Bavelas and others have performed extensive research in this area to provide the dynamic of simple tasks being best fit to hierarchies and complicated tasks to open communication structures, existing research does not give a precise notion of where the cooperative best-m-of-n task lies in that spectrum. Equivalently according to Steiner's Taxonomy of Tasks [24], further experiments are required to determine under what circumstances the cooperative best-m-of-n task is a disjunctive task (necessitating hierarchical coordination) or discretionary (allowing for decentralized team-based decision making). Our research aims to provide a definite classification of the cooperative best-m-of-n task using Bavelas' and Steiner's framework by measuring how latency, bandwidth, and connection losses affect organizational performance. Therefore we conduct experiments to empirically determine which small group structures are suitable for the best-m-of-n problem under various circumstances.

3   Problem Definition and Simulation Details

3.1   Organization Types

This research is centered around two organizational structures: hierarchies and fully connected teams.

This paper uses a tree-based communication model for the *hierarchical* organization. One hierarchy member is designated as the "leader" and all other members are considered "subordinates" . All subordinates provide information on their perceived state of the world to the leader. The leader then issues orders to coordinate the efforts of the subordinates. Subordinates then forward these orders, formulated by the leader, to each other according to a predetermined schedule.

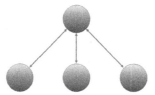

Fig. 1. Example of a communication network for a two layer hierarchy

As may be seen in Fig. 1, all communication is routed through a single member of the organization. Centralization allows for efficient aggregation and processing of information, but subjects the organization to a bottleneck because of the leader.

Figure 2 illustrates the organization topology for the *teams* considered in this paper. Note that every member is connected to every other member, meaning that the organization is fully connected. In the *team* organizational structure used in this paper, no leader is designated to coordinate the actions of the rest of the group. Teams instead rely on group members to intelligently take initiative. Unlike the hierarchy, communication is allowed between all members within a team and no single simulated human operator acts as an intermediary for the others. Team members declare their intended actions and share information about the world according to their individual best judgment. Once a team member has decided to take action, it will broadcast its intentions to its neighbors. This declaration will be respected and any team member that learns of this intention will adjust its plans accordingly to not interfere. If two team members broadcast to each other conflicting intentions, the team member that broadcasted its intentions first is given priority.

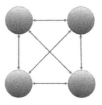

Fig. 2. Example of a team organizational network

Figure 2 shows the organization topology for the teams considered in this paper. Note that every team member is connected to every other team member, meaning that the organization is fully connected. (Unoptimized) teams require more messages to reach an optimal configuration of knowledge and group roles. They do, however, allow for nodes to communicate with exactly who they need to instead of routing through an intermediary.

3.2   Cooperative Best-M-of-N Overview

The task we use to measure the performance of the two different organizations is a variation of the best-of-n problem, a problem described in greater detail in other work [26]. Instead of only one hub-based swarm seeking out a high quality nest site, multiple swarms based out of separate spatially distributed hubs each seek to commit to a high quality nest site. As the name of this variant, cooperative best-m-of-n, suggests, these swarms are cooperative and seek to maximize the sum quality of sites selected by the entire group.

Figure 6 illustrates the best-m-of-n problem. Hubs are represented as hangars, swarm agents as drones, and sites of interest as cross symbols surrounded by incomplete circles. These associations of hubs, swarm agents, and sites are somewhat arbitrary and were chosen for convenience. Hubs and their swarms are grouped together by the color of the circle around them as the swarm agents search the environment for sites of interest.

Communication between simulated human operators is required to direct search efforts, share information about location and quality of nest sites found, and coordinate commitment to different sites. This last step is especially important, as a site which is committed to by two swarms only counts once towards the group's score.

Swarm agents are each associated with a hub and human operator based at that same hub. Swarm agents can only communicate at their hub. Swarm agents only share information about sites with other swarm agents based out of the

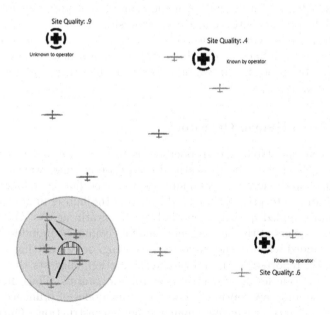

Fig. 3. One hub with a human operator, and set of agents in different swarm states (red-exploring, orange-assessing, turquoise-observing, green-dancing) (Color figure online)

same hub and with the human operator. Human operators can only influence swarm agents associated with their hub when those agents are at the hub.

Robotic swarm agents exist as small, point-sized agents in a 2-D rectangular world. Agents can perceive other sites and robotic swarm agents within a fixed radius around them. For a given instance of the simulation, all robotic swarm agents possess both the same state behavior and the same parameter values for movement and detection.

Hubs are the bases of operation for swarm robotic agents. Hubs are based on two primary assumptions: one, that swarm agents have a finite amount of fuel and will need refueling to continue mission operation; two, that hardware limits on bandwidth prevent communication between the simulated human operators and swarm agents beyond an extremely localized region around the hubs. Therefore, swarm agents return to the hub to refuel and exchange information with their human operator and other swarm agents. Hubs are the only locations from which human operators can directly influence the swarm.

The behavior of the simulated swarm agents are modeled after the honeybee nest site selection process in the manner of the honey bee model in [18] and the swarm agent behavior described in [7]. The state machine dynamic drives the aggregate behavior of the swarm and will generally follow a predictable overall pattern. Simulations begin with half of the swarm agents exploring the map to find high-value sites, and the other half of the swarm agents waiting at the hub in the observing state. Swarm agents then evaluate the sites that have been found through the dancing and assessment states. Once enough swarm agents dance for the same site, swarm agents begin the commitment processes for that site. The swarm then moves entirely to the selected site.

Depending on the communication dynamics of the simulated humans, the swarm may receive influence regarding site choice from human operators later in the simulation. If no such direction is received, the swarm will autonomously complete the process.

3.3 Simulated Human Operators

The role of the simulated human operator is to supervise and provide strategic management of the robotic swarm. Because we assume swarm agents lack the equipment and energy to communicate with the hub over long distances, human operator perception of the world outside the hub is limited to the site locations and sampled qualities reported by the swarm agents. Operators can only influence agents at the hub. Agents therefore cannot be individually or even collectively guided when in the exploring, assessing, or committing states.

Prior work, reported in the related works section, suggests that a humans should use strategic levels of control over robotic swarms. Thus, human commands may be more appropriately referred to as modes of influence, as swarm agents have a chance of ignoring simulated human instructions. Once a swarm agent has received a command, it ignores all other commands whether or not it accepted the original command for a period of time. The two human operator commands are:

- Promote site: This command influences observing swarm agents to investigate a site. If an observing swarm agent accepts this command, it will transition to the assessing state and visit the suggested site.
- Reject commit: A reject commit command will force all swarm agents considering a site to forget that site and convert to the resting or observing states. This command can be issued only once per simulation per hub, but it also cannot be rejected by agents. There is also no cooldown on accepting influence associated with this command as there are with others. This command permits a hub to delay the decision making process without taking absolute control over swarm agent behavior.

3.4 Human Communication

Human communication and action is split into two phases. In the first phase, simulated humans focus solely on processing information gathered by robotic swarm agents. This first phase is 35% of the total mission time. In the second phase, or the 65% portion of mission time remaining, the hub agents share information about sites they have discovered, decide on a course of action, and implement it. In this phase, leaders in *hierarchies* deliver orders to subordinates detailing which sites they should commit to. Subordinates act on this information as soon as it is received. By contrast, simulated humans in *team organizations* finish sharing information with each other until all agents' information is complete. Once a team agent has been updated by all of the other team members, it will act on the appropriate solution.

The primary interest of this research is to see how these human organizational structures fulfill their missions when subject to communications difficulties. *Latency* is the delay between sending and receiving of a message. *Bandwidth* describes the total number of messages that can be sent or received in a specified time interval by a human operator. For each instance of the simulation, the amount of latency and bandwidth is constant. Swarm agents use heuristics to determine how to communicate within their organizations and subject to these difficulties.

Importantly, when an operator can only send a message to one other operator at a time. Latency and bandwidth are expected to cause difficulties in the coordination of human operators.

3.5 Automation of Human Input

In the spirit of Steinfeld's work in [25], we automate human input to validate the hypothesis. This design decision allows us to conduct a larger number of tests over a broader spectrum of latency and bandwidth values than would be possible otherwise.

4   Performance Metric and Hypothesis

The key metric of performance is the probability of achieving the maximum score possible, given the information gathered by the cutoff point. This metric is called the *probability of optimal commit*, and is calculated by dividing (a) the number of successful trials in which a group of hubs committed to an ideal configuration given their knowledge by (b) the total number of trials; the ratio is defined for a given set of test parameters.

We hypothesize that worsening conditions, latency and bandwidth will cause both hierarchical and team performance to suffer, but also we anticipate that team performance will degrade more gracefully than hierarchical performance. The reason for the hypothesis is that, under stressful network conditions, a team is potentially a more effective organizational choice than a hierarchy due to the abundant and redundant communication links between operators.

Figure 3 helps demonstrate how the different metrics are applied. In the figure, there are three sites: one high quality site, one medium quality site, and one poor quality site. Swarm agents have discovered the two hubs on the right-hand side of the figure, returned to the hub, and reported the locations and qualities of the discovered sites. The hub is therefore aware of the poor and medium quality site, but is unaware of the high quality site. As the figure indicates, the swarm agents are focusing their attentions on the medium quality site. As time passes, the swarm agents will eventually commit to the medium quality site.

Using the *probability of optimal commit metric*, the trial illustrated in Fig. 3 and described in the paragraph would be recorded as successful, contributing to a higher average rate of optimal commitment, because the swarm committed to the better of the two known sites. Had the swarm committed to the worse of the two known sites, the trial would have been recorded as a failure and would have contributed to a lower probability of optimal commits. The purpose of this metric is *to determine how effective organizations are at distributing information instead of measuring how well they explore.*

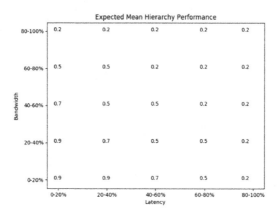

Fig. 4. Expected hierarchy performance

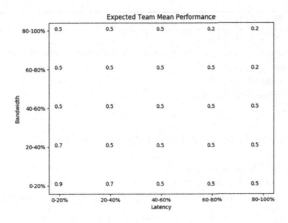

Fig. 5. Expected team performance

5 Human Organizational Algorithms

In the interest of managing algorithm complexity, both hierarchies and teams have been programmed to use a greedy approach for generating a solution to the best-m-of-n problem. Given enough bandwidth and low enough latency, both teams and hierarchies should reach optimal assignments. Especially because human operators are only capable of sending a message to only one operator at a time, differences in performance will arise as latency and bandwidth change.

Each simulated human operator uses Algorithm 1, to directly influence their swarm. Each simulated human operator – either a member of a hierarchy or a member of a team – will issue a *forbid* command for a site under two conditions. First, the operator will forbid a site chosen by the swarm if the site differs from the site selected by the operator. Second, an operator will forbid a site selected by the swarm if the site is claimed by another operator.

Once an operator has chosen a site, it will influence agents using the *promote* command to explore the site. Recall that a promote command influences agents at the hub to visit a site specified by the operator. About two thirds of the time, this command is ignored. If ignored, swarm agents must wait through a cool-down period before they can consider accepting another *promote* command.

5.1 Hierarchy Solution

The algorithm used to direct hierarchy operator logic is presented in Algorithm 2. Hierarchies have each human operator passively gather information by observing the reports delivered by swarm agents until the time for the first phase of the simulation runs out and the second phase of the simulation begins. When this occurs, all subordinates report their discovered sites to the leader. The leader assigns each of the best m of sites to whichever unassigned operator is nearest to

---

Algorithm 1. Basic Operator Functions

1: **function** CANSENDMESSAGE
2:     **return** $CurrentTime - LastMessageSendTime > Bandwidth$
3: **end function**
4: **function** MANAGESWARM
5:     **if** $GetSelectedSite() = null$:
6:         **return**
7:     **else**:
8:         $PromoteSiteToAgentsAtHub(GetSelectedSite())$
9:     **end if**
10:    $s_{swarm} \leftarrow GetSwarmCommit()$
11:    $s_{assigned} \leftarrow GetSelectedSite()$
12:    **if** $(s_{swarm} \neq null$ **and** $s_{assigned} \neq s_{swarm})$ **or** s_{swarm} in $GetClaims()$ **then**
13:        $ForbidSite(s_{swarm})$
14:    **end if**
15: **end function**

---

the site. The leader then informs the operators of the entire set of assignments one operator at a time.

Once a subordinate human operator receives information about its assignment, the subordinate operator begins informing other subordinate operators. The schedule for subordinates informing other subordinates is formed before the beginning of the simulation and is optimized so that the maximum number of human operators can be informed of their assigned sites in the shortest amount of time.

5.2   Team Solution

Algorithm 3 lists the steps used Team members also passively gather information until the time limit for the first phase is reached and the second phase of the simulation begins. Team members then start exchanging information via time-stamped messages. The simulated human operators lay claim to the best site they know of. They then immediately begin informing their neighbors of this decision. Team members inform other group members about their decision in order of proximity to each other, from nearest to farthest.

As long as the simulation is not over, if a team member has messaged all other neighbors, it will begin sending messages again in the same order as the first round of message passing. A team member will relinquish a site if it receives a message indicating another operator has selected the same site before it selected the site. Simulated operators "gossip" claims (and site locations and qualities) to each other, so simulated operators may learn of a claims from other operators with whom they never directly communicated.

Algorithm 2. Optimal Assignment Problem Hierarchy Algorithm

```
1: function DEFAULTHIERARCHYOPERATORBEHAVIOR
2:     ManageSwarm()
3:     if HasAssignments() and CanSendMessage() then
4:         nextOperator = GetUninformedOperatorFarthestFromAssignment()
5:         sendAssignments(nextOperator)
6:     end if
7:     if MessageIsReadyToBeProessed() then
8:         ProcessMessageQueue()
9:     end if
10: end function
11: function SUBORDINATEBEHAVIOR
12:     if Time = Phase1TimeLimit then
13:         SendReport(Leader)
14:     end if
15:     DefaultHierarchyOperatorBehavior()
16: end function
17: function LEADERBEHAVIOR
18:     if ReceivedMessagesFromAll() and !AssignmentsCreated() then
19:         for s in GetBestMSites():
20:             AssignOperatorToSite(GetClosestUnassignedOperatorToSite(s), s)
21:     end if
22:     DefaultHierarchyOperatorBehavior()
23: end function
24: function PROCESSMESSAGEQUEUE
25:     msg ← GetMessageFromQueue()
26:     if this.IsLeader():
27:         AddToKnownSites(msg.GetReportedSites())
28:     else:
29:         SetAssignment(msg.GetAssignment())
30: end function
```

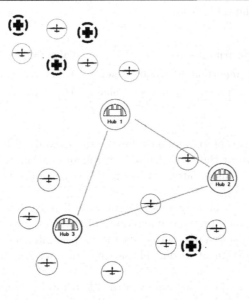

Fig. 6. Three hubs and four sites

Algorithm 3. Optimal Assignment Problem Team Algorithm

1: **function** TEAMBEHAVIOR
2:     $ManageSwarm()$
3:     **if** $Time > Phase1TimeLimit$ **and** $CanSendMessage()$ **then**
4:         **if** $GetSelectedSite() == null$ **then**
5:             $SetSelectedSite(GetBestUnclaimedSite()))$
6:         **end if**
7:         $nextNeighbor \leftarrow GetClosestUnmessagedNeighborToThisOperator()$
8:         $nextNeighbor.AddMessageToQueue(knownSites, knownClaims)$
9:     **end if**
10:    **if** $MessageIsReadyToBeProcessed()$ **then**
11:        $ProcessMessageQueue()$
12:    **end if**
13: **end function**
14: **function** PROCESSMESSAGEQUEUE
15:     $msg \leftarrow GetMessageFromQueue()$
16:     $knownSites.union(msg.reportedSites)$
17:     $UpdateKnownClaims(msg.knownClaims)$
18:     $ResolveConflicts()$
19: **end function**

---

6 Experiment Results

6.1 Experiment Structure

We developed and ran the simulation in the Unity engine over a series of parameters detailed in the table below:

Experiment parameters	Value range
Latency (proportion of second phase)	0.05, 0.15, ..., 0.85, 0.95
Bandwidth (proportion of second phase)	0.05, 0.15, ..., 0.85, 0.95

The most important parameters, latency and bandwidth, are measured in terms of the length of the second phase of the simulation, or 65% of the total simulation length. This is intended to provide a generalizable result from this work.

Note that in the table above, for latency the listed values describe the proportion of second phase mission time required between the sending and receiving of a message. For bandwidth, perhaps somewhat counter-intuitively, the values describe the proportion of second phase time an operator must wait between sending messages.

Initial tests focused on the performance of four randomly uniform distributed hubs among eight randomly uniform distributed sites. No minimum distance between any combination of hubs and sites was enforced. We varied latency and bandwidth delay each to be in the value ranges of 5% to 95% of mission time in the second phase of the simulation. We ran 30 tests for each block, where hub positions, site positions, and site qualities were each randomly generated for each trial.

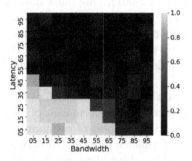

Fig. 7. Hierarchy results

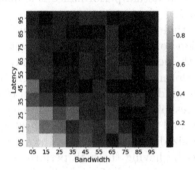

Fig. 8. Team results

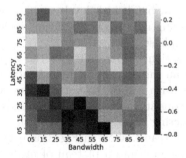

Fig. 9. Comparison results

6.2   Effect of Latency and Bandwidth on Hierarchy and Team Performance

A logistic regression analysis of the entire data set confirms the notion that a meaningful relationship exists among organization type, latency, bandwidth, and mission performance ($p < .0001$). One must note, however, that the differences between hierarchy and team performance for specific settings of latency and bandwidth are generally not statistically significant. We nevertheless use the heat-maps describing cell-by-cell performance of the hierarchy and team organizations to provide useful indications of where one organization outperforms the other.

Some features of the data are consistent with our hypothesis, other features are not. Recall that the predicted performance of the hierarchy organization anticipated high performance in the best of communication conditions, uniform and gradual decreasing performance in either direction of increasing latency or constricting bandwidth, and a sudden, diagonal drop-off along the a line stretching from constricted bandwidth and low latency to high bandwidth and high latency. Figure 7 shows that actual performance is similar to, but not identical to, predicted performance.

Hypothesized and actual performance of hierarchies are similar in the best and worst communication conditions (the lower left and upper right of Fig. 7). They are also similar in the possession of a straight, sharp threshold between high performance and low performance running diagonally from the middle of the left side of the graph to the middle of the bottom portion of the graph. They differ in the sense that the threshold between high performance and low performance occurs at lower latency and higher bandwidth values in comparison with the threshold of the hypothesized data (See Fig. 4). The actual data also differs from the hypothesized results by having the high performance side of the threshold be nearly uniform in quality instead of gradually degrading. Lastly, the actual data shows that hierarchies are able to tolerate higher amounts of bandwidth constriction than latency restrictions; this is seen in Fig. 7 the hierarchy achieves near perfect performance in bandwidth levels as high as 65% of second phase time as opposed to achieving near perfect performance with latency levels only as high as 45% of second phase time.

For the team organization, also recall that the hypothesized performance of the organization was an initial peak at high bandwidth and low latency, a uniform descent in score with respect to both latency and bandwidth, a large plateau at medium score quality, and a sudden drop in performance at the most extreme conditions restricting latency and bandwidth.

Actual performance of teams, show in Fig. 8, is marked by initial high performance and gradual slope off into a plateau of mediocre solutions. However, the plateau is much lower than anticipated: at best .3 or .4 in an area where .5 was expected (see Fig. 5). Furthermore, there was no sudden drop-off for the team organization. Performance smoothly transitioned from high to low as either latency increased or bandwidth decreased.

Most importantly, we compare the hypothesized and actual differences between the performances of the two organizations. The hypothesized differences can be inferred by taking the differences between Fig. 5 and Fig. 4. As expected from our previous discussion, at extremes there was no significant difference in performance between the hierarchy and team organization. This matches the expected outcome of the experiments. Like in the hypothesized differences for organizational performance, in the results there is a band of values next to the set of ideal conditions that favors hierarchical performance; this band is the set of dark cells in the lower-left quadrant of Fig. 9. Unlike the hypothesis, however, in this band the hierarchy is shown to be slightly better than expected while bandwidth is low and much better than expected when bandwidth is constricted. Beyond this band of values, the team is shown to be only slightly better or no different than the hierarchy in performance. This contrasts with the expected uniform band of superior performance by the team organization under conditions of high latency and constricted bandwidth.

7   Summary

This paper explored how effectively hierarchical and team organizations could manage swarm agents in the best-m-of-n task. Our desire was to see how human operators helped or hindered multiple semi-autonomous, hub-based swarms working together in this task. We designed and created a simulation that models human operator behavior, swarm agent behavior, and the problem environment. Greedy algorithms were employed for both hierarchy and team organizations. Hundreds of tests were run to evaluate the performance of simulated hierarchies and teams when subject to varying levels of latency and bandwidth, as well as other factors including hub and site distribution.

The data from the tests are consistent with our hypothesis that teams are a more suitable choice when communication difficulties exist, and hierarchies are more suitable for favorable communication settings. As expected, teams were shown to choose effectively who to share information with in order to avoid collisions or assist other hubs. Contrary to expectations, teams outperformed hierarchies instead of only equalling their performance in medium levels of latency and bandwidth.

These results suggest the conclusion that using Bavelas' and Steiner's classification of tasks, under favorable network conditions the best-m-of-n task is a simple or disjunctive task suitable for hierarchical structures, and a complicated or discretionary task when network conditions are unfavorable. This distinction is likely created by the abundance of information sharing under favorable network conditions and the siloing of information under unfavorable network conditions.

Acknowledgement. The work in this paper was supported by a grant from the US Office of Naval Research under grant number N000141613025. All opinions, findings, and results are the responsibility of the authors and not the sponsoring organization.

References

1. Bavelas, A.: Communication patterns in task-oriented groups. J. Acoust. Soc. Am. **22**(6), 725–730 (1950)
2. Bonabeau, E., Dorigo, M., Theraulaz, G.: Swarm Intelligence: From Natural to Artificial Systems, vol. 1. Oxford University Press, Oxford (1999)
3. Brown, D.S., Kerman, S.C., Goodrich, M.A.: Human-swarm interactions based on managing attractors. In Proceedings of the 2014 ACM/IEEE International Conference on Human-Robot Interaction, pp. 90–97. ACM (2014)
4. Castello, E., et al.: Adaptive foraging for simulated and real robotic swarms: the dynamical response threshold approach. Swarm Intell. **10**(1), 1–31 (2016)
5. Coppin, G., Legras, F.: Autonomy spectrum and performance perception issues in swarm supervisory control. Proc. IEEE **100**(3), 590–603 (2012). https://doi.org/10.1109/JPROC.2011.2174103. ISSN 0018–9219
6. Coppin, G., Legras, F.: Controlling swarms of unmanned vehicles through user-centered commands. In: AAAI Fall Symposium: Human Control of Bioinspired Swarms, pp. 21–25 (2012)
7. Crandall, J.W., et al.: Human-swarm interaction as shared control: achieving flexible fault-tolerant systems. In: Harris, D. (ed.) EPCE 2017. LNCS (LNAI), vol. 10275, pp. 266–284. Springer, Cham (2017). https://doi.org/10.1007/978-3-319-58472-0_21
8. Cummings, M.L., Guerlain, S.: Developing operator capacity estimates for supervisory control of autonomous vehicles. Hum. Factors **49**(1), 1–15 (2007)
9. Flap, H., Bulder, B., Beate, V., et al.: Intra-organizational networks and performance: a review. Comput. Math. Organ. Theory **4**(2), 109–147 (1998)
10. Garnier, S., Gautrais, J., Theraulaz, G.: The biological principles of swarm intelligence. Swarm Intell. **1**(1), 3–31 (2007)
11. Guetzkow, H., Simon, H.A.: The impact of certain communication nets upon organization and performance in task-oriented groups. Manage. Sci. **1**(3–4), 233–250 (1955)
12. Jung, S.-Y., Brown, D.S., Goodrich, M.A.: Shaping Couzin-like torus swarms through coordinated mediation. In: 2013 IEEE International Conference on Systems, Man, and Cybernetics (SMC), pp. 1834–1839. IEEE (2013)
13. Kolling, A., Sycara, K., Nunnally, S., Lewis, M.: Human swarm interaction: an experimental study of two types of interaction with foraging swarms. J. Hum.-Robot Interact. **2**(2), 103–129 (2013)
14. Leavitt, H.J., Mueller, R.A.H.: Some effects of feedback on communication. Hum. Relat. **4**(4), 401–410 (1951)
15. Lee, D., Franchi, A., Giordano, P.R., Son, H.I., Bülthoff, H.H.: Haptic teleoperation of multiple unmanned aerial vehicles over the internet. In: 2011 IEEE International Conference on Robotics and Automation (ICRA), pp. 1341–1347. IEEE (2011)
16. Miller, C.A., Funk, H.B., Dorneich, M., Whitlow, S.D.: A playbook interface for mixed initiative control of multiple unmanned vehicle teams. In: Proceedings of the 21st Digital Avionics Systems Conference, 2002, Proceedings, vol. 2, pp. 7E4–7E4. IEEE(2002)
17. Navarro, F.: An introduction to swarm robotics. ISRN Robot. **2013**, 1–10 (2012)
18. Nevai, A.L., Passino, K.M., Srinivasan, P.: Stability of choice in the honey bee nest-site selection process. J. Theor. Biol. **263**(1), 93–107 (2010)
19. Niku, S.B.: Introduction to Robotics: Analysis, Systems, Applications, vol. 7. Prentice Hall, Upper Saddle River (2001)

20. Pendleton, B., Goodrich, M.: Scalable human interaction with robotic swarms. In: AIAA Infotech@ Aerospace (I@ A) Conference, p. 4731 (2013)
21. Rubenstein, M., Ahler, C., Nagpal, R.: Kilobot: a low cost scalable robot system for collective behaviors. In: 2012 IEEE International Conference on Robotics and Automation (ICRA), pp. 3293–3298. IEEE (2012)
22. Schmickl, T., Hamann, H.: BEECLUST: a swarm algorithm derived from honeybees. In: Bio-Inspired Computing and Communication Networks. CRC Press, March 2011
23. Shaw, M.E.: Some effects of unequal distribution of information upon group performance in various communication nets. J. Abnorm. Soc. Psychol. **49**(4p1), 547 (1954)
24. Steiner, I.D.: Group Processes and Group Productivity. Academic Press, New York (1972)
25. Steinfeld, A., Jenkins, O.C., Scassellati, B.: The Oz of wizard: simulating the human for interaction research. In: Proceedings of the 4th ACM/IEEE International Conference on Human Robot Interaction, pp. 101–108. ACM (2009)
26. Valentini, G., Ferrante, E., Dorigo, M.: The best-of-n problem in robot swarms: formalization, state of the art, and novel perspectives. Front. Robot. AI **4** (2017). https://doi.org/10.3389/frobt.2017.00009
27. Wilson, S., et al.: Pheeno, a versatile swarm robotic research and education platform. IEEE Robot. Autom. Lett. **1**(2), 884–891 (2016)

The Current Status and Challenges in Augmented-Reality Navigation System for Robot-Assisted Laparoscopic Partial Nephrectomy

Akihiro Hamada[1], Atsuro Sawada[1], Jin Kono[1], Masanao Koeda[2], Katsuhiko Onishi[2], Takashi Kobayashi[1], Toshinari Yamasaki[1], Takahiro Inoue[1], Hiroshi Noborio[2], and Osamu Ogawa[1(✉)]

[1] Department of Urology, Graduate School of Medicine, Kyoto University, Kyoto, Japan
ogawao@kuhp.kyoto-u.ac.jp
[2] Department of Computer Science, Osaka Electro-Communication University, Osaka, Japan

Abstract. Robot-assisted surgeries have enabled surgeons to perform complex procedures more precisely and easily as compared with the conventional laparoscopic surgery. These new technologies have expanded the indications of the nephron-sparing surgery to cases that are anatomically more complicated. One of the challenging cases is that of the completely endophytic tumors because surgeons do not have any visual clues about tumor location on the kidney surface. In addition, these tumors pose technical challenges for their localization and resection, thereby likely increasing the possibility of perioperative complications. Since April 2014, we have been developing a visual support system for performing robot-assisted laparoscopic partial nephrectomy (RAPN) using the augmented-reality (AR) technology. The AR-based navigation system for RAPN can help identify the vasculature structure and tumor location easily and objectively. Moreover, image registration and organ tracking are critical to improving the accuracy of the system. Notably, tissue deformation, manual adjustment, and depth perception are the key elements for achieving precise image registration. Thus, console surgeons must effectively understand the properties and weak points of the AR navigation system and, accordingly, manipulate the laparoscopic camera and robot forceps to facilitate image registration and organ tracking. The cooperation of the console surgeon can result in a better collaboration between the real-time operation image and three-dimensional computer graphics models in the navigation system. We expect our system will offer significant benefits to both surgeons and patients.

Keywords: Robot-assisted laparoscopic partial nephrectomy (RAPN) · Augmented reality (AR) · Navigation system · Renal tumor

1 Introduction

The standard treatment for localized renal tumors is the nephron-sparing surgery [1]. The robot-assisted laparoscopic partial nephrectomy (RAPN) is an excellent and minimally

© Springer Nature Switzerland AG 2020
M. Kurosu (Ed.): HCII 2020, LNCS 12182, pp. 620–629, 2020.
https://doi.org/10.1007/978-3-030-49062-1_42

invasive treatment that can achieve both cancer control and renal-function preservation. Robot-assisted surgeries have enabled surgeons to perform complex procedures more precisely and quickly compared with the conventional laparoscopic surgery because of both the clear visual field provided by three-dimensional cameras and precise motion by articulated arms. These new technologies have expanded the indications of the nephron-sparing surgery to cases that are anatomically more complicated.

One of the challenging cases is that of the completely endophytic tumors because surgeons do not have any visual clues regarding the tumor location on the kidney surface (see Fig. 1) [2, 3]. In addition, these tumors pose technical challenges for localization and resection, thereby increasing the distinct possibility of perioperative complications. Recently, some reports asserted the safety and feasibility of RAPN for treating endophytic tumors; however, the operations were performed only by experienced surgeons in these reports. Although the use of intraoperative ultrasound is recommended [4], it is not always adequate in assessing the precise border when the tumor is either completely endophytic or appears relatively isoechoic. The misidentification of the tumor location may result in longer operative time, positive surgical margin, and unnecessary loss of normal kidney tissue. Therefore, to avoid predictable perioperative complications, surgeons, especially novice ones, must support the visualization of the tumor location.

Since April 2014, we have been developing a visual support system for RAPN using the augmented-reality (AR) technology. Appropriate image guidance using the AR navigation system can offer a potential clinical advantage for performing accurate anatomical identification and precise resection of tumors, reducing the possibility of perioperative complications.

In this report, we describe the current status of our navigation system and the underlying problems thereof via our in-vivo human experiences.

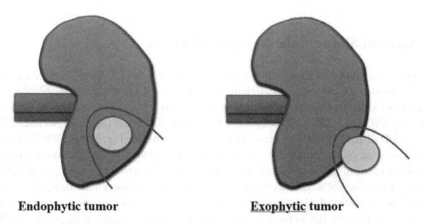

Endophytic tumor   **Exophytic tumor**

Fig. 1. Difference between an endophytic and exophytic tumor.

2   Surgical Technique of RAPN

We used either the transperitoneal or retroperitoneal approach depending on the tumor location. Patients were placed in the lateral position. After placing the robotic ports, the da Vinci Xi Surgical system (Intuitive Surgical, Inc., Sunnyvale, CA) was docked. The surgical procedures included the following: mobilization of the bowel, exposure of the kidney, identification of the hilum, and dissection of the renal artery and vein. Subsequently, the kidney was defatted, and the console surgeon identified the tumor depth and margin via robotic ultrasound. After identifying the tumor location and adequate margin of normal parenchyma, the hilum was clamped, following which the tumor was resected, and the defect was reconstructed by suturing the renal capsule (see Fig. 2).

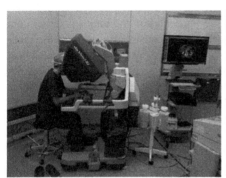

Fig. 2. Overview of the RAPN. (Left: console surgeon, Right: assistant surgeon)

3   Current Status of the Navigation System

We previously reported about our AR navigation system for RAPN [5]. Before surgery, we prepared three-dimensional computer graphics (3DCG) models that included the graphics of kidneys, arteries, veins, tumors, and urinary tracts, all of which were obtained from the DICOM images of computed tomography (CT) scans with SYNAPSE VIN-CENT (FUJIFILM Holdings Corporation, Tokyo, Japan) (see Fig. 3). The 3DCG models were projected on the console of the operator by using the Tilepro function and on the operating room monitor. An assistant doctor manually controlled the projected 3DCG model of the visceral structures during the surgery. The position and orientation of the 3DCG model were calculated using the optical flow of the endoscopic camera images, thereby enabling the 3DCG model to track the laparoscopic images semi-automatically.

We have applied this surgical navigation system for a total of 38 RAPN cases from November 2014 to June 2019. The main purpose of this system is to show the hilum structure and identify the tumor location, especially for endophytic tumors. However, some barriers exist toward achieving a practically useful navigation system for console surgeons.

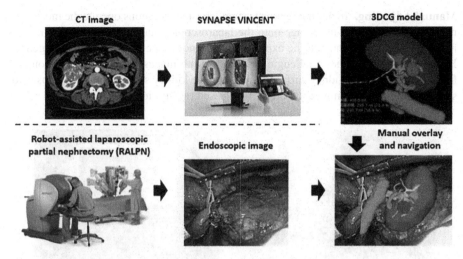

Fig. 3. Overview of our current AR navigation system.

4   Challenges to Overcome

Applying the 3DCG image onto intra-abdominal kidneys poses many challenges. The kidneys do not stay at the same position during the surgery relative to the surrounding organs. Moreover, the size and shape of the kidney during operation also varies both because of clamping the hilum and manipulation of the organ and dissection [6]. We describe the current problems by focusing on two steps, namely, image registration and organ tracking.

4.1   Image Registration

The registration of the 3DCG image to intraoperative organs is the first step to overlay. We intend to align the preoperative 3D image with laparoscopic image by matching corresponding locations such as hilar vasculature, kidney shape, kidney-surface characteristics, and surrounding anatomic structures. The registration must be highly accurate to indicate adequate margin from the tumor when determining the resection line.

We consider the following three reasons that decrease the accuracy of image registration: tissue deformation, manual adjustment, and depth perception.

Tissue Deformation. Tissue deformation is one of the major challenges during operation. The 3DCG model comprises preoperative CT images, which reflect the kidney shape for the prone position of the patient. However, during the actual operation, the kidney is deformed via several factors such as lateral position of the patient, pneumoperitoneum, surgical dissection, physiological cardiorespiratory pattern, and clamping renal vessels [6]. Therefore, to achieve precise image registration, the preoperative 3DCG models must reflect the real-time laparoscopic image that changes at every step of the surgery.

Manual Adjusting. In our navigation system, assistant surgeons operate the models to manually superimpose the image onto the laparoscopic image. Therefore, the image-matching quality depends on the experience and knowledge of the assistant surgeons. However, it is sometimes challenging to overlay the images because there are only a few landmarks on the kidney surface. Therefore, the kidney surface must be exposed to some extent for performing accurate surface-based registration (see Fig. 4).

Fig. 4. Assistant surgeon manually operating the 3DCG models. (Left: The console surgeon and assistant surgeon, Right: Controller of the 3D models)

Depth Perspective. The da Vinci surgical system is equipped with stereo cameras, which provide excellent 3D images. During the operation, we can feel depth perspective that is very useful for precise operation. However, overlay 3DCG models do not exactly reflect the same depth perspective as that reflected by the real operation image. Therefore, a depth perspective gap is formed depending on the distance from the laparoscopic camera to organs, for example, between the upper and lower poles of the kidney. To achieve complete image registration, the 3DCG models must reflect the same depth perspective in the real-time images. Therefore, the tumors in the lower pole are less effected by the depth-perspective gap (see Fig. 5).

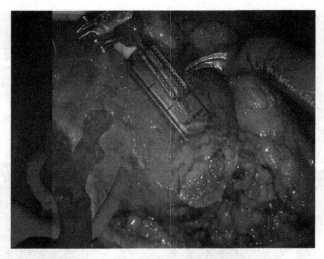

Fig. 5. The tumor in lower pole is easier to overlay.

4.2 Organ Tracking

Another issue that affects the accuracy of image registration is the insufficiency of the tracking performance. The overlaid registered image will be expected to lock to the operative view and synchronously move with the organ. We use the optical flow system of the endoscopic camera images; the system calculates the position and orientation of the 3DCG model and enables the 3DCG model to semi-automatically track the laparoscopic images. During the operation, the characteristic landmarks of the kidney change continuously as surgeons mobilize the neighboring organs and raise the kidney to dissect the vasculature. The surrounding fat and bleeding can also decrease the accuracy of organ tracking.

In robot-assisted surgeries, surgeons rely only on visual information because of the lack of haptic feedback. Therefore, the laparoscopic camera repeatedly moves back and forth to confirm the overview of the operation field and detailed structures such as small vasculatures. However, our tracking system cannot follow the quick motion of the camera, resulting in the failure of image registration.

5 Future Plans

5.1 Development of New Technology

Surface-Matching System. To overcome the challenges during image registration, we are developing a new registration method equipped with a surface-matching technique [7]. In this system, an object can be detected and localized by combining both intensity and depth data. This technique can assess the position and posture of the kidney by identifying the common features between 3D models obtained using real-time surgical images and 3DCG models obtained using preoperative CT images. The validation of the technique is presently in progress (see Fig. 6).

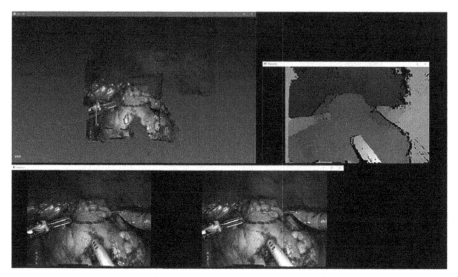

Fig. 6. Disparity map (upper right) and point cloud (upper left) generated from the stereo images simultaneously captured during surgery for the surface matching.

Simultaneous Localization and Mapping. Since April 2018, we have been testing the simultaneous localization and mapping (SLAM) technique to achieve a totally automatic tracking system [8]. The SLAM system imports the information of the characteristic features from the operation images, estimates its own location, and creates a map of its surrounding environment. The SLAM technique might improve the tracking ability of our navigation system. Thus far, models cannot follow the quick motion of the endoscopic camera even when the SLAM system is working, and when the camera returns to the endoscopic port, it resets the SLAM system. To overcome these problems, we are trying to install Stereo SLAM system. To utilize Stereo SLAM, we first conducted stereo endoscopic camera calibration and acquired the camera parameters (see Fig. 7a). Using this parameter, Stereo SLAM during surgery was tested in July 2019 and we confirmed that the tracking robustness was improved than the conventional SLAM (see Fig. 7b).

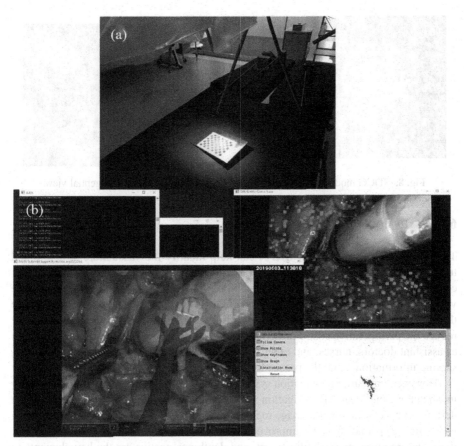

Fig. 7. (a) Stereo camera calibration in vitro setting. (b) Stereo SLAM during surgery.

5.2 Cooperation of the Surgeons

As describe previously, many challenges still exist to achieve a practical system. Thus far, the understanding of this system and corporation of the console surgeons is critical to achieving better collaboration.

The important points for achieving accurate image registration are as follows:

- remove the fat tissue surrounding the kidney as widely as possible;
- put the kidney on a flat position;
- see the kidney from the side view (not from the tangential direction) to reduce the depth-perspective gap when overlaying the 3DCG model on the real operative image (see Fig. 8).

The important points for achieving accurate organ tracking are as follows:

- move the camera slowly;
- do not pull the camera into the camera port.

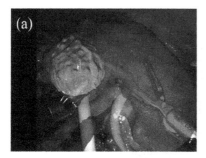 

Fig. 8. 3DCG model on a real operative image. (a) Side view. (b) Tangential view.

6 Discussion

The AR navigation system for RAPN can help identify the vasculature structure and tumor location easily and objectively. Consequently, we can expect better surgical outcomes such as short operative time, less blood loss, and reduced complications. The visually supporting system can compensate for less surgical experience and help improve the learning curve of novice surgeons. In addition, less invasiveness of the surgery may reduce the perioperative cost. Furthermore, as all the staffs in the operation room, such as assistant doctors, nurses, and other medical staffs, can see the projected 3D images, sharing information about the proceeding of the surgery.

However, our current navigation system still has some defects associated with tumor localization. The ideal AR navigation system would have the ability of flexible tissue deformation, fully automatic image registration, and organ tracking. Image registration is the first step that must be improved to achieve the accurate system. In addition, tissue deformation, manual adjustment, and depth perspective are the key elements to achieving precise image registration. Surface-matching system might adjust the image automatically. Accordingly, SLAM is a new technology for the intraoperative tracking of an image. However, even these new technologies cannot work smoothly when the operation view is changing significantly. Although there have been several reports that examined the AR system for RAPN, much work need be done before AR surgical systems can be used for performing accurate image-guided tumor resection [6]. Thus far, console surgeons must understand the properties and weak points of the AR navigation system and, accordingly, manipulate the laparoscopic camera and robot forceps to facilitate both image registration and organ tracking. In addition, the cooperation of the console surgeon can help achieve a better collaboration between the real-time operation image and 3DCG models in the navigation system.

Patients merit the utmost priority in any surgery; therefore, a time-consuming, inaccurate system is not practical. The "Trifecta" outcome is a concept that comprises the following three criteria: warm ischemia time < 25 min, negative surgical margin, and no perioperative complications [9]. To increase the Trifecta achievement rate is one of the goals for achieving better surgical results [10]. Although our current navigation system partially supports the identification of the tumor location, it must be improved to achieve higher accuracy and clinically validate the improvement of perioperative outcomes.

7   Conclusion

We developed a novel AR navigation system for RAPN. Our navigation system performed appropriately and partially helped to localize the tumor and determine the resection lines. However, the current challenge lies in improving both image-registration and organ-tracking performances. We expect our system will offer significant benefits to both surgeons and patients.

Acknowledgment. This study was supported in part by Grant-in-aid from the Ministry of Education and Science (to A.S. # 17K13035 and to M.K. # 18K11496). The authors thank all the past and present laboratory members in the Department of Urology, Kyoto University Graduate School of Medicine, Kyoto, Japan for their technical assistance. We would like to thank Editage (www.editage.com) for English language editing.

References

1. Ljungberg, B., Albiges, L., et al.: European association of urology guidelines on renal cell carcinoma: the 2019 update. Eur. Urol. **75**(5), 799–810 (2019)
2. Autorino, R., Khalifeh, A., et al.: Robot-assisted partial nephrectomy (RAPN) for completely endophytic renal masses: a single institution experience. BJU Int. **113**(5), 762–768 (2014)
3. Komninos, C., Shin, T.Y., et al.: Robotic partial nephrectomy for completely endophytic renal tumors: complications and functional and oncologic outcomes during a 4-year median period of follow-up. Urology. **84**(6), 1367–1373 (2014)
4. Assimos, D.G., Boyce, H., et al.: Intraoperative renal ultrasonography: a useful adjunct to partial nephrectomy. J. Urol. **146**(5), 1218–1220 (1991)
5. Sengiku, A., Koeda, M., et al.: Augmented reality navigation system for robot-assisted laparoscopic partial nephrectomy. In: DUXU: Design, User Experience, and Usability: Designing Pleasurable Experiences, pp. 575–584 (2017)
6. Hughes-Hallett, A., Mayer, E.K., et al.: Augmented reality partial nephrectomy: examining the current status and future perspectives. Urology. **83**(2), 266–273 (2014)
7. Drost, B., Ulrich, M., et al.: Model globally, match locally: efficient and robust 3D object recognition. In: 2010 IEEE Computer Society Conference on Computer Vision and Pattern Recognition, pp. 998–1005 (2010)
8. Mur-Artal, R., Tardós, J.D.: ORB-SLAM2: an open-source SLAM system for monocular, stereo and RGB-D cameras. IEEE Trans. Robot. **33**(5), 1255–1262 (2017)
9. Hung, A.J., Cai, J., et al.: "Trifecta" in partial nephrectomy. J. Urol. **189**(1), 36–42 (2013)
10. Furukawa, J., Kanayama, H., et al.: 'Trifecta' outcomes of robot-assisted partial nephrectomy: a large Japanese multicenter study. Int. J. Clin. Oncol. (2019). https://doi.org/10.1007/s10147-019-01565-0. [Epub ahead of print]

Database Semantics for Talking Autonomous Robots

Roland Hausser[✉]

Universität Erlangen-Nürnberg (em.), Erlangen, Germany
rrh@linguistik.uni-erlangen.de

Abstract. Database Semantics (DBS) models the cycle of natural language communication as a transition from the hear to the think to the speak and back to the hear mode (turn taking). In contradistinction to the substitution-driven sign-based approaches of truth-conditional semantics and phrase structure grammar, DBS is data-driven and agent-based. The purpose is a theory of semantics for an autonomous robot with language.

Propositions are content in DBS, instead of denoting truth values (Sects. 1–3). Content is built from the semantic kinds of referent, property, and relation, which are concatenated by the classical semantic relations of structure, i.e. functor-argument and coordination. To enable reference as an agent-internal cognitive process, language and nonlanguage contents use the same computational data structure and operation kinds, and differ mostly in the presence vs. absence of language-dependent surface values.

DBS consists of (i) an interface, (ii) a memory, and (iii) an operation component. (The components correspond roughly to those of a von Neumann machine (Neumann 1945): the (i) interface component corresponds to the vNm input-output device, the (ii) memory (database) component corresponds to the vNm memory, and the (iii) operation component performs functions of the vNm arithmetic-logic unit.) The interface component mediates between the agent's cognition and its external and internal environment, represented as raw data provided by sensors and activators (Sects. 4–7). The data of the agent's moment by moment monitoring are stored at the memory's now front. As part of the on-board control unit, the now front is the location for performing the procedures of the operation component, resulting in content.

Keywords: Data structure · Data base schema · Pattern matching · Turn taking · Type-token · Grounding · Sensory and processing media and modalities · Reference

1 Building Content in the Agent's Hear Mode

DBS defines a content in terms of concepts like **square** or **blue** connected with the classical semantic relations of structure such as subject/predicate and conjunct−conjunct. The concepts are supplied by the agent's memory and defined as types. In recognition, they are activated by matching raw data provided by the

© Springer Nature Switzerland AG 2020
M. Kurosu (Ed.): HCII 2020, LNCS 12182, pp. 630–643, 2020.
https://doi.org/10.1007/978-3-030-49062-1_43

interface component, resulting in tokens.[1] In action, a type is adapted to a current purpose as a token and realized as raw data (Sect. 7)

For concatenation, the concepts are embedded as core values into nonrecursive feature structures with ordered attributes, called proplets. Proplets serve as the computational data structure of DBS. The semantic relations between proplets are established by address. Consider the following example:

THE CONTENT OF The dog snored.

$$
\begin{bmatrix}
\text{sur:} \\
\text{noun: } \textbf{dog} \\
\text{cat: def sg} \\
\text{sem:} \\
\text{fnc: } \textbf{snore} \\
\text{mdr:} \\
\text{nc:} \\
\text{pc:} \\
\text{prn: 24}
\end{bmatrix}
\begin{bmatrix}
\text{sur:} \\
\text{verb: } \textbf{snore} \\
\text{cat: \#n' decl} \\
\text{sem: past ind} \\
\text{arg: } \textbf{dog} \\
\text{mdr:} \\
\text{nc:} \\
\text{pc:} \\
\text{prn:24}
\end{bmatrix}
$$

The proplets implement the subject/predicate relation by using the noun value **dog** of the first proplet as the arg value of the second, and the verb value **snore** as the fnc value of the first (bidirectional pointering).

In the hear mode, the above content results from the following derivation:

SURFACE COMPOSITIONAL TIME-LINEAR HEAR MODE DERIVATION

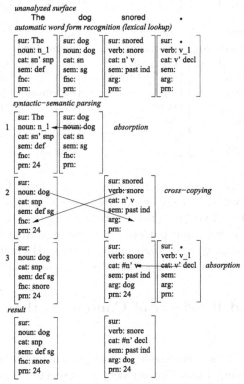

In DBS, hear mode derivations are time-linear and surface compositional.

---

[1] The type-token distinction was introduced by C. S. Peirce (CP 4:537).

There are three kinds of hear mode operations: (1) cross-copying, (2) absorption, and (3) suspension. Cross-copying encodes the semantic relations of structure such as SBJ×PRED (line 2). Absorption combines function words with content word such as DET∪CN (line 1). Suspension such as ADV∼NOM (TExer 3.1.3) applies if no semantic relation exists for connecting the next word with the content processed so far, as in Perhaps ∼ Fido (is still sleeping there now).

DBS operations consist of (i) an antecedent, (ii) a connective, and (iii) a consequent. Defined as proplet patterns, DBS operations are data-driven in that they are activated by content proplets matching part of the pattern as input. Consider the hear mode operation SBJ×PRED as it applies in line 2:

HEAR MODE OPERATION SBJ×PRED APPLYING BY CROSS-COPYING

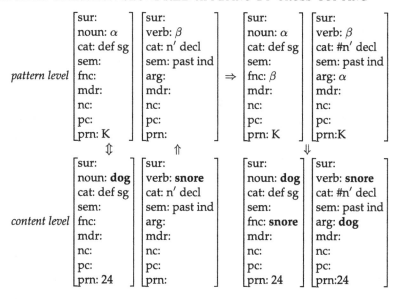

In the hear mode, the second proplet at the content level, here *snore*, resulted from automatic word form recognition. By *snore* matching the second input pattern at the pattern level (⇑), the operation is triggered to look for a content proplet matching its first input pattern (⇕) at the now front the special case of a sentence start consisting of a single lexical proplet. By binding α to dog and β to snore, the consequent produces the output as content proplets (⇓).

2   Storage and Retrieval of Content in the On-Board Memory

Contents derived in the hear mode and activated in the think-speak mode (Sect. 3) have in common that they are defined as sets of self-contained proplets, concatenated by proplet-internal address. As sets, the proplets of a content are order-free, which is essential for their storage in and retrieval from the agent's

A-memory (formerly called word bank). The database schema of A-memory is defined as follows:

TWO-DIMENSIONAL DATABASE SCHEMA OF A-MEMORY

- *horizontal token line*
  Horizontally, proplets with the same core value are stored in the same token line in the time-linear order of their arrival.
- *vertical column of token lines*
  Vertically, token lines are in the alphabetical order induced by the letter sequence of their core value.

The arrival order of the member proplets is reflected by (a) the position in their token line and by (b) their prn value. The *(i) member proplets* are followed by a free slot as part of the column called the *(ii) now front*, and the *(iii) owner.*[2]

A-MEMORY BEFORE STORAGE OF THE CONTENT AT THE NOW FRONT

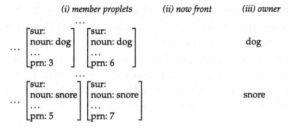

(i) member proplets	*(ii) now front*	*(iii) owner*
⎡sur: ⎤ ⎡sur: ⎤ ⎢noun: dog⎥ ⎢noun: dog⎥ ⎢... ⎥ ⎢... ⎥ ⎣prn: 3 ⎦ ⎣prn: 6 ⎦		dog
⎡sur: ⎤ ⎡sur: ⎤ ⎢noun: snore⎥ ⎢noun: snore⎥ ⎢... ⎥ ⎢... ⎥ ⎣prn: 5 ⎦ ⎣prn: 7 ⎦		snore

The owners equal the core values in their token line and are used for access in storage and retrieval. Proplets provided by current recognition, by A-memory, or by inferencing are stored at the now front in the token line corresponding to their core value:

STORAGE OF THE CONTENT AT THE NOW FRONT OF A-MEMORY

(i) member proplets		*(ii) now front*	*(iii) owner*
⎡sur: ⎤ ⎡sur: ⎤ ⎢noun: dog⎥ ⎢noun: dog⎥ ⎢... ⎥ ⎢... ⎥ ⎣prn: 3 ⎦ ⎣prn: 6 ⎦		⎡sur: chien⎤ ⎢noun: dog ⎥ ⎢... ⎥ ⎣prn: 14 ⎦	dog
⎡sur: ⎤ ⎡sur: ⎤ ⎢noun: snore⎥ ⎢noun: snore⎥ ⎢... ⎥ ⎢... ⎥ ⎣prn: 5 ⎦ ⎣prn: 7 ⎦		⎡sur: ronfler⎤ ⎢noun: snore ⎥ ⎢... ⎥ ⎣prn: 14 ⎦	snore

Once a content has been assembled as a proposition, the now front is cleared by moving it and the owners to the right into fresh memory space (loom-like clearance, Sect. 3). This leaves the proplets of the current content behind in

---

[2] The terminology of member proplets and owner values is reminiscent of the member and owner records in a classic network database (Elmasri and Navathe 1989[1]–2017[7]), which inspired the database schema of the A-memory in DBS.

what is becoming their permanent storage location as member proplets never to be changed, like sediment.

A-MEMORY AFTER NOW FRONT CLEARANCE

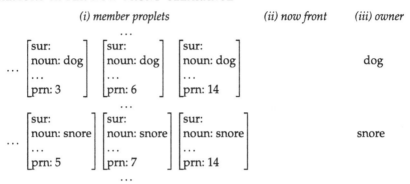

       (i) member proplets   *(ii) now front*   *(iii) owner*

Clearance of the current now front is triggered when its proplets have ceased to be candidates for additional concatenations. This is basically the case when an elementary proposition is completed (formally indicated by the automatic incrementation of the prn value for the next proposition). Exceptions are extrapropositional (i) coordination and (ii) functor-argument. In these two cases, the verb of the completed proposition must remain at the now front for cross-copying with the verb of the next proposition until the extrapropositional relation has been established (strictly time-linear derivation order).

3   Speak Mode Riding Piggyback on the Think Mode

The classical semantic relations of structure between the order-free proplets defined by address and stored in A-memory may be shown graphically as follows:

SEMANTIC RELATIONS GRAPH UNDERLYING THE CONTENT

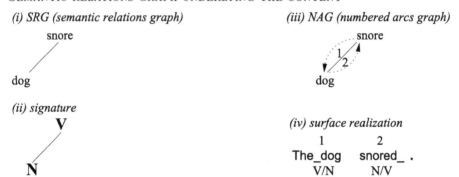

The *(iv) surface realization* shows the language-dependent production and is restricted to the speak mode riding piggy-back on the think mode navigation. The concepts dog and snore are provided by the agent's interface component as a declarative definition and an operational implementation (grounding, Sect. 7).

The arc numbers of the NAG are used for specifying (i) a think mode navigation and (ii) a think-speak mode surface production as shown by the *(iv) surface realization*. In the think mode, there are 14 kinds of traversal operations: (1) predicate/subject, (2) subject/predicate, (3) predicate\object, (4) object\predicate, (5) noun↓adnominal, (6) adnominal↑noun, (7) verb↓adverbial, (8) adverbial↑verb, (9) noun→noun, (10) noun←noun, (11) verb→verb, (12) verb←verb, (13) adnominal→adnominal, and (14) adnominal←adnominal.

The think mode operations driving the traversal of the NAG are V/N and N/V, and apply as follows:[3]

NAVIGATING WITH V/N FROM *snore* TO *dog* (arc 1)

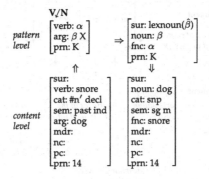

NAVIGATING WITH N/V FROM *dog* BACK TO *snore* (arc 2)

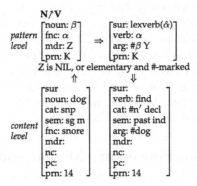

If the lexnoun rules in the sur slot of the output patterns are switched on (as assumed in the surface realization), they generate a language-dependent surface using relevant values of the output proplet.

---

[3] Because the Xfig graphics editor used here does not provide a satisfactory representation of arrows in the linear notation of speak mode operation names, the arrow heads are omitted in the *(iv) surface realization*. Nevertheless, the direction of a traversal is specified unambiguously by the arc number written directly above in the top line. For further detail see NLC 6.1.4 ff.; CLaTR Chap. 7.

4   Graphical Summary of the DBS Component Structure

The component structure of a DBS agent may be summarized graphically as follows:

TWO-DIMENSIONAL LAYOUT OF DBS COGNITION COMPONENTS

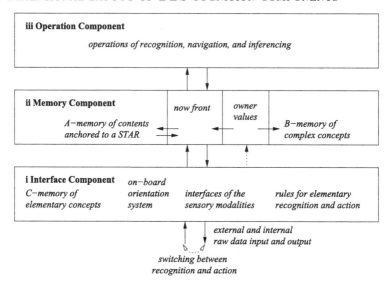

Cognitive content is processed at the now front. It gets proplets (a) from the interface component (aided by the owners) and (b) from A-memory. For processing, the now front provides proplets as input to (iii) the operations, which either replace the input with their output or add their output to the input. As the now front is cleared in regular intervals by moving into fresh memory space (Sect. 2), the processed proplets are left behind in A-memory like sediment (loom-like clearance). Processing may also result in blueprints for action, which may be copied to the interface component for realization.

5   Sensory Media, Processing Media, and Their Modalities

The functional equivalence required between the artificial agent and its natural prototype is defined at a level of abstraction which is above the distinction between different processing media, such as natural, mechanical, and electronic processing. Functional equivalence is shown, for example, by the basic operations of arithmetic: $3 + 4$ equals 7 no matter whether the calculation is performed by (i) a human,[4] (ii) a mechanical calculator, or (iii) a computer.

In addition to the processing media there are the sensory media. In natural language communication, there exist four, each of which has two sensory

---

[4] The operations of arithmetic as they are processed by the human brain are described by Menon (2011).

modalities.[5] For example, if the speaker chooses the medium of speech, the only sensory modality for production is vocalization ($\searrow$), which leaves the hearer no other option than using the sensory modality of audition ($\nearrow$). This asymmetry of modalities holds also for the other sensory media of natural language, namely writing, Braille, and sign language:

SENSORY MEDIA AND THEIR MODALITIES IN NATURAL LANGUAGE

In terms of human evolution, the primary sensory medium is speech.

While the sensory media must be the same in the natural prototype and the artificial counterpart, as required by functional equivalence, the processing media are fundamentally different between the two. For the natural prototype, neurology suggests an electrochemical processing medium, though much is still unknown.[6] In artificial DBS cognition, in contrast, the processing medium is a programming language; its processing modalities are (i) the declarative specification of commands for interpretation by the computer and (ii) their procedural execution by the computer's electronic operations.

PROCESSING MEDIA AND THEIR DUAL PROCESSING MODALITIES

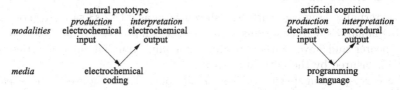

Utilizing a programming language as the processing medium of an artificial agent requires an interface component capable of efficiently mediating between raw data and an alphanumeric representation in recognition and action.

6 Reference as a Purely Cognitive Process

Sign-based philosophy defines reference as a relation between language (referring part) and the world (referred-to part).[7] Agent-based DBS, in contrast, confines reference to nouns (Hausser 2019, 1.5.3, 12.3.3) and distinguishes (1) between referring nouns with and without external surfaces and (2) between referred-to nouns

---

[5] In the literature, the term modality has a multitude of uses, such as the temperature (Dodt and Zotterman 1952), the logical (Barcan Marcus 1961), and the epistemic (Kiefer 2018) modalities.

[6] For an early overview see Benson (1994).

[7] Reimer and Michaelson (2014) extend the referring part from language to "representational tokens," which include cave paintings, pantomime, photographs, videos, etc. DBS goes further by generalizing the referring part to content per se, i.e. without the need for any external representation.

with and without external[8] counterparts. The two distinctions may be characterized by the binary features [±surface] and [±external], whereby [+external] reference is called *immediate*, while [−external] reference is called *mediated* (FoCL 4.3.1).

For example, identifying "the man with the brown coat" (Quine 1960) with
someone seen before, or identifying an unusual building with an earlier language
content, e.g. something read in a guide book or heard about, are [−surface +exter-
nal]. Talking about Aristotle or J.S. Bach, in contrast, is [+surface −external].

The four kinds of generalized DBS reference,[9] begin with the [+surface
+external] constellation between speaker and hearer:

IMMEDIATE REFERENCE IN LANGUAGE COMMUNICATION

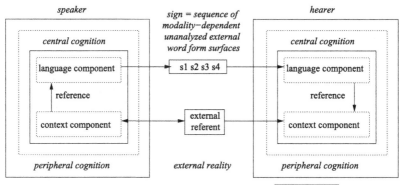

Agent-externally, language surfaces (shown here as s1 s2 s3 s4) are modality-
specific unanalyzed external signs (raw data) which are passed from the speaker
to the hearer and have neither meaning nor any grammatical properties, but
may be measured by the natural sciences.

The corresponding [+surface −external] constellation between the speaker
and the hearer is as follows:

MEDIATED REFERENCE IN LANGUAGE COMMUNICATION

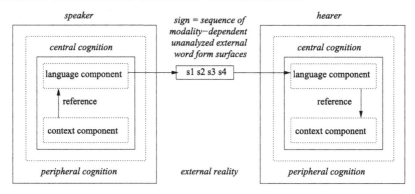

---

[8] Newell and Simon call the agent's external surroundings the *task environment* (Newell
and Simon 1972).

[9] The [±surface] and [±external] distinctions are not available in truth-conditional
semantics and generative grammar because their sign-based ontology provides neither for cognition nor for cognitive modes.

The reference relation begins with content in the memory of the speaker and ends as content in the memory of the hearer. The mechanisms of assigning surfaces to content in the speak mode and content to surfaces in the hear mode are the same in immediate and mediated language reference.[10]

The graphs show the speaker on the left, the sign in English writing order in the middle, and the hearer on the right. This is a possible constellation which is in concord with the naive assumption that time passes with the sun from left to right ($\rightarrow$) on the Northern Hemisphere. Yet it appears that the first surface s1 leaves the speaker last and the last surface s4 arrives at the hearer first, which would be functionally incorrect.

It is a pseudo-problem, however, which vanishes if each surface is transmitted individually and placed to the right of its predecessor, i.e. (((s1 s2) s3) s4). This *left-associative*[11] departure and arrival structure allows incremental surface by surface processing, provided the derivation order is based on computing possible continuations, as in Left-Associative grammar (LAG, Hausser 1992).

Nonlanguage reference differs from language reference in that it is [−surface]. Thereby nonlanguage immediate reference is [−surface [−surface +external] while nonlanguage mediated reference is [−surface −external]:

NONLANGUAGE IMMEDIATE VS. MEDIATED REFERENCE

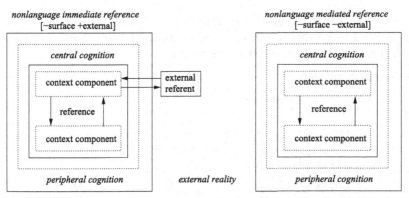

The referring content in the [−surface +external] constellation is a current nonlanguage recognition. In the [−surface −external] constellation of nonlanguage mediated reference, in contrast, the referring content is activated without an external trigger, for example, by reasoning. In both, the referred-to content is resonating (Hausser 2019, Sects. 3.2, 3.3) in memory.

---

[10] On the phone, the speaker may use an immediate reference which is mediated for the hearer and vice versa. For example, if the speaker explains to the hearer where to find something in the speaker's apartment, the speaker uses mediated reference and the hearer immediate reference.

[11] Aho and Ullman (1977), p. 47; FoCL 10.1.1.

Computationally, the conceptual view of reference as a vertical interaction between two separate components is implemented as a horizontal relation between two proplets in the same token line:

COMPARING THE NAIVE AND THE COMPUTATIONAL SOLUTION

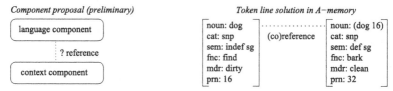

Because the semantic kind of referent is limited to nouns while that of adjs is property and that of transitive verbs is relation, (co)reference is restricted to nouns (Hausser 2019, 6.4.1, 6.4.4–6.4.6). The core value of the referring noun (shadow, copy) at the now front is always an address. The core value of the referred-to noun (referent, original) is never an address. The fnc and mdr values are free (identity in change, Hausser 2019, 6.4.7).

7   Grounding

The semantics of DBS is grounded (Barsalou et al. 2003, Steels 2008, Spranger et al. 2010). In recognition, concept types (supplied by the agent's memory) are matched with raw data (provided by sensors):

RECOGNITION OF square

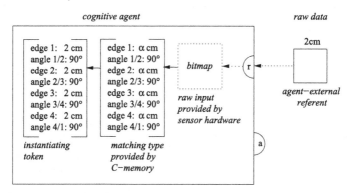

The raw data are supplied by a sensor, here for vision, as input to the interface component. The raw data are matched by the type, resulting in a token.

In action, a type is adapted to a token for the purpose at hand and realized by the agent's actuators as raw data:

ACTION OF REALIZING square

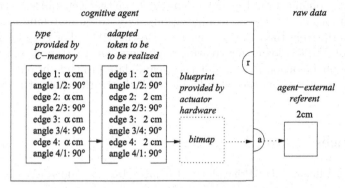

The token is used as a blueprint for action, (e.g. drawing a square).

Next consider the recognition of a color, here blue:

RECOGNITION OF blue

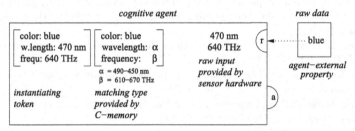

An example of the corresponding action is turning on the color blue, as in a cuttlefish using its chromatophores:

ACTION OF REALIZING blue

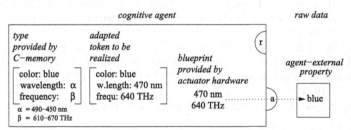

The concept type matches different shades of blue, whereby the variables α and β are instantiated as constants in the resulting token. Recognizing the color blue is a general mechanism which may be applied to all colors. It may be expanded to infrared and ultraviolet, and to varying intensity.[12]

Pattern matching based on the type-token relation applies to nonlanguage items and language surfaces alike. For example, in the surfaces of spoken

---

[12] Complementary approaches from cognitive psychology are prototype theory (Rosch 1975) and composition based on geons (Biederman 1987).

language the type generalizes over different pitch, timbre, dialect, and speaker-dependent pronunciation. In written language, the type generalizes over the size, color, and font of the letters. Computational type-token matching is more adequate descriptively than the nonbivalent (Rescher 1969; FoCL Chap. 20.5) and fuzzy (Zadeh 1965) logics for treating vagueness because type-token matching treats the phenomenon at the root (best candidate principle in pattern matching, FoCL Sect. 5.2) instead of tinkering with the truth tables of Propositional Calculus.

References

Aho, A.V., Ullman, J.D.: Principles of Compiler Design. Addison-Wesley, Reading (1977)

Barcan Marcus, R.: Modalities and intensional languages. Synthese **13**(4), 303–322 (1961)

Barsalou, W., Simmons, W.K., Barbey, A.K., Wilson, C.D.: Grounding conceptual knowledge in modality-specific systems. TRENDS Cogn. Sci. **7**(2), 84–91 (2003)

Benson, D.F.: The Neurology of Thinking. OUP, New York (1994). https://doi.org/10.1002/ana.410360535

Biederman, I.: Recognition-by-components: a theory of human image understanding. Psychol. Rev. **94**, 115–147 (1987)

Dodt, E., Zotterman, Y.: The discharge of specific, cold fibres at high temperatures. Acta Physiol. Scand. **26**(4) 358–365 (1952)

Elmasri, R., Navathe, S.B.: Fundamentals of Database Systems, 7th edn. (1st ed. 1989). Benjamin-Cummings, Redwood City (2017)

Hausser, R.: Complexity in left-associative grammar. Theor. Comput. Sci. **106**(2), 283–308 (1992)

Hausser, R.: Computational Cognition, Integrated DBS Software Design for Data-Driven Cognitive Processing, pp. i–xii, 1–237 (2019). lagrammar.net

Kiefer, F.: Two kinds of epistemic modality in Hungarian. In: Guentchéva, Z. (ed.) Empirical Approaches to Language Typology (2018). https://doi.org/10.1515/9783110572261-013

Menon, V.: Developmental cognitive neuroscience of arithmetic: implications for learning and education. ZDM (Zentralbl. für Didaktik der Math.) **42**(6), 515–525 (2011)

Von Neumann, J.: First draft of a report on the EDVAC. IEEE Ann. Hist. Comput. **15**, 27–75 (1945)

Newell, A., Simon, H.A.: Human Problem Solving. Prentice-Hall, Englewood Cliffs (1972)

Van Orman Quine, W.: Word and Object. MIT Press, Cambridge (1960)

Reimer, M., Michaelson, E.: Reference. In: Zalta, E.N. (ed.) The Stanford Encyclopedia of Philosophy, Winter 2014 edn. (2014). http://plato.stanford.edu/archives/win2014/entries/reference/

Rescher, N.: Many-Valued Logic. McGraw-Hill, New York (1969)

Rosch, E.: Cognitive representations of semantic categories. J. Exp. Psychol.: Gen. **104**, 192–253 (1975)

Spranger, M., Loetzsch, M., Pauw, S.: Open-ended Grounded Semantics (2010). https://csl.sony.fr/wp-content/themes/sony/uploads/pdf/spranger-10b.pdf

Steels, L.: The symbol grounding problem has been solved. So what's next?" In: de Vega, M. (ed.) Symbols and Embodiment: Debates on Meaning and Cognition. Oxford University Press, Oxford (2008)

Zadeh, L.: Fuzzy sets. Inf. Control **8**, 338–353 (1965)

Emotion Synchronization Method for Robot Facial Expression

Yushun Kajihara, Peeraya Sripian$^{(\boxtimes)}$, Chen Feng, and Midori Sugaya

Shibaura Institute of Technology, 3-7-5, Toyosu, Koto-Ku, Tokyo 135-8504, Japan
peeraya@shibaura-it.ac.jp

Abstract. Nowadays, communication robots are becoming popular since they are actively used in both commercially and personally. Increasing empathy between human-robot can effectively enhance the positive impression. Empathy can be created by syncing human emotion with the robot expression. Emotion estimation can be done by analyzing controllable expressions like facial expression, or uncontrollable expression like biological signals. In this work, we propose the comparison of robot expression synchronization with estimated emotion based on either facial expression or biological signal. In order to find out which of the proposed methods yield the best impression, subjective impression rating is used in the experiment. From the result of the impression evaluation, we found that the robot's facial expression synchronization using the synchronization based on periodical emotion value performs the best and best suitable for emotion estimated both from facial expression and biological signal.

Keywords: Emotion estimation · Empathy · Robot facial expression

1 Introduction

The communication robot market is expanded since they are used actively in many sites such as commercial facilities, medical or nursing care facilities, or even use personally at home. In order to improve the acceptance of communication robots, many aspects are considered. Nonverbal behavior is one of the essential factors for enhancing communication for human-human. Many robots could communicate; however, a few robots employ nonverbal behavior in communication such as using various facial expressions. The positive impression could be increased when the robot's expression is synchronized with human emotion, Misaki et al. [1]. Recently Kurono et al. [2] compared emotion estimation using facial expression and biological signals and found that biological signals result in a better concordance with the subjective evaluation. Also, Sripian et al. [3] compared subjective impression evaluation toward robots with expression based on emotions estimated from either source and found that impression like intellectual and is higher when the robot's expression is synchronizing with emotion estimated from the biological signal. The robot expression is shown only one time after the emotion is estimated for a certain period.

© Springer Nature Switzerland AG 2020
M. Kurosu (Ed.): HCII 2020, LNCS 12182, pp. 644–653, 2020.
https://doi.org/10.1007/978-3-030-49062-1_44

2 Background

To express emotion on robots, Hirth et al. [4] developed a robot "ROMAN," that can express six basic emotions consist of anger, disgust, fear, happiness, sadness, and surprise. The emotion state was calculated similarly to the method in Kismet-project [5]. However, the expressed emotion in the robot was not from the real understanding of human emotion at the time. There was no investigation for how human value robot's emotion expression in the communication.

Emotion estimation is the process of identifying human emotion. Typically, the estimation can be done through observable expressions, such as facial expression that includes eyes, mouth, and facial muscles [6], or speech tone [7]. These expressions are carried by the somatic nervous system, which is a voluntary nervous system, hence, controllable by the sender. Meanwhile, emotion can also be estimated through unobservable expressions such as biological signals. The sender could not control biological signals such as heart rate and brain waves because it is driven by the automatic nervous system, which is an involuntary nervous system, or the unconscious mind.

In recent years, the means of estimating emotions based on biological signals have been actively studied. For example, the PAD model by Mehrabian et al. [8] that evaluated emotion by Pleasure (the degree of comfortableness to a particular event), Arousal (the degree of how active and bored one feels), and Dominance (how much control one has or how obedient one is). There are many studies that rely on Russell's Circumplex Model of Affection [9], which related to Mehrabian's PAD model. This model suggests that emotions are plotted on a circle on a two-dimensional coordinate axis; the Arousal axis and the Valence axis. The model has been widely used, for instant, Tanaka et al. [10] estimate emotion by associating brain waves to the Arousal axis and nasal skin temperature to the Valence axis. Accordingly, Ikeda et al. proposed a method to estimate emotion by correlating the value obtained from pulse sensors rather than nasal skin temperature with the Arousal axis [11]. They used the pNN50 calculated from pulse measurement. Figure 1 shows Russel's Circumplex model of affection and emotion estimation used by works in [2, 3, 11].

Fig. 1. Emotion estimation on Russel's circumplex model of affection

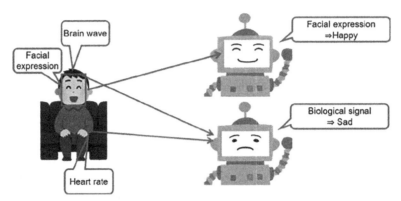

Fig. 2. The robot facial expression synchronization method. The emotion expressed on robot face is based on emotion estimated from biological signals (brain wave and heart rate) or from facial expression.

Kurono et al. [2] proposed the emotion classification method from biological signals and facial expression and compared with subjectively evaluated emotion. The emotion classification was based on the coordinate positioning of the Arousal and Pleasant axis on Russel's Circumplex Model of Affection. Although they found that biological signals performed better than facial expression, we concern that emotion mapping was not suitable. In many pieces of literature [10, 11], high arousal and high pleasant value are estimated as "Happy," while Kurono et al. [2] classified the emotion as "Surprise." Accordingly, low arousal and high pleasant are classified as "Happy," while other literature classified as "Relax." Therefore, the emotion mapping is corrected as shown in Fig. 1 in this work.

Also, the robot's facial expression did not synchronize in real-time with the user in Kurono et al. [2] Biological signals and facial expression are not static signals, and they tend to change many times within an event instantly. In order to achieve a real-time synchronization, we will verify the synchronization time interval for human facial expressions or biometric information about the timing to change the robot's facial expressions in time series.

3   Proposed Method

In order to achieve the final goal of creating empathy between humans and robots, we aim to develop the method proposed in [2, 3] by investigating methods for emotion synchronization with robot expression in this paper. Methods for emotion synchronization are proposed as follows;

1. Synchronization based on cumulative emotion value.
2. Synchronization based on one shot of emotion value.
3. Synchronization based on periodical emotion value.

All of the above methods are described in detail in the next section. In this work, we perform an experiment that compares subjective evaluation toward the robot's facial

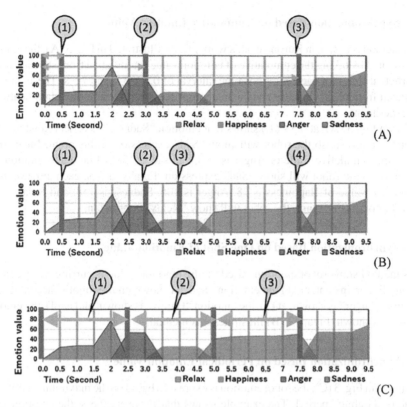

Fig. 3. Proposed methods for synchronization of estimated emotion with robot expression

expression, synchronized with the emotion estimated from biological signals or facial expression using one of the three proposed methods. Before starting the experiment, the participant will answer a questionnaire regarding personal interest and knowledge in the robot according to Okada and Sugaya's findings [12]. Also, a questionnaire about self-control or nonverbal skill is conducted before the experiment. Finally, we use the SD method [13] for subjective's impression evaluation toward the robot expression, similar to [2, 3].

Biological signals are measured from brain waves and heart rate, while facial expression is taken from a camera. The synchronization of robot facial expression is depicted in Fig. 2.

4 Proposed Method

We propose three synchronization methods for robot expression. Figure 3 illustrates each proposed method accordingly.

4.1 Synchronization Based on Cumulative Emotion Value

This method is based on Kurono et al.'s work [2]. As illustrated in Fig. 3 (A), the emotion is estimated by taking the cumulative of emotion value (cumulative from starting time to a particular time) for each emotion at the interval of 0.5 s, 3 s, and 7.5 s. These intervals are taken from [2, 3] since they yield an appropriate result for emotion classification in the experiment.

From Fig. 3 (A), at 0.5 s (1,) shows that emotion "Sadness" is observed while other emotions are zero, so the robot will show "Sad" expression at this point. Meanwhile, at 3 s, the cumulative value of Anger is 106, and sad is 158, while other emotions are still zero, so the robot will show "Sad" expression. Finally, at 7 s, each emotion has a cumulative value of Happiness is 78, Anger is 106, Sadness is 158, and Relax is 278 accordingly. At this point, the robot will show "Relax" expression.

4.2 Synchronization Based on One Shot of Emotion Value

This method show robot emotion based on the emotion value occurring at a particular timing. For an instant, at (1) the emotion "Sad" is shown on the robot's face, at (2), the emotion "Anger" is shown, at (3), the emotion "Happy" is shown, and at (4), the emotion "Relax" is shown. Figure 3 (B) illustrates this method.

4.3 Synchronization Based on Periodical Emotion Value

As shown in Fig. 3 (C), the robot emotion is expressed based on the maximum cumulative value of a defined period. The example shows that for every 2.5 s, the emotion value is calculated. For example, (1) calculates cumulative emotion occurring from 0.0 to 2.5 (The robot would express the emotion "Sad") (2) calculates cumulative emotion occurring from 2.5 to 5.0 (The robot would express the emotion "Happy"). Finally, (3) calculates cumulative emotion occurring from 5.0 to 7.5 (The robot would express the emotion "Relax").

5 Experiment

We conducted a preliminary experiment by presenting an 80 s video clip that evokes the emotion of "Happy" to evaluate which of the three proposed synchronization method yield a better subjective evaluation.

5.1 Subjects

Three students (two males and one female) age range from 18–21 participated in the experiment with a given consent.

5.2 Stimuli

The stimulus is an 80 s length of the video sequence, composed from 3 to 4 small video clips manually selected from annotated video clips database LIRIS-ACCEDE [14]. All selected small video clips have high scores in emotional and high alertness; therefore, they evoke "Happy" emotion. It is the largest video database currently in existence interpreted by an extensive population using induced emotional labels. The three synchronization methods are tested with all participants in a random manner. We prepared a total of 8 video sequences as stimuli.

5.3 Procedure

Before the experiment, the participants have to answer the pre-experiment questionnaire. The participant is asked to wear a brain wave sensor and a pulse sensor during the whole experiment. OMRON's OKAO^{TM} Vision is set on a table in front of the participant to detect the participant's facial expression. Figure 4 shows a photo taken from the experiment. After begin retrieving all input data from all sensors, the experimental procedure is as follows.

1. The participant stays still (Rest) for 30 s for baseline measurement.
2. One of the video clips (80 s) is presented on the screen as the stimulus.
3. During the video clip presentation, the robot changes its facial expression according to the synchronization method, estimated emotion from either facial expression or biological signal.
4. The participant is asked to evaluate the impression of the robot during that trial using the SD method.
5. Repeat steps 2 to 4 until all video clips are presented.

5.4 Subjective Evaluation

To evaluate the participant's impression on robot expression, we utilized the 12 adjective pairs that compose the Japanese property-base adjective measurement method [15, 16]. The impression rating on adjective pairs is done using Osgood's Semantic Differential (SD) method [13], which is usually used to measure opinions, attitudes, and values on a psychometrically controlled scale. Similar to [3], we use the three attributes "Intimacy," "Sociability," and "Vitality" and selected four corresponding property-based adjectives for each attribute.

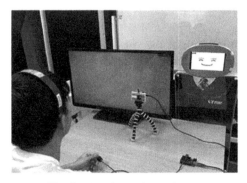

Fig. 4. The photo of experiment.

6   Results and Discussion

Figure 5 shows the average results of an impression evaluation questionnaire of the robot. From average impression evaluation scores, grouping into three main attributes. It can be implied that the robot's facial expression synchronized with facial expression is rated with a higher impression score in "Vitality" and "Intimacy" attributes for most of the methods. Overall, robot expression that synchronizes with the participant's facial expression appears to result in an overall higher impression rating score when the synchronization method B (moment) and C (5.0 cycle) were used.

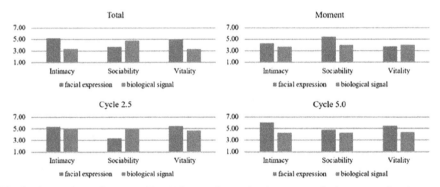

Fig. 5. Comparison of average (N = 3) impression evaluation scores of robot expression that synchronize with emotion estimated from facial expression and from biological signal. The impression evaluation scores are grouped into three attribute: intimacy, sociability, vitality.

However, the impression evaluation score is subjective. So we further investigate the individual impression rating score. Figure 6 shows the results of an impression evaluation questionnaire of the robot of the participant#2. For this participant, the robot's facial expression synchronized with facial expression is rated with a higher impression score in "Vitality" attributes for most of the methods. So, we look at the emotional value of the participant#2 (Fig. 7) for more in-depth analysis. It was found that the emotion "Sad" and "Anger" are estimated frequently. Meanwhile, there are many times that neutral facial expression is observed, which is estimated as "Relax" emotion, hence, the robot express "Relax" on its screen. In addition, the synchronization based on periodical emotion value (for every 2.5 s) results in a higher average score of impression rating when estimate emotion from facial expression. Similarly, the same synchronization method C, for every 5 s, results in a higher average score of impression rating when estimate emotion from biological signals.

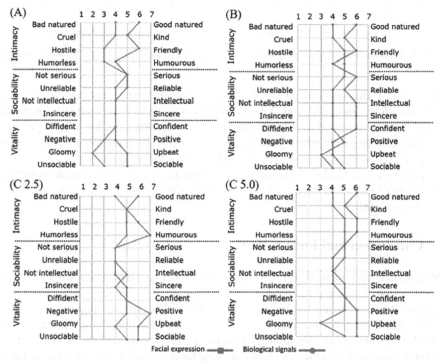

Fig. 6. Comparison of impression rating of participant#2 on the robot's expressed emotion estimated from facial expression and Biological signals. (A) shows the impression rating for emotion synchronized based on cumulative emotion value. (B) shows the impression rating result for emotion synchronized based on one shot of emotion value. (C) shows the impression rating result for emotion synchronized based on periodical emotion value, 2.5 s and 5.0 s, respectively.

From the experiment results, it may be possible to imply that the pleasant emotion like "Happy" and "Relax" is related to "Intimacy" attribute in the robot impression. Also, during the experiment, many unpleasant emotions are evoked by looking at the video clips even though we manually picked "Happy" emotion video from the database as the stimuli. This could be because all of our participants are Japanese. Therefore, cultural differences or language barriers could occur because some of the video clips contain English dialogues or events that are mutually understandable only in western culture. It could be assumed that the stimuli may not be suitable for Japanese participants.

For the cumulative emotion value used in the synchronization method A, it appears that if one of the emotion is frequently estimated, the result would be biased toward

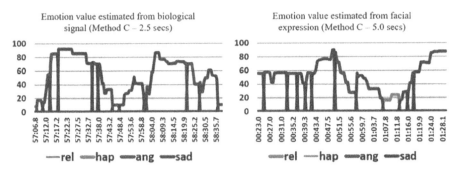

Fig. 7. Emotion value estimated from biological signal and facial expression for participant#2

that emotion. This could fix the robot's facial expression toward only one type of emotion. Therefore, "Intimacy" and "Vitality" attributes are rated lower than other methods. Meanwhile, we observed from the participants' free comments that the robot expression changes too quickly when synchronized with method B. Therefore, almost all items in the impression rating is given a rather low score for this method.

Based on these results, we consider that it is better to use the synchronization method C for robot facial expression with emotion estimated from both facial expression and biological signals.

7 Conclusion and Future Work

We proposed three methods for robot facial expression synchronization with estimated emotion from facial expression or biological signals. A preliminary experiment was performed to investigate the best suitable methods that gave the highest impression rating toward the robot expression. From the result of the impression evaluation, the robot's facial expression synchronization using the synchronization based on periodical emotion value performs the best, hence suitable for emotion estimated both from facial expression and biological signal.

There are several considerations during the experiment. For instant, the emotion-induced video database may not be suitable for Japanese participants due to cultural differences. The number of participants is low. Also, a non-verbal evaluation index (SAM [17]) could be used toward to robot in addition to the SD method. In the future, the main experiment could be performed with more participants, using more suitable stimuli and collect subjective evaluation from more post-experiment questionnaires.

References

1. Misaki, Y., Ito, T., Hashimoto, M.: Proposal of human-robot interaction method based on emotional entrainment. In: HAI Symposium (2008). (in Japanese)
2. Kurono, Y., Sripian, P., Chen, F., Sugaya, M.: A preliminary experiment on the estimation of emotion using facial expression and biological signals. In: Kurosu, M. (ed.) HCII 2019. LNCS, vol. 11567, pp. 133–142. Springer, Cham (2019). https://doi.org/10.1007/978-3-030-22643-5_10

3. Sripian, P., et al.: Study of empathy on robot expression based on emotion estimated from facial expression and biological signals. In: The 28th IEEE International Conference on Robot & Human Interactive Communication, New Delhi, India (2019). IEEE

4. Hirth, J., Schmitz, N., Berns, K.: Emotional architecture for the humanoid robot head ROMAN. In: IEEE International Conference on Robotics and Automation, pp. 2150–2155. IEEE (2007)

5. Breazeal, C., Scassellati, B.: A context-dependent attention system for a social robot. rn **255**, 3 (2003)

6. Ekman, P., Friesen, W.V.: Facial Action Coding System: Investigator's Guide. Consulting Psychologists Press, Palo Alto (1978)

7. Nwe, T.L., Foo, S.W., De Silva, L.C.: Speech emotion recognition using hidden Markov models. Speech Commun. **41**(4), 603–623 (2003)

8. Mehrabian, A.: Basic Dimensions for a General Psychological Theory: Implications for Personality, Social, Environmental, and Developmental Studies. Oelgeschlager, Gunn & Hain, Cambridge (1980)

9. Russell, J.A.: A circumplex model of affect. J. Pers. Soc. Psychol. **39**(6), 1161 (1980)

10. Tanaka, H., Ide, H., Nagashuma, Y.: An attempt of feeling analysis by the nasal temperature change model. In: SMC 2000 Conference Proceedings, 2000 IEEE International Conference on Systems, Man And Cybernetics. 'Cybernetics Evolving to Systems, Humans, Organizations, and Their Complex Interactions' (cat. no. 0. 2000. IEEE

11. Ikeda, Y., Horie, R., Sugaya, M.: Estimate emotion with biological information for robot interaction. In: 21st International Conference on Knowledge-Based and Intelligent Information & Engineering Systems (KES-2017), Marseille, France, pp. 6–8 2017

12. Okada, A., Sugaya, M.: Interaction design and impression evaluation of the Person and the active robot. In: Human Computer Interaction (HCI), pp. 1–6 (2016). (in Japanese)

13. Osgood, C.E.: Semantic differential technique in the comparative study of cultures. Am. Anthropol. **66**(3), 171–200 (1964)

14. Baveye, Y., et al.: LIRIS-ACCEDE: a video database for affective content analysis. IEEE Trans. Affect. Comput. **6**(1), 43–55 (2015)

15. Hayashi, F.: The fundamental dimensions of interpersonal cognitive structure. Bull. Fac. Educ. Nagoya Univ. **25**, 233–247 (1978)

16. Hayashi, R., Kato, S.: Psychological effects of physical embodiment in artificial pet therapy. Artif. Life Robotics **22**(1), 58–63 (2017). https://doi.org/10.1007/s10015-016-0320-7

17. Bradley, M.M., Lang, P.J.: Measuring emotion: the self-assessment manikin and the semantic differential. J. Behav. Ther. Exp. Psychiatry **25**(1), 49–59 (1994)

Human-Robot Interaction in Health Care: Focus on Human Factors

Lisanne Kremer$^{(\boxtimes)}$, Sumona Sen, and Monika Eigenstetter

Niederrhein University of Applied Sciences, Krefeld, Germany
{lisanne.kremer,sumona.sen,
monika.eigenstetter}@hs-niederrhein.de

Abstract. In-patient and out-patient care processes in the health care system are strongly affected by the effects of demographic change and a tense skill shortage. Digitization - both as a digitizing transformation process and as a process of implementing technical innovations such as robots - is intended to counteract these processes. Not only for safe interaction with a care robot, but also for its acceptance, humans must be able to understand and predict the robot's movements. The ability to make predictions about the movements of a robot/technology and to be willing to interact with it is linked to the construct of situation awareness.

In an experimental setting, a care situation was simulated in the full-scope simulator and the effects of the interaction on the situation awareness and the acceptance of the robot were investigated. The experiment was realized with 33 participants. The methods used were the SAGAT technique and an adapted UTAUT questionnaire.

Significant correlations between UTAUT predictors and added measures were found. A stepwise hierarchical regression model found Performance Expectancy and Attitude as significant predictors of acceptance, but none of the other UTAUT and added factors were identified to be significant predictors. There was no significant effect between situation awareness and acceptance. A descriptive analysis of the measures of situation awareness showed an average to good situation awareness across all participants.

Keywords: Health care · Situation awareness · UTAUT · Technology acceptance · Human-robot interaction

1 Introduction

The digitization process in the healthcare sector and the effects of demographic change, influence the healthcare sector and confront it with new challenges [1]. A tense personnel situation, high medical care costs, patient safety and infrastructural problems are some of the challenges already mentioned. Inpatient care is explicitly affected by the effects of demographic change. The number of new entrants to the nursing profession is falling, while older nursing staff is leaving the profession early due to the consequences of high physical and psychological stress. Medical staff and healthcare workers already have many days of absence due to mental illness and are generally ill more often than

© Springer Nature Switzerland AG 2020
M. Kurosu (Ed.): HCII 2020, LNCS 12182, pp. 654–667, 2020.
https://doi.org/10.1007/978-3-030-49062-1_45

members of other occupational groups. Digitization – as a digitizing transformation process as well as an implementation process of technical innovations such as robots – is intended to counteract these processes. The digitization process per se initially focuses on the purpose of improving the connectivity of the actors and the security of the data.

Besides better networking, the digitization of the health care system also offers economic opportunities. The health system contributes more than 12% of the German gross domestic product, more than 8 million employees work in the health sector. The German Federal Association for Health Information Technology estimates the monetary efficiency potential from the implementation of eHealth at approx. 39 billion per year worldwide [2]. At the same time, however, Germany scores particularly poorly in an international comparison regarding the digitization of the health care system. A study by Bertelsmann Foundation [3] puts Germany in penultimate place compared to 14 other EU and 3 OECD countries. With a Digital Health Index of 30.0 [3], Germany is one of the less developed countries concerning digitization in health care.

In addition to the economic opportunities offered by the implementation of new technologies, the focus of digitization processes is on improving patient care and working conditions. Strategies to improve both factors can be found in the implementation and improvement of established medical information systems, but for some time now also in the support of various processes by robot. There are several types of robots used and implemented in the health care sector. A large proportion of the robots used in healthcare can be assigned to service robots [4]. A distinction is made between surgery, therapy and care robots. The implementation of robot systems is most advanced in minimally invasive surgical procedures and neurological rehabilitation [5]. Transport robots also represent a large proportion. In this area, the health care system has learned from processes that have already been implemented in an industrial environment, e.g. from production. A beginning implementation of robotics in the health care system – especially in the hospital organization – is becoming apparent, which supports on the one hand basic off-patient care (logistics, medication) and on the other hand supports patient-oriented care optimization in high-risk areas (surgical robots, therapy robots). The challenges of the health care system – above all demographic change will, however, require a form of support for basic patient-oriented care in the near future. For this reason, further investigation and implementation of care robotics appears to be urgently necessary and highly relevant.

In order to implement robots on a large scale, especially in this patient-oriented area, it is necessary to take a closer look at human factors in the context of the interaction with the robot.

1.1 Human Factors in Human-Robot Interaction

Not only for safe interaction but acceptance of the robot, people must be able to understand and predict the movements of the robot. Being able to make predictions about the movements of a robot/a technology and to be prepared to interact with is associated with the construct of situation awareness (SA). Endsley [6] defines SA as the process of human's perception and mental representations of a great amount of information. The construct consists of three levels: Level 1 (perception), 2 (comprehension), 3 (prediction). Level 1 – perception – refers according to Endsley [6] to perceiving the status, attributes and dynamics of relevant elements in the closer environment. In our setting it would have been, besides the robot and its movements, several health care relating elements. Perception is as important as the following stages as it allows to know the status and dynamics of the current situation. Level 2 – comprehension – indicates a "synthesis of disjointed Level 1 elements" [6]. This level enables a holistic view of the situation in order to assess the relevance of individual elements in the associated situation. Endsley [6] defines prediction (level 3) as "the ability to project the future actions of the elements in the environment" (Table 1).

Table 1. SA-levels [6]

SA level	
1	Perception
2	Comprehension
3	Prediction

Referring to Endsley [6], there are several methods to examine SA including verbal protocols, psychophysiological measures, communication analysis and query techniques. In a recent review, Xu et al. [7] conducted a systematic review of the evaluation strategies of studies relating to relevant human factors in high fidelity simulations. The review concentrated on human-system interfaces (HSI) of industrial control systems. The review resulted in 42 studies measuring human performance across six different dimensions: task performance, workload, situation awareness, teamwork/collaboration, plant performance and other cognitive performance indicators. The concept of situation awareness was evaluated by only seven of the reviewed studies: The methodical quality of the measurement of SA was rather weak.

Nitsch [8] stated that SA in context of using service robots in personal households is a relevant construct. Until today robots aren't flexible enough to react appropriately in sudden and non-predictable situation. Main goal of the research project was to evaluate cognitive models concerning their predictive power of robotic movements.

Schuster and Jentsch [9] published a model that integrates the robot as a team member and explains SA in the team. Bolstad and Cuevas [10] address the same issue as they state that SA is in focus of performance measurement regarding the cooperation of human and robots.

The challenge of implementing new technologies into new application fields leads to the question how those technologies are accepted by users. Changes in Technology – like the implementation of robots – should have a positive impact on routines and processes. Technology acceptance is captured by many different theoretical approaches. Davis [11] developed the technology acceptance model (TAM) as a basis for upcoming technology acceptance research. The factors perceived usefulness and perceived ease of use were predict the attitude toward using and the behavioural intention to use. This leads to actual system use [11]. Several researchers developed and modified TAM in the following years. In 2003, Venkatesh et al. [12] released a synthesis and expansion of eight technology acceptance models. The result was a model called UTAUT (Unified Theory of Acceptance and Use of Technology) [12] that was found to surpass the predictability of the eight individual models with an adjusted R^2 of 70%. UTAUT has been applied in a large number of studies investigating the acceptance of new technologies and has already been investigated in first experiments in the context of human-robot interaction (HRI) [13, 14]. The UTAUT constructs are Performance Expectancy (PE), Effort Expectancy (EE), Social Influence (SI) and Facilitating Conditions (FC). The four constructs are direct determinants of Use Behaviour as well as three of them are determinants for Behavioural Intention. The effect is moderated by four moderator variables: gender, age, experience and voluntariness of use (Table 2).

Table 2. UTAUT constructs and definitions.

UTAUT factors	Definition [12]
Performance Expectancy (PE)	The degree to which an individual believes that the use of the system will help achieve gains in job performance
Effort Expectancy (EE)	The degree of ease associated with using the system
Social Influence (SI)	The degree to which an individual perceives that important others believe he or she should use the system
Facilitating Conditions (FC)	The degree to which the individual believes that organizational and technical infrastructure is available to support the use of the system

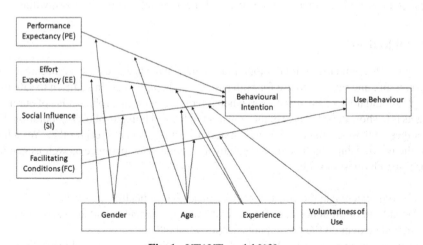

Fig. 1. UTAUT model [12].

Williams, Rana and Dwivedi [15] stated that the focus of UTAUT research was on the investigation of business systems as well as information systems in general. In most cases explored research methodologies are survey methods and cross-sectional designs. Performance Expectancy and Behavioral Intention are found to be the best predictors for Acceptance. A key result shows that UTAUT model is extended by a wide range of variables like Anxiety, Attitude, Perceived Risk and Trust [15] (Fig. 1).

Kremer, Sen and Breil [16] proposed an extension of UTAUT model by cognitive variables as they are influencing the perception of accepted technologies. The theoretical approach considers the relation between SA and Acceptance as well as Mental workload and acceptance.

In contrast to technology acceptance, psychological constructs as Anxiety and Insecurity, should be considered. Nomura, Kanda, Suzuki and Kato [17] showed some first results regarding the relation between Anxiety and robots as factor that influences the Attitude towards robots. Spielberger [18] defines Anxiety as something that "appears from the fear of being deprived of expected satisfaction although there is no clear evidence that the satisfaction will be deprived (p. 47).

Perceived insecurity deals with the subject's reaction to work with the robot whether the subject is sceptical or open-minded about the technology. Subjectively Perceived Insecurity is influenced by the approach speed and the atmosphere of the workplace, i.e. noise and proximity to the robot [19]. There are several approaches in literature that link Anxiety/Perceived Insecurity and UTAUT (TAM) model. Studies showed that anxiety affects Performance Expectancy [20], Perceived Usefulness (TAM [13]) and Effort Expectancy [21].

When considering the current research on robotics and human factors, it becomes clear that most studies refer mainly to an isolated construct. Besides method validation, the focus is more on basic research or theoretical approaches. Situation Awareness is therefore very often identified as the most important construct in robotics research.

In order to obtain a more holistic picture of the processes of HRI, however, a systemic approach based on the model of the sociotechnical model is certainly worthwhile [22].

1.2 Objectives

As a possible compensator for demographic change in the health care system, care robots must be safe and fearless to use for both patients and employees. In addition to safe use, people should not feel any discomfort when interacting with care robots. One of our main targets is to show the relevance of the construct of SA in a human-robot collaboration. We hypothesize that acceptance, SA and anxiety/insecurity relate to each other. We admit that the relationship could be moderated by age, previous experience as well as gender. Our research questions are:

1. To what extent can the construct SA be measured in health care setting?
2. What kind of influence does SA have on Acceptance and the added measures?
3. To what extent do the participant accept the robot?
4. Are Perceived Insecurity, Attitude, Anxiety and Self-efficacy possible predictors of Behavioural Intention (Acceptance)?

2 Methods

2.1 Sample

34 subjects consented to participate in the experiment. Because of safety reasons we set one exclusion criteria. People with a severe visual impairment were not allowed to participate. We excluded one participant because of non-responding to the questionnaires. The final sample included 33 participants aged between 18 and 52. The average age was 23,7 (SD = 5,78). 9 (27,27%) participants were female, 24 were male. Most of the participants were undergraduate students and were recruited via public announcement at university or personal address.

2.2 Experimental Setting and Conduction

The experiment was performed in a robotic laboratory at Niederrhein University of Applied Sciences in a full-scope simulation with controlled environmental conditions. The full-scope simulator was prepared as a simulated hospital room with a hospital bed, an overbed table, a robot as well as a flat screen and decoration objects relating to a hospital scene (Fig. 2). All objects in the Full-Scope Simulator are controlled by a programmable logic controller.

Before carrying out the experiment the participant undergoes a safety briefing by the test supervisor. For this purpose, the participant is informed about protective measures, such as the operation of the emergency stop switch, and that there is the possibility to stop and leave the experiment at any time. The instruction includes beside first information about the experiment some rules of behavior, which are aimed at the interaction between the collaborating robot Sawyer and the test person.

After the safety briefing the participants entered the simulation room and took place in the nursing bed. The supervisor arranged the over-bed table as seen in Fig. 2. As soon as the participant is placed in bed, a kind of cover story is shown on the TV to put the test person in the situation of a patient in hospital. At the same time, the test person is given a basic explanation of the course of the experiment ("A robot is used to assist during selected activities. This ensures that the medicine and the supply of water and snacks are always at your disposal. The robot "Sawyer" is used to hand you the medicine, water bottles and snacks").

On the side-table we placed a Sudoku booklet. The respondent is supposed to work on it with a pen according to an instruction that appears on the TV. At various times,

Table 3. Sample.

	n	Mean (age)	Experience
m	24	24,8	6
w	9	22,7	2
$\sum$	33	23,7 (SD = 5,78)	8

Fig. 2. Experimental setting. Simulated hospital room in a full-scope simulator. (1: Sawyer, 2: TV, 3: webcam, 4: swam, 5: over-bed table, 6: sudoku, 7: emergency stop, 8: nursing bed, 9: side-table, 10: pillbox, 11: biscuits, 12: water bottle, 13: mirror, 14: picture imitating view from hospital room.)

objects are provided to the subject by the collaborating robot Sawyer on the over-bed table. These objects are a pillbox, a water bottle and a tray with cookies. These can be removed by the test person and put back after use on the designated mark on the folding table. The participant has 30, 45 or 50 s to use the items before the collaborating robot Sawyer picks up the item from the over-bed table and proceeds. In addition, the SAGAT method is used in the test procedure, in which three questions are displayed on the television. The test person answers these questions verbally.

In order to find out how the test person reacts to unusual designs of the collaborating robot Sawyer; disturbing influences are integrated into the test procedure. The collaborating robot drops a water bottle on the floor, the lamp fails, and the simulation room darkens. The aim is to observe whether the test person activates the emergency stop switch. The total time of the experiment including instruction is 24 min and 30 s. After the experiment, the test person works on the questionnaire independently in the adjoining room.

2.3 Measures

UTAUT Questionnaire. Measures and Cronbach's alpha of an adapted UTAUT model and questionnaire are presented in Table 3. We used a questionnaire based on a translation by Vollmer [23] and adapted the questions to human-robot collaboration. The constructs were measured on a 6-point Likert scale ranging from "I do not agree at all" (1) to "I fully agree" (6).

The questionnaire contains questions concerning sociodemographic data. We asked for age, gender and previous experience with robots. In addition, we asked whether the participants knew of a possible disturbance during the experiment as it was relevant for pressing the emergency stop or not. Based on the work of Vollmer [23] and previous research items measuring anxiety, self-efficacy and perceived insecurity are added to the questionnaire (Table 4) .

Table 4. Cronbach's alpha of used scales.

Scale	Cronbach's alpha
Performance Efficiency	.866
Effort Efficiency	Single item
Social Influence	Single item
Facilitating Conditions	.861
Behavioural Intention	.897
Attitude	.744
Self-efficacy	.669
Anxiety	.811
Perceived Insecurity	.894

SAGAT. To measure situation awareness, one of the best-known instruments is the SAGAT technique (Situation Awareness Global Assessment Technique). It was developed to assess SA with all its levels [24]. With the help of SAGAT a simulation is used which is frozen at randomly selected times. In this process, all sources of information are also hidden, or the light is extinguished. During this freezing process the test persons are asked about their perception of the situation. As a global measure, SAGAT includes queries on all SA requirements, including the components of level 1 (perception of data), level 2 (understanding of meaning) and level 3 (projection of the near future). This includes a consideration of the system function and status as well as relevant characteristics of the external environment. To examine SA with SAGAT method, the questions displayed in Table 5 are questioned.

Table 5. Operationalization of SA-levels (SAGAT).

Levels of SA	Questions
Level 1	Which objects are located in your environment?
Level 2	In which direction did the robot arm move most recently?
Level 3	What will the robot do next: what do you suspect?

3 Results

3.1 Descriptive Statistics

All predictors of acceptance show relatively high average scores with moderate levels of standard deviation (M = 3.81–5.40, SD = .66–1.42). SAGAT level 1 has a moderate average (M = 6.67), but a quite high SD (SD = 3.35, range = 0–13) (Table 6) .

Table 6. Descriptive statistics: predictors of acceptance (6 level likert scale from 1 = strongly disagree to 6 = strongly agree) and SAGAT level 1.

	Mean	SD	Range	Minimum	Maximum
PE	4.28	1.06	4.0	2.0	6.0
Att	4.39	.81	3.4	2.4	5.8
FC	5.40	.66	2.33	3.7	6.0
BI	3.81	1.25	4.5	1.3	5.8
SI	4.06	1.30	5.0	1.0	6.0
SE	4.82	1.01	3.5	2.5	6.0
AX	3.84	1.13	4.3	1.5	5.8
PI	4.57	1.30	4.8	1.2	6.0
EE	4.24	1.42	5.0	1.0	6.0
SAGAT level 1	6.67	3.35	13	0	13

3.2 Technology Acceptance

Statistical analysis on technology acceptance referred to UTAUT measures as well as it referred to added measures anxiety, perceived insecurity, attitude and self-efficacy.

Based on previous studies, the mean value of acceptance was classified as low (1–2.34), moderate (2.35–3.67) or high (3.68–6). Acceptance of collaboration with robots was low to moderate on average (mean = 2.39, SD = 0.7; range 1–6). Almost half of the participants could be classified as high (51,5%, 17/33) acceptance; 36,4% (12/33) reported a moderate and 12.1% (4/33) a low acceptance (Table 7).

Table 7. Classification of acceptance [25].

	N	Percentage
1 (low)	4	12,1
2 (moderate)	12	36,4
3 (high)	17	51,5
Σ	33	100

There are strong positive correlations between performance expectancy (PE) and Behavioral Intention (BI) (r = .745, p < .01), attitude and BI (r = .538, p < .01), self-efficacy (SE) and Facilitating Conditions (FC) (r = .464, p < .01), perceived insecurity (PI) and FC (r = . 459, p < .01), PI and SE (r = .636, p < .01), PI and anxiety (AX) (r = .451, p < .01, Effort Efficiency (EE) and Att (r = .554, p < .01) and EE and SE (r = . 442, p < .01) (Table 8) .

A significant hierarchical stepwise regression model included 3 of 8 selected variables from one of two blocks in three steps (F(3,29) = 22,251, p < .01). There was no

Table 8. Correlations between UTAUT and added measures.

	Mean_PE	Mean_Att	Mean_FC	Mean_BI	Mean_SI	Mean_SE	Mean_AX	Mean_PI	Mean_EE
Mean_PE	1								
Mean_Att	.436*	1							
Mean_FC	−.096	.046	1						
Mean_BI	.745**	.538**	−.104	1					
Mean_SI	.252	.363*	.191	.306	1				
Mean_SE	.417*	.348*	.464**	.409*	.385*	1			
Mean_AX	.142	.064	.034	.350*	−.050	.176	1		
Mean_PI	.270	.281	.459**	.327	.400*	.636**	.451**	1	
Mean_EE	.377*	.554**	.146	.285	.327	.442**	.187	.340	1

* The correlation is significant at the level of 0.05
** The correlation is significant at the level of 0.01

evidence of strong multicollinearity. The model explained 66,6% of the variance of the effect ($R^2 = .66,6$, $F(1,29) = 6.26$, $p = .01$). The effect size for R^2 corresponds to a strong effect ($f^2 = 1.9$). The Inclusion of PE in step two resulted in a change of R^2 in the amount of 37,3%. Effect sizes for changes in R^2 were strong (PE, $f^2 = 1,39$) and moderate (Att, $f^2 = 0,29$).

Only two of eight possible predictors remained significant in the final model: PE as well as attitude toward collaboration with a robot. PE was the strongest predictor (ß = .584, p < .01), followed by attitude (ß = .337, p < .05). None of the other initial UTAUT predictors and none of the added factors became significant.

3.3 Situation Awareness

We conducted a descriptive analyses of SA measures. The Levels of SA are evaluated. The average reported number of objects for level one of SA was 6,67 (SD = 3,35). For level two, 25 participants registered the correct direction of the robot movement as well for level three. Eight participants mentioned the wrong direction. Although the results of level two and three are similar, the participants who answered the questions wrong weren't the same. Figure 3 shows the three different SAGAT-scores resulting from correct answers in percentage.

3.4 Situation Awareness and Acceptance

Next, we analysed relations between acceptance and SA. We couldn't find any significant effect between predictors of acceptance and SA as well as between SA and acceptance. A trend can be identified that participants with and without previous experience differ in their first level of SA (t (13.54) = −1.99, p = .06).

There is a significant correlation between level three of SA (prediction) and attitude (r = −.373, p < .05) as well as between prediction and anxiety (r = .384, p < .05).

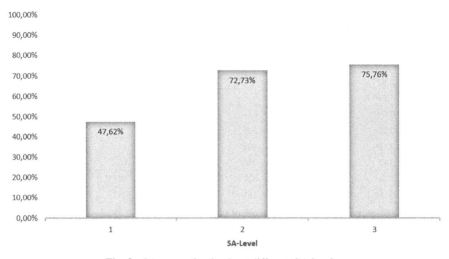

Fig. 3. SA scores for the three different SA levels.

4 Discussion

4.1 Human-Robot Interaction in Health Care: Human Factors

The results show interesting relationships between the constructs investigated. In general, the acceptance of the technology is on a moderate average. In a stepwise hierarchical regression model, PE and attitude are significant predictors of acceptance, but none of the other UTAUT factors could be replicated as significant predictors. There's a trend that shows that perceived insecurity as well as anxiety could play a role in predicting acceptance. As the UTAUT model already explains about 70% of the variance, it remains unclear if it useful to extend the model or adapt the model by excluding factors that don't become significant (especially FC and SI).

The SAGAT measurements show a medium to high situation awareness. No differences between age and gender can be determined here. There are also no correlations between the 3 levels of the SA. The measurement of SA shows differentiating results in the first level, in levels two and three the general level seems to be rather high. The applied SAGAT method was reasonably applicable in the described setting.

After a separate evaluation of the two constructs, the hypothesized relationship between SA and technology acceptance was analyzed. Unfortunately, no direct connection between these two constructs could be determined, since only few significant correlations between predictors of acceptance and SAGAT level three (prediction) occur. As described above, a trend can be identified that shows a connection between the first level of SA and the previous experience in collaborating with a robot. The higher the level of anxiety, the more accurate the assessment of the situation (SA) seems to be. On the other hand, the higher the positive attitude towards the robot, the less pronounced the SA. With regard to the present sample, this effect is not surprising.

4.2 Limitations

Since our study was exploratory in nature, there are some limitations to the results that should be considered. We found high levels of SA in comprehension and prediction levels. This could be due to the fact that the sample was highly selective in terms of prior experience with technology and therefore highly likely to have an affinity for technology. The sample was also very young and had a relatively high level of education. Both of these factors ensure that the test persons seem to be generally familiar with technology but mean a low ability to differentiate and a lack of external validity for the results. On this basis, a generalisation of the results is not possible without further investigation.

Beside the high degree of selectivity, the experimental design did not include a longitudinal comparison of participants neither compared an intervention to a control group. For this reason, the internal validity also appears to be limited.

In addition, all three SA levels were examined by one item only. Endsley, however, suggests several questions per level. An extension of the SAGAT would be useful in this sense.

4.3 Implications and Future Work

The results seem a little contradictory. On the one hand, perceived insecurity and anxiety are related to acceptance and thus confirm the suspected results. On the other hand, uncertainty and anxiety are not related to the objective data of the SA, contrary to what was predicted. This indicates that there is a discrepancy between the subjective evaluation of the situation (uncertainty, anxiety) and the actual ability of the user (SA) to interact safely and effectively with the robotic system. This is possibly influenced by the positive attitude and PE towards collaborative robotics.

It might be useful to go deeper in future research to understand what leads to this positive attitude and PE, as they are not necessarily justified in the current situation. Is it the belief that this technology could be successful in the future (PE = the degree to which an individual believes that the use of the system will help achieve gains in job performance)? PE should be operationalized on several dimensions "currently" and "in the future".

An emerging aspect during the investigations is mental workload. Besides SA and technology acceptance, mental workload can be another construct to investigate the collaboration between humans and robots. Just like a low SA level, excessive workloads can lead to accidents or dangerous situations. New technologies often lead to people being overburdened, although this may not be reflected in their statements about technology acceptance.

5 Conclusion

Attitude and perceived insecurity could play an important role concerning the prediction of acceptance of HRI. Obviously, UTAUT model is applicable to HRI, but not all predictors of the acceptance model seem to be relevant in this context. SAGAT method is a useful methodological approach to measuring SA in HRI, but surprisingly showed no relation to acceptance measures.

References

1. Lux, T., Breil, B., Dörries, M.: Digitalisierung im Gesundheitswesen — zwischen Datenschutz und moderner Medizinversorgung. Wirtschaftsdienst **97**(10), 687–703 (2017). https://doi.org/10.1007/s10273-017-2200-8

2. Bernnat, R., Bauer, M., Schmidt, H., Bieber, N., Heusser, N., Schönfeld, R.: Effizienzpotenziale durch eHealth (2017). https://www.strategyand.pwc.com/de/de/studie/effizienzpotentiale-durch-ehealth.pdf. Accessed 30 Jan 2020

3. Thiel, R., et al.: #SmartHealthSystems: Digitalisierungsstrategien im internationalen Vergleich (2018)

4. Bendel, O.: Surgical, therapeutic, nursing and sex robots in machine and information ethics. In: van Rysewyk, S.P., Pontier, M. (eds.) Machine Medical Ethics. ISCASE, vol. 74, pp. 17–32. Springer, Cham (2015). https://doi.org/10.1007/978-3-319-08108-3_2

5. Klein, B., Graf, B., Schlömer, I.F., Rossberg, H., Röhricht, K., Baumgarten, S.: Robotik in der Gesundheitswirtschaft: einsatzfelder und potenziale. Medhochzwei, Heidelberg (2018)

6. Endsley, M.R.: Toward a theory of situation awareness in dynamic systems. Hum. Factors **37**(1), 32–64 (1995). https://doi.org/10.1518/001872095779049543

7. Xu, J., Anders, S., Pruttianan, A., et al.: Human performance measures for the evaluation of process control human-system interfaces in high-fidelity simulations. Appl. Ergon. **73**, 151–165 (2018). https://doi.org/10.1016/j.apergo.2018.06.008. (PMID: 30098630)

8. Nitsch, V.: Situation awareness in autonomous service robots. In: 10. Berliner Werkstatt Mensch-Maschine-Systeme (2013)

9. Schuster, D., Jentsch, F.: Measurement of situation awareness in human-robot teams. In: Proceedings of the Human Factors and Ergonomics Society Annual Meeting, vol. 55, no. 1, pp. 1496–1500 (2011). https://doi.org/10.1177/1071181311551311

10. Bolstad, C.A., Cuevas, H.M.: Integrating situation awareness assessment into test and evaluation. ITEA J. **31**, 240 (2010)

11. Davis, F.D.: Perceived usefulness, perceived ease of use, and user acceptance of information technology. MIS Q. **13**(3), 319–340 (1989). https://doi.org/10.2307/249008

12. Venkatesh, V., Morris, M.G., Davis, G.B., Davis, F.D.: User acceptance of information technology: toward a unified view. MIS Q. **27**(3), 425–478 (2003). 10.2307/30036540

13. Heerink, M., Krose, B., Evers, V., Wielinga, B.: Measuring acceptance of an assistive social robot: a suggested toolkit. In: The 18th IEEE International Symposium on Robot and Human Interactive Communication, pp. 528–533. IEEE (2009)

14. Benmessaoud, C., Kharrazi, H., MacDorman, K.F.: Facilitators and barriers to adopting robotic-assisted surgery: contextualizing the unified theory of acceptance and use of technology. PLoS One **6**(1), e16395 (2011). https://doi.org/10.1371/journal.pone.0016395. (PMID: 21283719)

15. Williams, M.D., Rana, N.P., Dwivedi, Y.K.: The unified theory of acceptance and use of technology (UTAUT): a literature review. J. Enterp. Inf. Manag. **28**(3), 443–488 (2015). https://doi.org/10.1108/JEIM-09-2014-0088

16. Kremer, L., Sen, S., Breil, B.: Relating factors for acceptance of health care technology: focus on mental workload. Stud. Health Technol. Inform. **264**, 1953–1954 (2019). https://doi.org/10.3233/SHTI190730. (PMID: 31438424)

17. Nomura, T., Kanda, T., Suzuki, T., Kato, K.: Prediction of human behavior in human–robot interaction using psychological scales for anxiety and negative attitudes toward robots. IEEE Trans. Robot. **24**(2), 442–451 (2008). https://doi.org/10.1109/TRO.2007.914004

18. Spielberger, C.D.: Anxiety and Behavior. Elsevier Science, Saint Louis (2014)

19. Shen, Y.: System für die Mensch-Roboter-Koexistenz in der Fließmontage. Herbert Utz Verlag GmbH, München (2015)

20. Carlsson, C., Carlsson, J., Hyvonen, K., Puhakainen, J., Walden, P.: Adoption of mobile devices/services – searching for answers with the UTAUT. In: Proceedings of the 39th Annual Hawaii International Conference on System Sciences (HICSS 2006), p. 132a. IEEE (2006)
21. Bröhl, C., Nelles, J., Brandl, C., Mertens, A., Schlick, C.M.: Entwicklung und Analyse eines Akzeptanzmodells für die Mensch-Roboter-Kooperation in der Industrie. Soziotechnische Gestaltung des digitalen Wandels – kreativ, innovativ, sinnhaft, Frühjahrskongress 2017, Brugg und Zürich: Gesellschaft für Arbeitswissenschaft e.V., Dortmund (2017)
22. Smith, M.J., Sainfort, P.C.: A balance theory of job design for stress reduction. Int. J. Ind. Ergon. 4(1), 67–79 (1989)
23. Vollmer, A.: Entwicklung und Anwendung eines Modells zur Untersuchung soziotechnischer Faktoren bei der Einführung neuer Informationssysteme im klinischen Bereich, Dissertation, Friedrich-Alexander-Universität Erlangen-Nürnberg (2015)
24. Endsley, M.R.: The application of human factors to the development of expert systems for advanced cockpits. Proc. Hum. Factors Soc. Annu. Meet. 31(12), 1388–1392 (1987). https://doi.org/10.1177/154193128703101219
25. Hennemann, S., Beutel, M.E., Zwerenz, R.: Drivers and barriers to acceptance of web-based aftercare of patients in inpatient routine care: a cross-sectional survey. J. Med. Internet Res. 18(12), e337 (2016). https://doi.org/10.2196/jmir.6003. PMID: 28011445

Evaluating a Mouse-Based and a Tangible Interface Used for Operator Intervention on Two Autonomous Robots

Andreas Mallas[1]([⊠]) [iD], Michalis Xenos[1] [iD], and Maria Rigou[2] [iD]

[1] Computer Engineering and Informatics Department, Patras University, Patras, Greece
{mallas,xenos}@ceid.upatras.gr
[2] Department of Management Science and Technology, Patras University, Patras, Greece
rigou@upatras.gr

Abstract. This paper presents an experiment where participants used two different interfaces of an application designed for controlling the movements of two vineyard spraying agricultural robots. The goal of the application was to evaluate users' efficiency and perceived satisfaction while controlling the robots' movements using a mouse-based and a tangible interface. In a controlled experiment conducted at the Software Quality and Human-Computer Interaction Laboratory of the Computer Engineering and Informatics Department of Patras University 32 participants, experienced in using mouse-based interfaces, used both interfaces. During the experiment, the users interacted with a simulation of the robot movements, without moving and colliding the actual robots, while the robot speed and behavior were based on actual data from our field experiments. The experiment followed a within-group design and for the tangible interface, the Wizard of Oz method was used. For data collection, eye-tracking glasses were used to capture the interaction with the tangible interface combined with recording devices. The hypotheses tested included efficiency measured in time to complete a task, accuracy measured in unsprayed or double-sprayed areas and robot collisions, and perceived user satisfaction measured with a short custom questionnaire. Results indicated that no statistically significant differences were found related to interface efficiency and accuracy, but users liked using the tangible version of the application the most.

Keywords: Human-Robot Interaction · Interface efficiency · Tangible interface · Agricultural robots · Eye-tracking

1 Introduction

In all interactive systems, the design of the graphical user interface (GUI) and the selection of the interaction mode in terms of input and output devices is crucial for determining the usability as perceived by users. This also stands for Human-Robot Interaction (HRI) and the field of remotely controlling multiple autonomous robots in scenarios with a high human operator intervention ratio. There have been empirical studies concerning

© Springer Nature Switzerland AG 2020
M. Kurosu (Ed.): HCII 2020, LNCS 12182, pp. 668–678, 2020.
https://doi.org/10.1007/978-3-030-49062-1_46

design guidelines for HRI applications [1] targeted at increasing operator awareness of robots and their surroundings, and more recent studies also address the use of various alternative input devices (mouse, haptic, gestures, tangibles, etc.) [2, 3] in an effort to investigate specific design guidelines while assuring their compliance with more general HCI design guidelines that have long proved their value and practical applicability for guaranteeing effectiveness, efficiency, satisfaction, error tolerance, and learnability [4].

Remote operator control in HRI settings has traditionally been based on 2D user interfaces (UIs) using mouse and keyboard for input, but there are certain limitations inherent in this approach (despite the familiarity of the average computer user with these devices) [5]: the motor skills required for efficient use of a mouse and mainly a keyboard are not intuitive to learn and it takes considerable practice and effort to type fast without looking at the keys. In such cases, there is a substantial amount of time that the attention of the operator is drifted away from the robot control task at hand hindering overall performance. Moreover, the typical 2D representation used on trivial UIs limits people's spatial abilities when controlling robots that move in the 3D environment or interacting with three-dimensional objects. One of the prevailing approaches to overcome these limitations of traditional UIs is Tangible User Interfaces (TUIs). A TUI (initially referred to as 'Graspable User Interface') is defined as "... a UI in which a person interacts with digital information through the physical environment ... taking advantage of the human ability to grasp and manipulate physical objects and materials" [6].

The position of a physical object in relation to its surroundings along with the spatial orientation give the human operator intuitive interaction insight and task awareness: we easily interact with physical objects and there is no need for instruction, training, specific knowledge or memorization to be able to move and manipulate a physical object in a physical environment [7]. This makes TUIs a promising approach for HRI as they make effective use of physical object affordances [8].

Research in the field of HRI is rather inconclusive on the benefits of tangible inter-faces compared with traditional ones (mouse and keyboard). Tangible inter-faces have been found to improve efficiency (navigation time), accuracy (fewer user mistakes) and user satisfaction [5], or simply improve efficiency but not accuracy [9, 10], while some studies [11] found that the quantitative results were inconclusive with only positive qualitative results. Lucignano et al. [12] compared a tangible tool with a GUI implementation using eye-tracking data for gaining more insight into the user experience and concluded that TUIs require lower mental effort suggesting some cognitive advantages in them. Besançon et al. [3] evaluated the comparative performance and usability of mouse-based, touch-based, and tangible interaction for manipulating objects in a 3D virtual environment. Melcer et al. [13] presented a comparison between the efficacy of tangible and mouse design approaches for improving key learning factors in educational programming games. Results showed that while both game versions were successful at improving programming self-beliefs, the tangible version was considered as more enjoyable. In fact, many research approaches focus on using TUIs for educational purposes based on the assumption that they can provide hands-on experience, which may have positive learning outcomes [14–16], like for instance when manipulating 3D chemical molecules [17] or learning heart anatomy [18]. Nevertheless, there are reservations about the features of TUIs that offer a learning advantage over a virtual material equivalent [16].

In our case, the focus is on investigating the use of a TUI for navigating two agricultural robots for vineyard spraying and comparing the TUI with an equivalent simple GUI approach. Robots operating in agricultural environments face specific technical challenges imposed by the physical environment they operate in (e.g. weather damage, occlusion of sensors by dirt, variable light conditions, etc.), as well as restrictions in automatic robotic grasping. Another factor that may implicate robot control tasks is when an operator must coordinate efficiently multiple robots, as is in the case examined in this paper.

The designed experiment evaluates two alternative versions of a simple screen that users interacted with using a traditional (mouse-based) and a tangible interface for positioning and manipulating two autonomous robots. This screen is intended to be part of a complex interface since the rationale is that in the future such interfaces would allow users to focus on the content of their human-robot interaction tasks, rather than on the micro-scale operations needed to accomplish these tasks [5]. For this experiment, the focus was on the operator intervention in an emergency case (the two robots heading towards a collision) and on other operator's errors (e.g. allowing the robots to spray the same area of the vineyard twice, or leaving an area of the vineyard unsprayed).

The rest of the paper is structured as follows. Section 2 presents the research questions, the robots, the user application, and the experiment setup as well as the tools used for data collection. Section 3 presents the data analysis and outlines the results, while Sect. 4 summarizes the main findings and discusses limitations and future work.

2   The Research Questions and the Experiment Setup

2.1   The Research Questions

This study aimed to compare the two different interfaces of the application in terms of users' efficiency, spraying accuracy and perceived users' satisfaction. For evaluating efficiency, the time to complete a task was selected as the dependent variable. For evaluating accuracy, three potential user errors were used: a) a user will fail to guide the robots to spray all the required areas resulting in some parts of the vineyard to be left without spraying, b) a user will allow the robots to spray an area of the vineyard more than one time, and c) a user will fail to prevent the collision of robots. For error (a) the percentage of the vineyard left unsprayed was used as the dependent variable, while for error (b) the percentage of the vineyard sprayed by both robots. To measure error (c), the application has been designed to lead into a situation that the two robots will collide without the user's intervention, therefore it was examined if the collision was prevented by the user or not. Finally, for evaluating the perceived user's satisfaction a short questionnaire was used. Based on the dependent variables selected, the research questions were formulated as follows:

- RQ_1: Is there any difference in users' time to complete a specific task while using each interface?

- RQ$_2$: Is there any difference in the percentage of the vineyard left without spraying while using each interface?
- RQ$_3$: Is there any difference in the percentage of the vineyard that was sprayed with both robots while using each interface?
- RQ$_4$: Is there any difference in preventing the collision of the robots while using each interface?
- RQ$_5$: Is there any difference in users' satisfaction while using each interface?

For each of these research questions the null hypotheses and the alternative hypotheses were tested, using the appropriate statistical tests and the results are presented in Sect. 3.

Fig. 1. Agrirobot (on the left) and SAVSAR (on the right)

2.2 The Robots and the Application

The two robots simulated in this experiment, named "Agrirobot" and "SAVSAR" are shown in Fig. 1. Both robots are based on the Summit XL mobile platform by Robotnik[1]. Agrirobot [7] is equipped with a non-movable electric sprayer and spraying is performed according to a pre-programmed algorithm [19], considering timing, duration, intensity, etc. SAVSAR [20] is equipped with an OUR-1[2] light-weight robotic arm, allowing selective target spraying and using a laser scanner and a camera placed on the end-effector sprayer nozzle. Since Agrirobot is spraying in a large area, whilst SAVSAR selects targets to spray, Agrirobot can move faster (2.23 m/s). The speed used in the

---

[1] http://www.robotnik.eu.

[2] http://www.our-robotics.com.

case simulated in the application was based on actual data from field experiments, so the SAVSAR speed was set at 42% of the Agrirobot's speed.

The application simulated a scenario created explicitly to facilitate the experiment. In this scenario, both robots operate in the same field working in a fully autonomous mode, spraying and moving each one at their own speed. The interface comprises a vineyard representation (static) and the representations of the two robots (moveable elements leaving a trail). In the scenario used in the experiment, the Agrirobot started at the bottom right corner of the vineyard as shown in the operator's screen, while the SAVSAR started at the top left corner. Both robots moved autonomously on their path, while a collision was imminent. The scenario was designed specifically to lead into a collision since the goal of the experiment was for the operator to intervene to prevent the collision by stopping the robots and then moving one of them (or both) to new positions and continue the process of spraying the vineyard.

2.3 Participants and Experiment Setup

The experiment was carried out at the Software Quality and Human-Computer Interaction Laboratory of the Computer Engineering and Informatics Department of Patras University. Participants were recruited after a short interview having as a requirement to be experienced in using mouse-based computer interfaces (at least for 3 years and at least two hours per day). Overall 38 participants selected for the experiment, 4 of them used in the piloting phases for equipment calibration, 2 removed due to errors in the measurement process, and thirty-two participants (n = 32), 14 females, accounted for the experiment. Their ages ranged from 18 to 34 years old (mean = 24.28, median = 22.5, SD = 3.86).

Following a period of trial experiments with various users (not accounted as participants in this experiment) the experiment protocol was finalized as follows: First, participants were informed about the experiment, without being given crucial information of the process, and filled in an appropriate consent form along with a questionnaire about demographic information. Then, the experiment followed the within-subject design, with each participant being exposed to both experimental conditions: tangible user interface and mouse-based interface. The starting user interface rotated for each participant (i.e., half of the subjects started with the tangible UI, and the other half started with the mouse-based UI). To randomize the experiment, a list defining the starting order was created, and when the participants entered the laboratory, using a random function, they were assigned to a place in the list. At the end of each session, the participants filled in a short questionnaire (5 questions about the user interface they had just used) used to measure perceived user satisfaction [21]. The questionnaire aimed to record participants' evaluation of how easy, efficient, accurate, and enjoyable the interface was and included the following items:

1. I found the interface easy to use.
2. I considered the time needed to complete the task satisfactorily.
3. The interface helped me to avoid making mistakes.
4. I liked the interface.
5. I could use the interface daily if that was required for my job.

Reliability analysis was carried out for both mouse-based and tangible interface questionnaires. For the mouse-based interface, Cronbach's α showed the questionnaire to have acceptable reliability, α = 0.799. For the tangible interface, Cronbach's α was found to be marginal α = 0.682, but with all items appearing to decrease the α value when deleted. Despite having high reliability for both mouse-based and tangible questionnaires, since the value of α was under 0.7 for one case in the analysis in the following section, we haven't used the overall questionnaire score but focused on each question instead.

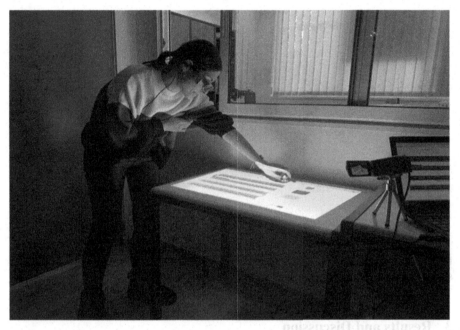

Fig. 2. A user wearing eye-tracking glasses while interacting with the tangible interface

For the mouse-based interface, the users used a typical desktop computer and their data were recorded using screen capturing. For the tangible interface, the Wizard of Oz technique [22] was used. The screen was projected on a clean surface, and the users could control the robots by picking up miniatures and placing them on the surface. Each movement of the miniatures on the surface corresponded to a simulated movement of the robots. Additionally, the user could stop any robot at any time by picking up its miniature. Our initial plan was to 3D print actual robot miniatures to use in the experiments, but during the early trial experiments (before engaging the final 4 users for piloting the entire experiment) miniature toys from a well know cartoon were used. Since the participants in these trial experiment seem to had a lot of fun working with these toy miniatures, and since "participating in HCI studies should be fun and engaging whenever possible: by making our studies positive experiences, we encourage people both to participate and to provide useful feedback" [23] we decided to keep these toy miniatures for the actual experiments too. Considering that in the trial experiments in some cases the eye-tracking glasses were disconnected, we also used a camera to record the experiment and keep track of user actions and time. The experiment setup is shown in Fig. 2. For the Wizard of Oz part of the experiment, the operator response time was kept to a minimum and disregarded in the times measured. As aforementioned, data from 2 participants were not accounted for since the evaluator (Wizard of Oz) failed to perform accurately the participants' actions.

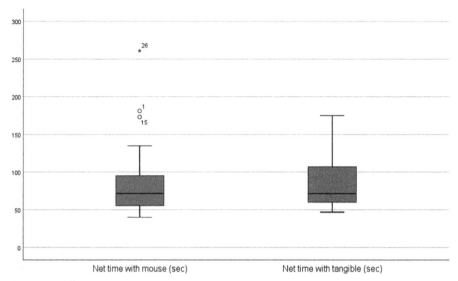

Fig. 3. Boxplots of the time of completion for both interfaces. The mouse-based interface is shown on the left and the tangible interface on the right

3   Results and Discussion

Following the data collection and the data cleaning (i.e. removing from the 34 initial participants the 2 ones where the operator failed to accurately simulate their movements), the final dataset still contained an equal number of participants starting with each interface. The collected data were organized and pre-processed using Microsoft Excel 365 ProPlus and were analyzed using IBM SPSS Statistics v26.0. The results from the statistical analysis of the five research questions are presented hereinafter.

3.1 RQ_1: Time to Complete a Task

For RQ_1, the time to complete a task was measured in seconds as shown in Fig. 3. A Shapiro-Wilk test showed a significant departure from normality on time measurements for both the mouse-based ($W(32) = 0.765$, $p < 0.001$) and the tangible ($W(32) = 0.851$, $p < 0.001$) interfaces, and thus only non-parametric tests were con-ducted. A Wilcoxon Signed Rank Test showed that there was no significant difference in completion time between the mouse-based interface (Min = 40, Max = 261, Median = 71.5, Mean =

84.47, SD = 46.86) and the tangible interface (Min = 47, Max = 175, Median = 71.5, Mean = 83.97, SD = 34.35), n = 32, Z = 0.505, p = 0.614. The results indicate that regarding RQ_1, there is no statistical difference in users' time to complete a specific task while using each interface.

3.2 RQ_2: Percentage of Unsprayed Areas

For RQ_2, the percentage of unsprayed area was measured. A Shapiro-Wilk test showed that the percentage of the unsprayed area is not normally distributed for both the mouse-based (W(32) = 0.242, p < 0.001) and the tangible (W(32) = 0.411, p < 0.001) interfaces. A Wilcoxon Signed Rank Test showed that there was no significant difference in percentage of unsprayed areas between the mouse-based interface (Min = 0, Max = 12.5, Median = 0, Mean = 0.6, SD = 2.22) and tangible interface (Min = 0, Max = 0.7, Median = 0, Mean = 0.51, SD = 0.17), n = 32, Z = −1.352, p = 0.176. The results reveal that regarding RQ_2, there is no significant difference in the percentage of the vineyard left without spraying while using each interface.

3.3 RQ_3: Percentage of Double Sprayed Areas

For RQ_3, the percentage of the area sprayed by both robots was measured. A Shapiro-Wilk test showed that the percentage of the area sprayed by both robots is not normally distributed for both the mouse-based (W(32) = 0.695, p < 0.001) and the tangible (W(32) = 0.629, p < 0.001) interfaces. A Wilcoxon Signed Rank Test showed that there was no significant difference in percentage of double sprayed areas for the mouse-based interface (Min = 0, Max = 25, Median = 0.3, Mean = 3.66, SD = 5.61) and the tangible interface (Min = 0, Max = 37.5, Median = 0, Mean = 5.03, SD = 8.73), n = 32, Z = 0.7, p = 0.484. Based on the results concerning RQ_3, there is no significant difference in the percentage of the vineyard that was sprayed with both robots while using each interface.

3.4 RQ_4: Preventing the Collision of the Robots

For RQ_4, the number of collisions was measured. Since there were no cases recorded of more than one collision, the results were classified as "having a collision" and "avoiding the collision". A Shapiro-Wilk test revealed that the normality hypothesis was violated for both the mouse-based (W(32) = 0.511, p < 0.001) and the tangible (W(32) = 0.540, p < 0.001) interfaces. A Wilcoxon Signed Rank Test showed that there was no significant difference in number of collisions between the mouse-based interface (Min = 0, Max = 1, Median = 0, Mean = 0.22, SD = 0.42) and the tangible interface (Min = 0, Max = 1, Median = 0, Mean = 0.25, SD = 0.44), n = 32, Z = 0.333, p = 0.739. The results indicate that regarding RQ_4, there is no significant difference in preventing the collision of the robots while using each interface.

3.5 RQ_5: Users' Satisfaction

Finally, for RQ_5, a survey was distributed among the 32 participants following the use of the two interfaces (see Sect. 2.3). After following the appropriate statistical procedures,

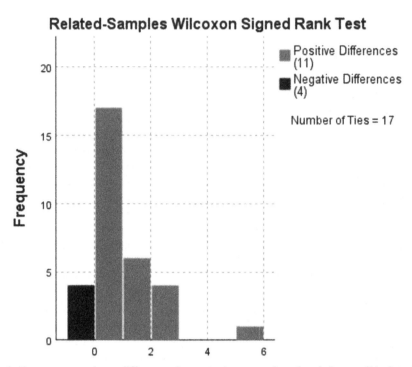

Fig. 4. Frequency graph on differences between the mouse-based and the tangible interface concerning RQ4

the data of items 1, 2, 3, and 5 of the questionnaires showed no statistical differences between the mouse-based interface and the tangible interface. In contrast to the previous findings, item 4, which is related to perceived user satisfaction, showed a significant difference between the two interfaces. Initially, a Shapiro-Wilk test showed that the questionnaire data were not following the normal distribution for both the mouse-based $(W(32) = 0.796, p < 0.001)$ and the tangible $(W(32) = 0.736, p < 0.001)$ interfaces. Consequently, a Wilcoxon Signed-Ranked test revealed that there is a significant difference in perceived user satisfaction for the mouse-based interface (Min = 2, Max = 7, Median = 6, Mean = 5.94, SD = 1.24) and the tangible interface (Min = 4, Max = 7, Median = 7, Mean = 6.41, SD = 0.8), n = 32, Z = 2.239, p = 0.025, r = 0.4. Because the standardized test statistic is positive (Z = 2.239), the opinion of the users regarding user satisfaction is more positive about the tangible interface compared to the mouse-based interface. Additionally, Fig. 4 shows that there were far more positive differences (11) between mouse-based and tangible interface as opposed to negative differences (4) with the rest being ties (17), which also shows that overall opinions were more positive for the tangible interface. Based on the results concerning RQ5, we can conclude that there is a significant difference in users' satisfaction while using each interface.

4 Conclusions, Limitations and Future Goals

The results from the experiments revealed that participants' performance was the same regardless of the interface they were using. Since there was a learning effect, which is a typical problem for the within-group design, participants performed better in their second attempt, regardless of the ordering of the alternative interfaces. This effect was controlled by using a randomly assigned order in the use of the interfaces. For the experiment protocol, this limitation was much easier to control rather than adopting a between-group design, since in this case, the noise added by the individual differences of such a generic group would be much more difficult to handle. Nevertheless, future goals include experiments with more specific groups (e.g. farmers) to investigate if the findings are the same in a group of agricultural professionals.

Another limitation is that the results might be dependent on the scenario, although this was a scenario required a high degree of operator intervention to robot movements. Scenarios such as this one, are the ones expected to reveal differences among various interface designs, should any of these exist. Towards this, a future goal is to investigate more complex scenarios.

Finally, the results revealing that the tangible interface was the one that the participants liked the most could also be attributed to the fun factor related to the experiment as well as to the novelty effect introduced by the tangible interface. Still, the observation that users performed similarly with both interfaces despite their high familiarity with the mouse-based one, could be considered as a positive indicator for the use of tangible interfaces in settings of remote control of more than one robot. These conclusions need to be investigated further in future experiments.

Acknowledgement. The authors would like to thank the participants in this survey and Mrs. Dimitra Fountzoula for developing the user interface and helping in the experiments as the Wizard of Oz.

References

1. Goodrich, M.A., Olsen, D.R.: Seven principles of efficient human robot interaction. In: SMC 2003 Conference Proceedings. 2003 IEEE International Conference on Systems, Man and Cybernetics. Conference Theme-System Security and Assurance (Cat. No. 03CH37483). IEEE (2003)
2. Kruse, T., et al.: Human-aware robot navigation: a survey. Robot. Auton. Syst. **61**(12), 1726–1743 (2013)
3. Besançon, L., et al.: Usability comparison of mouse, touch and tangible inputs for 3D data manipulation. arXiv preprint arXiv:1603.08735 (2016)
4. Nielsen, J.: Usability Engineering. Morgan Kaufmann, San Francisco (1994)
5. Guo, C., Sharlin, E.: Exploring the use of tangible user interfaces for human-robot interaction: a comparative study. In: Proceedings of the SIGCHI Conference on Human Factors in Computing Systems, Florence, Italy, pp. 121–130. ACM (2008)
6. Ishii, H.: Tangible user interfaces. In: Human-Computer Interaction: Design Issues, Solutions, and Applications, pp. 141–157 (2007)

7. Adamides, G., et al.: HRI usability evaluation of interaction modes for a teleoperated agricultural robotic sprayer. Appl. Ergon. **62**, 237–246 (2017)
8. Faisal, S., Cairns, P., Craft, B.: Infovis experience enhancement through mediated interaction (2005)
9. Randelli, G., Venanzi, M., Nardi, D.: Tangible interfaces for robot teleoperation. In: Proceedings of the 6th International Conference on Human-Robot Interaction. ACM (2011)
10. Randelli, G., Venanzi, M., Nardi, D.: Evaluating tangible paradigms for ground robot teleoperation. In: 2011 RO-MAN. IEEE (2011)
11. Lapides, P., Sharlin, E., Costa Sousa, M.: Three dimensional tangible user interface for controlling a robotic team. In: Proceedings of the 3rd ACM/IEEE International Conference on Human Robot Interaction. ACM (2008)
12. Lucignano, L., et al.: My hands or my mouse: comparing a tangible and graphical user interface using eye-tracking data. In: Proceedings of the FabLearn Conference 2014 (2014)
13. Melcer, E.F., Hollis, V., Isbister, K.: Tangibles vs. mouse in educational programming games: influences on enjoyment and self-beliefs. In: Proceedings of the 2017 CHI Conference Extended Abstracts on Human Factors in Computing Systems (2017)
14. Xie, L., Antle, A.N., Motamedi, N.: Are tangibles more fun? Comparing children's enjoyment and engagement using physical, graphical and tangible user interfaces. In: Proceedings of the 2nd International Conference on Tangible and Embedded Interaction (2008)
15. Horn, M.S., Solovey, E.T., Jacob, R.J.: Tangible programming and informal science learning: making TUIs work for museums. In: Proceedings of the 7th International Conference on Interaction Design and Children (2008)
16. Marshall, P.: Do tangible interfaces enhance learning? In: Proceedings of the 1st International Conference on Tangible and Embedded Interaction, Baton Rouge, Louisiana, pp. 163–170. ACM (2007)
17. Gillet, A., et al.: Tangible interfaces for structural molecular biology. Structure **13**(3), 483–491 (2005)
18. Skulmowski, A., et al.: Embodied learning using a tangible user interface: the effects of haptic perception and selective pointing on a spatial learning task. Comput. Educ. **92**, 64–75 (2016)
19. Berenstein, R., et al.: Grape clusters and foliage detection algorithms for autonomous selective vineyard sprayer. Intel. Serv. Robot. **3**(4), 233–243 (2010)
20. Adamides, G., et al.: Design and development of a semi-autonomous agricultural vineyard sprayer: human–robot interaction aspects. J. Field Robot. **34**(8), 1407–1426 (2017)
21. Xenos, M., Christodoulakis, D.: Software quality: the user's point of view. In: Lee, M., Barta, B.-Z., Juliff, P. (eds.) Software Quality and Productivity. IAICT, pp. 266–272. Springer, Boston, MA (1995). https://doi.org/10.1007/978-0-387-34848-3_41
22. Hudson, S., et al.: Predicting human interruptibility with sensors: a Wizard of Oz feasibility study. In: Proceedings of the SIGCHI Conference on Human Factors in Computing Systems. ACM (2003)
23. Lazar, J., Feng, J.H., Hochheiser, H.: Research Methods in Human-Computer Interaction. Morgan Kaufmann, Amsterdam (2017)

On Positive Effect on Humans by Poor Operability of Robot

Mitsuharu Matsumoto[✉]

The University of Electro-Communications,
1-5-1 Chofugaoka, Chofu-shi, Tokyo, Japan
mitsuharu.matsumoto@ieee.org
http://www.mm-labo.org

Abstract. This paper describes positive effect on humans by poor operability of a robot. In recent years, we can find many robots to help users' daily life. Although many robots are designed to fully assist users in their daily lives, this approach sometimes leads users to a passive life. On the other hand, some researchers developed incomplete robots. In such approaches, users need to be active to assist the robots. Robots that make people convenient are effective in reducing human effort, but on the other hand, they feel bored and tired of robots. In this study, we investigate the effects of inconvenience on the operation of robots on humans to solve the problems.

Keywords: Inconvenience · Poor operability · Robot design

1 Introduction

In this paper, we discuss positive effect on humans by poor operability of a robot. With the spread of life support robots such as home robots and nursing robots, many studies have been reported on how humans interact with robots [1–3]. However, some studies reported that full support from humans and robots has not only advantages but also disadvantages. For example, it is known that physical and mental decays of elderly people progress rapidly when they lost something to do and live a bleak life after reaching the mandatory retirement age [4,5]. Other researchers have reported that people who require nursing care feel strong stress even if they receive good skilled care because they feel loss of independence due to their passive lives [6]. Some researchers noted the importance of works, that is, to have some tasks to be done in daily life. These types of tasks give people a purpose in life [7]. Based on the above prospects, some authors have developed the robots that need humans' assists. The robots cannot work without users' help unlike typical life supporting robots. For example, Kano et al. developed a baby-like robot named Babyloid [8]. Babyloid cannot do anything like baby and waits users' help by doing some actions such as changing its facial expression and crying. Users intend to have active interaction with Babyloid due to its ineffectuality. Okada et al. have developed a trash box type robot

© Springer Nature Switzerland AG 2020
M. Kurosu (Ed.): HCII 2020, LNCS 12182, pp. 679–687, 2020.
https://doi.org/10.1007/978-3-030-49062-1_47

named Sociable Trash Box [9]. Although Social Trash Box can move and bow its body, it cannot take garbage. Social Trash Box only bows when users pick up the garbage and dump it to Social Trash Box. Social Trash Box requires users' help and aim to encourage users' active support by using the robot ineffectuality. They labeled this concept power of weakness and confirmed its availability. We have also investigated the positive effects of robots that can sometimes be annoying [10,11]. In this study, we focus on how much human attachment and interest to a robot can be aroused by increasing the complexity of the operation.

2   Interaction Design

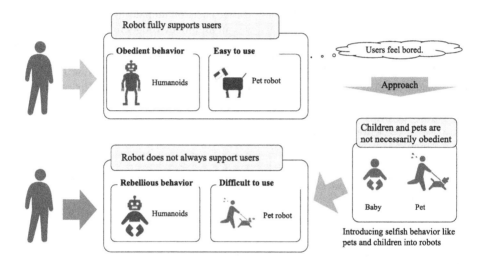

Fig. 1. Concept of robot design

With the spread of life support robots such as home robots and nursing robots, many studies have been reported on how humans interact with robots. These life support robots have a wide variety of appearances and support methods. Many of them focus on how to help the subject without error and how to perform the job perfectly according to the subject's intentions. On the other hand, some studies show that it is not always an advantage for humans that robots fully support humans. In addition, there are many people who feel tired of robots that only follow the commands of the subjects. Our aim is to solve this problem by introducing a kind of selfishness to the robot. The concept of this research is shown in Fig. 1

Many researchers have been researching interfaces for robot operation. Basically, to improve operability, they have been developing interfaces that enable simpler operations. However, people often have more interest in more time-consuming tasks than simple tasks. For example, there are automatic transmission vehicles (AT vehicles) and manual transmission vehicles (MT vehicles).

Because MT cars take more time than AT cars in normal driving, many people currently use AT cars in Japan. However, there are a certain number of people who prefer MT cars. This is an example of increasing intimacy to things due to the complexity of operations. In this study, we focus on this fact and aim to increase the user's interest in the robot by deteriorating the operability.

3 Experiment

3.1 Experimental Setup

Fig. 2. Prepared robot used for experiments.

Fig. 3. Wii remote controller: prepared controller for the experiments.

Figure 2 shows the prepared robot for the experiment. Figure 3 shows Wii remote controller, that is, the prepared robot controller for the experiment. Figure 4 shows the experimental setup.

Eight subjects attended the experiments. In the experiment, the subjects experienced five operation methods with different operability. Through experiments, Beauto Rover, a small wheel robot, was used for the robot, and a Wii remote control was used for the operation. Users were asked to direct the robot to bring a small ball to the goal by using five operation methods. The work time limit was set to 3 min. Beauto Rover is wirelessly connected to the notebook computer via Bluetooth and can be controlled from the notebook computer. Microsoft Visual C# was used to control the Beauto Rover and Wii remote control. After the experiments, we asked the subjects to answer the questionnaires such as "joy of operation", "difficulty of operation", and "attachment to robots".

3.2   Robot Behaviors

In this section, prepared behaviors are explained.

– Normal operation

This is the most basic operation using the cross key. When the up and down buttons are pressed with the cross button, the front, back, right and left buttons will advance to the right and left respectively.

Fig. 4. Experimental setup.

– Two press operation

This is a slightly complicated operation that requires another operation. For example, when moving the robot forward, it is necessary for users to press the up button and the A button. When moving the robot back, it is necessary to press the down button and the B button.

– Operation of broken specifications

This is an operation with pseudo malfunction. If the robot is operated a certain number of times, the robot stops operating as a pseudo failure effect. Users can restore the robot by performing a preset operation. In this operation, we aim to create the attachment of the subject to the robot as a result of the tasks of the subject to the robot. In this operation, the user can operate the robot using the cross button as in the normal operation. However, if the user performs the operation five times, the robot stops moving. When the user presses the home button for recovery, the robot is initialized and cured. After the cure, the robot breaks again when the user operates five times, and the robot heals when the home button is pressed. In order to explain the situation to the subject, the robot made a voice saying "It's broken. Please press the home button".

– Operation of fuel refill specifications

This is an operation with a pseudo refueling. When the user operates the robot a certain number of times, the robot operation stops due to pseudo fuel shortage. The aim is to confirm the difference between the pseudo malfunction and pseudo refueling. If the user continues to operate the robot, the robot will run out of fuel. The robot cannot be operated without refueling. In order to explain the situation to the subject, the robot made a voice saying "Fuel is exhausted. Press the home button."

– Operation of random control

This is an operation in which the robot does not follow the subject. We aimed to check whether such operation could arouse users' attachment to the robot. The user operates using the cross button as in normal operation. However, the direction in which the robot moves is not fixed in this operation.

3.3 Experimental Process

We asked the examinees to answer a questionnaire after the operation was completed. Eight contents were set for the questionnaire as follows:

1. Did you feel fun?
2. Did you feel bored?
3. Did you feel it was easy to use?
4. Did you get attached?
5. Did you feel you wanted
6. Did you get interested?
7. Please tell us your impressions

For questions (1) to (6), the evaluation was set in five stages, and (7) was a free description. When 4 or 5 of 5 grades is given, the user is positive for the question. When 1 or 2 of 5 grades is given, the user is negative for the question.

3.4 Experimental Results

Figure 5 shows the positive answers regarding questionnaire 1 (Did you feel fun?).

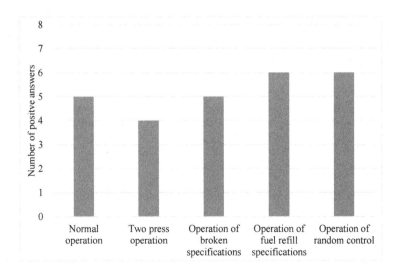

Fig. 5. Number of positive answers regarding questionnaire 1: Did you feel fun?

Figure 6 shows the positive answers regarding questionnaire 2 (Did you feel bored?). In this case, the figure shows the number of people who did not get bored with the robot.

Figure 7 shows the positive answers regarding questionnaire 3 (Did you feel it was easy to use?).

Figure 8 shows the positive answers regarding questionnaire 4 (Did you get attached?).

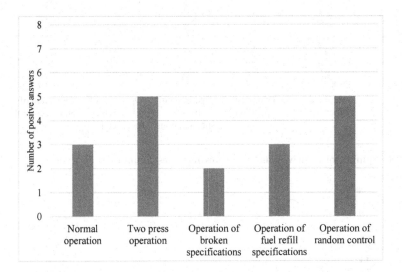

Fig. 6. Number of positive answers regarding questionnaire 2: Did you feel bored?

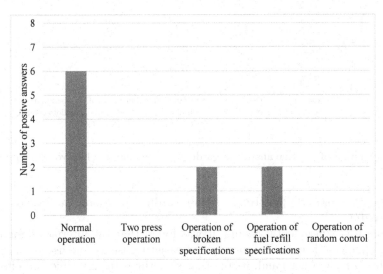

Fig. 7. Number of positive answers regarding questionnaire 3: Did you feel it was easy to use?

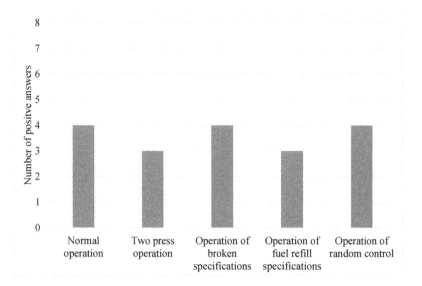

Fig. 8. Number of positive answers regarding questionnaire 4: Did you get attached?

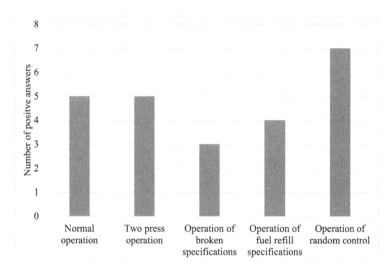

Fig. 9. Number of positive answers regarding questionnaire 5: Did you get interested?

Figure 9 shows the positive answers regarding questionnaire 5 (Did you get interested?).

From the experimental results, it was found that the interface design with simple operation is easier to operate and easier to use for the user, as normally thought. On the other hand, robots that sometimes require time and effort are arousing user enjoyment and attachment.

While there is users who have much attachment to broken specifications, there are users who do not have much attachment to refueling and vice versa. It was suggested that the difference in the behavior of the robot affects the user's attachment to the robot even in the same time-consuming action.

4 Conclusion

In this paper, we described some concept of poor operability of a robot and reported some experimental results related to the concepts. We conducted some experiments to check our concept. Although the experiments are an early stage, we obtained some positive feedbacks from users regarding our concept. As a future prospect, we would like to examine more detailed conditions to realize our concept.

References

1. Hiroi, Y., et al.: A patient care service robot system based on a state transition architecture. In: The 2nd International Conference on Mechatronics and Information Technology, pp. 231–236 (2003)
2. Iwata, H., Sugano, S.: Design of human symbiotic robot TWENDY-ONE. In: IEEE International Conference on Robotics and Automation, pp. 580–586 (2009)
3. Matsuyama, Y., Fujie, S., Taniyama, H., Kobayashi, T.: Psychological evaluation of a group communication activation robot in a party game. In: Interspeech 2010, pp. 3046–3049 (2010)
4. Iguchi, A.: Incoming Geratology. The University of Nagoya Press, Nagoya (2002)
5. Takenaka, H.: Loss Experience and Rebirth of Elderly People. Seitosha Publishing, Tokyo (2005)
6. Tanaka, K., et al.: Geratology isagoge. Nihon Hyoron Sha, Tokyo (1997)
7. Kamiya, M.: On a Purpose of Life. Misuzu Shobo, Tokyo (2004)
8. Kanoh, M., Shimizu, T.: Developing a robot Babyloid that cannot do anything. J. Robot. Soc. Japan **29**(3), 76–83 (2011)
9. Yoshida, Y., Yoshiike, Y., Okada, M.: Sociable Trash Box: a robot collecting trashes with children. J. Hum. Interface Soc. **11**(1), 27–36 (2009)
10. Yasuda, H., Matsumoto, M.: Psychological impact on human when a robot makes mistakes. In: Proceedings of 2013 IEEE/SICE International Symposium on System Integration, pp. 335–339 (2013)
11. Matsumoto, M.: On positive effect to human impression by a forgetful robot. Int. J. Soc. Sci. Humanity **7**(9), 650–654 (2017)

Human-Drone Interaction: Using Pointing Gesture to Define a Target Object

Anna C. S. Medeiros$^{(\boxtimes)}$, Photchara Ratsamee, Yuki Uranishi,
Tomohiro Mashita, and Haruo Takemura

Osaka University, Osaka, Japan
anna@lab.ime.cmc.osaka-u.ac.jp,
{photchara,uranishi,mashita}@ime.cmc.osaka-u.ac.jp,
takemura@cmc.osaka-u.ac.jp

Abstract. This paper focuses on exploring the optimal gesture interface for Human-Drone Interaction in a firefighting scenario. For this purpose, we conducted a Preliminary Interview and User Study with seven subjects from the Kobe Firefighting Brigade, Japan. As a drone's flight and locomotion properties significantly affect the user's mental and physical expectations, differently compared to other grounded robots, a careful investigation of user-defined design preferences and interactions is required. This work proposes an examination and discussion, with experienced firefighters, about Human-Drone Interactions when relying solely on the drone's monocular camera, without relying on other devices such as GPS or external cameras. The User Study had three main elements: A drone, a building, and the volunteering firefighters. During the Study, each firefighter should specify a window to the drone. The drone would theoretically use that window to enter the building and perform some designed tasks, like information gathering, thus saving the firefighter time and effort. Results show that the subjects always chose Pointing Gestures and voice commands as a means to communicate to the drone a target window. We built A prototype application with the resulting gesture from this investigation. In the prototype, a drone can understand to which object the user is pointing.

Keywords: Human-Drone Interaction · Pointing gesture · Natural interaction

1 Introduction

In recent years, robots have been taking advantage of developments in Hardware and Software Technologies; this continuous improvement prompts the expansion in the potential use of robotics, which leads to crescent visibility of robots in everyday lives. A specific type of robot that has been gaining popularity is Unmanned Aerial Vehicles (UAVs). Also known as drones, UAVs are flying robots that can be remotely controlled or operated autonomously; it has diverse applications: cinematography, disaster monitoring [1], surveillance, journalism

© Springer Nature Switzerland AG 2020
M. Kurosu (Ed.): HCII 2020, LNCS 12182, pp. 688–705, 2020.
https://doi.org/10.1007/978-3-030-49062-1_48

[2], military reconnaissance [3], and others. Given the wide variety of applications and multiple degree of freedom, it is challenging to design a natural interaction namely, Human-Drone Interaction (HDI), for effectively control UAVs.

The most basic feature of Human-Drone Interaction is a user or system signaling a drone to change its position [4]. In the traditional form, the user directly controls the flight path using a device like a joystick. With more intelligent systems, how one controls the drone changes. For example, the user can define targets for the drone to reach autonomously [5]. They are thus allowing for applications where the drone could position itself relative to a goal, which in turn would make more complex tasks possible, for example, signaling a drone to grab and drop blocks, stacking them until the drone can build a wall. The scenario just described can be referred to as a Task-Oriented scenario [4].

On Task-Oriented scenarios, drones might need to interact and make decisions based on human input. In order to create user interfaces for human-drone interaction, it is necessary to control the drone, know where the drone is, and provide communication between the drone and other systems [4].

Controlling the drone in interactive systems depends on the available resources and requirements of the task at hand. For example, wearable devices might not be the optimal solution for long jobs where they would run out of batteries [6], or tasks that involved a high number of human participants. Other options could be the traditional Command-Line: every time the drone required a human input in the middle of a task, they could provide it via typing a command. But the downsides to it are clear, seeing as the human might need to interrupt their activities to communicate with the drone. One possible solution to avoid wearable devices, or interrupting human activities to input commands to a system, would be the use of Gesture Input.

Fig. 1. Possible scenario for the system presented here

Gesture refers to any bodily motion or states, particularly any hand motion or face motion [7]. It is a form of visual communication that, in the case of drones, could be especially convenient in cases that computer vision substitutes GPS on determining the drone position, which is the case of indoor environments. It would also benefit situations where computer vision and GPS, or other localization technologies, could cooperate to create a more robust system.

Gestures are also a natural form of human communication. Imagine the following scenario (Fig. 1): drones are supporting a firefighter unit by entering a building and providing some assessment on the situation inside. In this scenario, a possible approach would be for the drone to wait for a human command, as to which window or entrance it should take to enter the building mentioned above. The firefighter could point to the desired window, and the drone, now with a target entrance, could carry on with some designed task inside, like scanning the room for victims.

There are many possible scenarios were drone systems, and humans would benefit from collaboration in the course of a task. This paper studies about guidance for natural Human-Drone Interactions when relying solely on the drone camera, without external devices, non-dependant on GPS systems, and without the use of external tracking of the drone (for example, external cameras are pointing to the drone), and in the firefighting scenario. We performed an User Study with a fire brigade, during which the firefighters often chose to use pointing gestures and voice commands.

2   User Study

In the scenario depicted in Fig. 1, the hypothesis was that the pointing gesture would be used to indicate the target window. In order to be certain that this gesture was the most appropriate for this scenario, we performed an User Study in a Fire Brigade in Kobe, Japan. In this Study it was questioned how the fireman would interact with the drone, that is, how the fireman would indicate a window as an entering point to the drone.

Seven firefighters participated in the Study. The position of the subjects on the fire brigade varied from officer to chief. We asked the subjects opinion on using drones to aid firefighters, if they felt that drones could be useful, and if so, what type of interface would they prefer to control it.

2.1   Environment

The first part of the User Study consisted of the following scenario: a drone hovering next to a building. Each subject stood between the drone and the building (Fig. 2). Each subject was requested to signal the drone, in whichever way they preferred, to enter a window. Afterward, in the second part of the Study, an interview was conducted with each firefighter. We collected their opinions on future applications of drones in firefighting, and interfaces for drones control systems.

We tested the scenario using four different positionings between subject and drone (Fig. 3). In the first setup, the drone was two meters far from the subject

Fig. 2. User Study: How to indicate a window to a drone?

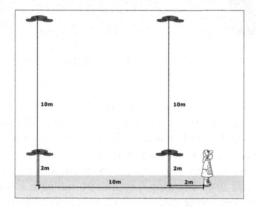

Fig. 3. We tested four different positionings between subject and drone

and hoovered two meters high. In the second setup, the drone was two meters far from the subject and hoovered ten meters high. In the third setup, the drone was ten meters far from the subject and hoovered two meters high, and on the fourth, the drone was ten meters far from the subject and hoovered ten meters high. The distance between a subject and the building was always 40 m.

2.2 Results

All subjects wished for a fully autonomous drone that could quickly arrive in the fire scene and gather useful data for First Responders such as building type, source of fire, type of fire, victims present.

An important observation made was that in dealing with drones, the firefighters would like to be always kept in touch with how the task performed by the drone was evolving, that is, quality and timed feedback to ensure the firefighter the drone was not derailing from the defined task.

Fig. 4. Experiment: Indicating a window to the drone

When describing the scenario, the word "pointing" was not mentioned. We didn't give any suggestions to the Pointing gesture, verbally or otherwise. In the results (Fig. 4) it was observed that to indicate a window, the firefighters always used Pointing Gesture and Verbal commands.

Given the results of this User Study we became interested in building a gesture interface that used Pointing Gestures to indicate a window to a drone. Besides the scenario here presented, there are many possible scenarios were drone systems would benefit from interaction with humans in the course of a task. This paper aims to provide guidance for natural Human-Drone Interactions when relying solely on the drone camera, without external devices, non-dependant on GPS systems, and without the use of external tracking of the drone (for example, external cameras pointing to the drone). Pointing Gestures are studied as a means to estimate the correct Target Object.

3   Related Work

There is multiple research on using gestures to navigate a drone [8–10]. But what we investigate here is a collaboration between drone and human, in order to relieve human task load and reduce drone error by processing periodical human-input.

We conducted a User Study with a fire brigade, and the fireman always used Pointing Gesture and voice commands to interact with the drone during the scenario proposed. We then decided to develop an application to put those results into real practice.

Pointing is a ubiquitous gesture formed by extending the arm, hand, and index finger to specify a direction from a person's body, usually indicating a location, object, thing, or idea. Many works used a Pointing Gesture as a means to specify a target for a robot. The scenario is the following: human points to a particular location or object, robot process it, and determines the point of interest, proceeding to perform a predefined desired action. This section provides insight as to how that scenario is handled.

The work of Tölgyessy et al. [11] relies on a 3D sensor (1st generation Kinect device) mounted on the robot for controlling an autonomous mobile robot with a referential pointing gesture. The design included state machines of the algorithm, using the point of view of the operator, as well as the point of view of the robot. Tölgyessy et al. [11] also provided a literature review on pointing gestures, providing a good perception as to where Human-Robot Interaction stood at the time on Gesture Input for Target Object Estimation on robots. In order to detect gesture through visual input, a wide range of devices could be observed, a Time of Flight camera [12–14], fish-eye camera [15], single camera using a skin-color blob tracker [16], 1st generation Kinect sensor [17–19]. Most of these works aimed at terrestrial operating robots. The Pointing Gestures were more commonly detected through the use of depth sensors. The works reviewed usually focused on the correct identification of the target, not the actual robot movement.

Gromov et al. [20] uses data from two Inertial Measurement Units (IMU) to estimate pointed locations and detect the pointing event, the task in question was landing a drone. The results fair better than a joystick, although during long time operations the users might suffer from gorilla arm syndrome due to fact that the users need to hold the Pointing Gesture for as long as it takes for the drone to get to the desired location, then hold it for an extra 3 second to confirm landing.

Azari et al. [21] detects pointing gestures in individual RGB-D frames. A CNN-based detector is used to find hands and faces in the images, then the corresponding depth channel pixels is examined to obtain full 3D pointing vectors. It can be noticed how many works rely on sensors other than a monocular camera (RGB) to detect gestures and guide drones on tasks. But drones usually are already equipped with RGB cameras, adding extra sensors like depth cameras or scanning lasers range-finders might be impossible due to weight limits on UAVs, especially on lightweight drones, or even financial constraints.

The work of Mirri et al. [22] shows a recent review (2019) about Human-Drone Interaction. It categorizes the paper based on the following dimensions: The drone role (e.g., sensing tool), the context of use (e.g., helping in rescue missions), indoor VS outdoor usage, the interaction mode (e.g., gestures). The present work is being developed to work on the scenario presented in Fig. 1, in the future. Therefore it would fit the dimensions as exemplified before (sensing tool, help in rescue missions, using gestures).

The work of Mirri et al. [22] also mentions that scenarios like the one presented in the Fig. 1 opens challenges in the way the operator can interact with the drones considering that he/she is not fully dedicated to the drones, but involved in search and rescue tasks. Then, the way to develop a Pointing Gesture Interface that diminishes the effort required by the operator, and at the same time allows the drone to support the mission effectively, is one of the utmost importance. Given that there are lots of other issues to consider here, such as ethics and privacy concerns [22], this scenario might even require a particular methodology for the development of effective systems in this scope. Hence, it is for now, out of the reach of this work in the present state.

4   Methodology

The present work uses available software resources and no hardware addition on drones or humans, thus creating a system with few device requirements, to estimate target objects using pointing gestures.

4.1   System Architecture

Regarding the applicability of the present work, any computational system where depth cameras were not feasible due to constraints, could profit from the results presented here. Some common constraints are weight limit and lack of financial resources, but access to RGB cameras are widespread, therefore widening the applicability of the present work.

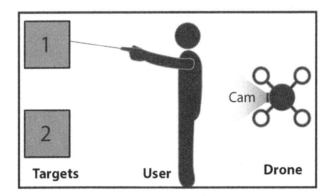

Fig. 5. Basic elements of System

There are four essential elements in the system presented here (Fig. 5): The User, the Targets, the Camera, the Processing Unit. The User is the human who will interact with the Camera, this interaction will be in the form of pointing towards the desired Target. The Targets are types of visual content, for example, an object that the Processing Unit has been trained to recognize by using object detection algorithms like YOLO [23]. The Processing Unit is any computational system that processes the images from the Camera and sends signals to the drone or robot. The Camera is the image feed in the moving robot or drone.

The Pointing Gesture detection uses Openpose [24] to detect two points on the User's forearms, this two points are used to calculate the equation of a line, extending the line segment until the borders of the image, hereby defined as Extended Pointing Segment.

The Target detection uses YOLO, here a total of 400 images were used in the training of each Target Object. The work presented relies on the input of Openpose and YOLO to get the Pointing Gesture and Target Objects' Bounding Box points, then if the Extended Pointing Segment and the Bounding Box of a Target Object are overlapping, this means that Target Object was selected. The drone now can interact with this Target, for example getting closer to it.

4.2   Pointing Gesture Interaction

Besides the four basic elements described above, its worth mentioning the importance of Pointing as a Gesture for interacting with the environment, and for communication in general. The Pointing Gesture is one of the first means of communication that humans develop [25], thus in order to facilitate interaction with humans, machines should be improved on that aspect. Pointing is also an universal gesture to determine a Region of Interest, therefore its importance in this study.

Regarding other gestures for Drone Interaction, there are many Wizard of Oz elicitation studies that try to determine good gestures for Human-Drone Interaction [26,27], however other gestures may face challenges when considering the preferences from persons with cultural differences and other background and personal divergences. For estimating a Target Object through gestures, the Pointing Gesture is the most appropriate choice.

5   Experiment

In order to test the aforementioned Methodology an application was developed and an experiment was conducted. The environment and details of the experiment will be described bellow.

5.1   Tangible Resources

The Parrot Bebop 2 [28] was the chosen drone for the experiments, it is a quadricopter that weights around 500 g, offers 25 min of autonomous flight time, can film in 1080p full HD with its wide-angle 14 megapixel lens. But for the sake of performance the image size was limited to 856 × 480. There is an available SDK by the name of bebop_autonomy, for ROS-supported system.

Bebop 2 interfaced via wifi with a laptop. The used notebook was an Alienware 13 R3 (the Processing Unit), graphics card NVIDIA GTX 1060, 8GB RAM and a I7-7700hq processing unit. Other than the Bebop 2 and the Laptop, no other electronic devices were used. They interfaced using ROS (Robot Operating System) [29].

5.2   System Application

As mentioned before, Openpose [24] is the basis for detecting the pointing gesture. Openpose was ported to a ROS environment and it publishes human joint-points based on multiple models available, the chosen model was Body25. Openpose Body25 model uses non-parametric representations called Part Affinity Fields to regress joint positions and body segment connections between the joints [24].

From this model, there can be obtained two points on a forearm, this two points are used to calculate the equation of a line, making possible to extend the forearm's line segment until the borders of the image, hereby referenced as Extended Pointing Segment.

The Target Object detection relies on YOLO, which is also used inside ROS environment. For each detected object it creates a Bounding Box, the Bounding Box consists in two points, the top left and top right points of an object. In order to Select an Target Object there is a check to see if the Extended Pointing Segment and the Bounding Box are overlapping, the details of how this check was performed will be described bellow.

A Bounding Box has four line segments that together form a rectangle. The Pointing Gesture is a line segment that originates in the User's elbow, passing by User's wrist and is extended until the margins of the image. The check performed is whether or not the Pointing Gesture's line segment (Extended Pointing Segment) crosses with any of the Bounding Box's four line segments. To better

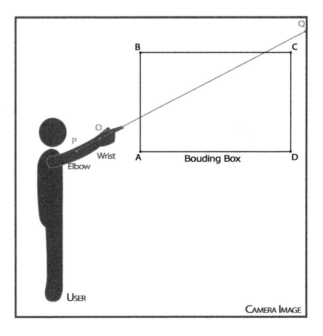

Fig. 6. Target Object Estimation using Pointing Gesture

visualize what was said, Fig. 6 depicts the Extended Pointing Segment as the line segment from point P until point Q, and the Bounding Box as a rectangle with vertices ABCD.

In order for the Object delimited by the ABCD bounding box be selected, the Extended Pointing Segment PQ has to the crossing either AB, BC, CD or AD. There is an approach to this problem that uses Vector Cross Products [30]. Define the 2-dimensional vector cross product $\vec{v} \times \vec{w}$ to be $\vec{v}_x \vec{w}_y - \vec{v}_y \vec{w}_x$. Considering P and Q the points that stand the end of vectors $\vec{p}$ and $\vec{p} + \vec{r}$, respectively. Also, consider A and B the points that are located in the end of vectors $\vec{a}$ and $\vec{a} + \vec{s}$, as shown in Fig. 7.

Then any point on the line segment PQ can be represented as $\vec{p} + t\vec{r}$ (for a scalar parameter t) and any point on the line segment AB as $\vec{a} + u\vec{s}$ (for a scalar parameter u). The two lines intersect if there is a t and u such that $\vec{p} + t\vec{r} = \vec{a} + u\vec{s}$, as shown in Fig. 8.

In order to isolate t we cross both sides with $\vec{s}$ (1), and to isolate u we cross with both sides with $\vec{r}$ (2).

$$(\vec{p} + t\vec{r}) \times \vec{s} = (\vec{a} + u\vec{s}) \times \vec{s} \tag{1}$$

$$(\vec{p} + t\vec{r}) \times \vec{r} = (\vec{a} + u\vec{s}) \times \vec{r} \tag{2}$$

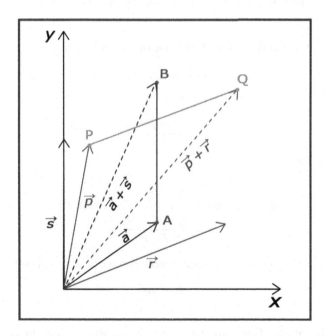

Fig. 7. Vector Cross Products approach to verify if two line segments are crossing each other

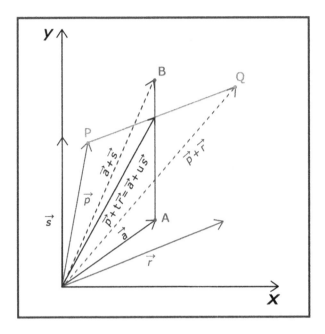

Fig. 8. If $\vec{p} + t\vec{r} = \vec{a} + u\vec{s}$ then the two lines intersect.

Since $\vec{r} \times \vec{r} = 0$ and $\vec{s} \times \vec{s} = 0$, this means the following:

$$(\vec{p} + t\vec{r}) \times \vec{s} = (\vec{a} + u\vec{s}) \times \vec{s}$$
$$(\vec{p} \times \vec{s}) + t(\vec{r} \times \vec{s}) = (\vec{a} \times \vec{s}) + u(\vec{s} \times \vec{s})$$

$$t = \frac{(\vec{a} - \vec{p}) \times \vec{s}}{\vec{r} \times \vec{s}} \tag{3}$$

Similarly, for u:

$$(\vec{p} + t\vec{r}) \times \vec{r} = (\vec{a} + u\vec{s}) \times \vec{r}$$
$$(\vec{p} \times \vec{r}) + t(\vec{r} \times \vec{r}) = (\vec{a} \times \vec{r}) + u(\vec{s} \times \vec{r})$$
$$u = \frac{(\vec{p} - \vec{a}) \times \vec{r}}{\vec{s} \times \vec{r}}$$

Given that $\vec{s} \times \vec{r} = -\vec{r} \times \vec{s}$, it is convenient to rewrite u as follows:

$$u = \frac{(\vec{a} - \vec{p}) \times \vec{r}}{\vec{r} \times \vec{s}} \tag{4}$$

Given the above, there are four cases to consider, first, in the case that $\vec{r} \times \vec{s} = 0$ and $(\vec{a} - \vec{p}) \times \vec{r} = 0$, then the two lines (PQ and AB) are collinear. In this case, it is possible to express the endpoints of the AB segment ($\vec{a}$ and $\vec{a} + \vec{s}$) in terms of the equation of the PQ line segment ($\vec{p} + t\vec{r}$), as shown in Fig. 9.

Developing the equation for t_0 (5):

$$\vec{p} + t_0\vec{r} = \vec{a}$$
$$\vec{p} + t_0\vec{r} = \frac{\vec{a} \cdot \vec{r}}{\vec{r}}$$
$$\vec{r} \cdot (\vec{p} + t_0\vec{r}) = \vec{a} \cdot \vec{r}$$
$$t_0\vec{r} \cdot \vec{r} = (\vec{a} - \vec{p}) \cdot \vec{r}$$

$$t_0 = \frac{(\vec{a} - \vec{p}) \cdot \vec{r}}{\vec{r} \cdot \vec{r}} \tag{5}$$

Developing the equation for t_1 (6):

$$\vec{p} + t_1\vec{r} = \vec{a} + \vec{s}$$
$$\vec{p} + t_1\vec{r} = \frac{(\vec{a} + \vec{s}) \cdot \vec{r}}{\vec{r}}$$
$$\vec{r} \cdot (\vec{p} + t_1\vec{r}) = (\vec{a} + \vec{s}) \cdot \vec{r}$$
$$t_1\vec{r} \cdot \vec{r} = (\vec{a} + \vec{s} - \vec{p}) \cdot \vec{r}$$

$$t_1 = \frac{(\vec{a} + \vec{s} - \vec{p}) \cdot \vec{r}}{\vec{r} \cdot \vec{r}} = t_0 + \vec{s} \cdot \frac{\vec{r}}{\vec{r} \cdot \vec{r}} \tag{6}$$

It can be observed that if the interval between t_0 and t_1 intersects the interval $[0, 1]$ then the line segments AB and PQ are collinear and overlapping, otherwise

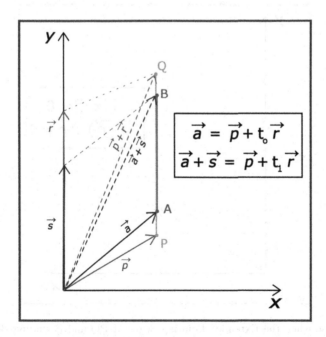

Fig. 9. Case when the Extended Pointing Segment PQ and Bounding Box segment AB are collinear.

they are collinear and disjoint. In the case that $\vec{s}$ and $\vec{r}$ are pointing in opposite directions, the interval to be checked are $[t_1, t_0]$ rather than $[t_0, t_1]$. The Target Object would not be considered selected if they were disjoint.

The second case of the four possible cases would happen if $\vec{r} \times \vec{s} = 0$ and $(\vec{a} - \vec{p}) \times \vec{r} \neq 0$, then the two line segments AB and PQ are parallel and non-intersecting (Fig. 10), therefore the Target Object wouldn't be selected.

The third case happens when $\vec{r} \times \vec{s} \neq 0$ and $0 \leq t \leq 1$ and $0 \leq u \leq 1$, then the two line segments AB and PQ would meet at the point $\vec{p} + t\vec{r} = \vec{q} + u\vec{s}$. In this situation, regarding just the line segment AB of the Bounding Box ABCD, the Target Object delimited by it would be considered selected. Therefore, for a Target Object given by a Bounding Box ABCD to be considered as selected, the Extended Pointing Segment PQ only have to be crossing with one of the four segments of the ABCD Bounding Box.

The fourth and last case would happen in a three-dimensional environment, when the two line segments are not parallel but do not intersect. Which, for the moment would be out of scope of this work, given that the estate of the present work is, for the moment, dealing with Target Object selection with only two dimension coordinates, but the expansion of the present work for 3D is already in sight for future works.

With the Extended Pointing Segment and the Bounding Box are overlapping, a Target Object is now defined and selected. A flowchart of the whole system can be seen on Fig. 11.

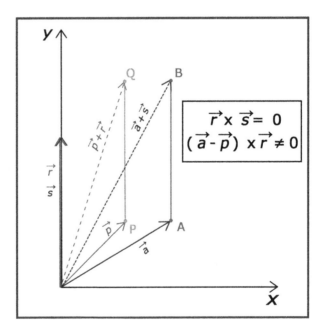

Fig. 10. Case when the Extended Pointing Segment PQ and Bounding Box segment AB are parallel and non-intersecting.

The drone uses a PID controller to reach the Target Object, using only 2D coordinates from the drones's monocular camera. In order to do that, the center of the image and the center and area of the Target Object is taken into account. On the drone image feed, if the center of the Target Object is to the right of the middle point of the image, than the drone should go right. Likewise for the left, up and down sides. Here it should be mentioned that the bebop 2 camera stabilization of the image influences the movements going up and down, because the motion effect on those directions are masked by it. Therefore the disabling of this feature is suggested. Lastly, to calculate the approximation to the Target Object, its area is taken into account, we know that this is not optimal, because it needs to take into account the real size of the Target Object, but it should be fixed on future works.

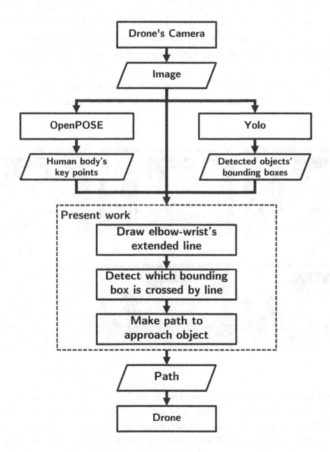

Fig. 11. Flowchart of the present work

5.3   Experimenting the Application

In this session the experiments on the Application will be reported. First the User starts the application without any target selected, the forearms of the User are highlighted with a green line and two small circles, there is a line extending from the elbow until the image borders, this line is the Extended Pointing Segment.

If the User points to a Target Object it will be selected, after the selection of a Target Object the Application will show a green point on its middle. There is no need for the User to keep pointing to the desired Target Object. The reasoning for this is that after selecting a target, the drone should carry on with any task it was required to do on the selected Target Object, until further notice. This is also a positive point for the User, who wont tire easily.

In the case of this experiment, after selecting a Target Object the Bebop's task was to get closer to it. In order to achieve that a simple PID controller was build using the drone's SDK. The Fig. 12 shows the summary of the whole experiment. The frames per second for the Application was around 12 fps, the most demanding component was Openpose, if it was shutdown the fps would rise to 35 fps.

The experiment was carried on using only one person as the User, but more subjects and a more complex experimentation will be considered on future versions of the system.

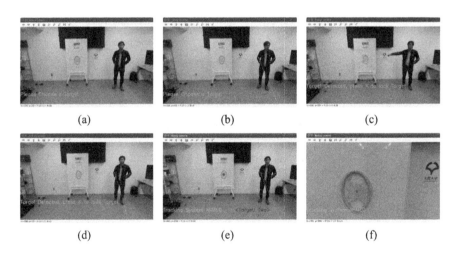

(a)   (b)   (c)

(d)   (e)   (f)

Fig. 12. Experiment summary: Sequential from (a) to (f). (a) The drone waits the selection of a target, (b) Body points are detected, (c) The crossing of the Pointing Gesture and Bounding Box of one of the recognized objects in the scene is detected, that object become the Target Object until further notice, (d) Drone system responds to the selection of the object by asking permission to start approaching the Target Object, (e) After permission is given, the point in the middle of the Target Object turns red to indicate the approach, (f) Drone gets close to the desired Target Object successfully.

6   Conclusion

This paper presented an investigation of the firefighters' preferences regarding user interfaces in a collaborative environment for UAVs in a firefighting scenario. A total of seven firefighters were interviewed and participated in a User Study. Pointing Gesture and Voice commands were the most popular choice when communication with the drone.

The objective of the present work was to make available new options of Human-Drone Interactions when relying solely on the drone camera, usually of the monocular camera type. The reason for that is that there might be situations where the use of external devices is not possible; for example, areas were onboard tracking systems like GPS are not available. Other possibilities would be integration with GPS systems in environments where depth cameras are not feasible.

Based on an investigation result, we developed an application that used Pointing Gestures as a means to estimate the correct Target Object. Here it is argued that while other gestures may face challenges when considering the preferences from persons with cultural differences and other background divergences, for estimating a Target Object through gestures the Pointing Gesture was the most popular choice.

The experiment showed that relying on very few devices, like a drone and a laptop, is sufficient to accomplish many tasks. Of course the system is working only with 2D coordinates but there is a possibility to extend that to 3D if the size of all elements of the scene is known. Which is not very feasible in real time applications, that is why as a future work this paper is thought to be extended to SLAM as a way to overcome that.

References

1. Reich, L.: How drones are being used in disaster management?. http://geoawesomeness.com/drones-fly-rescue/
2. Azevedo, M.A.: Drones give journalists a new way to report news. https://newsroom.cisco.com/feature-content?articleId=1851973
3. Smith, S.: Military and civilian drone use - The future of unmanned aerial vehicles. https://www.thebalancecareers.com/military-and-civilian-drone-use-4121099
4. Funk, M.: Human-drone interaction: let's get ready for flying user interfaces!. ACM Interact. **25**, 78–81 (2018)
5. Kim, J., et al.: Autonomous flight system using marker recognition on drone. In: 21st Korea-Japan Joint Workshop on Frontiers of Computer Vision (FCV), p. 1–4. IEEE (2015)
6. Al-Eidan, R.M., Al-Khalifa, H., Al-Salman, A.M.: A Review of wrist-worn wearable: sensors, models, and challenges. J. Sensors **2018**, 20 (2018)
7. Alsheakhal, M., Skaik, A., Aldahdouh, M., Alhelou, M.: Hand gesture recognition system. In: Information Communication and Systems, p. 132 (2011)
8. Obaid, M., et al.: How would you gesture navigate a drone? a user-centered approach to control a drone. In: Proceedings of the 20th International Academic Mindtrek Conference (2016)

9. Nagi, J., Giusti, A., Di Caro, G.A., Gambardella, L.M.: Human control of UAVs using face pose estimates and hand gestures. In 9th ACM/IEEE International Conference on Human-Robot Interaction (HRI), pp. 1–2. IEEE, March 2014

10. De Marsico, M., Spagnoli, A.: Using hands as an easy UAV joystick for entertainment applications. In: Proceedings of the 13th Biannual Conference of the Italian SIGCHI Chapter: Designing the Next Interaction (2019)

11. Tölgyessy, M., Dekan, M., Duchoň, F., Rodina, J., Hubinský, P., Chovanec, L.: Foundations of Visual Linear Human–Robot Interaction via Pointing Gesture Navigation. Int. J. Soc. Robotics 9(4), 509–523 (2017). https://doi.org/10.1007/s12369-017-0408-9

12. Droeschel, D., Stückler, J., Behnke, S.: Learning to interpret pointing gestures with a time-of-flight camera. In: Proceedings of the IEEE International Conference on Human-robot Interaction, pp. 481–488 (2011)

13. Fransen, B.R., Lawson, W.E., Bugajska, M.D.: Integrating vision for human-robot interaction. In: Proceedings of the IEEE Computer Society Conference on Computer Vision and Pattern Recognition, pp. 9–16 (2010)

14. Li, Z., Jarvis, R.: Visual interpretation of natural pointing gestures in 3D space for human-robot interaction. In: Proceedings of the IEEE International Conference on Control, Automation, Robotics and Vision, pp. 2513–2518 (2010)

15. Yoshida, K., Hibino, F., Takahashi, Y., Maeda, Y.: Evaluation of pointing navigation interface for mobile robot with spherical vision system. In: Proceedings of the IEEE International Conference on Fuzzy Systems, pp. 721–726 (2011)

16. Pateraki, M., Baltzakis, H., Trahanias, P.: Visual estimation of pointed targets for robot guidance via fusion of face pose and hand orientation. In: Proceedings of the IEEE International Conference on Computer Vision Workshops, pp. 1060–1067 (2011)

17. Van Den Bergh, M., et al.: Realtime 3D hand gesture interaction with a robot for understanding directions from humans. In: Proceedings of the IEEE International Symposium on Robot and Human Interactive Communication, pp. 357–362 (2011)

18. Pourmehr, S., Monajjemi, V., Wawerla, J., Vaughan, R., Mori, G.: A robust integrated system for selecting and commanding multiple mobile robots. In: Proceedings of the IEEE International Conference on Robotics and Automation, pp. 2874–2879 (2013)

19. Abidi, S., Williams, M., Johnston, B.: Human pointing as a robot directive. In: Proceedings of the IEEE International Conference on Human–Robot Interaction, pp. 67–68 (2013)

20. Gromov, B., Gambardella, L.M., Giustin, A.: Video: landing a drone with pointing gestures. In: Companion of the 2018 ACM/IEEE International Conference on Human-Robot Interaction, p. 374 (2018)

21. Azari, B., Lim, A., Vaughan, R.T.: Commodifying pointing in HRI: simple and fast pointing gesture detection from RGB-D images. arXiv preprint arXiv:1902.02636 (2019)

22. Mirri, S., Prandi, C., Salomoni, P.: Human-Drone Interaction: state of the art, open issues and challenges. In: Proceedings of the ACM SIGCOMM 2019 Workshop on Mobile AirGround Edge Computing, Systems, Networks, and Applications, pp. 43–48 (2019)

23. Redmon, J., Farhadi, A.: YOLO9000: better, faster, stronger. In: Proceedings of the IEEE Conference on Computer Vision and Pattern Recognition, pp. 7263–7271 (2017)

24. Cao, Z., Hidalgo, G., Simon, T., Wei, S.E., Sheikh, Y.: OpenPose: real-time multi-person 2D pose estimation using part affinity fields. arXiv preprint arXiv:1812.08008 (2018)
25. Colonnesi, C., Stams, G.J.J., Koster, I., Noom, M.J.: The relation between pointing and language development: a meta-analysis. Dev. Rev. **30**, 352–366 (2010)
26. Jane, L.E., Ilene, L.E., Landay, J.A., Cauchard, J.R.: Drone and Wo: cultural influences on human-drone interaction techniques. In: Proceedings of the 2017 CHI Conference on Human Factors in Computing Systems, pp. 6794–6799 (2017)
27. Cauchard, J.R., E, J.L., Zhai, K.Y., Landay, J.A.: Drone and me: an exploration into natural human-drone interaction. In: Proceedings of the 2015 ACM International Joint Conference on Pervasive and Ubiquitous Computing, pp. 361–365 (2015)
28. Parrot Bebop 2 drone. https://www.parrot.com/us/drones/parrot-bebop-2
29. Robot Operating System: Robot Operating System - Documentation. http://wiki.ros.org/Documentation
30. Goldman, R.: Intersection of two lines in three-space. In: Graphics Gems, p. 304. Academic Press Professional, Inc., San Diego. ISBN 0-12-286169-5 (1990)

Enhancing Drone Pilots' Engagement Through a Brain-Computer Interface

Tracy Pham, Dante Tezza$^{(\boxtimes)}$, and Marvin Andujar

University of South Florida, Tampa, FL 33620, USA
dtezza@mail.usf.edu

Abstract. Drones are becoming ubiquitous in society, and as their use continues to grow, it becomes important to research new approaches to provide a better user experience and safer flights. In this paper, we propose the use of brain-computer interfaces (BCI) to measure the drone pilot's engagement from the brain while piloting drones. We hypothesize that relaying on a quantified measurement, the pilot will be encouraged to increase their focus, leading to higher engagement and possible safer flights. Our first contribution is a technical description of the system, which allows the pilots to control a virtual first-person view (FPV) drone while receiving feedback on their engagement level measured with a BCI. Secondly, we present the results of a user study with 10 participants, in which their feedback stated that receiving engagement level feedback increased their engagement as they tried to raise their focus in the activity.

Keywords: Brain-computer interfaces · Brain-controlled drones · Brain-controlled games · Human-Drone Interaction · Passive BCI

1 Introduction

Recently, drones have increased in popularity and now are commonly used for many applications [19]. Although current technologies allow fully autonomous drone flights, there are use cases in which a pilot is still necessary. For instance, drone racing has emerged as a competitive sport in which pilots test their skills flying drones through obstacle courses [6]. Therefore, it can be beneficial to explore new approaches to enhance the pilot's experience, such as increasing their engagement when flying. In this paper, we evaluate the use of a brain-computer interface (BCI) to measure the user's engagement levels during the activity of piloting a simulated first-person view (FPV) racing drone. Engagement can be defined as the user's ability to focus on a task, in this case, the activity of flying a virtual drone. We also provide this measurement as feedback to possibly increase users' engagement when flying simulated FPV drones. We hypothesize that relaying on a quantified score of a pilot engagement level from the brain will invoke self-regulation. We expect that providing such a score will encourage pilots to increase their focus when piloting, leading to higher engagement levels.

© Springer Nature Switzerland AG 2020
M. Kurosu (Ed.): HCII 2020, LNCS 12182, pp. 706–718, 2020.
https://doi.org/10.1007/978-3-030-49062-1_49

In this paper, we present how BCIs can be used to measure pilots' engagement when flying drones. Additionally, our main contribution is the results of a within-subject study with 10 participants evaluating users' perception towards using BCIs to measure their engagement and to receive engagement level feedback when flying a simulated drone.

To explore the concept, we integrated a popular drone racing simulator (DRL Sim) with a BCI to measure and visualize the user's engagement level. Modern drone simulators provide a realistic flying experience while providing advantages to pilots. For instance, it allows them to practice at a lower cost, without risks of crashing, and do not require special authorizations (e.g. FAA regulations in the USA) [20]. Our system acquires the users' brain activity (EEG signals) in the frontal lobe using the g.Nautilus EEG headset (shown in Fig. 1)[1]. This data is post-processed to the EEG waves (α, β, and θ) to calculate the user engagement score using the formula $\beta/(\alpha + \theta)$ [4]. Our system provides visual feedback (engagement level) to pilots in real-time as they control the virtual drone. The feedback is provided in the form of a numerical value and a horizontal bar graph. An example of the first-person view displayed to the pilot, as well as the engagement level feedback can be seen in Fig. 2.

Fig. 1. g.Tec Nautilus EEG headset.

In this paper, we also present the results of a user study to evaluate users' perception towards receiving engagement level feedback when flying drones. Each participant flew the virtual drone for 10 rounds, receiving feedback on one half of the rounds. Our results indicate a positive attitude towards the system, and participants indicated that the engagement feedback was useful in motivating them to improve their focus when flying the simulated FPV drone.

---

[1] Figure 1 acquired from g.Tec Nautilus user manual.

Fig. 2. First-person view image displayed to the pilot (top), and engagement level feedback (numerical value and bar graph).

2 Related Work

The Federal Aviation Administration (FAA) reported that approximately 900,000 drones were registered in 2018 with an average increase of 8000–9000 registrations every month. Additionally, by analyzing industry sales the FAA predicts that unregistered drones increase such numbers by 40% [3]. Such an increase in drone usage has lead to numerous studies investigating how humans interact with drones, a field known as Human-Drone Interaction (HDI). More relevant, state-of-the-art topics include the variations of drone models, exploration of the role of humans in HDI, interaction distances, and novel control methods [19]. Studies have observed instinctive human responses to different physical attributes of drones, such as the distance and height they approach [2], or the ability to portray emotion through their flight patterns [8]. The results of these studies are important to coherently integrate drones further into society. Current examples of drone usage include assistance with rescues during natural disasters [5], precision agriculture [15], and assistance during mass sports events like the Olympics [13].

The increase in drone usage is proportional to the increase in accidents bound to occur with such systems. Even with more sophisticated systems and anti-collision technology, drones are still prone to accidents [7]. The United States went through at least 79 drone accidents in 2010. The top suspected cause is human error, which is evident for example, in one common case where flying unregulated drones within proximity to airports compromised flight operation [7]. Further criticism revolves around flying commercial drones in domestic areas where even small mishaps such as crashing into infrastructures like electricity poles could create dangerous situations, jeopardizing the health, well-being, and property of the public [16]. Therefore, it is important to study and evaluate systems that aid users in safely piloting drones. From research on control designs to training models, increasing situational awareness of drone pilots is one approach that has proven to be effective for minimizing accidents and other promising benefits [10]. One technique to increase monitoring skills is to add more viewpoints. Temma et al. used an additional drone to add an interactive third-person perspective, which also supported operations of the primary drone [18], and Hing showed improved performance of UAV operators when generating a chase viewpoint [10].

Previous work in HDI has focused on integrating drones with BCI's, allowing pilots to control flight with their brain-waves. For instance, Tezza et al. present a brain-controlled drone racing game where the player controls a virtual drone by performing motor imagery [20]. Another example demonstrates how brain-controlled drones can be used to aid users with disabilities [22], and Nourmohammadi et al. presents a survey on the topic [14]. However, such studies have an active BCI element, where users intentionally manipulate their thoughts to control the drone. This approach differs from ours since our application falls within the passive BCI category. In other words, we monitor the user's brain activity to measure engagement without requiring them to perform a mental task.

BCIs have been used to measure engagement levels and provide these measurements as real-time feedback. Additionally, previous work has studied the correlation between an increase in attention and its effect on overall performance. For instance, AttentivU combines Electrooculography (EOG) and EEG in a pair of glasses to provide audio and haptic feedback when attention falls below a desired threshold to refocus the wearer in a work and school environment [12]. Another example, EngageMeter is a tool for presenters to observe real-time attention data of the audience and record it for later self-improvement [9]. Andujar et al. present how a BCI can be used to measure engagement to provide feedback and enhance user experience during a reading task [4]. Such work has motivated us to evaluate this concept with the activity of flying drones. Therefore, in this study we expand previous work of using BCIs to measure engagement and explore the concept of relaying engagement levels feedback directly to drone pilots during the flight.

3   System Description

3.1   Equipment

EEG Headset. The EEG headset used to measure the participants' EEG signals was the g.Nautilus manufactured by g.Tec. This device is a non-invasive cap with 16 EEG dry electrodes that can be placed at any location specified by the 10–20 International System [11]. For this study, the electrodes were positioned at channel locations: FP1, FP2, AF3, AF4, FZ, F3, F4, F7, F8, FG6, FG5, T7, T8, P7, P8, OZ as displayed in Fig. 3. However, previous work has stated that electrodes placed on the frontal lobe is an adequate placement for obtaining cognitive information from the brain [1], therefore signals from P7, P8, and OZ were excluded from the analysis.

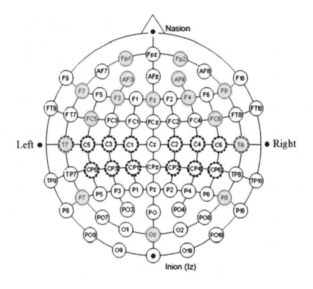

Fig. 3. International 10–20 system for EEG electrode placement.

Drone Racing Simulator. To simulate drone flying, we integrated our system to the Drone Racing League (DRL) simulator version 3.0. We chose this simulator as it is a popular choice among professional drone racing pilots. This software provides a realistic FPV flying experience. For this study, the "Morning Cruise" map was selected as it is classified as a "beginner" level map. Similarly, the "DRL Racer 3" drone (shown in Fig. 4a) was selected for all participants.

Controller. To control the simulator and race the virtual drone, the simulator can be integrated with most standard Bluetooth controllers. In this study, we used the Xbox controller showed in Fig. 4b due to its similarities to drone controllers.

3.2   System Architecture

While pilots fly the virtual drone, the system calculates (and optionally displays) their engagement level using the EEG signals acquired with the g.Tec Nautilus.

DRL Racer 3 virtual drone.   XBox Controller

Fig. 4. Equipment used during user study.

To process the EEG signals we used the OpenVibe software (see Appendix for script). This software is a standard tool for processing brain signals in real-time. The script saves the raw EEG signals, select desired channels, filter and process the raw signals to calculate the α, β, and θ band powers. Using the engagement formula described in [4], a single value is calculated and exported to a python script using the LabStreamingLayer (LSL). LSL is a standard software for transferring and synchronizing data among different software processes, and it is commonly used by BCI researchers to exchange data among applications. The python script receives the engagement level and updates both the numerical value (0–100 range) and the bar graph (see Fig. 2) at the end of each round. This BCI cycle is presented in Fig. 5.

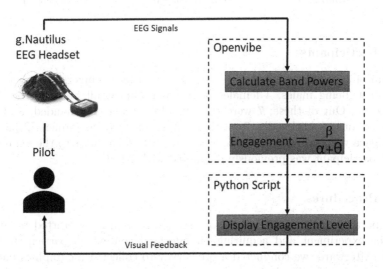

Fig. 5. BCI cycle. EEG signals are used to calculate engagement score, which is provided as a visual feedback to the pilot.

4   Study Design

We conducted a within-subject user study to evaluate the system and users' perception towards receiving engagement level feedback. This engagement was processed as described in Sect. 3.2. Prior to controlling the game, each participant was asked to perform an Alpha calibration phase (i.e. clear their mind). Following, they controlled the virtual drone during 10 rounds (2 min each), and received engagement level feedback during 5 of them. Five of the ten participants received feedback for their first five laps, and the other five received it on their last five laps as shown in Table 1.

A pre-experiment survey was included to gather general demographic information, as well as study-specific information such as gaming experience, caffeine consumption, and whether or not the participant has been diagnosed with any attention disorder. These questions were included to explore possible correlations between these factors and the participants' engagement level. Additionally, the standardized Positive and Negative Affects Schedule (PANAS) [21] was completed twice by each participant, once before and once after their flying experience, so that the effect of the experience on their affective state can be analyzed. Lastly, a short post-experiment questionnaire was also included to receive open-ended feedback from participants.

Table 1. Order in which engagement score was displayed to participants during user study.

	Participants	Laps 1–5	Laps 6–10
Group 1	5	Score not displayed	Score not displayed
Group 2	5	Score displayed	Score not displayed

4.1   Participants

A total of 10 participants were recruited from a local university for the study, 5 of them being males, 4 females, and 1 non-binary, all between the ages of 18 and 24. Out of these, 7 were right-handed, 2 were left-handed, and 1 was ambidextrous. Additionally, 7 participants reported to be gamers, 2 had prior experience with drone simulators, 2 consumed caffeine prior to the experiment, and 1 participant was previously diagnosed with ADHD.

4.2   Procedures

Each participant attended a one-hour session, in which we started by explaining the experiment and acquiring an informed consent to participate in the study. Afterward, we conducted a pre-survey to collect demographics data and determine their familiarity with drones and BCIs. During this step, we also conducted the Positive and Negative Affect Schedule (PANAS) survey [21]. Then, we assisted participants in wearing the g.Nautilus EEG headset. At this point, we instructed them on how to use an XBOX controller to control the simulation and allowed them to freely fly the virtual drone for two minutes. Following, we performed an alpha calibration phase in which we asked the participant to close their eyes and relax for five minutes. Next, we asked the participant to control the drone around a race track for ten rounds, each round lasting two minutes. The first-person view of the map (as displayed to the participant) can be seen in Fig. 6. As the participant flew the drone within the simulation, the system processed the raw EEG signals obtained with the BCI to calculate their engagement level, as described in Sect. 3.2. The engagement score was only provided as feedback to the participant at the end of five out of ten racing rounds, following the order displayed in Table 1. We recorded the participants' EEG signals and calculated engagement scores for post-analysis. Lastly, we asked the participants to complete a post-experiment survey to provide qualitative feedback and answer questions related to how the engagement score feedback impacted their gameplay experience. In this step, participants also completed the post-experiment PANAS survey.

Fig. 6. First-person view of the Morning Cruise map used during the study.

5   Results and Discussion

Our results demonstrate a positive user perception towards receiving engagement level feedback measured with a BCI As shown in Fig. 7, eight out of ten participants declared that having engagement level feedback impacted their performance in controlling the simulated drone, the remaining two participants neither agreed or disagreed with this statement. Furthermore, qualitative data reinforces these results, as participants provided feedback such as:

– *I think the feedback added stakes to the game and made me want to perform better.*
– *It made me more competitive against myself.*
– *I was focusing on my score and trying to raise it.*

These responses confirm our hypothesis that providing a quantified engagement measure encourage pilots to focus on the activity of controlling the simulated drone and raise their score. It also suggests that participants felt challenged to increase their engagement score, which increased the gamification aspect of the activity. Additionally, seven participants stated that they would buy a BCI to obtain engagement level feedback, as shown in Fig. 8. Seven participants also stated that the visual engagement feedback was easy to comprehend, and two participants noted that they felt uncomfortable when they scores dropped.

Fig. 7. Participants answer to "Did the attention level feedback influenced your performance in the game?"

Analysis from the PANAS survey also strengthen the above results as it shows an increase in participants' attention levels throughout the experiment. Participants' PANAS attention score increased from an average score of 3 to 4.1 (1–5 scale), with a p-value of 0.011. Additionally, the overall positive affect score increased from 31.1 to 36.3 (1–50 scale) with a p-value of 0.031, and the average score for inspiration increased from 2.8 to 3.6 (p = 0.036).

The above results validate our hypothesis that having their engagement level displayed encouraged pilots to be more engaged while controlling the simulated drone. This also shows the potential in passive BCI applications to enhance human-drone interaction, as previous studies focused on the active BCI category. One concern with BCI applications, is that wearing EEG headset can cause user discomfort. However, when asked if they felt any discomfort during the experiment, only one participant stated a slight discomfort in wearing the device.

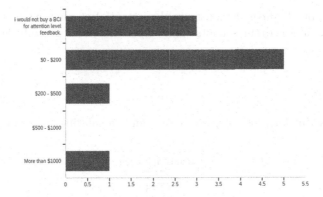

Fig. 8. Participants answer to "How much would you pay for a BCI headset to obtain attention level feedback?"

5.1 Future Work

Our system provides the participants feedback every two minutes, but the system may be customized to allow calculated scores to be displayed at any interval. Therefore, we propose a future study to find the optimal interval to update the pilot's engagement level in the user-interface. For example, updating the feedback score every thirty seconds may allow the user to perform self-regulation more often and focus better. However, continuously updating the engagement score in real-time may become a distraction to the pilot. Furthermore, the system can then be upgraded to alarm the pilots if their engagement score falls below a threshold.

At the current stage, our system is integrated with a drone racing simulator. We propose future studies to evaluate engagement level feedback when flying drones to validate that similar results are found when flying physical systems. Additionally, monitoring skills of a flight crew can increase situational awareness and its effect on flight safety [17]. Therefore, the system could also be adapted and used for manned aircraft systems. In this case, a similar approach (simulation first, followed by a physical system) could be used to evaluate engagement score feedback to manned aircraft pilots.

6   Conclusion

In this paper, we explored the use of brain-computer interfaces to measure a drone pilot's engagement when flying an FPV drone simulator. We first presented our system, which integrates a popular drone simulator with a BCI application designed to measure and display engagement levels. We hypothesized that relaying such measurement as feedback to the pilot would encourage them to increase their focus to achieve higher scores. Throughout a user study with 10 participants, we found that providing such feedback encouraged participants to focus on the activity to increase their engagement, which validated our hypothesis.

Concluding, our findings demonstrate the potential of using passive BCI applications to enhance drone's pilots' user experience, and possibly lead to safer flights.

Appendix

OpenVibe script for processing EEG data and calculating engagement.

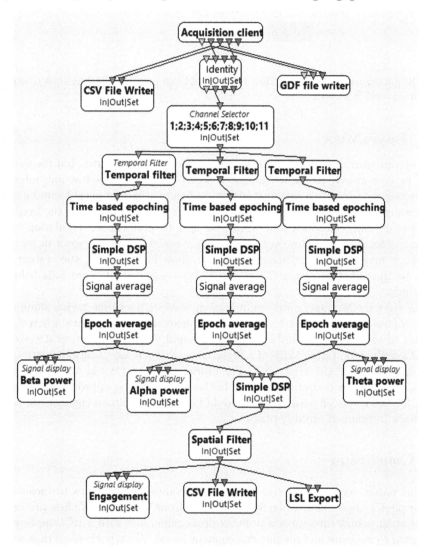

References

1. Abdelrahman, Y., Hassib, M., Marquez, M.G., Funk, M., Schmidt, A.: Implicit engagement detection for interactive museums using brain-computer interfaces. In: Proceedings of the 17th International Conference on Human-Computer Interaction with Mobile Devices and Services Adjunct, pp. 838–845 (2015)
2. Abtahi, P., Zhao, D.Y., E, J.L., Landay, J.A.: Drone near me: exploring touch-based human-drone interaction. Proc. ACM Interact. Mob. Wearable Ubiquit. Technol. **1**(3), 1–8 (2017)
3. Federal Aviation Administration: Unmanned aircraft systems forecast (2019). https://www.faa.gov/data_research/aviation/aerospace_forecast. Accessed 27 Jan 2020
4. Andujar, M., Gilbert, J.E.: Let's learn! Enhancing user's engagement levels through passive brain-computer interfaces. In: CHI 2013 Extended Abstracts on Human Factors in Computing Systems, pp. 703–708. ACM (2013)
5. Apvrille, L., Tanzi, T., Dugelay, J.L.: Autonomous drones for assisting rescue services within the context of natural disasters. In: 2014 XXXIth URSI General Assembly and Scientific Symposium (URSI GASS), pp. 1–4. IEEE (2014)
6. Barin, A., Dolgov, I., Toups, Z.O.: Understanding dangerous play: a grounded theory analysis of high-performance drone racing crashes. In: Proceedings of the Annual Symposium on Computer-Human Interaction in Play, pp. 485–496. ACM (2017)
7. Boyle, M.J.: The race for drones. Orbis **59**(1), 76–94 (2015)
8. Cauchard, J.R., Zhai, K.Y., Spadafora, M., Landay, J.A.: Emotion encoding in human-drone interaction. In: 2016 11th ACM/IEEE International Conference on Human-Robot Interaction (HRI), pp. 263–270. IEEE (2016)
9. Hassib, M., Schneegass, S., Eiglsperger, P., Henze, N., Schmidt, A., Alt, F.: EngageMeter: a system for implicit audience engagement sensing using electroencephalography. In: Proceedings of the 2017 CHI Conference on Human Factors in Computing Systems, pp. 5114–5119 (2017)
10. Hing, J.T., Sevcik, K.W., Oh, P.Y.: Improving unmanned aerial vehicle pilot training and operation for flying in cluttered environments. In: 2009 IEEE/RSJ International Conference on Intelligent Robots and Systems, pp. 5641–5646. IEEE (2009)
11. Klem, G.H., Lüders, H.O., Jasper, H., Elger, C., et al.: The ten-twenty electrode system of the international federation. Electroencephalogr. Clin. Neurophysiol. **52**(3), 3–6 (1999)
12. Kosmyna, N., Sarawgi, U., Maes, P.: AttentivU: evaluating the feasibility of biofeedback glasses to monitor and improve attention. In: Proceedings of the 2018 ACM International Joint Conference and 2018 International Symposium on Pervasive and Ubiquitous Computing and Wearable Computers, pp. 999–1005 (2018)
13. Nadobnik, J., et al.: The use of drones in organizing the Olympic games. Handel Wewnętrzny **365**(6), 288–299 (2016)
14. Nourmohammadi, A., Jafari, M., Zander, T.O.: A survey on unmanned aerial vehicle remote control using brain-computer interface. IEEE Trans. Hum.-Mach. Syst. **48**(4), 337–348 (2018)
15. Puri, V., Nayyar, A., Raja, L.: Agriculture drones: a modern breakthrough in precision agriculture. J. Stat. Manag. Syst. **20**(4), 507–518 (2017)
16. Rao, B., Gopi, A.G., Maione, R.: The societal impact of commercial drones. Technol. Soc. **45**, 83–90 (2016)

17. Sumwalt, R.L., Thomas, R., Dismukes, K.: Enhancing flight-crew monitoring skills can increase flight safety. In: Annual International Air Safety Seminar, vol. 55, pp. 175–206. Flight Safety Foundation 1998 (2002)

18. Temma, R., Takashima, K., Fujita, K., Sueda, K., Kitamura, Y.: Third-person piloting: increasing situational awareness using a spatially coupled second drone. In: Proceedings of the 32nd Annual ACM Symposium on User Interface Software and Technology, pp. 507–519 (2019)

19. Tezza, D., Andujar, M.: The state-of-the-art of human-drone interaction: a survey. IEEE Access **7**, 167438–167454 (2019)

20. Tezza, D., Garcia, S., Hossain, T., Andujar, M.: Brain eRacing: an exploratory study on virtual brain-controlled drones. In: Chen, J.Y.C., Fragomeni, G. (eds.) HCII 2019. LNCS, vol. 11575, pp. 150–162. Springer, Cham (2019). https://doi.org/10.1007/978-3-030-21565-1_10

21. Watson, D., Clark, L.A., Tellegen, A.: Development and validation of brief measures of positive and negative affect: the PANAS scales. J. Pers. Soc. Psychol. **54**(6), 1063 (1988)

22. Yu, Y., et al.: FlyingBuddy2: a brain-controlled assistant for the handicapped. In: Ubicomp, pp. 669–670. Citeseer (2012)

The Effects of Different Robot Trajectories on Situational Awareness in Human-Robot Collaboration

Sumona Sen[✉], Hans-Jürgen Buxbaum, and Lisanne Kremer

Robotics and Human Engineering Lab, Niederrhein University of Applied Sciences,
Reinarzstr. 49, 47805 Krefeld, Germany
{sumona.sen,hans-juergen.buxbaum,lisanne.kremer}@hsnr.de
http://www.hs-niederrhein.de

Abstract. This paper describes an experiment, to answer the question whether and how different trajectories from robotic path planning are perceived in a differentiated way from the perspective of the collaborating human being, with regard to situation awareness. This is done with the help of reliable proband experiment, in a HRC Full-Scope Simulator. Only if the human being in a human-robot-collaboration is able to recognize early, what the robot is doing or will do, an ad hoc task distribution can be reasonably realized. The long-term goal of this research is to develop a recommendation for the path planning, in the context of the construction of HRC systems, which enables a simple and fast programming of safe robot movements.

Keywords: Human-robot collaboration · Trajectory path planning · Situational awareness

1 Introduction

Flexible manufacturing is one of the buzzwords of Industry 4.0. The important areas of application for robots today are mainly in large-scale production, with the automotive industry still being the pioneer [1,2]. A high degree of automation is achieved in parts production, car body construction and paint shops. The often mentioned flexibility of production lines in automotive engineering, is mainly realized in downstream processes, e.g. in assembly. There are still many non-automated or only partially automated operations; the degree of automation is significantly lower and the proportion of manual operations correspondingly higher. It would also be desirable to relieve workers of physical stress or monotonous work, but early experience in the development of assembly automation has shown, that fully automated assembly is neither economically viable nor technologically feasible [3].

HRC systems offer a new approach with the aim to combine the skills and intellectuality of human workers, with the power and the accuracy of industrial robots. Instead of autonomous mechanical tasks, which always require human

© Springer Nature Switzerland AG 2020
M. Kurosu (Ed.): HCII 2020, LNCS 12182, pp. 719–729, 2020.
https://doi.org/10.1007/978-3-030-49062-1_50

intervention. e.g., in case of a failure, collaboration systems are planned from the beginning in a way, that human worker and collaborative robot are involved in the process in a common workspace, spatially and temporally parallel. Of course, this will work only, if there are no separating devices, such as protective fences. Collaborative robots for this purpose must be completely re-evaluated, especially in the aspect of safety and have to fulfill different requirements than the classic industrial robots, which work isolated behind fences or barriers. Standards such as DIN (2017) ISO/TS 15066 [4] and corresponding certification procedures have already been established for this purpose.

Flexible manufacturing systems are required, especially in the area of small and medium-sized enterprises (SMEs). SMEs usually have to deal with smaller batch sizes and with fluctuating capacity utilization. For SMEs, flexible automation technology therefore makes sense in theory, provided, however, that the engineering effort remains controllable. Flexible solutions often place high demands on set-up processes and programming activities, for which both, manpower and know-how, are lacking in SMEs. Especially for the interaction between the human worker and the collaborating robot in a HRC, solutions are required, which make the cooperation user friendly and intuitive. In order to achieve a broad user acceptance, in this target group of SMEs, the operating characteristics of an HRC system have to be adapted to the qualification level of the employees. Therefore, the usable design of the systems is of enormous importance here. The operation has to be intuitive and safe, the programming simple and efficient.

The actions of the robot must be comprehensible and perceptible for a human being. This is the only way to prevent accidents, e.g., caused by collisions or other disturbances [5]. Another aspect results from the flexible distribution of tasks. By varying the movements and rearranging the distribution of tasks between humans and robots, no learning effects can occur [6]. The consequence is a higher demanded on situational awareness of humans for accident prevention [7].

2   Path Planning in HRC

Motion controls of robot systems can be classified according to different path types as shown in Fig. 1. The following standard movements are used in typical robot controllers [8]:

- Point-to-point movement (PTP):
  The movement of the robot is described by the initial and final position of the axes and is independent of the geometric position of the end effector in space during the movement. Since the movement of the individual axes is independent of each other and therefore uncoordinated, the movement path of the end effector from the start to the end position is not geometrically defined. It is deterministic, but does not follow a pattern and is therefore not predictable for a collaborating human being. The advantage of the PTP movement is that the target position is reached in the fastest possible way. The

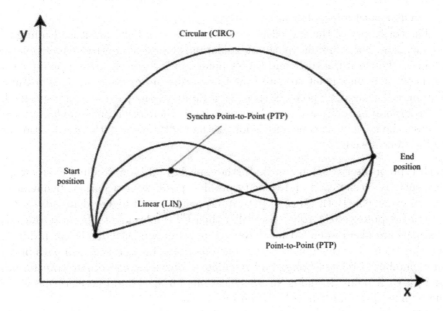

Fig. 1. Robot Standard Path Types for Movements from a Start Position towards an End Position: Linear (LIN), Circular (CIRC) and two different Point-To-Point (PTP) Modes

axis with the longest travel distance is decisive for the total movement duration. With the so-called Synchro-PTP type, there is an interaction between the axis movements in terms of time. The axes are controlled in their speed profile so that they reach the end position at the same time. The already mentioned axis with the longest travel distance determines the default travel time. This allows the other axes to move to their respective target position at a lower speed. PTP movements are used where previously defined points have to be approached without the resulting path of the end effector from the start to the target point playing a role. For many applications in robotics the PTP movement is sufficient, e.g. for pick-and-place tasks or spot welding.

– Linear path interpolation:
If the trajectory is also important in robot processes, the path of the end effector from the start to the target point must be interpolated by the robot controller. Typically, path interpolation is used in path welding processes or when viscous lubricants are applied by robots. Here, another obvious requirement is a given, and frequently constant path speed. A linear path is a straight line between the starting and target points. Linear path interpolation calculates such linear paths with a given velocity profile. The advantage of linear trajectories is that the shortest path from the start to the target point is selected. In any case, the travel time is longer than with a comparable PTP movement from start to destination.

- Circular path interpolation:
  The trajectory of the end effector between start and end point is also important here. For a circular path interpolation, the robot controller interpolates an arc between the start and target points, also regularly with a preset path speed. It is important to note that to describe an arc from start to destination, either another point in space or a radius of the path must be specified. Programming a circular path interpolation is therefore more complex. In any case, the movement time here is longer than with linear path interpolation at the same speed.

Each type of interpolation can be further specialized by individual characteristics, such as acceleration and velocity profiles, positioning accuracy, behavior in case of error, etc. Both types of path interpolation need higher demands on the computing power of the robot controller than PTP movements, because the axis positions are also in defined local and temporal dependence in the path during the movement. For this purpose, the controller must break down each path into a large number of related points and calculate a Cartesian coordinate transformation for each point. In doing so, specifications for speed and acceleration along the planned path must also be taken into account.

The conceptually slower movement times of the path interpolation play a rather subordinate role in applications of the HRC, because in collaboration scenarios the maximum movement speed has to be reduced anyway and the maximum speed of a PTP movement is not available here. In common robot applications, away from collaboration scenarios, the choice of an interpolation is either made according to technical aspects (e.g. glue application in an interpolated circular path) or optimized according to speed (e.g. PTP in cycle time oriented logistic processes). In today's robot controllers, the two path interpolation modes presented are implemented in addition to one or more PTP modes, so that the programmer has a choice here and can select the different interpolation modes to suit the application. Occupational psychological criteria for such a selection in HRC-scenarios are still missing, however, so that plant constructors and programmers do not necessarily select an optimal motion profile.

3   Situational Awareness

According to Endsley [9], Situation Awareness (SA) is the perception of the elements in the environment within a volume of time and space, the understanding of their meaning and the projection of their status into the near future.

Situation Awareness is a construct that consists of three levels. Level 1 describes the perception of the elements of the environment. Due to inadequate representation and cognitive abbreviations, this can lead to misperceptions and thus to an incorrect understanding of the situation. Level 2 describes the understanding of the situation and deals with errors in the correct integration of the information recording. A lack of mental models or blind trust can lead to false predictions and thus to a wrong decision. Level 3 refers to the prediction of future events. This depends on the expert status of the person [9].

4 Situation Awareness Global Assessment Technique

There are various methods for recording situation awareness. According to Endsley, various process measures can be used to investigate situation awareness. These include verbal protocols (thinking aloud), psychophysiological measures such as ECG and heart rate for example or communication analyses. However, such process measures are rarely used because these methods allow subjective interpretations or require very complex measurement techniques to record psychophysiological measures. In objective processes, the person's knowledge of the current situation is queried and thus the measure of situational awareness is formed.

One of this measurement method is called the Situation Awareness Global Assessment Technique (SAGAT). As a precondition for this method, a realistic simulation environment is required, which is called full scope simulation. The SAGAT measurement method involves stopping the simulation in the full-scope simulator at randomly appearing times. In doing so, all sources of information are switched off, the test room is darkened if necessary and the proband is questioned about his perception of the situation. This procedure is called freezing [10]. The three levels of situational awareness are taken into account in the survey. The questions should not deal with the derivation of behavioural patterns or contexts, but should refer directly to the dynamic process of the situation. Thus, in the end one receives a concrete statement about the situation awareness and no subjective conclusions [11].

5 Full-Scope Simulation in HRC

Experiments involving humans, which are necessary for the design of HRC, require a special procedure in experimental design and execution. Especially distraction of the proband by situational influences, which are not part of the experiment, have proven to be problematic in the past and often question the reliability of the results. Also non-situational influences, such as environmental conditions like room temperature or noise contamination have to be considered.

With the HRC-Full-Scope Simulator of the Niederrhein University of Applied Sciences [12] a closed room-in-room experimental system is available, with which processes in HRC systems including robots and handling objects and including all operator functions can be completely reproduced. This real simulation can then be used for experiments with any number of test persons. It is also possible to simulate situational influences (distractions) or environmental conditions by the use of loudspeaker and video technology in the same way and at the same time, thus creating identical test conditions for each test person.

Full-scope simulators have been used in power plant engineering, especially in nuclear technology. A typical definition is as follows (quote) [13]:

"A full scope simulator is a simulator incorporating detailed modeling of systems of Unit One with which the operator interfaces with the control room environment. The control room operating consoles are included. Such a simulator demonstrates expected plant response to normal and abnormal conditions."

Accordingly, a full-scope simulator is a simulator that simulates the behavior of the modeled reference system (power plant technology: Unit One) in order to investigate the operator's interaction with the system. The controls of the reference system are part of the full scope simulation. With such a simulator, the operators are trained in the handling of the regular and irregular operating conditions of the reference system.

In power plant operation, continuous and effective operator training is required. The aim is to operate the power plants safely and efficiently. Many important parts of the training programs are carried out by such full scope simulators. These training programs are designed to increase the decision-making and analytical skills of the operators and prepare them for problems that may occur during operation of the actual plant [14]. Full scope simulators are recognized as an effective tool for operator training and are used in particular for nuclear power plants.

Through the use of a multitude of different human-machine interfaces, humans are directly involved in the simulation processes. There is a causal relationship between human actions and the resulting system states. In addition to improving operator performance through training programs, full scope simulators are also used to improve the safety and reliability of plant and personnel and to reduce operating costs. Furthermore, industrial and psychological aspects (human factors) are also part of full scope simulations. These include, for example, attention control and situation awareness. [12] show that full-scope simulation can also be used in the field of HRC to conduct and evaluate experiments involving humans.

6   Objectives

The experiment is intended to show a possible connection between the depicted standard movement paths of robotics and situation awareness in proband trials and to demonstrate whether the respective movements differ in this respect. For this particular experiment only Linear Path Interpolation (LIN) and Point-to-Point movement (PTP) is taken to account. An according hypothesis is formulated for this purpose as follows.

Hypothesis: Linear interpolated movements and PTP movements differ in the level of situational awareness.

For this purpose, an experiment with a KUKA lightweight robot LBR iiwa will be set up in a full-scope simulator. The background of the experiment is a HRC workstation for picking small parts for distribution.

7 Methods

7.1 Sample

The experiment is carried out with 40 probands, 32 men and 8 women. The probands are aged between 19 and 31 (M = 25,15, SD = 4,10). All of them are students. The probands are divided into two experimental groups, both groups with a balanced number of 16 men and 4 women each. For the first group only PTP movements of the robot LBR iiwa are used, for the second experimental group only linear paths. This design avoids habituation effects that can occur when all probands would get both movement types.

7.2 Experimental Design

As mentioned before, an HRC workstation for picking small parts for distribution is set up to investigate the research question and hypothesis. The probands are given an introductory explanation of their task and a safety briefing. Then the experiment starts. The robot LBR iiwa picks the small parts to be commissioned from a magazine according to an electronic order picking list and places them on predetermined deposit positions at the assembly station. The magazine used in the experiment is a conveyor chute, from which the robot LBR iiwa can pick different parts for the commission. The depositing positions are located in the common working area of human and robot, so there is a possibility of unintentional collisions. Figure 2 illustrates the complete working area and positions.

Simultaneously with the provision of the parts by the robot, the proband, in his role as a packer, takes one part at a time from his depositing positions, packs it individually in packing paper and positions the packed part in a shipping carton. The packer repeats this process until the commission is completely packed.

A maximum of 6 parts can be packed in the shipping boxes, but the commissions are flexible, i.e. neither the number of parts nor the selection of parts is identical. There are 6 stacking positions available, so that the robot can prepare a complete commission. The packer can work autonomously from the robot, but it is recommended that the packer and the robot work in parallel in order to reduce packing times.

When all parts of the order are packed into the dispatch carton, the packer confirms the packing list on his screen, takes a barcode, positions it on the outside of the dispatch carton, glues the carton and places it on a trolley for collection by dispatch. During this manual activity, the robot already starts with the next order picking and again places up to 6 parts on the stacking positions. Neither the order of this positioning nor the exact composition of the commission is known to the packer at this time. Therefore the packer does not know, what exactly the robot is doing at the moment and how many parts are positioned in which order. One run takes approx. 22 min.

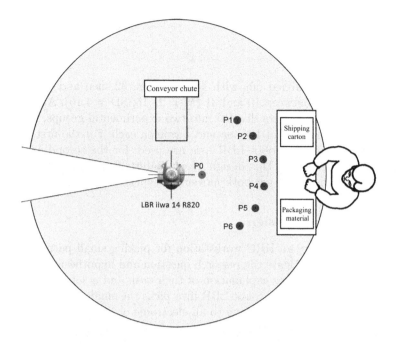

Fig. 2. Experimental design

7.3   Measures

Three freezings are performed for each subject according to the SAGAT method and corresponding surveys are conducted. For reasons of comparability, these freezings will always take place at the same time and in the same commission. The exact control of the freezings will be done by the Full-Scope Simulator. All probands are instructed to attend to their tasks as they normally would, with the SAGAT queries considered as secondary. For each question the probands have 30 seconds to answer. After this time everything continues as before. According to the three levels of situational awareness, the following questions will be asked:

1. Which objects are located in your environment? Can you describe them?
2. What specific task is the robot carrying out at the moment? Where is the gripper located? What is in the gripper?
3. What specific action do you think the robot will perform next? What will be the goal of this action? What is in the gripper then?

The first question refers to the first level of situational awareness. All things placed in the environment have to be listed to have an 100% score. The following 13 objects are placed in the simulation:

– Robot
– Gripper
– Magazine with small parts (cartons) or conveyor chute

- Empty cartons
- Tape
- Scissor
- Waterbottle
- Small parts for commissioning
- Tablet
- Foil
- Assembly carton
- Pen
- WD40 bottle

The second questions belong to the second level of situational awareness. As described, the questions are designed to investigate the comprehension of the situation of each proband. The focus is on the robot and the gripper. Here it is only possible to distinguish between right and wrong. With this data the score for level 2 is now generated.

The same procedure is used in question three for the 3rd level of situational awareness. The future system status is queried here.

In the end all scores are summed up to one overall SA score for both groups.

8   Results

The data, provided by the SAGAT queries, are evaluated. For each of the 3 levels a separate score is build. Figure 3 shows the results. It can be seen that there is not much difference between level 1 and level 2 of situational awareness in both movement types. In level 1 the SA score for the PTP movement is 62,3%, for the LIN movement 59,6%. The PTP movement in level 2 has a SA score of 58,3% and the LIN movement 63,3%.

Remarkable, however, is the larger difference in level 3. Here the two values differ more from each other. The SA score for the PTP movement is 46,7% and the SA score for the LIN movement is 78,3%. The delta is greater here than in the other levels. The overall SA score for PTP movements is 55,76% and 67,06% for LIN movements.

9   Discussion

As the results show the level 1 of SA, Perception, barely differs between the two movement types. Most of the probands can name 8–9 objects in their environment, no matter what type of trajectory is used.

In level 2 of SA, Comprehension, there is also no appreciable difference between PTP and LIN movements. Thus it can be said that those two types of movement do not cause a difference in the understanding of the current situation.

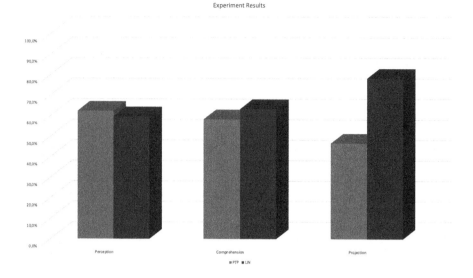

Fig. 3. SA scores of the two movement types

This does not apply to level 3 of SA in this experiment. Here a large difference between the two movements is remarkable. In the case of PTP movements, probands can not give as good a projection of the future system status as with LIN movements. Because PTP movements do not follow a logical path, unlike LIN movements, it is harder to predict a direction or the next action of the robot.

With regard to level 3, the stated hypothesis can be confirmed. The overall SA score also shows a difference in the two trajectory types. However, looking at levels 1 and 2, it becomes clear that the result from level 3 is the main factor for this finding.

10   Conclusion

At HRC, plant designers and programmers are confronted with the question of whether and how different robot trajectories are perceived in a differentiated way from the perspective of the collaborating human being in terms of situation awareness. This is investigated here with the help of a reliable proband experiment.

Certain classes of trajectories, namely point-to-point (PTP) movements and linear (LIN) movements, are investigated with respect to SA in two groups of probands. The score of the two movement categories is compared. It can be shown that, although no significant difference can be seen in the first levels of SA, the difference becomes significant in the third level. Therefore the overall SA score is different. Linear movements are to be preferred if there are requirements in the SA.

What remains open in this study is, to what extent the circular motion profile also shows advantages over the PTP profile. It would also be interesting whether the circular or the linear profile leads to a better SA. This is where future investigations will start and further experiments are planned. The long-term goal ois to develop a recommendation for the path planning, in the context of the construction of HRC systems, which enables safe robot movements with a simple and fast programming.

References

1. Roboter-Absatz in fünf Jahren verdoppelt - World Robotics Report. https://ifr.org/downloads/press2018/2018.pdf. Accessed 4 Oct 2019
2. Roboterdichte steigt weltweit auf neuen Rekord - International Federation of Robotics. https://www.presseportal.de/pm/115415/3861707. Accessed 10 Oct 2019
3. Heßler, M.: Die Halle 54 bei Volkswagen und die Grenzen der Automatisierung. Ueberlegungen zum Mensch-Maschine-Verhaeltnis in der industriellen Produktion der 1980er Jahre. Studies in Contemporary History 11
4. DIN ISO/TS 15066:2017–04; DIN SPEC 5306:2017–04 DIN SPEC 5306:2017–04 Roboter und Robotikgeräte - Kollaborierende Roboter (ISO/TS 15066:2016), Berlin, Beuth Verlag (2017)
5. Wischniewski, S., Rosen, P. H., Kirchhoff, B.: Stand der Technik und zukünftige Entwicklungen der Mensch-Roboter-Interaktion. In: Presented on the 65. Congress der Gesellschaft für Arbeitswissenschaft, Dresden (2019)
6. Tausch, A.: Aufgabenallokation in der Mensch-Roboter-Interaktion. 4. Workshop Mensch-Roboter-Zusammenarbeit. Bundesanstalt für Arbeitsschutz und Arbeitsmedizin, Posterpräsentation, Dortmund (2018)
7. Sen, S.: Erwartungskonformität von Roboterbewegungen und Situationsbewusstsein in der Mensch-Roboter-Kollaboration. In: Buxbaum, H.-J. (ed.) Mensch-Roboter-Kollaboration, Chapter 12. Springer, Wiesbaden (2020). https://doi.org/10.1007/978-3-658-28307-0_12
8. Weber, W.: Industrieroboter, 3rd edn. Carl Hanser Verlag, Leipzig (2017)
9. Endsley, M.R.: Design and evaluation for situation awareness enhancement. In: Proceedings of the Human Factors Society 32nd Annual Meeting, vol. 32, pp. 97–101 (1988)
10. Endsley, M.R.: Measurement of situation awareness in dynamic systems. Hum. Factors **37**, 65–84 (1995)
11. Endsley, M.R., Smith, R.P.: Attention distribution and decision making in tactical air combat. Hum. Factors **38**, 232–249 (1996)
12. Buxbaum, H., Kleutges, M., Sen, S.: Full-Scope simulation of human-robot interaction in manufacturing systems. In: IEEE Winter Simulation Conference, Gothenburg (2018)
13. National Nuclear Regulator: Requirements for the full scope operator training simulator at Koeberg nuclear power station. Licence-Document-1093 (2006)
14. Tavira-Mondragon, J., Cruz-Cruz, R.: Development of power plant simulators and their application in an operators training center. In: Ao, S.I., Amouzegar, M., Rieger, B. (eds.) Intelligent Automation and Systems Engineering. Lecture Notes in Electrical Engineering, vol. 103. Springer, New York (2011)

Author Index

Printed in the United States
by Baker & Taylor Publisher Services